HumanFactors
Enhancing Pilot Performance

Dale Wilson

AVIATION SUPPLIES & ACADEMICS
NEWCASTLE, WASHINGTON

Human Factors: Enhancing Pilot Performance
by Dale Wilson

Aviation Supplies & Academics, Inc.
7005 132nd Place SE
Newcastle, Washington 98059-3153
asa@asa2fly.com | asa2fly.com

See the ASA website at **asa2fly.com/reader/human** for the "Reader Resources" page containing additional information and updates relating to this book.

ASA-HUMAN
ISBN 978-1-61954-927-2

Additional formats available
Kindle   ISBN 978-1-61954-929-6
eBook ePub   ISBN 978-1-61954-928-9
eBook PDF   ISBN 978-1-61954-930-2
eBundle   ISBN 978-1-61954-931-9 (print + eBook PDF download code)

Printed in the United States of America
2024   2023   2022   2021   2020   9 8 7 6 5 4 3 2 1

Library of Congress Cataloging-in-Publication Data:

Names: Wilson, Dale, author.
   Title: Human factors : enhancing pilot performance / Dale Wilson.
Description: Newcastle, Washington : Aviation Supplies & Academics, Inc., [2020] |
   Includes bibliographical references and index.
Identifiers: LCCN 2019055364 | ISBN 9781619549272 (trade paperback) |
   ISBN 9781619549289 (ebook) | ISBN 9781619549296 (kindle edition) | ISBN
   9781619549302 (pdf) | ISBN 9781619549319 (eBundle)
Subjects: LCSH: Airplanes—Piloting—Human factors. | Airplanes—Piloting—
   Safety measures. | Aeronautics—Human factors. | Flight—Physiological aspects.
   | Aircraft accidents—Prevention.
Classification: LCC TL710 .W545 2020 | DDC 629.132/52—dc23
LC record available at https://lccn.loc.gov/2019055364

Contents

Foreword

When Dale asked me to write the Foreword for his new textbook, *Human Factors: Enhancing Pilot Performance*, I was honored but not excited, because I have never had a good relationship with textbooks. I am a "get to the point and let's move on" type of person, and most of the textbooks I have had the misfortune of being forced to read were not of that persuasion, as they often seemed to have little to do with reality and a lot to do with big words that normal people don't use. I had a particularly rough time with accounting textbooks, as I really didn't care at all what happened to the XYZ Corporation that seemed to be featured in all their examples.

This would be a particular challenge in a textbook about human factors, as the very word "human" means that it has to relate to people and their feelings and performance. I often fought this battle in my consulting with major corporations, as they usually wanted to count things. I kept stressing that human factors analysis requires human factors metrics, and that too much emphasis on numbers will scare people off and distract them from the truly important issues. This is why, in the many articles on human factors in aviation I wrote for *Flying* magazine, I always used stories other pilots could relate to, and terminology that would not send them to their computers to try to find out what something meant.

As I read Dale's new book, I was happy to discover that he has the same philosophy that I have. He starts each chapter with a brief synopsis of several accidents caused by a lack of knowledge or application of the information in that chapter. This immediately pulls the reader into the topic and sets the scene for the factual information that follows, making it clear why this information is important to a pilot. Because it is a textbook, Dale does provide comprehensive coverage of each subject, but continually relates that information to actual accidents, thus always reinforcing the fact that a working knowledge of this topic could literally save the reader's life.

If a pilot finds a particular topic especially interesting, Dale has included a "Helpful Resources" section at the end of each chapter, with up-to-date URLs and other information, along with extensive notes. Both include web addresses when those are available. The book also has an extensive Glossary and a list of Abbreviations and Acronyms making this an excellent reference tool.

While anyone interested in human factors in aviation could benefit from this book, Dale's target audience are pilots attending a collegiate aviation program with a desire to fly professionally, and I feel that he has achieved a wonderful balance by providing a wealth of detailed information, while always relating that information to actual operational considerations. I care deeply about the safety of pilots in general, and especially those flying small aircraft, so I am relieved to know that such a comprehensive yet practical guide will be available to students in collegiate aviation programs and anyone else who seeks a deeper understanding and working knowledge of this important topic.

—*Jay Hopkins*
Founder and president of the Error Prevention Institute, Inc., and former contributing editor on Human Factors to *Flying* magazine

Acknowledgments

It takes a team to publish a book like this. That is why I am extremely grateful for the contribution made by the following professionals who agreed to serve as its reviewers. Along with safety educators and experienced pilots representing several different airlines, these reviewers include experts in aerospace physiology, experimental psychology, cognitive psychology, advanced flight deck design, and human factors education. Their detailed feedback—especially within their areas of expertise—was invaluable and most of their suggestions were incorporated into the final manuscript.

Bruce Chase, M.A.S. Professor and Chair, Department of Flight Science, LeTourneau Univeristy

Eric David, Captain, Boeing B-777, Air Canada

Harold Faw, Ph.D., Professor Emeritus, Psychology, Trinity Western University

Maelene Fodor, First Officer, Boeing B-787, Air Canada

Bryce Hansen, M.D., Flight surgeon and civil aviation accident investigator (retired) and author of *Flying is Safe—Are You?*

Dan Hargrove, M.S., Pilot USAF (retired); Professor and Director, Aviation, Rocky Mountain College

Jay Hopkins, Founder, Error Prevention Institute, Inc.; former Human Factors Contributing Editor, *Flying* magazine

Joe Hopkins, Founder, Mission Safety International, Inc.

David Hunter, M.S., Lieutenant Colonel, USAF (retired); Ph.D. Candidate, Aviation Safety and Human Factors

Ruggero Ienna, Captain, Boeing B-737, United Airlines

Scott Macpherson, Chair, International Business Aviation Council (IBAC) Governing Board and Founder of TrainingPort.net®

Jim Norton, Ph.D., U.S. Naval Aerospace Physiologist (retired)

Robert Nullmeyer, Ph.D., Professor, Aviation, Arizona State University

Arne Olson, Check Pilot (ACP), Boeing B-767, Air Canada (retired)

Mason Peterson, First Officer Boeing B-757, FedEx Express

Michael Prevost, Ph.D., U.S. Naval Aerospace Physiologist (retired);
Former Director, Human Performance Laboratory, U.S. Naval Academy.

Joshua Tobin, Captain, Airbus A320, JetBlue Airways

Kathleen Van Benthem, Ph.D., Cognitive Scientist, Institute of Cognitive
Science, Carleton University

Erik Vogel, Pilot and Firefighter (retired)

Andrew Walton, Director of Safety and Adjunct Professor, Liberty
University School of Aeronautics

Thanks to Jackie Spanitz at Aviation Supplies and Academics, Inc.,
for taking on this project. A special thanks is due to Alex Lorden
(Production Editor) and Kelly Burch (Graphic Designer) for their excellent
work. I especially thank Jay Hopkins for providing valuable feedback and
writing the foreword to this work. Jay is the founder and president of
Error Prevention Institute, Inc., a two-decade writer of the *Human Factors*
column for *Flying* magazine, an accomplished pilot (ATP, CFI), and one
of the most down-to-earth and insightful flight-safety communicators I
know. If you have read any of his more than 250 human factors articles
in *Flying* magazine, I think you would agree.

My highest gratitude belongs to my family who have supported me in
my career—my two wonderful adult children who I am very proud of,
and my beautiful wife of more than 40 years whose support in my life
and my work has been unwavering.

About the Author

Dale Wilson, M.S., is Emeritus Professor of Aviation at Central Washington University in Ellensburg, Washington, where he has taught courses in aviation weather, aerospace physiology and psychology, and threat and error management since 1996. He holds a master's degree in aviation safety from the University of Central Missouri and a bachelor's degree in psychology from Trinity Western University in British Columbia, Canada. Professor Wilson has been a pilot for 40 years, logging several thousand hours in single- and multi-engine airplanes in the United States and Canada. He holds several professional FAA pilot certifications, including Airline Transport Pilot, Certified Flight Instructor, Advanced Ground Instructor, and Instrument Ground Instructor. While in Canada, he held the Airline Transport Pilot License and Class 1 Flight Instructor Rating—the highest of four levels of flight instructor certification.

At Central Washington University, he received several awards for outstanding teaching and scholarship in the Department of Aviation, including the *Excellence in Teaching* award from the College of Education and Professional Studies. He was also nominated for the Central Washington University Faculty Senate *Distinguished Professor of Teaching* award. He earned the biennial *Master Flight Instructor* designation seven times (1999 through 2013), and the *Master Ground Instructor* from 2013 through 2017, from the National Association of Flight Instructors. He also served as an Aviation Safety Counselor and later as an FAA Safety Team Representative for the FAA's Spokane Flight Standards District Office.

His primary research interests include visual limitations of flight, pilot decision making, and VFR flight into instrument meteorological conditions. He has authored (or co-authored) more than 20 articles related to flight crew human factors in scholarly journals and professional aviation magazines, and has given numerous safety-related presentations at conferences and seminars in the U.S. and Canada. Published by ASA, Inc., in 2014, his co-authored book *Managing Risk: Best Practices for Pilots* describes many of the major threats to safe flight operations, offers insights on how and why pilots make errors that exacerbate them, and provides best practice countermeasures needed to successfully manage them (available at asa2fly.com). You can reach the author on *LinkedIn* or at Dale.Wilson@cwu.edu.

Introduction

It was after midnight when I got the call. Two of our school's airplanes were overdue. After daybreak, our worst fears were confirmed—both aircraft had collided in mountainous terrain south of our airport, killing all six occupants. As you can imagine, these deaths shattered the families of all those aboard—five aviation students and a flight instructor—and devastated the flight school staff and instructors who knew them.

The return from their multi-day trip had been delayed a couple of times because of weather. In fact, they were already late for the beginning of their spring semester at the college that housed our flight program. They resumed their trek when the weather cleared, and in spite of receiving information that indicated the weather would likely remain VFR conditions, as they neared our home airport they encountered unexpected deteriorating weather in the form of snow showers and clouds. They continued VFR flight, with the radar tapes indicating that one airplane followed the interstate highway, while the other stayed closer to a navigation (Victor) airway. However, the sun had set and it was very dark. Investigators determined that the cause of these accidents were the decisions by the pilots to continue VFR flight into instrument meteorological conditions and their failure to maintain proper altitude clearance from the mountainous terrain. Contributing factors were the darkness of night, adverse weather, and terrain conditions.

If you knew the pilots, you would know that they were not prone to risk-taking, nor were they incompetent. They progressed well in their flight training and were otherwise conscientious aviators. Neither of them suffered from any psychological disorders—they were normal people like you and me. A witness at a fixed base operator overheard one in their group say that they were not going to just sit around the airport waiting for a marginal weather report that would allow "scud running" to the next stopping point. So, rather than wasting their time at the airport waiting for the slightest hint of improvement that might tempt them to launch in questionable weather, they instead called it quits for the day and elected to go into town to participate in other recreational activities. The pilot-in-command of one of the flights was an experienced flight instructor who was providing instruction to his private-pilot student. One of my students was in the other airplane. She was a commercial pilot and I was teaching her how to be a flight instructor. Though she was not the pilot-in-command of the flight, she occupied the front right seat and, according to the accident report, was the designated safety pilot.

It has been almost 30 years, and I have never gotten over these two accidents. Though I have a better understanding today of some of the causal factors involved in these types of accidents than I did back then, the unanswered questions still haunt me: Why didn't they turn around? Why did my flight-instructor colleague elect to fly lower when he was an accomplished instrument pilot and reportedly had the appropriate instrument charts on board his aircraft? What role did a rather somewhat optimistic weather forecast play in their decision making? For example, the accident report indicates that, with the exception of the possibility of marginal weather en route, about 40 minutes before these accidents a flight service specialist expressed doubt that the weather would drop below VFR conditions. Pilot witnesses reported unexpected local snow showers in the area that day and evening: How difficult was it for them to visually detect this weather at night, especially a dark one? Finally, what part did their previous delays play in their thinking? A witness for the fueling service company they used stated "everyone was most anxious to get going." Was it possible their desire to get home—with less than 25 miles to go—clouded their judgment?

Sadly, statistics indicate that the majority of aircraft accidents are caused by the actions of the pilots who fly them (*see* Chapters 1 and 2). After these two accidents, I changed the direction of my career and began a pursuit that was to occupy most of the remainder of my professional life: to discover *why* we pilots do the things we do. I reasoned that, just as we cannot prescribe a cure for an illness if we don't know its cause, we cannot reduce the incidence of flight crew errors if we don't know what causes them. Perhaps if I had a better idea, I might be able to help other pilots avoid the same fate.

Since the topics of visual perception, decision making, and human error—all apparent factors in these two accidents—fall primarily within the domain of cognitive psychology, I completed an undergraduate degree in psychology to better understand the limitations of human sensation, perception, attention, memory, and decision making. I also gained an appreciation for the subtle, yet profound, role that other people often play in our decision making. My graduate studies also helped me understand the risk management principles necessary to counter the threats and errors that are an inevitable aspect of everyday flight operations. Since then, I have spent thousands of hours in my teaching, speaking, and writing, helping pilots understand their "humanness," and how human "factors" pose an ever-present threat to safe flight operations.

A large body of research from several human-factors-related disciplines clearly indicates that we are subject to physiological, psychological, and psychosocial limitations when it comes to operating aircraft. For example, as pilots, not only do we experience physiological limitations common to most earth-bound individuals (illness, colds, sleep deprivation, fatigue, poor physical fitness, etc.), we are also subject to physiological threats that are unique to the flight environment. For example, when flying above altitudes as low as 10,000 feet, we will fall victim to hypoxia, a malady that causes us to become indifferent to our surroundings and that could lead to total incapacitation (Chapter 4). If we fly at high enough altitudes (in an unpressurized cabin), we will also experience what deep-sea divers do when they rise to the surface too quickly: decompression sickness, a condition that also physically incapacitates its victims (Chapter 5). Even though the human eye is equipped with a remarkable dual-visual system—one for day, the other for night—when flying in the dark or in poor visual conditions we may fail to detect adverse weather and/or terrain (Chapter 6). Alternatively, we may succumb to a visual illusion that tricks us into misperceiving the outside world (Chapters 12), or fall victim to a vestibular or somatosensory illusion that leads to spatial disorientation and possible loss of control of our aircraft (Chapter 9). In perfectly clear daylight conditions, we may think we are conducting an adequate visual lookout for other aircraft, when in fact we are not (Chapter 6).

Likewise, cognitive and social factors may impede our ability to make informed decisions on the flight deck. While paying attention to one aspect of the flight environment, we may completely miss another, such as the airspeed indicator, possibly leading to an unusual attitude or undesired aircraft state (Chapter 14). Similarly, distraction may keep us from monitoring the altimeter, resulting in overshooting our altitude assignment. Alternatively, we may accept a clearance intended for another aircraft that has a similar call sign as our aircraft, possibly leading to an incident or an accident (Chapter 7 and 13). Because human memory is not perfect, pilots forget things. In spite of injunctions to "not forget," pilots still do; like obtaining a clearance, or lowering the landing gear before landing, or forgetting to remove a myriad of things before flight such as control locks, pitot and static port covers, tow bars, and fuel caps (Chapter 16).

Many accidents are the result of pilots making wrong decisions. Unfortunately, research indicates that the complex process of decision making is often subject to error and bias (Chapter 17). For example, we may make an inappropriate decision to continue an approach-to-landing in the face of poor weather and attempt a landing with a tailwind, adverse crosswind, or in marginal visibility. Most pilots, even experienced ones, are reluctant to conduct a go-around when conditions clearly warrant it. As was the case with the two accidents previously discussed, sometimes VFR pilots decide to continue flying into less-than-VFR weather conditions, resulting in either loss of control in flight (LOC-I), due to spatial disorientation, or controlled flight into terrain (CFIT). Finally, other people—customers, supervisors, other pilots—sometimes have an influence on our decision making, even when we think they do not. This *social* influence can sometimes result in others making our decisions for us; in effect, *they* are flying our aircraft instead of us (Chapter 18).

Even though today's aviation industry enjoys a remarkable safety record—primarily because it has learned from the mistakes of its past—aircraft accidents, such as CFIT, LOC-I and loss of control on the ground, midair collisions, and other deadly accidents, still occur and the hazards of flight remain. Some aircraft accidents occur because of mechanical failure, improper maintenance or hazardous weather; but as this book attests to, the vast majority are caused by the actions (or inaction) of pilots who fly them. The majority of these are not intentional, nor are they the result of some psychological deficiency or mental disorder. Rather, most are caused by inadvertent errors made by pilots—errors that arise from normal physiological, psychological, and psychosocial limitations inherent in the human condition. For those who primarily move about on the earth's surface, the consequences of such human errors are often benign. For we who fly, these normal everyday human attributes operating in the non-normal environment of flight can be deadly. This book thoroughly explores the nature of these human limitations, describes how they often manifest themselves on the flight deck, and most importantly, provides best practice countermeasures designed to help you minimize their influence in your own flight performance.

This old adage is universal, applying to aviators everywhere: Learn from the mistakes of others; you will not live long enough to make them all yourself. This book is written to help you accomplish that learning. Whether you are a fair-weather private pilot, a new-hire first officer at a regional airline, or a seasoned pilot with thousands of hours under your belt, this book will help you better understand why we pilots make the mistakes we do. More importantly, it will arm you with the knowledge you need to successfully avoid or mitigate them.

This book is divided into four parts. Part I (Chapters 1–3) includes a discussion of the aircraft safety record, human error, and the discipline of human factors—all essential elements for the discussion of flight crew human factors that occupies the remainder of the book. Part II (Chapters 4–11) and Part III (Chapters 12–18) thoroughly explore the physiological and psychological aspects of pilot performance, respectively. Part IV (Chapters 19–20) concludes this book with a discussion of two major approaches used on today's flight deck for reducing or mitigating human error—crew resource management (CRM) and threat and error management (TEM).

Each topic is written not for the human factors or safety specialist, but for you, the pilot. While each chapter covers a topic in depth—so that you discover not only the *what* but the *why*—each also includes several examples of accidents or incidents that have occurred because of the human limitation or error discussed. Important terms are in highlighted in bold and are further defined in the extensive Glossary found in Appendix C. With the exception of two introductory chapters, each concludes with a "Helpful Resources" section that provides a list of web sites, videos, courses, documents, and other references for further study.

A Note About the Accident and Incident Citations in this Book

Numerous aircraft accident reports are used in this book to illustrate many of the human factors concepts discussed. These reports— primarily from the National Transportation Safety Board (NTSB) and the Transportation Safety Board of Canada (TSB), and incident reports from the National Aeronautics and Space Administration's (NASA) Aviation Safety Reporting System (ASRS)—contain a wealth of information about how and why accidents and incidents occur. NTSB and TSB reports can be accessed at www.ntsb.gov and www.bst-tsb.gc.ca, respectively, and ASRS incident reports can be accessed at asrs.arc.nasa.gov. The following are examples of typical accident and incident report citations used in this book and how they are coded:

NTSB/AAR-07/05
The fifth (05) major NTSB aircraft accident report (AAR) issued in 2007 (07).

NTSB-AAR-75-9
The ninth (9) major NTSB aircraft accident report (AAR) issued in 1975 (75). Note: In 1983, the NTSB changed the report number format from hyphens (e.g., NTSB-AAR-82-16) to slash/hyphen/slash (e.g., NTSB/AAR-83/01). Both of these formats are used for major accidents published in Blue Cover Reports, so named because of their blue and white covers.

NTSB Identification No: LAX90LA116
The Los Angeles (LAX) NTSB office filed the accident report, which occurred during the 1990 fiscal year (90). It was a limited aviation accident investigation (LA), the 116th in fiscal year 1990. If the identification number is appended with a final letter, another aircraft was involved in the accident. All NTSB accidents are assigned an accident case number such as this one; however, most major aircraft accidents, especially those involving commercial flights carrying passengers, are identified using the format in the first example above and are published as Blue Cover Reports.

TSB Report No: A04Q0089
A TSB of Canada aviation (A) accident report from the year 2004 (04) in the Quebec (Q) region, which was the 89th accident or incident (0089) in fiscal year 2004.

ASRS Report No: 763177
The report ascension number (ACN) is 763177, which is the 736,177th incident report submitted to the National Aeronautics and Space Administration's (NASA) Aviation Safety Reporting System (ASRS) since the program began in 1976.

Part I
The Human in the Cockpit

1

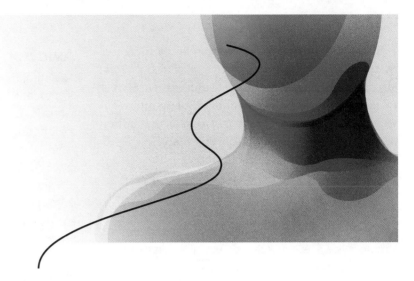

Is flying safe?
The Aviation Safety Record

A friend of mine, who lived near Vancouver, Canada, often went on winter vacations to Disneyland in Southern California with his family during his children's Christmas break. If you thought he would choose to enjoy the three-hour journey southbound in the comfort of a modern Boeing passenger jetliner, you would be mistaken. Instead, he loaded up the minivan with his family and belongings and drove over 20 hours and more than 1,300 hundred miles at a time of year when winter road conditions could quickly become treacherous. Why did he do this? Because, according to him, it was safer than flying. What he didn't know was that, statistically, he and his family were at least 100 times more likely to die on the trip because he refused to go by air.

Before we thoroughly explore the main focus of this book—*human factors* and what they are in the aviation environment—it is important to first understand the safety context out of which the discipline arises. The first chapter of this book, therefore, compares the aviation safety record to other modes of transportation and between sectors within aviation, provides a brief overview of the various types of aircraft accidents that occur, and highlights some of the major causes of aircraft accidents.

Transportation Safety

The answer to the question in this chapter's title, "Is flying safe?" depends on how you define safe. Flight safety is defined differently by different people, as evidenced, for example, by our Disneyland traveler. If he defines it as the total absence of danger, then his assessment would be correct: flying is not safe.

However, he, along with all of us, surely realizes that practically every human endeavor, let alone activities involving movement on the earth's surface—or above it—involves some degree of risk. For example, in the first decade of this millennium (2000 through 2009 inclusive), an average of 43,239 people died each year in transportation accidents (e.g., bicycles, cars, trucks, motorcycles, buses, aircraft, trains) in the United States making the annual risk of dying in a transportation accident about 1 in 6,800 per U.S. resident. In fact, transportation accidents are the number one cause (at almost 40 percent) of accidental deaths (often termed **unintended injury deaths**) in the United States, which is the equivalent to the number of people killed by falls and poisonings, the next two highest causes of accidental deaths.[1]

Compared to non-highway **transportation modes** (aviation, rail, maritime, etc.), road methods of human transport (cars, trucks, motorcycles, buses, bicycles, etc.) claimed by far the most lives during the 10-year period accounting for 95 percent of all transportation fatalities. Conversely, U.S. aircraft accidents claimed the lives of only 646 people annually during the period—less than 0.15 percent of all transportation deaths—with 85 percent of those occurring in the **general aviation (GA)** sector and the remaining 15 percent resulting mostly from only four scheduled **air carrier** (commercial airline) accidents during the entire decade.[2]

In fact, a look at the statistics clearly indicates that, in comparison to all other modes, commercial air-carrier flying is the safest mode of passenger transport in the United States. For example, if we compare the 0.07 passenger deaths per billion passenger-miles traveled[3] on commercial flights with passenger deaths on commuter trains, ferry-boats, and cars and light trucks (see Table 1-1), we see the odds of dying when traveling using these modes increase by factors of more than 6 (.43/.07 = 6.14), 45, and 104, respectively. The odds of dying while riding a motorcycle are 29 times greater than riding in a car or light truck, and an astonishing 3,000 times greater than flying on a commercial air carrier!

Table 1-1. Passenger fatalities per billion passenger-miles for selected modes for ten year period 2000–2009.[4]

Transportation mode	Passenger fatalities per billion passenger-miles
Motorcycle	212.57
Car or light truck	7.28
Local ferryboat	3.17
Commuter rail and Amtrak	0.43
Urban mass transit rail (2002–2009)	0.24
Bus holding more than 10 passengers—transit, inter-city, school, charter.	0.11
Commercial aviation	0.07

The good news for all U.S. travelers is that accidents and accident fatality rates for most modes of transportation—including aviation—have gradually trended downward over the past several decades. For example, highway fatalities per 100 million vehicle miles dropped from 3.35 in 1975 to 1.11 by 2010, a 300 percent improvement.[5] For large truck accident fatalities, the improvement was even better: fatalities per 100 million vehicle miles dropped from 5.51 in 1975 to 1.26 by 2008, more than a four-fold improvement. Other modes, such as railroad and maritime (both commercial vessels and recreational boating) have also seen significant fatality rate reductions over the years. But the fact still remains that the most dangerous part of the flight in a commercial air carrier is the drive to the airport, especially if you are on a motorcycle!

Aviation Operations

As noted, most U.S. **aircraft accident** fatalities (about 85 percent) during the ten-year period involved GA aircraft. Civil aviation is generally divided into two major groups: air carriers and GA.

U.S. air carriers are commercial operators certificated under Parts 121 and 135 of Title 14 of the Code of Federal Regulations (14 CFR) to carry passengers or cargo for hire. In 2018 the U.S. air carrier fleet consisted of almost 7,500 airplanes (mostly turbofan-powered) used by mainline and regional passenger air carriers and cargo carriers, to transport passengers and cargo.[6] U.S. commercial carriers conducted more than nine million domestic and international flights, flew more than 17 million flight hours, carried a record 849 million passengers (called *enplanements*) and delivered more than 18 million tons of cargo in 2017. The U.S. commercial aviation industry directly employs more than 700,000 people and is responsible for creating over 10 million jobs (7.3 percent of U.S. jobs) and more than 5 percent of the gross domestic product in the United States.[7, 8, 9]

General aviation, or "gen av" as some call it, comprises all civilian flight operations other than scheduled commercial air carrier passenger and cargo service. With approximately 210,000 aircraft (more than 416,000 worldwide), GA accounts for more than 90 percent of the U.S. civil aircraft fleet and includes piston- and turbine-powered, single- and multi-engine airplanes (almost 80 percent of the GA fleet) and rotorcraft (e.g., helicopters), balloons, airships, and gliders. As you can imagine, GA does just about every type of flying there is, some of which includes: personal/recreational flights in piston-powered single-engine airplanes; instructional training flights (most U.S. commercial airline pilots learned to fly in GA); business and corporate transport in light, medium, or even heavy twin-engine jets; on-demand charter (air taxi) flights in piston- or turbine-powered airplanes; helicopter emergency medical (air ambulance) service; sight-seeing flights; and a variety of aerial observation/application flights, including highway traffic reporting, mapping, patrol, surveillance, search-and-rescue, crop production, and fire suppression. GA aircraft fly into more than 5,000 U.S. public-use airports (scheduled airlines fly to less than 400 U.S. airports), log more than 24 million hours per year—with about 65 percent conducted for business and public services—and transport an estimated 166 million passengers annually. The U.S. GA industry supports $219 billion of economic output and 1.1 million jobs. Of the almost 600,000 certified pilots in the United States, about 500,000 fly GA aircraft.[10, 11, 12]

Aviation Accidents

A distinction should be made between the *number* of accidents, or fatal accidents (in which at least one person died as a result of the accident), and the *rate* of accidents (or fatal accidents). For example, if the number of accidents in a given year dropped from the previous year you might conclude the safety record was improving. In one sense, that is certainly an improvement in safety because fewer unwanted outcomes—accidents and accidental deaths—occurred. But the improvement could have been because there were fewer aircraft operations. Let's say there were zero accidents because there was zero flying during a given time period. This tells us nothing about the safety of flying, only the safety of not flying. It's like having no private automobile acci-

dents because everyone stopped driving their cars. What is needed, in order to determine and compare levels of flight safety (or highway, boating, or other modes of safety) over time and between aviation sectors, is some kind of rate. A rate is a ratio of the number of events compared to the exposure to them. You've already seen an example of rates in this chapter (*see* Table 1-1) expressed as the number of passenger fatalities per billion passenger-miles. Because these values are the easiest to obtain, it's common for the denominator in aviation accident rates to be the number of hours flown (e.g., x/million hours), the number of departures (e.g., x/100,000 departures), the number of aircraft-miles flown (e.g., x/million aircraft-miles), and the number of passenger-miles flown (e.g., x/million passenger-miles).

GA Accident Record

Looking at both the number and rate of accidents for the most recent available five-year period (2013 through 2017), you can see in Table 1-2 a stark difference between the safety record of Part 121 air carriers and GA.

Table 1-2. Number of accidents, fatal accidents and fatalities, and accident and fatal accident rates for U.S. GA aircraft and 14 CFR §121 air carriers for 2013 through 2017.[13]

		Number of accidents	Number of fatal accidents	Fatalities	Accident rate per 100,000 flight hours	Fatal accident rate per 100,000 flight hours
2017	GA	1,233	203	331	5.672	0.935
	Air carrier	32	0	0	0.172	0.00
2016	GA	1,267	213	386	5.934	0.984
	Air carrier	31	0	0	0.164	0.00
2015	GA	1,210	230	378	5.851	1.098
	Air carrier	30	0	0	0.162	0.00
2014	GA	1,223	257	424	6.230	1.300
	Air carrier	29	0	0	0.175	0.00
2013	GA	1,224	222	390	6.259	1.118
	Air carrier	23	2	9	0.129	0.011
Total	GA	6,157	1,125	1,909	--	--
	Air carrier	145	2	9	--	--
Yearly average	GA	1,231	225	382	5.989	1.087
	Air carrier	29	0.4	1.8	0.160	0.002

Notice that there were only two fatal Part 121 accidents resulting in nine fatalities over the five-year period. Compare that with the 1,125 fatal GA accidents that claimed the lives of 1,909 people during the same time frame. The average GA accident and fatal accident rates during the five years were 5.99 and 1.09 per 100,000 hours, respectively. Some improvement has occurred during the past two decades, but unfortunately, very little: the GA accident and fatal accident rates averaged 6.82 and 1.28 per 100,000 hours, respectively, for the 10 years from 2005 through 2014, and 7.04 and 1.27 per 100,000 hours, respectively, for the 10 years prior to that (1995 through 2004).[14]

The GA record is much the same in other countries. In Australia for example, 206 accidents in 2015 claimed the lives of 30 people in general- and recreational-aviation operations, while no lives in scheduled airline operations have been lost in that country since 1975.[15] In Canada, 31 people in 240 aircraft accidents in 2017 died, but only one of those deaths involved scheduled passenger airline operations. In fact, for the 11-year period between 2007 through 2017 inclusive, only two fatal accidents in commercial airline operations occurred in that country and, for the four-year period of 2014 through 2017 inclusive, no fatal commuter accidents occurred.[16]

Of course, you can probably think of several reasons why the GA sector has a higher accident rate than scheduled airline operations. Not only do airlines and commercial cargo operators use sophisticated multi-engine turbine-powered airplanes that are certified and typically maintained to the highest standards in the industry, but each airplane is piloted by at least two experienced crew members who are also highly trained and usually certified to the highest standards in the business. Crews also benefit from sophisticated (and expensive) life-saving technology, such as forward-looking Doppler weather radar inclusive of ground and in-flight wind shear detection, **terrain awareness and warning systems (TAWS)**, and **airborne collision avoidance systems (ACAS)**.

Airlines also operate in a stricter regulatory environment and enjoy a support system that is the envy of others in the business, including such benefits as company dispatch, weather and flight monitoring services, refueling and ground personnel, and air traffic control (ATC) services for almost all phases of flight. As part of their **safety management systems (SMS)**, airline safety departments also use a variety of organizational safety tools such as **aviation safety action programs (ASAP)**, **line operations safety audits (LOSA)** and **flight operational quality assurance (FOQA)** to help achieve their high levels of safety.[17]

However, in spite of these safety benefits, the airlines recognize that even experienced pilots sometimes make mistakes—they may get distracted and forget important items, they may execute the wrong action, or they may take the correct action too late. To compensate for these limitations, airline flight crews are trained to engage in best practice risk-reduction strategies during all flights. Some of these include adhering to **standard operating procedures (SOPs)** that are spelled out in detail for every phase of flight; conducting memorized procedural flow checks and using written checklists for normal, non-normal (abnormal), and emergency operations; verbalizing procedures—using callouts—during key points during their execution in order to reduce the possibility of miscommunication; complying with what is commonly called the **sterile cockpit rule** (14 CFR §§121.542 and 135.100) by avoiding nonessential activities (including extraneous conversations) that could distract them from completing the essential duties required for the safe operation of their aircraft during the critical phases of flight (generally below 10,000 feet); and practicing behaviors that are designed to effectively manage automation, distractions, and stress. These are effective tactics that professional and amateur pilots alike can use to avoid or mitigate errors on the flight deck. To help you effectively overcome the human limitations that are often involved in aircraft accidents, we will revisit some of these in greater depth, along with two other particularly effective strategies—crew resource management and threat and error management—in the last two chapters of this book.

Airline Accident Record

The safety record in scheduled commercial airline flying has not always been stellar and accidents still occur both at home and abroad. Boeing compiles a yearly accident *Statistical Summary* that includes the worldwide fleet of commercial turbojet airplanes—made by Boeing and other manufacturers—that have a maximum certificated takeoff weight of more than 60,000 pounds. Their analysis, therefore, excludes all commercial operations using lighter turboprop and piston-engine airplanes, a segment responsible for most accidents in commercial aviation.[18] According to Boeing, 41 accidents involving commercial jet airplanes worldwide took the lives of 304 people in 2018, with 301 of the 304 lost in two major scheduled passenger airline flights; one involving the loss of all but one occupant of a Boeing B-737-200 that crashed after takeoff from Cuba's José Martí International Airport and the other involving the loss of all crew and passengers on board Lion Air Flight 610, a Boeing B-737-8 MAX, that crashed shortly after takeoff from Soekarno-Hatta International Airport, near Jakarta, Indonesia. Between 1959 and 2018, the worldwide fleet experienced 2,030 accidents, 632 fatal accidents,

30,330 onboard fatalities, and 1,255 external fatalities. External fatalities refer to people on the ground or from another aircraft that were also involved in the accident. During the same time period, U.S. and Canadian operators experienced 590 accidents, 183 fatal accidents, and 6,584 total onboard and external fatalities.[19]

The safety record has significantly improved for the worldwide commercial fleet since 1959. Boeing's *Statistical Summary* indicates that the percentage of accidents that involve fatalities (the **lethality rate**) was 35 percent between 1959 and 2018 but averaged only 13 percent for the 2009–2018 decade—a more than 60 percent drop.

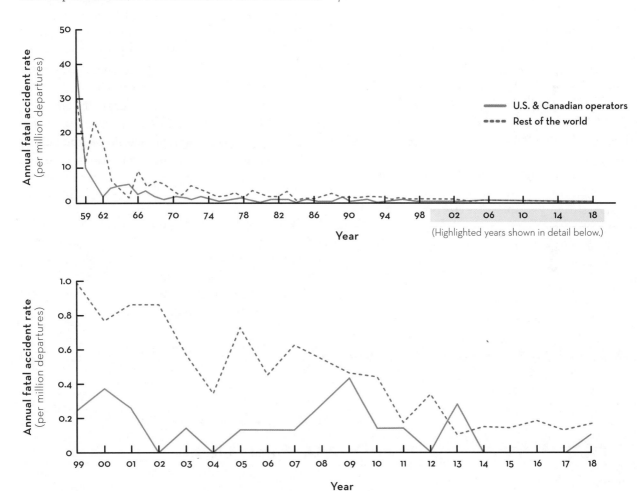

Fig 1-1.

American and Canadian commercial jet fatal accident rate (per million departures) compared to the rest of the world for the periods 1959 to 2018 and 1999 to 2018.[20]

The average U.S. air carrier accident rate and fatal accident rate over the most recent 10 years where complete data are available (2008 through 2017), were 0.31 and 0.007 per 100,000 departures (takeoffs), respectively. This represents a 21 percent drop in the accident rate and a 65 percent drop in the fatal accident rate over the previous 10 years (1998 through 2007) where it was 0.39 and 0.02 per 100,000 departures, respectively.[21]

Types and Causes of Aircraft Accidents

Accident data reveal relatively predictable types and causes of both GA and airline accidents. The U.S. National Transportation Safety Board (NTSB) often uses one event, called the **defining event**, to describe the type or category of accident that occurred. Some examples of defining events are loss of control in flight, controlled flight into terrain, and fuel related. The NTSB also identifies the probable cause or causes of an accident and its contributing factors—those situations or circumstances that are central to the accident cause.[22]

From 2008 through 2017, most U.S. GA accidents—at just over 80 percent—involved personal flight operations (flying for pleasure, recreation, or other personal reasons) and instructional flights. Personal flights accounted for 67 percent of all GA accidents and 63 percent of fatal accidents, and instructional flights accounted for 13 percent and 6 percent of all GA accidents and fatal accidents, respectively. This was followed by aerial applications, and depending on the year, positioning, public use, business, aerial observations, flight tests, skydiving, banner towing, air race/show, external load, ferrying, glider towing, executive/corporate, and unknown.[23]

An earlier U.S. Government Accountability Office (GAO) analysis for the 12 years between 1999 to 2010 found the percentage of fatal accidents involving personal flying was disproportionate to the number of hours it was responsible for—it accounted for only an estimated 40 percent of GA activity yet was responsible for 77 percent of the accidents. Similarly, the GAO noted an estimated 14 percent of GA flight hours involved corporate flight operations, a GA sector that was responsible for less than 1 percent of fatal accidents.[24] Corporate flight departments often

make use of airline-type flight crew training, require annual or semi-annual recurrent training in simulators, possess greater levels of operational support, and conform to a variety of safe operating practices that are often required by their respective insurance companies.

According to a recent U.S. Federal Aviation Administration (FAA) GA Safety *Fact Sheet*, the following are the five leading defining events involved in fatal U.S. GA accidents over the past several years. The acronyms that accompany these aviation **occurrence**[25] categories were developed by the Commercial Aviation Safety Team (CAST)/International Civil Aviation Organization (ICAO) Common Taxonomy Team (CICTT). The taxonomy consists of common definitions designed to assist the world's aviation safety community by using standard definitions to classify accidents and **aircraft incidents**. A list of these categories (defining events) and their definitions is included in Appendix B.

1. Loss of aircraft control in flight (LOC-I).
2. Controlled flight into terrain (CFIT).
3. System/component failure—powerplant (SCF-PP).
4. Fuel related (FUEL).
5. Unknown or undetermined (UNK).

System/component failure—non-powerplant (SCF-NP), unintended flight in **instrument meteorological conditions (IMC)**, **midair collisions (MAC)**, low-altitude operations, and other (OTHR)—in that order—are the remaining five types of GA accidents.[26]

The top five accident categories (or defining events) are responsible for the majority of fatal accidents in GA, especially in the highest risk category of personal flight operations. In 2015, for example, they were responsible for 44 percent of all U.S. GA fatal accidents and 74 percent of all fatal accidents involving personal flying operations.[27]

GA Safety Alerts

Concerned about the more than 1,400 GA accidents per year in which more than 400 passengers and pilots died annually, the NTSB—for the first time ever—listed the entire GA sector on its **Most Wanted List of Transportation Safety Improvements** in 2011. They also, for the first time, began addressing some of the major safety issues associated with GA flight operations by publishing safety alerts that were historically published primarily for commercial flight operations. The first few GA safety alerts[28] were published in 2013 and targeted the top three types of fatal GA accidents: loss of aircraft control in flight, controlled flight into terrain, and system/component failure—powerplant.

Loss of control in flight (LOC-I) involves an unintended departure of an aircraft from controlled flight. Since LOC-I is the most common defining event for fatal GA accidents, the NTSB Safety Alert SA-019, *Prevent Aerodynamic Stalls at Low Altitude*, addresses a major cause of LOC-I accidents. According to the safety alert, accident pilots typically fail to avoid the conditions that lead to an aerodynamic stall, to recognize the symptoms of an approaching stall and to use proper stall-recovery procedures.

The safety alert also reveals that these types of accidents arise from a variety of circumstances that tend to repeat themselves in GA flight operations— becoming distracted while maneuvering in the traffic pattern (*circuit* in Canada), fixating on ground objects, and coping with emergencies. For example, applying excessive rudder after overshooting the extended runway centerline while turning base to final, attempting a 180 degree turn back to the runway after losing engine power at low altitude, and losing control when distracted by a spectator while conducting a low altitude pass over the ground.

Another NTSB safety alert, *Reduced Visual References Require Vigilance* (SA-020), underscores the threat of reduced visual references, a condition that has contributed to fatal commercial and military accidents but is particularly problematic among GA flights, many of which are conducted under **visual flight rules (VFR)**. Outside visual references (e.g., horizon, terrain) needed to safely fly under VFR are diminished when visibility is near or below **visual meteorological conditions (VMC)** and during dark-night conditions (overcast and/or moonless). The NTSB says that accidents involving reduced visual references generally are involved in GA's two biggest killers—LOC-I and **controlled flight into terrain (CFIT)**. The safety alert highlights typical scenarios: VFR pilots fly into IMC and either collide with nearby terrain or lose control of their aircraft due to spatial disorientation (SD); instrument-rated pilots experience SD (discussed in Chapter 9) while flying in IMC; and pilots lose control of their aircraft as a result of SD or are involved in

a CFIT accident as a result of a visual illusion while attempting to rely on inadequate outside visual references during dark-night conditions.

The good news is the rate of GA CFIT accidents has decreased in recent years, and the General Aviation Joint Steering Committee, an FAA/Industry program, speculates that this may be due to the proliferation in GA aircraft of moving map displays in avionics and **electronic flight bags (EFB)**.[29]

System/component failure-powerplant (SCF-PP) is generally the third most common type of fatal GA accident, but in 2015 it crept ahead of CFIT to second place behind LOC-I. The GA sector relies heavily on the use of single-engine piston-powered airplanes (over 80 percent of the U.S. GA fleet), and piston engines are generally less reliable than turbine engines. The fastest growing segment of the GA fleet—experimental-amateur built (E-AB) aircraft (often called "homebuilts")—is responsible for a disproportionate share of accidents (4 percent of fight hours, 21 percent of fatal accidents), in part because "most E-ABs are simple aircraft that may incorporate previously untested systems and modified airframes and instruments."[30]

NTSB safety alerts *Is Your Aircraft Talking to You? Listen!* (SA-021), addressed to pilots, and *Mechanics: Manage Risks to Ensure Safety* (SA-022), appropriately targeting aircraft maintenance personnel, indicate that the circumstances involved in fatal accidents involving system or component failures are "remarkably similar to those of previous accidents" and that pilots and mechanics are not taking advantage of the lessons learned from previous accidents. For example, too often pilots attempt a flight even though they are aware that something is not quite right mechanically with their aircraft.

Finally, according to Safety Alert SA-067, *Flying on Empty*, there was a yearly average of 50 GA fuel mismanagement accidents (FUEL) between 2011 and 2015. Fuel exhaustion (the aircraft completely runs out of fuel) and fuel starvation (fuel is present but isn't delivered to the engine) accounted for more than 90 percent of all fuel-related accidents. Fuel system malfunctions were cited in less than 5 percent of these accidents—pilot inexperience, complacency, overestimation of flying abilities, and improper operation of fuel systems caused, or were contributing factors, in over 95 percent of fuel-related accidents.

Causes of and Contributing Factors to GA Accidents

As with fuel-related accidents, most GA accidents are caused by some type of pilot error. In fact, the Aircraft Owners and Pilots Association (AOPA) concluded that the "overwhelming cause of accidents is pilot error, which has consistently caused 75 percent of accidents for decades."[31] Pilots, like all humans, are prone to error and mistakes. Some of these involve, at least in part, errors of skill as witnessed by the fact that the highest number of pilot-caused accidents occur during landings. Fortunately—as indicated in AOPA's Air Safety Institute's recent *Joseph T. Nall Report* and seen in Figure 1-2—these also involve the fewest fatalities: there were 262 landing accidents involving U.S. GA aircraft in 2015, but only three resulted in fatalities.

Also seen in Figure 1-3, the most common type of landing accident involves loss of directional control suggesting that they are caused, or at least partially caused, by skill errors. There were 115 landing accidents in 2015 involving loss of control, one of which involved a fatality. Other likely skill-related causes include airspeed control issues, stalls, and landing short or long on the runway.

Fig 1-2.

Types of pilot-related GA accidents, including number of accidents and fatal accidents for each type in 2015.[32]

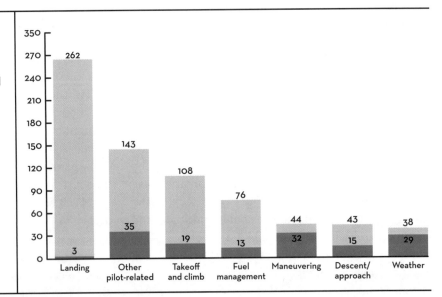

Fig 1-3.

Types of GA landing accidents, including number of accidents and fatal accidents for each type in 2015.[33]

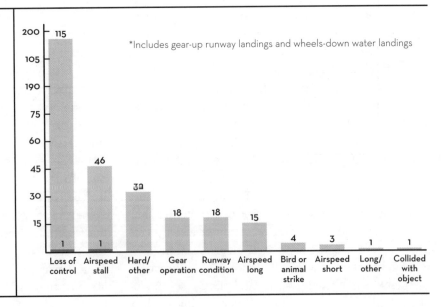

*Includes gear-up runway landings and wheels-down water landings

Of course there are other types of errors, besides stick-and-rudder skill errors, that contribute to landing accidents. The *Nall Report* highlights two major types of errors that GA pilots consistently make: flight planning errors and decision-making errors. These higher level cognitive errors can also lead to landing accidents if a pilot makes a decision to attempt a landing in weather conditions (crosswind, tailwind, turbulence, poor visibility) or runway conditions (short or downsloped runway, or water, snow, ice contamination) that exceed her or his skill level.

One particularly vexing decision error involves pilots' decisions to continue **VFR flight into IMC**. Notice in Figure 1-2 that the lowest number of accidents in 2015 were weather-related accidents, yet they involved the highest proportion of fatal accidents—29 out of 38—producing a lethality rate of 76 percent. That's because the majority of these fatal accidents involved attempted VFR flight into IMC. (The others involved thunderstorms, airframe icing, poor instrument flying technique and turbulence.) In these accidents, VFR pilots either depart into existing adverse weather or, more typically, continue VFR flight into gradually deteriorating weather, and while attempting to make it to their destination they inadvertently fly into IMC (weather conditions below VFR weather minimums) and lose sight of their outside visual references. If they are VFR-only pilots, or pilots with inadequate instrument flying skills, as pointed out previously in NTSB Safety Alert SA-020, pilots either fly under controlled flight into nearby terrain (CFIT) or experience SD and lose control of their aircraft (LOC-I). The latter results in **uncontrolled flight into terrain (UFIT)** or in-flight structural failure due to the pilot overstressing the aircraft while recovering from an unusual attitude. In fact, a study conducted by the University of Illinois in the 1950s found that pilots who lack sufficient instrument flying ability lose control of their airplane in an average of only 178 seconds once they lose outside visual references.[34] It's no wonder that 95 percent of these types of accidents in 2015, like most previous years, were fatal.[35]

Types of Air Carrier Accidents

Figure 1-4 portrays the most common CAST/ICAO CICTT accident categories and associated fatalities from 2009 through 2018 for the worldwide commercial jet fleet.

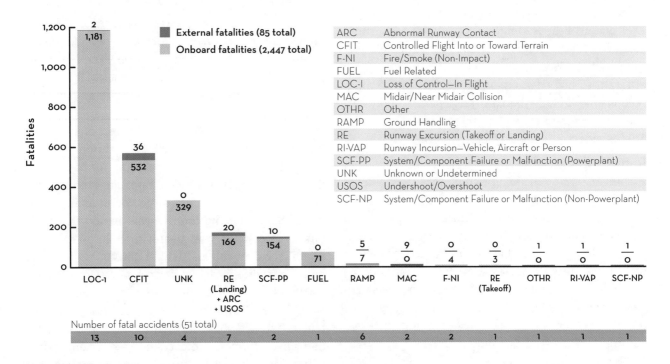

Fig 1-4.

CAST/ICAO CICTT accident categories (defining events) and fatalities for worldwide commercial jet fleet, 2009 through 2018.[36]

Loss of Control in Flight

Like GA, the biggest killer for air carriers was LOC-I at 1,183 deaths for the 10-year period. According to the International Air Transport Association, world-wide, LOC-I was responsible for less than 10 percent of commercial jet and turboprop aircraft accidents from 2011 through 2015, yet was responsible for 45 percent of all fatal accidents.[37] That's because LOC-I in airline operations, as for GA flights, are fatal 90 percent of the time.[38] In-flight LOC has held the top spot since 2006 where its 10-year average first over-took CFIT as the leading cause of fatalities in the worldwide commercial jet airplane fleet.

Similar to GA accidents, CFIT, SCF-PP, FUEL, and UNK occupy the remaining top categories or defining events for fatal accidents.

Controlled Flight into Terrain

Worldwide, CFIT is currently responsible for only 5 percent of airline accidents, yet 16 percent of all fatalities.[39] CFIT has historically been the number one cause of aviation fatalities in commercial airline accidents. A study conducted in the 1990s found that it had claimed the lives of more than 9,000 passengers and airline crew members since commercial passenger jet operations began in the mid-1950s.[40] CFIT was still the leading cause of worldwide airline fatalities between 1987 and 2005—responsible for the loss of 3,735 lives[41]—but since then the number of fatalities has been gradually decreasing, coming second only to LOC-I thanks in large part to improved education, better awareness, and the use of improved CFIT-avoidance technology (e.g., TAWS).

Runway Excursions

A category that you might expect for large, heavy, and fast airplanes, that are required to take off and land on runways with limited lengths, are **runway excursions (RE)**. An RE occurs when an aircraft departs the end (overrun) or the side (veers off) of the runway during a takeoff or landing. A Flight Safety Foundation study discovered that 29 percent of 1,429 major and substantial damage accidents involving worldwide turboprop and turbojet commercial transport aircraft from 1995 through 2008, were REs.[42] For a recent five-year period (2012 through 2016) they were the number one cause of worldwide commercial air transport turbojet and turboprop accidents—responsible for 26 percent

of all accidents. The good news is they accounted for only 6 percent of fatal accidents and less than 1 percent of all fatalities.[43]

From 2009 through 2018, 98 percent of airline REs occurred during landing. As for GA accident statistics—where landing accidents are the number one type of accident—landing excursions point out a major fact of piloting an aircraft: no matter how experienced a pilot you are, the approach and landing are the most difficult phases of flight to safely accomplish. The aircraft must be correctly aligned—both laterally and vertically—and at the correct speed, configuration and position at the touchdown zone in order for a successful landing to occur. In addition, proper control inputs during landing are needed to compensate for runway conditions such as cross-winds or runway surface contamination; otherwise the consequences could be catastrophic.

The elevated level of risk during the approach and landing is visibly illustrated in Figure 1-5 which reveals that just under one-half of the world's fatal commercial jet airplane accidents between 2009 and 2018 occurred during the final approach and landing phases of flight—phases that occupied only about 4 percent of flight time! In fact, 61 percent of fatal accidents and 43 percent of all fatalities for Western-built commercial turbojet aircraft occurred during takeoff, initial climb, final approach, and landing—phases which occupy only 6 percent of flight time. These 10-year average figures have remained relatively the same for decades.

The statistics reveal another aspect of safety we haven't yet discussed. The last two columns in Table 1-2 indicate the disparity between U.S. air carrier and GA accident and fatal accident rates. For example, U.S. passenger air carriers and cargo operators in 2013—the only year during the five-year period that their fatal accident rate was greater than zero—recorded a fatal accident rate of .011 per 100,000 flight hours and GA experienced a fatal accident rate of 1.118 per 100,000 flight hours—more than 100 times the air carrier rate. However, these figures may belie the true difference between them because the denominator used to measure accident rates is number of hours, instead of departures. It can be argued that if the latter was used, the disparity between the two sectors would be reduced. The reasoning goes like this: Larger scheduled commercial airplanes typically fly for a longer duration each flight than do smaller GA aircraft. Consequently, for a given flight time period—let's say four hours—a typical light GA aircraft may actually accomplish several flights (takeoffs and landings) for each flight a commercial airliner does. Therefore, since smaller GA aircraft are exposed to the riskiest stages of flight—takeoff, initial climb, final approach, and landing—more often per given flight-hour, then measuring fatal accidents per departures would narrow the gap slightly between the airline and GA safety record because each departure has the same exposure to these risky phases. Unfortunately, accurate departure statistics for GA aircraft are impossible to obtain, so the FAA, NTSB, and other organizations use information they can obtain: the number of flight hours.

Causes of and Contributing Factors to Airline Accidents

As is true in GA, the majority of airline accidents result from errors committed by the flight crew. Estimates vary widely, depending on what sector, time frame, or region being measured. For example, an evaluation of 329 major U.S. airline accidents and 1,627 commuter/air taxi crashes for the 14 years from 1983 through 1996, found that pilot error was a probable cause in 38 percent of the major airline accidents and 74 percent of commuter/air taxi accidents.[45] However, statistics compiled by Boeing found that flight crew errors were the primary cause of 66 percent of worldwide commercial jet accidents from 1991 through 2000. This was followed by airplane malfunctions (13 percent), adverse weather (8 percent), mainte-

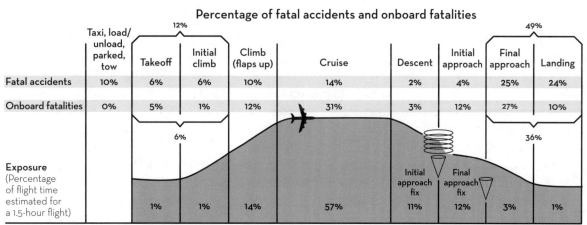

Note: Percentages may not sum to 100% due to numerical rounding.

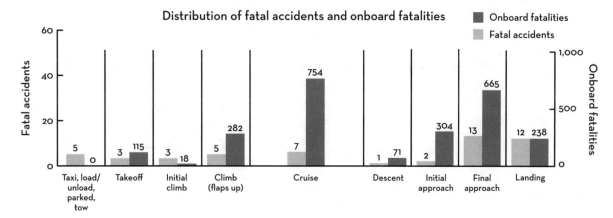

Fig 1-5.

Fatal accidents and onboard fatalities by phase of flight for worldwide commercial jet fleet, 2009 through 2018.[44]

nance (5 percent), miscellaneous/other (5 percent), and airport/ATC (3 percent). There was an improvement for the 10-year period from 1996 through 2005: flight crew errors were the primary cause of only 55 percent of the accidents. This was followed by airplane malfunctions (17 percent), adverse weather (13 percent), miscellaneous/other (7 percent), airport/ATC (5 percent), and maintenance (3 percent).[46, 47] Unfortunately, 2005 was the last year Boeing classified accidents by *primary cause* in their annual statistical summary. During approximately the same time frame, however, the FAA asserted that human error was a contributing factor in 60 to 80 percent of air carrier incidents and accidents.[48]

Two types of airline accidents were previously highlighted: LOC-I (which occurs infrequently yet is the number one cause of fatalities) and RE (which is the most frequent, but leads to fewer casualties). Both, however, are primarily caused by the actions or inactions of the pilots involved.

Poor weather/environmental conditions are involved in many airline LOC-I accidents (e.g., low visibility, IMC, thunderstorms, turbulence, airframe icing, wing-tip vortices), but so too are errors made by pilots. For example, about half of air carrier LOC-I accidents involve an aerodynamic stall/spin, and the percentage is even higher in GA. Contributing factors include improper handling of the flight controls, poor monitoring and cross-checking, and failure to adhere to SOPs. Other errors include incorrect use of systems, radios and automation; improper checklist usage or non-usage; failure to conduct required verbal call-outs; unnecessary penetration of adverse weather; and poor internal (pilot-to-pilot) communication.[49] Flight crews are often caught unaware in LOC-I incidents/accidents because they fail to complete a task (or tasks) they were supposed to do, like noticing diminishing airspeed (monitoring failure) or activating the anti-ice equipment. They often experience a startle reflex, a surprised reaction that results in an involuntary delayed response, no response or even an incorrect one.[50] Crews have failed to notice decreasing airspeed while troubleshooting minor malfunctions, and have failed to properly detect and/or recover from stall/spin scenarios.

Adverse runway conditions are involved in many REs (tailwind, crosswind, runway contamination), but the vast majority are caused by improper actions of the flight crew. The top contributors to landing excursions—the most prevalent type of RE—include an unstable approach (speed high or fast; angle shallow, steep, or variable; long, hard, or fast touchdown), poor pilot technique during landing (directional control, braking), and the failure to conduct a go-around during an obvious unstable approach.

Human Causes vs. Machine Causes

Only two types of accidents have been the primary focus in this chapter: LOC-I and landing accidents in the GA sector, and LOC-I and RE accidents in commercial air transport. As noted, these accidents result from a combination of skill and decision errors made by pilots, and only very few involve aircraft malfunctions. Unfortunately, this is the case for most other categories of aircraft accidents, including CFIT, MAC, unintended flight in IMC, **runway incursions (RI)** abnormal runway contact (ARC), loss of control on the ground (LOC-G), airframe icing (ICE), collisions with obstacles during takeoff or landing (CTOL), FUEL, and landing off the runway (undershoot/overshoot, USOS).

Air transportation has evolved into the fastest and safest mode of transporting people and goods over long distances. Its enviable safety record hasn't come about by chance, however. The trail of tragic accidents that troubled the industry—especially in its early days—motivated society, through accident investigation agencies such as the NTSB and the Transportation Safety Board of Canada, and regulatory bodies like the FAA and Transport Canada, to learn what happened and take measures to reduce their reoccurrence. The following are just some of the outcomes these measures have produced:

- Increased powerplant, airframe, and systems reliability;
- Sophisticated onboard safety technologies, such as airborne weather radar, flight management systems, global positioning system navigation, head-up displays and guidance systems, synthetic vision systems, ACAS, and TAWS;
- Safety-supportive infrastructure, such as increased dispatch capabilities, flight monitoring/tracking systems, better-designed airports, and improved weather information delivery, ATC and air navigation systems;

- Organizational practices designed to enhance safety, such as supportive incident reporting systems (ASAP) and safety management systems (SMS), Line Operation Safety Audits (LOSA) and Flight Operations Quality Assurance (FOQA) programs;
- Better education, not just for flight crew, but others involved in a supporting role; and
- A stricter regulatory environment.

Yet, despite these continuing improvements, aviation accidents still occur. And pilots—even well-trained and experienced ones—are primarily responsible for them. What we've witnessed during aviation's evolutionary history is that aircraft design and reliability have significantly improved, but the people who fly them haven't evolved nearly as quickly. As David Beaty writes in his provocatively titled book, *The Naked Pilot*, "the machine, the technology, has advanced more in a hundred years than man's brain has in a hundred thousand."[51] So, even as the overall number and rate of accidents have fortunately decreased, and the safety performance of flight crews has improved with time (*see* Figure 1-1), the result of the rapid improvement in the reliability of aviation technology has, by default, elevated the relative proportion of accidents caused by human failure on the flight deck (Figure 1-6).

In spite of the fact that human failure looks high in Figure 1-6, pilot performance on the flight deck has actually significantly improved—as evidenced by the reduction in the pilot-caused accident rate over the years—but it has been painfully slow, and especially so in parts of the world where the aviation industry is still emerging from its developing stage.

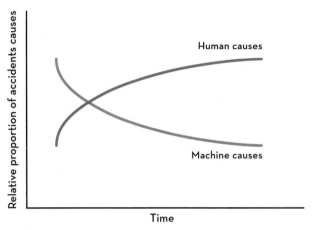

Fig 1-6.

The relative proportion of accidents caused by human and machine failure.[52]

You've learned in this chapter that flying—especially scheduled commercial passenger transport—is the safest mode of transportation. But you've also learned that fatal and non-fatal accidents involving aircraft still occur—especially in GA—and that the primary cause of the majority of these involve errors made by the pilots who fly them. Chapter 2 introduces some of the reasons pilots make errors and Chapter 3 describes how the discipline of human factors helps crew members and others involved in aviation safety understand, recognize, and take measures designed to mitigate the impact of these errors.

Endnotes

1. Ian Savage, "Comparing the Fatality Risks in United States Transportation Across Modes and Over Time," *Research in Transportation Economics* 43 (July 2013): 9–22.

2. Ibid. The lives lost from the hijacking of four U.S. passenger airplanes on September 11, 2001, are not included in aviation accident deaths or airline fatal accident statistics because these were deliberate criminal acts of sabotage and terrorism.

3. There are various ways to measure accident rates in aviation. Using passenger miles traveled accounts for the number of people and their level of exposure, which seems to be the easiest way to compare statistics between different transportation modes. A passenger mile is 1 passenger traveling 1 mile: 1,000 passenger-miles could be 5 passengers traveling 200 miles or 20 passengers traveling 50 miles.

4. Information adapted from Savage, "Comparing the Fatality Risks in United States," 14.

5. Savage, "Comparing the Fatality Risks in United States."

6. Federal Aviation Administration, *FAA Aerospace Forecast: Fiscal Years 2019–2039* (Washington, DC: 2019).

7. Airlines for America, *The Airline Industry* (n.d.). Available at www.airlines.org/industry/.

8. U.S. Bureau of Transportation Statistics, *U.S. Air Carrier Traffic Statistics through May 2018* (Washington, DC: U.S. Bureau of Transportation Statistics). Available at www.transtats.bts.gov/TRAFFIC/.

9. U.S. Bureau of Transportation Statistics, *2017 Annual and December U.S. Airline Traffic Data* (Washington, DC: U.S. Bureau of Transportation Statistics). Available at www.bts.dot.gov/newsroom/2017-annual-and-december-us-airline-traffic-data.

10. General Aviation Manufacturers Association, *2016 General Aviation Statistical Databook & 2017 Industry Outlook* (2017).

11. General Aviation Manufacturers Association, *The Wide Wings and Rotors of General Aviation: The Industry's Economic and Community Impact on the United States* (2015).

12. Pricewaterhouse Coopers, *Contribution of General Aviation to the US Economy in 2013* (February 11, 2015).

13. National Transportation Safety Board (NTSB), *Summary of US Civil Aviation Accidents for Calendar Years 2013, 2014, 2015, 2016 and 2017.* Available at www.ntsb.gov/investigations/data/Pages/aviation_stats.aspx.

14. U.S. Bureau of Transportation Statistics, *National Transportation Statistics 2017: Table 2-14: U.S. General Aviation Safety Data* (Washington, DC: U.S. Bureau of Transportation Statistics, 2017). Available at www.bts.gov/content/us-general-aviationa-safety-data.

15. Australia Transport Safety Bureau, *Aviation Occurrence Statistics, 2006 to 2015* (Canberra City, Australia: ATSB, January 11, 2017). Australia makes a distinction between high-capacity and low-capacity regular public air transport (RPT) operations. The former is the closest to the U.S. definition of scheduled air carriers.

16. Transportation Safety Board of Canada, *Statistical Summary: Air Occurrences in 2017* (last modified June 28, 2018). *See* Table 2, *Occurrences involving Canadian-registered aircraft 2007–2017*, and Table 4, *Aircraft accident fatalities 2007–2017*. Available at www.tsb.gc.ca/eng/stats/aviation/2017/ssea-ssao-2017.asp.

17. See descriptions of these reporting/monitoring programs in the *Glossary* at the end of this book. Three of these have been simply described as what the crew is saying (ASAP), what the airplane is saying (FOQA), and what a fly on the wall on the flight deck would say (LOSA).

18. Airplanes manufactured in the Commonwealth of Independent States or the Union of Soviet Socialist Republics are excluded because of the lack of operational data.

19. Boeing Commercial Airplanes, *Statistical Summary of Commercial Jet Airplane Accidents: Worldwide Operations, 1959–2018* (Seattle, WA: September 2019). The most recent summary can be found at www.boeing.com/resources/boeingdotcom/company/about_bca/pdf/statsum.pdf.

20. Boeing Commercial Airplanes, *Statistical Summary of Commercial Jet Airplane Accidents: Worldwide Operations, 1959–2018* (Seattle, WA: Boeing, September 2019). Used with permission.

21. Calculated from U.S. Bureau of Transportation Statistics, "Table 2-9: U.S. Air Carrier Safety Data," *National Transportation Statistics 2018* (Washington, DC: U.S. Bureau of Transportation Statistics, 2018.). Available at www.BTS.gov/bts/bts/bts-publications/national-transportation-statistics/national-transportation-statistics-previous.

22. United States Government Accountability Office (GAO), *General Aviation Safety: Additional FAA Efforts Could Help Identify and Mitigate Safety Risks.* Report to Congressional Committees, Report No. GAO-13-36 (Washington, DC: U.S. GAO, October 2012).

23. Analysis of data presented in "General Aviation Data Spreadsheet in MS Excel format (data updated on October 31, 2019)," National Transportation Safety Board, *Aviation: Data & Stats, 2017 NTSB US Civil Aviation Accidents Statistics.* Available at www.ntsb.gov/investigations/data/Pages/AviationDataStats2017.aspx#.

24. United States GAO, *General Aviation Safety: Additional FAA Efforts Could Help Identify and Mitigate Safety Risks.*

25. The definition of an aviation occurrence varies slightly between countries, but is generally defined as an accident or an incident. 49 CFR §830.2 defines an accident as an occurrence associated with the operation of an aircraft which takes place between the time any person boards the aircraft with the intention of flight and all such persons have disembarked, and in which any person suffers death or serious injury, or in which the aircraft receives substantial damage. An incident is defined as an occurrence other than an accident, associated with the operation of an aircraft, which affects or could affect the safety of operations.

26. Federal Aviation Administration, *Fact Sheet – General Aviation Safety* (July 30, 2018). Available at www.faa.gov/news/fact_sheets/news_story.cfm?newsId=21274.

27. NTSB, *Aviation: Data & Stats, 2015 NTSB US Civil Aviation Accidents Statistics.* Available at www.ntsb.gov/investigations/data/Pages/AviationDataStats2015.aspx#.

28. National Transportation Safety Board Safety Alerts are available at www.ntsb.gov/safety/safety-alerts/Pages/default.aspx.

29. General Aviation Joint Steering Committee (GAJSC), *SCF-PP Working Group System Component Failure – Powerplant Report* (June 23, 2016).

30. United States GAO, *General Aviation Safety: Additional FAA Efforts Could Help Identify and Mitigate Safety Risks*, 12.

31. AOPA Air Safety Institute, *26th Joseph T. Nall Report: General Aviation Accidents in 2014* (Frederick, MD: AOPA Air Safety Institute, 2017).

32. AOPA Air Safety Institute, *27th Joseph T. Nall Report: General Aviation Accidents in 2015* (Frederick, MD: AOPA Air Safety Institute, 2018). Used with permission.

33. Ibid. Used with permission.

34. Leslie A. Bryan, Jesse W. Stonecipher and Karl Aron, "180-Degree Turn Experiment," *Aeronautics Bulletin* 52.11 (Urbana, IL: University of Illinois, 1954).

35. AOPA Air Safety Institute, *27th Joseph T. Nall Report: General Aviation Accidents in 2015* (Frederick, MD: AOPA Air Safety Institute, 2018).

36. Boeing Commercial Airplanes, *Statistical Summary of Commercial Jet Airplane Accidents: Worldwide Operations*, 1959–2018 (Seattle, WA: Boeing, September 2019). Used with permission.

37. International Air Transport Association (IATA), *Environmental Factors Affecting Loss of Control In-Flight: Best Practice for Threat Recognition & Management* (Montreal, Canada: 2016).

38. International Air Transport Association, *Annual Review 2017* (Montreal, Canada: 2017).

39. IATA, *Annual Review 2017*.

40. Federal Aviation Administration, *Controlled Flight Into Terrain Education and Training Aid* (Washington, DC: FAA, September 1997).

41. Boeing Commercial Airplanes, *Statistical Summary of Commercial Jet Airplane Accidents: Worldwide Operations*, 1959–2005 (Seattle, WA: Boeing, May 2006).

42. Flight Safety Foundation, *Reducing the Risk of Runway Excursions* (Alexandria, VA: May 2009).

43. International Air Transport Association, *Safety Report 2016*, 53rd ed. (Montreal, Canada: April 2017).

44. Boeing Commercial Airplanes, *Statistical Summary of Commercial Jet Airplane Accidents: Worldwide Operations*, 1959–2018 (Seattle, WA: Boeing, September 2019). Used with permission.

45. Guohua Li, Susan P. Baker, Jurek G. Grabowski, and George W. Rebok "Factors Associated with Pilot Error in Aviation Crashes," *Aviation, Space, and Environmental Medicine* 72 (January 2001): 52-58.

46. Boeing Commercial Airplanes, *Statistical Summary*, 1959–2005.

47. Boeing Commercial Airplanes, *Statistical Summary of Commercial Jet Airplane Accidents: Worldwide Operations*, 1959–2000 (Seattle, WA: Boeing, June 2001).

48. Federal Aviation Administration, *Crew Resource Management Training*, AC 120-51E (Washington, DC: FAA, January 22, 2004).

49. IATA, *Environmental Factors Affecting Loss of Control In-Flight*.

50. Wayne L. Martin, Patrick S. Murray and Paul R. Bates, "The Effects of Startle on Pilots During Critical Events: A Case Study Analysis," *Proceedings of 30th EAAP Conference: Aviation Psychology & Applied Human Factors-Working Towards Zero Accidents* (Sardinia, Italy: September 2012): 388–394.

51. David Beaty, *The Naked Pilot: The Human Factor in Aircraft Accidents* (Shrewsbury, U.K.: Airlife Publishing, 1995): 10.

52. Adapted from International Civil Aviation Organization, *Accident Prevention Manual*, ICAO Doc 9422-AN/923, 1st ed. (Montreal, Canada: 1984), and reproduced by permission from ICAO.

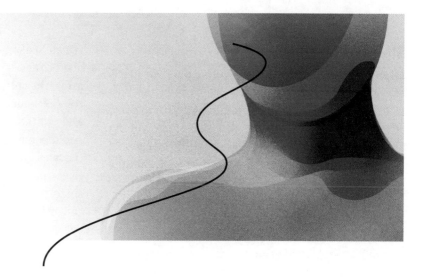

2

A sampling of headlines recently gleaned from news sources highlights the focus of this chapter:

- *NTSB blames pilot error for plane that skidded off snowy LaGuardia runway*—ABC News
- *Japan blames pilot error for 2015 Black Hawk crash off Okinawa*—Stars and Stripes
- *TSB (Canada) blames pilot error, bad weather for deadly B.C. float plane crash*—Globe and Mail
- *Army blames pilot error in 2015 helicopter crash in Colorado*—U.S. News & World Report
- *Pilots Blamed For Canadian Helicopter Crash In Afghanistan 4 Years Ago*—Huffington Post
- *NTSB blames Delta pilots for wrong-airport landing*—Fox News
- *NTSB blames pilot error for Ohio jet crash that killed 9*—Associated Press

In the previous chapter we established that the majority of aviation accidents are due to pilot errors—about 75 percent for GA and anywhere from 55 to 80 percent for commercial air carriers. In this chapter we explore the nature of these errors and briefly outline the possible reasons that pilots make them.

Human Error Defined

There are several definitions of error, but at the most basic level an **error** occurs when a person fails to perform the correct action or performs the wrong action for a particular circumstance. In the context of aviation, flight crew error is more specifically defined as an "action or inaction that leads to a deviation from crew or organizational intentions or expectations."[1]

To err is human.

Flight Crew Error

If not caught and corrected for, errors of commission and omission, as they are sometimes called, could lead to an **undesired aircraft state (UAS)**. The latter is just what it sounds like: an undesired aircraft position, condition, or attitude that compromises safety and, if not corrected, could lead to an **aircraft incident** or an accident. Examples of such states include an incorrect flap or landing gear setting, penetration of adverse weather, an unstable approach (too high, low, fast, or slow), or unintentionally taxiing across an active runway.

Basic Error Types

There are also various ways to classify errors and several categories and types have been identified. Three common errors humans make are mistakes, slips, and lapses.

Mistakes

According to renowned error researcher James Reason, a **mistake** occurs when you fail to formulate the correct assessment and/or action needed for the situation. This may result from misdiagnosing a situation or problem, such as misinterpreting weather reports, or misperceiving visual cues during a night visual approach resulting in inadvertently flying the airplane too low to the ground.

Slips and Lapses

Slips and **lapses** occur when you have properly understood the situation and determined the best course of action, but you unintentionally fail to carry out the action correctly (slip) or forget to carry it out altogether (lapse). An example of the former would be inadvertently raising the landing gear handle instead of the flap handle. Actions prone to slip errors are often well-rehearsed skills that are conducted without much conscious thought, and are therefore more susceptible to being captured by similar well-learned actions, such as raising the lever for the gear instead of the flaps, or setting the incorrect missed approach altitude in the mode control panel (MCP).[2]

An example of a lapse—the failure to implement the chosen action—would be forgetting to listen to the automatic terminal information service (ATIS) to determine recent weather conditions at your landing airport, forgetting to reset the altitude to the missed approach altitude in the MCP, or forgetting to set the flaps to the appropriate flap setting before takeoff. As will be discussed in our chapter on memory (Chapter 16), this latter error is an example of a prospective memory failure and is responsible for several departure accidents that have claimed the lives of hundreds of people in the United States and elsewhere.

Human Factors Analysis and Classification System

A helpful framework in which to better understand human error—especially in the context of aviation flight operations—is the **human factors analysis and classification system (HFACS)**, developed by researchers Scott Shappell and Donald Wiegmann. Based on the findings of aircraft accident investigations and human error research—including those of James Reason—the classification system was developed to assist investigators to more accurately determine the human causes of aviation accidents. The HFACS model includes errors made not only by front end operators such as pilots, air traffic controllers, and mechanics, but by others in the system including those made by management. From a pilot's perspective, understanding management error is important since the actions of others within an organization can influence a pilot's own behavior on the flight deck. We will refer to the model throughout this chapter, but the immediate discussion below briefly describes the categories of errors made by pilots.[3]

The classification system identifies two types of **unsafe acts** flight crews commit that could jeopardize safety: errors and violations.[4] Errors are those unintended mistakes, slips, and lapses that afflict all humans. The HFACS model also identifies three basic types of error that pilots generally make: perceptual, skill-based, and decision errors. Violations, on the other hand, involve intentional noncompliance with regulations and procedures that are designed to ensure safe flight operations. The categories of errors and violations identified in the HFACS model are summarized in Figure 2-1 and are used in this chapter as a basic framework in which to elaborate and expand upon the topic of human error.

Perceptual Errors

When we fail to correctly interpret stimuli (inputs) received from the outside world through our eyes, ears, and other senses, we may commit a **perceptual error**. For example, we may fail to take evasive action because we missed important visual cues indicating that our aircraft is on a collision course with another aircraft. Or, we may allow our airplane to fly too low because we misperceived our approach angle while

Fig 2-1.

Categories of operator error in the HFACS model.[5]

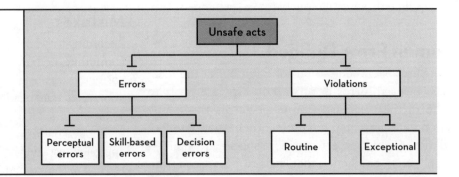

conducting a visual approach in impoverished visual conditions such as in poor visibility, at night, or over featureless terrain. Perceptual errors also involve other senses, such as our auditory and somatosensory senses. For example, we may misunderstand a verbal clearance from ATC resulting in inadvertent unauthorized airspace penetration. Or, while flying in IMC, we may allow the aircraft to enter an unusual attitude because we succumbed to spatial disorientation. The topics of visual, auditory, and spatial perception are addressed in separate chapters in this book.

Skill-Based Errors

Another type of error in the HFACS model involves psychomotor performance, such as stick-and-rudder skills and what is sometimes known in aviation vernacular as *knobology* skills—the ability to correctly manipulate knobs, dials, and controls to achieve a desired outcome. These **skill-based errors** involve improper operation of flight controls, aircraft systems, and other components, including automated systems. The model delineates three kinds of skill-based errors—attention, memory, and technique errors.

Attention Errors

Since most psychomotor stick-and-rudder skills involved in flying an aircraft are well-learned, and even overlearned, they usually occur at a subconscious level. However, any breakdown in conscious attention could lead to errors such as failure to notice diminishing airspeed on the airspeed indicator, or incorrectly inputting information into the flight management system, or not executing the correct input using knobs or dials, a phenomenon sometimes called *finger trouble* (e.g., wrong frequency on radio). The topic of attention is addressed in Chapter 14.

Memory Errors

Forgetfulness can also lead to skill-based errors. An example of this type of error noted previously is a lapse: the failure to implement the chosen action. Forgetting to lower the landing gear or flaps before landing or missing a checklist item are examples of skill-based errors induced by a failure in memory. This topic is addressed in Chapter 16.

Technique Errors

The final type of skill-based error involves what usually comes to mind when thinking about skills—faulty technique. Imprecise control inputs, over- and under-controlling aircraft controls, failure to properly use automation, and the failure to effectively manipulate the flight controls and power/thrust to achieve a stabilized approach are just a few examples of technique errors. An example of a skill-based technique error, or handling error, recently occurred in New York while landing a Boeing B-737 at LaGuardia Airport. Eastern Air Lines Flight 3452, carrying then U.S. vice-presidential candidate Mike Pence, overran Runway 22 and came to a stop 170 feet past the end of the runway after transiting a bed of crushable concrete in the runway's **engineered materials arresting system**. Even though decision making and other factors contributed to this accident, the NTSB found that the first officer (FO), who was the pilot flying, flared too high, was slow to reduce thrust to idle, and failed to get the jet's wheels on the ground within the first third of the runway. He allowed it to float too long before touching down more than 4,200 feet past the threshold of the 7,000-foot runway, leaving less than 2,800 feet of runway surface remaining for the aircraft to decelerate and stop (NTSB Identification No: DCA17IA020).

Decision Errors

In this RE overrun incident, skill-based errors morphed into a decision error when the FO failed to conduct a go-around. Flawed decision making by flight crews of commercial transport jets and pilots of GA aircraft is responsible for numerous aircraft accidents. **Decision errors** were the second leading cause of pilot-error-induced commercial air-taxi accidents in the United States between 1983 and 2002.[6] A recent study of 2,801 U.S. GA accidents also found the pilot's actions, decision making, or cockpit management was the cause of 70 percent of fatal airplane accidents.[7] According to the HFACS framework, decision errors include procedural decision errors, poor decisions, and problem solving errors. Decision making is addressed at greater length in Chapter 17.

Procedural Decision Errors

Flight operations are highly procedural, especially on the flight decks of scheduled commercial airliners. Standard operating procedures (SOPs), memorized procedural flow checks, and written or electronic checklists are all designed to assist crew members in accomplishing tasks in a certain defined way to enhance safety. Procedural decision errors occur when pilots incorrectly follow these procedures. For example, the FAA examined data for a 10-year period and found that improperly following or not using checklists was implicated in 279 U.S. civilian Part 91, 135, and 121 aircraft accidents.[8]

Poor Decisions

Poor decisions can occur when you have to make a choice among options for which there is no clear-cut SOP or checklist guidance to aid you. For example, when choosing whether to continue, return, or divert elsewhere in the face of deteriorating weather conditions, you might misdiagnose the actual weather situation and choose the wrong action, or you may be influenced by unconscious biases and continue the flight even though you are not entirely sure it is the right decision. Poor decisions made by GA pilots often reveal themselves in pre- and in-flight planning and when flying in conditions beyond their ability and experience. Both airline and GA pilots demonstrate poor decision making when failing to conduct a missed approach or go-around when weather and other conditions indicate it is the most prudent thing to do.

In 2014, US Airways Flight 1702, an Airbus A320, received substantial damage and came to rest on the edge of the runway at Philadelphia International Airport, in Philadelphia, Pennsylvania, after the captain rejected the takeoff (RTO) following rotation on Runway 27L. It should be noted that pilots of transport category airplanes should not abort a takeoff above V_1 speed (sometimes called takeoff decision speed), which is at or below rotation speed (V_R), and that conducting an RTO above V_1 will almost certainly result in an RE (overrun). Since the crew received a confusing electronic centralized aircraft monitoring (ECAM) message during the takeoff roll and a RETARD aural alert telling the crew to reduce thrust levers to idle, the captain deemed it was unsafe to continue the departure. However, the airplane was performing as it should have. The reason for their troubles, according to the NTSB investigation, was the crew's failure to follow SOPs. The captain's decision to reject the takeoff after the airplane had rotated, the crew's failure to verify the correct departure runway before pushback from the gate, and the captain's failure to move the thrust levers to the takeoff/go-around detent in response to the ECAM message, were all contrary to the airline's SOPs. The captain also fell victim to skill-based technique errors when his erratic pitch control inputs caused the aircraft to bounce into the air after the throttle levers had been returned to idle (NTSB Identification No: DCA14MA081).

Problem Solving Errors

On rare occasions a pilot may face a situation for which not only is there no SOP or checklist procedure available, but a proper diagnosis and solution may be difficult to determine. These *ill-defined problems* as they are often called can be very challenging for pilots. In these situations pilots must rely on their previous knowledge, skill, and experience to effectively resolve the issue. A problem-solving error occurs when they can't. An example of an exceptionally successful resolution of an ill-defined problem occurred when captain "Sully" Sullenberger and his co-pilot landed their A320 on the Hudson River three minutes after losing both engines after flying through a flock of birds at 2,800 feet above ground level on departure from Runway 04 at LaGuardia Airport. The checklists really couldn't resolve this for them. For example, the dual-engine failure checklist was written for such a catastrophe to occur above 20,000 feet and required a minimum engine relight speed of 300 knots, neither of which they had nor, given the altitude at which the aircraft was at, would possibly acquire. The crew had few landing locations their airplane could possibly glide to, but fortunately they made the right decision, ultimately choosing the best one under the circumstances (Report No: NTSB/AAR-10/03).

Communication Errors

Some errors may encompass two or more of the three major HFACS error types. For example, communication failures can involve perceptual errors and decision errors, which can manifest themselves in skill-based errors. Though not specifically categorized as a major error type within the HFACS model, both internal (crew-to-crew) and external (crew-to-others) communication errors have contributed to aircraft accidents. These involve messages with incomplete or inaccurate content, ambiguous phraseology, confusing messages, and outright failure to communicate (e.g., failure to make appropriate verbal callouts). For example, in the early morning hours at Birmingham-Shuttlesworth International Airport, in Birmingham, Alabama, United Parcel Service Flight 1354, an Airbus A300 cargo flight, crashed short of Runway 18 during a nonprecision instrument approach, killing both pilots. The crew intended to conduct a *profile approach* using a glide path generated by the flight management computer to provide vertical path guidance from the final approach fix to the decision altitude (DA), as opposed to the step-down method (sometimes called the "dive and drive" method) that does not provide vertical guidance and requires the crew to refer to the altimeter to ensure that the airplane remains above the minimum crossing altitude at each of the approach fixes. The NTSB identified several communication errors that contributed to the accident: The company dispatcher, though aware of a runway closure, approach limitations, and low ceilings, failed to discuss these items with the captain; the captain failed to re-brief the approach after switching the autopilot from the profile final approach mode to the vertical speed mode, reducing the FO's awareness of what was going on; and the existence of variable ceilings on final approach—which the NTSB concluded may have influenced the captain's decision making—was not communicated to the flight crew because the *Remarks* section of the weather report (where this information was found) was automatically deleted in the dissemination system used by the airline and was not entered into the ATIS by the air traffic controllers (Report No: NTSB/AAR-14/02). The multi-faceted aspects of auditory perception and communication are specifically addressed in Chapters 7, 13, and 19.

Violations

An important distinction needs to be made between errors and violations. The former are unintentional errors or mistakes (the pilot may not know better) while **violations**, sometimes called *willful noncompliance*, are decisions that intentionally involve noncompliance with regulations, rules, and procedures that are designed to ensure safe flight operations (the pilot knows better but still refuses to comply). Violations can be routine or exceptional.

Routine Violations

Routine violations involve somewhat habitual noncompliance with rules and regulations. For example, a pilot may "push the weather" to get her passengers to their destination, and as long as they arrive safely, the company's management may turn a blind eye and overlook such behavior. Or, because he has gotten away with it before, a pilot may routinely operate his aircraft above its maximum certificated takeoff weight to avoid having to deal with the headache of off-loading passengers or baggage. Or, an experienced instrument pilot may make a habit of descending slightly below the DA or minimum descent altitude/height without acquiring adequate outside visual references. Other examples include performing unauthorized aerobatic maneuvers or unnecessary low flying. Routine violations often point to the negative influence that other people—company management, passengers, etc.—can sometimes play in a pilot's behavior (*see* Chapter 18). One of the advantages of the HFACS model is it can help identify these influences.

Exceptional Violations

Unlike routine violations, exceptional violations are just that: rare. An otherwise responsible, conscientious pilot, who may even take pride in doing things by the book may, for whatever reason, decide not to follow that book. These may include any of the behaviors indicative of routine violations. A private pilot may skip a weather briefing because it's getting dark and he needs to hurry, or a pilot may continue flight in marginal weather because she doesn't want to miss an important appointment. An airline pilot may fail to request a second deicing before departing from a snowy airport, fail to comply with the sterile flight deck rule (*see* Chapter 14), or fail to execute a missed approach when SOP parameters are not met. Whatever the nature of the intentional violation, the reason it is exceptional is the pilots involved would normally never think of breaking the rules, but for whatever reason—sometimes even unknown to themselves—in certain circumstances, they do.

It should be noted that, except in extremely rare cases of sabotage or suicide, intentional violations are not done to deliberately cause an accident. Pilots sometimes deliberately fail to follow a rule or procedure because they don't think that doing so will do any harm—their risk assessment is faulty. Or, they commit a violation because they believe it will better facilitate the accomplishment of the flight, even if they may know it likely involves an elevated level of risk. Fortunately, most pilots avoid intentional noncompliance with safety rules and procedures, but when they don't it's usually because of other situational factors or influences in their social or working environment. For example, a deliberate violation of a rule may be necessary (and acceptable according to 14 CFR §91.3) during an emergency, such as breaking the 250-knot indicated airspeed limit rule below 10,000 feet above mean sea level (MSL) to expedite a landing as soon as possible because of an onboard fire or medical emergency. Apart from this, however, it is important to know how situational and social factors can influence your decision making. We discuss these kinds of pressures throughout this book, particularly in Chapter 18.

Why do Pilots Err?

Since errors and violations committed by pilots are responsible for the majority of aircraft accidents, we need to know what causes them in order to reduce their frequency. Just as we cannot prescribe a cure for an illness if we don't know what's causing it, we cannot reduce flight crew errors if we don't know what causes them.

Several error models and attempts at modeling human error have developed over the years. What you may have guessed is there are numerous reasons why people err. The following discussion summarizes six basic frameworks identified by the creators of HFACS which attempt to explain the reasons why people make errors.[9]

The Aeromedical Perspective

The aeromedical approach to human error suggests that some errors may be linked to a medical or physiological condition. Just as driving performance (perception, reaction time, etc.) is degraded when the driver is suffering from an illness, a cold, sleep deprivation, hangover, and the like, so too is pilot performance adversely affected when these types of maladies are present.

But pilots are also susceptible to unique physiological phenomena that earth-dwellers normally do not experience. For example, because of the drop in atmospheric pressure at higher altitudes, pilots must fly in pressurized cabins or breathe supplemental oxygen when flying above 10,000 feet MSL for any appreciable length of time. Should a rapid decompression occur at airline cruising altitudes, pilots must also react quickly because their time of useful consciousness is short. They must also be wary of decompression sickness, especially above 25,000 feet MSL.

Pilots are also sometimes subject to excessive noise and extremes in temperature and, in pres-surized cabins, low humidity levels that contribute to dehydration and fatigue (the latter discussed at length in Chapter 10). Additional challenges unique to the flight environment include jet lag (circadian dysrhythmia) from crossing several time zones and SD, a phenomenon whereby conflicting signals are communicated to the brain when a pilot lacks adequate outside visual references—in IMC, at night, or both—that provide cues as to which way is up.

Any of these physiological factors could lead to pilot incapacitation, the inability to carry out the duties required to fly an aircraft, which may manifest itself in skill-based, perceptual, or decision errors.

The Cognitive Perspective

Humans also make errors because of psychological limitations. These are not psychological (mental) disorders, but rather normal limitations inherent in human thinking and information processing. Cognitive psychology, the study of human thought and behavior, uses the information processing approach to describe and study human thought processes. Using the analogy of computer inputs, processing, and outputs, we receive stimuli (inputs, information) from the outside world through our senses (eyes, ears, etc.) that are processed at several stages before we make a decision and act upon them (outputs). We first must sense the stimulus, then perceive what it is means before we can act upon it, if we act on it at all. The information likely relates to something that is previously stored in our long-term memory, so we may pay attention to the information to retain it in our working memory before we decide what to do with it. Finally, we will make an assessment of the situation upon which to base our subsequent decision(s).

Errors occur when there is a breakdown in any of these information processing stages—sensation, attention, perception, memory, assessment, decision making, etc. For example, you may fail to see (sense) another aircraft on a collision course with yours because you were not conducting an adequate visual scan (attention). Or you may see it but misinterpret (perception) its trajectory thinking it is not on a collision course. Or you may see it, make an accurate assessment that it poses a threat, and decide (decision making) to take evasive action, but turn the aircraft in wrong direction. Or you may decide to turn in the correct direction but improperly execute the chosen action. An error in any step along the way could lead to a UAS.

The Psychosocial Perspective

Airline pilots not only interact with fellow crew members in the front of the airplane and cabin crew in the back, but they work with several other important players who also contribute to the safe arrival of any given flight. These include dispatchers, maintenance personnel, ground personnel (marshalling agents, tug operators, wing walkers, line-service fueling and de-icing personnel), ATC, and flight service specialists. Other people, including passengers and even people who are not directly involved in the flight (e.g., people at your destination), can also influence your behavior. Though not as extensive, single-pilot and private pilot flight operations also are influenced by a network of operational personnel and other people.

The psychosocial perspective on human error suggests that breakdowns in interactions with other people lead to flight crew errors. As noted previously, a major source of error involves **intra-cockpit communication** (crew-to-crew) and **extra-cockpit communication** (crew-to-others). In fact, during a five-year period communication deficiencies were involved in more than 70 percent of 28,000 reports submitted by pilots and air traffic controllers to the National Aeronautics and Space Administration Aviation Safety Reporting System (NASA ASRS).[10] For example, a pilot incorrectly reads back a clearance from ATC and the controller doesn't catch it, resulting in each having a different mental model of the situation. Alternatively, a controller misidentifies an aircraft that has a similar call sign as another aircraft in the vicinity. Sadly, sometimes these communication errors contribute to accidents.

Communication is a critical component of **crew resource management (CRM)**, a set of behaviors used extensively by airline crews that promotes coordination and teamwork for the purpose of facilitating safe and efficient flight operations. Unfortunately, CRM errors have also contributed to accidents and incidents. For example, inadequate crew coordination, monitoring/cross-checking, and communication—all important elements in CRM—were contributing factors in 72, 41, and 33 percent of approach and landing accidents involving turbojet business airplanes between 1991 and 2002, respectively.[11] A

recent study of 113 Part 121 air carrier accidents and incidents that occurred between 2002 and 2012, found 61 percent of accidents and 39 percent of incidents involved breakdowns in CRM.[12]

The Behavioral Perspective

Behaviorism is a branch of psychology premised on the assumption that human behavior is primarily learned and reinforced through rewards. The behavioral perspective then, according to the creators of HFACS, suggests that people make errors because they are rewarded for doing so. If a person is rewarded and feels satisfaction from doing things a certain way, then she or he will be motivated to continue that behavior. Unfortunately, as was briefly alluded to earlier, sometimes pilots are rewarded for deliberate unsafe acts (violations) or even punished for not breaking or bending the rules to get the job done. This type of atmosphere within an organization only reinforces willful noncompliance in the form of routine violations by flight crews.

The Organizational Perspective

Management personnel do not have to encourage or turn a blind eye to deliberate violations to foster error-making by its front-line workers. In fact, they may seemingly do all they can to encourage and reward safe behavior, yet by their organization's unintentional and imperfect actions (or inaction) they can still reduce safety margins. The organizational perspective notes that fallible decisions and errors made by upper-, mid-, and lower-level management within an organization can unintentionally lead to errors made by front-line personnel. For example, the simple act of rewarding flight crews and line personnel for on-time performance—a desireable goal for any airline business—may have the unintended effect of prompting flight crews to take actions that may violate safe operating practices

Several models describing the role organizational structure and management play in accidents have appeared over the years, but none has caught the attention of safety experts working in complex technological systems more than James Reason's organizational accident model, often called the **Swiss cheese model**.

Reason proposes that active failures (errors and violations) made by front-line operators (e.g., pilots, air traffic controllers, mechanics) are the result of latent conditions that reside within an organization. These conditions lie dormant until they combine with local circumstances and active failures to penetrate the defenses an organization has built to prevent an accident. Organizations often use multiple barriers, or defenses—called **defenses-in-depth**—to reduce the chances of an accident or incident: if one fails, there are several more to guard against an accident or incident. Such defenses in aviation usually include training; safety regulations; safe procedures (SOPs, checklists, etc.); safety technology such as warning horns and lights ("bells and whistles"), TAWS, ACAS; and other safeguards such as dispatch, ground support, and ATC services.

Latent conditions are created by fallible decisions made by people higher up in the system who are removed in both time and space from the *sharp end* of the organizational spear. These decisions by chief executive officers and managers involve such tasks as budgeting, forecasting, allocating resources, planning, scheduling, communicating, managing, and auditing. The impact of these decisions spread throughout an organization shaping its **corporate culture** and can create error-producing conditions at the front line of the operation. Examples of such conditions include maintenance failures; inadequate personnel selection, training, and supervision; understaffing, low pay, and poor morale; ambiguous or incomplete procedures; poor communication; inadequate management oversight; and inadequate organizational and regulatory surveillance.

In contrast to what Reason calls *individual accidents*, which are relatively frequent, limited in their defenses and consequences, and often caused by only one individual, *organizational accidents* in high-technology industries like commercial air transportation are rare, have multiple defenses, are often catastrophic involving large numbers of people, and are usually caused by not only the actions of a single front line operator, but by others within the organization who are removed from the accident.[13] You will see some examples of this throughout this book, including the tragic breakup of the space shuttle Challenger discussed in Chapter 18.

Organizational accidents originate from fallible decisions made by those at the top of an organization and deficiencies in line management that create latent conditions (the precursors of unsafe acts) that contribute to, and combine with, active

failures (unsafe acts) made by front-end workers. People began to call Reason's model the Swiss cheese model from the idea that an accident or incident occurs because holes (deficiencies or weaknesses) in the barriers (defenses-in-depth) that are designed to protect an organization from an accident, allow latent conditions and active failures to penetrate them (Figure 2-2).

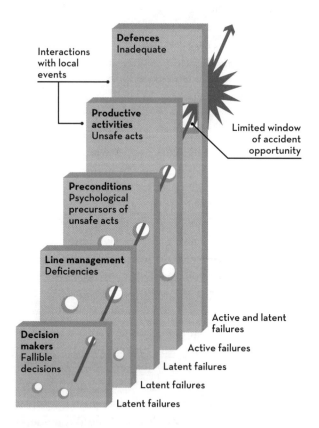

Fig 2-2.

Modified graphical representation of James Reason's Swiss cheese model of accident causation.[14]

The organizational aspects of Reason's framework have been captured and operationalized in the HFACS model, as diagrammed in Figure 2-3. Organizational influences created by decision makers at the top of an organization can lead to unsafe supervision of flight operations creating preconditions for unsafe acts by those on the front line.

The model specifies three types of organizational influences that can create the preconditions for unsafe acts: organizational influences, unsafe supervision and preconditions for unsafe acts. Organizational influences include inadequate resource management such as inappropriate allocation of resources—people, money, facilities, or equipment—to realize the safety needs of a flight organization. Organizational climate includes inadequate policies and a poor corporate culture. And organizational processes contribute to latent conditions when procedures, schedules, and other policies, including safety oversight, are substandard.[15]

The HFACS model also identifies four ways in which supervisors may contribute to unsafe outcomes (Figure 2-3). Inadequate supervision includes fail-ures in training, observing, guiding, tracking, and correcting performance deficiencies. Some organizations may deliberately or inadvertently plan inappropriate flight operations such as scheduling flights with inadequate time for proper briefings or rest periods between flights. Supervisors can also fail to correct a problem by not reporting or correcting unsafe behavior. Unfortunately, to accomplish the profit goals of their organization, some managers may deliberately commit supervisory violations by allowing an unqualified crew to fly a flight, by tolerating crew violations, or by fudging required paperwork.

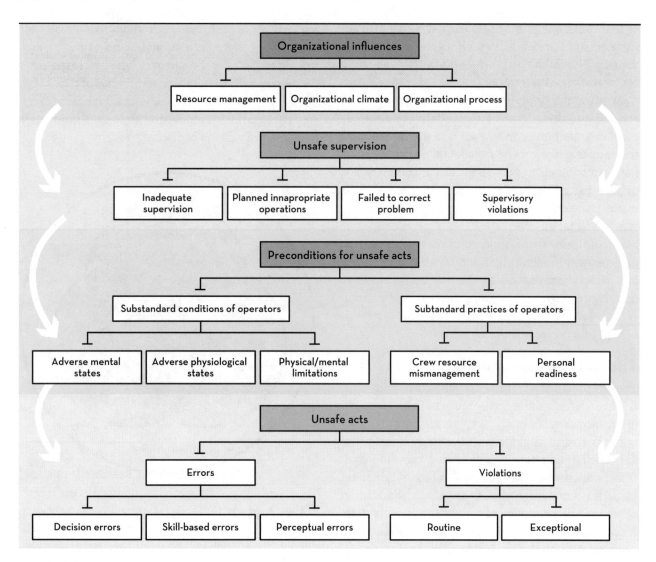

Fig 2-3.

Types of organizational influences, unsafe supervision, and preconditions that can contribute to unsafe acts in the HFACS model.

Finally, these organizational and management shortcomings can create preconditions for unsafe acts in the form of substandard conditions (or states) or substandard practices of flight crew members. A pilot may suffer from an adverse mental state such as stress, task and attention overload, complacency, overconfidence, or other unsafe condition; an adverse physiological state such as a cold or influenza, hypoxia, jet lag, SD, and fatigue; or a physical/mental limitation such as a vision problem, lack of experience, or poor flight skills.

Substandard practices of the operator—the pilot—include his or her failure to effectively practice CRM skills such as communication, assertiveness, or teamwork. Pilots may also exhibit deficiencies in their personal readiness, such as self-medicating, abusing alcohol or drugs while off duty, or showing up for work not fully rested.

It may not be evident that management has anything to do with the substandard condition or practices of flight crews until you dig deeper and find out that the airline's inadequate training may have contributed to poor flight skills, complacency, or poor distraction management; or that crew scheduling practices may have contributed to jet lag, stress, and fatigue.

All of these organizational and management deficiencies are preconditions for a variety of unsafe acts (errors and/or violations) made by flight crews (*see* Figure 2-1 and accompanying discussion). Fortunately, not all unsafe acts lead to an accident, but they do increase the risk of one.

The Systems Perspective

The discussion of a systems approach to human error has been left until the end because such an approach often incorporates many of the error models previously discussed. A **system** is set of components that act together as a whole to achieve a common goal. It includes several subsystems—people, equipment, facilities, tools, procedures—in which the human operator is just one component in the overall system. A failure in one of these subsystems affects the performance of the overall system, including the performance of the human operator at the front end of it.

5M model

Several systems approaches to human error and accident causation have been used in the aviation field. One used by the U.S. Air Force is the **5M model**: man, machine, medium, mission, and management.[16] The *man* is the human operator of the aircraft with all of his or her physiological and psychological limitations; the *machine* is the aircraft with its inherent design, reliability, and operating limitations; the *medium* is the environment the aircraft flies in—time of day (dark or light), weather conditions, cabin temperature/humidity, terrain, etc.; the *mission* is the purpose of the flight and how that may elevate risk levels e.g., a low-level, high-speed, nap-of-the-earth flight at night carries with it greater risk than a local VFR flight on a sunny day); and *management* are those CEOs and managers who are responsible for managing the overall system, including the safety of flight operations. Figure 2-4 is a graphical representation of the 5M model and shows the interaction between the various components of this system.

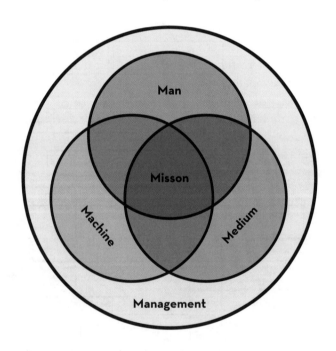

Fig 2-4.

The 5M systems model.[17]

SHELL model

Another popular systems approach used in aviation is the **SHELL model**. Table 2-1 summarizes its main components. Similar to the 5M model, the SHELL approach identifies several components—not just the pilots—that make up the entire system. Similar to other systems models, a mismatch, or deficiency, in one subsystem can induce errors by front end operators.

For example, several components of the SHELL model were evident in the accident of Delta Air Lines Flight 1141. The crew failed to extend the flaps and slats for takeoff which resulted in a violent rolling motion shortly after liftoff from Runway 18L at Dallas-Fort Worth International Airport in Texas. The Boeing B-727 then struck an instrument landing system localizer antenna array approximately 1,000 feet beyond the end of the runway and came to rest about 3,200 feet beyond its departure end. The crew clearly erred by forgetting to properly configure the aircraft for takeoff—a *liveware-crew* problem. However, the NTSB also cited a *hardware* problem— the takeoff configuration warning system failed to alert the crew that the airplane was not properly configured for the takeoff. Other factors contributed to the accident, which killed 14 of the 108 people aboard. For example, the NTSB cited the airline's slow implementation by the company (a *liveware-others* problem) of SOP and checklist changes (also a *software* problem) and the FAA's inadequate oversight (another *liveware-others* problem) in correcting known flight crew deficiencies as contributing factors to the accident (Report No: NTSB/AAR-89/04).

Despite the fact that aircraft design has improved significantly over the years, deficiencies in *hardware* design may still contribute to errors made by pilots. An example of a serious hardware problem involved the poor placement of a fuel selector valve—it was located behind the pilot's left shoulder—in an amateur-built Long-EZ airplane flown by singer-songwriter John Denver, who lost his life after crashing into the Pacific Ocean near Pacific Grove, California. While on a local VFR flight the aircraft ran out of fuel in one tank, and according to the NTSB, the location of the fuel selector handle forced the pilot to turn in his seat to locate and manipulate it, diverting his attention from the operation of the airplane, which in turn likely caused him to inadvertently apply right rudder resulting in loss of aircraft control in flight. The NTSB concluded the pilot should have re-fueled the airplane before departure (a *liveware-crew* error) but the placement of the fuel control valve, along with unmarked fuel quantity sight gauges (a *hardware* deficiency) also led to the accident (NTSB Identification No: LAX98FA008).

Table 2-1. The SHELL systems model.

Designation	Description and examples	Interface mismatch issues
Software	Information—SOPs, checklists, manuals, charts.	Incomplete SOPs, poorly designed checklists, charts difficult to read, instrument approach charts difficult to interpret, etc.
Hardware	Aircraft—design, ease of operation, limitations, maintenance.	Poorly designed cockpit layout and flight instruments, control knobs difficult to reach and displays not easily interpreted, control-display incompatibility, etc.
Environment	Environment—cabin, weather, time of day, terrain, airspace, airports.	Hazardous or unsuitable weather, night, hot or cold cabin temperatures, high terrain, lack of emergency landing spots, irregular runways/helipads, approach obstacles, etc.
Liveware-others	Employer, manager, maintenance technicians, cabin crew, passengers, ATC.	Employer expectations, poor corporate safety culture, passenger expectations, crew scheduling and dispatch deficiencies, ATC (talks too fast, uses non-standard phraseology), etc.
Liveware-crew	Physical, physiological, and psychological condition of flight crew.	Hypoxia, SD, visual illusions, communication problems, forgetfulness, decision making, etc.

PAVE model

Perhaps the simplest systems model to understand (and remember) is the FAA's **PAVE model**: the **P**ilot, **A**ircraft, en**V**ironment, and **E**xternal pressures.[18] The model incorporates most of what the other systems models do and, as opposed to forensic analysis and classification, is somewhat more practical for pilots to actually use in their everyday flying. For example, you as a pilot can assess beforehand how each of these four elements could influence the safety of any given flight:

- **P**ilot. What is your condition? This involves assessing your physiological and mental state, currency, proficiency, etc.
- **A**ircraft. Is the aircraft airworthy and ready for flight? This entails an evaluation of required maintenance, minimum equipment list, aircraft performance capabilities, determining adequate fuel quantity and reserves, a preflight inspection, etc.
- En**V**ironment. How will the environment affect this flight? This involves obtaining a thorough weather briefing and determining if the actual and/or forecast conditions meet company or personal weather minimums, assessing airport and runway suitability, and taking appropriate cautions if flying in potentially hazardous environmental conditions such as at high altitude, at night, or over mountainous terrain.
- **E**xternal pressures. Finally, are there external pressures that might affect your decision to complete a flight? These can be time (e.g., delayed flight) and other pressures that, as we have seen from other models, often arise from other people's expectations—employer, passengers, etc.

In many ways a systems approach to explaining human error is much like the organizational approach. Both look at *all* the elements in the overall system—not just errors committed by front-line operators—to identify factors that may contribute to errors committed by those at the sharp end of the system. The difference between the two approaches is that the systems approach extends its look even further—to designers, manufacturers, and regulators—than does the organizational approach.

Such was the case in a landmark accident investigation into the crash of Air Ontario Flight 1363 in Dryden, Ontario, that killed 24 of the 69 people aboard, including both pilots and one flight attendant. The Fokker F-28 stalled and crashed just beyond the departure end of the slush-covered Runway 29, after the crew attempted to takeoff with snow and ice on the wings. Even though the 24,000-hour captain prided himself on flying by the book, he uncharacteristically committed several errors and violations by conducting hot fueling operations (fueling with an engine running) with passengers aboard, by failing to deice the airplane while snow was falling and ice was accumulating on the wings, and by making the decision to depart in such conditions.

It turns out the crew members faced a dilemma during their intermediate stop at Dryden. Company policy prohibited ground deicing procedures with one or more engines operating (for safety reasons). However, since Flight 1363 had been dispatched with an unserviceable auxiliary power unit and ground-start equipment was unavailable at Dryden, had they shut down the engines, they and their passengers would have been stranded at Dryden. The pilots chose to keep one engine running rather than deice the aircraft before takeoff.

The airline also had no written policy about hot refueling while passengers were aboard, a practice that is considered unsafe. The crew also only had to refuel at Dryden because they were dispatched with 10 unexpected additional passengers at Thunder Bay. This added to the aircraft's weight, which required the captain to offload fuel to remain within legal limits—the captain wanted to offload the additional passengers at Thunder Bay, but dispatch decided against that.

The accident investigation—likely the most extensive in Canadian history—documented in its four-volume, 1,700-page report, uncovered *systemic* failures not only within Air Ontario, but with its parent airline Air Canada, Transport Canada, and the aviation industry at large. Besides citing Air Ontario's inadequate operational control of Flight 1363, the report also concluded that lack of involvement by Air Canada in Air Ontario's flight operations procedures allowed the smaller feeder airline to operate at a lower level of safety than its parent airline. It also concluded that the regulatory body in that country—Transport Canada—failed in its obligation to conduct a proper audit of Air Ontario's F-28 flight operations. Finally, it also placed blame on the entire aviation industry for its somewhat permissive attitude regarding flight operations in icing conditions. In short, investigators concluded that this accident was not only the result of the captain's failure to abort the flight, but was the result of a "*failure in the air transportation system.*"[19]

Quantifying Human Error

It was noted in Chapter 1 that even though the aircraft safety record has been steadily improving, the rise in aircraft reliability has, by default, elevated the proportion of aircraft accidents caused by human (pilot) failure. One of the reasons for these technological improvements is the practice of **engineering reliability analysis (ERA)**, the process of testing the failure rates of aircraft airframe and powerplant systems (and all their individual sub-systems and components) to predict overall reliability. If the system's predicted reliability is unacceptable, then design and manufacturing measures can be taken to improve it. For example, manufacturers conduct static and fatigue testing to determine the load factor at which airframe components will break and the number of cycles (i.e., pressurization and depressurization that occurs every flight) an airframe can withstand before failure. Engine manufacturers also test their products under varying start and operating conditions to assess reliability.

There are those who believe that, just as you can quantify the reliability of machines, you can do the same—at least to a degree—for the human operators of those machines. Such an assessment involves using various qualitative and quantitative task and error analysis techniques to determine probabilities of certain types of errors occurring within the human-machine system, an endeavor called **human reliability assessment (HRA)**. Such an assessment assists systems designers in ascertaining the overall probability of human-machine failure,[20] which in turn provides guidance in developing systems that could compensate for any deficiencies in human reliability.

Let's assume, for the sake of simplicity, that a careful and thorough ERA determines that the probability that a particular machine (or one of its subsystems) will *not* fail over a given time period is 0.99 (its failure probability is .01, or 1%), while an HRA deter-

mines that the probability the human operator will not fail during the same time period is 0.90 (failure probability is 0.10, or 10%). This is represented in Figure 2-5. Lined up serially—meaning if one component fails the whole system does—the probability of the entire human-machine system not failing, and failing, is 0.89 (89%) and 0.11 (11%), respectively. If lined up in parallel, however—meaning if one component fails the system continues to operate—the probability of the entire human-machine system not failing, and failing, is 0.999 (99.9%) and 0.001 (0.1%), respectively.

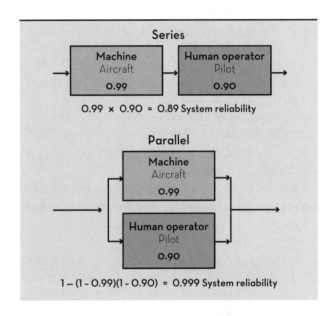

Fig 2-5.

Hypothetical system reliability analysis with individual and overall system reliability probabilities indicated.

Such an analysis, if accurate, would greatly assist systems designers and aircraft manufacturers in creating safer human-machine systems. But how reliable is HRA? It turns out that most researchers conclude it isn't that reliable. Why? Because, after more than a century of scientifically studying human behavior, we still do not fully understand what makes people tick and why they make errors. Therefore, we are unable to predict human failure to the extent we can with machines and technology. One insightful observation can be made if, at the bottom diagram in Figure 2-5, you were to replace the machine component with another human being on the fight deck: no matter what probabilities you plug into the equation, you can see the significant gain in reliability (and safety) by having more than one flight crew member on board.

"To err is human"

—Seneca the Younger

Nothing has really changed since these insightful words were first spoken two-thousand years ago. For a variety of reasons, and in a variety of ways, humans still err. These errors are ubiquitous in normal everyday human experience. We tolerate them readily enough when operating on terra firma, because the consequences are usually not severe. Forgetting to flick a switch in your house (or even your car), may not amount to much. The flight environment, however, is not so forgiving—forgetting to move the flap switch on takeoff on a jet could kill you and hundreds of passengers.

We certainly identify with those early pioneers who ignored, and even mocked the naysayers who claimed that if "God had wanted man to fly, He would have given him wings." Yet there is a kernel of truth in the doubters' sentiment: Hurtling through three-dimensional space at hundreds of miles per hour, sometimes at night, sometimes in clouds, sometimes in ice and turbulence, and at altitudes inhospitable to supporting human life, and in a machine whose sophistication sometimes baffles our understanding, is unnatural. We may be able to fly higher, faster, and longer than the hawk, eagle, or duck, but flight is their natural environment, not ours. The fact, as was previously noted in Chapter 1, that the machine has advanced more in a hundred years than the human brain has in a hundred thousand, led James Reason decades before he expounded on human error to conclude that:

> ...our position and motion senses as well as our capacity for processing information remain those of a self-propelled animal designed to travel at around three to four miles per hour through a mainly two-dimensional world under conditions of normal terrestrial gravity. In short, man was intended to walk, run and climb the occasional tree; but no more.[21]

Also previously noted, up to 80 percent of all aviation accidents are attributed to errors or mistakes made by pilots; and this chapter has suggested almost as many reasons as there are errors. The remainder of this book will include more. From your reading thus far, perhaps you've caught a glimpse into the reasons why people make mistakes or engage in risky behaviors. By the time you read the final pages of this book, you may come to the same conclusion that many designers, manufacturers, human factors engineers, and safety specialists have also arrived at: errors made by pilots are inevitable and are a result of *normal* physiological, psychological, and sociological processes operating in the *abnormal* environment of flight.

Although this perspective may seem depressing, burying your head in the sand like the proverbial ostrich will do nothing to make you a safer pilot. In fact, it will make matters worse. Acknowledging the inevitability of errors is actually the essential first step in learning how to effectively manage them. Only when we acknowledge the pervasiveness of errors and learn all we can about why and under what circumstances they are likely to manifest themselves, will we be adequately equipped to take the actions necessary to eliminate or reduce their number or mitigate their impact.

Fortunately, you are not alone in this quest. Using a systems approach to design a better, safer, and more efficient system—thereby reducing or mitigating the errors made by those at its front end—the interdisciplinary field of human factors has for several decades aided aircraft designers, engineers, physiologists, psychologists, manufacturers, and safety specialists in applying their expertise in designing not only aircraft, but the overall system in which they operate, making them more error-tolerant, more reliable, safer, and easier to fly. As a result, the industry has steadily reduced the number and rate of most types of accidents.

Fully Autonomous Flight

Before discussing in the next chapter what the discipline of human factors is, we must briefly explore an idea that has recently garnered significant attention—the idea of completely eliminating pilot error by removing the pilot from the flight deck altogether. As with self-driving automobiles, considerable effort and resources are currently being expended in developing pilotless airplanes for passenger transport. The logic used by those advocating for this is simple: If the majority of aircraft accidents are the result of errors made by pilots, then we should remove them from the flight deck and let the computers do the flying. They reason—incorrectly in the author's view—that since computers on most modern jetliners currently do most of the flying anyway, it should not be a big jump to fully autonomous flight. To bolster their argument they point to the fact that to achieve fuel savings and reduce flight crew workload it has been the common practice of airlines and flight departments to encourage, and even require, their pilots to use the automated systems as much as possible.

However, another reason for moving in this direction is the forecast worldwide pilot shortage. Just as advances in cockpit technology did away with the need for a flight engineer in the 1980s, further advances in autonomous capabilities could allow the removal of one or both pilots from the cockpit. In fact, Boeing recently began testing automated systems to determine the feasibility of removing one pilot from the flight deck, while another one monitors from the ground. Using incremental steps, they are currently exploring ways in which aircraft can auto-taxi to and from the runway completely autonomously. In 2019 they hoped to test autonomous auto-start, taxi, and takeoff using a Boeing B-787 with autonomous in-flight operations to follow sometime later.[22]

According to some in the industry, advances in technology, artificial intelligence (AI), and machine learning will eventually lead to fully self-flying, passenger-carrying aircraft and the complete removal of the pilot from the flight deck. Critics argue, however, that this accomplishment will take several decades to arrive, if it arrives at all. Apart from the likely unwillingness of passengers to even board a pilotless airplane, and the unfathomable consequences of an aircraft's computer systems being hacked and its control systems being remotely sabotaged—U.S. Department of Homeland Security officials recently were able to remotely hack into a Boeing B-757 at Atlantic City Airport—[23] many believe that the computer, even with significant advances in AI, will likely never rise to the level needed to match the level of safety currently enjoyed by human-piloted aircraft.

However, assuming that autonomous flight is eventually successful in achieving an equivalent level of safety while at the same time removing one crew member from the flight deck, is removing the remaining pilot from the flight deck really the right approach? Many argue that if our goal is to remove pilot-error-caused accidents, we are looking at it the wrong way. While it is true that a small fraction of airline flights result in accidents—with most attributable to the behavior of pilots—you could also say that the very high percentage of the millions of flights that occur each year do not result in accidents because in each case the pilots flying them prevented them from crashing. This is especially true when something goes wrong with the aircraft's propulsion systems, its hardware or its software. Is the machine going to be able to fix or safely land itself when it breaks?

Developing autonomous passenger airplanes is an admirable attempt to reduce pilot-caused accidents. However, if human error on the flight deck is such a persistent problem, what makes us think it won't rear its ugly head in the humans that design and program the software of an autonomous aircraft? It is naive to believe that the humans involved in creating autonomous aircraft are immune to the same types of errors that the humans who currently fly them are subject to. Yes, errors committed by human operators would clearly disappear, but many believe calamitous errors won't completely go away—they instead would be transferred to the humans who design, program, manufacture, and maintain them.

Whether we like it or not, we cannot completely avoid human error in flight operations; whether it occurs by the pilots who fly the aircraft or the engineers who design and program them. The best we can do is to continue to conduct research into how and why human error occurs and take measures—better design, better procedures, better training—to reduce them or mitigate their impact.

The next chapter—our final introductory chapter—provides a brief overview of the field of human factors as it applies to aviation, and summarizes how its many disciplines increase our understanding of human error.

Endnotes

1. Federal Aviation Administration, "Appendix 1. Threat and Error Management," in *Line Operations Safety Audit*, AC 120-90 (Washington, DC: April 27, 2006): 2.

2. Donald A. Norman, *The Design of Everyday Things* (New York: Currency-Doubleday, 1988).

3. Scott A. Shappell and Douglas A. Wiegmann, *The Human Factors Analysis and Classification System–HFACS*, DOT/FAA/AM-00/7 (Washington, DC: FAA Office of Aviation Medicine, February 2000).

4. James Reason, *Human Error* (New York: Cambridge University Press, 1990).

5. Scott A. Shappell and Donald A. Wiegmann, *The Human Factors Analysis and Classification System–HFACS*, DOT/FAA/AM-00/7 (Washington, DC: Federal Aviation Administration, Office of Aviation Medicine, February 2000).

6. Guohua Li, Jurek G. Grabowski, Susan P. Baker and George W. Rebok, "Pilot Error in Air Carrier Accidents: Does Age Matter?" *Aviation, Space, and Environmental Medicine* 77 (July 2006): 737–741.

7. United States Government Accountability Office, *General Aviation Safety: Additional FAA Efforts Could Help Identify and Mitigate Safety Risks*, Report to Congressional Committees, Report No. GAO-13-36 (Washington, DC: GAO, October 2012).

8. Federal Aviation Administration, *Human Performance Considerations in the Use and Design of Aircraft Checklists* (Washington, DC: FAA Safety Analysis Division, January 1995).

9. The six different frameworks are from Douglas A. Wiegmann and Scott A. Shappell, *A Human Error Approach to Aviation Accident Analysis: The Human Factors Analysis and Classification System* (Burlington, VT: Ashgate 2003).

10. Charles E. Billings and William D. Reynard, "Dimensions of the Information Transfer Problem," *Information Transfer Problems in the Aviation System*, NASA TP-1875, eds. C.E. Billings and E.S. Cheaney (Moffett Field, CA: NASA-Ames Research Center, September 1981): 9–14.

11. Patrick R. Veillette, "Controlled Flight Into Terrain Takes Highest Toll in Business Jet Operations," *Flight Safety Digest* 23 (May 2004): 1–47.

12. Frank Wagener and David C. Ison, "Crew Resource Management Application in Commercial Aviation," *Journal of Aviation Technology and Engineering* 3 (April 2014): 2–13.

13. James Reason, *Managing the Risks of Organizational Accidents* (Burlington, VT: Ashgate Publishing Company 1997).

14. International Civil Aviation Organization, *Human Factors Digest* No. 7, ICAO Circular 240-AN/144 (Montreal, Canada: ICAO, 1993). Reproduced with the permission of ICAO.

15. Wiegmann and Shappell, *A Human Error Approach to Aviation Accident Analysis*.

16. U.S. Air Force, *Risk Management (RM) Guidelines and Tools*, AFPAM 90-803 (February 11, 2013).

17. The 5M model used for trouble-shooting, by Davidjcmorris, June 11, 2017 (https://commons.wikimedia.org/wiki/File:The_5M_model_used_for_trouble-shooting.png); WC CC BY-SA 4.0

18. Federal Aviation Administration, *Pilot's Handbook of Aeronautical Knowledge*, FAA-H-8083-25B (Washington, DC: 2016).

19. Virgil P. Moshansky, *Commission of Inquiry Into the Air Ontario Crash at Dryden, Ontario: Final Report*, Volume I (Ottawa, ON: Minister of Supply & Services, Canada, 1992): xxi, 5.

20. Christopher D. Wickens, *Engineering Psychology and Human Performance*, 2nd ed. (New York: HarperCollins, 1992).

21. James Reason, *Man in Motion: The Psychology of Travel* (New York: Walker and Company, 1974): 1.

22. Guy Norris, "Boeing's Plan for Autonomous Flight," *Aviation Week & Space Technology* (June 9, 2017). Available at www.aviationweek.com/optimizing-engines-through-lifecycle/boeings-plan-autonomous-flight.

23. Calvin Biesecker, "Boeing 757 Testing Shows Airplanes Vulnerable to Hacking, DHS Says," *Avionics* (November 8, 2017). Available at www.aviationtoday.com/2017/11/08/boeing-757-testing-shows-airplanes-vulnerable-hacking-dhs-says/

3

What's a human factor?

Aviation Human Factors

It shocked both passengers and crew. A few moments after successfully landing on Runway 22 at Homer Airport in Alaska, the nose and main landing gear of the Beechcraft 1900 suddenly collapsed. The airplane slid on its belly to a stop on the runway, resting on the lower fuselage, wings, and engine nacelles. Fortunately, there was no fire and all 13 passengers and both pilots walked away from the damaged commuter turboprop without injury. It turns out the FO of Flight 878, who had logged almost 2,400 total hours with 400 in this make and model, had inadvertently raised the landing gear after touchdown when he intended to raise the flap handle instead (NTSB Identification No: DCA14FA002). Subsequent to the accident, two lawsuits were filed by three passengers: one alleges the company, ERA Aviation, failed "to properly screen, evaluate, train and select pilots and that it crewed the flight with pilots who did not know how to perform proper landing procedures."[1]

The FO in this story is not alone in selecting the wrong handle. Decades earlier, pilots flying airplanes used in World War II made the same mistakes. In fact, more than "400 planes were lost in a 22 month period because pilots confused the landing gear and flaps controls."[2] It was this phenomenon that triggered some of the first major attempts at applying psychological principles to solving human-machine interface problems in aviation, eventually giving rise to the discipline of human factors. Psychologist Alphonse Chapanis, working at Wright Field near Dayton, Ohio, discovered that pilots of Boeing B-17s, Republic P-47s,

and other airplanes easily confused these two controls because they were located in close proximity to one another and their shape and size were identical. He also noticed that pilots were generally not prone to selecting the wrong handles in other airplanes, like the Douglas C-47, because they were located further away from one another and each had to be activated differently in order to work. Chapanis significantly reduced the number of inadvertent gear retractions by attaching a small rubber tire to the end of the landing gear switch and a triangular flap-shaped device on the flap actuation knob, thereby allowing pilots to identify them using their tactile sense, or sense of touch.[3]

After the war, other shape and color control coding changes were made—and standardized—to help pilots better discriminate between cockpit controls, such as power/thrust and propeller control knobs. Figure 3-1 shows the current standards for designing the shape of six common cockpit controls for transport category airplanes. You may have also noticed on some aircraft that the carburetor heat control for reciprocating engines is shaped like a box (carburetor heat box) while the fuel mixture control knob is usually colored red (aviation gasoline, or AVGAS, used to be red).

Fig 3-1.

Standard shapes of six cockpit controls for transport category airplanes required for United States airworthiness standards (14 CFR §25.781).

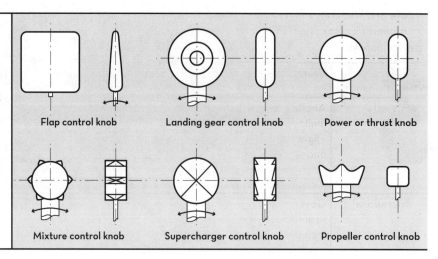

Flap control knob   Landing gear control knob   Power or thrust knob

Mixture control knob   Supercharger control knob   Propeller control knob

Human Factors Defined

It was also during WWII that the capabilities and complexity of newly designed airplanes began to exceed the abilities of the pilots who flew them. They operated at higher altitudes where the partial pressure of oxygen is insufficient for sustaining human life; their range and endurance significantly increased and they flew at least four times faster than previous World War I aircraft, challenging the navigation and visual detection abilities and response times of their pilots; some could withstand high-G forces for aerial combat, which, unfortunately, induced visual disturbances and loss of consciousness in their pilots;[4] and the number of instruments, knobs, and dials used to monitor and control the complex systems and equipment needed for war operations grew considerably. They were also noisy, hampering communication. It was, therefore, no longer acceptable to design the human to *fit the machine*, primarily through pilot selection and training, as it was prior to WWII; a different approach—designing the machine to *fit the needs of the human operator*—was needed.[5]

In the previous chapter we defined a system as a set of components that act together as a whole to achieve a common goal, and suggested that aviation safety—and pilot error—is best understood when you look not only at deficiencies in pilot performance, but weaknesses in the various components that make up the entire system. We also pointed out that no matter how you describe an aviation system (using 5M, SHELL, PAVE, etc.), a failure in any one component—

pilot, other people, training, environment, aircraft, information, procedures, etc.—affects the performance of the overall system, including the performance of the operator/user at the front end of it.

The human-operator problems that arose in aviation during WWII accelerated the growth of **human factors**, a multidisciplinary field that seeks to optimize the effectiveness of human-machine systems through design that accommodates the limitations and capabilities of the human operator, thereby reducing human error and maximizing human performance, safety, efficiency, and comfort.

Also called *ergonomics* (*ergo*=work; *nomos*=law, or rule), the field was commonly defined as the scientific study of humans in their working environment with the goal of optimizing the relationship between the two.[6] The field has since expanded its focus to areas beyond one's work environment. For our purposes, a sufficient and succinct definition of human factors for pilots is *the scientific study of flight crew and the flight environment with the goal of optimizing the relationship between the two*. The **flight crew** includes the physical, physiological, psychological, and psychosocial limitations and capabilities of the pilots who fly the aircraft. And, as indicated in the various systems models discussed previously, the **flight environment** includes all of the system components other than the pilot(s). For simplicity, we can distinguish between the physical, operational, and social environments, as indicated in Table 3-1.

Table 3-1. The crew's flight environment consists of numerous components that can affect their performance.

Flight environment	Examples
Physical	Aircraft design, maintenance, limitations, and airworthiness. Flight deck temperatures, humidity, and workstation layout. Weather conditions, time of day, and terrain. Airspace, navigation aids, and airports.
Operational	Government air regulations. Company requirements and procedures, including information in standard operating procedures, checklists, manuals, charts, etc.
Social	Employer, supervisors, trainers, maintainers, dispatchers, schedulers, cabin crew, ground crew, ATC, passengers, corporate culture, etc.

It should be pointed out that some confusion arises when using the term human factors to describe the design of human-machine systems that accommodate the limitations and capabilities of the human operator. It was noted that the term ergonomics is essentially the same as human factors, the former generally favored by those in the United Kingdom and other countries, the latter by those in the United States. The Human Factors Society even changed its name to the Human Factors and Ergonomics Society to accommodate this ambiguity. In addition, the phrase human factors—especially for non-professionals outside of the field, including pilots—often means the human limitations or faults that affect the safety of flight, not necessarily the flight environment side of the equation. If that is your intuitive understanding of the field, the good news is you are not necessarily wrong in thinking this way, because the physical, physiological, psychological, and psychosocial limitations—the *human factors* (or aspects) in flight operations—are major areas of study in the formal overall discipline of human factors/ergonomics. Its goal is to identify what these limitations (and capabilities) are and to design human-machine systems that fit the needs of the user/operator in order to enhance their performance. Accomplishment of this objective in aviation operations, in turn, enhances safety.

The Multidisciplinary Nature of Human Factors

Human factors and ergonomics involve the design of human-machine systems that are user-centered; that is, design that accommodates the limitations and capabilities of the human operator. As you might surmise, then, the field encompasses several disciplines—some from the design side of the equation, primarily engineering, but most from the human side, primarily physiology and psychology. Many of the disciplines that fall under the umbrella of human factors are listed in Figure 3-2, with only some applicable to flight operations briefly introduced in the discussion that follows.

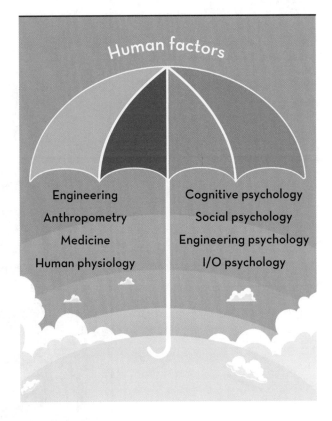

Fig 3-2.

Some of the major disciplines that fall under the umbrella of human factors.

Anthropometry

A major area in which human factors principles are applied is in workstation design. As a pilot, this primarily involves the layout of the flight deck including seat comfort and adjustability, control manipulation access, and the ease at which visual displays can be seen and interpreted. For example, if a pilot cannot reach the rudder pedals, all because the seat won't accommodate his or her stature, then his or her ability to operate safely is impaired.

Anthropometry (*anthropos* = human; *metron* = measure) is the study of the measurement of the size and shape of the human body. It is an important discipline within the field of **physical ergonomics**, the scientific study of human "anatomical, anthropometric, physiological and biomechanical characteristics as they relate to physical activity."[7] You have likely seen the application of this branch of human factors in the design of computer workstations. Figure 3-3 diagrams what people often call an "ergonomically designed" workstation using human factors design principles in computer workstations to minimize the possibility of suffering from a work-related musculoskeletal disorder.

Fig 3-3.

An example of designing user interaction with equipment and workplaces that fit the anatomical, anthropometric, physiological, and biomechanical characteristics of the user.[8]

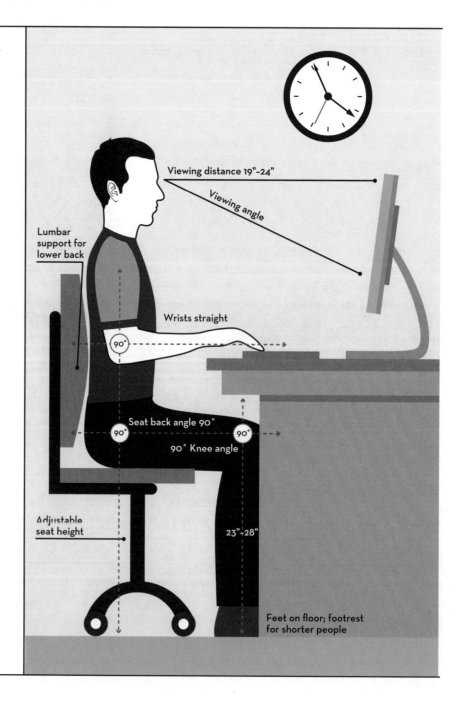

Unfortunately, mostly due to cost factors, the design of some aircraft cockpits in the past only accommodated the body types of certain human populations that fell within a specific range of anthropomorphic dimensions. For example, U.S. Air Force (USAF) aircraft were customarily designed to fit 90 percent of the American male population,[9] making it difficult, if not impossible, for taller or shorter than "average" men and women to safely operate them. Anthropometric data assist flight deck workspace designers by providing information about average stature (height), torso length, sitting height, and other data applicable to different human body types. A pilot's workstation should allow you to sit in the **design eye reference point (DERP)**—also known as the *design eye position*—a point in space where the position of your eyes are located when the seat is adjusted accordingly and which provides not only the best access to the flight controls, but also an optimum viewing angle for both cockpit instrumentation and the outside environment. If your eyes are not positioned at this point in space your ability to adequately reach the controls and see outside the flight deck will be hampered.

It was noted in the last chapter that poor design of the fuel display and the location of the fuel control selector valve played a role in the tragic accident involving John Denver's Long-EZ homebuilt aircraft. A study of GA airplane design conducted by the Civil Aeronautics Board's Bureau of Safety, predecessor to the NTSB, found that in one popular model four fuel starvation accidents involved pilots of smaller stature who could not see, or in some cases even reach, the fuel selector from the normal sitting position.[10] The study also discovered that nonstandard design and positioning of fuel selector controls also contributed to fuel starvation accidents, with the fuel tank in use indicated by the long handle of the selector in some aircraft models and by the short handle in others.

In an incident involving an airline flight on a non-directional beacon (NDB) instrument approach, the pilots lost their positional awareness because of the placement of the NDB control panel. It was located directly below the landing gear handle, so when the captain put the gear down his hand brushed against the tuning knob and he inadvertently changed the frequency. Fortunately, the aircraft broke out of instrument meteorological conditions (IMC) in time for the crew to make a safe landing.[11]

Poor anthropometric design is only one issue related to the design of flight deck workstations. Chapter 15 looks more closely at the difficulties of interpreting analog and digital instrument displays, including the traditional three-pointer altimeter, and the problem of control-display pairings that can confuse pilots.

Physiology and Medicine

As a branch of biology, **physiology** is the study of the ways in which the human body and its various systems function. It is also the basis for modern medicine, the study and practice of disease prevention and treatment. The field of aviation/aerospace physiology and medicine examines the effects of the flight environment and other factors on normal physiological functioning and flight crew performance. These include factors common to all people, such as the effects of illness, colds, influenza, sleep deprivation, fatigue, alcohol and drugs, and poor physical fitness. But, as mentioned in the previous chapter, they also include unique physiological phenomena that most normal earthlings are not afflicted with, such as hypoxia, decompression sickness, jet lag, and spatial disorientation.

Some of the earliest aviation problems that contributed to the development of the discipline of human factors involved physiology. Long before the Wright brother's achievement at Kitty Hawk in 1903, efforts had been directed at documenting the problems of high-altitude flight in aviation's first aircraft—hot-air and gas-filled balloons. At lower altitudes these early pilots encountered problems with trapped gas in their ears, but as these flying machines ascended to greater heights they experienced the effects of not only cold temperatures, but balloon sickness; what we now know as hypoxia, the effects of insufficient partial pressure of oxygen reaching the brain. This physiological phenomenon, along with altitude decompression sickness, was studied by Paul Bert, one of the early pioneers of altitude physiology, in experiments he conducted in a hypobaric (altitude) chamber which he also built. In April 1875, three daring French aeronauts set out to break James Glaisher's altitude record of approximately 36,000 feet in their gas-filled balloon, the *Zenith*. They knew enough to carry oxygen to offset the effects of hypoxia, but were warned by Paul Bert that they needed more for the proposed duration of their flight. Unfortunately, his letter arrived too late: only one of them survived the flight to 28,000 feet; two of them lost consciousness and later died of hypoxia.[12,13]

William Wilmer postulated in 1918 that most British military pilot deaths in World War I were due to accidents, not combat, with up to 90 percent killed because of some type of human limitation.[14] Recent research challenges his claim, suggesting it might have been only as high as about 42 percent.[15] In either case, research labs in both the military and civilian sectors began to spring up to investigate the human origins of aircraft accidents. As newer aircraft began to fly faster and higher after the Great War, specialists in the military began to study the physiological aspects of human performance, not only in high altitude environments, but in high-G environments using a centrifuge. Engineers designed a rudimentary pressure suit to combat the decompression sickness pilots experienced at high altitudes. Wiley Post was the first to fly with one, attaining a height of 50,000 feet.[16]

Some pilots lost complete control of their otherwise perfectly airworthy aircraft upon entering clouds or fog because of the inadequacy of the vestibular apparatus in determining orientation, a phenomenon known as spatial disorientation (SD). On September 24, 1929, Lieutenant James Doolittle demonstrated that flight by sole reference to aircraft flight instruments could be accomplished when he successfully conducted the first *blind* flight in a Consolidated NY-2 biplane operating out of Mitchel Field in Garden City, New York. With his safety pilot riding in the back, and his own canopy completely covered by a hood up front, he conducted a 15-minute flight, including a takeoff and landing, solely by reference to the flight instruments and radio navigation aids (radio range and fan markers) without being able to see any references outside the airplane. Though pilots will always be subject to SD, even when flying by reference to the flight instruments—a topic discussed thoroughly in Chapter 9—Doolittle's achievement paved the way for so-called *all-weather flying* in the commercial airline industry.[17]

Upon entry into WWII, the U.S. Army and USAF embarked on programs that provided extensive mandatory physiology and high altitude training for all of their aircrews, including such topics as oxygen equipment, cabin decompression procedures, trapped gas disorders, night vision, G-forces, and thermal stress.[18] As time went on, significant work on several other physiological stresses affecting pilot performance was accomplished, including research into SD, vision, hearing and noise, vibration, sleep, fatigue, circadian dysrhythmia, shift work, alcohol, drugs, health maintenance, stress, nutrition, and exercise.

Since human physiology has not changed, the problems of hypoxia, SD, G-induced loss of consciousness, fatigue, and other physiological issues still contribute to accidents and incidents in both civil and military aviation. Therefore, Part II—a major portion of this book—presents eight chapters that delve into the different physiological stresses that flight crews often face and must learn to effectively manage.

Psychology

Another major human factors discipline applicable to flight operations is **psychology**, traditionally defined as the scientific study of the human mind and behavior (*psyche* = spirit; *ology* = study of), but nowadays defined differently by different specialists in the field. For example, some define it as the study of human behavior, while others define it as the study of human thought and behavior. While it is easy to see how physiological incapacitation can lead to suboptimal flight crew performance, or even an accident, the parallel impact of psychological limitations may be less evident. We are not talking here about mental illness or a psychiatric disorder that could obviously affect pilot performance.

Though certain psychological disorders prohibit a pilot from attaining and maintaining a valid medical certificate (*see* Chapter 11), efforts by regulatory bodies, airlines, airline unions, aviation medical examiners, and others are currently underway to help, not censure, pilots who may be suffering from certain forms of mental illness, including depression (Chapter 19 outlines some of these measures). Though recent research suggests that commercial airline pilots may experience depression as frequently as the general population,[19] such a condition has rarely resulted in an aircraft accident due to deliberate sabotage or suicide by a crew member. Even though authorities are currently re-evaluating their approach to mental health issues of airline flight crews—in part due to the aircraft-assisted murder-suicide committed by the FO of Germanwings Flight 9525 on March 24, 2015—less than 0.3 percent of 2,758 civilian fatal aircraft accidents in the United

States during a recent ten-year period were caused by suicide. All involved GA flights, none were commercial airline operations.[20]

As established in the previous two chapters, it is true that the actions of pilots have historically been responsible for the majority of aircraft accidents, but not because of any adverse mental or psychological disorder that may have afflicted them. Rather, flight-crew-caused aircraft accidents are mostly the result of inadvertent errors that they make—errors that arise from the normal physiological and psychological limitations inherent in the human condition.

The field of psychology is vast, but there are several branches, or approaches, that are particularly relevant when seeking to understand human performance on the flight deck. These are briefly summarized in Table 3-2.

Of all the branches listed, two stand out as particularly helpful when it comes to explaining the major aspects of flight crew behavior: cognitive psychology and social psychology.

Cognitive Psychology

The scientific study of how humans think and process information is the domain of **cognitive psychology**. It uses the scientific method to study mental processes like perception, memory, reasoning, problem solving, and decision making—all processes that have been implicated in flight crew error. Understanding human error arises from an understanding of human thinking, which is primarily the domain of cognitive psychology. As briefly discussed in the previous chapter, it is also called the **information processing** approach to understanding human thought and behavior, and uses the computer as a

Table 3-2. Some of the major branches of psychology applicable to aviation human factors.

Psychology branches	Description	Applicable to aviation
Behavioral	Study of observable human behavior (not thought), which is believed to be learned and reinforced primarily through rewards in a person's environment.	A major approach to studying human behavior. Its rigorous scientific methodology provides a solid empirical foundation for the discipline and its findings are foundational to an understanding of human behavior.
Cognitive	Using the scientific method to study mental processes like perception, memory, reasoning, problem solving, and decision making, it is the study of how humans think and process information.	Has a wider breadth of perspective compared to other approaches (e.g., behaviorism) and has produced useful insights into the everyday normal human behavior, including that of pilots.
Experimental	Uses experiments to learn about human thought and behavior.	Uses rigorous scientific methodology to learn about human thought and behavior, increasing the credibility of findings in behavioral, cognitive, and other branches of psychology.
Engineering	Study of human behavior, capabilities, and limitation as it relates to the design and operation of systems.	Draws from cognitive psychology and is directly applicable to the human factors discipline (often called *human factors engineering*).
Industrial/ organizational	Study of human behavior at work.	Directly applicable to human factors in that it attempts to optimize human performance of an organization and individuals (and pilots) who work there.
Personality	Study of individual differences.	Applicable in flight crew hiring and selection.
Educational	Study of psychological principles to improve learning and teaching.	Flight crew members require significant training and extensive learning to master their craft.
Social	Study of how people's thoughts and behaviors are influenced by others.	Other people—supervisors, ATC, dispatch, customers—have a profound influence on pilot decision making and behavior.

metaphor postulating that inputs (stimuli, or information) from the environment are received by the senses and are processed before a response (output) is made (Figure 3-4). The model assumes that information processing takes time as inputs travel from left to right (sometimes referred to as *bottom-up processing*), but also rejects the strictly behaviorist notion that humans are merely passive responders to external **stimuli**; rather, people actively seek information, often processing information from right to left (often called *top-down processing*).

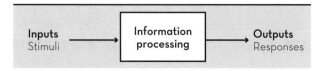

Fig 3-4.

A simple information processing model.

A more elaborate version, developed by one of the world's foremost researchers in the field of aviation human factors, Christopher Wickens, is found in Figure 3-5.

Bottom-up information processing begins with stimulation of sensory receptors located in the eyes, ears, skin, vestibular apparatus, etc., that is stored for only milliseconds (*see* Table 3-3).

It is generally agreed that some sort of attentional mechanism filters these stimuli (inputs), often limiting the type and amount of information that is perceived, or interpreted, by the brain. These perceptions are influenced by previous experience (long-term memory) and current inputs (short-term memory, or working memory). Higher level cognitive functioning, such as decision making and problem solving, is also memory dependent and influenced by the accuracy of one's perception of the situation, or one's *situational awareness*. Finally, the model recognizes that the human brain, like a computer, has limited processing capacity, and if overloaded with inputs (task saturation) the attentional resources allocated to the various mental operations needed to effectively perform a task will significantly diminish.

Experimental psychologists often study these processes in isolation but recognize that they are interdependent. For example, a distraction (e.g., a wing flap anomaly) may lead to a breakdown in voluntary attention, causing a pilot to focus too much on the flap indication, which in turn could lead to forgetting to accomplish a checklist item such as lowering the landing gear before landing. Also, research shows that any distortions upstream in the model (e.g., sensory processing and/or perception) will adversely affect downstream cognitive functions such as decision making and response selection and execution.

Fig 3-5.

Human information processing model showing the various mental operations involved in processing information before a response is made (adapted after Christopher Wickens).[21]

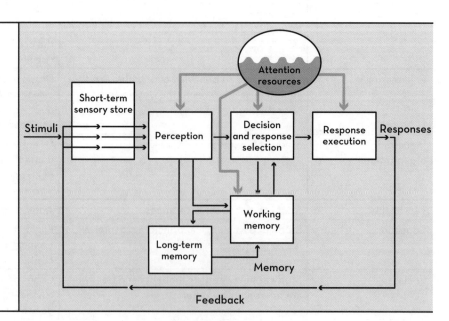

Table 3-3. Major human senses involved in piloting an aircraft.

Human sensation	Description
	Specialized senses detect specific types of stimuli, each of which are important for pilots in obtaining accurate information about their external world. Some rank higher when it comes to flying: vision and hearing are crucial for flight while gustation (sense of taste) is not.
Vision	Sense of sight. Photoreceptors in the retina of each eye are stimulated by light causing a chemical reaction that converts light energy into neural signals that are sent to the visual cortex via the optic nerve.
Audition	Sense of hearing. Hair-like receptors located in the cochlea of the inner ear are stimulated by sound waves and create neural impulses that are sent to the auditory cortex via the auditory nerve.
Tactile/cutaneous	Sense of touch. Different kinds of receptors in the skin sense different inputs—pressure, temperature, or pain.
Olfaction	Sense of smell. Olfactory receptors located in the nasal cavity chemically react to variety of odors. Specific receptors detect specific smells.
Vestibular	Sense of balance. Receptors located in the semicircular canals in the inner ear move in response to angular acceleration while the membrane located in the adjacent otolith bodies moves in response to linear acceleration.
Somatosensory	Sense of overall position and movement of body parts in relation to each other. Receptors in the body's skin, muscles, and joints respond to gravitational acceleration providing sense of body position and movement. Sometimes called kinesthetic or postural sensation, but more commonly referred to as the "seat-of-the-pants" sensation because accelerations experienced in flight can be confused with gravity.

Lessons learned from aircraft accident investigations reveal how normal everyday human cognitive limitations in perception, attention, memory, and decision making can play a significant causal role. The following highlight some of these.

Perceptual Errors

In perfectly clear flying weather, flight crews have completely missed or misperceived visual cues necessary to avoid a midair collision in daylight conditions and CFIT at night. They've also failed to detect or correctly perceive vital auditory cues from ATC communications. For example, numerous incidents (and some accidents) have occurred as a result of call-sign confusion, which occurs when controllers issue, and/or pilots respond to, a clearance intended for another aircraft with a similar call sign.

Attention Failures

Misperceptions are often the result of breakdowns in selective attention. Pilots attend to the wrong stimulus while failing to pay attention to the correct one. CFIT, loss of control in flight, and other types of fatal accidents have occurred because pilots were preoccupied with nonessential tasks, or were saturated with important tasks that their diminished attentional resources were unable to cope with.

Memory Failures

Successful flight performance is memory-dependent, but pilots sometimes forget previously learned information (retrospective memory) or forget to execute an important task in the future (prospective memory). A common example of the latter includes forgetting to lower the landing gear before landing or to raise it after takeoff. Another is forgetting to change fuel tanks. For example, all three passengers were killed when a Cessna 206 struck terrain in Greenville, Maine, after the pilot failed to move the fuel selector to the right tank before takeoff resulting in fuel starvation during the initial climb (NTSB Identification No: NYC03FA197). If maximum performance is needed on takeoff, air transport pilots will sometimes conduct a *packs-off* takeoff that involves turning off the engine intake bleed air needed to run the environmental control systems (cabin pressurization, air conditioning). However, if they forget to turn the packs back on during the climb (prospective memory failure), the cabin pressure altitude may exceed 10,000 feet causing subsequent deployment of the oxygen masks.

Decision-Making Errors

One of the most complex of mental operations is decision making. As already noted, any deficiencies upstream—sensory processing, perception, attention, or memory—can lead to poor decision-making outcomes downstream. However, decision making itself comes with its own inherent limitations. For example, biases are often evident in the decision making of GA—and sometimes commercial—pilots who attempt VFR flight into IMC. Compared to an overall GA fatal accident rate of less than 18 percent, 95 percent of U.S. GA VFR flight-into-IMC accidents in 2015 resulted in fatalities.[23] Empirical studies and accident investigations indicate that decision biases such as invulnerability, optimistic and ability bias, overconfidence, framing, and escalation biases have been operable in pilots' decisions to continue VFR flight into IMC.[24]

Since cognitive psychology has made a substantial contribution to the field of human factors and its findings have significantly expanded our understanding of normal everyday human behavior, Part III—the other major section in this book—presents several chapters that explore the different stages of information processing and how they can affect pilot performance on the flight deck.

Social Psychology

In the previous chapter we also noted that one of the major attempts at explaining human error was the psychosocial perspective. This perspective derives its findings from **social psychology**, the scientific study of how people's thoughts and behaviors are influenced by others.

Social influence—the actual or perceived influence exerted by other people on us to feel, think or behave in a certain manner—whether obvious or subtle, begins at, or even before, birth and continues throughout our lifespan. Our social environment, especially during childhood and adolescence, profoundly affects our thoughts, beliefs, opinions, attitudes, and our behavior. What other people, especially family and friends, do and say impacts our overall worldview—what we believe about life, how the world works, faith, other people, politics, and a host of other things. Everything we do is shaped by others: from how we dress, eat, and drive, to how we respond to other people in our communities.

Social psychology seeks to understand these influences, in part, by studying the thoughts and behaviors of individuals in groups. For example, researchers have discovered that social norms—unwritten rules of expected behavior—regulate how we behave in groups. Other factors such as one's role and status, and group cohesiveness, also affect the degree to which individual members of a group conform to the group's expectations.

Interacting with people is very important for our day-to-day functioning. The information and guidance others provide us helps to clarify our ideas, attitudes and beliefs. For example, when starting a new position as an FO at a regional airline, such verbal and non-verbal feedback is essential in learning how to do your job effectively. This *conformity*, or compliance, to group expectations at work, whether explicit or implied, can be very positive in other ways. For example, if you are flying for an airline whose chief pilot, flight operations training instructors, line check pilots, captains, and FOs place the safety of flight operations above all other considerations, including profit, on-time performance, or even passenger approval, it will be easier for you to do the same. But if such is not the case, psychosocial research indicates that either begrudgingly or willingly, the odds are you will likely *do as they do*. As evidenced in the Air Ontario accident in Dryden, Ontario (discussed in the previous chapter), the expectations of other people, including passengers, company dispatch, and upper airline management can influence you—consciously or unconsciously—to take unnecessary risks, even if you pride yourself on flying by the rules.

Social psychology studies other topics, such as interpersonal relationships and group decision making. For example, just as an individual's decisions can be positively or negatively influenced by the group, a group's decision making can be positively or negatively influenced by its individual members and even by its own dynamics. Research has discovered, for example, that such dynamics can foster polarization of positions, often leading to a suboptimal group decision, if not a stalemate. Group undercurrents can also involve conformity to a group decision even when some individual group members strongly disagree with it. Whether it is because of bystander apathy, diffusion of responsibility, social loafing, or some other phenomena, such *groupthink* has led to poor decisions with sometimes catastrophic results.

Since a **crewed flight deck** is a group, which consists of at least a captain and an FO, it shouldn't surprise you that some of the shortcomings of group behavior have exhibited themselves in aircraft accidents and incidents. In fact, in response to several fatal airline accidents in the 1970s and 1980s involving poor group performance in the cockpit, the airline industry implemented crew resource management (CRM) principles into their pilot training curricula. CRM is a practical example of using the findings of social psychology (and industrial-organizational psychology) to optimize flight crew performance and safety. It consists of a set of behaviors designed to overcome the limitations of flight crew performance—including cognitive and psychosocial shortcomings—by practicing skills such as communication, assertiveness, and teamwork to facilitate safe and efficient flight operations.

Since other people have a profound influence on our own behavior, we devote an entire chapter to the psychosocial aspects of flight crew performance (*see* Chapter 18). And because effective interaction with other people is an important component in achieving safe flight operations, Chapter 19 explores the fundamental principles of CRM.

Human Factors for Pilots

As this chapter has demonstrated, the formal discipline of human factors is actually several disciplines that seek to optimize the effectiveness of human-machine systems through design that accommodates the limitations and capabilities of the human operator. This in turn reduces human error and maximizes human performance, safety, efficiency, and comfort. We have also seen that the discipline is defined somewhat differently by some people, especially those outside of the formal academic discipline. From a pilot's point of view, for example, human factors are seen as those human limitations or shortcomings that contribute to unsafe flight operations and accidents.

Even though the engineering side of human factors/ergonomics has contributed greatly to the reduction of operator error on the flight deck—through the design of seats, workstations, controls, flight instruments, avionics, and other aircraft components to better fit the needs and limitations of the human operator—it is the human side of the field that most pilots are interested in, and therefore what this book is primarily about. Drawing mostly from the fields of medicine, physiology, and psychology, the aim of this book is to help you to better understand the physiological, psychological, and psychosocial aspects of individual pilot performance. The engineering disciplines have contributed significantly to the reduction of operator error on the flight deck, and will continue to do so as new advances are implemented, but they are beyond your control as a pilot. What you can control, however, is your own thinking and behavior. What you need to acquire is a solid understanding of how, when, and why you make mistakes, and more importantly, how you can implement strategies that are designed to eliminate, reduce, or mitigate their effects. That is what the remainder of this book hopes to achieve. After all, since pilots are the first to arrive at the scene of an accident, you have a vested interest in avoiding and reducing the errors that may lead to one.

Helpful Resources

The FAA Human Factors Division has produced a ten-module web-based course that describes the most salient concepts of human factors research and engineering. Designed for FAA employees, the Human Factors Awareness Course is an excellent introduction to the discipline of human factors and is available for anyone to use. (www.hf.faa.gov/training.aspx)

Even though it is written for specialists and is highly technical, lengthy, and can be expensive (even used), *Engineering Psychology and Human Performance*, written by Christopher Wickens and others (depending of the edition), is a good book for those who want to delve deeper into the cognitive aspects of human factors design.

Another excellent work of similar character as Wickens et al. that is slightly more readable for the layperson and contains a broader coverage of the discipline is the *Handbook of Aviation Human Factors*, second edition, edited by John Wise, David Hopkin, and Daniel Garland.

A very short video clip of the first "blind flight" conducted by Lieutenant James "Jimmy" Doolittle and his safety pilot on September 24, 1929. (www.gettyimages.com/detail/video/james-jimmy-doolittle-performs-first-blind-flight-news-footage/145012946)

Endnotes

1. Michael Armstrong, "Pilot Error Caused 2013 ERA Crash, NTSB Says," *Homer News* (October 30, 2015).

2. "Control Coding – Shape," *FAA Human Factors Awareness Web Course*," eds. Rebecca R. Gray and Glen Hewitt (Washington, DC: FAA Human Factors Division). Available at www.hf.faa.gov/webtraining/controls/ControlsFinal016.htm.

3. Stanley N. Roscoe, "The Adolescence of Engineering Psychology," *Human Factors History Monograph Series, Volume 1*, ed. Steven M. Casey (Santa Monica, CA: Human Factors and Ergonomics Society, 1997).

4. Jefferson M. Koonce, "A Historical Overview of Human Factors in Aviation," *Handbook of Aviation Human Factors*, eds. Daniel J. Garland, John A. Wise and V. David Hopkin (Mahwah, NJ: Lawrence Erlbaum Associates, 1999): 3–13.

5. Christopher D. Wickens and Justin G. Hollands, *Engineering Psychology and Human Performance*, 3rd ed. (Upper Saddle River, NJ: Prentice Hall, 2000): 3.

6. K.F.H. Murrell, *Human Performance in Industry* (New York: Reinhold Publishing, 1965).

7. International Ergonomics Association, *Definition and Domains of Ergonomics: Physical Ergonomics* (n.d.). Available at www.iea.cc/definition-and-domains-of-ergonomics/.

8. Cleanup of File:Computer Workstation Variables.jpg, by Yamavu, August 1, 2013 (https://commons.wikimedia.org/wiki/File:Computer_Workstation_Variables_cleanup.png); WC CC0 1.0 Public Domain Dedication

9. Kenneth W. Kennedy, *International Anthropometric Variability and Its Effects on Aircraft Cockpit Design*, ADA027801 (Wright-Patterson AFB, OH: USAF Aerospace Medical Research Lab, July 1976): 50.

10. U.S. Bureau of Safety, Civil Aeronautics Board, *Aircraft Design-Induced Pilot Error* (Washington, DC: July 1967).

11. National Aeronautics and Space Administration, *NASA Aviation Safety Reporting System: Second Quarterly Report, July 16—October 14, 1976*, NASA Technical Memorandum NASA TM X-3494 (Moffett Field, CA: NASA Ames Research Center, December 1976): 60.

12. John Mackenzie Bacon, *The Dominion of the Air: The Story of Aerial Navigation* (New York: Cassell & Company, 1902): 223–228.

13. J. Colin, *Paul Bert, Translation of "Paul Bert", Science (French Edition of Scientific American)*, No. 12, Oct. 1978, pp. 27–33, NASA Technical Memorandum NASA TM-75599 (Washington DC: NASA, December 1978).

14. Jean Paries and Brent Hayward, "Human Factors and Ergonomics Practice in Aviation: Assisting Human Performance in Aviation Operations," *Human Factors and Ergonomics in Practice: Improving System Performance and Human Well-Being in the Real World*, eds. Steven M. Casey and Claire Williams (Boca Raton, FL: CRC Press, 2017): 203–218.

15. David R, Jones, "Flying and Dying in WWI: British Aircrew Losses and the Origins of U.S. Military Aviation Medicine," *Aviation, Space, and Environmental Medicine* 79 (2008): 139–46.

16. Koonce, "A Historical Overview of Human Factors in Aviation."

17. "First Blind Takeoff, Flight and Landing, 1929," *Engineering and Technology History Wiki* (December 31, 2015). Available at www.ethw.org/Milestones:First_Blind_Takeoff,_Flight_and_Landing,_1929.

18. Irena Farlik, *U.S. Military Aerospace Physiology* (February 26, 2015). Available at www.goflightmedicine.com/usaf-aerospace-physiology/.

19. Terouz Pasha and Paul R.A. Stokes, "Reflecting on the Germanwings Disaster: A Systematic Review of Depression and Suicide in Commercial Airline Pilots," *Frontiers in Psychiatry* 9 (Mar 20, 2018): 86.

20. Russell J. Lewis, Estrella M. Forster, James E. Whinnery, Nicholas L. Webster, *Aircraft-Assisted Pilot Suicides in the United States, 2003–2012*, DOT/FAA/AM-14/2 (Washington, DC: FAA Office of Aviation Medicine, February 2014). Available at www.faa.gov/data_research/research/med_humanfacs/oamtechreports/2010s/2014/.

21. "Wickens' Model," *FAA Human Factors Awareness Web Course*, eds. Rebecca R. Gray and Glen Hewitt, (Washington, DC: FAA Human Factors Division). Adapted from Christopher D. Wickens, Engineering Psychology and Human Performance, 2nd ed. (New York: HarperCollins, 1992).

22. Experts believe that humans possess more than five basic senses. For example, within the broad category of touch, there are separate types of sensory receptors for pressure, temperature and pain.

23. AOPA Air Safety Institute, *27th Joseph T. Nall Report: General Aviation Accidents in 2015* (Frederick, MD: AOPA Air Safety Institute, 2018).

24. Dale R. Wilson and Gerald Binnema, "Pushing Weather" (Chapter 4), in *Managing Risk: Best Practices for Pilots* (Newcastle, WA: Aviation Supplies and Academics, 2014).

Part II
Physiological Aspects of
Flight Crew Performance

4

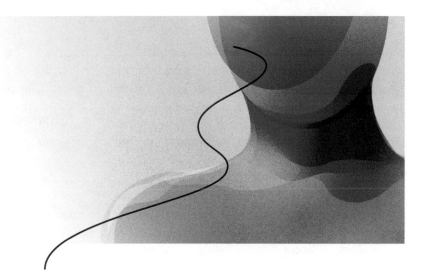

How high can I fly?
Hypoxia and Hyperventilation

Imagine you're the commander of a Lockheed Martin F-16 fighter jet and you receive a call to intercept a Boeing B-737 that isn't responding to calls from ATC. When you arrive you find the airplane is flying at FL340 (34,000 feet) in a holding pattern over the VOR (very high frequency omnidirectional range). You try to get the crew's attention by using standard interceptor signals and by making radio calls on the area control center and emergency frequencies, but to no avail. You maneuver closer to see if you can see inside the cabin and you are shocked to discover that no one is flying the airplane—the captain's seat is empty and the FO is slumped unconscious over the controls! You're unable to see any movement whatsoever in the aircraft and the few passengers you do see in the cabin are sitting motionless in their seats wearing oxygen masks over their faces.

After about 15 minutes you notice something moving inside the airplane. Someone wearing a light blue shirt enters, sits down in the captain's seat, and puts on a pair of headphones. A few moments later, the left engine of the commercial jet flames out from fuel starvation and the aircraft begins to turn and descend. You try to get the attention of the person in the captain's seat and finally, at about 7,000 feet, he acknowledges you by making a hand motion. You signal back that he should follow you to the airport, but as the right engine also flames out, he just points his hand downwards and fails to follow your turn. You then watch helplessly as the airplane descends and crashes into the ground.

You don't have to imagine such a scenario because, unfortunately, it really did happen. Helios Airways Flight 522, on a flight from Larnaca, Cyprus, to Athens,

Greece, was climbing through 12,000 feet when the cabin altitude warning horn—which warns the crew that the aircraft **cabin altitude** (the pressure in the cabin expressed as an altitude) exceeds 10,000 feet—sounded. However, the cabin altitude warning horn on this B-737 also doubled as a takeoff configuration warning, signifying the aircraft was improperly configured for takeoff. Unfortunately, the crew misinterpreted this warning as the latter (the captain told dispatch they had a "takeoff configuration warning on") and continued to climb to FL340. While the aircraft was passing through 18,000 feet, and while they were troubleshooting their problems with the help of a company ground engineer on the radio, the passenger oxygen masks deployed at 14,000 feet cabin altitude. However, the flight crew was unaware of this in spite of the PASS OXY ON light illuminating on the flight deck. As they continued the climb the crew lost consciousness; the last radio transmission the captain made occurred while passing through FL290, about eight minutes after the cabin warning horn activated.

The B-737 leveled off at FL340 and, flown by the autopilot, continued en route for almost three hours. It then dutifully went through all the motions programmed into its flight management system by its crew: it conducted an approach, a missed approach, and then entered a hold at the VOR, but it remained at FL340. It turns out the person who entered the flight deck while the aircraft was in the hold was a young cabin attendant who also held a commercial pilot license. Investigators don't exactly know how he remained, or regained, consciousness, but it appears he made a last-ditch attempt to save the airplane. Unfortunately, it wasn't enough: it was destroyed and all 121 of its occupants were killed when it impacted hilly terrain near a village about 20 miles northwest of the Athens International Airport.[1]

Almost four years to the day after this accident an experienced pilot embarked on a VFR cross-country flight on a warm August morning in 2009 from Rantoul, Illinois. Unfortunately, he never made it to his destination of O'Neill, Nebraska. ATC-radar data indicate the Air Tractor AT-802 was on a west-northwest course flying toward a line of thunderstorms. The pilot climbed as high as 17,700 feet MSL in an apparent attempt to clear those cells. The agricultural aircraft then reversed course to an easterly heading and descended to 15,200 feet, then climbed to 16,300 feet, and then descended on a southeast course—at a rate of more than 12,000 fpm—until it impacted an open field about eight miles east of Corning, Iowa (NTSB Identification No: CEN09LA527).

What these two tragic accidents have in common is the pilots of both airplanes suffered from debilitating **hypoxia**—a lack of sufficient oxygen—that rendered them mentally and physically incapable of controlling their aircraft. Accident investigators concluded that the primary causes of the Helios Airways accident were: the flight crew's failure to recognize that the cabin pressurization mode selector was in the manual (MAN) mode, their failure to correctly identify the cabin altitude warnings while continuing the climb, and their incapacitation due to hypoxia. National Transportation Safety Board investigators in Iowa discovered the 32,000-hour commercial pilot operated the unpressurized AT-802 airplane above 12,000 feet MSL for approximately 24 minutes, and above 15,000 feet MSL for at least 14 minutes of that time. They concluded the LOC-I was due to the pilot's impairment as a result of hypoxia and his decision to operate the unpressurized airplane at an altitude requiring supplemental oxygen without having any oxygen available to him (NTSB Identification No: CEN09LA527).

Without adequate protection, flying at higher altitudes will eventually lead to flight crew incapacitation. **Incapacitation** involves any physiological or psychological condition that renders a flight crew member incapable of performing his or her normal flight duties, including the ability to safely control the aircraft. In these two accidents incapacitation was due to hypoxia from insufficient oxygen. In the Helios accident, the aircraft cabin never properly pressurized because the crew failed to notice the pressurization mode selector was set to MAN—it had been left in that position after maintenance personnel conducted a routine check earlier that morning—and, despite three opportunities to do so during the required preflight and checklist procedures, they never reset it to automatic (AUTO) which would have automatically pressurized the aircraft cabin as altitude was gained. In a non-pressurized aircraft hypoxia is prevented through the use of fixed or portable oxygen systems. It's almost certain the experienced aviator piloting the AT-802 in Iowa knew about the phenomenon of hypoxia, but for whatever reason, he chose to fly at hypoxic-inducing altitudes without carrying any oxygen on board.

Hypoxia and Pilot Performance

Hypoxia adversely affects pilot performance in a number of ways. A quick search through the NASA ASRS database for the period covering the first decade of this millennium indicates how. Besides turning to wrong headings, leveling off at wrong altitudes, entering the wrong airspace, and dialing in the wrong frequencies on the radio, pilots suffering from hypoxia have started instrument approaches without an ATC clearance, unintentionally flown from VMC into IMC, flown 6,000 feet below the minimum **instrument flight rules (IFR)** en route altitude in mountainous terrain while in IMC, mismanaged fuel controls leading to engine failures, and misread altimeters by as much as 10,000 feet. Pilots have also reported losing their hearing (a pilot was unable to hear the cabin altitude warning horn), their memory (one pilot forgot an entire portion of the flight), and even their ability to move an arm to press the push-to-talk switch on the control column!

All of these ASRS incident examples fortunately had happy endings: the pilots involved lived to talk about them. Unfortunately, many others haven't. A search of the NTSB's accident database over the same period reveals that hypoxia accidents have a high lethality rate, with 14 out of the 16 hypoxia accidents resulting in fatalities. Rather than just making mistakes that only affected or potentially could have affected the safety of flight (i.e., an incident), hypoxic pilots involved in these accidents were either mentally unable to make the decisions needed to safely fly their aircraft or, like the pilots involved in the two accidents discussed at the beginning of this chapter, were rendered completely unconscious.

This chapter and the next investigate the physiological effects of altitude on the human body. This chapter discusses hypoxia and other physiological issues related to respiration, while Chapter 5 looks at the physiological effects of trapped and evolved gases on pilot performance. To understand the physiological phenomena discussed in both chapters you must first understand the nature of the air we breathe.

Characteristics of Earth's Atmosphere

Even though the cold temperature of high altitudes creates an inhospitable environment for human survival, pilots and passengers are mostly shielded from its effects in today's aircraft from capable onboard environmental heating systems. The focus of this chapter and the next, therefore, is on another atmospheric characteristic that poses a threat to proper physiological functioning: the effects of reduced atmospheric pressure at higher altitudes.

Atmospheric Composition

What we call air consists of several gases that make up the life-sustaining gaseous envelope that surrounds Earth. As Figure 4-1 illustrates, the atmosphere (*atmos* = vapor; *sphere* = sphere) is made up of nitrogen (78 percent), oxygen (21 percent), argon (0.9 percent), and trace gases (0.1 percent), primarily carbon dioxide. These fixed constituents in the atmosphere are well mixed and maintain the same percentages within the homosphere, which reaches up to about 80 kilometers (km) (50 miles or 262,000 feet). This is close to the *Kármán line*, named after the early 20th-century aeronautical scientist Theodore von Kármán, who calculated the approximate altitude—about 100 km or 62 miles or 328,000 feet—at which the air is too thin for conventional aircraft to produce aerodynamic lift to sustain controlled flight. Above these altitudes in the heterosphere, the composition of atmospheric gases changes with its constituents stratifying into layers based on their molecular mass, with the heaviest molecules concentrated in the lower regions. Water

vapor (water in gaseous form), considered a variable constituent that is concentrated within the troposphere (see later section in this chapter), ranges from close to zero (in dry climactic regions) to as high as four percent (mostly in the tropics) by volume.

Although nitrogen is important to life, the molecular nitrogen in the atmosphere—diatomic nitrogen (N_2)—is generally not used by the human body. We breathe it in and exhale most of it back out, although some is absorbed by the cells and tissues of the body which poses a problem at high altitudes (to be discussed in our next chapter).

Atmospheric oxygen (O_2) is, however, essential to life. It combines with nutrients in the blood from the food we eat, and through the process of respiration is delivered to every cell in the body, creating the energy our bodies need to function. Without oxygen we wouldn't be able to live much longer than about three minutes.

| N_2 78% Nitrogen | O_2 21% Oxygen | ● 1% Argon & other |

Fig 4-1.

The permanent gases in the atmosphere consist of 78% nitrogen, 21% oxygen, and 1% argon and other gases. Not included in the figure is water vapor, which can reach up to 4% by volume.

Atmospheric Pressure

Atmospheric pressure—the force of the air over a given area—at any point on the earth's surface consists of the weight, or total mass, of the air above it. The international standard atmosphere (ISA) represents the average conditions in the lower 80 km (50 miles or 262,000 feet) of the atmosphere at 45 degrees latitude.[2] The ISA sea-level pressure is 14.7 PSI (pounds per square inch). Using other units of measurement, it is also 29.92 in Hg (inches of mercury), 1013.25 mb (millibars), or 1013.25 hPa (hectopascals).

As you ascend in the atmosphere the pressure decreases until it reaches zero at its top (an altitude that is not well defined). But the change is not linear, it is logarithmic. For example, just as blankets of equal thickness placed at the bottom of a stack of blankets are compressed because of the weight of the blankets above them, so too is the air at the bottom of the atmosphere compressed because of the weight of the air above it. Figure 4-2 illustrates that 99.9 percent of the atmosphere's mass lies below approximately 164,000 feet (31 miles), 90 percent lies below 53,000 feet (10.5 miles) and half the weight of the earth's atmosphere lies below 18,000 feet MSL (3.5 miles). This means the reduction in atmospheric pressure sufficient to create oxygen problems for flight crews occurs at very low altitudes compared to the overall height of the atmosphere. It also means that atmospheric pressure changes more rapidly at lower altitudes (a concept that relates to trapped gases in the body discussed in the next chapter).

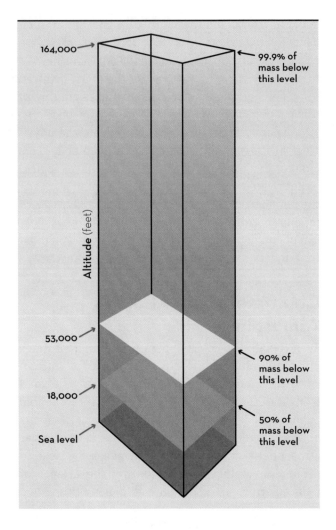

Fig 4-2.

Atmospheric mass and pressure at various altitudes.

Atmospheric Layers

The atmosphere is also divided into layers that are based primarily on temperature. Of the four major layers indicated in Figure 4-3, the lowest layer is the most applicable to flight crews. The average ISA height of the troposphere is about 36,000 feet above MSL; however, since cold and warm air mass volumes differ, it extends from the surface to about 25,000 to 30,000 feet at the colder poles and 55,000 to 65,000 feet at the warmer equator. The troposphere (*tropos* = change; *sphere* = sphere) is the layer in which most water vapor exists and most of the earth's weather occurs. It is also the layer in which virtually all flight activity takes place.

Since the troposphere is heated primarily from radiation emitted from the earth's surface, air temperature lowers as you ascend in the troposphere—at an ISA lapse rate (rate of temperature change with altitude) of 1.98 degrees Celsius (°C) per 1,000 feet—and reaches an ISA temperature of –56.5°C, or –70 degrees Fahrenheit (°F), at the tropopause (or *trop*, pronounced *trope*). The cooling rate abruptly stops and remains the same at the tropopause, an isothermal (*iso* = equal; *thermal* = temperature) layer where most upper-level jet streams—fast flowing winds—are located. Most commercial jet aircraft fly at or near the tropopause, and as we mentioned, occupants are protected from these intolerable temperatures by effective cabin heating systems.

Warming occurs in the next layer above the troposphere—the stratosphere—because the presence of ozone absorbs energy from the ultraviolet radiation of the Sun, shielding life on Earth from the worst of its harmful effects. After warming to slightly less than sea level temperatures at the stratopause, cooling begins again in the mesosphere located between two energy absorbing layers. The warming in the layer above the mesopause—the thermosphere—occurs primarily because of high-energy solar radiation splitting diatomic oxygen (O_2) and nitrogen (N_2) molecules apart into atomic oxygen (O) and nitrogen (N).

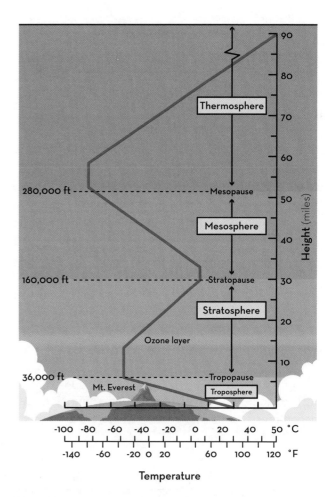

Fig 4-3.

Atmospheric layers with temperature changes depicted by the red line.

Physiological Zones of the Atmosphere

Up to now, we have looked at some basic *physical* characteristics of the atmosphere. The atmosphere can also be divided into three *physiological layers*, or zones, as indicated in Table 4-1. Humans can generally tolerate activity in the **physiological efficient zone**, which lies between sea level and 10,000 feet MSL. Pilots flying in the lower regions of this zone may experience problems with trapped gas in body cavities such as the ears, sinus, and gastrointestinal (GI) tract (discussed in the next chapter), and in the upper regions they may experience mild hypoxia and fatigue, especially when flying for long durations at these altitudes. Night vision is also affected by reduced oxygen pressures at or above 5,000 feet MSL.

Most commercial flight activity occurs in the **physiological deficient zone**, between 10,000 and 50,000 feet MSL. Without adequate equipment or countermeasures, pilots and passengers flying in this zone will experience hypoxia and altitude decompression sickness (DCS), the latter discussed in the next chapter.

The **space equivalent zone**, extending from 50,000 feet MSL to space is completely hostile to human survival. For example, at or above the **Armstrong line** (63,000 feet MSL) the atmospheric pressure is so low that, unless crew members are flying in a completely sealed cabin or wearing pressurized space suits, their bodily fluids will change from a liquid state to a gaseous state—i.e., their blood will boil!

Several laws governing the behavior of gases—including air—were discovered by scientists more than two centuries ago. One relevant to this chapter is **Dalton's Law**, which states that *the total pressure of a mixture of gases is equal to the sum of the partial pressures of each individual gas*. Table 4-2 describes the partial pressures (P) of the individual gases if the total pressure of the atmosphere at a given point at sea level is 1,000 hPa (mb).

The percentage of O_2 does not decrease with increasing altitude—it remains at approximately 21 percent right up to altitudes in the thermosphere—but its partial pressure does. For example, if the partial pressure (PO_2) of oxygen at sea level is 210 hPa as Table 4-2 indicates, and total atmospheric mass

Table 4-1. The three physiological zones of the atmosphere.[3]

Physiological zones	Altitudes	Pressure (mb)	Characteristics
Physiological efficient zone	Sea level–10,000 feet	1,013–700	Functioning is generally not affected with the exception of trapped gas problems (ears, sinus, GI tract, etc.) and mild hypoxia and fatigue in the upper regions, especially during long flights. Night vision is also affected by reduced O_2 pressures at or above 5,000 feet MSL.
Physiological deficient zone	10,000–50,000 feet	700–116	Reduced atmospheric pressure causes two major physiological problems: hypoxia and DCS.
Space equivalent zone	50,000 feet–1,000 miles	116–0	This zone is completely inhospitable to humans. Unprotected exposure above 63,000 feet (Armstrong line) causes body fluids to boil. A fully pressurized space suit and/or sealed cabin is required.

Table 4-2. The total pressure of atmospheric gases is the sum of the partial pressures of each individual gas ($P_{Total} = PN_2 + PO_2 + PA/T$).

Constituent gas	Composition (%)	Partial pressure hPa (mb)
Nitrogen (N_2)	78	$PN_2 = 780$
Oxygen (O_2)	21	$PO_2 = 210$
Argon/Trace (A/T)	1	$PA/T = 10$
Total (P_{Total})	100%	1,000 hPa (mb)

and pressure at 18,000 feet is half that of sea level (*see* Figure 4-2), it is the PO_2 of oxygen that is halved (105 hPa), not its percentage.

Respiration and Circulation

The process by which a living organism exchanges gases with its environment is known as **respiration**. This gas exchange involves the delivery of O_2 to, and the removal of carbon dioxide (CO_2) from, the body's cells. The process is divided into three types of respiration: external, internal, and cellular. The respiratory system is responsible for delivering O_2 from the atmosphere to the lungs (external respiration), to the blood (internal respiration), then to the body's cells (cellular respiration). Glucose (blood sugar) in the blood produced from the nutrients in the food we eat and drink combines with O_2 and is delivered to the cells where chemical reactions take place, producing the energy needed to sustain life in a process known as *metabolism*. One of the byproducts of these chemical reactions is CO_2, which is mostly offloaded back to the blood then through the lungs and into the atmosphere.

External Respiration

External respiration involves the exchange of O_2 and CO_2 between the atmosphere and the lungs. It begins by simply breathing: inhaling (inspiration) and exhaling (expiration) air, a process that occurs automatically about 12 to 20 times a minute when resting, almost always unconsciously, and with very little effort, due in part to the assistance of physics.

This automatic breathing occurs when CO_2 levels in the blood build up sending a signal to the brain to begin inhalation. The reason for this is to maintain an ideal body acid-alkaline pH (potential of hydrogen) level of about 7.35 to 7.45.[4] Values higher (too alkaline) or lower (too acidic) than these upset the body's delicate chemical balance, causing alkalosis or acidosis that adversely affects all major systems of the body leading to a variety of deleterious symptoms.

The lungs are pyramid-shaped organs made up of spongy tissue that fills up the *thoracic cavity* (chest cavity). During inhalation, as illustrated in Figure 4-4, the respiratory muscles contract causing the top-to-bottom and front-to-back size of the chest cavity to enlarge.

Inhaling air is almost effortless, thanks to **Boyle's Law**, which states that *the volume of a gas is inversely proportional to the pressure exerted on it*. Since the volume of the lungs has increased, the pressure of the air inside lowers creating a slight negative pressure differential between the outside air and the lungs. According to **Graham's Law**, *a gas under high pressure will flow toward a low pressure*; therefore, air automatically flows from the outside into the lungs. During expiration the muscles relax, the cavity returns to its smaller size, and air is expelled, this time because of a positive pressure differential.

After passing through the nose and/or mouth, the trachea (windpipe), and the two bronchial tubes (one for each lung), the air travels into tiny tubes called bronchioles that open up into millions of little air sacs

Fig 4-4.

The mechanics of breathing.
Contraction of the respiratory muscles during inhalation increases the volume of the lungs, creating a pressure differential that draws outside air into the lungs. The opposite occurs during exhalation.

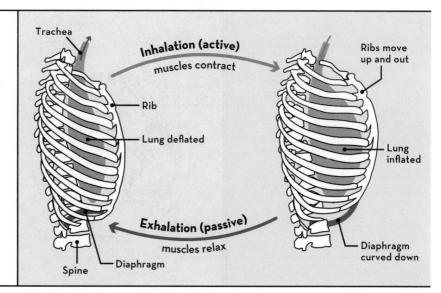

called *alveoli*. Each alveolus is covered by numerous capillaries, the smallest of blood vessels, and it is at this interface where the exchange of gases between the lungs and the blood takes place (*see* Figure 4-5). In order to exchange as much gas as possible (i.e., O_2 from alveoli to blood and CO_2 from blood alveoli)—especially to accommodate varying levels of physical activity—the lungs need a sufficient quantity of alveoli.[5] Fortunately, the design of the lungs does just that. Though relatively small in size, a typical pair of adult lungs (depending on person's body size) contain an average of 480 million alveoli.[5] And, if spread out flat they would cover an area of about 750 square feet.[6]

Internal Respiration

Internal respiration involves the exchange of gases between the alveoli in the lungs and the blood. Blood is pumped by the heart through the arteries to your body's cells and returns through the veins. Each alveolus in the lungs is encircled by capillaries connected

Fig 4-5.

The human respiratory system. Inhaled air travels through the trachea, two bronchi, and bronchioles, ultimately arriving at the alveoli. Each alveolus is covered by capillaries where gases in the lungs and the blood are exchanged.

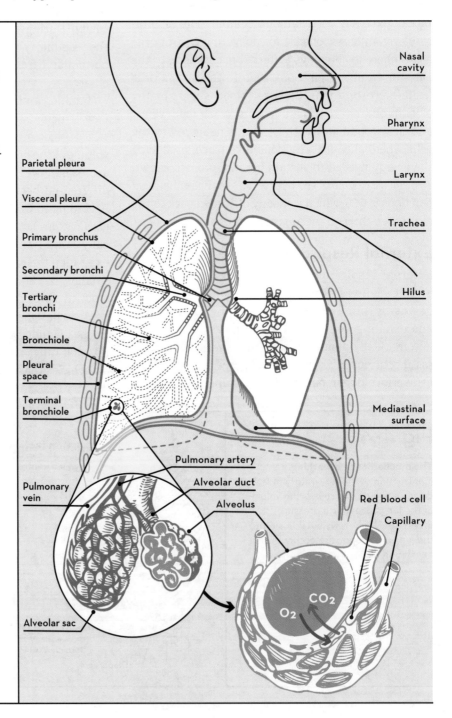

Parietal pleura

Visceral pleura

Primary bronchus

Secondary bronchi

Tertiary bronchi

Bronchiole

Pleural space

Terminal bronchiole

Pulmonary vein

Alveolar sac

Nasal cavity

Pharynx

Larynx

Trachea

Hilus

Mediastinal surface

Pulmonary artery

Alveolar duct

Alveolus

Red blood cell

Capillary

CO_2

O_2

to these veins and arteries and consists of a very thin membrane that is only about 1/50,000th of an inch thick.[7] Liquid cannot pass through the capillaries but gaseous molecules (O_2, CO_2) can. The actual exchange can be described using Graham's Law and **Fick's Law**, which states that *molecules of high-concentration passively move to areas of low-concentration*. Because there is a greater pressure and quantity (concentration) of O_2 in the alveoli than there is in the blood in the capillaries after inhalation, O_2 diffuses (passes) through the alveolar and capillary walls into the blood. Similarly, since the pressure and quantity of CO_2 in the blood is greater than that in the lungs, CO_2 diffuses through the capillary and alveolar walls into the lungs. Figure 4-6 illustrates this. The blood is only in the lung area for about one to two seconds, yet this is sufficient for the O_2 to pass through the walls of the alveoli and capillaries into the blood and for the CO_2 to pass from the blood through the capillaries and alveolar walls into the lungs.

Cellular Respiration

Cellular respiration involves the exchange of gases between the blood and the body's cells. After O_2 moves from the alveoli to the capillaries, the oxygen-rich blood is pumped through the heart and transported to the body's cells through the arteries. The same gas exchange process used during internal respiration is at work for cellular respiration: Because the quantity and pressure of O_2 in the blood is greater than the quantity and pressure of O_2 in the body's cells, the O_2 diffuses into the cells. As mentioned previously, a chemical reaction takes place as O_2 is used to metabolize food in the cells, producing the energy needed to sustain life. One of the byproducts of this reaction is CO_2. Since the quantity and pressure of CO_2 in the cells is now greater than that in the blood, CO_2 diffuses into the blood, and in turn is carried back through the veins to the heart and lungs then into the atmosphere.

Role of Hemoglobin

Blood consists of about 55 percent plasma, the fluid portion of blood (mostly water, but also proteins, CO_2, and other compounds), and about 45 percent red blood cells, the cellular component.[8] Very little O_2 is transferred in the blood in solution as diatomic molecules (O_2); more than 95 percent of it is piggy-backed on **hemoglobin** (Hb)—an iron-rich protein in the red blood cells that magnetically attracts O_2 molecules and gives the red blood cells their color—to form oxyhemoglobin. The oxyhemoglobin compound (HbO_2) enables the blood to carry about 70 times the amount of oxygen that would normally occur if O_2 was in simple solution in the blood.[9] Since there are approximately 250 million Hb molecules in each red

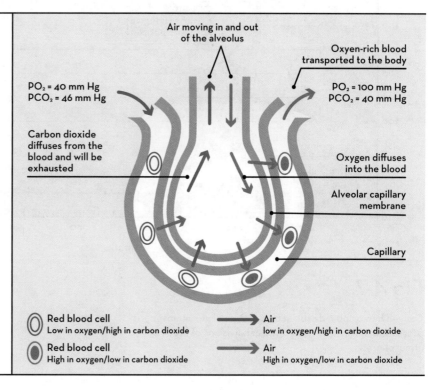

Fig 4-6.

The exchange of carbon dioxide and oxygen between an alveolus and a capillary. Since the partial pressure of inhaled O_2 in the alveolus ($PO_2 = 100$ mm Hg) is greater than in the capillary ($PO_2 = 40$ mm Hg) it diffuses through the alveolar and capillary walls into the capillary. Since the partial pressure of CO_2 in the capillary ($PCO_2 = 46$ mm Hg) is greater than in the alveolus ($PCO_2 = 40$ mm Hg) it diffuses through the capillary and alveolar walls into the lungs.

Air moving in and out of the alveolus

Oxyen-rich blood transported to the body

$PO_2 = 40$ mm Hg
$PCO_2 = 46$ mm Hg

$PO_2 = 100$ mm Hg
$PCO_2 = 40$ mm Hg

Carbon dioxide diffuses from the blood and will be exhausted

Oxygen diffuses into the blood

Alveolar capillary membrane

Capillary

Red blood cell
Low in oxygen/high in carbon dioxide

Red blood cell
High in oxygen/low in carbon dioxide

Air
low in oxygen/high in carbon dioxide

Air
High in oxygen/low in carbon dioxide

blood cell, and each Hb molecule can carry four O_2 molecules, each red blood cell can transport approximately 1 billion O_2 molecules.[10] Multiply that by the number of red blood cells in the body—approximately 26 billion for the average adult male[11]—and, well, you get the idea.

When oxyhemoglobin molecules carry their maximum of four O_2 molecules per Hb molecule, the blood is considered 100 percent saturated with oxygen. However, as the partial pressure of O_2 decreases with altitude, the ability of Hb to "hold on" to these O_2 molecules decreases, reducing blood-oxygen saturation. The relationship is not linear though, because the Hb molecule actually changes in such a way that its affinity (attraction force) for O_2 decreases (by about 1.7 times) when less than four O_2 molecules are bound to it.[12] The red line in Figure 4-7 is the *oxygen-hemoglobin dissociation curve*

portrayed as the percentage of O_2 combined with Hb for various altitudes. You can see it is not a straight line: it is sigmoidal in shape with only a slight drop in O_2 saturation from sea level to 10,000 feet MSL, but a substantially steeper drop (slope) above that altitude because of hemoglobin's decreased affinity for oxygen.

Hypoxia

Hypoxia (*hyp* = low; *oxia* = oxygen) is not the absence of oxygen—that would be *anoxia*—but a state of oxygen deficiency in the blood, tissues, and cells sufficient to cause an impairment of body functions. There are four types of hypoxia that are briefly described in Table 4-3: hypoxic, hypemic, stagnant, and histotoxic hypoxia.

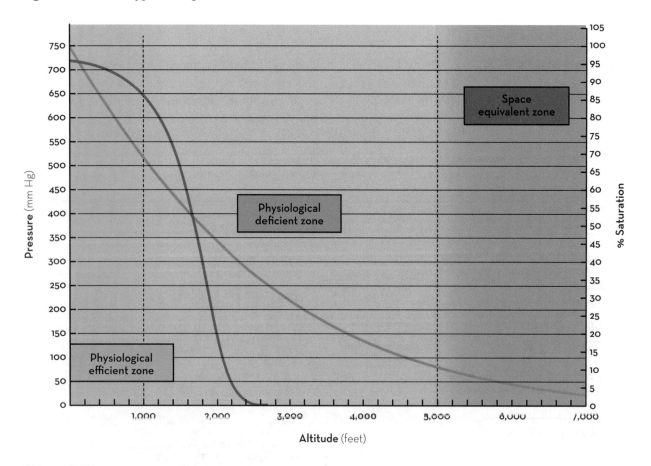

Fig 4-7.

Oxygen hemoglobin dissociation curve (red line), atmospheric pressure (blue line), and physiological divisions of the atmosphere.

Hypoxic (Altitude) Hypoxia

Sometimes called *altitude* hypoxia, or *hypobaric* (*hypo*=low; *baric*=pressure) hypoxia because flying at higher altitudes is the major cause of this type of hypoxia, **hypoxic hypoxia** is usually the type that a pilot will encounter. It is caused by a reduction in the partial pressure of oxygen (PO_2) that occurs when one ascends into the atmosphere. Altitude hypoxia can generally be described by four stages as summarized in Table 4-4: the indifferent, compensatory, disturbance, and critical stages.

Indifferent Stage

About 90 percent blood-oxygen saturation is maintained at 10,000 feet MSL (*see* Figure 4-7), which is generally the upper limit for sufficient body and brain functioning in the physiological efficient zone.

Below this altitude the body is generally unaffected in the **indifferent stage** of hypoxia, except that the pulse and breathing rates increase slightly and night vision is degraded. Since the retina of the eye has the "highest oxygen demand and the lowest deprivation tolerance of any human structure" it is the first organ to be negatively affected by the reduced partial pressure of oxygen.[15] This *visual hypoxia* occurs at altitudes as low as 4,000 to 5,000 feet MSL, seriously degrading visual acuity, peripheral vision, and object brightness in low-light conditions common at night. Chapter 6 discusses visual hypoxia in greater detail.

Even though the body and brain are relatively *indifferent* to the effects of reduced O_2 below 10,000 feet MSL (with the exception of vision), that doesn't mean they are unaffected. Given a sufficient length of time, you may still be susceptible to mild symptoms of hypoxia when flying at or near 10,000 feet.

Table 4-3. Four types of hypoxia.[13]

Common Name	Location of impediment	Explanation
Hypoxic (altitude hypoxia)	Lungs	Any condition that interrupts adequate flow/quantity of O_2 to the lungs. This type of hypoxia is encountered at altitude due to the reduction of the partial pressure of O_2.
Hypemic hypoxia	Blood	Any condition that interferes with the ability of the blood to carry oxygen. Anemia and CO poisoning are two conditions that can keep the O_2 from attaching to the Hb in the red blood cells.
Stagnant hypoxia	Blood transport	Any condition that interferes with the normal circulation of the blood arriving to the cells (e.g., heart failure, shock, and positive G accelerations [$+G_Z$]).
Histotoxic hypoxia	Cells	Any situation that interferes with the normal utilization of O2 in the cells. Alcohol, narcotics, and other drugs can interfere with the cell's ability to use the O_2 in support of metabolism.

Table 4-4. Four stages of hypoxia.[14]

Stage	Percent O_2 saturation	Approximate altitude (feet MSL)	Symptoms
Indifferent	90–98	Sea level–10,000	Decreased night vision at or above 5,000 feet. Mild hypoxia for long durations at or near 10,000 feet.
Compensatory	80–98	10,000–15,000	Drowsiness; poor judgment; impaired coordination and efficiency.
Disturbance	70–79	15,000–20,000	Impaired flight control, handwriting, speech, vision, intellectual function, and judgment; decreased coordination, memory, and sensation to pain.
Critical	60–69	20,000–25,000	Unconsciousness from circulatory or central nervous system failure; convulsions; cardiovascular collapse; death.

I remember experiencing one of the symptoms of hypoxia—euphoria (a feeling of well-being)—after flying for almost four hours in a small airplane at only 9,500 feet MSL. I looked at my passenger, who was also a pilot, with a wide grin and said, "Hey, I'm feeling pretty good right now. I think I'm getting hypoxia." My passenger looked back at me with an equally large grin and said, "Yeah, me too." "Do you think we should descend?" I said, still feeling very happy with that big smile on my face, to which my pilot-friend replied, "Yeah, probably a good idea." We did descend, and within a couple of thousand feet we were our normal not-so-overly happy selves again.

Compensatory Stage

As seen in Figure 4-7, blood-oxygen saturation drops precipitously above 10,000 feet—the lower limit of the physiological deficient zone—because of a decrease in hemoglobin's affinity for oxygen. The body tries to *compensate* for reduced oxygen in the **compensatory stage** of hypoxia by significantly increasing the rate and depth of breathing, and by increasing the pulse rate, blood circulation rate, and cardiac output. This will *compensate* for the reduced oxygen intake only if exposure is of short duration and the person is not requiring more oxygen through increased physical activity (a flight attendant (FA) is likely to be more active). It should be noted that just because your body is trying to compensate for the reduction in the partial pressure of oxygen, it doesn't mean it is succeeding.

As Table 4-4 indicates, you will still experience negative symptoms between 10,000 and 15,000 feet, especially if exposed to longer durations at the upper limit of this altitude range. This is the reason regulations limit exposure to only 30 minutes when flying between 12,500 feet MSL and 14,000 feet MSL in the United States and between 10,000 feet MSL and 13,000 feet MSL in Canada. A search of the NTSB's accident database for a recent 10-year period shows that pilots in about half of fatal hypoxia accidents in the United States failed to comply with these basic rules. For example, a 700-hour pilot recently lost control of his Cessna 182T and died after impacting terrain near Ludlow, California. Thirty minutes after leveling off at 14,600 feet the Skylane began a meandering descent. Air traffic questioned the pilot as to his intentions but his responses were garbled and unintelligible. Radar data indicate the aircraft had flown at altitudes exceeding 12,500 feet MSL for about 40 minutes, with much of that time spent at 14,600 feet MSL. The NTSB concluded that the pilot's LOC-I was due to his impairment as a result of hypoxia (NTSB Identification No: WPR12FA154).

Disturbance Stage

The name used to describe this stage—the **disturbance stage** of hypoxia—is somewhat of a misnomer since hypoxic disturbances, or symptoms, as we have seen, can also occur below the 15,000-foot bottom threshold of this stage. It should also be noted that even though general altitude ranges are used to describe these stages, they are not necessarily restricted to them. For example, your body still uses compensatory mechanisms (increased pulse and respiratory rate) at disturbance-stage altitudes. However, between 15,000 feet and 20,000 feet, the automatic physiological mechanisms designed to compensate for oxygen deficiency are insufficient—even for relatively short durations—to prevent the onset of hypoxia. But, if flight crews are able to quickly don their oxygen masks and breathe supplemental oxygen, they will very likely avoid the deleterious symptoms of hypoxia. As indicated in Tables 4-4 and 4-5, a variety of physiological and mental disturbances can occur.

Critical Stage

This **critical stage** of hypoxia is where consciousness is lost within about three to 10 minutes due to circulatory or nervous system failure. With sufficient exposure, death can occur. Though investigators concluded that the occupants of Helios Airways Flight 522 died from impact forces sustained in the crash near Athens, Greece, they also concluded that all on board were in a "deep non-reversible coma due to their prolonged exposure (over 2.5 hours) to the high hypoxic environment."[16]

Signs and Symptoms of Hypoxia

Hypoxia *signs* are those symptoms that are usually detectable by others; hypoxia *symptoms* include the subjective symptoms that can usually only be detected by the victims of hypoxia. Table 4-5 lists some of the major signs and symptoms one may experience when hypoxic. The number and type of signs/symptoms varies between individuals, and may not occur in any particular order. Alarmingly, the first symptom of hypoxia can also be unconsciousness.

Table 4-5. Some of the signs (usually detectable by others) and symptoms (usually detectable only by the victim) of hypoxia.[17]

Hypoxia signs	Hypoxia symptoms
Rapid breathing	Air hunger (breathlessness)
Cyanosis	Apprehension
Reduced reaction time	Fatigue
Lethargy	Nausea
Muscle incoordination	Headache
Impaired judgment	Lightheaded or dizziness
Mental confusion	Hot and cold sensations
Unconsciousness	Tingling or numbness
Euphoria	Visual impairment

Physiological Effects of Hypoxia

A mixture of physiological and mental effects may present themselves. Cyanosis (or the *blueberry effect*) is a bluish color in the extremities (lips, fingernails, skin) that results from the low number of O_2 molecules binding with hemoglobin in the blood. One's sensory perception may also be affected. For example, focal (central) visual acuity and peripheral vision may be impaired. The sense of touch, pain, and hearing may be also be diminished. Psychomotor functions, such as muscle co-ordination and fine muscular movements may also be negatively affected and a person may have trouble speaking and may stammer.

Mental Effects of Hypoxia

One of the most dangerous aspects of hypoxia is its effect on mental functioning, and it's no wonder: the average adult brain accounts for about two percent of a person's body weight yet it needs at least 20 percent of the body's O_2 intake to function effectively.[18] A person may experience basic personality traits and emotions that are similar to what they experience from alcohol intoxication (happy, overconfident, sad, aggressive, etc.). As with alcohol intoxication, memory, thinking, judgment, decision making, and reaction time are adversely affected. Probably the most dangerous symptom of hypoxia—besides unconsciousness—is **euphoria**, a feeling of well-being and confidence that contributes to one's own inability to recognize its onset.

Hypoxia's Insidious Onset

If one of hypoxia's most dangerous symptoms is euphoria, then its most dangerous characteristic is its insidious onset. That is, it can sneak up on you, and if you're not aware of it, like the crew of Helios Airways Flight 522, it can completely incapacitate you in a matter of minutes, or even seconds. In hypobaric (altitude) chamber tests people who claim they are experiencing no physiological or psychological impairment do so, not because they haven't been affected, but because they simply are unable to recognize it. For example, when subjects were simulating 12,000 feet in a chamber, they noticed the lights go brighter after breathing in a few breaths of oxygen, but they didn't previously notice the lights going dimmer as they were experiencing hypoxia's subtle effects.[19] Combine this general inability to diagnose the presence of hypoxia with its most dangerous symptom—euphoria—and you can see how difficult it may be to recognize hypoxia and, most importantly, take the necessary measures to correct for it.

The previous chapter briefly mentioned the deaths of two French aeronauts brought on by hypoxia—the first recorded attributed to a physiological limitation—while flying their gas-filled balloon, the *Zenith*, almost a century-and-a-half ago. The lone survivor, Gaston Tissandier, recounted his experience with euphoria:

> About the height of 25,000 feet the condition of stupefaction which ensues is extraordinary. The mind and body weaken by degrees, and imperceptibly, *without consciousness of it*. No suffering is then experienced; on the contrary, *an inner joy is felt* like an irradiation from the surrounding flood of light. One becomes *indifferent*. One thinks no more of the perilous position or of danger. One ascends, and is *happy to ascend*.[20]

Effective Performance Time (Time of Useful Consciousness)

Compounding the problem of its insidious onset, and the difficulty of recognizing its effects, is the fact that there is only a limited time period in which you are capable of making sound decisions, including the decision to take effective measures to combat hypoxia. **Effective performance time** (EPT), also referred to as the **time of useful consciousness** (TUC), is not the maximum time available before you become unconscious, but the time of available *useful* consciousness before you succumb to the deleterious effects of hypoxia rendering you incapable of making and executing the decisions needed to combat it (i.e., descend to non-hypoxic altitude and/or use oxygen). As Figure 4-8 indicates, EPTs (or *TUC times*) are drastically reduced when flying at altitudes above 12,500 feet MSL and range from about 20 minutes at 18,000 feet to only about 20 seconds at 37,000 feet.

The EPT/TUC times in Figure 4-8 are averages and do not reflect the wide variation between individuals. Factors such as body size, diet, physical activity, physical fitness, overall health, and a variety of other factors will affect these times (see discussion later in this chapter). Therefore, it is prudent to treat these published times as maximum, not minimum, values.

Hyperventilation

It was mentioned that when flying at hypoxic altitudes the body attempts to compensate for reduced oxygen (compensatory stage and higher) by increasing its rate and depth of breathing. This **hyperventilation** (*hyper* = over; *ventilation* = breathing) is somewhat effective in combating its symptoms, but only for short exposures at the lowest range of hypoxic altitudes. However, when a person's rate of breathing is greater than is normally required, excess CO_2 is expelled by the lungs. This decreased carbon dioxide (called *hypocapnia*) raises the pH level in the blood increasing its alkalinity, a condition known as *alkalosis*. This imbalance in the acid-alkaline balance in the blood reduces proper functioning of the body's cells, and in response the brain defends itself from this pH level by restricting blood flow to it causing a variety of possible negative symptoms, many of which are similar to hypoxia.

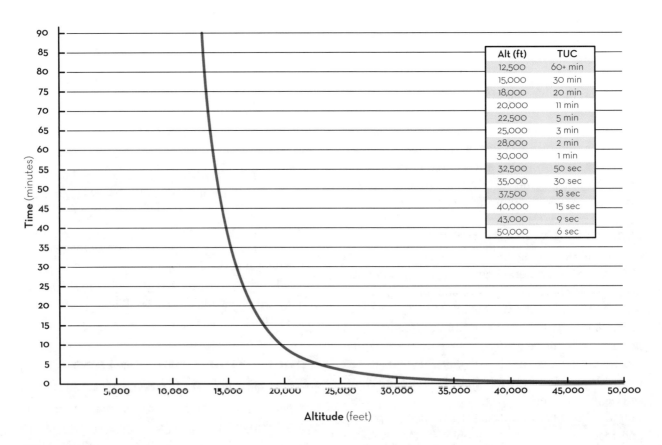

Alt (ft)	TUC
12,500	60+ min
15,000	30 min
18,000	20 min
20,000	11 min
22,500	5 min
25,000	3 min
28,000	2 min
30,000	1 min
32,500	50 sec
35,000	30 sec
37,500	18 sec
40,000	15 sec
43,000	9 sec
50,000	6 sec

Fig 4-8.

Effective performances time (EPT), or time of useful consciousness (TUC), breathing air at various altitudes.

Causes of Hyperventilation

Hyperventilation has several causes. As mentioned, one cause is the automatic compensatory response to reduced oxygen partial pressures. The pulse and breathing rates reflexively increase in an attempt to compensate for the reduced oxygen. Unfortunately, diagnosis of hyperventilation under these circumstances may be confused with hypoxia, especially when flying at hypoxic altitudes. Since hyperventilation symptoms often are similar to the symptoms of hypoxia (*see* next section), a pilot who mistakenly believes his or her hyperventilation symptoms are actually those of hypoxia (because of awareness of flying at hypoxic altitudes) could actually increase the severity of hyperventilation symptoms by attempting to increase oxygen intake by deliberately overbreathing.

Hyperventilation can also be caused by fear or anxiety by a pilot experiencing an in-flight emergency, or more likely, by a passenger who is apprehensive about the flying environment. In this situation, matters could become worse for the person who is unaware of hyperventilation symptoms since manifestation of these symptoms could actually increase a person's anxiety level, further causing even higher rates of overbreathing. In an accident involving a Schweizer SGU-2-22, the pilot was experiencing difficulty controlling his glider due to extreme turbulence and thermals. He stated that he was frustrated and nervous and started "breathing really hard because [he] was scared." He began to "feel strange," his face and hands "felt numb," he began to see "a lot of little dots," then he "passed out." The aircraft flew under some powerlines, then landed in a field, and struck a pole embedded in the ground. The NTSB determined the probable cause of the accident was pilot incapacitation (loss of consciousness) due to dehydration and hyperventilation (NTSB Identification No: DEN99LA102).

Symptoms of Hyperventilation

Any of the symptoms in Table 4-4 and 4-5 could be experienced by one who is hyperventilating—the same symptoms which hypoxic individuals experience. However, there are two symptoms that a hyperventilating person could experience but a hypoxic individual will not: the skin will appear pale and clammy (vs. cyanosis with hypoxia) and, given sufficient exposure, muscles will be spastic (vs. flaccid with hypoxia). The most telling distinguishing symptom for one experiencing hyperventilation is a tetany, or muscle spasm (*tetanus* = spasm). One type of tetany is a *carpopedal* spasm, where the fingers curl together and back toward the wrist. In extreme cases a generalized tetany, where the entire body stiffens up, has also been reported. Another distinguishing aspect of hyperventilation is symptom onset is usually slower, and dissipation after treatment usually takes longer than hypoxia.

Oxygen Paradox

There is another situation involving hyperventilation that, though rare, you should be aware of. The standard treatment for hypoxia is to breathe 100 percent pure oxygen (discussed later in this chapter). In almost all situations, doing so will clear up any symptoms after only a few breaths. However, there are occasions, particularly during a prolonged altitude hypoxia episode, that the immediate response to breathing 100 percent oxygen may result in a temporary worsening of symptoms, such as headache, dizziness, nausea, loss of vision, and possibly even temporary unconsciousness. It is believed that this **oxygen paradox** occurs because of reduced carbon dioxide in the blood from prolonged compensatory hyperventilation and a temporary decrease in blood pressure that occurs when oxygen is first administered. This phenomenon, which has been witnessed during altitude chamber hypoxia training in individuals who have been allowed to become hypoxic well beyond their EPT/TUC time, may last up to 60 seconds. The standard treatment for oxygen paradox, therefore, is to remain on oxygen as recovery will be forthcoming.

Other Types of Hypoxia

The most likely type of hypoxia a pilot will experience—hypoxic, or altitude, hypoxia—results from reduced partial pressure of O_2 when flying at altitudes near or above 10,000 feet MSL. Table 4-3 lists three other types: hypemic, stagnant, and histotoxic hypoxia.

Hypemic Hypoxia

A reduction in the blood's oxygen-carrying capacity, either from contamination of the blood from other gases or from a low red blood cell count, creates **hypemic hypoxia**. Sufficient O_2 reaches the lungs, but something interferes with the blood's ability to carry it to the cells. Although the word hypemic (*hyp* = low; *haima* = blood) more accurately describes this type of hypoxia, a synonym people are more familiar with is anemia (*a* = without; *haima* = blood), a major cause of this type of hypoxia. Hypemic (anemic) hypoxia results from blood loss, a low hemoglobin or red blood cell count, or an iron deficiency. Another major culprit is carbon monoxide poisoning.

Carbon monoxide (CO) has an affinity for hemoglobin that is approximately 200 to 300 times greater than oxygen.[21] It combines with hemoglobin at the exact sites that O_2 normally would to form carboxyhemoglobin (COHb). Because of its considerably greater attraction to hemoglobin, it prevents O_2 from binding to it, preventing it from being transported in the blood

Even though CO is an odorless, colorless, and tasteless gas, if you inhale exhaust fumes from an aircraft powerplant, or smoke from burning oil or some other type of fire, you are also inhaling CO. Smoke from cigarettes also produce CO. If you have COHb in your blood, your physiological altitude is higher than the cabin altitude of the aircraft. For example, Table 4-6 indicates that if the COHb level in your blood is 10 percent your physiological altitude will be 7,000 feet higher than a 6,000-foot cabin altitude (i.e., 13,000 feet).

Table 4-6. Approximate physiological altitude at a given carboxyhemoglobin (COHb) level.[22]

Cabin altitude (feet)	0% COHb	5% COHb	10% COHb
6,000	6,000	10,500	13,000
7,000	7,000	11,000	13,500
8,000	8,000	12,000	14,000

Apart from causing hypoxia in individuals at lower altitudes than hypoxia would normally be experienced, CO poisoning poses a threat to life. You can see from Table 4-7 just how harmful CO poisoning can be.

Table 4-7. Physiological responses to different CO concentrations in the blood.[23]

Percent CO in blood	Typical symptoms
<10	None
10–20	Slight headache
21–30	Headache, slight increase in respiration, drowsiness
31–40	Headache, impaired judgment, shortness of breath, increasing drowsiness, blurring of vision
41–50	Pounding headache, confusion, marked shortness of breath, marked drowsiness, increasing blurred vision
>50	Unconsciousness, eventual death if victim is not removed from source of CO

The FAA analyzed toxicology samples from fatal aircraft accidents between 1967 and 1993 and found that at least 360 people had been exposed to sufficient CO before or after the crash to impair their abilities.[24] In 2005, a Cessna 170 was destroyed and the pilot, the sole occupant, died after it crashed near Portland, Oregon. Investigators discovered the engine heat was on, exhaust residue was present on the heater hose, and the muffler which is located inside the heater shroud was cracked around its entire circumference. Toxicology tests revealed a 50 percent CO concentration in the pilot's blood. They determined that the cause of death was "carbon monoxide toxicity (hypemic hypoxia) and positional asphyxia" (NTSB Identification No: SEA05FA090).

More recently, in February 2017, a Mooney M20 crashed in an open field in Ellendale, Minnesota, after the pilot became incapacitated. Fortunately, he was able to extricate himself from the wreckage and walk to a nearby house for help. This was his third flight of the day and he used the heater to stay warm each time. He recalls that he experienced an intermittent headache and occasional "butterflies" in his stomach near the end of each flight. The last thing he remembered was being cleared to 6,000 feet on a heading of 240 degrees, yet controllers said he tried to contact departure control on the incorrect (tower) frequency and radar tapes indicate the airplane climbed higher than 12,000 feet and was off course. NTSB investigators found the exhaust muffler had several cracks which allowed exhaust gases to enter the cockpit. They concluded the accident was caused by the pilot's incapacitation from carbon monoxide poisoning in flight—he had an estimated 28 percent CO concentration in his blood at the time of the accident (NTSB Identification No: CEN17LA101).

If your aircraft isn't already equipped with one, it's a good idea to install a CO detector in the cockpit. To stop CO from entering the cabin you need to eliminate its source by conducting a careful preflight inspection of heating and exhaust manifold equipment before flight. If you suspect it while airborne in an aircraft that uses the exhaust manifold to provide heat to the heating system, you should turn off the cabin heat and try to get fresh air into the cabin. If you suspect CO poisoning you should also breathe 100 percent pure oxygen, land as soon as possible, and seek medical attention. Carbon monoxide poisoning not only hinders O_2 from attaching to Hb in the red blood cells, inducing hypemic hypoxia at lower altitude thresholds, it also stays in the cells for several days, or even weeks, and must be flushed out of your system. Medical personnel will have you breathe 100 percent oxygen for several hours to help eliminate CO from your body. But if COHb blood saturation is high enough they will also administer 100 percent oxygen in a hyperbaric (*hyper*=high; *baric*=pressure) chamber which increases the partial pressure of O_2 to higher-than-sea-level values. The former reduces the half-life (removes 50 percent) of COHb from about 5.5 hours to 1.3 hours; the latter reduces it to about 20 minutes.[25]

Stagnant Hypoxia

The oxygen-carrying capacity of hemoglobin in the blood is adequate when experiencing **stagnant hypoxia**, but blood flow is reduced because of failure of the circulatory system to pump an adequate amount of blood, and therefore oxygen, to the tissues. Heart failure, shock, blood vessel restrictions, and positive G accelerations can cause this type of hypoxia. Significant positive G accelerations ($+G_z$) that occur during steep turns, rapid recoveries from dives, or other aerobatic maneuvers can cause the blood to stagnate, reducing O_2 flow to the brain. These and other effects of acceleration are discussed in Chapter 8.

Histotoxic Hypoxia

Impaired cellular respiration results when the body's cells fail to efficiently utilize the oxygen brought to them. Oxygen delivered to the cells by the hemoglobin in the blood is adequate, but the cells/tissues themselves, due to alcohol, drugs, or poisons, fail to utilize the oxygen. With **histotoxic hypoxia** the tissues (*histo*) become toxic due to some outside contaminant. Though CO contributes primarily to hypemic hypoxia by interfering with hemoglobin's ability to carry oxygen, it can also work its way into the body's cells contributing to histotoxic hypoxia.

Hypoxia Severity Factors

It was noted earlier that several factors influence the severity of hypoxia. These can be classified as environmental factors and individual factors.

Environmental Factors

Environmental factors such as altitude attained, duration at altitude, rate of ascent, and cabin temperature and humidity, can affect the degree of hypoxia and the severity of its symptoms.

Altitude Attained

The higher the altitude the faster the onset of hypoxic hypoxia and the greater the severity of its symptoms. For example, as Figure 4-8 indicates, your EPT/TUC at 15,000 feet may be as long as 30 minutes, but 10,000 feet higher it is reduced to no more than three minutes.

Duration at Altitude

The same goes for length of exposure at any given hypoxic altitude: you only have a specified EPT/TUC time before incapacitation sets in.

Rate of Ascent

The faster you climb to altitude, the quicker the symptoms will manifest themselves resulting in shorter EPT/TUC times. A rapid cabin decompression at high altitude (*see* discussion later in this chapter) causes the inside cabin pressure to equalize with the outside air pressure exposing you to severe hypoxic altitudes in just a matter of seconds.

Cabin Temperatures and Humidity

Any extremes in temperature and/or humidity can affect O_2 partial pressures and your body's demand for O_2.

Individual Factors

Several individual factors, some of which can be controlled by the pilot, also affect the degree of hypoxia and the severity of its symptoms.

Physical Activity

Increased physical activity requires higher amounts of oxygen for the body to properly function, lowering the altitude at which hypoxic symptoms will first manifest themselves. A survey of Australian Army helicopter aircrews involved in flight operations up to 10,000 feet MSL found that loadmasters reported more symptoms of hypoxia than did flight crews.[26] American Trans Air Flight 406, a Boeing B-727, experienced a decompression at FL330 near Indianapolis, Indiana. The lead FA was on the flight deck serving meals and, at the captain's request, she walked back to the cabin to see if the passenger oxygen masks had dropped. While returning to the flight deck she made it as far as the cockpit door then passed out and slumped to the floor. As they were troubleshooting the problem the captain and flight engineer (FE) also eventually passed out, but fortunately the FO was able to control the airplane because he immediately donned his oxygen mask after the decompression. The accident report doesn't specifically say so, but the FA may have succumbed to hypoxia sooner than the others because of her increased physical activity (NTSB Identification No: CHI96IA157).

Minor Illnesses

Flying with a cold, influenza, or infections also increases susceptibility to hypoxia. Even with a minor illness, the body will utilize increased amounts of O_2 to fight the illness.

Emotional State

A person experiencing any emotional extremes (fear, anger, etc.) requires more oxygen, thereby aggravating hypoxia's effects.

Physical Fitness

A physically fit person has a greater lung capacity, greater blood oxygen content, and a more effective circulatory system than one who is not physically fit. Therefore, a fit person functions better at marginal altitudes. Experiments conducted in hypobaric chambers found that nonsmoker pilots who regularly exercised and watched their diet experienced significantly longer EPT/TUC times than smokers who were not physically fit.[27]

Smoking

Besides all the health problems and cancer risks associated with smoking cigarettes and cigars, smoking increases a person's susceptibility to hypoxia at lower-than-normal altitudes. The main culprit is CO in the inhaled smoke which reduces the blood's ability to carry oxygen to the tissues. As noted previously, CO has about 200 to 300 times the attraction to hemoglobin than oxygen, combining with Hb to form COHb and inhibiting O_2 from being transported in the blood. Figure 4-9 illustrates the average smoker has approximately 8 to 10 percent COHb in their blood placing them at a physiological altitude of 5,000 feet higher than their actual altitude. This creates hypemic hypoxia that, when added to hypoxic hypoxia that naturally results when flying at higher altitudes, lowers a smoker's altitude tolerance and intensifies the symptoms of hypoxia. It also lowers EPT/TUC times for smokers.

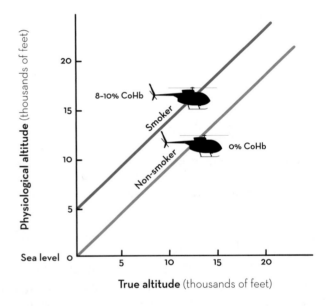

Fig 4-9.

Physiological altitudes for average smoker is 5,000 feet higher than the average non-smoker.

Anemia

It was noted that hypemic, or anemic, hypoxia can result from blood loss, low hemoglobin, or a low red blood cell count. This can be due to surgery, menstruation, pregnancy, disease, a nosebleed, or from an iron or vitamin deficiency. Another cause of this type of hypoxia is loss of blood from blood donations. The FAA's *Pilot's Handbook of Aeronautical Knowledge* states that it takes several weeks for blood levels to return to normal after donating blood; therefore, during that time your body may not be able to function at its peak capacity.

Medication, Alcohol, and Drugs

Some drugs and medications, including over-the-counter (OTC) medications, can interfere with oxygen transport in the blood by creating dyshemoglobin (*dys*=bad) impairing oxygen's ability to bind to and release from hemoglobin.[28] They can also impair the ability of the body's cells, including those in the brain, to effectively utilize oxygen. Alcohol contributes to histotoxic hypoxia by interfering with the cells' ability to use oxygen. It is estimated that every ounce of alcohol consumed raises a person's physiological altitude by about 2,000 feet. Alcohol use and misuse is discussed in Chapter 11.

Oxygen Systems

Hypoxia is prevented in non-pressurized aircraft by breathing oxygen from onboard fixed or portable oxygen systems. For light GA aircraft the most common system is a portable tank containing compressed gaseous oxygen, valves, a regulator to control the O_2 flow, pressure and flow gauges, hoses, and a mask (or nasal cannulas). Tank pressures are usually between 1,800 and 2,200 PSI. Less common are systems that use low pressure storage systems (400–450 PSI) or store oxygen in liquid or solid form. Solid-state oxygen—oxygen created through a chemical reaction from oxygen generators—is commonly used in transport category aircraft, but is also used in some GA operations. Fixed installations consist of fixed oxygen tanks which can be filled from an external valve with a built-in system of tubes to deliver the oxygen to the pilots' and passengers' masks.

Continuous Flow System

The two main oxygen systems used in civil aviation today are the continuous flow and diluter demand systems. The continuous flow system delivers 100 percent oxygen continuously to the mask even when the user is exhaling. Some continuous flow systems require the O_2 flow rate to be set by manually adjusting the regulator while others automatically adjust the oxygen flow rate appropriate to the altitude being flown. Some systems use nasal cannulas to deliver oxygen, but these are usually only effective up to 18,000 feet. Those that use a full face mask are usually equipped with an attached plastic bag, called a rebreather bag, which allows the wearer to reuse some of the exhaled oxygen thereby reducing some of the wastage inherent in a continuous flow system. This system is usually adequate for altitudes up to 25,000 feet MSL.

Diluter Demand System

Demand systems, introduced in World War II, deliver oxygen only when the pilot is inhaling (on demand) thereby reducing the O_2 wastage common in continuous flow systems. This has generally been replaced by the more sophisticated diluter-demand system that is even more economical than the basic demand system since at the lower altitudes it dilutes the oxygen with some of the outside air. The oxygen regulator increases the percentage of pure oxygen with increasing altitude until at 34,000 feet MSL (or 34,000 feet cabin altitude) no dilution occurs and the pilot is breathing 100 percent pure oxygen. Breathing 100 percent pure oxygen at 34,000 feet in an unpressurized cabin is the physiological equivalent, as far as oxygen is concerned, of sea level.

Pressure Demand System

Breathing 100 percent pure O_2 in an unpressurized cabin above 34,000 feet raises one's physiological altitude to the equivalent of about 10,000 feet when flying at 40,000 feet MSL. We know that flight at 10,000 feet MSL provides for about 90 percent blood O_2 saturation (see red line in Figure 4-7) and that above this altitude significant impairment begins. Therefore, for flights above 40,000 feet MSL in an unpressurized cabin, oxygen must be delivered to the lungs at a pressure that is higher than the ambient pressure using a pressure-demand system. More common in military applications, these systems deliver 100 percent O_2 to a tightly sealed mask under high pressure, which, in effect, pressurizes the lungs, increasing the partial pressure of oxygen. These systems can be of the continuous flow variety, resulting in oxygen wastage and difficulty exhaling and talking into the oncoming high-pressure oxygen flow. Or, they are more likely to be the on-demand type where high pressure oxygen is delivered only when inhaling. Using the latter becomes more of a passive exercise, increasing the likelihood that a pilot may experience hyperventilation.

Pressure-demand oxygen systems are only good up to approximately 43,000 to 45,000 feet. Pressure breathing at higher altitudes causes the lungs to expand to the point where circulation is impaired and the risk of total circulation failure is likely. Above these altitudes, a pressurized cabin, or a partial or full pressure suit (i.e., a space suit) is needed to stave off these harmful effects. The pressure exerted on the body counterbalances internal lung pressures and eliminates problems associated with lung expansion. If the cabin can be pressurized to 10,000 feet or lower, flights can be accomplished up to 50,000 feet, without the use of a pressure suit. Flight at and above a cabin altitude of 50,000 feet however, requires a sealed cabin or the crew must wear pressure suits.[29]

Cabin Pressurization

Most physiological problems associated with high-altitude flight, including hypoxia, are prevented through aircraft cabin pressurization. Though some manufacturers are re-introducing electrical, rather than pneumatic systems to power aircraft environmental control systems (ECS), including cabin pressurization systems (e.g., Boeing B-787 Dreamliner),[30] most of today's aircraft cabins are pressurized using compressed intake air from the engines (bleed air), and the air's expulsion from the cabin is controlled through the adjustment of outlet valve settings.

A cabin altimeter, which indicates cabin pressure expressed as an equivalent altitude, and cabin rate-of-climb/descent indicator are used by pilots to monitor the cabin altitude and rate of altitude change within the cabin. 14 CFR §25.841 requires that the air in the cabin of commercial airliners be compressed to a cabin pressure altitude of not more than 8,000 feet when the airplane is flying at its maximum operating altitude. This is a compromise between maintaining safety and comfort (i.e., avoiding hypoxic cabin altitudes above 10,000 feet) and keeping increased weight and subsequent reduction of aircraft performance to a minimum.

Sudden Decompressions

Even though hypoxia is generally prevented in pressurized cabins, if an in-flight decompression occurs crew and passengers alike will suffer from hypoxia's effects unless corrective measures are implemented quickly. Though relatively rare, loss-of-cabin-pressure events through system or structural failure do occur. Citing data provided by Airbus and Boeing, the FAA reports in its final rule regarding extended operations of multi-engine airplanes that between 1959 and 2001 there were almost 3,000 depressurization events in transport category airplanes weighing more than 60,000 pounds. For Boeing airplanes alone there were 73 events between 1980 and 2000.[31] The FAA estimates the odds of experiencing a loss-of-cabin-pressure event in a large transport category airplane is between one in a million and one in 10 million per flight-hour. The vast majority of these depressurization events were the result of pressurization system failures (pressure controllers, valves, etc.), followed by structural failures (door seals, etc.), and very rarely by **uncontained engine failures**. Using Airbus data, the FAA estimates the probability of experiencing a decompression due to pressurization system failure alone is about 3.5 decompression events for every million flights.

Some decompressions are gradual while others are more sudden. A gradual decompression usually takes longer than 10 seconds for the cabin pressure to equalize with that of the outside environment. **Sudden decompressions** are classified as either rapid or explosive: A rapid decompression takes 0.5 to 10 seconds to occur, while an explosive one takes less than 0.5 seconds. With the latter, air in the lungs is unable to escape as fast as the air in the cabin and lung damage could occur, especially if a person's airway is closed due to swallowing or is holding their breath. According to incident data, the majority of decompressions are gradual, few are rapid, and fewer still are explosive.[32]

Airplanes with larger cabins are less likely to experience explosive decompressions, because given the same circumstances, larger cabin volumes take longer to decompress than those with smaller volumes. According to FAA AC 61-107 on high-altitude flight, the cabin volume of a Boeing B-747 is about 59,000 cubic feet compared to a Learjet at about 265 cubic feet, yielding a cabin volume ratio between the two of 223 to 1. Therefore, given the same type of depressurization, the Learjet will decompress 223 times faster than a B-747.

Depending on the rate of pressure equalization, the phenomena experienced during the decompression itself could range from relatively negligible to downright frightening. During a sudden—rapid or explosive—decompression, you will hear a loud bang or noise, feel the rushing wind, and see flying dust and debris as it escapes from the cabin. You will also likely experience the uncomfortable sensations of air escaping from the various orifices of your body, and any excess pressure in your ears will quickly clear. Fog could form from water vapor condensing as a result of the rapid expansion of air. As warm cabin air is displaced by cold outside air, the cabin air temperature will also drop substantially, causing significant discomfort. Finally, passengers will feel anxious and fearful, and so will you as you quickly try to ascertain what just happened. It should be noted that very rarely has someone involuntarily exited the airplane because they were located near the opening and were unsecured by a safety harness.

As harrowing as it might be perceived by crew or passengers, in the vast majority of decompressions the major threat to health and safety does not occur during the decompression event itself, but after it takes place—and that threat is hypoxia. Since air escapes from the body's tissues very rapidly during a sudden decompression, a degassing effect occurs lowering EPT/TUC times by about half. That means you (and your fellow crew members), who would normally have about one minute (see Figure 4-8) to take the required measures to secure your safety, have only about a maximum of 30 seconds following a sudden decompression at 30,000 feet.

Four passengers were on a chartered Part 135 flight from Orlando, Florida, to Dallas, Texas, when ATC lost communication with the crew of the Learjet 35. The airplane veered off course, and after several unsuccessful attempts to re-establish radio contact, ATC scrambled military jets to have a look. What they found was disturbing: no movement whatsoever of people inside the airplane, including the crew. The airplane continued en route (reaching a maximum altitude of 48,900 feet) under control of the autopilot until it ran out of fuel, entered a spiral dive and crashed near Aberdeen, South Dakota. The accident killed the captain, copilot, and all four passengers, including U.S. professional golfer William Payne Stewart. The NTSB determined the crew became incapacitated as a result of its failure to receive supplemental oxygen after a loss of cabin pressur-

ization. Investigators were unable to determine why the pressurization system failed (NTSB Identification No: DCA00MA005).

Important Altitude Thresholds

Various altitudes relating to hypoxia have been referenced throughout this chapter. Table 4-8 summarizes some important altitude thresholds related to hypoxia that every pilot should know.

Table 4-8. Important altitude thresholds.

Cabin altitude (feet)	Significance
5,000	Supplemental O_2 recommended above this altitude due to impaired night vision.
8,000	§25.841 requires cabin air be compressed to a cabin altitude of not more than 8,000 feet when the airplane is flying at its maximum operating altitude.
10,000	Upper threshold for normal functioning in physiological efficient zone with blood O_2 saturation at 90%. U.S. commercial flight crews must use supplemental O_2 at cabin altitudes above 10,000 feet (§121.327) or when flying in excess of 30 minutes (§135.89) between 10,000 and 12,000 feet.
12,500	§91.211 requires pilots to use supplemental O_2 between cabin altitudes of 12,500 to 14,000 feet (10,000 to 13,000 feet in Canada, Canadian aviation regulation (CAR) 605.31) when flying in excess of 30 minutes.
14,000	§91.211 requires pilots to use supplemental O_2 above a cabin altitude of 14,000 feet (13,000 feet in Canada, CAR 605.31).
15,000	§91.211 requires passengers be provided with supplemental O_2 above 15,000 feet (13,000 feet in Canada, CAR 605.31).
22,000	Occupants experience loss of consciousness at this approximate altitude.
34,000	Breathing 100% O_2 at FL340 is the equivalent of sea-level blood O_2 saturation.
40,000	Breathing 100% O_2 at FL400 is the equivalent of 10,000 feet blood O_2 saturation.
43,000	Positive pressure breathing and pressure suit required above this altitude.
50,000	Flight at and above 50,000 feet MSL requires sealed cabin or pressure suit.

Avoiding Hypoxia

It should be obvious that pilots and passengers cannot fly at high altitudes without proper protection. Flying in a pressurized cabin or using supplemental oxygen allows you to fly higher, but you still need to know what to do if these systems fail. Therefore, whether or not your aircraft is equipped with these systems, it is essential you know what measures to take to prevent hypoxia from sneaking up on you.

Be Careful at Marginal Altitudes

As Table 4-8 indicates, oxygen use in the United States is not required for pilots operating under Part 91 regulations when flying at or below 12,500 feet MSL. However, it is required after flying for more than 30 minutes between 12,500 and 14,000 feet MSL and at all times when flying above 14,000 feet MSL. In Canada, it is not required when flying at or below 10,000 feet MSL, but is after flying more than 30 minutes between 10,000 and 13,000 feet MSL and at all times when flying above 13,000 feet MSL. However, you may erroneously think that because it's legal to operate an aircraft up to these altitudes without using supplemental oxygen, it must be safe. Remember, at these altitudes the body tries to compensate for reduced oxygen by increasing both the heart and breathing rate, and it can only do so for a limited period of time before the symptoms of hypoxia take hold. To avoid its insidious effects, you should limit time at these marginal altitudes. If you have to remain there because of terrain or weather, be on your guard for hypoxia's signs, and if present, descend to a lower altitude or begin to supplement your breathing with oxygen.

Pilots tend to hyperventilate at these altitudes as the body attempts to compensate for reduced oxygen (i.e., compensatory stage). As mentioned, the symptoms can sometimes be confused with those of hypoxia. Symptoms experienced below 10,000 feet MSL are likely those of hyperventilation; those experienced above 10,000 feet are probably hypoxia. However, if you are experiencing symptoms and you have oxygen available, it is recommended that you begin using it, and if hypoxia is the cause, the symptoms should clear up within a few breaths. If symptoms continue, in addition to breathing 100 percent pure oxygen, deliberately slow your rate of breathing and the hyperventilation symptoms should clear up within a few minutes. It is recommended that you do not try and diagnose for hyperventilation, but treat the symptoms as if they were the symptoms of hypoxia for at least two reasons. First, if for some reason you misread your altimeter (a common problem; see discussion in Chapter 15) and are at a higher altitude than you think you are, time is of the essence—you have a limited EPT/TUC time before incapacitation so you do not want to waste valuable time diagnosing your condition. Second, pilots rarely experience hyperventilation. As mentioned previously, fear or anxiety is the major cause of hyperventilation; therefore it is more likely to occur among your inexperienced and uninformed passengers.

If it is certain you are not at a hypoxic altitude and it appears a passenger is hyperventilating, help him or her re-establish their normal breathing rate by asking them to talk or count out loud. If he or she is too anxious and seems unable to do this then get them to breath in and out of a bag that is sealed over the nose and mouth. Re-breathing the expired air will increase the body's CO_2 content, which will restore the pH balance in the blood and eliminate the symptoms of hyperventilation.

Finally, some pilots use a pulse oximeter—usually placed on a fingertip—to monitor their blood-oxygen saturation levels while flying at or above 10,000 feet MSL. This inexpensive device measures and displays the percentage of O_2 saturation in the hemoglobin using transmitted light passing through the blood. Maintaining above 90 percent is ideal. However, be aware the device will be fooled into reading the same if you are being poisoned by carbon monoxide because hemoglobin turns just as red with CO attached to Hb (COHb) as it does with O_2 attached (O_2Hb) to it. To detect the presence of CO in your blood, you need a different device called a CO-oximeter.

Consider Hypoxia Training

Not everyone experiences hypoxia the same way. Some encounter easily recognizable symptoms such as headaches, nausea, hot and cold flashes, or tingling of the skin. These are considered "good" symptoms because they are easily noticeable and you are therefore more likely recognize them as symptoms of hypoxia. Others experience symptoms such as indifference, apathy, or euphoria—what are considered "bad" symptoms because they are not so noticeable. The FAA recommends pilots discover their own personal hypoxia symptoms by participating in hypobaric (altitude) chamber or portable reduced oxygen training enclosure (PROTE) training. That way, if hypoxia sneaks up on you, you will be ready since you know what to look for ahead of time. The FAA provides physiology training to civilian pilots, including simulation to FL250 in a hypobaric chamber, at their Civil Aerospace Medical Institute in Oklahoma City. Up until recently, it also offered such training at selected military installations throughout the country. There are universities and private contractors who provide this training to pilots as well. Keep in mind, that incidents have occurred in which crew members who've participated in such training have been incapacitated from hypoxia, so participating in altitude chamber training to discover your own unique symptoms won't automatically prevent you from succumbing to hypoxia—but it should reduce your odds.

Decrease Your Susceptibility

As indicated previously, certain factors increase your susceptibility to hypoxia. Some of these include smoking, use of alcohol, and use of OTC medications such as antihistamines and pain relievers. Be aware that the underlying conditions requiring such medications can also reduce your tolerance. Of course, anemia and loss of blood through blood donations significantly reduce the blood's ability to carry needed oxygen to the body's tissues. Since it takes several weeks for blood levels to return to normal after donating blood, your body will not be able to function at its peak capacity. This may not be a problem at sea level, but the negative effects of reduced oxygen in the blood at altitude are likely to be significant. This is why active U.S. Navy pilots are prohibited from donating blood more than every four months and within four weeks prior to flying in combat, flying in a shipboard environment, or flying operational missions. Permission is required for other types of flying within four days of a blood donation.[33] The U.S. Air Force restricts their aircrew from flying within 72 hours after donating blood or plasma.[34]

Nothing in the regulations prohibits civilian pilots from donating blood. However, the Transport Canada *Aeronautical Information Manual* recommends that active pilots not donate blood at all. If you do donate, however, it recommends that you wait at least 48 hours before resuming flying activities. The FAA recommends that you not fly for 24 hours if you give one unit (about a pint) of blood, or 72 hours if you give more than one unit.[35]

Follow the Regulations

Table 4-8 includes some of the basic altitude restrictions for GA pilots flying without oxygen: Pilots in the United States are required to breathe supplemental oxygen at all times when flying above cabin altitudes of 14,000 feet MSL (13,000 feet in Canada) and when flying for more than 30 minutes between 12,500 and 14,000 feet (between 10,000 and 13,000 feet in Canada). Simply following these regulations could have gone a long way to keeping a pilot and her three passengers trying to get to Las Vegas, Nevada, out of trouble. The Piper PA-28R wasn't pressurized, it wasn't equipped with a supplemental oxygen system, and there is no evidence the pilot took a portable supplemental oxygen unit on the airplane with her. It appears she was either unaware of these regulations or she disregarded them. The engine quit due to fuel starvation, and the subsequent forced landing proved unsuccessful. The Piper Arrow crashed near La Sal, Utah, killing all four aboard. Radar data indicate the pilot flew at an altitude of approximately 16,000 feet MSL for an estimated 45 minutes, above 14,000 feet for 1 hour and 49 minutes, and above 12,500 feet for 2 hours and 17 minutes (NTSB Identification No: DEN03FA038).

Of course, the regulations are even more stringent for commercial passenger-carrying flights. Thresholds for mandatory oxygen use are lowered to cabin altitudes of 10,000 feet for flight crews flying under Part 121 (scheduled airline) and for no longer than 30 minutes between cabin altitudes of 10,000 and 12,000 feet for pilots flying under Part 135 regulations (commuter and on-demand). These rules also apply should an aircraft lose pressurization. There is an extensive list of other regulations regarding oxygen requirements for flight crew, cabin crew and passengers; you must fully understand the applicable U.S. FARs, or CARs in Canada, if you fly commercially.

Know Your Oxygen System

Whether you need oxygen to take advantage of the benefits of high-altitude flight (higher true airspeed, greater tailwind, etc.) in an unpressurized aircraft, or need it in the event of a rapid decompression in a pressurized one, it's crucial that you receive training and fully understand the oxygen system in your aircraft. Whichever system is installed—a portable or fixed system that stores O_2 in gas, liquid, or solid form that delivers oxygen via a continuous flow or diluter-demand system—you should be thoroughly familiar with it. Since EPT/TUC time at higher cruise altitudes may be as little as 15 to 20 seconds following a rapid decompression, it is crucial that you also receive practice in quickly donning your oxygen mask and ensuring the O_2 is adequately flowing.

A commonly used acronym to check for proper functioning of the equipment is the **PRICE check**. You should first check the *pressure* gauge to confirm there is enough pressure and an adequate oxygen supply. Next is the pressure *regulator*, which reduces pressure and regulates oxygen flow. Confirm the system is set properly and delivering oxygen. You can check the oxygen flow rate on the *indicator*. Ensure that all *connections*, including face mask, are not leaking or twisted and are properly connected. Finally, you should have an *emergency* supply of oxygen in the cockpit (regulations for airline flights require this).

It's important to ensure the system is working properly, but it's just as important to determine if you have enough oxygen for the proposed flight. Keep in mind that the higher you go, the more oxygen you will use and the more frequently you will need to check your supply. Most systems increase the amount of oxygen delivered to the mask with altitude until at approximately 34,000 feet MSL it is providing 100 percent oxygen to the user. It is not known whether the pilot of a turbocharged Beech Baron conducted these checks or not, but if he did, it might have prevented his incapacitation due to hypoxia. He was flying from Glendive, Montana, to St. Paul, Minnesota, at altitudes up to FL270 and he was using oxygen. However, at some point in the flight he ran out of oxygen and became unconscious. Though military jets were dispatched to intercept and provide assistance, there was nothing they could do to rouse his attention. The airplane continued on autopilot, overflew St. Paul, and eventually descended and crashed in Winfield, West Virginia. The NTSB determined the cause of the crash was the "pilot's inadequate preflight preparation to ensure an adequate supply of supplemental oxygen, and his inadequate in-flight planning and decision making,

which resulted in exhaustion of his oxygen supply" (NTSB Identification No: NYC06FA079).

When servicing oxygen equipment you should make sure you use **aviator's breathing oxygen**. This type of oxygen meets standards required for flying at high altitudes and is purer than oxygen used for other purposes and is also drier, which precludes the possibility of the system freezing at the cold temperatures found at higher altitudes. A Cessna 337 entered an uncontrolled descent and crashed near Hickory, Pennsylvania, after the pilot lost consciousness at 27,700 feet. According to the surviving passenger, the portable oxygen system used by the Skymaster pilot appeared to be functioning properly. However, according to the NTSB investigation, the bottle was not filled with 100 percent oxygen but with compressed air that provided only 21 percent oxygen (NTSB Identification No: IAD97FA060).

Finally, be very careful with oxygen. Since it is a necessary component of combustion— along with heat and fuel in what is known as the fire triangle— it goes without saying that smoking is prohibited in its presence. You should also avoid using flammable oil- or petroleum-based products (the "fuel" in the fire triangle), such as lip balms, when using oxygen.

Know Your Pressurization System

If you fly in a pressurized cabin it is vital to understand not only how the ECS in your aircraft works but also how to properly operate it. Several self-induced decompressions have occurred because flight crews have improperly managed this system. In the fatal Helios Airways accident mentioned in the introduction to this chapter, the crew failed to recognize that the cabin pressure mode selector was left in the MAN mode after an earlier ground check of the system by maintenance personnel. It should have been set to AUTO. In MAN mode the system does not automatically control the desired pressurization for flight but requires the crew to manually adjust the cabin pressurization settings. Also mentioned was the rapid decompression to FL330 in an American Trans Air Boeing B-727 near Indianapolis, Indiana. The FE inadvertently opened the pressurization outlet valve when troubleshooting the system. The FA initially lost consciousness, followed by the captain and FE. But the catastrophe was averted by a sharp FO who, although he had only 10 hours of initial operating experience in the airplane, immediately donned his oxygen mask and conducted an emergency descent to a safe altitude (NTSB Identification No: CHI96IA157).

Finally, in several cases crew members have confused the cabin altitude warning horn—designed to activate when cabin pressure exceeds 10,000 feet—for some other warning. In some airplanes, especially older ones, this is understandable since the same horn is used to signify other anomalies, most commonly a takeoff warning. This is what happened in the Helios Airways accident: the captain mistook the cabin altitude warning for a takeoff warning. For many airplanes this warning is not tied into the master warning/caution system, and the horn is the only warning of excessive cabin altitude; the crew must look at the cabin altitude instruments to confirm if the horn signifies an excessive cabin altitude. Numerous occurrences, including the Helios accident, prompted the FAA to issue a *Safety Alert for Operators* (SAFO) for B-737 aircraft, advising crew members to be aware of this confusion and to immediately don their oxygen masks as soon as the warning horn sounds in flight while they troubleshoot the problem.[36]

Follow Proper Decompression Procedures

In the unlikely event of a sudden or even gradual cabin decompression, you need to know what to do. The crucial point to remember is you will become incapacitated if you don't act quickly. Several accidents and incidents have occurred because pilots did not follow the proper procedures quickly enough. For example, while climbing to FL330 near Salt Lake City, Utah, the crew discovered their McDonnell Douglas DC-9 wasn't properly pressurizing. The captain ordered the FO, who was the pilot flying, not to level off at 16,000 feet MSL as the FO had suggested, but continue the climb to their assigned altitude of FL330 while he left the flight deck, using the portable oxygen

system, to troubleshoot the problem. Unfortunately, the captain never returned: he was later found unconscious in the forward cargo hold with his oxygen mask on and the portable storage tank still full of oxygen. Pathologists determined that he died from hypoxic hypoxia and the NTSB concluded it was due to his improper flight planning and decision making and his improper use of the portable oxygen system (NTSB Identification No: FTW89MA047).

As soon as the decompression occurs, or is recognized, you should follow the recommended emergency procedures published in the approved aircraft flight manual for your aircraft. The general procedure is for you and your crew to immediately don oxygen masks, ensuring they are delivering a 100 percent supply of oxygen, then initiate a maximum rate emergency descent—spoilers, landing gear, and flaps deployed as appropriate—to 10,000 feet MSL or lower (or the minimum safe IFR altitude if higher). As a result of the Payne Stewart crash, the NTSB looked at 129 ASRS reports over a 10-year period and found many pilots did not immediately don their oxygen masks while troubleshooting cabin pressure altitude problems. In its *Safety Recommendation* (A-00-109 through -119), the NTSB stresses the absolute necessity of donning oxygen masks as soon as the cabin altitude warning horn sounds or when the decompression is first recognized.

There are also other reasons to quickly initiate an emergency descent: It precludes those who, for whatever reason, might not be successful in receiving oxygen from their masks from experiencing serious hypoxia; it reduces the demand for oxygen since regulations require only a limited supply of oxygen be carried for passengers; and, if the decompression occurs above 25,000 feet, it reduces the chance of you and your passengers experiencing altitude decompression sickness, a topic fully discussed in the next chapter.

Helpful Resources

The FAA's Civil Aerospace Medical Institute has produced several short but very informative flight physiology videos available in English, and some also in Spanish and/or Japanese, at www.faa.gov/pilots/training/airman_education/physiologyvideos/. The following relate to the contents of this chapter:

- *Physics of the Atmosphere*
- *Respiration and Circulation*
- *Flying & Hypoxia*
- *Understanding Aviation Oxygen Equipment*
- *Hyperventilation: When Flying Takes Your Breath Away*
- *The Ups and Downs of Cabin Pressurization*

The FAA has also published several helpful brochures related to the topics in this chapter available at www.faa.gov/pilots/safety/pilotsafetybrochures/.

- *Carbon Monoxide: A Deadly Menace*
- *Hypoxia: The Higher You Fly...The Less Air In The Sky*
- *Oxygen Equipment Use in General Aviation Operations*

Chapter 17, "Aeromedical Factors," in the FAA *Pilot's Handbook of Aeronautical Knowledge* (FAA-H-8083-25B, 2016) provides an excellent overview of hypoxia. (www.faa.gov/regulations_policies/handbooks_manuals/aviation/phak/)

Aeromedical Training for Flight Personnel. A great reference that provides in-depth coverage of a variety of physiological aspects related to flying, including hypoxia and DCS, published by the U.S. Department of the Army and is available to the public through booksellers and from other publishers.

Aircraft Operations at Altitudes Above 25,000 Feet Mean Sea Level or Mach Numbers Greater Than .75 (FAA AC 61-107). This updated Advisory Circular provides physiological and aerodynamic information for pilots upgrading to complex, high-performance aircraft capable of operating at high altitudes and high airspeeds. (www.faa.gov/regulations_policies/advisory_circulars/index.cfm/go/document.information/documentID/1020859)

Endnotes

1. Greek Air Accident Investigation and Aviation Safety Board (AAIASB), *Aircraft Accident Report: Helios Airways Flight HCY522, Boeing 737-31S, at Grammatiko, Hellas on 14 August 2005* (Hellenic Republic Ministry of Transport & Communications, Athens, Greece: November 2006).

2. International Civil Aviation Organization, *Manual of the ICAO Standard Atmosphere*, 3rd ed., Doc 7488/3 (Montreal, Canada: ICAO, 1993).

3. Adapted from Federal Aviation Administration, *Introduction to Aviation Physiology* (Oklahoma City, OK: FAA Civil Aerospace Medical Institute, n.d.). Available at www.faa.gov/pilots/training/airman_education/.

4. United States Department of the Army, *Aeromedical Training for Flight Personnel*, TC No. 3-04.93 (Washington, DC: August 31, 2009).

5. Matthias Ochs, Jens R. Nyengaard, Anja Jung, Lars Knudsen, Marion Voigt, Thorsten Wahlers, Joachim Richter, Hans Jørgen G. Gundersen, "The Number of Alveoli in the Human Lung," *American Journal of Respiratory and Critical Care Medicine* 169 (February 2004).

6. Ryan W. Maresh, Andrew D. Woodrow and James T. Webb, *Handbook of Aerospace and Operational Physiology*, 2nd ed. (Wright-Patterson AFB, OH: U.S. Air Force School of Aerospace Medicine, October 2016).

7. Federal Aviation Administration, *Introduction to Aviation Physiology* (Oklahoma City, OK: FAA Civil Aerospace Medical Institute, n.d.).

8. U.S. Department of the Army, *Aeromedical Training for Flight Personnel*.

9. Linda S. Costanzo, *Physiology* (Hagerstwon, MD: Lippincott Williams & Wilkins, 2007).

10. Ibid.

11. Maresh, Woodrow and Webb, *Handbook of Aerospace and Operational Physiology*.

12. Jeremy M. Berg, John L. Tymoczko, and Lubert Stryer, Section 10.2, Hemoglobin Transports Oxygen Efficiently by Binding Oxygen Cooperatively, in *Biochemistry*, 5th ed., (New York: WH Freeman, 2002). Available at www.ncbi.nlm.nih.gov/books/NBK22596/.

13. Adapted from FAA, *Introduction to Aviation Physiology*.

14. Adapted from U.S. Department of the Army, *Aeromedical Training for Flight Personnel*.

15. Warner D. Fan, "Night Vision: Question and Answer Column," *Aviation, Space, and Environmental Medicine* 62 (March 1991): 274–275.

16. AAIASB, *Aircraft Accident Report: Helios Airways Flight HCY522*, 57.

17. Adapted from U.S. Department of the Army, *Aeromedical Training for Flight Personnel*; and, Maresh, Woodrow and Webb, *Handbook of Aerospace and Operational Physiology*.

18. Marcus E. Raichle and Debra A. Gusnard, "Appraising the Brain's Energy Budget," *Proceedings of the National Academy of Sciences of the United States of America* 99 (August 6, 2002): 10237–10239.

19. Robert J. Del Vecchio, *Physiological Aspects of Flight* (New York: Dowling College Press, 1977).

20. John Mackenzie Bacon, *The Dominion of the Air: The Story of Aerial Navigation* (New York: Cassell & Company, 1902): 223–228.

21. U.S. Department of the Army, *Aeromedical Training for Flight Personnel*.

22. Maresh, Woodrow and Webb, *Handbook of Aerospace and Operational Physiology*.

23. G.J. Salazar, "Carbon Monoxide: A Deadly Menace," *Medical Facts for Pilots* (brochure), OK05-0270 (Oklahoma City, OK: FAA Civil Aerospace Medical Institute, n.d.).

24. Ibid.

25. Maresh, Woodrow and Webb, *Handbook of Aerospace and Operational Physiology.*

26. Adrian M. Smith, "Hypoxia Symptoms Reported During Helicopter Operations Below 10,000 Feet: A Retrospective Survey," *Aviation, Space, and Environmental Medicine* 76 (August 2005): 794–798.

27. Federal Aviation Administration, *Aircraft Operations at Altitudes Above 25,000 Feet Mean Sea Level or Mach Numbers Greater Than .75,* AC 61-107B (Washington, DC: September 9, 2015).

28. Maresh, Woodrow and Webb, *Handbook of Aerospace and Operational Physiology.*

29. Federal Aviation Administration, *Aircraft Operations at Altitudes Above 25,000 Feet Mean Sea Level and/or Mach Numbers (MMO) Greater Than .75,* AC 61-107A (Washington, DC: January 2, 2003).

30. Mike Sinnett, "787 No-Bleed Systems: Saving Fuel and Enhancing Operational Efficiencies," *AeroMagazine* 7 (2007): 6–11.

31. Federal Aviation Administration, "Extended Operations (ETOPS) of Multi-Engine Airplanes: Final Rule," *Federal Register* 72.9 (January 16, 2007): 1807–1887.

32. Federal Aviation Administration, *Interim Policy on High Altitude Cabin Decompression,* Memo No. ANM-03-112-16 (Washington, DC: March 24, 2006).

33. U.S. Department of the Navy, *Naval Air Training and Operating Procedures Standardization (NATOPS), General Flight and Operating Instructions Manual,* CNAF M-3710.7 (Washington, DC: May 5, 2016).

34. Maresh, Woodrow and Webb, *Handbook of Aerospace and Operational Physiology.*

35. Federal Aviation Administration, *Amateur-Built Aircraft and Ultralight Flight Testing Handbook,* AC 90-89B (Washington, DC: FAA, April 27, 2015).

36. Federal Aviation Administration, "Boeing 737 (B-737) Cabin Altitude Warning Horn Confusion," *Safety Alert for Operators,* SAFO 08016 (Washington, DC: FAA, July 7, 2008).

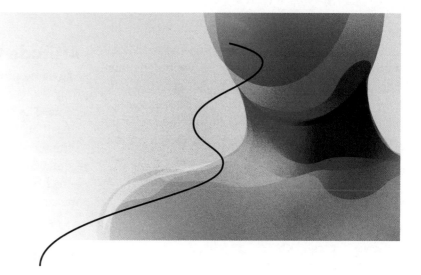

5

You must pass that gas—either fore or aft.
Trapped and Evolved Gases

U.S. Air Force Lieutenant Colonel Kevin Henry was flying alone in his Lockheed U-2 spy plane on a combat mission in the Middle East when he began to experience the symptoms. It started with pain in both knees then spread to his ankles. At first he didn't think too much of it, but as the flight progressed he experienced other problems: extreme fatigue, headache, nausea, loss of color vision, blindness in half of his visual field (hemianopsia), and hearing loss. He even began to hallucinate. His ability to think and remember things was so impaired that that controllers even had to help him remember how to fly the airplane. At one point the airplane stalled then recovered, and after five attempts at landing on the wrong runway he was able to safely land. He immediately received medical treatment but continued to suffer until his release from the hospital seven days later. He continued to experience a variety of physiological symptoms several months later and was eventually disqualified from flying.[1, 2]

Even though the *Dragon Lady*, as it was affectionately nicknamed, was flying at FL700 (70,000 feet), and the cabin was pressurized to a cabin altitude of 28,000 feet, the pilot's incapacitation was not the result of hypoxia; rather, it was the result of **altitude decompression sickness (DCS)**. As with scuba divers who return to the surface too quickly, Lieutenant Colonel Henry's prolonged exposure to the low atmospheric pressure associated with a cabin altitude of 28,000 feet exposed him to the dangerous symptoms of DCS.

The previous chapter explored a major physiological phenomenon—hypoxia—that poses a threat when flying at high altitudes. This chapter looks at two more physiological hazards associated with flight at higher altitudes: decompression sickness caused by the evolving of gases in the body and a variety of other ills resulting from trapped gases in the body. Since these conditions arise from changes in air pressure the term **altitude dysbarism** (*dys* = ill; *barism* = reduced barometric pressure) is sometimes used to describe them.

Decompression Sickness

Have you noticed that right after opening a bottle of carbonated soda that gas bubbles form and rise to the surface? This is because the CO_2 gas, which is dissolved in solution (in liquid form) under pressure in the soft drink container, is released, or *evolved*, when the pressure is reduced to the outside ambient pressure. Molecules in liquid solution evolve into a gaseous state if the temperature is increased or the pressure is decreased. **Henry's Law**, which states that *the amount of gas dissolved in solution is directly proportional to the pressure of the gas over the solution*, explains why elements in solution in your body evolve into gaseous form at the low ambient pressures that occur at high altitudes in an unpressurized aircraft cabin or after a sudden decompression in a pressurized one. This can result in altitude DCS, sometimes called *altitude sickness*, which, as our U-2 pilot discovered, can lead to a number of very serious incapacitating symptoms.

Some of the first to notice the problems associated with significant pressure changes were construction workers who emerged from high-pressure caissons—watertight structures filled with compressed air lowered into the water—used to build the foundations of bridges and other structures. In fact, the construction of the Eads Bridge in St. Louis, Missouri, and the Brooklyn Bridge in New York City in the mid-1800s were the first to use caisson technology in the United States. Unfortunately, some of these workers were also among the first casualties of *caisson disease*, what we now call DCS.[3]

Deep sea divers also noticed problems associated with significant pressure changes. After diving to greater depths, exposing themselves to greater pressures, they reported an increasing number and severity of physiological problems after returning to the surface. In fact many reported that they felt better when they were "down below."

When divers breathe air under pressure the oxygen is utilized (metabolized) by the body but the remaining nitrogen (N_2) is not: it remains inert and goes into solution, or dissolves, in the body's fluids and tissues. When a diver reaches two atmospheres at approximately 33 feet (or 10 meters) the amount of nitrogen that goes into solution increases by a factor of two. If a diver returns to the surface too quickly, especially from a deep dive, the supersaturated nitrogen in the body's tissues is unable to return back to the atmosphere through the lungs quickly enough and, like a can of soda, gas bubbles form. These escaping bubbles in turn can lead to a wide variety of detrimental symptoms, the most common being the **bends** (called the "bends" because of the bent posture which results from the pain from the nitrogen bubbling into the joints and muscles).

Divers have learned to prevent the bends by using charts which tell them how long they need to stop (decompression stops) while ascending to the surface to allow for safe N_2 elimination. Many commercial operations now use decompression chambers that the diver enters while at depth. The pressure in the diving chamber is left at the dive-depth pressure while it is returned to the surface. Divers then decompress in more comfortable surroundings at a more controlled and safer rate.

Altitude DCS Symptoms

The same process that occurs during rapid ascents from a dive are responsible for DCS experienced by pilots. The symptoms of altitude DCS are generally classified into two types: **Type I DCS** (pain-only symptoms) and **Type II DCS** (severe symptoms). The former includes physiological symptoms such as the bends and skin manifestations (sometimes called the *creeps*); the latter includes the *chokes* and neurological disturbances (sometimes called the *staggers*). Type I DCS is less serious than Type II DCS, but is still considered a medical emergency and both need to be treated by qualified medical personnel.[4, 5]

Type I DCS—The Bends

The most common altitude DCS symptom, at almost 75 percent frequency when exposed to a cabin altitude of 28,000 feet for two hours (*see* Table 5-1), is joint pain caused by the *bends*. As mentioned previously, the bends are caused by nitrogen bubbling into the joints and muscles of the body. The body parts which are most affected, in order of decreasing occurrence, are the knees, shoulders, elbows, wrists or hands, ankles or feet, and, rarely, the hips.[6] The pain usually progresses from mild to severe with increasing altitude and time aloft. It also tends to spread from a specific area to an entire limb (arm or leg).

Table 5-1. Relative percentage of DCS symptoms after a two-hour exposure at 28,000 feet and 37,000 feet cabin altitude.[7]

Symptom	Gas bubble location	Percentage (%) incidence for 2-hour interval	
		28,000 feet	37,000 feet
Bends	Limb joints and muscles	73.9	56.5
Creeps	Skin	7.0	1.6
Chokes	Lungs	4.5	7
Staggers	Brain, eyes, spinal cord, or peripheral nerves	3.0	4.8
Collapse	Central nervous or circulatory system	9.0	25.8
Misc.		2.5	4.8

Type I DCS—The Creeps

Less common are the **creeps**, the sensations arising from nitrogen bubbling near the nerves of the skin. The symptoms include paresthesia—a prickling, tingling, or itching of the skin—skin rashes, cold/warm sensations and *formication* (sensation of tiny insects crawling on your skin). It's no wonder they call these symptoms, especially the last one, the creeps! A less common, but more serious, type of the creeps involves mottled or marbled skin lesions. The creeps are generally not debilitating. However, it does mean that you are in an unprotected environment and immediate action is necessary.

Type II DCS—The Chokes

Nitrogen bubbles in the lungs can also create a respiratory problem known as the **chokes**. Though not as common as the bends, the chokes can involve greater incapacitation. Symptoms begin with a burning sensation under the sternum and progresses to a stabbing pain with increasing altitude and time aloft. Taking deep breaths makes matters worse and shorter breaths are the only way to avoid the severe pain associated with this phenomenon. An unproductive (dry) cough develops and the sensation of suffocation and can occur. Unconsciousness will occur with prolonged exposure.

Type II DCS—The Staggers

Although our U-2 pilot experienced loss of color vision, partial blindness, and other neurological disturbances, symptoms that affect the brain, eyes, spinal cord, and peripheral nerves—sometimes called the **staggers**—are a relatively rare occurrence with altitude DCS. However, such symptoms are serious and require an immediate descent and medical attention. Common nervous system disturbances involve vision: tunnel vision, blurred vision, double vision, or a loss of vision in part of the visual field known as a *scotoma*. Other neurological symptoms include mild to severe headaches, dizziness, confusion, memory loss, personality changes, anxiety, unusual sensations, aphasia (inability to use or understand words), loss of orientation, unilateral (on one side only) paresthesia or numbness, fatigue, seizures, muscle weakness, urinary and rectal incontinence, and even partial paralysis.[8, 9]

Collapse

Severe DCS can result in temporary, partial, or total loss of consciousness. This can be caused by bubbling nitrogen interfering with the circulatory system (primary collapse) or as a result of symptoms associated with prolonged bends, chokes, or staggers (secondary collapse).[10] You will notice in Table 5-1 that the incidence of the bends and the creeps is actually less at 37,000 feet than at 26,000 feet when exposed for two hours at these altitudes: that's because 25 percent of the symptoms at the higher altitude will be some form of collapse. Type II DCS is a serious medical emergency that can lead to permanent disability or death. It requires an immediate descent and transport of the victim to the nearest medical facility to receive treatment from medical personnel experienced with DCS.

Predisposing Factors for Altitude DCS

Several environmental and personal factors affect the severity of DCS symptoms. These include altitude attained, the rate of ascent, duration at altitude, physical activity, age and body type, frequency of exposure, and scuba diving.

Altitude

The threshold for experiencing altitude DCS is generally a cabin altitude of 25,000 feet; but symptoms can also occur as low as 18,000 feet MSL. Figure 5-1 reports the incidence of decompression sickness over a four-hour exposure for 193 people (113 males, 80 females) performing mild exercise and breathing 100 percent oxygen. The entire curve will be skewed to the right for lower exposure times and for persons resting quietly, which is usually the case for flight crew. Less than 1 percent of DCS symptoms occurred at 18,000 feet; yet, from the chart you can see the percentage of incidence rises rapidly above that altitude.

Rate of Ascent

A rapid climb to DCS altitudes will generally increase the onset and, to some extent, the severity of symptoms. Like opening a can of soda quickly, bubble formation is accelerated with a rapid climb to altitudes above 18,000 feet, leaving the body less time to expel excess nitrogen through the lungs normally.

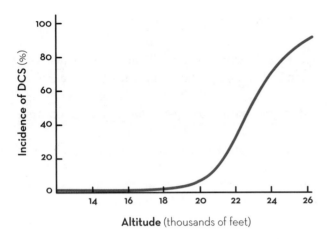

Fig 5-1.

Incidence of decompression sickness over four-hour exposure for 193 people performing mild exercise and breathing 100 percent oxygen.

Time at Altitude

Prolonged exposure at DCS altitudes increases the probability and severity of symptoms.

Physical Activity

Just as shaking a can of soda before opening it increases CO_2 bubble formation, physical activity increases the probability and severity of DCS symptoms. It also lowers the altitude at which DCS symptoms will occur. Heavy exercise effectively increases your physiological altitude by about 5,000 feet, thereby significantly lowering altitude thresholds at which symptoms will be experienced.[11]

Age and Body Type

Approximately half of all N_2 dissolved in the body is in fat, which stores about five times more N_2 than that dissolved in other tissues. Therefore, those with high body fat and a higher body mass index are at a greater risk of experiencing altitude DCS. Symptoms also increase with age: Compared to 18- to 21-year-olds, people over 42 years of age are three times more likely to experience DCS.[12]

Age and body weight may have been a factor for a captain who experienced DCS while he was troubleshooting a pressurization problem. The flight engineer of Connie Kalitta Flight 861 could not get the McDonnell Douglas DC-8 to pressurize during the climb and the captain ordered the FO to continue the climb to FL330 while he went back to examine the forward overwing emergency exit. When reaching altitude the captain became incapacitated and the FO initiated a descent to 10,000 feet and diverted to another airport to get medical assistance for him. According to an FAA aviation medical examiner (AME), the captain's obesity may have contributed to his incapacitation from severe DCS symptoms (NTSB Identification No: NYC94LA062).

Frequency of Exposure

There is also evidence that the more frequent a person is exposed to cabin altitudes greater than 18,000 feet—especially within a relatively short time period—the more likely they are to experience DCS symptoms.[13]

Scuba Diving

Altitude DCS can occur at altitudes much lower than 18,000 feet if a pilot or passenger has recently been scuba diving (scuba = self-contained underwater breathing apparatus). The amount of excess nitrogen dissolved in the body depends upon the depth and length of the dive, and the probability of experiencing altitude DCS depends on how soon after the dive one flies and how high the cabin altitude is.

Trapped Gas

Another physiological threat that arises from changes in atmospheric pressure, besides hypoxia and altitude DCS, is **trapped gas**. As pointed out in the previous chapter, and as seen in Figure 5-2, as you ascend into the atmosphere pressure decreases logarithmically. For example, even though 99.9 percent of the Earth's atmospheric mass lies below approximately 164,000 feet, half of it (and half its pressure) lies below 18,000 feet MSL (see Figure 4-2 in Chapter 4).

As noted in the previous chapter, the volume of a gas expands with increasing altitude in accordance with Boyle's Law, which states that the volume of a gas is inversely proportional to the pressure exerted on it. Therefore, as you ascend in the atmosphere the volume of gas trapped in the various cavities in the body will also expand. Figure 5-3 illustrates that trapped gas will dramatically expand with increasing altitude until it is about six times its volume at approximately 43,000 feet MSL.

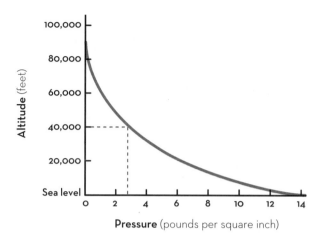

Fig 5-2.

Atmospheric pressure decreases with altitude. The pressure at sea level is 14.7 PSI, while at 40,000 feet, as the red dotted lines show, the pressure is only 2.72 PSI.

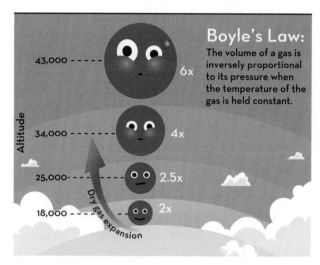

Boyle's Law: The volume of a gas is inversely proportional to its pressure when the temperature of the gas is held constant.

Fig 5-3.

Expansion of trapped gas with increase in altitude.

Barotrauma, consisting of discomfort, pain, and possible incapacitation, will result if the gases in the body are unable to escape. The areas that are affected the most are the middle ear, sinuses, teeth, and the GI tract. Trapped gas in the teeth and GI tract are more likely to occur during the climb to altitude, while middle ear and sinus problems are more likely to occur during the descent.

Ear Block

Difficulty clearing the ears is probably the most common problem associated with trapped air during altitude changes. Figure 5-4 diagrams the outer, middle and inner ear. Pain and possible ear damage occurs when trapped air in the middle ear cannot escape and the pressure cannot be equalized with that of the outside ambient pressure in the outer ear,

Fig 5-4.

Outer, middle and inner ear.

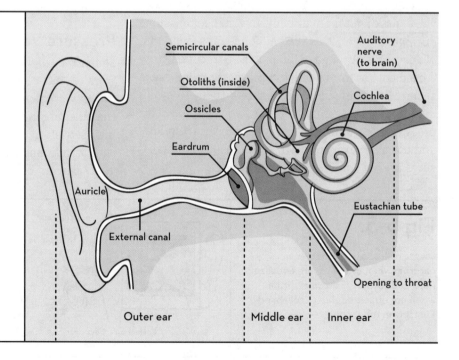

a condition known as **barotitis media**. Symptoms may include mild discomfort, minor hearing loss, ringing in the ears (tinnitus), severe pain, dizziness, and even eardrum rupture.

As its name implies, the middle ear is a cavity that lies between the outer and inner ear. The eardrum separates it from the outer ear (external auditory canal) and a thin wall of bone separates it from the inner ear. Inside the middle ear are the bones (auditory ossicles) which transmit sound waves to the inner ear. The Eustachian tube is a canal about an inch-and-a-half long that extends from the middle ear to the back of the throat.

Equalizing Pressure on Ascent

As altitude is gained, the expansion of air inside the middle ear exerts outward pressure on the eardrum causing it to bulge slightly outward. When the middle ear pressure exceeds the outside pressure by about 0.3 PSI, air escapes through the Eustachian tube down to the throat. This is felt and heard as a faint popping in the ear as the eardrum returns to its normal position.

Equalizing Pressure on Descent

During a descent from altitude the increased ambient (atmospheric and/or cabin) pressure in the outer ear exerts pressure on the eardrum causing it to bulge inward. Unfortunately for fliers, air passes down the Eustachian tube to the throat easier than going up back up to the middle ear from the throat. This is because the tube is essentially a one-way valve, making it more difficult to equalize pressures during a descent. This is compounded if a rapid rate of descent is initiated or if one has an infection from a head cold or from allergies: associated membranes secrete extra mucus which causes them to swell, making air passages narrower and equalization of air pressures more difficult. Severe pain, hearing loss, and possible eardrum rupture will result if the pressures are not equalized during descent.

Figure 5-5 illustrates the mechanisms involved when the ear is able to clear during a descent and when it is not because of an ear block from a collapsed Eustachian tube.

Since the density of the atmosphere is greater at lower altitudes, the rate of atmospheric pressure change with altitude is also greater (*see* Figure 4-2 in Chapter 4, and Figure 5-2). For example, the change in atmospheric pressure per 1,000 feet is greater between 5,000 feet MSL and sea level than it is between 20,000 feet and 15,000 feet MSL. Therefore, pressure build-up in the middle ear will occur faster and difficulty clearing the ears will be greater when descending in the lower altitudes. Various methods used to clear the ears on descent are discussed later in this chapter.

Oxygen Ear

It should be noted that a delayed ear block can occur after landing from breathing 100 percent oxygen in flight. Because the oxygen is slowly absorbed by the tissues in the middle ear, a partial vacuum is created causing the eardrum to bulge inward which causes ear pain. Usually the *Valsalva maneuver* (discussed shortly) is sufficient to equalize pressure and restore the slight temporary hearing loss caused by **oxygen ear**. However, the problem could be compounded if the oxygen absorption takes place while the person is asleep. Pressure differentials can reach higher levels since the sleeping person does not naturally perform activities which clear the ears (e.g., talk or swallow).

Pressure Vertigo

Sometimes higher-than-normal middle ear pressures from an ear block, or from performing a Valsalva maneuver, can stimulate the vestibular apparatus in the inner ear inducing temporary dizziness or a spinning sensation. This **pressure vertigo**, called *alternobaric vertigo*, has been experienced by approximately 10–17 percent of the pilot population.[14]

Fig 5-5.

Diagram illustrating no strain on eardrum when pressures are equalized (left) and severe strain on eardrum when not equalized due to collapsed Eustachian tube (right).

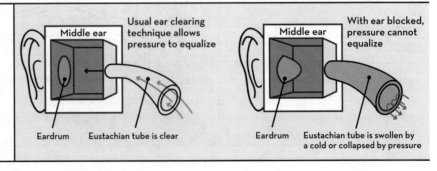

Sinus Block

The paranasal sinuses are small air-filled cavities located in the bone of the skull which give the skull its strength and light weight. The sinuses of concern are the two frontal sinuses located above the eyes in the forehead, the two ethmoid sinuses located just above the nasal cavity and the two maxillary sinuses located within the cheekbones (Figure 5-6).

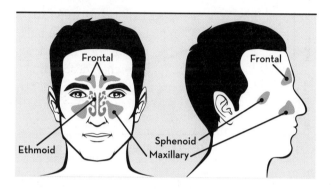

Fig 5-6.

Location of sinuses.

Normally these sinuses do not pose a problem on ascent or descent, since equalization of pressure occurs through small openings into the nasal cavity, but if the sinus openings are blocked because of membrane swelling due to infection from a cold or allergy, severe pain could be experienced on ascent or descent, a condition known as **barosinusitis** (or *aerosinusitis*). Trapped air in the sinuses generally equalizes easier on ascent, and if sinus congestion is involved, with greater difficulty on descent. The partial vacuum in the sinuses as the descent progresses could cause fluid accumulation and bleeding into the sinus, resulting in incapacitating pain. The greatest pain is likely to be encountered at the lower altitudes since this is where the rate of pressure change is the most. Pain in the frontal sinuses feels like an ice pick has been pushed into your forehead.

Tooth Block

The onset of a toothache with altitude gain rarely occurs in flight. It is caused by trapped gas in a tooth, a condition known as **barodontalgia**. Sometimes caused by a tooth abscess, a tooth block is more likely the result of imperfect dental work, such as from a loose filling or an improperly filled root canal that allows air to be trapped.

The most likely cause of barodontalgia, however, is referred pain from the sinuses during descent. Sinusitis in the maxillary sinuses can induce pressure on the nerves of the teeth sufficient to produce pain in the teeth of the upper jaw.

Gastrointestinal Tract

A common problem is trapped gas in the GI tract. As Figure 5-3 indicates, trapped gas expands significantly at higher altitudes, and if not allowed to escape you could experience excruciating pain or even lose consciousness through fainting. How and what you eat before flight can have an effect on the severity of GI gas problems. For example, eating quickly, eating large quantities of food, and drinking large quantities of fluids—especially carbonated beverages—involves swallowing large volumes of air, a major source of trapped gas in the GI tract. High fiber foods, gas-forming foods (such as onions, apples, melons), and high-fat foods also contribute to gas formation in the GI tract.

Managing Evolved and Trapped Gas Problems

Reduced atmospheric pressures at high altitudes and rapidly changing atmospheric pressures encountered during climbs and descents are responsible for the evolution of gases that cause DCS and trapped gases and their accompanying painful and incapacitating conditions. Fortunately, there are a number of strategies you can use to either avoid these physiological threats or safely manage them should they occur.

Avoid Flight at High Altitudes in Unpressurized Aircraft

Since the probability of altitude DCS increases at or above 25,000 feet (MSL altitude or cabin altitude), with an even lower likelihood at 18,000 feet, avoiding flights above these altitudes will keep you from experiencing symptoms. Of course, you can also avoid DCS by flying in a pressurized cabin. As mentioned in the previous chapter, most transport aircraft are required to be pressurized to a cabin pressure altitude of not more than 8,000 feet when the airplane is flying at its maximum operating altitude—an altitude below the hypoxia threshold of 10,000 feet and well below the lowest DCS threshold.

Avoid Scuba Diving Before a Flight

It was noted that DCS can occur at altitudes much lower than 18,000 feet if you participate in scuba diving before a flight. In a dive to only 33 feet below the surface the external pressure exerted on the body, and subsequently the amount of nitrogen absorbed in the body's tissues and fluids, increases by a factor of two (14.7 PSI atmospheric pressure + 14.7 PSI water = 29.4 PSI). Before you embark on a flight, sufficient time must be allowed for the excess nitrogen to escape at a normal rate through the lungs, otherwise you will experience DCS at lower-than-DCS-threshold altitudes. This is why if you plan on flying at or below 8,000 feet MSL—both the FAA and Transport Canada *Aeronautical Information Manuals* recommend waiting at least 24 hours after a dive if it involved a controlled ascent (i.e., decompression-stop dive) and at least 12 hours if it did not require a controlled ascent. Due to the possibility of a sudden decompression, they also recommend waiting at least 24 hours if flying above 8,000 feet MSL (not pressurized cabin altitude), regardless of the type of dive.

Denitrogenation

A practice not common in civilian aviation—because most high altitude flying is conducted in pressurized aircraft—but in military operations and in preparation for hypobaric (altitude) chamber training, is **denitrogenation** (or *preoxygenation*). One way to reduce, but not eliminate the probability of experiencing DCS if flying at or above DCS altitudes in an unpressurized cabin is to remove as much N_2 as possible from the body's tissues and fluids before flight begins. This can be done by prebreathing 100 percent O_2 for at least 30 minutes. Since oxygen is utilized by the body, and since no additional N_2 is added to its tissues and some preexisting N_2 is also being expelled from your system during the time of prebreathing O_2, operations at higher altitudes are possible without the side effects of N_2 bubbling into the body's tissues. You can see in Figure 5-7 the incidence of DCS decreases the longer one prebreathes oxygen. There are limits to the altitude attained, however, and longer denitrogenation times are needed for higher altitudes or if greater levels of physical activity are anticipated.

However, as you can see in the figure, the relationship between prebreathing time and protection from DCS is not linear; there are diminishing returns the longer one prebreathes oxygen.

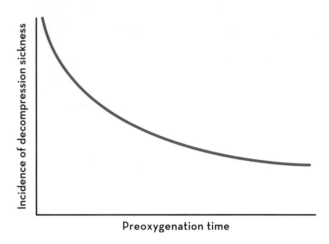

Fig 5-7.

The incidence of DCS decreases the longer one prebreathes oxygen, but at a diminishing advantage the longer oxygen is prebreathed.

As noted, denitrogenation is generally not practiced by civilian pilots. The following quotation from the FAA's *Introduction to Aviation Physiology* booklet addresses this:

> Although 100 percent oxygen prebreathing is an effective method to provide individual protection against altitude DCS, it is not a logistically simple nor an inexpensive approach for the protection of civil aviation flyers (commercial or private). Therefore, at the present time it is only being used by military flight crews and astronauts for their protection during high altitude and space operations.[15]

Follow Proper Decompression Procedures

The importance of knowing what to do in the unlikely event of a sudden or gradual cabin decompression was stressed in the previous chapter. It's important you take proper corrective measures as soon as possible; failure to do so could result in incapacitation that will jeopardize the safe continuance of flight.

Besides hypoxia, the other threat after a sudden decompression is altitude DCS. Since decompression procedures require an emergency descent to 10,000 feet MSL (or the minimum safe IFR altitude if higher) to effectively deal with the effects of hypoxia, such a procedure automatically reduces or eliminates the probability of DCS since the thresholds of 18,000 to 25,000 feet are much higher. Such a descent will clear up most, if not all, symptoms by dissolving N_2 gas back into solution.

Take Precautions if You Experience DCS

Most altitude DCS symptoms go away by the time you land. However, whether you have been exposed to DCS altitudes or have experienced it after a gradual or sudden cabin decompression, symptoms will sometimes manifest themselves even after returning to the surface. You should take precautions to avoid this. For example, it is strongly recommended that you avoid exercise for at least 24 hours after being exposed to DCS altitudes.[16] Just as shaking a can of soda increases CO_2 bubble formation, physical activity also increases the probability that N_2 will evolve into gas bubbles, even after returning to ground level. Also, after exposure to DCS altitudes, and certainly if you experienced symptoms at altitude, you should avoid drinking alcohol for at least 12 hours.[17] The symptoms of alcohol may mask the symptoms of altitude DCS, and you, and those around you, may erroneously think your symptoms are only those of alcohol intoxication.

The serious nature of DCS has been noted throughout this chapter. Therefore, whether you experience Type I or Type II DCS—during or after a flight—or you experience something unusual as a result of flying at a higher altitude but are not entirely sure of its origin, you should seek immediate medical attention from an FAA AME, a Transport Canada civil aviation medical examiner (CAME), or a hyperbaric medicine specialist. Even if symptoms disappear after landing, you should still see qualified medical personnel in case there is damage that isn't easily readily noticeable. Since a regular physician may not be familiar with this type of medical problem you need to be your own advocate to ensure you receive proper and timely treatment. Treating DCS often involves breathing 100 percent pure oxygen. However, if symptoms are of the Type II variety—the chokes, neurological distur-

bances, or mottled or marbled skin lesions—you must immediately be treated with compression therapy which involves breathing 100 percent oxygen delivered under high pressure in a hyperbaric chamber operated by specially trained medical personnel.[18]

Consider High Altitude Physiology Training

Three major tasks you must engage in after a rapid decompression at high altitude are donning your oxygen mask, ensuring 100 percent O_2 is being delivered to the mask, and initiating an emergency descent to a non-hypoxic altitude. This type of training protects you from the adverse effects of hypoxia and altitude DCS. It is recommended, therefore, that you take such training from a qualified organization in actual conditions in a real airplane or, as we mentioned in the previous chapter, in simulated conditions in a hypobaric (altitude) chamber or portable reduced oxygen training enclosure. This will help you not only recognize your own personal symptoms of hypoxia, but learn the procedures to follow in the event of a rapid decompression, which will also help you avoid altitude DCS.

Follow Procedures to Clear an Ear or Sinus Block

Swallowing, chewing, yawning, and moving your jaw forward and from side to side (sometimes called the *aviator's jaw jut*) will usually maintain adequate pressure equalization between your middle ears and the outside air, preventing an ear blockage during a climb or descent. During a descent, you can also periodically employ the **Valsalva maneuver**, ideally before it feels like an ear is being blocked, to force air up into the Eustachian tube. The Valsalva maneuver is performed by pinching your nose shut with your fingers and quickly and sharply exhaling while not allowing any air to escape from your mouth or nose. You should feel and hear a popping sound, and your hearing will likely also improve. Make sure to hold your head straight up or slightly back, and if only one ear is blocked, tilt your head in the opposite direction of the affected ear to assist airflow up the Eustachian tube. Be careful not to blow extremely hard, too long or too often, otherwise you will overpressure the middle ear or possibly cause ear damage or fainting.

How often you use perform Valsalva maneuvers during a descent depends on altitude, rate of descent, and how quickly your ears seem to be affected. Since the rate of pressure increase is greater at lower altitudes (e.g., from 5,000 feet to sea level than from 15,000 feet to 10,0000 feet), you should perform them more often to prevent excessive pressure build-up in the middle ear. You should do the same if the rate of descent is steep and if you feel your ears are plugging up frequently.

If these measures fail to clear the ears you should level off, consider climbing back to an altitude that equalizes the ears, and then initiate a more gradual descent and perform Valslavas more frequently. As you do this you should also consider administering a liberal dose of nose spray which can be very effective in opening up the Eustachian tube. You should be able to taste it at the back of the throat.[19] Even though many nose sprays contain antihistamines which cause drowsiness and are, for the most part, medically disqualifying, and even though prolonged use can lead to rebound sinusitis after you stop using them, most agree that it is appropriate to keep some in your flight bag in case of a severe ear block emergency. Better this than a ruptured eardrum.

The same procedure should be used if you are experiencing pain from a sinus block: level off from the descent and try Valsalvas. Failing that, reascend to an altitude where the sinus pain is less, administer nose spray, perform Valsalvas, and resume descent and perform Valsalvas. If no sinus relief is experienced, land as soon as possible and seek medical assistance from an FAA AME or Transport Canada CAME.

Since any ear block that develops during a climb involves higher pressure in the middle ear than in the ambient environment, you should never use the Valsalva maneuver to clear your ears during a climb—you will only increase middle ear pressure by doing so, thereby exacerbating the problem. An ear block on an ascent indicates you have severe congestion and will almost certainly experience a block on descent. It is also advisable to wake up a sleeping passenger during a descent since the normal swallowing reflex is absent during sleep. And, oh yes, it's alright for that baby to scream during a descent for landing: she is only protecting her middle ear!

You should also consider periodically performing Valsalvas after landing—especially if you experienced an ear block in flight or were breathing oxygen in flight—to prevent or correct a delayed ear block or oxygen ear. Finally, it goes without saying that to reduce your odds of experiencing a serious ear block or sinus block you should avoid flying when you have a head cold or upper respiratory infection.

Descend and Land if You Experience a Tooth Block

Barodontalgia is rare in flight, but if a toothache from trapped gas develops after climbing into lower atmospheric pressures found at higher altitudes then the treatment is to return to higher pressures found at lower altitudes. Tooth pain will often disappear at the same altitude it began.[20] Pain from a toothache generally begins to occur between 5,000 feet and 15,000 feet, but can occur lower. After landing you should see a dentist. As was noted, you should also be aware that upper tooth pain could actually be referred pain from the maxillary sinuses. If this is the case, you should follow the procedures for clearing a sinus block.

Be Careful What You Eat

To reduce the possibility of experiencing debilitating pain from trapped gas in the GI tract, you should follow the advice regarding diet in the FAA's old *Medical Handbook for Pilots*:

1. Don't eat too quickly before a flight.
2. Don't eat too much (swallowed air increases with each bite).
3. Avoid large quantities of fluid, especially cokes, pop, and beer.
4. Don't eat gas-forming foods (beans, cabbage, onions, raw apples, cucumbers, melons, or any greasy foods).
5. Avoid chewing gum on the way up—it may result in swallowing a great deal of air.[21]

When it comes to trapped gas in the GI tract you should also follow the advice given in an old U.S. military training video: "Now is not the time for the niceties of social convention—you must pass that gas, either fore or aft." If you're unable to pass the gas through flatulence or belching you could try to move the bubbles towards your colon by pushing the heel of your hand from the upper right area of your lower abdomen to the lower left. Certainly, if you receive no relief you should descend to a lower altitude or land as soon as possible.

Helpful Resources

The FAA's Civil Aerospace Medical Institute has produced several short but insightful flight physiology videos available in English, but some also in Spanish and/or Japanese, at www.faa.gov/pilots/training/airman_education/physiologyvideos/. The following relate to the contents of this chapter:

- *Altitude-Induced Decompression Sickness*
- *Trapped Gas*
- *Physics of the Atmosphere*
- *The Ups and Downs of Cabin Pressurization*

The FAA also has published a helpful brochure titled *Altitude-Induced Decompression Sickness* (Publication AM-400-95/2) available at www.faa.gov/pilots/safety/pilotsafetybrochures/.

Chapter 17 (*Aeromedical Factors*) in the FAA *Pilot's Handbook of Aeronautical Knowledge* (FAA-H-8083-25B, 2016) provides a good overview of trapped gas issues. (www.faa.gov/regulations_policies/handbooks_manuals/aviation/phak/)

Aeromedical Training for Flight Personnel. A great reference providing in-depth coverage of a variety of physiological aspects related to flying, including hypoxia and DCS, is published by the U.S. Department of the Army and is available to the public through booksellers and from other publishers.

Aircraft Operations at Altitudes Above 25,000 Feet Mean Sea Level or Mach Numbers Greater Than .75 (AC 61-107). This updated Advisory Circular provides physiological and aerodynamic information for pilots upgrading to complex, high-performance aircraft capable of operating at high altitudes and high airspeeds. (www.faa.gov/regulations_policies/advisory_circulars/index.cfm/go/document.list/parentTopicID/119)

Endnotes

1. Sean L. Jersey, Robert T. Baril, Richmond D. McCarty and Christina A. Millhouse, "Severe Neurological Decompression Sickness in a U-2 Pilot," *Aviation, Space, and Environmental Medicine* 81 (January 2010): 64–68.

2. Mark Betancourt, "Killer at 70,000 Feet: The Occupational Hazards of Flying. the U-2," *Smithsonian Air & Space Magazine* (May 2012).

3. W.P. Butler, "Caisson Disease During the Construction of the Eads and Brooklyn Bridges: A Review," *Undersea and Hyperbaric Medical Journal* 31 (Winter 2004): 445–459.

4. United States Department of the Army, *Aeromedical Training for Flight Personnel*, TC No. 3-04.93 (Washington, DC: August 1, 2018).

5. A.J.F. Macmillan, "Decompression Sickness," *Aviation Medicine* (2nd ed.), eds. John Ernsting and Peter King (London: Butterworths, 1988): 19–26.

6. Ibid.

7. Adapted from Federal Aviation Administration, *Introduction to Aviation Physiology* (Oklahoma City, OK: FAA Civil Aerospace Medical Institute, n.d.), and A.J.F. Macmillan, "Decompression Sickness," *Aviation Medicine*.

8. FAA, *Introduction to Aviation Physiology*.

9. U.S. Department of the Army, *Aeromedical Training for Flight Personnel*.

10. Macmillan, "Decompression Sickness," *Aviation Medicine*.

11. Ibid.

12. Z.M. Sulaiman, A.A. Pilmanis and R.B. O'Connor, "Relationship Between Age and Susceptibility to Altitude Decompression Sickness," *Aviation, Space, and Environmental Medicine* 68 (August 1997): 695–698.

13. Ryan W. Maresh, Andrew D. Woodrow and James T. Webb, *Handbook of Aerospace and Operational Physiology*, 2nd ed. (Wright-Patterson AFB, OH: U.S. Air Force School of Aerospace Medicine, October 2016).

14. A.J. Benson, "Spatial Disorientation—Common Illusions," *Aviation Medicine* (2nd ed.), eds. John Ernsting and Peter King (London: Butterworths, 1988): 297–317.

15. FAA, *Introduction to Aviation Physiology*.

16. Ibid.

17. Maresh, Woodrow and Webb, *Handbook of Aerospace and Operational Physiology*.

18. FAA, *Introduction to Aviation Physiology*.

19. Maresh, Woodrow and Webb, *Handbook of Aerospace and Operational Physiology*.

20. U.S. Department of the Army, *Aeromedical Training for Flight Personnel*.

21. Federal Aviation Administration, *Medical Handbook for Pilots*, AC 67-2 (Washington, DC: FAA Civil Aerospace Medical Institute, May 1974): 18.

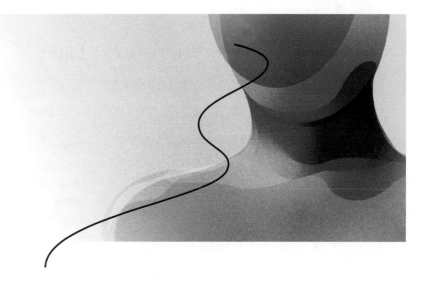

6

I can't see a thing!

Vision

You think they would have seen it. It was a clear sunny day and visibility was 10 miles when ATC informed the Boeing B-727 crew of the Cessna 172's location several times. In fact, after the FO said "Got 'em," the captain told ATC that they had the traffic "in sight." But a minute later the two aircraft collided three miles northeast of Lindbergh Field in San Diego, California, killing all 137 people aboard both airplanes and seven people on the ground (Report No: NTSB-AAR-79-5).

Almost eight years later, it happened again in the sunny skies of Southern California: An Aeromexico McDonnell Douglas DC-9 collided with a Piper Archer that had inadvertently entered the Los Angeles terminal control area (TCA)[1] without a clearance. The collision killed all 68 people aboard the two airplanes and 15 people on the ground in the town of Cerritos (Report No: NTSB/AAR-87-07). The weather was clear with 15 statute miles (SM) visibility.

Eight years later still, a Trans World Airlines DC-9 collided while taking off on Runway 30R with a Cessna 441 located on the same runway at taxiway Romeo at St. Louis Lambert International Airport in Bridgeton, Missouri, killing both occupants of the Cessna. The sky was clear, the visibility 25 SM, but it was dark (Report No: NTSB/AAR-95/05). A decade later, a Med Flight Air Ambulance Learjet 35 crashed into mountainous terrain shortly after takeoff from Brown Field Municipal Airport near San Diego, California, killing all five people aboard. While waiting for an IFR clearance and maintaining night visual flight rules (NVFR) flight below a cloud deck, the airplane flew into the side of Otay Mountain at an elevation of 2,256 feet MSL (NTSB Identification No: LAX05FA015).

What these tragic accidents—and numerous others like them—have in common is they all occurred, at least in part, because of inherent limitations in human vision. The midair collisions (MACs) in Southern California during the day and runway incursion accident in Missouri at night—all in clear weather conditions—occurred because of the failure to see and avoid the other aircraft, and the CFIT accident near San Diego at night in VMC, because of the inability of the eyes to adequately see in the dark.

Of all the senses needed to accurately perceive our environment to achieve safe flight operations, none ranks higher in importance than our sense of vision. The eye is undoubtedly the most remarkable and intricate organ in the human body. Functioning properly, the various components of this organ work together to convert light energy to chemical energy and then into electrical energy to enable us to see stimuli in the outside world.

However amazing these abilities are, the eyes are subject to certain limitations that can sometimes affect the safety of flight. For example, most aircraft collisions are the result of the failure of pilots to adequately see each other's aircraft. Pilots also have trouble seeing terrain, adverse weather, and airports during the hours of darkness—even in clear atmospheric conditions. And even when pilots think they are seeing their outside world correctly, sometimes conditions are such that their perception of it is wrong—without knowing it, they are under the influence of a visual illusion (a misperception of visual reality), with its sometimes-deadly consequences. The topic of visual illusions will be explored in depth in Chapter 12.

As a pilot, therefore, you must not only fully understand the nature of these visual limitations and the situations in which they are most likely to present themselves in the flight environment, but you must also be able to take measures designed to reduce their adverse effects. A basic understanding of vision is necessary before an understanding of these limitations can be appreciated.

Light

The physiological and psychological experience of vision requires the physical stimulus of reflected light from objects around us. What we call light is actually the visible portion of the electromagnetic spectrum. The wavelengths of light, which determine the color of objects, fall between about 400 and 700 nanometers (nm), and comprise only a small fraction of the electromagnetic spectrum (see Figure 6-1). The amplitude of the wave determines the intensity (or brightness) of the light.

Fig 6-1.

Visible light consists of a small portion of the electromagnetic spectrum.[2]

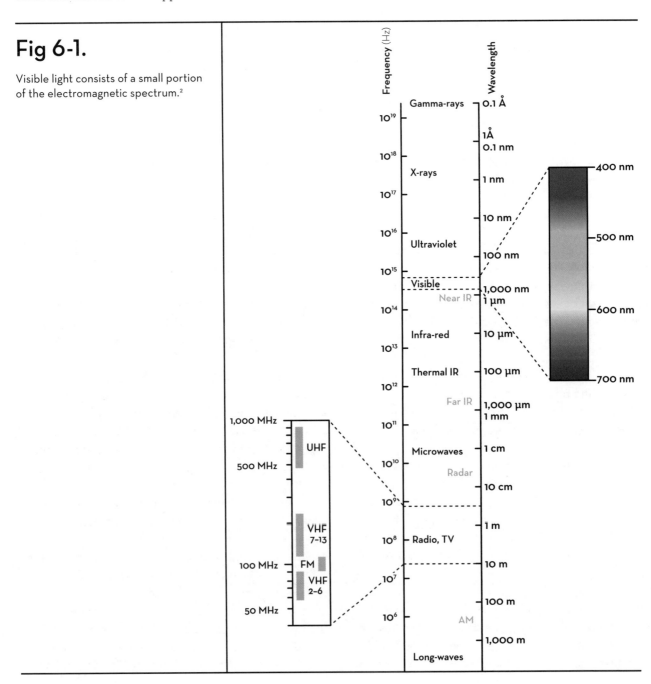

The Visual System

Translating the physical energy of light into visual images is the role of the eye. As noted, the eye is an intricate and complex organ. The eyelashes protect the eye from particulate matter and sunlight. Blinking of the eyelid cleans the surface of the eyeball as well as regulates the amount of incoming light. The eyeball itself is a sphere about an inch in diameter located within the eye sockets (spaces in the skull). The hard, outer shell (sclera) of the eye is mostly white and supports the entire eyeball (see Figure 6-2). Under this layer lies the choroid membrane that contains blood vessels that provide nutrients and oxygen to the organ. The inner layer located around the sides and back of the eyeball is called the retina. The retina contains photoreceptors—the **rods** and **cones**—which convert the incoming light energy into neural impulses which are sent to the brain via the optic nerve. This nerve leaves the retina about 18 degrees from the center of vision. Neural impulses travel along the optic nerve to the visual cortex where the signals are processed and interpreted by the brain. The bulk of the eye consists of a clear jelly-like substance called the vitreous humor. Light passes through here and strikes the retina.

The mechanical moving parts of the eye are located at the front. The outermost structure is the half-inch clear dome-shaped cornea. Clear fluid (*aqueous humor*) lies between the cornea and the iris. The iris is the circular portion of the eye that determines a person's eye color. This muscle regulates the amount of incoming light by contracting (making pupil diameter as small as 2 millimeters) under conditions of bright light and dilating (making pupil diameter as large as 8 millimeters) under conditions of dim light. The pupil is simply the hole in the iris which light passes through. The aperture of a camera functions in the same way as the iris/pupil arrangement. The lens, located behind the pupil, focuses light on the retina.

Process of Vision

Light entering the cornea is refracted (bent) as it passes through the aqueous humor. The light-sensitive iris contracts and dilates to allow for maximum visual efficiency under varying light intensities. In order to focus clearly on objects that vary in distance from the eye, the shape of the lens changes. By changing its degree of sphericity, the lens further refracts the light waves by focusing the image on the

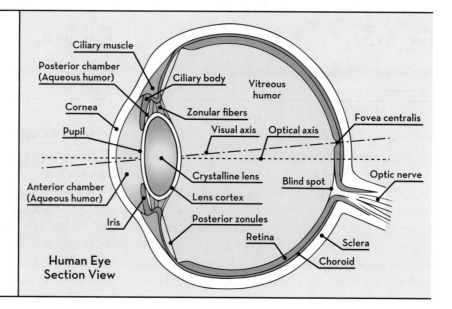

Fig 6-2.

The human eye.

Human Eye Section View

Ciliary muscle
Posterior chamber (Aqueous humor)
Ciliary body
Vitreous humor
Cornea
Zonular fibers
Visual axis
Optical axis
Fovea centralis
Pupil
Crystalline lens
Blind spot
Optic nerve
Anterior chamber (Aqueous humor)
Lens cortex
Iris
Posterior zonules
Retina
Sclera
Choroid

retina. This process of **accommodation** is controlled by the ciliary muscles which flatten the lens for long-distance focusing and allow the lens to return to a more spherical shape for short-distance focusing (*see* Figure 6-3).

The image which strikes the retina is actually reversed and inverted. Exactly how the brain switches the image around so it makes proper sense is still a question which remains unresolved.

nerve exits the eye at approximately 18 degrees from the fovea, there are no rods or cones at this location also. The presence of different pigments within the rods and cones are partly responsible for their unique abilities. When light energy strikes these photoreceptors, a chemical reaction occurs which breaks down (bleaches) the pigment. The chemical reaction is what changes the light energy into electrical energy that the brain receives via the optic nerve.

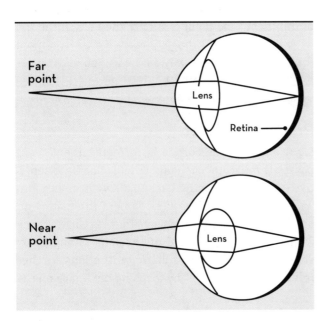

Fig 6-3.

Accommodation is the process of focusing.

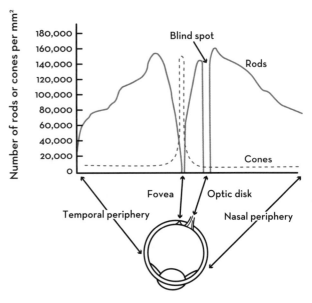

Fig 6-4.

Distribution of cones and rods along retina.[3]

Day and Night Vision

The human eye employs a dual vision receptor system: one for day and one for night. The design of these photoreceptors and the nature of the different pigments within them are responsible for the dual visual system located within the same retina. About six million cones located primarily at the center of the retina (*see* Figure 6-4) are responsible for providing color vision during daylight conditions. This is known as **photopic vision** (day vision). Approximately 120 million rods located in the periphery of vision, with the densest concentration about 15 to 25 degrees off the center of vision, provide black-and-white vision under conditions of low light. This is called **scotopic vision** (night vision). Figure 6-4 shows there are no rods located at the center of vision (called the *fovea*) and, since the optic

Visual Acuity

Visual acuity refers to the clarity of vision. Good **visual acuity** is the ability to discriminate fine detail. Figure 6-5 indicates the greatest visual acuity occurs, not in the periphery, but when an image falls within the center of vision on the fovea; in other words, when looking directly at an object in daylight conditions. The further out from this arc an object is, the less the ability to see fine detail.

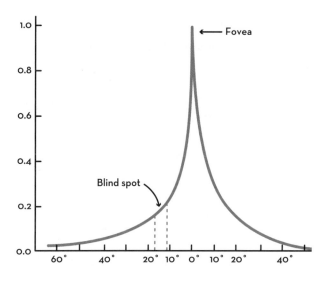

Fig 6-5.

Daylight visual acuity along the retina.[4]

Peripheral vision, or **ambient vision**, is good at detecting motion and is crucial in determining our orientation in space. For example, try walking in a straight line while only looking through two paper towel rolls: it is difficult to do without ambient vision. Figure 6-6 illustrates the total extent of normal binocular (two-eye) vision, or **field of view**, is about 200 degrees horizontal (side-to-side) and about 120 degrees vertical (up and down).

However, as stated previously, the ability to clearly identify an object in our peripheral vision becomes more difficult the further away its image is located from the center of vision. To better see an object in our peripheral vision, we instinctively turn our gaze toward it so its image falls on the fovea. Only then are we able to identify it. **Foveal vision**, also called *focal* or *central* vision—during daylight conditions—provides the greatest possible acuity for several reasons. First, the density of peripheral cones is significantly less than in the fovea, where the cone receptors are most densely packed (*see* Figure 6-4). Second, a secondary layer of retinal cells is folded away in the foveal depression (or pit), allowing for maximum stimulation of light energy on the foveal cones. Third, each foveal cone is connected to its own optic nerve fiber, communicating significantly more information to the brain than peripheral cones which share single optic nerve fibers with other cones. Finally, about half of the visual cortex in the brain processes information from the fovea, an area comprising only about 1 percent of the retina.[5]

From this basic understanding of eye physiology, you may be able to deduce the nature of some of the visual limitations that could exhibit themselves in the flight environment. First, we will look at how some of these make it difficult to see and avoid an in-flight collision. We will then look at how they make it difficult to see in the dark.

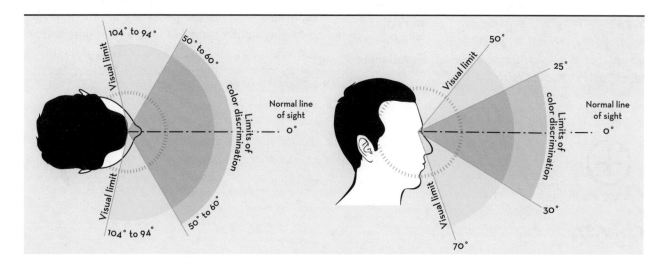

Fig 6-6.

Normal horizontal and vertical range of visual field.

Vision Problems in Midair Collision Avoidance

According to the U.S. right-of-way rules published in 14 CFR §91.113(b), "When weather conditions permit, regardless of whether an operation is conducted under instrument flight rules or visual flight rules, vigilance shall be maintained by each person operating an aircraft so as to *see and avoid* other aircraft." (emphasis added) A cursory glance at **near midair collision (NMAC)** reports indicates that many in-flight collisions were averted because one or more pilots saw the other in time to take evasive action; yet the most common cause of MACs cited by accident investigators is still the failure of pilots to *see and avoid* other aircraft. For example, in a study of 329 U.S. MACs, 88 percent of the pilots failed to see the other aircraft in time to avoid the collision.[6] The overwhelming evidence from accident investigations and safety studies indicates, therefore, that the see-and-avoid concept has significant limitations, and relying on this practice as the sole means of avoiding a collision is not enough.

Accommodation Lag

Figure 6-3 illustrates that to focus clearly on objects that vary in distance, the shape of the eye's lens must change. This accommodation process takes time, so when attempting to focus outside to look for possible conflicting air traffic after looking inside at the instrument panel, there is a time lag before proper focusing takes place. Even though this may only be a fraction of a second to two seconds in duration, the results could be significant if the time available to take evasive action is minimal.

Empty-Field Myopia

As its name suggests, **empty-field myopia** (also called *empty-sky myopia*, *night myopia*, or *dark focus*) is a near-sightedness that occurs when looking outside into an empty visual field. An empty visual field can occur when flying at high altitudes where terrain and cloud features are absent, flying in conditions of reduced visibility, such as in mist or haze, or flying during the hours of darkness. The absence of distinctive objects in one's visual field of view causes the eyes to focus at their resting state which, depending on the individual observer, ranges from only about two feet to two yards away. The result is that objects farther away than this distance are blurred or even imperceptible.[7] In these conditions, you might be under the false impression that you're conducting an adequate visual lookout for other traffic when in fact you're not. This *looking-without-seeing* is further aggravated by the fact that this phenomenon makes distant objects appear smaller and farther away than they actually are—certainly not something that is conducive to avoiding a MAC. Windscreen posts and frames, and dirty windscreens, also tend to pull eyes' focal distance inward.

Blind Spot

There are no visual photoreceptors where the optic nerve exits the eye (*see* Figures 6-2, 6-4, and 6-5). This **visual blind spot** is usually unnoticeable since one eye fills in what the other can't see. However, if vision from one eye is blocked (by a windscreen post, for example), a target in the periphery of vision may be completely undetectable. In fact, a jumbo jet will be undetectable as close as 1.5 miles away if its image falls on the blind spot. *See* Figure 6-7 to discover the existence of the blind spot in your own eyes.

Fig 6-7.

Visual blind spot. Hold the page close to your face with your left eye closed. Stare at the center of the circle with your right eye while slowly moving the page away from you; the image of the airplane in your peripheral vision will disappear when its image falls on the blind spot.[8]

Peripheral Vision

The best visual acuity is only good up to a maximum of one to two degrees from the center of the fovea, in daylight conditions (*see* Figure 6-5). This roughly corresponds to the area of a quarter held at arm's length. Beyond this visual arc acuity sharply drops, until at only about 15 to 20 degrees of arc the maximum possible visual acuity attained is approximately 20/200 using the Snellen visual acuity scale (named after the 19th century Dutch opthamologist Herman Snellen). Therefore, the farther out an object is located from the foveal field of view, the more difficult it is to perceive. In fact, the FAA's *AIM* states that an aircraft at a distance of seven miles that appears in sharp focus when looking directly at it with foveal vision would need to be as close as seven-tenths of a mile away in order to be recognizable when not being looked at directly.

As previously mentioned, ambient (peripheral) vision is important in maintaining spatial orientation and detecting moving targets. However, it does not detect targets that appear stationary on the retina. In a recent MAC involving a Piper PA-25 Pawnee and a Cirrus SR20 near Boulder, Colorado, the NTSB determined that the probable cause was the failure of both pilots to "see and avoid" each other, in part because there was no perceived visual relative motion of each airplane by the pilots; both aircraft remained stationary in each other's windscreen right up to the time of the accident (NTSB Identification No: CEN10FA115C).

Central Vision Blindness at Night

During pure night vision the cones are shut down and only the rods are active. Since there are no rods in the fovea (*see* Figure 6-4), and the foveal cones are shut down, **central vision blindness** occurs when staring directly at a dim light source when using scotopic vision. For example, the image of a dimly lit object on the retina at night (e.g., a star, distant tower light) will disappear when staring directly at it using foveal vision. Therefore, during pure night vision there are two blind spots in each eye.

How good are you at seeing other airplanes in flight?

The Massachusetts Institute of Technology conducted a study to determine the ability of pilots to detect other aircraft on a near-collision course. Twenty-four volunteers—half of whom held commercial pilot certificates—each flew a 45-minute cross-country in a Beech Bonanza with an observer/safety pilot. Participants were told the objective of the study was to measure pilot workload and, among other things, were instructed to immediately notify the observer whenever they saw another aircraft, whether it appeared to conflict with their flight path or not. Once established at cruising altitude, and unbeknownst to the pilots beforehand, a Cessna 401 flew by their airplane within a few tenths of a mile horizontally and at 500 feet above or below their altitude—once from head-on, once from directly behind and once at an angle from the side. *Even though they knew one of their tasks was to point out any air traffic, only 56 percent of the target aircraft were detected by the pilots!*

Source: J.W. Andrews, *Unalerted Air-to-Air Visual Acquisition*, Report No. DOT/FAA/PM-87/34 (Lexington, MA: MIT Lincoln Laboratory, November 26, 1991).

There are several other human factors issues that increase the risk of experiencing a MAC. For example, although the relative size of an approaching aircraft doubles whenever its distance from the viewer is reduced by half, its apparent size (i.e., visual angle on the retina) remains relatively small until it is quite close. Figure 6-8 shows that its size then increases exponentially and appears to blossom. This **blossom effect** has been the experience of many who have survived a MAC or NMAC. Despite maintaining what they thought was an adequate visual lookout, pilots have reported that they were surprised to find an airplane appear out of nowhere "filling up" their windscreen. One pilot got so close he could actually see the other pilot; he said he "wore a blue shirt and what looked like aviator Ray-Bans!" (ASRS Report No: 787228).

Finally, your ability to respond to the threat of a MAC is not only impeded by the visual difficulties in detecting other aircraft, it is delayed by the relatively long time needed to take effective evasive action. According to AC 90-48, *Pilots' Role in Collision Avoidance,* to recognize a target as an aircraft, become aware of the collision course, make a decision to take evasive action, and implement that action takes a minimum of 12.5 seconds (*see* Figure 6-8). This reaction time is based on military data, so it would likely be even longer for less maneuverable GA or transport aircraft. It certainly isn't enough time if aircraft closing speeds are high, or if the other aircraft is only recognized after it blossoms in the windscreen.

Fig 6-8.

Relative size of approaching target and pilot reaction times for avoidance.

Hold this illustration at arm's length in front of you. From that position, the silhouettes represent a T-33 aircraft as it would appear to you from the distances indicated in the table on the left. The time required to cover these distances is given in seconds for combined speeds of 360 and 600 mph.

The blocks on the lower left mark the danger area, for the speeds quoted, when aircraft are on a collision course. This danger area is based on the recognition and reaction times shown in the table on the lower right.

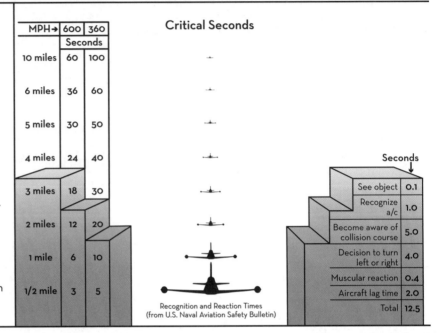

Critical Seconds

MPH→	600	360
	Seconds	
10 miles	60	100
6 miles	36	60
5 miles	30	50
4 miles	24	40
3 miles	18	30
2 miles	12	20
1 mile	6	10
1/2 mile	3	5

	Seconds
See object	0.1
Recognize a/c	1.0
Become aware of collision course	5.0
Decision to turn left or right	4.0
Muscular reaction	0.4
Aircraft lag time	2.0
Total	12.5

Recognition and Reaction Times
(from U.S. Naval Aviation Safety Bulletin)

Environmental Factors in MACs

Table 6-1 provides examples of environmental factors that increase the risk of experiencing a MAC.

Table 6-1. Environmental factors in MAC avoidance.

Conspicuity
A bright (or dark) aircraft in front of a bright (or dark) sky, or an aircraft positioned in front of a cluttered background (buildings), reduces contrast and is more difficult to detect. The NTSB noted that an overcast sky condition in a recent MAC involving a Piper PA-25 and a Cirrus SR20 near Boulder, Colorado, likely "made it difficult for the Piper pilot to detect the primarily white-colored Cirrus" (NTSB Identification No: CEN10FA115C).

Glare
Glare from the early morning Sun hampered the ability of an instructor and student aboard a Grob G-115 to see a Tobago TB-10 ahead on final approach at Parafield Airport in South Australia. The two collided, but fortunately no one was seriously injured.[9]

Reduced visibility
Reduced visibility reduces the time available to detect another aircraft. A military twin turbojet trainer collided with a single-engine Air Tractor AT-502B in cruise flight. A contributing factor in the accident was reduced visibility due to haze (NTSB Identification No: CHI05FA055B).

Aircraft blind spots
A high-wing Cessna 172 and a low-wing Piper PA-28 collided in midair killing all four occupants. The accident report stated that "as the flights converged and rolled out of their simultaneous turns, structure from both airplanes would have blocked the pilots' visibility and prevented them from seeing the other airplane and avoiding the collision" (NTSB Identification No: WPR13FA254A/B).

Though there are other factors that play a role in MACs, it is beyond the scope of this book to fully explore them. *See* the Helpful Resources listed at the end of this chapter that provide more information about MACs and guidance about how to avoid them.

Vision-Physiology Problems at Night

According to the AOPA Air Safety Institute, the odds of experiencing a fatal accident in a GA aircraft are more than doubled when flying at night—and increase even more depending on the type of flight operation. For example, night IMC has the highest lethality rate, increasing the probability of a fatal accident fivefold.[10] Visual flight at night is also a threat; so much so that the NTSB issued Safety Alert SA-013 warning pilots about the risks of visual flight operations at night—whether conducted under VFR flight or during the *visual* portions of IFR flight.[11]

Dark Adaptation

When quickly traveling from a well-lit environment into darkness (into a darkened theater, for example), the ability to see is initially severely impaired, but improves with time. That's because as light levels drop after sunset to that of moonlight when at about half-moon, the cone receptors responsible for day vision gradually cease functioning while the rod receptors continue to increase their sensitivity until full **dark adaptation** is complete. Dark adaptation usually takes about 30 minutes but can take considerably longer in the case of previous exposure to extreme lighting conditions. With higher light intensities, the pigment *rhodopsin* in the rods is broken down (or bleached), and with lower illumination it is replenished. If the rods are even momentarily exposed to high-intensity light levels, then excessive bleaching will occur, rod sensitivity will decrease, and it will take additional time (usually 30 minutes) for your eyes to re-adapt (or dark-adapt) to low light levels as the rhodopsin regeneration process begins all over again.

What happens if you lose your dark adaptation?

A study conducted by the FAA's Civil Aerospace Medical Institute found that glare, flash blindness, and afterimages caused by exposure to bright lights when the pilots' eyes were dark-adapted to low-light levels, were partly responsible for 30 accidents and 28 incidents in the United States between 1978 and 2005. The culprits ranged from approach and runway lights that were too bright, landing lights that reflected back (by fog, snow, etc.) into the cockpit, improperly located ramp lights, emergency vehicle lights and laser lights that flashed into pilots' eyes. The effects ranged from landing short or long, damaging landing gear from poor landings, colliding with other aircraft on the apron, colliding with approach light structures or obstacles near the runway end, and hitting power lines.

A relatively new phenomenon that poses a threat to flight safety is laser targeting, either inadvertently or deliberately, of aircraft. The FAA reports that no accidents have been attributed to the illumination of crewmembers by lasers, but the number of reported laser events in the United States has increased dramatically from less than 400 in 2006 to more than 7,000 in 2016. This is especially hazardous at low altitudes during takeoff, climb, approach and landing. A laser illumination of a pilot's eyes can at best startle and distract a pilot; at worse it can cause flash blindness, the complete destruction of dark adaptation rendering their vision useless until the dark-adaptation process begins again. The popularity and the power of laser pointers means the problem is not going to go away—in spite of stiff penalties for offenders. The FAA provides several recommended actions pilots can take to mitigate the hazard of laser illuminations in their aeromedical safety brochure, *Laser Hazards in Navigable Airspace* (see Helpful Resources in this chapter for more information).

Source: Van B. Nakagawara, Ron W. Montgomery and Kathryn J. Wood, *Incidents Associated With Visual Disturbances From Bright Lights During Nighttime Flight Operations*, DOT/FAA/AM-06/28 (Oklahoma City: FAA, November 2006).

At dusk (or artificial-light equivalent) and during the darkness that follows, there is a shift in sensitivity to the blue-green end of the visible color spectrum as the rods take over visual functioning. This change in sensitivity, known as the **Purkinje shift**, is illustrated in Figure 6-9. The rods, unlike the cones, are insensitive to light frequencies above 640 nm that correspond to the color red.[12]

Therefore, using red light (or wearing red goggles) in a brightly lit environment before a night flight will enhance your dark adaptation. Though this was often the practice during combat briefings before stealthy night flying missions during WWII, and though meteorologists, star gazers, and pilots who need their dark-adaptation during specialized flight operations at night may do this today, it is likely not necessary for most pilots since they will lose full dark-adaptation in the well-lit environment of an airport during their walk to their aircraft. Also, there are problems with the use of red light as the sole source of cockpit illumination during flight. Color discrimination for charts, maps, and the instrument panel is severely hampered, and anything colored red, like magenta lines or shading found on air navigation charts, is virtually impossible to see. This, along with the fact that it is difficult to focus in red light (especially for older pilots), is why a low-density white light is generally recommended for interior cockpit lighting. The resulting **mesopic vision**, where both rods and cones are activated at the same time, is a compromise between preserving dark adaptation and maintaining an adequate degree of color discrimination.

There is one situation in which it may be advantageous for you to fly with the interior cockpit lights at full-bright settings: when flying in the vicinity of thunderstorms. The intensity of momentary lightning flashes can completely destroy your dark adaptation, making subsequent vision extremely difficult in a darkened cabin. Some aircraft have a separate switch, called a *storm light*, to turn up all interior flight deck lights to full bright.

Monochromatic Vision

The discoverer of Purkinje shift, physiologist Johann Evangelist Purkinje, reasoned that there must be two systems for vision—one for day and one for dusk/dawn—after noticing that the colors of his favorite flowers changed from a bright color in the daylight to gray during dusk and dawn.[13] During bright daylight, using photopic (cone) vision, the geranium in Figure 6-10 (top photograph) appears in its full red color. Using scotopic (rod) vision it appears gray as in the bottom photograph. Using mesopic (*meso* = middle) vision, where both rods and cones are activated, the geranium is likely to look more like the middle photograph. To be able to discriminate colors, two or more types of retinal cone receptors (and pigments) are required. There are three different types of cones but only one type of rod receptor; hence the loss of color vision when using pure night (scotopic) vision. Colors, therefore, are seen as various shades of gray.

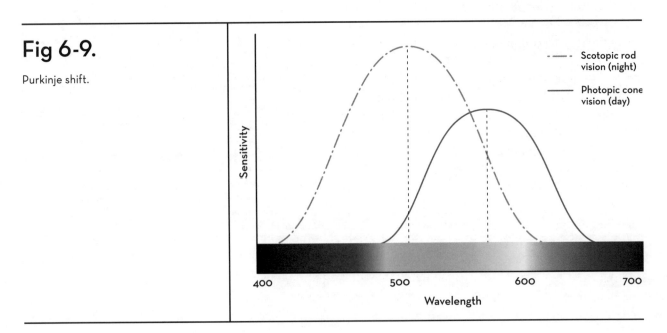

Fig 6-9.

Purkinje shift.

Scotopic rod vision (night)

Photopic cone vision (day)

Sensitivity

400   500   600   700

Wavelength

Fig 6-10.

Appearance of red geranium using photopic vision (top), mesopic vision (middle), and scotopic vision (bottom).[14]

Central Vision Blindness and Reduction in Visual Acuity

You have already learned that visual acuity is best during daylight conditions up to a maximum of only about two degrees from either side of the fovea (center of vision). And since there are no rods in the fovea (see Figure 6-4), and the foveal cones are shut down during scotopic (rod) vision, you will be unable to see an object when staring directly at it using pure night vision.

You have also learned that peripheral vision is poor in daylight conditions. This is in part because of the high synaptic ratio of cones to optic nerve fibers in the peripheral retina. The ratio is even higher for rods during night vision: As many as 100 to 1,000 rods (which make up the bulk of the periphery) share a single optic nerve fiber, communicating less information to the brain.[15] It is estimated that the best visual acuity during pure scotopic vision is about 20/200 using the Snellen visual acuity scale.[16] However, this high rod-to-fiber ratio also contributes to the rods' greater sensitivity to weak light, a fact that enables healthy, fully dark-adapted eyes to see candlelight from as far away as 15 to 20 miles. Finally, the high ratio of rods to nerve fibers is also partly responsible for the reduction in your depth perception during night vision. Because visual input from many rods funnels into only one neuron to the brain, there is "ambiguity in the exact direction and size of retinal images."[17] Therefore, your judgments of distance are adversely affected.

Dark-Focus (Night Myopia)

As previously noted, in the absence of a target to focus on when looking outside the cockpit during empty-field conditions—high altitude, reduced visibility, or at night—your eyes will not focus on optical infinity but will instead focus at their resting state of about two feet to two yards ahead. During the hours of darkness this empty-field myopia—also called **dark-focus**—creates a nearsightedness that blurs objects in the distance, making them appear smaller, farther away, and obviously less detectable.

Visual Hypoxia

The use of supplemental oxygen is mandatory in most countries for commercial flights at altitudes above 10,000 feet MSL in unpressurized aircraft. However, its use is also recommended for altitudes at or above 5,000 feet MSL when flying at night. This recommendation is not made because the composition of night air is any different than day air, but because hypoxia seriously degrades visual abilities—especially at night in low-light conditions—in part because of the oxygen requirements of the retinal rod receptors. We mentioned in Chapter 4 that the retina has the highest oxygen demand and lowest oxygen deprivation tolerance of any other organ in the body. Because of this, degraded color vision during the day and a delay in dark adaptation at night occurs as low as 4,000 to 5,000 feet. With increasing altitudes visual acuity and object brightness are reduced, and night vision (*scotopic* vision) ability is reduced by 20 percent and 35 percent at 10,000 feet and 13,000 feet, respectively.[18] Another consideration is the phenomenon of corneal hypoxia. Since the cornea is removed from the blood supply, oxygen must be directly diffused into it from the outside atmosphere. Therefore, low illumination combined with visual structures that are sensitive to even mild degrees of hypoxia can drastically reduce your visual acuity at night. Carbon monoxide from inhaled cigarette smoke or other sources produces similar effects, since overall oxygen intake from the blood to the retina is reduced (*see* hypemic hypoxia discussion in Chapter 4).

Autokinetic Effect

A phenomenon that can lead to potentially fatal consequences is the **autokinetic effect,** or autokinesis. In a very dark environment, a small stationary light will actually appear to move about a person's field of view when stared at directly. The exact mechanisms involved are not clearly understood, though it may be due to the retinal fatigue that occurs when staring at a stationary light source in the absence of other reference points.[19]

I remember a story related to me by an experienced pilot about this phenomenon. He was flying westbound at night over the Cascade Mountain Range in Washington State when he spotted what looked like an airplane flying on a collision course with his airplane. He immediately conducted a steep right turn to avoid the collision, but when he looked over his shoulder to see if he was clear of the aircraft he realized to his astonishment that he had just taken evasive action to avoid a collision with the light of a lookout tower located about 20 miles away!

Hazards That Lurk in the Dark

Statistics indicate that just as there is a greater risk of certain types of automobile accidents that occur at night; so too is there a higher risk of certain types of aircraft accidents that occur after the sun goes down. Pilots who rely solely on outside visual references at night while flying under VFR, or under IFR in VMC, are particularly vulnerable. The following accidents, all of which occurred in VMC during the hours of darkness, illustrate the risks apply to all phases of fight—ground operations, takeoff, cruise, and landing.

Ground Operations
Reduced lighting, combined with the *sea-of-blue effect* created by the maze of blue taxiway lights, hampers a crew's ability to safely navigate to and from the runway in the dark, increasing the probability of a runway incursion:
- A B-727 landing on Runway 26R at William B. Hartsfield International Airport in Atlanta, Georgia, struck a King Air that had just landed on the same runway, killing its two occupants (Report No: NTSB/AAR-91/03).
- A B-737 landing on Runway 24L at Los Angeles International Airport, struck a Fairchild Metroliner that was waiting on the runway for its takeoff clearance. All 12 people aboard the Metro and 22 aboard the B-737 were killed, making this the worst runway incursion accident in the U.S. (Report No: NTSB/AAR-91/08).

The flight crews of the Boeing jets reportedly didn't see the other airplanes on the runway ahead of them until their aircraft's landing lights illuminated them.[1]

Takeoff

Reduced ambient light has contributed to wrong surface—taxiway and wrong-runway—departures in VMC:

- A B-737 reached 60 knots before the captain aborted takeoff at Phoenix Sky Harbor Airport after realizing he was attempting a takeoff on Taxiway Foxtrot (ASRS Report No: 622348).
- A CRJ-100 crashed during takeoff at Blue Grass Airport in Lexington, Kentucky, killing 49 of the 50 people aboard, after the crew attempted a takeoff on the short Runway 26 instead of the longer Runway 22. The accident occurred in VMC about one hour before sunrise with no illumination from the moon (Report No: NTSB/AAR-07/05).

En route

- Sixteen people aboard an Air Canada B-767 were injured after it dropped 400 feet to avoid what the FO thought would be a crash with an opposite direction U.S. Air Force Boeing C-17. The Air Canada pilot initially mistook the light of the planet Venus for the C-17 (TSB Report No: A11F0012).
- While flying below the San Diego Class B airspace, and waiting for an IFR clearance, the crew of a Hawker Siddeley HS-125 flew under CFIT near Brown Field Municipal Airport, killing all aboard, including eight members of country singer Reba McEntire's band: It was a clear, moonless night, with a visibility of 10 miles (NTSB Identification No: LAX91FA132). Tragically, the crew of an air ambulance Learjet flew into the same unseen terrain near Brown Field 13 years later (see introduction to this chapter). It was this accident, and many others like it, that prompted the NTSB to issue Safety Alert SA-013, CFIT in *Visual Conditions: Nighttime Visual Flight Operations Are Resulting in Avoidable Accidents*, in 2008 warning pilots of the dangers of NVFR flight.

Approach and Landing

- A B-737 impacted terrain about 150 feet short of the runway threshold of Runway 06 at San Andres Island-Gustavo Rojas Pinilla Airport, in Colombia. The airplane broke up, skidding to a halt just past the runway threshold. Of the 131 people aboard, two passengers died. With the runway in sight, the captain disconnected the autopilot and flew the approach by hand. However, heavy rain and black-hole conditions during the night approach caused the pilot to believe the aircraft's approach angle was too high, which led him to fly an approach that was too low.[2]

Sources:

1. Dale R. Wilson, "Darkness Increases Risks of Flight," *Human Factors and Aviation Medicine* 46 (Nov–Dec 1999): 1–8.
2. Flight Safety Foundation, Aviation Safety Network, Accident Description: AIRES Colombia, Boeing 737-73V (WL), Flight 8250, San Andres Island-Gustavo Rojas Pinilla International Airport, Colombia (August 16, 2010).

Flicker Vertigo

Another phenomenon that poses a threat to safe flight, which can occur day or night, is **flicker vertigo**. A student pilot flying a Grumman American AA-5B lost directional control and collided with an airport sign on landing at Bridgeport, Connecticut. The NTSB said the pilot was suffering from the symptoms of flicker vertigo, which began while he was flying on a westerly heading in the late afternoon, looking through the propeller (NTSB Identification No: ERA09CA034). Sunlight passing through an airplane propeller or helicopter rotor blades can create a strobe-light, or flicker, effect at low RPM. Aircraft strobe and beacon lights, especially in cloud, can also create flicker. Symptoms can include "nausea, dizziness, headaches, grogginess, and unconsciousness or confusion, uneasiness, nervousness, hypnosis, gastrointestinal discomfort, and a feeling of severe panic."[20] Though very rare, it seems that in certain individuals, the presence of flicker in the frequency range of between 4 and 20 Hertz (Hz; one Hz is equal to one cycle per second) is sufficient to induce epileptic seizures.[21] Changing rotor- or propeller-blade RPM, or turning off the offending lights, will usually remedy problems associated with flicker.

Eye Disorders

A variety of eye disorders can interfere with the ability to engage in safe flight operations. Some may be medically disqualifying for flight crews, while others can be treated or corrected.

Color Vision Deficiency

In the early morning darkness of July 26, 2002, a Federal Express B-727 struck trees on final approach at Tallahassee Regional Airport. Since Runway 09 was not equipped with an instrument landing system, the FO, who was the pilot flying, was relying on the precision approach path indicator (PAPI)—a series of four lights used to determine if the aircraft is on the glide path—to judge the approach angle. The NTSB concluded that the accident, which seriously injured the captain, FO, and flight engineer and completely destroyed the airplane from impact forces and a post-crash fire, was caused in part by the FO's color vision deficiency that interfered with his ability to discern the differences between the white and red lights of the PAPI. He continued descending on the approach even though all four PAPI lights were red indicating that the airplane was too low (Report No: NTSB/AAR-04/02).

People with normal-functioning eyes have trichromatic vision; that is, their retinas contain the three different types of cones (and their photopigments sensitive to the three primary colors red, green, and blue) necessary to see the full range of colors. However, some lack one or more of these types of cones. Approximately 8 percent of men and 0.5 percent of women of Northern European ancestry suffer from a red-green color deficiency.[22] This, the most common type of **color vision deficiency** (often called *color blindness*, though few people are fully color blind), is most frequently caused by an inherited recessive gene on the X chromosome. Females have two X chromosomes, so if one has the defect the other usually corrects for it; males have only one X chromosome, so they are more prone to color blindness. There are different versions of this: some have a deficiency in red cone photopigments, others have a deficiency in green cone photopigments.

U.S. medical certification standards require that pilots be able to "perceive those colors necessary for the safe performance of airman duties" (14 CFR §67.103(c)). Unfortunately, the two colors most color-deficient individuals have the most trouble with—red and green—are two common colors used in flight operations (*see* Table 6-2): for example, runway threshold (green) and end (red) lights, visual approach slope indicator systems (red/white), stop bar lights (red), flight deck flight instrument and warning lights, and ATC tower light gun signals for communicating to aircraft that are operating NORDO (equipped with no communication radio or an improperly functioning one).

Table 6-2. ATC light gun signals (from 14 CFR §91.125).

Air traffic control tower light gun signals		
Color & type of signal	Aircraft on the ground	Aircraft in flight
Steady green	Cleared for takeoff	Cleared to land
Flashing green	Cleared for taxi	Return for landing (to be followed by steady green at proper time)
Steady red	Stop	Give way to other aircraft and continue circling
Flashing red	Taxi clear of the runway in use	Airport unsafe, do not land
Flashing white	Return to starting point on airport	Not applicable
Alternating red and green	Exercise extreme caution	Exercise extreme caution

Aviation medical examiners use a variety of tests to ascertain the extent of a pilot's color deficiency—whether it is mild or severe—such as the Ishihara Color Test (*see* Figure 6-11). If a pilot fails to meet the color vision standard using one type of test, there are others that may be taken. If, after taking alternate tests, a U.S. pilot still fails to meet the color vision standard, a color restriction statement will be placed on their medical certificate (e.g., "Not valid for flights requiring color signal control during daylight hours," or "Not valid for night flying or by color signal control," etc.).

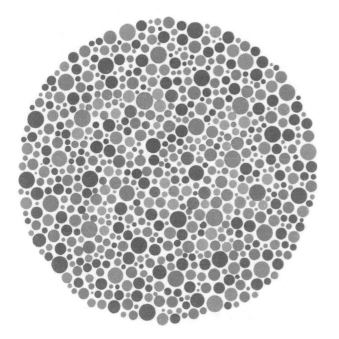

Fig 6-11.

Example of an Ishihara color test plate. What number do you see?

However, U.S. pilots do have options to get such restrictions removed from their medical certificate. They should contact their local FAA Flight Standards District Office (FSDO) to determine if they are eligible to take an operational color vision test, and in some cases a medical flight test with an FAA aviation safety inspector. The nature of the tests varies (signal light test, identifying colors on aeronautical charts, etc.) according to the class of medical held and the nature of the color deficiency. Successful completion of specified tasks may result in the issuance of a medical certificate and/or a Statement of Demonstrated Ability (SODA), or Letter of Evidence (LOE).[23]

Nearsightedness/Farsightedness

First class medical certification for U.S. pilots requires distant visual acuity of 20/20 or better in each eye separately, with or without corrective lenses (14 CFR §67.103(c)). An eye test typically involves looking at rows of letters at a distance of 20 feet (or the equivalent when using a mirror in a doctor's office) on a Snellen chart. A person who can read the eighth line

on a Snellen chart (*see* Figure 6-12) at 20 feet is said to have normal 20/20 vision. A person with 20/40 vision can see at 20 feet what the normal person can see at 40 feet. Some jurisdictions use meters with 6/6 being the equivalent of 20/20. Fractional units are also used with 0.5 equaling 20/40, 1.0 equaling 20/20, and 2 equaling 20/10, etc.

People who do not meet the 20/20 standard (uncorrected) are said to possess *refractive errors*, either from an irregularly shaped eyeball (usually long or short) or cornea, or because of problems with the flexibility of the eye's lens. **Nearsightedness** (or *myopia*) occurs when the image is focused in front of the retina, causing clear vision for close objects and

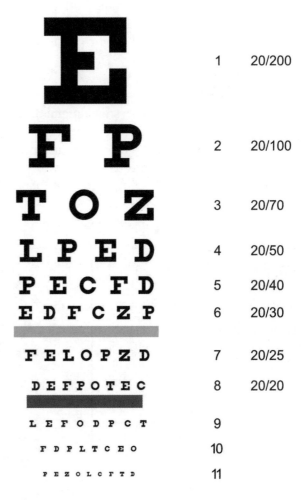

Fig 6-12.

Snellen chart for measuring visual acuity.[24]

blurred vision for distant objects (*see* Figure 6-13a). **Farsightedness** (or *hyperopia*) occurs when the image is focused behind the retina, causing blurred vision for close objects and clear vision for distant objects (*see* Figure 6-13b).

Fortunately, most of these refractive errors can be mended with corrective lenses (glasses or contact lenses), which is sufficient for pilots to meet the 20/20 vision standard for a first class medical certificate. If corrective lenses are necessary for 20/20 vision, regulations require pilots to wear them while exercising the privileges of their pilot certificate (14 CFR §67.103(c)). Contrary to most other countries, including Canada, the rules do not require that U.S. pilots carry an extra pair while flying in the United States. Nevertheless, the FAA states that, "Pilots who require corrective lenses *should* carry a spare set of lenses for use within the U.S. and they must carry a spare pair of lenses while flying internationally."[27]

Astigmatism

Another type of refractive error is **astigmatism**. It is caused by an irregularly shaped cornea or lens, which causes blurred vision from the image focusing unevenly on the retina, instead of at a single point. Corrective lenses or other procedures can usually correct for this.

Presbyopia

Near-focus acuity begins to deteriorate for almost everyone—even those who normally do not require vision correction—beginning at about age 40. Sometimes called *old-sightedness*, **presbyopia** (*presby* = elder; *opia* = vision) primarily involves difficulty in focusing on items that are close due to the hardening of the lens with age. The lens becomes brittle when the oldest cells (in the middle of the lens) become further and further removed from the nutrients of the blood supply and die, resulting in near-focus images being focused behind the retina. Presbyopia can usually be corrected by the use of reading glasses or bifocal lenses, the latter correcting for both distant and near refraction errors.

There are several other visual decrements associated with aging. For example:

- Dark adaptation time at night increases and light sensitivity decreases (by as much as 300 times).
- Due to increased light scattering, sensitivity to glare increases by as much as 30 times.
- Because the clear crystalline lens takes on a bit of a yellow hue with age, reduced sensitivity to the shorter wavelengths of the visible spectrum (blue) also occurs.
- A significant reduction of peripheral vision.[28]

Fig 6-13.

A. Nearsightedness and its correction.

B. Farsightedness and its correction.[25, 26]

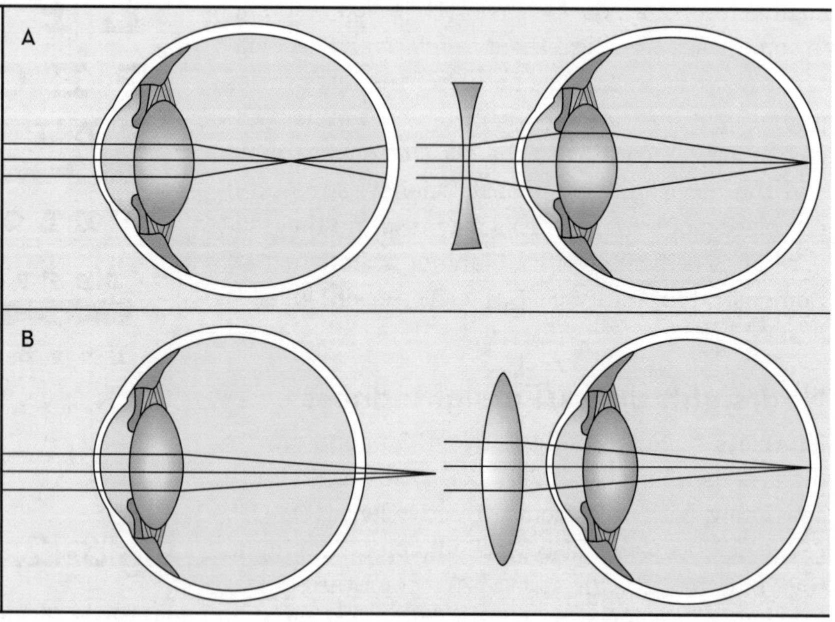

Night Blindness

A variety of factors, such as cataracts, untreated nearsightedness, drugs, and a Vitamin A deficiency can cause **night blindness**—not complete, but functional blindness—during low light conditions at night.[29] Studies have shown that night blindness can be induced within 60 days in normal individuals who have been put on a diet lacking Vitamin A.[30] That's because rhodopsin, the pigment found in the rod receptors, is made up of Vitamin A and *opsin*. Most types of night blindness are treatable, but some are not. You should consult an ophthalmologist if you suspect you have a problem.

Corrective Eye Surgery

Nearsightedness, farsightedness, astigmatism, and other eye disorders can now be corrected using surgical procedures such as photorefractive keratectomy (PRK) and laser-assisted in situ keratomileusis (LASIK). Though these types of procedures are relatively safe, they are not risk-free. The decision to partake in such a procedure should not be made until you have consulted the FAA literature on the subject (*see* the Helpful Resources for more information) and an experienced eye surgeon.

Compensating for Visual Limitations

In spite of the amazing abilities that of a set of healthy human eyes possess, there are limitations that, in some circumstances, increase the risk of an aircraft accident. For example, we don't always see conflicting aircraft in flight—even when ATC notifies us of its location or even if we are looking directly at it. We also have trouble seeing in the dark. Fortunately, there are a variety of strategies you can use to mitigate these limitations.

Midair Collision Strategies

Using an effective visual scanning technique to detect possible conflicting air traffic will overcome many of the physiological limitations of vision. It brings possible targets out of our periphery and into our best focal vision and allows time for adequate focusing. You should avoid wide sweeping eye movements since our eyes need to momentarily stop to avoid visual blurring and achieve proper focusing. An AOPA *Safety Advisor* recommends you scan the entire outside visual field by dividing the sky into 10 to 15 degree "blocks" and then pause at each one, looking approximately 10 degrees above and below your flight path for at least one to two seconds to allow for proper refocusing and the utilization of foveal vision. It also recommends starting from one side and working your way across to the other (side-to-side scan), or looking directly ahead and scanning all the way to one side before returning to the center and scanning to the other (front-to-side scan).

AOPA's Air Safety Institute also found that contrary to popular belief, only a small percentage of MACs involve head-on collisions; most—*82 percent*—involve faster aircraft overtaking a slower one from behind.[31] Even though it is important to scan the entire sky, studies show that most pilots don't—their gaze tends to default directly ahead with many glances to only a few degrees to either side.[32] Therefore, it's crucial to scan your entire field of view and move your head as far left and right as you can during the scan. Also, if you see your aircraft's shadow on the ground or on top of a cloud layer, keep an eye out for other shadows that may be converging on yours.

To see what may be located in an aircraft structural blind spot, you should also periodically perform gentle turns and/or momentarily level off during prolonged climbs or descents. Be sure to clear the area (by raising a high-wing or lowering a low-wing) before every turn and perform clearing turns before conducting any type of training or other maneuvers.

If you are flying in empty-field conditions (high altitude, haze, or night), you should refocus your eyes on distant objects (e.g., the ground or even a wingtip) about every two minutes since it takes approximately that long for your eyes to return to their resting state. Ensure the aircraft's windscreen is clean to assist distant focusing.

You can improve your ability to see in bright sunlight and when encountering glare by wearing good quality sunglasses, but be aware that some make it more difficult to see reflected light off other aircraft—this is one of many reasons why polarized lenses are not recommended for aviators. Choosing the right type of lens is not always as easy as it sounds, so consult an ophthalmologist who is knowledgeable about the advantages and disadvantages of a particular type for the flight environment. Use the aircraft's glare shield and the bill of a baseball hat to shield your eyes from bright sunlight.[33]

Night Vision Strategies

Make sure to allow enough time for proper dark adaptation to occur before a flight at night takes place (at least 30 minutes). Once you attain proper dark adaptation, it's important to maintain it. Keep interior cockpit lights low during flight, but not so low as to reduce your ability to accurately read your instruments. Try to avoid exposure to bright lights. If you can't avoid them, allow only one eye to be exposed; this will at least preserve dark adaptation in the other. To enhance dark adaptation, avoid bright-light conditions during the day beforehand (e.g., beach, snow-covered terrain) and wear sunglasses during a day spent at the beach or snow skiing if a night flight follows. Out of courtesy to others, momentarily turn off your taxi lights should they shine into someone else's cockpit. Use an airport taxi diagram to help you successfully navigate to and from the runway and don't hesitate to request progressive taxi instructions if you are unfamiliar with the airport layout.

For easier identification of dimly lit objects at night, you should use off-centered vision; looking slightly to the side of an image (about 20 degrees from center) will project it onto the location of maximum peripheral rod density (*see* Figure 6-4), thus making identification easier. However, developing this off-centered viewing takes some effort since we are strongly conditioned to look directly at objects.

Since it is difficult to maintain visual separation from terrain in the dark, fly at minimum safe obstruction clearance altitudes and, if possible, over well-lit terrain. If flying IFR, fly at or above the applicable minimum IFR altitude. Adhere to minimum en route altitudes as shown on IFR charts and, if flying off an airway, minimum off-route obstruction clearance altitudes. If you don't have an instrument rating, learn how to find the maximum elevation figure on VFR sectional charts for the quadrant over which you are flying and add at least 1,000 feet (2,000 feet in the mountains) to that figure, since it only provides about 100 to 300 feet of obstruction clearance.

Make sure you know your position at all times and supplement your vision of the outside environment using radio navigation aids and ATC assistance if necessary. Many aircraft, including smaller GA aircraft, are now equipped with terrain awareness and warning systems. These systems, which co-locate your global positioning system (GPS) position with a terrain and obstacle database, can help you maintain your positional awareness and provide you with terrain avoidance information as well. But don't become complacent and lose your ability to navigate using other tried-and-true pilotage and dead reckoning methods.

Since it is also difficult to see adverse weather in the dark, your **personal weather minimums** during NVFR flight should be higher than they are in the day. However, they mean nothing if you are not resolved to stick to them when weather conditions drop below them. Pay particular attention to visibility and cloud reports and forecasts, and be aware that you can't always count on your vision to avoid inadvertent entry into IMC. It's always best to fly in high lighting conditions, which the FAA *AIM* defines as either flight over surface lighting that provides for the lighting of prominent obstacles, the identification of terrain features (shorelines, valleys, hills, mountains, slopes) and a horizontal reference by which you can control the aircraft, or a sky condition with less than broken (5/8th) cloud coverage and a moon with at least 50 percent illumination. This lighting could be a result of extensive cultural (human-made) lighting found over metropolitan areas or limited cultural lighting combined with a high level of natural reflectivity of celestial illumination, such as that provided by a snow-covered or desert surface. Finally, if you don't have extensive mountain flying experience and knowledge of local terrain, you should definitely avoid flying VFR over mountainous terrain at night.

Finally, consider following the recommendation to use supplemental oxygen when flying at or above 5,000 feet MSL at night and engage in behaviors that help you to maintain good night vision. For example, maintain an adequate diet and avoid cigarette smoke, since reduced blood sugar, reduced Vitamin A, and carbon monoxide can negatively affect night vision.

Helpful Resources

The FAA's Civil Aerospace Medical Institute provides a variety of resources related to pilot vision:

- Three aeromedical safety brochures titled *Laser Hazards in Navigable Airspace* and *Laser Eye Protection (LEP) Perceptual Effects on Aviation*, with suggestions on how to mitigate a laser illumination encounter, and *Sunglasses for Pilots: Beyond the Image*, with guidance on what to look for in quality sunglasses. (www.faa.gov/pilots/safety/pilotsafetybrochures/)
- A 15-minute video (in English or Spanish) titled, *Vision in Aviation—To See or Not To See.* (www.faa.gov/pilots/training/airman_education/physiologyvideos/)

Chapter 13, "Night Operations," in the FAA's latest *Helicopter Flying Handbook* provides excellent coverage of physiological and perceptual aspects of night flying, including practical suggestions on how overcome these limitations when flying at night. (www.faa.gov/regulations_policies/handbooks_manuals/aviation/helicopter_flying_handbook/)

Chapter 2, "The Big Sky Is Not So Big," in *Managing Risk: Best Practices for Pilots*, by Dale Wilson and Gerald Binnema, explains the factors that increase the risk of a MAC and provides an extensive list of best practice strategies you can use to mitigate the risk. (www.asa2fly.com/Dale-Wilson-C565.aspx)

Two helpful resources from the FAA for pilots contemplating undergoing surgical procedures, such as laser eye surgery (LASIK) to improve vision: "The Eyes Have It," by Susan Parsons, *FAA Safety Briefing* (January/February 2013), available at (www.faa.gov/news/safety_briefing/2013/) and "Information for Pilots Considering Laser Eye Surgery," FAA pamphlet OK-06-148. (www.faa.gov/pilots/safety/pilotsafetybrochures/)

Answers for Pilots: Vision—How Different Vision Issues Can Impact Your Airman Medical Certification, by Kathleen Dondzila King, published by the AOPA Air Safety Institute, provides information about a variety of vision issues as they may relate to your medical certification. (www.aopa.org/news-and-media/all-news/2013/january/01/answers-for-pilots-vision)

Endnotes

1. As part of its airspace reclassification in the early 1990s, the term *terminal control area* (TCA) in United States was replaced by the term *Class B airspace*. Federal Aviation Administration, "Airspace Reclassification; Final Rule," *Federal Register* 56.242 (December 17, 1991): 65638–65665.

2. Electromagnetic spectrum, by Victor Blacus, October 2012 (https://commons.wikimedia.org/wiki/File:Electromagnetic-Spectrum.svg) WC CC BY-SA 3.0

3. Robert Sekuler and Randolf Blake, *Perception*, 2nd ed. (New York: McGraw-Hill, 1990): 54. Used with permission. ISBN 0-07-056065-X

4. Approximation of the acuity of the human eye, horizontal cross section, by Vanessa Ezekowitz, July 2009 (https://commons.wikimedia.org/wiki/File:AcuityHumanEye.svg) WC CC BY-SA 3.0

5. Jeff Johnson, "Our Peripheral Vision is Poor," Chapter 6, *Designing With the Mind in Mind: Simple Guide to Understanding User Interface Design Rules* (New York: Morgan Kaufmann, 2010).

6. Robert C. Matthews, "Characteristics of U.S. Midairs," *FAA Aviation News* 40 (May/June 2001): 1–3.

7. H.W. Leibowitz and D.A. Owens, "Anomalous Myopias and the Intermediate Dark Focus of Accommodation," *Science* 189 (1975): 646–648.

8. Dale Wilson and Gerald Binnema, *Managing Risk: Best Practices for Pilots* (Newcastle, WA: Aviation Supplies and Academics, Inc., 2014).

9. Australian Transport Safety Bureau, *Midair Collision, Parafield Airport, VH-TGM Grob, Burkhaart Flugzeugbau G-115 Grob VH-YTG S.O.C.A.T.A. Groupe Aerospatiale TB-10 Tobago, February 7, 2009*, Transport Safety Report No. AO-2009-005 (Canberra City, Australia: ATSB, July 2009).

10. AOPA Air Safety Institute, *2008 Nall Report: Accident Trends and Factors for 2007* (Frederick, MD: AOPA ASI, 2009).

11. National Transportation Safety Board, *NTSB Safety Alert, Controlled Flight Into Terrain in Visual Conditions: Nighttime Visual Flight Operations are Resulting in Avoidable Accidents*, SA-013 (Washington, DC: January 2008). Available at www.ntsb.gov/safety/safety-alerts/pages/default.aspx.

12. Warner D. Fan, "Night Vision: Question and Answer Column," *Aviation, Space, and Environmental Medicine* 62 (March 1991): 274–275.

13. Nicholas J. Wade, Josef Brozek and Jiri Hoskovec, *Purkinje's Vision: The Dawning of Neuroscience* (Mahwah, N.J.: Lawrence Erlbaum Associates, 2001).

14. Simulation of mesopic and scotopic visual appearance from a photopic (full-color) original of a red geranium with greenery and blue in the background, to illustrate the Purkinje effect or Purkinje shift, by Dick Lyon of original by Lewis Collard, June 2009 (https://commons.wikimedia.org/wiki/File:Red_geranium_photoic_mesopic_scotopic.jpg) WC CC BY-SA 3.0

15. Fan, "Night Vision: Question and Answer Column."

16. Van B. Nakagawara, Ron W. Montgomery and Kathryn J. Wood, *Incidents Associated With Visual Disturbances From Bright Lights During Nighttime Flight Operations*, DOT/FAA/AM-06/28 (Oklahoma City: FAA Civil Aerospace Medical Institute, November 2006).

17. Fan, "Night Vision: Question and Answer Column," 147.

18. Ryan W. Maresh, Andrew D. Woodrow and James T. Webb, *Handbook of Aerospace and Operational Physiology*, 2nd ed., (Wright-Patterson AFB, OH: U.S. Air Force School of Aerospace Medicine, October 2016).

19. Richard L. Gregory, *Eye and Brain: The Psychology of Seeing*, 5th ed. (Princeton, N.J.: Princeton University Press, 1997).

20. Maresh, Woodrow and Webb, *Handbook of Aerospace and Operational Physiology*, 2nd ed., 7–59.

21. International Civil Aviation Organization, *Manual of Civil Aviation Medicine*, Doc 8984, AN/895, 3rd ed. (Montreal: ICAO, 2012).

22. National Eye Institute, *Color Blindness* (July 3, 2019). Available at www.nei.nih.gov/health/color_blindness/facts_about.

23. FAA, "Section 1 Issuance of a Medical Certificate and/or a Statement of Demonstrated Ability, or Letter of Evidence," in *Chapter 8 Conduct a Special Medical test—Title 14 CFR Part 167; Volume 5 Airman Certification; Flight Standards Information Management System*, FAA Order 8900.1 CHG 18 (April 14, 2008).

24. A typical Snellen chart, by Jeff Dahl, July 2008 (https://commons.wikimedia.org/wiki/File:Snellen_chart.svg) WC CC BY-SA 3.0

25. Vector illustration for myopia and it's correction with lens, by Gumenyuk I.S., May 2014 (https://commons.wikimedia.org/wiki/File:Myopia_and_lens_correction.svg) WC CC BY-SA 4.0

26. Hypermetropia lens correction, by Гуменюк И.С., July 2014 (https://commons.wikimedia.org/wiki/File:Hypermetropia_color.svg) WC CC BY-SA 4.0

27. Federal Aviation Administration, "Use of Corrective Lenses and Possession of a Spare Set of Lenses," *Information for Operators*, InFO 12008 (April 24, 2012).

28. Donald H. McBurney and Virginia B. Collings, *Introduction to Sensation/Perception* (Englewood Cliffs, N.J: Prentice-Hall, 1984): 288.

29. Marissa Selner, "*Everything You Need to Know About Night Blindness*," *Healthline* (July 22, 2019). Available at www.healthline.com/symptom/night-blindness.

30. Stanley Coren, Clare Porac and Lawrence M. Ward, 2nd ed. (Orlando. FL: Academic Press, 1984): 152.

31. AOPA Air Safety Institute, *Safety Advisor: Collision Avoidance Strategies and Tactics, Operations & Proficiency* No. 4 (Frederick, MD: August 2006).

32. Kurt Colvin, Rahul Dodhia and R. Key Dismukes, "Is Pilots' Visual Scanning Adequate to Avoid Mid-air Collisions?" *Proceedings of the 13th International Symposium on Aviation Psychology* (Oklahoma City, OK: 2005): 104–109.

33. Nakagawara, Montgomery and Wood, *Incidents Associated With Visual Disturbances From Bright Lights*.

7

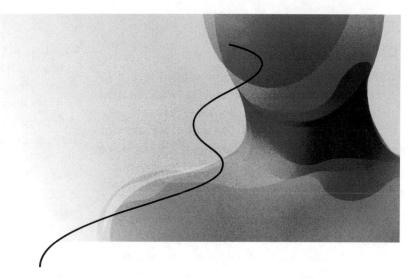

The pilots were confused. ATC cleared Henson Airlines Flight 1517 for an ILS approach to Runway 04, terminated radar coverage, and authorized the crew to switch frequencies to universal communications (UNICOM), the common traffic advisory frequency for traffic advisories at Shenandoah Valley Airport in Weyers Cave, Virginia. However, ATC was puzzled to hear back from them a full 12 minutes later asking ATC for radar clarification of their position. Minutes later, while in level flight at 2,400 feet MSL, the Beechcraft B99 Airliner flew under controlled flight into terrain six miles east of the airport killing both crew members and all 12 passengers.

The NTSB concluded that the crew was likely navigating off the Montebello VOR on the 045 degree radial instead of an inbound course of 045 degrees on the Shenandoah ILS. The probable cause of the accident was "a navigational error by the flight crew resulting from their use of the incorrect navigational facility and their failure to adequately monitor the flight instruments." The NTSB also cited, as one of several contributing factors, "intra-cockpit communications difficulties associated with high ambient noise levels in the airplane" (Report No: NTSB/AAR-86/07). Investigators concluded from a prior accident that the interior flight deck noise levels in the Beechcraft B99 were excessive. In fact, they discovered that flight crews often resorted to using hand signals to communicate with each other. This, combined with the fact the airplane was not equipped with a crew intercom/interphone system, led them to conclude the crew experienced difficulties communicating verbally with each other as they were trying to determine their geographical location.

Say again?
Hearing and Noise

Noise can be defined as any loud, unpleasant, or unwanted sound. It is a problem for both flight and cabin crews. Noise in aircraft cabins can, as in the Henson Airlines accident, interfere with communication between flight crew members (intra-cockpit communication) and between controllers and pilots (extra-cockpit communication). For example, a recent ASRS query found that excessive noise on the flight deck caused pilots to miss or mishear ATC clearances that have led to altitude busts, near midair collisions, and runway incursions (ASRS Report No: 509170; 920128; 1065118; 869403). Captains have had to turn off air conditioning systems on the airplane, and controllers have had to do the same in ATC control cabs/rooms, because excess noise interfered with verbal communications (ASRS Report No: 707312; 813904; 1017630).

Aircraft noise has other consequences: It contributes to pilot fatigue and can produce both short- and long-term (permanent) hearing loss. Even though modern design has helped to mitigate its impact compared to the craft of yesterday, noise will likely always will be a problem in the aviation environment. Therefore, pilots must be able to recognize the hazards associated with noise and be able to take protective measures to reduce its effects. A basic understanding of the topics of sound and hearing are necessary before an appreciation of the adverse effects of noise can be gained.

Physics of Sound

Vibrations (alternating compression and expansion) of air produced by vibrating objects (vocal chords, aircraft engine, etc.) travel in all directions in pressure waves and reach our ears as sound. The speed at which sound waves travel depends on the nature of the medium (solid, liquid, gas). Sound travels at about 1,100 feet per second in air at 0°C and increases about 2 feet per second for every 1°C temperature rise.

Two major characteristics of sound are frequency and intensity. **Sound frequency** is the physical characteristic of sound which creates the physiological and psychological sensation of pitch (how low or high a tone is). The frequency of sound refers to the number of vibrations within a given time period and is measured in Hertz (Hz), where one Hz is equal to one cycle per second. The notes of a piano range from a low of 27 Hz to a high of 4,000 Hz. The frequency range for normal human hearing is between about 20 Hz and 20,000 Hz. Children usually (and some animals certainly) are able to hear frequencies higher than those of adults. Pitch for most speech ranges from about 500 to 4,000 Hz.

Sound intensity is of greater significance to the discussion of the negative effects of noise. Intensity is the physical characteristic of sound that creates the physiological and psychological sensation of loudness. It refers to the amplitude (up and down distance) of a sound wave and is measured in decibels (dB; after Alexander Graham Bell). Since the highest sound intensity/energy a person can hear without experiencing pain (pain threshold) is about 10 million times greater than the quietest sound a person can detect (hearing threshold), it is more convenient to use this nonlinear logarithmic scale for its measurement. A small increase in dB, therefore, indicates a large increase in sound intensity. In fact, a rule of thumb for perceived loudness is that it doubles for every 10 dB increase in sound intensity. Table 7-1 indicates some of the effects, examples, and relative perception of different sound intensity levels.

The Auditory System

Hearing is likely second only to vision when it comes to safely flying an aircraft. The ability to hear is needed to identify normal and abnormal sounds emanating from the aircraft's structure and its systems, and to enable two-way verbal messages with passengers, ATC, and fellow crew members. The recognition of sound in the brain starts with the reception of the physical vibratory stimulus in the ear. As pointed out in Chapter 5, the human auditory system consists of the outer, middle, and inner ear. It also includes the cochlear (auditory) nerve which extends to the auditory cortex of the brain.

The Outer Ear

The outer ear consists of the ear flap (*auricle* or *pinna*), the external part of the ear that others can see, and the auditory canal. The ear flap directs sound waves into the external auditory canal to the eardrum (*tympanic membrane*). Wax is produced just inside the

Table 7-1. Effects and examples of different sound intensity levels.

Sound intensity (dB)	Effects & examples	Sensation
0	Hearing threshold	Almost imperceptible
20	Quiet room	Very quiet
40	Soft whisper	Quiet
60	Human conversation	Moderate
80	Freight train (100 feet away)	Somewhat loud
85	NIOSH* Maximum for 8 hrs work	Loud
90	Loud car horn	Loud
110	Night club	Very Loud
120	Discomfort threshold	Extremely loud, somewhat painful
140	Jet airplane takeoff (100 feet away)	Very painful
160	Eardrum rupture	Pain, no pain, hearing loss, and/or tinnitus

* *National Institute for Occupational Safety and Health*

opening of the canal and, along with the presence of tiny hairs near the entrance, provides protection for the sensitive eardrum by functioning as a screen which intercepts dust particles, small insects, etc.

The Middle Ear

The eardrum is the dividing line between the outer and middle ear (see Figure 7-1). A series of bones (*auditory ossicles*) lie within the air-filled middle ear (*tympanic cavity*) and are connected to each other. The *malleus*, attached to the eardrum, is connected to the *incus*, which in turn is connected to *stapes*. These three bones are also called the hammer, anvil, and stirrup, respectively. The design of the middle ear is such that sound transmission is actually enhanced as it travels from the outer to the inner ear. Since sound wave energy is substantially reduced when passing from a gas (air in outer ear) to a liquid (fluid in inner ear; see the next section), much of the sound reaching the inner ear from the outer ear would be lost if it weren't for the mechanical design of the middle ear. First, the bones of the middle ear are directly connected to the eardrum; so when the eardrum vibrates, so too do the bones (hammer, anvil, stirrup) which are connected to it. Second, the arm of the hammer (malleus) is longer than the arm of the anvil (incus), thereby providing greater displacement of the oval window of the fluid-filled cochlea in the inner ear. Finally, sound is further amplified because of the difference in size between the ear drum and the oval window, the oval window being smaller allowing for a greater displacement. This unique mechanical arrangement amplifies the sound energy by as much as 25 dB.

The Inner Ear

The stirrup (stapes) acts like a plunger which vibrates in and out as it acts on the oval window. The movement of the oval window sets up vibrations in the fluid-filled cochlea (cochlea means snail- or spiral-shaped). The cochlea is the most important part of the inner ear as far as the process of hearing is concerned. Other parts of the inner ear include the organs of balance: the vestibule (which detects linear acceleration) and three semi-circular canals (which detect angular acceleration). These will be looked at in Chapter 9 when we examine spatial disorientation. At either end of the closed cochlear canal lies the oval and round windows. The back-and-forth displacements at the oval window causes the round window to bulge out when the oval wind is pushed in, and bulge in when the oval window is pulled back by the stirrup. The fluid-filled cochlea houses a membrane containing the organ of Corti which contains thousands of sensitive nerve fibers. These tiny hair cells move back-and-forth in response to vibrations in the fluid, and in turn communicate information in the form of neural (electrical) impulses to the auditory cortex of the brain via the cochlear (auditory) nerve.

Fig 7-1.

Anatomy of the human ear.[1]

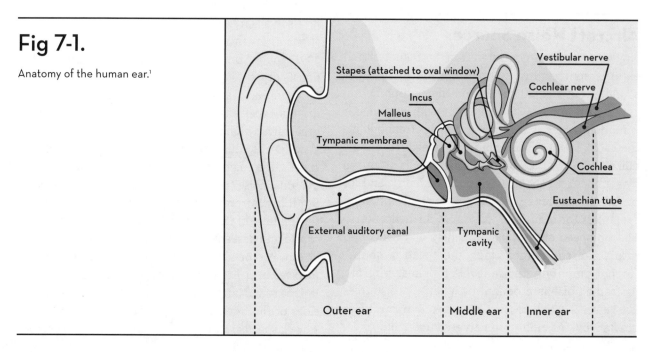

In summary, our sense of hearing occurs because of a remarkable system that enables us to hear both the intensity (loudness) and frequency (pitch) of various sounds. Vibrating motions of the eardrum, caused by sound waves funneled through the ear canal, are amplified by the mechanical arrangement of the auditory ossicles in the middle ear. These small bones transfer vibratory motion to the fluid in the organ of hearing (the cochlea), stimulating tiny hair cells which convert this motion into neural impulses that are sent to the brain. These signals are processed by the brain giving us the ability to sense various types of sounds. It should be obvious that any physical impairment or medical condition affecting these structures will affect the quality of hearing.

There are two other ways in which sound can reach the inner ear. One way is through vibration of the secondary eardrum which overlies the round window. Any sound vibrations entering the middle ear stimulate back-and-forth movement of the round window which causes similar motion in the fluid-filled cochlea and the hearing receptors in the organ of Corti. The other way in which sound can reach the inner ear is through bone conduction. Since part of the inner ear is connected directly to the skull, vibrations of the bone can also set up vibrations in the cochlea. Sound from humming and the dentist's dreaded drill are examples of this. These two phenomena explain how people with ruptured eardrums can still have relatively good hearing.[2]

Aircraft Noise Sources

Flight deck noise is generated from both interior and exterior sources. Internal noise primarily includes sounds from aircraft radios and the environmental control systems (ECS)—cabin pressurization, air conditioning, etc. The greatest source is from outside the cabin and is divided into two categories: engine noise and airframe noise. Engine noise is produced by sounds from the engine and its exhaust, and for piston- and turbine-propeller powered aircraft from propellers (or main and tail rotors for helicopters). The tip-speed of airplane propellers and helicopter rotors can sometimes reach the speed of sound, further amplifying noise levels for these aircraft. Airframe noise is produced by a variety of sources (*see* Figure 7-2) and consists of all aerodynamic noise created by the non-propulsive components of an aircraft, including airflow turbulence noise from air traveling past the fuselage, wings, control surfaces, high lift devices (trailing edge flaps, leading edge slats, etc.), and landing gear.

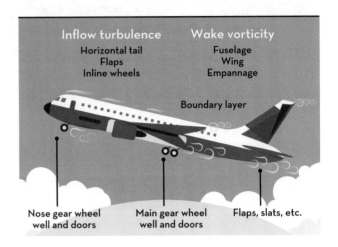

Fig 7-2.

Potential sources of airframe noise.

Airframe noise is partly a function of indicated airspeed—what physicists call dynamic air pressure—expressed as $1/2\rho V^2$, where ρ (rho) is the density of the air and V is the true airspeed. Therefore, the faster the airspeed and lower the altitude (greater air density), the greater the aerodynamic noise created around the aircraft's fuselage. For example, noise levels in a Harrier GR5 military jet during high speed flight at low altitude (more dense air) are at least 10 dB louder than when flying at high altitude (less dense air).[3]

Engine and airframe noise is analogous to what drivers experience in an automobile. Engine noise is greatest at higher throttle settings, usually during slow speeds while the car is accelerating. At highway speeds, the engine noise is usually lower but the aerodynamic noise from airflow around the car increases. Similarly, aircraft engine noise is usually highest during takeoff (high power/thrust) and lower during cruise and descent. Airframe noise, however, is lower at slower speeds and higher at the faster speeds involved in cruise and descent (although airflow circulation around landing gear, landing gear doors, and the sides of flaps generates significant airframe noise at slower speeds). Unlike a car, aircraft manufacturers usually use minimal noise insulation to keep costs and weight to a minimum. This explains why, according to the FAA, GA aircraft noise levels are often a hundred times more intense than automobile noise.[4] A study was conducted comparing interior cockpit/flight deck noise levels in 44 different types of aircraft commonly used in Australian civil aviation. These were classified into three broad categories:

- GA (single and twin piston-engine airplanes).
- Regular passenger transport (RPT; tail/fuselage- and wing-mounted turbojets).
- Rotary wing (light single- and turbine-engine and heavy turboshaft).

Not surprisingly, the research revealed cockpit noise levels were the highest for rotary-wing aircraft, averaging approximately 105 dB for almost all phases of flight. Noise levels for GA airplanes averaged only slightly below rotary-wing aircraft at approximately 100–103 dB for all phases of flight (except takeoff which averaged 110 dB). Regular passenger transports produced the lowest flight deck noise levels (see Figure 7-3) for all phases of flight (climb, cruise, descent, and landing), averaging less than 85 dB for most flight phases except takeoff (<100 dB) and descent/landing (≈90 dB).

Early piston-powered propeller aircraft produced significant noise levels; as much as 120 dB in WWII fighter airplanes.[6] The advent of jet engines, and their placement towards the back of the fuselage on some aircraft, helped to significantly reduce noise levels on the flight decks of commercial passenger transport aircraft. Further gains have been attained in modern jet passenger transport aircraft equipped with high bypass ratio (BPR) turbofan engines. One hundred percent of inlet air in an older turbojet engine passes through the engine core and exits the engine at a high speed after combustion, causing considerable turbulence and noise. A high proportion of inlet air (as much as 90 percent) in a modern high-BPR turbofan engine, however, passes through a large thrust-producing fan located at the front of the engine, bypassing the engine core where a smaller proportion of inlet air passes through to produce the thrust that drives the fan. The slower exit speed of the combined bypass air and engine core exhaust air increases engine efficiency and reduces overall noise.

Advances in propulsive noise reduction have meant that airframe noise for these airplanes is almost the same, or even greater than engine noise during the decent and landing phases of flight.[7] Helicopters generally still rank highest in noise, while propeller-driven piston and turboprop airplanes also still produce significant levels of noise. For example, a recent study comparing the noise levels of a Cessna 172 and a Piper Seminole—two popular GA aircraft used in the United States—found that noise levels exceeded the National Institute for Occupational Safety and Health (NIOSH) standard of 85 dB for eight hours exposure.[8]

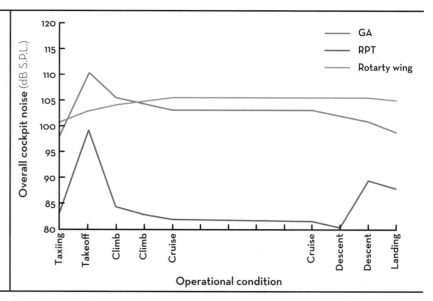

Fig 7-3.

Noise profiles for GA, regular passenger transport (RPT), and rotary-wing aircraft in dB for different phases of flight.[5]

Effects of Noise

As mentioned in the introduction to this chapter, noise can impair verbal communication, produce both short- and long-term permanent hearing loss, and contribute to fatigue.

Impaired Communication

Verbal **communication** on the flight deck involves the exchange of information between people using speech. Information transfer using written words and body language—two other ways of communicating—are also used, but to a much lesser degree between pilots. External noise from the airframe and powerplant, and internal noise from the ECS and communication and navigation radios, can interfere with intra- and extra-cockpit communication, thereby jeopardizing safety. If the noise is too loud, communication will be severely hampered. In fact, the FAA believes that crews will experience voice communication problems if the flight deck noise intensity levels are above 88 dB.[9]

When many sounds from different sources are presented, usually the loudest sound is perceived the most while the others are said to be **masked** (resulting in diminished perception/intelligibility). Speech is composed of various sounds, some of which can be masked quite easily. For example, since consonants—especially those that begin a word—are verbalized at lower frequencies and intensities than most speech, they are more easily masked and therefore can be easily missed by the hearer. This is especially true if the consonants sound similar (e.g., b, c, d, t, v, and the vowel e sound the same). One is reminded of the co-pilot's response after the Captain said "Cheer up!"

A comparison of speech intensity to noise intensity is called the **signal-to-noise ratio (SNR)**. Speech intelligibility is greater when the SNR is higher. For example, a speech signal 9 dB above the background noise level yields approximately 80 percent word recognition or better.[10] When SNR is lower (<1), verbal messages are masked by the louder noises, making speech intelligibility difficult or even impossible. This can be a problem on the flight deck where the flight crew's seats do not directly face each other, leaving the captain and FO unable to take full advantage of non-verbal communication cues such as lip movement, gestures, and facial expressions.

When both speech and noise levels are about the same (SNR = 1/1 = 1), most speech communication

is understood because of the context in which the individual words are used and because of the redundancy of the English language. For example, if you hear part of a sentence, you usually have no difficulty determining its meaning because of the context. Redundancy means the language itself possesses more information than is necessary for comprehension and arises out of built-in constraints to the English language. For example, since the 26 letters in English alphabet are not equiprobable (e.g., a, e, r, and n are more probable than w, x, y, and z) and because of sequential constraints (e.g., words ending in ed, th, and nt), the English language is highly redundant (or easier to understand). This fact helps make abbreviated messages possible, a common practice in aviation communications (see Table 7-2).

Table 7-2. Examples of abbreviated messages in aviation.[11]

Abbreviated message	Meaning
BACK-TAXI	Taxi an aircraft on the runway opposite to the traffic flow.
CLEARED AS FILED	Cleared to proceed in accordance with the route of flight filed in the flight plan.
GO AROUND	Instructions for a pilot to abandon his/her approach to landing.
NEGATIVE CONTACT	Used by pilots to inform ATC that previously issued traffic is not in sight or they were unable to contact ATC on a particular frequency
OUT	The conversation is ended and no response is expected.
OVER	My transmission is ended; I expect a response.
ROGER	I have received all of your last transmission.
SQUAWK	Activate specific modes/codes/functions on the aircraft transponder.
WILCO	I have received your message, understand it, and will comply with it.

Suggestions on how to improve speech communication in the noisy environment of the flight deck are provided at the end of this chapter. We delve deeper into the complex topic of communication in Chapter 13, where we focus on specific auditory perception and communication problems, and again in Chapter 19, where we discuss this topic in the context of crew resource management (CRM).

Temporary Hearing Loss

Commercial flight crews and GA pilots are exposed to elevated levels of noise and are at greater risk of developing noise-induced hearing loss (NIHL). NIHL can be either short- or long-term, the latter being permanent and irreversible.

Conductive Hearing Loss

Conductive hearing loss (CHL) arises out of complications in the outer and middle ear. Middle ear infections (otitis media) or calcium deposits on the ossicles can hamper bone movement necessary for efficient sound conduction and transmission. Conditions creating CHL can often be treated with medication or surgery.

Barotrauma of the Ear

Another type of temporary hearing loss occurs when unequal pressure between the middle- and outer- ear causes deformation of the eardrum, usually during the descent phase of flight. Proper equalization (through the Valsalva maneuver, etc.; see Chapter 5) will eliminate the problem.

Oxygen Ear

It was also noted in Chapter 5 that a delayed ear block can occur after a descent while breathing 100 percent oxygen. It can also cause short-term hearing loss. If pressure equalization does not take place after landing, the absorption of oxygen inside the middle ear causes the eardrum to bulge inward creating pain and noticeable hearing impairment. Usually the Valsalva maneuver is enough to equalize pressure and restore the temporary hearing loss caused by oxygen ear.

Auditory Fatigue

Auditory fatigue is a common type of temporary hearing loss that can occur after exposure to elevated noise levels. A long cross-country flight in a noisy light aircraft, for example, can cause the hair-like receptors in the organ of Corti in the cochlea to be overstimulated to the point that they become fatigued. This **auditory fatigue**, which may last for several minutes to several hours, causes a temporary decibel threshold shift impairing the ability to hear sounds below that threshold. Sometimes a person will also experience **tinnitus**, a perception of a ringing or buzzing sound in the ears even when no external sounds are present. If high noise levels are avoided while the hearing receptors are recovering, then permanent hearing loss is unlikely. However, repeated exposure to loud noises will cause a permanent threshold shift leading to permanent hearing loss.

Permanent Hearing Loss

Sensorineural NIHL occurs when the tiny nerve fibers (hairs) in the Cochlea are damaged due to excessive noise. In this case, NIHL is irreversible and cannot be corrected by surgery or medications. High frequencies are the first to be affected by NIHL. Unfortunately, since these are above those of the normal speaking range early hearing loss will usually not be detected by someone experiencing it and is normally only discovered by a hearing specialist.

Damage to the hearing receptors is primarily a function of noise intensity and the duration one is exposed to the noise. This relationship (intensity × exposure) is sometimes called the noise immission level (NIL). NIOSH has set a recommended daily (five days a week) exposure limit (REL) of eight hours at an 85-dB noise level.[12] Prolonged exposure at or above these limits increases the risk of permanent hearing damage. NIOSH has also determined that the probability of developing occupational NIHL over a forty-year working career is 8 percent with a REL of eight hours at 85 dB—which is less than the 25 percent probability of the Occupational Safety and Health Administration (OSHA) standard of 90 dB. They also use the "equal-energy rule" to calculate safe NIL values. For example, an equivalent level of noise energy can occur with short exposures (or doses) to high-intensity sounds or longer exposures to low-intensity sounds. Table 7-3 also illustrates the maximum noise dose levels using a 3 dB time-intensity tradeoff (i.e., for every 3 dB increase in intensity, maximum recommended noise exposure should be reduced by half)[13].

Table 7-3. Average sound exposure levels needed to reach the maximum allowable daily dose of 100 percent.

Time to reach 100% noise dose	Noise level per NIOSH REL
8 hours	85 dB
4 hours	88 dB
2 hours	91 dB
60 minutes	94 dB
30 minutes	97 dB
15 minutes	100 dB

Finally, it should be mentioned that even if pilots use hearing protection, NIHL as a function of age may be unavoidable. Hearing loss due to advancing age is called **presbycusis** (*presby* = elder; *cusis*, from *akousis* = hearing).

Fatigue

Prolonged exposure to noise is just one of many factors which contribute to pilot fatigue (others are discussed in Chapter 10). Noise fatigue—a feeling of tiredness or exhaustion—develops when specific muscles are not able to rest due to noise. Sound is simply another form of vibration (speech is produced by the vibration of the vocal chords), which at high enough intensities and certain frequencies, causes an involuntary reflex action whereby the muscles respond by contraction. Certain low frequency sounds in an aircraft cabin preclude muscle relaxation, leading to fatigue and its accompanying deterioration of both mental and physical abilities. The severity of fatigue increases with higher noise immission levels and is compounded by the presence of other fatigue-inducing environmental factors, such as engine and airframe vibration, cabin temperature extremes, dehydration, and hypoxia.

Noise Protection

Protection from the adverse effects of noise can be accomplished by reducing noise levels at the source or by using personal protection devices.

Reduction at Source

Reducing noise levels at the source is done by the manufacturer during an aircraft's design stage. Some aircraft are equipped with **active noise reduction (ANR)** systems to reduce noise (and usually vibration) caused by the aircraft engines and airframe. Microphones are strategically placed throughout the flight deck, passenger cabin, and high-noise areas. Using these inputs, a computer continuously analyzes aircraft noise frequencies then triggers actuators that transmit sound waves of the same frequency and amplitude of the original noise, but 180 degrees out of phase (antiphase). This mirror image of unwanted noise cancels out the original primary wave, resulting in lower noise levels in the aircraft (*see* Figure 7-4).

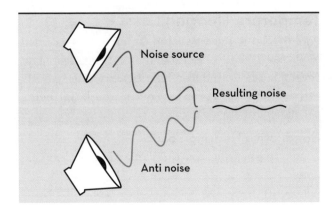

Fig 7-4.

Active noise reduction (ANR). A secondary wave of the same amplitude, but 180 degrees out of phase, is transmitted to cancel the primary wave.[14]

Personal Protection Devices

If an aircraft is not equipped with an ANR system, or the system isn't functioning to its full capability, pilots should wear personal protective hearing devices to avoid NIHL. These involve passive protection, active protection, or both.

Passive systems, such as earplugs that are inserted into the auditory canal, or earmuffs/earphones that fit over the ears, use sound-blocking materials (foam, silicone, etc.) to reduce the level of noise reaching the eardrum. Active personal protection hearing devices work in the same way as aircraft ANR systems, only all the electronic apparatus is contained within the headset itself.

Earplugs

Earplugs come in a variety of shapes and designs. Basic foam earplugs are pre-molded and must be compressed before being placed into the outer ear so they can expand when inside. Others are made of moldable materials (putty-like substances, foams, etc.) that usually provide a better fit than pre-molded foam earplugs. These are all inexpensive and provide good hearing protection in most cases. You might think their use would decrease communication abilities, but just the opposite occurs: the SNR is raised and the frequencies they block (mid- and high-frequencies) actually enhance verbal communication.

Earplugs provide varying levels of protection—some have a U.S. Environmental Protection Agency noise reduction rating (NRR) as high 33 dB. This does not mean, however, that noise reaching the eardrum will be 33 dB less than the ambient noise level. The NRR is obtained in laboratory conditions with participants wearing the devices properly. Since promulgation of this standard, OSHA and NIOSH have learned that the NRR actually overstates the level of protection for most people in real-world situations. For example, a U.S. Navy study found that only about 13 percent of flight deck crews who used insert-type earplugs inserted them into their ears properly (deeply) to achieve maximum noise reduction.[15] OSHA and NIOSH, therefore, use different formulas (depending on the type of decibels measured and the type of insert-type-earplug) to de-rate these values to calculate realistic noise exposure. So, for example, using one of the formulas, the average person wearing earplugs with an NRR of 25 dB for eight hours in a 98-dB noise environment will actually be exposed to about 89 dB, not 73 dB (98dB–25dB).

To get the maximum benefit from insert-type foam earplugs, NIOSH recommends roll, pull, and hold: *roll* it into a thin tube, *pull* the top of the ear up and back, insert the earplug, then hold the earplug in place for 20–30 seconds while waiting for the plug to expand (*see* Figure 7-5)[16]. If they are properly inserted they should feel uncomfortable, especially the longer they are in the ear.

Designed to fit the unique shape of a person's ear, custom-fit earplugs are made from a molded impression of your outer ear. Some can even be fitted to allow for radio/intercom communication through a small hose connected directly to the earplug. You might think that custom-fit earplugs would provide maximum protection and comfort while still providing for acceptable verbal communication. According to an FAA Civil Aerospace Medical Institute (CAMI) study, this conclusion is not always warranted—many are "more expensive, less comfortable, and less effective than premolded or moldable types."[17]

Earmuffs/Headsets

Hearing protection can also be achieved by wearing earmuffs, telecommunication headsets, or ANR headsets. Even though passive hearing protection is provided when wearing ear-muffs (headsets that

Roll
the earplug up into a small, thin "snake" with your fingers. You can use one or both hands.

Pull
the top of your ear up and back with your opposite hand to straighten out your ear canal. The rolled-up earplug should slide right in.

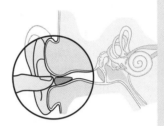

Hold
the earplug in with your finger. Count to 20 or 30 out loud while waiting for the plug to expand and fill the ear canal. Your voice will sound muffled when the plug has made a good seal.

Fig 7-5.

Recommended roll-pull-hold method to obtain maximum hearing protection from foam earplugs.

do not have built-in communication capability), intra- and extra-cockpit communication is hampered. That's why most pilots use headsets with built-in intercom earphones and microphone for communication with ATC and fellow crew members. Noise levels are reduced by the muffs over the ears and the source of communications is brought nearer to the ears. Though there are many models available, you should be aware they provide varying levels of protection. What some gain in reduced weight (which can be a very important comfort factor in long duration flights) they may lose when it comes to adequate noise protection. A quick survey indicates that most headsets **attenuate** noise by no more than 24 dB (NRR). Since NRRs are somewhat lower for headsets than for earplugs, many pilots wear both, especially in cockpits with high noise levels.

ANR headsets are gaining more popularity in aviation, especially among pilots flying small and louder aircraft. These hearing protection devices work in the same way as aircraft ANR systems, only the microphones used to measure ambient noise, and the speaker used to transmit sound waves to cancel the noise, are all contained within the earphone unit itself. Significant noise reductions have been reported by pilots, especially lower-frequency noises. However, according to an FAA *Information for Operators* notice, pilots and aircraft operators should be aware that under certain aircraft noise/frequency combinations, some units may attenuate important environmental sounds and alarm warnings.[18] Just as it is important to detect unusual smells (battery acid, electrical smoke, engine fumes, etc.), so too is it important to be able to detect both normal sounds (e.g., landing gear and flap extension sounds, and non-interphone voice communications between flight and cabin crew) and non-normal sounds (e.g., abnormal mechanical, airframe, and engine noises, and audio warnings such as landing gear horns). In fact, the FAA's suspicions have proved correct in some instances. A pilot of a Beechcraft D35 forgot to extend the landing gear before landing on Runway 18 at Sunriver, Oregon. The private pilot reported that he could not hear the gear warning horn annunciate while he was wearing his noise-canceling headset (NTSB Identification No: GAA15CA124). A corporate pilot (9,000+ hours) also landed with the landing gear retracted after being distracted by the co-pilot's door opening after liftoff. The shoulder harness, which was making loud noises while banging against the side of the fuselage, distracted him, causing him to forget to lower the gear. He also said the gear warning horn "was inaudible" through the noise-canceling headsets he was wearing (ASRS Report No: 217285).

Hearing Above All the Noise

Not only does noise contribute to fatigue and communication difficulties on the flight deck, numerous studies have confirmed what most pilots already know: the louder the aircraft, the longer the flying career and the less the noise protection, the greater the likelihood of suffering from permanent hearing loss. GA and helicopter pilots, and those flying propeller-driven piston and turboprops, are particularly vulnerable. For example, personnel at the FAA's CAMI have never tested a crop duster pilot who *did not* have hearing loss, and a study of 3,019 U.S. commuter air carrier and air taxi pilots found that the percentage of those with hearing deficits went from 2 percent to 19 percent over a ten-year period.[19, 20] There are, therefore, several best practice strategies you can use to reduce the negative effects of noise on both communication and your hearing.

Communication Strategies

You should properly enunciate and pronounce your words when speaking to crew members and others when using a microphone. The *Aeronautical Telecommunications* (Annex 10, Volume II) and the *Manual of Radiotelephony* (Doc 9432)—both published by the International Civil Aviation Organization (ICAO)—along with the FAA *AIM*, provide **radiotelephony** guidance on how to pronounce certain words and phrases, including the phonetic alphabet and numbers. If others are having trouble understanding what you are saying, you may have to spell out words using the phonetic alphabet.

Using personal hearing protection will not only help protect against hearing loss but will also help increase SNR for speech and enhance overall communication ability. Keep in mind that when wearing certain types of hearing protection, you should project your voice. An FAA Advisory Circular reminds pilots when wearing earplugs or earmuffs to speak louder and with more vocal effort.[21] That's because the noise level is reduced for the wearer and the temptation is to speak softly, precluding others from hearing your speech. Chapter 13 digs deeper into the topic of speech perception: it contains several recommendations for improving overall communication on the flight deck. Chapter 19 revisits the topic, focusing on some of the higher-level aspects of communication.

Hearing Protection Strategies

Not only should you use some type of personal hearing protection device every time you fly, but to gain maximum protection you should ensure it is fitted properly. Follow the *roll-pull-hold* technique outlined by NIOSH for insert-type earplugs and make sure the ear cushions on headsets are the correct size, completely cover each ear, and fit snugly. Do not use plain absorbent cotton balls as a substitute for earplugs: they don't work. Adjust headphone speaker volumes accordingly, but recognize that loud volumes can negate the reduction of noise levels provided by the ear protection device. If using noise-canceling headsets, the FAA also recommends that you check that environmental sounds and audible alarms in the aircraft you fly can be heard while electronic noise attenuation is on and active. For maximum protection in high noise environments, consider doing what many pilots do: use both earplugs and telecommunication headsets. Also, since NIHL doesn't discriminate, you should wear hearing protection and/or reduce your exposure to loud sounds when you are outside of the flying environment (loud music, loud sporting events or concerts, lawn mowers, vacuum cleaners, etc.).

For other types of temporary hearing loss, use the Valsalva maneuver (see Chapter 5 for instructions on how to perform this properly) to reduce temporary hearing impairment caused by oxygen ear or from unequal middle- and outer-ear pressures during climb or descent. Finally, to avoid further hearing damage after prolonged exposure to high noise levels (even when wearing hearing protection), you should avoid further exposure to give your hearing receptors time to recover.

Helpful Resources

Noise and Vibration in Aviation (in English or Spanish) is an informative short video produced by the Airman Education Programs branch at the FAA's CAMI that focuses on the effects of noise and vibration in the flight environment. (www.faa.gov/pilots/training/airman_education/physiologyvideos/)

The Siemens Corporation has published some excellent information in two short animated videos on how hearing works, noise and hearing loss—"How Hearing Works" and "Hearing Loss". (www.signia-hearing.com/hearing-and-hearing-loss/)

The FAA has several other resources that deal with noise and communication:

- Safety pamphlet, *Hearing and Noise in Aviation* (P-AM-400-98/3) (www.faa.gov/pilots/safety/pilotsafetybrochures/)
- Two Advisory Circulars—*Noise, Hearing Damage, and Fatigue in General Aviation Pilots* (AC 91–35); and *Cockpit Noise and Speech Interference Between Crewmembers* (AC 20-133). (www.faa.gov/regulations_policies/advisory_circulars/)
- "Radio Communications Phraseology and Techniques" (Chapter 4, Section 2) in the FAA *AIM*.

How To Buy a Headset: A Guide to Get you Started, by Elizabeth Tennyson, published by the AOPA Air Safety Institute, provides advice regarding both passive and active noise reduction aviation headsets. (www.aopa.org/news-and-media/all-news/2001/april/pilot/how-to-buy-a-headset)

"An Overview of Aircraft Noise Reduction Technologies," published in the June 2014 edition of the *AerospaceLab Journal*, is an absolutely fascinating article about current and future technologies used to reduce aircraft engine and airframe noise. (www.aerospacelab-journal.org/al7/overview-of-aircraft-noise-reduction-technologies)

Endnotes

1. A diagram of the anatomy of the human ear, by Chittka L, Brockmann, 2009 (https://commons.wikimedia.org/wiki/File:Anatomy_of_the_Human_Ear_en.svg); WC CC BY 2.5

2. Elsa Blackburn, *Medical Terminology: A Learning Adventure* (Trafford Publishing: October 15, 2002).

3. M.S. James, "Defining the Cockpit Noise Hazard, Aircrew Hearing Damage Risk and the Benefits Active Noise Reduction Headsets Can Provide," Paper 5, in *Personal Hearing Protection Including Active Noise Reduction Meeting Proceedings*, RTO-EN-HFM-111 (Neuilly-sur-Seine, France: RTO, June 2005): 5–1 to 5–24.

4. Federal Aviation Administration, *Noise, Hearing Damage, and Fatigue in General Aviation Pilots*, AC 91-35 (Washington, DC: March 28, 1972).

5. From Figure 5, p. 279 ("Noise flight profiles-3 aviation classes") in the following paper presented at the Speech Science and Technology Conference (SST1988): P.J. Kennedy and J.E. Clark, "Ambient Noise in the Cockpit/Flightdeck Communication Environment of Australian Civil Aviation Aircraft," in *Proceedings of the Speech Science and Technology Conference*, SST 1988, Sydney, Australia: 274–281. Used with permission.

6. James, "Defining the Cockpit Noise Hazard," 5-2.

7. Laurent Leylekian, Maxime Lebrun and Pierre Lempereur, "An Overview of Aircraft Noise Reduction Technologies," *Aerospace Lab Journal* 7 (June 2014): 4.

8. Ernesto Lamm and Nancy Lawrence, "Interior Sound Levels in General Aviation Aircraft," *Occupational Health & Safety, Exclusively Online* (July 12, 2010).

9. Federal Aviation Administration, *Cockpit Noise and Speech Interference Between Crewmembers*, AC 20-133 (Washington, DC: March 22, 1989).

10. Lightspeed Staff, "ANR 101: A Tutorial on Active Noise Reduction Headsets (Section 5—Optimizing Your Flying Experience)," *AVweb* (December 8, 1998).

11. Information taken from Federal Aviation Administration, *Pilot/Controller Glossary* (Washington, DC: January 30, 2020).

12. Chuck Kardous, Christa L. Themann, Thais C. Morata and W. Gregory Lotz, *Understanding Noise Exposure Limits: Occupational vs. General Environmental Noise* (February 8, 2016). Available at blogs.CDC.gov/niosh-science-blog/2016/02/08/noise/

13. Ibid.

14. Graphical Depiction of Active Noise Reduction, by Marekich, 2012, (https://commons.wikimedia.org/wiki/File:Active_Noise_Reduction.svg), WC CC BY-SA 3.0

15. Valerie S. Bjorn, Christopher B. Albery, CDR Russell Shilling and Richard L. McKinley, "U.S. Navy Flight Deck Hearing Protection Use Trends: Survey Results," Paper 1, in *New Directions for Improving Audio Effectiveness Meeting Proceedings* RTO-MP-HFM-123 (Neuilly-sur-Seine, France: RTO, April 1, 2005): 1–1–1–20.

16. From National Institute for Occupational Safety and Health (NIOSH), Mining Safety and Health Content, *How To Wear Soft Foam Earplugs*. Available at www.cdc.gov/niosh/mining/content/earplug.html.

17. Federal Aviation Administration, *Introduction to Aviation Physiology* (Oklahoma City, OK: n.d.): 12–4.

18. Federal Aviation Administration, "Noise Attenuation Properties of Noise-Cancelling Headsets," Information for Operators, InFO 07001 (January 5, 2007).

19. FAA, *Introduction to Aviation Physiology*, 12-3.

20. Yandong Qiang, George W. Rebok, Susan P. Baker and Guohua Li, "Hearing Deficit in a Birth Cohort of U.S. Male Commuter Air Carrier and Air Taxi Pilots," *Aviation, Space, and Environmental Medicine* 79 (November 2008): 1051-1055.

21. FAA, *Noise, Hearing Damage, and Fatigue.*

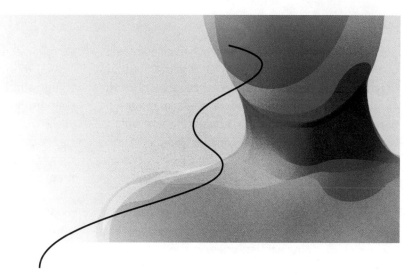

8

Do you want to be an aerobatic pilot?
Accelerations in Flight

Imagine this. You open your eyes, thinking you just woke up from a pleasant night's sleep in the comfort of your own bed, and to your astonishment you find you are in the driver's seat of a Lockheed Martin F-16 Fighting Falcon with your nose pointed down toward the ground in a 135-degree steep bank angle traveling faster than the speed of sound with full thrust and afterburners on. You don't have to imagine it; that's what happened to a U.S. Air Force (USAF) pilot in May 2016 while engaged in his first high-aspect air-to-air basic air combat maneuvers training flight (i.e., dog fight) against another F-16 flown by his flight instructor.

The exercise required significant maneuvering under high G-force conditions. As he passed the other fighter jet, he banked his aircraft pulling more than eight positive Gs ($+8 \, G_Z$). This rendered him completely unconscious leading to his perilous high-speed descent toward the ground. Fortunately, moments after waking up from his G-induced slumber, a new technology used in USAF F-16s since 2014—called *Auto-GCAS* (automatic ground collision avoidance system)—took over control and returned his airplane to straight-and-level flight at about 3,000 feet AGL. The pilot said it took him about 30 seconds to a minute to get everything under control, after which his first thoughts were "my girlfriend, and then my family, and then my friends back home, and the thought of them basically getting a call (that I had perished)."[1]

In a related incident, an Extra Flugzeugbau EA-300 operated by the Canadian Northern Lights Aerobatic Team was substantially damaged and the pilot was seriously injured, after colliding with the ground near Chenoa, Illinois. The pilot was practicing aero-batic maneuvers when he lost control of his aircraft. A pilot-witness saw it enter a knife-edge spin, but just when it looked like the aerobatic airplane was going to recover from the maneuver it continued to descend toward the ground. The pilot apparently made a last-ditch effort to recover, but it wasn't quite enough: the aircraft impacted the ground in a wings-level attitude. The pilot said he experienced "grayout" and "G-induced loss of consciousness" during the pullout from the maneuver. In addition, the NTSB cited fatigue as a factor that led to his loss of consciousness (NTSB Identification No: CHI98LA121).

The pilots in both of these events deliberately exposed themselves and their aircraft to the dynamic forces of a high-G environment, and both were incapacitated by G-induced physiological impairment. However, if you think such outcomes only affect aerobatic and fighter pilots, think again. For example, while on a VFR flight en route to Fort Lauderdale, Florida, a pilot lost control of his Cirrus SR22 while cruising at 15,400 feet. The single-engine airplane stalled and entered a rapid descent losing 13,000 feet of altitude in about 40 seconds before the pilot was able to recover. Data downloaded from the flight displays after the event indicate that during the recovery the airplane sustained a vertical load of more than 4 Gs for more than 20 seconds. The NTSB concluded that the private pilot likely experienced G-induced loss of consciousness (G-LOC) or near G-LOC, which, because amnesia is a common symptom of G-LOC, may also explain why he failed to accurately recall the events of the flight. The airplane was substantially damaged by aerodynamic forces, but fortunately he was able to land at a nearby airport in McRae, Georgia, saving himself and his two passengers (NTSB Identification No: ATL06LA134).

In aviation, the study of the body's response to dynamic forces imposed upon it—sometimes called **biodynamics**—specifically refers to the physiological effects of changing accelerations on the body. These accelerations, commonly called G *forces*, can be small or of short duration producing virtually no ill effects, or they can be large or of longer duration causing structural damage to an aircraft and/or physiological incapacitation of the pilot or flight crew.

Extensive G-force training is usually only provided for flight operations where excessive G is expected to be encountered. However, a basic appreciation of human tolerance to acceleration is important for all pilots—not just aerobatic and fighter pilots—since you are likely to occasionally experience a degree of G-acceleration during regular operations from strong updrafts or downdrafts or from steep turns. Also, as you saw with the Cirrus SR22 pilot, you may inadvertently find yourself in an unusual attitude which could involve pulling significant G during recovery.

One of the first reported incidents regarding the physiological effects of adverse G occurred in 1918 when a British pilot flying a single-seat Sopwith Triplane, an early fighter airplane used during World War I, reported the sky appeared to turn gray just before he "fainted in the air," or passed out, after pulling 4.5 Gs.[2] The pilot woke up to find he and his airplane were over a village about a mile away from where he originally was before the incapacitating event took place.[3] The first recorded example of G-LOC in the United States involved the 1922 Pulitzer Trophy air race winner who lost consciousness from acceleration forces during the race. The following year's air race winner experienced the same phenomenon, completing an unnecessary extra lap in a dazed state.[4] Also, in the early 1920s, as part of his studies at the Massachusetts Institute of Technology, Jimmy Doolittle mounted a new instrument, called an *accelerometer*, to a Fokker Pursuit PW-7 biplane and conducted a series of aerobatic maneuvers for the purpose of measuring structural loads on aircraft.

He reported that in one instance he pulled 4.7 Gs and "began to lose his sight, and for a short time everything went black except for an occasional shooting star similar to those seen when one is struck on the jaw."[5]

As aircraft were able to withstand greater structural G-loads, the pilots who flew them began to report more serious cases of G-induced physiological problems. For example, in the years leading up to World War II, the U.S. Navy developed the technique of dive-bombing for dropping ordnance on targets. This involved a steep dive toward the target, releasing the bomb, then employing a high-G pullout from the dive. On some of these dive-bombing runs pilots began to experience diminished vision and sometimes complete loss of consciousness.[6] In the 1930s, the first centrifuges were built in the United States, and in 1950 the U.S. Navy built the world's largest centrifuge, which enabled physiologists to study the effects of various types of acceleration on the human body under controlled conditions.[7, 8]

The number of G-induced physiological impairment events in civil aviation is difficult to determine. However, their incidence in the world's military sector is somewhat easier to obtain. For example, G-LOC was responsible for several mishaps, including the loss of 24 USAF pilots between 1982 and 2002.[9] A survey of experienced USAF pilots also discovered that about 227 of them (12 percent of those surveyed) lost consciousness at one time or another due to maneuvers involving greater than 1 G. Similar numbers were obtained for the U.S. Navy, with 14 percent experiencing G-LOC. The United Kingdom Royal Air Force reports similar findings with 19 percent of pilots reporting G-LOC.[10] Only 9 percent of Royal Australian Air Force (RAAF) fighter pilots surveyed reported experiencing G-LOC, yet more than 50 percent reported experiencing near G-LOC symptoms including disorientation and confusion. This latter survey also revealed that 98 percent of RAAF fighter pilots reported experiencing at least one visual or cognitive disturbance when flying in a high-G environment.[11]

Types of Acceleration

Acceleration is the rate of change of velocity. Velocity refers to both the magnitude (speed) and direction of a moving object. There are generally three types of acceleration. Linear acceleration occurs whenever there is a change in the speed of an object moving in a straight line, such as during a takeoff or landing roll, or when changing airspeed in flight. Extreme linear decelerations are often involved in aircraft crash landings. Biodynamics also concerns itself with the study of crash forces on the human body, including *crashworthiness*, the degree to which an aircraft's structure protects the occupants from injury during a crash. Radial acceleration occurs when there is a change in the direction of an object, such as occurs during a turn, or during a push into, or a pullout from, a dive. Finally, angular acceleration occurs when there is a change in both the speed and direction of a moving object. Most turning maneuvers and dive recoveries are more precisely called angular accelerations since a simultaneous change in both direction and speed is often involved.

Measurement of Acceleration

For simplification, multiples of the G unit are used when measuring accelerations in aviation flight operations. The small letter g usually refers to the acceleration produced by gravity, and a capital G is used to indicate the ratio of applied acceleration (a)—or aircraft-maneuver-induced acceleration—over the acceleration of gravity (g), and is used to describe the total acceleration on an aircraft and its pilot (G=a/g). Even though it is an *acceleration*, we sometimes use the term "G-force" to describe this ratio.

The gravitational acceleration (g) of positive one (+1 g) is what an object at rest on the earth's surface experiences: which is 9.8 meters per second per second (m/s^2), or 32 $feet/s^2$. Since an object's weight is the product of its mass and gravitational acceleration (W=mg), its weight would double if the earth's gravitational acceleration were to double to 19.6 m/s^2 (+2 g). Or, put another way, since G=a/g, if you were to accelerate an airplane at twice (2a) the gravitation acceleration (1 g), you would feel like your weight was doubled (2 G).

In relation to the pilot and aircraft (*see* Figure 8-1), positive (+) and negative (–) accelerations are measured along three axes: G_X (longitudinal axis), G_Y (lateral axis), and G_Z (vertical axis). Vertical acceleration is in the vertical axis and is either +G_Z (headward acceleration, or *eyeballs down*) or –G_Z (footward acceleration, or *eyeballs up*). Transverse acceleration in the longitudinal axis is considered as either +G_X

(forward acceleration, or *eyeballs in*) or –G_X (backward acceleration, or *eyeballs out*). Finally, lateral acceleration along the lateral axis is either +G_Y (acceleration to the right, or *eyeballs left*) or –G_Y (left acceleration, or *eyeballs right*).

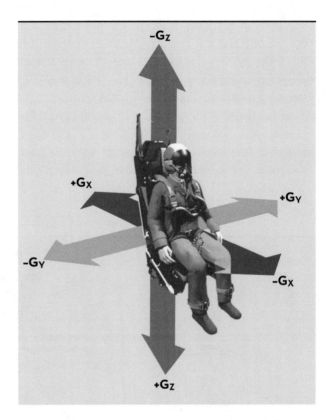

Fig 8-1.

The three dimensions of acceleration.

Lateral accelerations (±G_Y) seldom occur in normal flight. With the exception of crash landings and aircraft carrier operations, significant transverse accelerations (±G_X) are also rare (although, as discussed in the next chapter, significant positive transverse acceleration during takeoffs and go-arounds (+G_X) can contribute to a false climb illusion at night or in instrument meteorological conditions).

The type of accelerations most commonly encountered in flight, which are the primary concern of this chapter, are +G_Z and to a lesser extent –G_Z accelerations. We occasionally experience –G_Z acceleration during a rapid downdraft (or, if you are an aerobatic or military pilot, during a deliberate nose-over when conducting certain maneuvers). However, in most normal flight situations we usually experience $+G_Z$ acceleration in the vertical axis; rarely from pull-ups from dives in unusual attitude recovery, sometimes from rapid updrafts, but mostly from the increased load factor involved in turns.

When an airplane turns it changes direction because of the inward component of lift (sometimes called the centripetal force). Lift (L) equals weight (W) when an airplane is flying in straight-and-level (constant altitude) flight in a 1 g environment, but its lift is greater than its weight in a level turn. This is because lift generated by an airplane is perpendicular (90 degrees) to the wings, so more lift must be created to counteract the weight (or gravitational acceleration) of the aircraft during a level turn (see Figure 8-2).

In fact, twice the lift is necessary to counteract the airplane's weight in a level 60-degree bank turn. This extra wing loading, or *load factor* (n), is the ratio of lift over weight (n = L/W) which is equal to the resultant of the aircraft's weight and centrifugal force (*see* Figure 8-3).

A load factor of 2 on the airplane is also imposed on the human body during a 60-degree bank and can be expressed as positive 2 G in the z axis, or $+2\ G_Z$ (pronounced "*positive two gees*"). The amount of $+G_Z$ in a turn is equal to 1/cosine φ, where φ (Greek letter *Phi*) is the bank angle in degrees. The amount of $+G_Z$ in a level turn varies inversely with the radius of turn (i.e., smaller radius requires steeper bank) and $+G_Z$ rise sharply above the $+2\ G_Z$ bank angle of 60 degrees (*see* Figure 8-4).

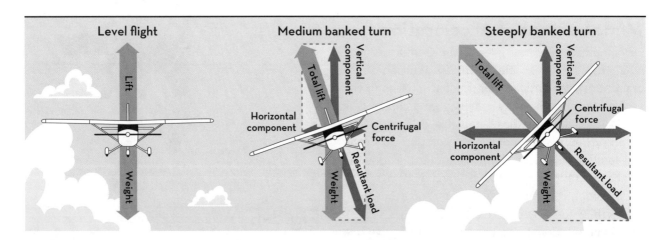

Fig 8-2.

Total lift must increase to maintain level flight (altitude) in a turn.

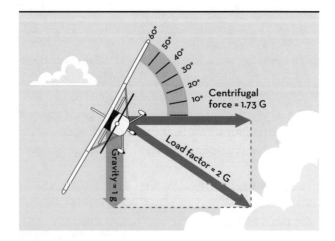

Fig 8-3.

Gravity and centrifugal force create load factor during level turns.

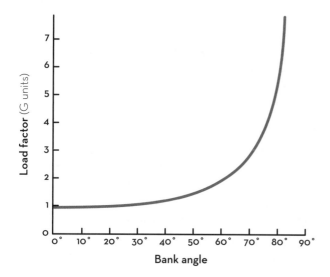

Fig 8-4.

The load factor (n) increases significantly with an increase in bank angle of more than 60 degrees in level flight.

G_Z Limitations in Aircraft

Most light aircraft, operating in the normal category, have a maximum maneuver operating limit range between 3.8 $+G_Z$ and 1.52 $-G_Z$. Purely aerobatic airplanes require almost double these limits. Even though aircraft are designed to withstand G_Z which are 50 percent higher than these values, the operating limits published in the aircraft flight manual (AFM) should never be exceeded, either purposely, through unauthorized aerobatic maneuvers, or inadvertently, from excessive bank angles or from excessive pull-ups from dives. Even short-duration exposure to $\pm G_Z$ values that are close to operational limits reduces the structural integrity of the aircraft and increases the risk of in-flight damage or break-up. Therefore, overstressing the aircraft by exceeding design operating load limits or through exposure at or near these limits, must be avoided.

Physiological Responses to G_Z Acceleration

It stands to reason that if excessive G_Z can result in aircraft structural failure it can also cause incapacitation of its human operator—just as there are definite G limitations for a particular aircraft, so too are there G limitations for a particular pilot. The level of tolerance in flight crew members depends on the magnitude and duration of the imposed G and varies between individuals. Even though the latter is true, a progression of common symptoms usually occurs with increasing G levels.

Symptoms of G_Z Acceleration

Symptoms vary between positive and negative accelerations. For example, $+G_Z$ involve a feeling of increasing weight, while $-G_Z$ involve a feeling of weightlessness and all that entails. However, the most significant symptoms for both types of G_Z accelerations involve the deleterious effects on the circulatory system.

Positive G_Z

Since every action creates an equal and opposite reaction (Newton's Third Law), the opposite reaction to acceleration is inertia. When you experience $+G_Z$ acceleration (toe-to-head) during a pull-up from a dive, an inside loop, or during a steep turn, inertia pushes you back down (head-to-toe) into your seat. If you have performed a level turn of 45 degrees of bank or greater you have definitely felt these effects. The most serious consequences of increased levels of $+G_Z$ on your body, besides the increased pressure on your buttocks, the drooping of your skin, and the difficulty raising your arms and legs, is the pooling of blood in the lower parts of your body and extremities due to inertia and a reduction in blood pressure where it is needed the most—your brain (*see* Figure 8-5).

Fig 8-5.

The effect of positive G ($+G_z$) on blood flow during a pull-up from a dive, an inside loop, or a steep turn.

As you learned in Chapter 4, the blood is responsible for carrying oxygen to the cells and tissues in your body, including your eyes and brain, and that even though these vital organs account for only about two percent of your body weight they need at least 20 percent of your body's oxygen intake to function effectively. The reduction of blood flow and pressure to these organs brought on by significant levels of $+G_z$ is responsible for the detrimental physiological effects and cognitive disturbances.

Just as the pressure of a column of water is less at the top than it is at the bottom because of the effect of gravity, so too in a column of a person's blood is the blood pressure near their head less than it is near their feet (when standing erect). For example, assuming the arterial blood pressure—the average pressure of blood leaving the heart to the arteries—is about 120 millimeters of mercury (mm Hg) for an average pilot in a sitting position, in conditions of $+1 G_z$ the blood pressure at the brain and feet would be approximately 96 mm Hg and 170 mm Hg, respectively (see Figure 8-6). This hydrostatic balance is usually not a problem for the brain in a 1 G environment. However, as seen in the right side of Figure 8-6, at $+5 G_z$ the blood pressure in the brain drastically decreases to 0 mm Hg and increases to 370 mm Hg at the feet.[12] These extremely low positive-vertical-G-induced blood pressures above heart-level are insufficient to deliver the oxygen partial pressure needed

for the brain and eyes to function properly. In fact, at approximately $+5 G_z$, without any natural physiological compensatory mechanisms or human-designed protection measures, you will lose your vision and your consciousness within only a few seconds of G-onset.

Visual Disturbances

As you learned in Chapter 4, the retina of the eye has the highest oxygen demand and the lowest deprivation tolerance of any human structure. It stands to reason, then, that the eyes are the first organs to be negatively affected by the reduced partial pressure of oxygen. This *visual hypoxia*, a form of stagnant hypoxia, brought on by $+G_z$-induced blood stagnation, takes on a variety of forms depending on the magnitude of the offending $+G_z$.

Grayout

The internal (intraocular) pressure of the eye is about 15 to 20 mm Hg, so when the blood pressure reaching the eye falls below this value, the ability to properly see suffers and you experience **grayout**. This involves a dimming of vision (making it hard to see lights, especially at night), reduced color vision (making things look grayer), visual blurring and other effects that generally occur between about $+3 G_z$ and $+4 G_z$, depending on the rate of G-onset and individual tolerance. In addition, since oxygen is delivered by the retinal artery that enters each eye at the optic disk, and radiates outward delivering oxygen to the retina via smaller arteries to its periphery, with sustained or increasing positive G-levels the peripheral receptors are the first to cease functioning, leading to tunnel vision that narrows until you can see only using central vision. In order to avoid the more serious symptoms of blackout and G-LOC, experienced aerobatic and fighter pilots often use the onset of grayout to warn them to relax the amount of G they are pulling. When they do this grayout disappears almost immediately.

Blackout

Depending on individual tolerance and G-onset rate, at about $+3.5 G_z$ to $+4.5 G_z$ you are likely to experience **blackout**, a complete loss of vision. Blood pressure reaching the eye falls below the eye's intraocular pressure, causing oxygen starvation in the receptors. Since the reduced oxygen flow hasn't yet affected the brain, you are still conscious and possess mental functioning even though your vision is lost. Since

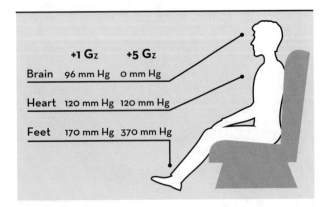

Fig 8-6.

Hydrostatic pressure of a human's column of blood while sitting at $+1 G_z$ and $+5 G_z$. As positive vertical Gs are increased, blood pressure, and consequently oxygen partial pressure, above heart-level decreases until at the brain it reaches zero (0 mm Hg) at about $+5 G_z$.[13]

blood pressure/oxygen required for the brain to function does not need to be as high as it does for the eyes to function (i.e., to overcome the 15 to 20 mm Hg intraocular pressure), blackout occurs about 0.7 G_Z before loss of consciousness.[14] Again, if you reduce the magnitude of G_Z your vision will usually rapidly return.

Loss of Consciousness

The most dangerous symptom associated with moderate to high levels of +G_Z is **G-induced loss of consciousness (G-LOC)**. Blood and oxygen flow to the brain is virtually nil at levels at or above approximately +4.5 G_Z to +5.5 G_Z, which leads to unconsciousness from severe stagnant hypoxia. G-LOC is generally divided into two stages, or types. *Absolute incapacitation* (Type I) involves total unconsciousness that, depending on the G-onset rate and individual tolerance, lasts for about 12 to 20 seconds.[15] A minority of pilots experience mostly pleasant dream-like states during this time, and a majority experience involuntarily muscle and skeletal movements with arms and legs flailing (sometimes called the "funky chicken") for a period of about 4 seconds just prior to regaining consciousness.[16, 17, 18] This latter condition could obviously cause problems if switches or controls are contacted.

Absolute incapacitation is followed by *relative incapacitation* (Type II) after the pilot regains consciousness. Like the experience of the USAF pilot upon waking up from G-LOC with his F-16 pointed toward the ground and flying at a high speed (*see* the introduction to this chapter), after waking up from G-LOC you will experience mental confusion, disorientation, and a general lack of understanding of what is going on that, for about another 12 to 16 seconds, will render you unable to function normally. In one study, the following symptoms (and percentages), in addition to confusion (69 percent), were reported by crew members during the relative incapacitation period in centrifuge training: surprise (52 percent), relaxation (42 percent), embarrassment (39 percent), euphoria (38 percent), apathy (36 percent), frustration (36 percent), anger (22 percent), denial (15 percent), fright (13 percent), and sadness (11 percent).[19] Compounding the problem of recovery is that 29 percent of participants experienced **retrograde amnesia** upon awaking from the absolute stage of G-LOC; they didn't remember the G-LOC event or typically the circumstances leading up to it.[20]

The obvious hazard of G-LOC is loss of aircraft control in flight (LOC-I). Like the aerobatic Extra EA-300 VFR pilot who lost consciousness during a knife-edge spin, and was fortunate to awake just before the collision (*see* introduction to this chapter), this is clearly an extreme hazard to safety. If there is any good news at all it is the fact that when unconsciousness occurs a pilot will usually (though not always) relax his or her grip on the controls, which will reduce +G_Z and return the flow of oxygen to the brain. However, even that may not be enough since it takes 12 to 20 seconds to regain consciousness (absolute incapacitation) and another 12 to 16 seconds to regain normal cognitive functioning and the ability to take corrective measures to extricate yourself from the hazardous situation (relative incapacitation), for a total incapacitation time of about 24 to 36 seconds.[21] This is certainly plenty of time for your aircraft to crash, especially if you are close to terrain before the G-LOC event occurs. Fortunately for the USAF pilot whose G-LOC episode was described earlier, the F-16 fighter jet he was commanding was equipped with an automatic recovery system (Auto-GCAS) that successfully engaged about the same time he regained consciousness and was still mentally struggling to figure out what was going on.

It should be noted that with short rapid onset exposures to relatively high positive G values, some aircrew have experienced G-LOC symptoms without losing consciousness. The symptoms of **almost loss of consciousness (A-LOC)** mostly include the cognitive deficits (confusion, stupor, memory loss, amnesia, etc.) associated with the relative incapacitation stage of G-LOC, but are usually of somewhat lesser intensity. A major problem pilots experience with both A-LOC and the relative incapacitation stage of G-LOC is their inability to act upon their cognitions (thoughts).[22]

The G-Time Tolerance Curve

Fortunately, the body possesses physiological mechanisms that compensate for—to a limited degree at least—the extremely low blood pressure in the brain and eyes when subjected to significant positive G_Z. The G-time tolerance curve (*see* Figure 8-7), adapted from a study conducted in the 1950s by Alice Stoll (hence it is also called a *Stoll curve*), depicts approximate thresholds for predicting G-induced physiological symptoms as a function of G_Z-level.[23]

The horizontal axis of the curve illustrates that no matter the +G$_Z$ level, you will be spared from symptoms for about 4 to 5 seconds after G-onset because of the residual storage of oxygen dissolved in the brain and eye tissues (the oxygen storage buffer in Figure 8-7). In fact, the green dotted line (A) indicates that you will not be subject to symptoms during rapid onset of high positive G if it is followed by a rapid reduction within 4 to 5 seconds to +G levels that are below symptom threshold levels. However, as the red dashed line (B) indicates, if a positive G level is not immediately relieved you won't be able to escape the symptoms but will instead go straight into G-LOC without ever experiencing the visual symptoms of grayout and blackout. The orange line (C) shows that with a moderate +G-onset rate, you will first experience the visual symptoms (grayout then blackout) before G-LOC.

The vertical dip in the curve reflects average thresholds for experiencing visual symptoms (grayout and blackout); however, these thresholds increase after about 12 to 15 seconds (the right of the curve) because of physiological mechanisms designed to compensate for low blood pressure and oxygen. Our bodies have a built-in cardiovascular reflex that increases, to a degree, blood/oxygen pressure to the head. The heart beats harder and faster, and the walls of peripheral blood vessels narrow resulting in higher blood (and oxygen) pressure reaching the eyes and brain. But as you can see from the curve, there is about a 15-second lag after the G

is applied for the reflex to become fully effective. If the +G$_Z$ onset rate is slow enough, you will bypass the dip, raising the threshold at which you begin to experience visual symptoms; and if you do, as indicated in the blue dashed line (D), you can also use that as a warning to reduce +G$_Z$-levels.

Negative G$_Z$

Mathematically, vertical G$_Z$ below one, but greater than zero is a positive number. However, since normal human functioning occurs in a +1 G$_Z$ environment it is not considered positive G$_Z$ because *any* G$_Z$ below +1 G$_Z$ has the same (though lesser) physiological effects as G$_Z$ below zero. Some researchers delineate separate terms to describe values between +1 G$_Z$ and 0 G$_Z$ (*relative* –G$_Z$) and below 0 G$_Z$ (*negative* – G$_Z$),[24] but this chapter simply uses –G$_Z$ to refer to any G$_Z$ below +1 G$_Z$. Also, you should note that because our normal gravitational environment is +1 G$_Z$ (and not 0 G$_Z$), when a pilot experiences –1 G$_Z$ it is the twice the magnitude (but in opposite direction) as +1 G$_Z$.

With increasing levels of –G$_Z$, such as would occur in an outside loop, a rapid nose-down push into a dive, or during inverted flight, blood rushes into the upper body and head (*see* Figure 8-8). This significantly increases blood pressures making tolerance to –G$_Z$ generally lower than for +G$_Z$. Head pressures quickly progress from feeling uncomfortable to unbearable. The fluid accumulation in the head causes facial swelling (edema). Considerable sinus

Fig 8-7.

The G-time tolerance curve. *See text for explanation.*

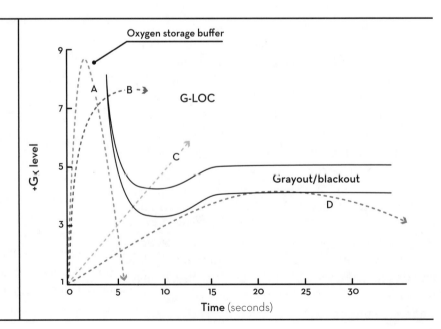

congestion and headache develops. Eye pain and the feeling that your eyes are bulging occurs. You may experience hearing loss, and a reddish rash or spots may develop on the facial skin (petechiae) from burst capillary blood vessels.[25]

At about –2.5 G_Z to –3 G_Z visual blurring and **redout** may also occur.[26] Since post-examination of those who have experienced this phenomenon indicates no retinal damage, this reddening of the visual field does not occur from the bursting of blood vessels in the eyes. However, since it has never been observed in controlled conditions (e.g., in a centrifuge), scientists are not entirely certain what causes it. Many believe it occurs when enough –G_Z causes the lower eyelid to move up slightly over the eye which allows light to filter through the blood-filled (and red-colored) eyelid, causing you to see things with a reddish veil. Others believe that the increased blood pressure at the optic nerve and retina may have something to do with it.[27] This is not to say that eye damage cannot occur in conditions of high –G_Z. Tiny fragile blood vessels below the eye's conjunctiva, a clear thin layer above the sclera of the eyeball (*see* Figure 6-2 in Chapter 6), can burst at –3 G_Z causing bleeding (subconjunctival hemorrhage).[28] However, even a severe sneeze or cough can cause this. This is evidenced by a red area on the white sclera of your eye which usually goes away after a couple of weeks.

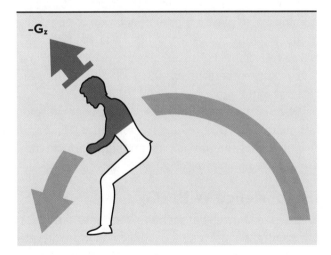

Fig 8-8.

The effect of negative vertical G (-G_z) on blood flow during inverted flight, an outside loop, or a rapid push into a dive.

The opposite cardiovascular reflex to +G_Z occurs when –G_Z is applied: In an attempt to reduce excessive blood pressure in the brain, the heart beats slower and the walls of peripheral blood vessels dilate resulting in lower blood pressure reaching the head. Sometimes the heart rate drops dramatically to values lower than 60 beats per minute, a condition called *bradycardia* (*bradus*=slow; *cardia*=heart). In some cases, unconsciousness occurs, and in extreme cases the heart has been known to completely stop for several seconds.[29]

Fortunately for normal flight operations, negative vertical accelerations are not often encountered, and when they are they are mostly limited to momentary downdrafts. The very nature of the flight environment (direction in which gravity acts, upright seating position, etc.) makes it more likely that any G_Z encountered will be positive (toe-to-head).

G Tolerance

The ability to withstand the adverse effects of G acceleration depends upon the nature of the acceleration involved and the physical/physiological attributes of the person experiencing it. The absolute level, or magnitude of G, its direction (positive or negative) and duration, and the rate of onset and decline are all factors which determine tolerance levels. Tolerance to G also depends on individual factors. For example, one experiment found that the +G_Z required to produce blackout varied from +2.7 G_Z and +7.8 G_Z between individuals.[30] Obviously individual tolerance levels are important factors when considering resistance to G-induced stress. Not all the variables that affect G-tolerance have been precisely determined, but since many have it would be prudent to be aware of them. With regard to +G_Z (our primary concern) the following factors usually lower tolerance levels and decrease grayout, blackout, and G-LOC thresholds.

Increased Height

You can see in Figure 8-6 that the hydrostatic pressure in a column of blood is the least at a person's head and greatest at their feet. In fact, the hydrostatic pressure in conditions of +1 G decreases by about 1.9 mm Hg for each inch above the heart. Therefore, if the average person's heart-to-brain distance is 12 inches, the decrease in blood pressure from the heart to the brain will be about 22 mm Hg.[31] Taller-than-average pilots have a greater heart-to-brain distance than people of shorter stature, so their blood pressure (and oxygen partial pressure) at head-level in a +1 G_Z environment will be less and their cardiovascular compensatory response that occurs after +G_Z is applied will be less effective. This in turn will lower the +G_Z level required to produce visual symptoms and G-LOC.

Altitude Hypoxia

Most of the visual symptoms and G-LOC caused by excessive +G_Z are the result of diminished oxygen delivery to the eyes and brain. If you are already hypoxic (or slightly hypoxic) from flying at a high altitude in an unpressurized cabin, the threshold for experiencing the negative effects of +G_Z will lower considerably.

Body Factors

Anything that interferes with the body's circulatory system (and hence its delivery of oxygen to the tissues) will reduce +G_Z tolerance and lower +G_Z levels required to experience symptoms. For example, low blood pressure, generally a good sign when it comes to reducing the chance of experiencing heart disease, will lower your +G_Z tolerance. So too will any blood-related factors that reduce altitude thresholds for experiencing hypoxia such as anemia, hypoglycemia (low blood sugar), medication, alcohol, drugs, and the presence of carbon monoxide (e.g., from smoking).

Other factors that increase susceptibility to hypoxia will also reduce +G_Z tolerance. For example, colds, influenza, and other illnesses require increased amounts of oxygen for the body to fight them. A physically unfit person also has a lower lung capacity, lower blood oxygen content, and a less effective circulatory system than one who is physically fit. Research has shown that anaerobic conditioning (weight training) can improve +G_Z tolerance. On the other hand, aerobic training has not been found to improve +G_Z tolerance but has also not been found to decrease it either. High levels of aerobic training (e.g., marathon training) have not been experimentally tested for G-effects but caution may be merited concerning tolerance limits.

Fatigue

In addition to impaired blood circulation and elements that contribute to hypoxia, other fatigue-inducing factors reduce a person's tolerance to +G_Z. For example, poor eating habits and poor nutrition, including missing meals (hypoglycemia), lower your tolerance. Dehydration lowers blood plasma volume reducing the efficiency of your blood to transport oxygen. The NTSB noted that the lack of food and water, along with fatigue, contributed to the accident mentioned in the introduction to this chapter involving the pilot who survived the crash of his Extra EA-300 after experiencing G-LOC. Besides its effects on cognitive performance, a hangover from alcohol consumption also reduces G-tolerance, primarily from its contribution to dehydration, but also from hypoglycemia.[32]

Environmental conditions, such as excessive noise and vibration and extreme temperatures, contribute to fatigue that can also lower the thresholds at which +G_Z symptoms manifest themselves. For example, an Australian Army Sikorsky Blackhawk helicopter pilot experienced tunnel vision (grayout) in both eyes after pulling only about +2.5 G_Z during a steep turn during a low-level tactical maneuver at about 200 feet AGL. The symptoms disappeared a few seconds after he reduced the bank angle. The pilot later reported that he was dehydrated and fatigued, and investigators also concluded that extreme cabin temperature and humidity also played a role. In addition to the heat-producing military gear the pilot was wearing (e.g., flame-retardant flight suit, gloves, survival vest) the outside air temperature was 35°C (95°F) and the estimated cabin temperature was 42°C (108°F).[33]

Of course, lack of sleep is another major cause of fatigue that can also reduce +G_Z tolerance. The negative effects of fatigue on overall flight performance are explored in greater depth in Chapter 10.

Inexperience With +G_Z

There is evidence that lack of experience, and lack of recent exposure to +G_Z, reduces tolerance levels lowering grayout, blackout, and G-LOC thresholds.

Certainly, if any one of these factors are present a person's individual tolerance will be affected. Also, even if deviations from the ideal physiological and environmental conditions are minimal, the cumulative effects of many variables working together can significantly affect one's response to G-accelerations.

Negative G_Z Followed by Positive G_Z

Another situation that has been shown to reduce $+G_Z$ tolerance, making you more susceptible to the adverse effects of positive acceleration, is pulling significant levels of $+G_Z$ immediately after pulling $-G_Z$. The body's physiological response to $-G_Z$ is to pump blood back down from the head region to the lower extremities. However, this is the exact opposite of what you need when exposed to $+G_Z$, where blood is pooling in the lower extremities and needs to be pumped back up to your head. Your tolerance to $+G_Z$ (during a pull-out from a dive) immediately after exposure to $-G_Z$ (rapid nose over to a dive) will be significantly reduced because of this.

Avoiding G-Induced Incapacitation

If you are an aerobatic pilot or an air-to-air combat pilot, or aspiring to be either, knowledge of how acceleration forces affect your physical and mental performance, and hence flight safety, is crucial. If you are a GA pilot or a professional commercial pilot you may have only experienced occasional minor accelerations greater than normal gravity, so you may think that this chapter is really not applicable to you. However, as we mentioned in the introduction, an understanding of human response to acceleration is important for all pilots since it is possible you may inadvertently experience an unusual aircraft attitude that could require significant levels of G-force during recovery from it.

G Avoidance

Fortunately for most professional pilots, the very nature of passenger transport precludes encountering significant levels of G. Passenger comfort and flight safety dictate the necessity of both flying smoothly and avoiding extreme flight attitudes which could involve adverse G. Also, for most aircraft, avoidance of the manufacturer's G limits (published in the AFM) will normally protect you from experiencing G symptoms. However, if for whatever reason you end up in an unusual attitude—in other words you fail in your primary duty to fly the aircraft (aviate, before navigate and communicate), you fail to monitor instruments, you allow airframe ice to build up to levels that could contribute to aircraft loss of control, etc.—you must make sure to carry out the proper recovery procedure,

including avoiding excessive G-loads that can damage the airframe or physiologically incapacitate you.

Get Training

If you want to become an aerobatic pilot, do it right and get the proper training. Take lessons from an experienced aerobatic pilot in a properly certified airplane. The more you practice, the better you will become at executing acrobatic maneuvers and the more you will understand how your body reacts to the G-forces involved in them. Military fighter pilots receive vertical G-training in a centrifuge. This helps them not only recognize their G-tolerance thresholds, but also aids them in practicing an anti-G straining maneuver.

Anti-G Straining Maneuver

The **anti-G straining maneuver (AGSM)** is a technique used by pilots to physically increase the level of $+G_Z$ that they can withstand before experiencing G-symptoms. Sometimes called *grunt breathing*, the AGSM involves muscle tensing and cyclic breathing. Deliberately contracting the muscles in the arms, legs, buttocks, and abdomen constricts the blood vessels in the lower body reducing the amount of blood that pools in the lower extremities. Cyclic breathing involves forceful breathing at regular intervals against either a closed glottis (L-1 maneuver, named after Dr. Sidney Leverett) or a partially closed glottis (M-1 maneuver, named after the Mayo Clinic). This in turn increases chest pressure creating an artificial pumping action that raises blood pressure to the head. Combined breathing and muscle tensing can raise $+G_Z$ tolerance by as much as $+4$ G_Z.[34]

Recognize Signs of Excessive $+G_Z$

If G-onset is fast and $+G_Z$ is high while deliberately performing aerobatic maneuvers, your first symptom of excessive $+G_Z$ could easily be G-LOC (line B in Figure 8-7), a very undesirable situation indeed. If $+G_Z$ onset is relatively low, it is very likely you will experience visual symptoms of grayout and blackout before you experience G-LOC. Therefore, should you experience any visual symptoms while pulling $+G_Z$, you should ease off on the G-load to help you to avoid G-LOC (line D in Figure 8-7). You can also expect lower tolerance if you haven't conducted aerobatics for a while. Therefore, you should begin with simpler and less challenging maneuvers until you are acclimated to the G environment again.

Anti-G Pressure Suits

Introduced during WWII and used by military fighter pilots and some civilian aerobatic pilots today, anti-G suits consist of inflatable air bladders that fit over the legs and lower abdomen. When G-forces exceed +1 G_Z a pressure G-valve inflates the bladders in proportion to the magnitude of the positive vertical G. Somewhat analogous to squeezing a tube of toothpaste from the bottom, these suits squeeze the lower body creating an upward internal pressure that counteracts the effects of the downward blood flow. A gain of up to +2 G_Z tolerance can be attained using an anti-G suit.[35]

Positive Pressure Breathing

Enhancing the effectiveness of an AGSM and the use of an anti-G suit is positive pressure breathing. The practice of pressure breathing at high altitudes was introduced in Chapter 4. These oxygen systems deliver 100 percent oxygen to a tightly sealed mask under high pressure, which, in effect, pressurizes the lungs and increases the partial pressure of oxygen. This has also been used by the military, usually in combination with other countermeasures, to assist in raising eye-level blood pressure and oxygen flow in conditions of high +G_Z. Using these combinations has the added benefit of reducing fatigue, increasing +G_Z tolerance, and lengthening endurance times in a high-G flight regime.[36]

Seat Configuration

As was noted earlier, because of the greater heart-to-eye distance than others, taller-than-average individuals experience reduced +G_Z tolerance even at +1 G_Z. This is explained by the laws of hydrostatic equilibrium discovered more than three-and-a-half centuries ago by French mathematician, scientist, and theologian Blaise Pascal. One aspect of Pascal's Law states that pressure in a static fluid increases with depth; hence the reduced blood pressure at eye-brain-level when a person is upright. Figure 8-6 illustrates that, as positive vertical Gs are increased,

blood pressure (and oxygen partial pressure) above the heart decreases until it reaches 0 mm Hg at the brain at approximately +5 G_Z. However, another aspect of Pascal's Law states that static fluid pressure is the same in the horizontal, so if a person is lying down there is no loss in blood pressure to the brain. In other words, the blood pressure at brain- and heart-levels (and feet) are the same since there is no vertical distance between them.

Even though it is impractical for pilots to fly an aircraft while lying down in a fully supine position, seats in some fighter and aerobatic aircraft have been designed to take advantage of Pascal's Law. The greater the seat tilt-back angle, the shorter the vertical eye-heart distance. For example, using the cosine of the seat angle, a seat tilt of 30 degrees will decrease the eye-to-heart distance by about 15 percent, and a 45-degree tilt will decrease it by about 30 percent. The USAF F-16 employs seats that are tilted at approximately at 30 degrees. This raises predicted blackout and G-LOC thresholds by approximately +0.7 G_Z and +0.8 G_Z, respectively. If seats could be tilted back to 60 degrees, thresholds double, increasing predicted blackout thresholds from +4.3 G_Z to +8.6 G_Z, and predicted G-LOC thresholds from +5.1 G_Z to +10.3 G_Z.[37]

As discovered in this chapter, the application of significant positive vertical G_Z on the human body primarily involves diminished vision, G-LOC, and cognitive deficits associated with A-LOC or post-G-LOC recovery. However, even small increases in vertical (G_Z) or transverse (G_X) acceleration can produce other physiological effects that have not been addressed in this chapter. Though these contribute to a relatively small proportion of accidents, G-induced illusions are often deadly. These will be discussed in the overall topic of spatial disorientation in the next chapter.

Helpful Resources

Watch a short video of the automatic ground collision avoidance system (Auto-GCAS) saving an F-16 (discussed in this chapter's introduction) from LOC-I after the pilot experienced G-LOC. (www.nasa.gov/centers/armstrong/features/auto-gcas_performs_fourth_confirmed_save.html)

Acceleration in Aviation is 23-minute FAA CAMI video in English or Spanish that illustrates various aspects of the G environment and G-induced incapacitation. There are some nice fighter jet shots, too! (www.faa.gov/pilots/training/airman_education/physiologyvideos/)

The FAA also has two helpful publications regarding addressing this topic:

- *A Hazard in Aerobatics: Effects of G-Forces on Pilots* (FAA AC 91-61). This advisory circular provides physiological information for pilots who desire to engage in aerobatic flying. (www.faa.gov/regulations_policies/advisory_circulars/index.cfm/go/document.information/documentID/22429)
- *Acceleration in Aviation: G-Force* (AM-400-09/4). This brochure provides a concise summary of the physiological effects of positive and negative vertical accelerations. (www.faa.gov/pilots/safety/pilotsafetybrochures/)

Endnotes

1. Matt Kamlet, *NASA-Supported Collision Avoidance System Saves Unconscious F-16 Pilot In Fourth Confirmed Rescue* (NASA Armstrong Flight Research Center, September 20, 2016). Available at www.nasa.gov/centers/armstrong/features/auto-gcas_performs_fourth_confirmed_save.html.

2. Federal Aviation Administration, *A Hazard in Aerobatics: Effects of G-Forces on Pilots*, AC 91-61 (Washington, DC: February 28, 1984).

3. Carl C. Clark, James D. Hardy and Richard J. Crosbie, "A Proposed Physiological Acceleration Terminology with An Historical Review," *Human Acceleration Studies*, Pub. 913, Panel on Acceleration Stress (Washington, DC: National Academy of Sciences, National Research Council, 1961): 7–65.

4. Russell R. Burton, "G-Induced Loss of Consciousness: Definition, History, Current Status," *Aviation, Space, and Environmental Medicine* 59 (January 1988): 2–5.

5. J.H. Doolittle, *Accelerations in Flight*, Report No. 203 (Cambridge, MA: Massachusetts Institute of Technology, 1925): 381.

6. FAA, *A Hazard in Aerobatics: Effects of G-Forces on Pilots.*

7. Burton, "G-Induced Loss of Consciousness: Definition, History, Current Status."

8. Mark Wolverton, "The G Machine: Riding an Atlas Into Space Was a Piece of Cake Compared to Pulling 32 Gs on the Johnsville Centrifuge," *Air & Space Magazine* (May 2007). Available at www.airspacemag.com/history-of-flight/the-g-machine-16799374/.

9. Lloyd D. Tripp, Joel S. Warm, Gerald Matthews, Peter Y. Chiu and R. Bruce Bracken, "On Tracking the Course of Cerebral Oxygen Saturation and Pilot Performance During Gravity-Induced Loss of Consciousness," *Human Factors* 51 (December 2009): 775–784.

10. North Atlantic Treaty Organization AMP Working Group No. 14, Advisory Group for Aerospace Research & Development (AGARD), *High G Physiological Protection Training*, AGARDograph No. 322 (Neuilly-sur-Seine, France: December 1990).

11. Caroline A. Rickards and David G. Newman, "G-induced Visual and Cognitive Disturbances in a Survey of 65 Operational Fighter Pilots," *Aviation, Space, and Environmental Medicine* 76 (May 2005): 496–500.

12. Salvadore A. Rositano, *Objective Measurement of Human Tolerance to $+G_Z$ Acceleration Stress*, NASA Technical Memorandum 81166 (Moffett Field, CA: NASA Ames Research Center: February 1980).

13. Data from Salvadore A. Rositano, *Objective Measurement of Human Tolerance to $+G_Z$ Acceleration Stress*, NASA Technical memorandum 81166 (Moffett Field, CA: NASA Ames Research Center: February 1980).

14. Naval Aerospace Medical Institute, *U.S. Naval Flight Surgeon's Manual*, 3rd ed. (Washington, DC: Department of the Navy, 1991).

15. James E. Whinnery, "Converging Research on $+G_Z$-Induced Loss of Consciousness," *Aviation. Space, and Environmental Medicine* 59 (January 1988). 9–11.

16. Estrella M. Forster, *A Database to Evaluate Acceleration $(+G_Z)$ Induced Loss of Consciousness (G-LOC) in the Human Centrifuge*, Final Report, No. NAWCADWAR-93089-60 (Naval Air Warfare Center, Warminster, PA: June 20, 1993).

17. Estrella M. Forster and James E. Whinnery, "Recovery from G_Z-Induced Loss of Consciousness: Psychophysiologic Considerations," *Aviation, Space, and Environmental Medicine* 59 (June 1988): 517–522.

18. Ryan W. Maresh, Andrew D. Woodrow and James T. Webb, *Handbook of Aerospace and Operational Physiology*, 2nd ed. (Wright-Patterson AFB, OH: U.S. Air Force School of Aerospace Medicine, October 2016).

19. Forster, *A Database to Evaluate Acceleration (+G$_Z$) Induced Loss of Consciousness (G-LOC) in the Human Centrifuge.*

20. Ibid.

21. James O. Houghton, Dennis K. McBride and Ken Hannah, *Performance and Physiological Effects of Acceleration Induced (+G$_Z$) Loss of Consciousness*, Final Report, No. NADC-86130-60 (Naval Air Development Center, Warminster, PA: October 1986).

22. Barry S. Shender, Estrella M. Forster, Leonid Hrebien, Han Chool Ryoo and Joseph P. Cammarota Jr., "Acceleration-Induced Near-Loss of Consciousness: The 'A-LOC' Syndrome," *Aviation, Space, and Environmental Medicine* 74 (October 2003): 1021-1028.

23. Alice M. Stoll, "Human Tolerance to Positive G as Determined by the Physiological End Points," *Journal of Aviation Medicine* 27 (August 1956): 356–367.

24. Robert D. Banks, James W. Brinkley, Richard Allnutt and Richard M. Harding, "Human Response to Acceleration," Chapter 4, in *Fundamentals of Aerospace Medicine* (4th ed.), eds. Jeffrey R. Davis, Robert Johnson, Jan Stepanek and Jennifer A. Fogarty (Philadelphia, PA: Lippincott Williams & Wilkins, 2008).

25. Naval Aerospace Medical Institute, *U.S. Naval Flight Surgeon's Manual.*

26. United States Department of the Army, Aeromedical Training for Flight Personnel, TC No. 3-04.93 (Washington, DC: August 31, 2009).

27. Maresh, Woodrow and Webb, *Handbook of Aerospace and Operational Physiology.*

28. U.S. Department of the Army, *Aeromedical Training for Flight Personnel.*

29. Maresh, Woodrow and Webb, *Handbook of Aerospace and Operational Physiology.*

30. D.H. Glaister, "The Effects of Long Duration Acceleration," *Aviation Medicine*, 2nd ed., eds. John Ernsting and Peter King (London: Butterworths, 1988): 139–158.

31. Naval Aerospace Medical Institute, *U.S. Naval Flight Surgeon's Manual.*

32. Naval Air Training Command, *Joint Aerospace Physiology Student Guide*, CNATRA P-204, Rev. 03-02 (Corpus Christi, TX: March 2002).

33. Terry W. McMahon and David G. Newman, "G-Induced Visual Symptoms in a Military Helicopter Pilot," *Military Medicine* 181 (November/December 2016): 1696–1699.

34. Naval Aerospace Medical Institute, *U.S. Naval Flight Surgeon's Manual.*

35. D.H. Glaister, "Protection Against Long Duration Acceleration," *Aviation Medicine*, 2nd ed., eds. John Ernsting and Peter King (London: Butterworths, 1988): 159–165.

36. Ulf I. Balldin, "Acceleration Effects on Fighter Pilots," Chapter 33, *Medical Aspects of Harsh Environments, Volume 2*, eds. Kent B. Pandolf and Robert E. Burr (Washington, DC: Walter Reed Army Medical Center, Borden Institute, 2002): 1014–1027.

37. Maresh, Woodrow and Webb, *Handbook of Aerospace and Operational Physiology.*

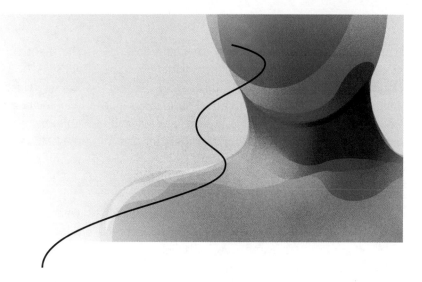

9

Which way is up?

Spatial Disorientation

It was a hot and humid dark August night, but the weather was CAVOK (Ceiling and Visibility OK)[1] and the pilots had no problem seeing the airport. They were conducting a VOR/DME approach for Runway 12 at Bahrain International Airport, but they got behind the airplane and failed to achieve a stabilized approach—the aircraft was 87 knots too fast at the final approach fix, and 62 knots too fast at 500 feet above the ground and 1.7 miles from the runway. The Airbus A320 climbed and circled for another try at the approach but it overshot the extended runway centerline on final. A second go-around was initiated and the controller instructed the crew to climb to 2,500 feet and fly a heading of 300 degrees for vectors for another approach. The crew used maximum TO/GA (takeoff/go-around) thrust, but only pitched the nose up to about 9 degrees instead of the 15 degrees required by the standard operating procedures. After raising the landing gear and gradually retracting the flaps, the flap overspeed aural warning annunciated indicating the airspeed was too fast for the amount of flaps left extended.

Then, according to the flight data recorder, something totally unexpected occurred: climbing through about 1,000 feet, the captain of Gulf Air Flight 072 pushed his side stick control forward for 11 seconds during which time the airplane's pitch angle changed from +5 degrees nose-up to –15 degrees nose-down (the maximum pitch-down angle allowed by the A320 flight control system). The airspeed accelerated from 193 knots to 234 knots and the vertical acceleration went from +1 G to +0.5 G. In spite of repetitive ground proximity warning system (GPWS) aural warnings— "whoop whoop, pull up"—right until the moment

of impact, the airplane continued to accelerate and descend, crashing into the shallow sea just three miles northeast of the airport, killing all 143 people aboard.[2]

Accident investigators concluded the captain experienced spatial disorientation which led to the devastating crash. In spite of good visibility and clear weather, and despite the fact that the flight deck instruments worked properly, the rapid acceleration during the go-around conducted in dark-night conditions—there were no lights over the water, no lights visible on the horizon through the haze, and the moon had not yet risen in the sky—created a strong sensation that the aircraft was pitching up and the captain erroneously responded by pitching the nose down. This further increased the acceleration and only strengthened the *somatogravic illusion*, more commonly known as the **false climb illusion**. In fact, the parameters of this accident were studied by the U.S. Naval Aerospace Medical Research Laboratory, in Pensacola, Florida. They concluded that when the captain began his 11-second nose-down push on the side stick he likely experienced a 12 degree pitch-up sensation.[3]

Spatial disorientation (SD) is an incorrect perception of your orientation with respect to the position of your aircraft in space. Specifically, it is an inaccurate perception of the aircraft's attitude, direction or motion as a result of faulty or inadequate information provided by your senses—or as FAA AC 60-4, *Pilot's Spatial Disorientation*, puts it, it is "the inability to tell which way is up." This phenomenon usually occurs in the absence of adequate outside visual references while flying in cloud, in poor visibility or, as in the case of the accident in Bahrain, in the dark. Without sufficient input from our visual system, our brain relies more heavily on our vestibular organs and postural sensations to discern our orientation and motion. Unfortunately, when relied upon alone, these sensations can lead to a false perception of the aircraft's position in space.

According to the ATC radar tapes, a Piper PA-32R descended to 2,200 feet while in a right turn, then climbed to 2,600 feet and entered a left turn. It then entered another descending right turn and the airspeed, descent rate, and turn rate rapidly increased. Descending at more than 4,700 fpm, with the airspeed exceeding redline (V_{NE}; never exceed speed), the airplane struck the water seven miles off the coast of Martha's Vineyard in Massachusetts, killing all three of its occupants—John F. Kennedy Jr., his wife, Carolyn, and her sister, Lauren Bessette. The weather was VMC on that warm July evening, but it was dark, hazy, and the pilot—Kennedy—elected to fly his Saratoga on a 30-mile direct route over open water, making it difficult for him to see a horizon that had imperceptibly blended in with the ocean. Though conspiracy theorists speculate otherwise, the NTSB determined the probable cause of this tragic accident was "the pilot's failure to maintain control of the airplane during a descent over water at night, which was a result of spatial disorientation" (NTSB Identification No: NYC99MA178).

Though inexperienced pilots are particularly vulnerable to SD—Kennedy had slightly more than 300 hours—this phenomenon can afflict experienced pilots as well. An airline transport captain and commercial FO fell victim to SD while flying in IMC, causing their Learjet to impact terrain after departing Ithaca Tompkins Regional Airport in Ithaca, New York. Both pilots died in the crash. According to the NTSB, the crew failed to maintain a proper climb rate, which was the result of SD (NTSB Identification No: NYC01FA214). During a flight in IMC at night (NIMC), the experienced crew of Air Transport International Flight 805, a scheduled air cargo flight, completely lost control of a McDonnell Douglas DC-8 due to SD while conducting a missed approach at the Toledo Express Airport in Swanton, Ohio. All four people aboard were killed. The captain had more than 16,000 hours, the FO more than 5,000 hours, and the flight engineer almost 22,000 hours (Report No: NTSB-AAR-92-05). Finally, SD was a major cause of Russia's third-worst aircraft accident to date. All 145 people aboard Vladivostokavia Flight 352 died when an experienced flight crew, conducting an approach in NIMC, allowed their Tupolev Tu-154 passenger jet to enter a stall and flat spin near Irkutsk, Russia.[4]

Though SD is not usually a major cause of U.S. and Canadian airline accidents, it's still a problem elsewhere. During the first decade of this century alone, almost 1,000 people lost their lives in airline accidents involving SD.[5] Data gathered by Boeing indicate that loss of control in flight (LOC-I)—often caused by SD, claiming more than 1,300 lives between 2007 and 2016 alone—is now the leading category of fatal worldwide accidents involving Western-built commercial turbojet aircraft weighing more than 60,000 pounds maximum certificated takeoff weight.[6] Military operations are also not immune. For example, SD was involved in 20 percent of U.S. Air Force fatal accidents between 1991 and 2000, and accounted for 11 percent of all accidents between 1990 and 2004, with 69 percent of these involving fatalities.[7, 8]

Even though SD accidents still occur in commercial flight operations, it has taken its greatest toll in the GA sector. For example, it was a cause or causal factor in 16 percent of fatal U.S. GA accidents between 1970 and 1975 and was responsible for 2,355 deaths over a 17-year period between 1976 and 1992.[9, 10] More than 70 percent of the latter occurred in IMC, half of them occurred at night and slightly more than half involved pilots with fewer than 500 hours of flight experience. The AOPA Air Safety Institute also found that attempted VFR flight into IMC is the number one cause of fatal GA spatial disorientation accidents in the United States.[11] Though the accident rate has gradually improved—likely the result of better education and technology—SD is still responsible for 5 to 10 percent of all GA accidents in the United States.[12]

What makes SD accidents particularly threatening is that they are almost always fatal. In fact, according to FAA statistics, more than 90 percent of GA spatial disorientation accidents result in fatalities.[13] That's because pilots who experience SD and lack the necessary instrument flying skills to safely pilot their aircraft without outside visual references either lose control of their aircraft and fly uncontrolled into terrain, or experience in-flight breakup by exceeding the design stress limits of their aircraft while attempting to recover from an unusual attitude. Unfortunately, this was the case for the airline transport pilot (ATP) and his passenger in a Cessna 525 Citation in a 2016 accident near Cedar Fort, Utah. Radar data indicate that during the 10 minutes after departure from Salt Lake City International Airport, the business jet conducted a series of climbs and descents with large variations in airspeed. It reached an altitude of 21,000 feet before it began a rapidly descending and tightening turn. Rolling into a partially inverted attitude the airplane reached a peak descent rate of 36,000 fpm and subsequently broke up in flight. The NTSB concluded the accident was caused by the "pilot's loss of control due to spatial disorientation while operating in instrument meteorological conditions, which resulted in an exceedance of the airplane's design stress limitations, and a subsequent in-flight breakup" (NTSB Identification No: WPR16FA054).

A study conducted by the Institute of Aviation at the University of Illinois back in the 1950s confirmed how pilots with minimal instrument flying skills can lose control of their aircraft when flying in IMC. Twenty VFR pilots, who represented a wide range of ages and flying experience but who lacked any simulated or actual instrument flight experience, flew into simulated IMC in a Beechcraft Bonanza with a qualified instructor on board. While one pilot lasted eight minutes before losing control, all of them eventually allowed the airplane they were flying to enter a dangerous flight attitude—most often a spiral dive (the graveyard spiral is discussed later in this chapter)—within an average of 178 seconds.[14]

A more recent Australian Transport Safety Bureau (ATSB) study concluded the probability of a pilot experiencing at least one episode of SD during his or her flying career was 90 to 100 percent. You've probably heard the old adage that goes, *"There are two types of pilots—those who've landed with the gear up, and those who will."* The ATSB study concluded, *"There are those who've experienced SD and those who will."*[15] Whether you are an experienced commercial pilot or just beginning to spread your wings, if that conclusion is correct, it's crucial that you understand the nature of SD, how to avoid it and, just as importantly, how to effectively overcome it should you experience it.

What Is Spatial Disorientation Anyway?

The three primary sensory systems that provide the information you need to correctly orient yourself in space are the visual, vestibular, and somatosensory systems (*see* Figure 9-1). To a lesser degree, the auditory sense is also helpful for determining our orientation in space. When you are spatially disoriented you may experience illusions corresponding to one or more of these three major systems in the form of visual illusions, **vestibular illusions**, or **somatosensory illusions**. Visual illusions are thoroughly discussed in Chapter 12; in this chapter we explore the major vestibular and somatosensory illusions resulting from SD.

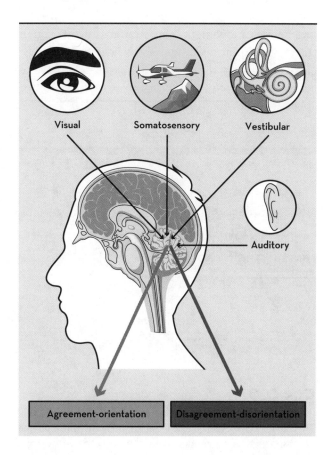

Fig 9-1.

The major sensory systems that help us to determine our orientation in space.

The study of SD began more than a century ago when the Austrian physicist Ernst Mach discovered that self-motion could be perceived not only visually but also through the vestibular organs located in the inner ear. Figures 5-4 and 7-1 in Chapters 5 and 7 show the **vestibular apparatus**, located in the bony labyrinth of the non-auditory portion of the inner ear. This organ consists of three semicircular fluid-filled canals that respond to angular acceleration and the otolith bodies (*saccule* and *utricle*) that respond to linear acceleration. The semicircular canals are arranged approximately at right angles to each other and closely correspond to the three flight axes of pitch, yaw and roll. A slight bulge in each canal (the ampulla) contains receptor hairs that protrude upward into the gelatinous *cupula* that occupies the diameter of the canal (*see* Figure 9-2). Since the fluid (endolymph) has inertia and resists movement, the cupula flows through the fluid with acceleration of the head or body (i.e., canals) in any of the three axes. The bending of the hairs in the cupula triggers the receptor cells, which in turn communicate to the brain that acceleration in a particular plane is occurring.

The same principle of inertia applies to the otolith organs of the saccule and utricle located just below the semicircular canals (*see* Figure 9-3); however, a different structure is at work. A dense, flat, plate-like membrane containing small calcium carbonate crystals overlies an array of tiny sensory hairs that, when deflected by head tilt or forward acceleration or deceleration, activate the sense receptors that lie underneath them.

Figure 9-4 indicates that the movement of the otolith membrane, and the sensory hairs below it, is the same when the head is tilted backward or when it is upright during forward linear acceleration. (It moves in the opposite direction when the head is either tilted forward or is upright during rearward linear deceleration.)

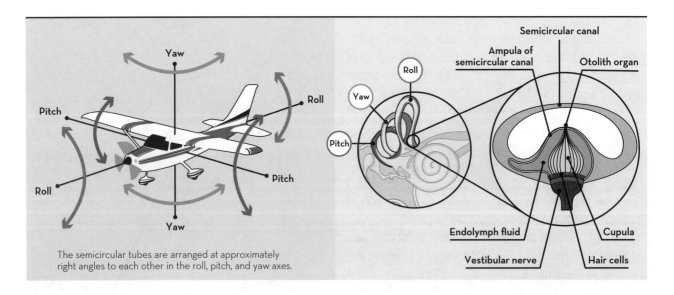

The semicircular tubes are arranged at approximately right angles to each other in the roll, pitch, and yaw axes.

Fig 9-2.

The semicircular canals in the inner ear lie in the three planes of rotation and sense motion about the roll, pitch, and yaw axes of the aircraft.

It's important to understand that these organs of balance can only detect angular and linear *acceleration*. For example, Figure 9-5 illustrates that once the angular acceleration stops and a steady state is maintained, the speed of the fluid in the semicircular canals catches up to the speed of the canal walls and the tiny hairs are no longer deflected. Once

established for about 15 to 20 seconds in a prolonged turn, therefore, a pilot will eventually "feel" that he or she is flying straight and level. This is the same phenomenon you will experience if someone were to spin you on a piano stool with your eyes closed. At first you would sense that you were turning, but after 15 to 20 seconds of a constant rotational

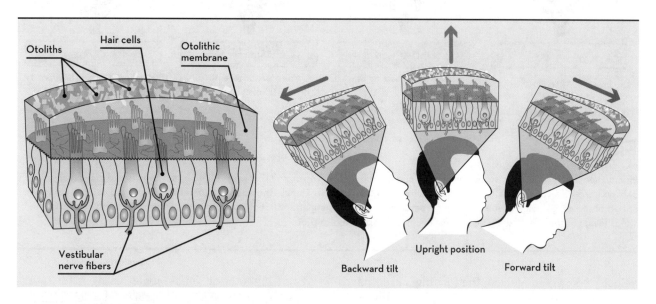

Fig 9-3.

Above—The weight of the crystals in the membrane move tiny sensory hairs in the saccule and utricle (otolith organs) in response to head tilt or linear acceleration and deceleration.

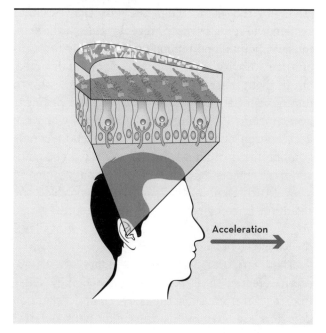

Fig 9-4.

The sensation of backward (nose-up) head tilt also occurs with the head erect during forward linear acceleration such as during takeoff or a go-around.

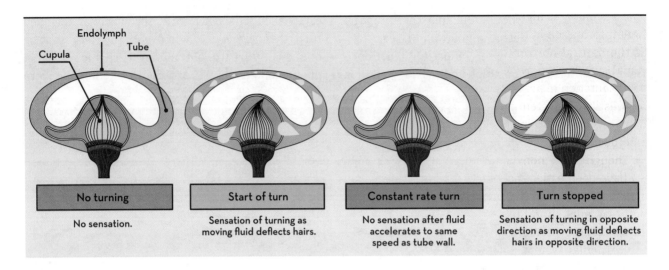

Endolymph
Tube
Cupula

No turning	Start of turn	Constant rate turn	Turn stopped
No sensation.	Sensation of turning as moving fluid deflects hairs.	No sensation after fluid accelerates to same speed as tube wall.	Sensation of turning in opposite direction as moving fluid deflects hairs in opposite direction.

Fig 9-5.

Human sensation of angular acceleration. The cupula deflects when you roll the aircraft into a bank angle and it is usually sensed correctly. However, after a prolonged turn at a constant bank angle the speed of the endolymph fluid catches up to the speed of the canal wall and you no longer "feel" like you are turning and will feel like the wings are level. When you return the wings level you will "feel" that you are turning in the opposite direction.

velocity you would feel like the turning had stopped. A piano stool is somewhat like a **Barany chair**, named after an early researcher into the vestibular system who used it to demonstrate to blindfolded subjects a variety of disorientation scenarios. Aerospace physiologists still use Barany chair's today to demonstrate several vestibular illusions.

Figure 9-5 also shows that once motion in the plane of rotation (e.g., a turn) is stopped, the fluid, which is still moving due to inertia, will initially deflect the upright cupula in the opposite direction giving the pilot a sensation of turning in the opposite direction. The same sensations occur to you in a Barany chair while blindfolded after rotating at a constant rate for about a half minute; if someone stopped the chair from turning, you would feel that you had begun to turn in the opposite direction. It is the same with the otolith bodies; the membranes return to their upright position once acceleration stops and a steady forward speed is maintained, but once you reduce the forward speed the membranes move in the opposite direction giving you the sensation of deceleration. As a result, we sense linear acceleration and deceleration, but not steady-state motion.

The third major way in which you perceive orientation in space is through the **somatosensory system**. Sometimes referred to as the propriocep-

tive or kinesthetic sense, when using it for orientation in flight it is commonly known by pilots as "flying by the seat of the pants." Like the vestibular system, the somatosensory receptor cells of the skin, muscles, joints, and tendons respond only to accelerations. Gravity is the major acceleration detected, but in flight these postural sensations are unable to distinguish between gravity and angular or linear accelerations (or G-forces). For example, when the acceleration detectors in the semicircular canals equilibrate in a prolonged level turn, only the somatosensory sense is detected. The centrifugal force in a level turn combines with gravity to produce one resultant force; depending on how steep the bank, you will perceive that you are now in a wings-level *climb* in straight flight.

The vestibular and somatosensory senses are often referred to as *body senses* since they sense information from *within* the body. Their acceleration detectors are often quite accurate for normal earth-bound activities that usually involve a series of accelerations and decelerations. Also, while maintaining a constant velocity in an automobile or aircraft, our visual system is dominant and overrides the limited inputs provided to the brain from these two major body senses, giving us an accurate perception of our speed and movement. However, when flying in poor visibility, at night or in cloud, there is insufficient information in the external environment (such as the natural horizon or terrain features) for our visual system to provide an accurate perception of our orientation in space. It is in these situations that our vestibular system and seat-of-the-pants sensations can create SD in the form of false perceptions and illusions.

Though many nonvisual illusions resulting from SD have been experienced by pilots, only the major ones will be discussed here. Some illusions involve both systems simultaneously, while most involve either the semicircular canals or the otolith bodies of the vestibular system. Some illusions—mostly those involving the otolith organs—also involve sensations provided by the somatosensory system.

Somatogyral Illusions

Though the otolith bodies are also involved in some of these, illusions involving primarily the semicircular canals are often referred to as **somatogyral illusions** (*soma* = body; *gyral* = circle). These generally include the leans, graveyard spin, graveyard spiral, and the Coriolis illusion.

The Leans

One of the most common vestibular illusions is known as the **leans**. In fact, a USAF survey of 2,582 pilots, representing experience in 34 different aircraft types, revealed that 76 percent experienced the leans at one time or another while flying their current aircraft type.[16] Since the hairs in the cupula are unable to sense rolling motion below a threshold of about two degrees per second, an inadvertent rolling movement below this threshold will go unnoticed. When you eventually detect this motion with your eyes through input provided by the flight instruments, you will likely correct for the resultant bank angle by rolling the wings level at a roll rate that is above the two-degree detection threshold. This will now deflect the cupula in the semicircular canals, giving a strong sensation of rolling into a turn in the *opposite* direction.

This is possibly what the captain of a Kenya Airways Boeing B-737 experienced shortly after takeoff from Douala International Airport in Cameroon just after midnight on May 5, 2007. All 114 people aboard Flight 507 perished after the B-737

crashed into a swamp in a steep bank and pitch angle only a few miles from the airport. Climbing through 1,000 feet the captain commanded the FO to engage the autopilot; however, there is no evidence it ever was. Left on its own, the aircraft began a very slow roll to the right which was not perceived or noticed by either crew member until the "bank angle" warning sounded 55 seconds later when the aircraft was in a 34 degree right climbing turn. The captain was startled when he took the controls and he initially moved the control column to the right. Realizing his mistake he then moved it to left but then rolled the airplane back 40 degrees to the right, then 11 degrees back to the left. Eventually the bank angle returned to a 50 degree right bank and continued rolling right to a bank angle that exceeded 90 degrees.[17] The post-accident investigation found the flight instruments were working properly, but because it was a dark night the crew had no outside references to gauge the airplane's attitude. The captain's maneuvers are indicative of the conflict described in the previous paragraph. Because the roll rate was less than 2 degrees per second, the slow roll was undetectable by the semicircular canals, and when the captain rolled the aircraft left (back towards wings-level) at a normal roll rate (above the detection threshold) the cupulae in the semicircular canals deflected creating a very strong sensation of entering a bank in the *opposite* direction. Feeling he was now turning left, he may have returned the airplane to a right bank angle to reconcile this sensation. The accident report concluded the aircraft crashed because the crew lost control as a result of "spatial disorientation...after a long slow roll...in the absence of external visual references in a dark night."[18]

Of course, not all pilots succumb to these sensations as the captain in Flight 507 did. If you recognize the conflict between these body sensations and the instrument indications, you can still use the instruments to level the wings. However, when you do, you might instinctively try to resolve it by *leaning* your body in the direction of the original bank. For example, when established in a left turn, the speed of the fluid in the semicircular canals eventually catches up to the speed of the canal walls and the cupula no longer deflects. You will therefore "feel" that you are flying straight and level (*see* Figure 9-6A). When you roll back to the right to level the wings (Figure 9-6B), the hairs in the cupula deflect from the neutral position giving you the sensation that you are rolling to the right, but also in a right bank—even after you have leveled the wings (Figure 9-6BC). This sensation will continue until the semicircular canals equilibrate; however, in an attempt to fight off this false-bank sensation until they do, you may find yourself leaning in the direction of the original turn to what you perceive is the gravitational vertical (Figure 9-6C).

I clearly remember my first experience with this illusion. It happened on my first instrument flight test with a Transport Canada inspector—which by the way was also the first time I ever flew in clouds (actual IMC)! While tuning the radio and listening to the automatic terminal information service, the Piper Warrior I was flying entered a slow roll (below the 2-degree-per-second threshold). After redirecting my gaze to the flight instruments, I realized I had entered a left turn but was dumbfounded as to why I hadn't "felt" this. After rolling the airplane back to a wings-level attitude (above the 2-degree roll threshold) I felt a strong sensation of turning to the right. Even though my flight instruments indicated I was flying straight and level, my body wanted to lean back to the left to reconcile these conflicting sensations. This happened two more times during the flight, and in case you're wondering, I did manage to overcome it and successfully pass my checkride.

Head Tilt Reflex

Research has discovered that the leans can also be caused or exacerbated during entry into a banked attitude and while established in a banked turn by our natural human tendency to align our head; not vertically with the aircraft's vertical (or *normal*) axis, but with the visible (or perceived) horizon. It is believed that this automatic unconscious reflexive response helps us maintain spatial orientation by keeping a stable visual image of the horizon on the retina.[19] In the case of a confusing visual horizon such as a sloping cloud layer or a false horizon, or when flying in and out of IMC while turning, this **optokinetic cervical reflex**—also known as *head tilt reflex*—conflicts with the actual alignment of both the aircraft and earth which in turn can contribute to or exacerbate the leans.

Graveyard Spin and Spiral

Since the semicircular canals only react to accelerations and not steady velocities, false sensations can be experienced during prolonged angular motions such as turns, spins, or spirals. After about 15 to 20 seconds of constant angular motion, the fluid in the semicircular canals catches up to the speed of the canal walls and the cupula returns to its neutral resting state, giving the sensation of zero motion or acceleration.

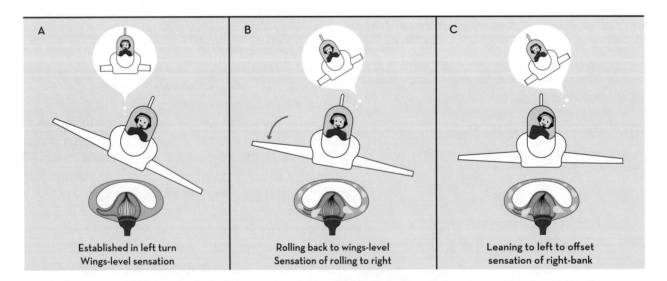

A	B	C
Established in left turn Wings-level sensation	Rolling back to wings-level Sensation of rolling to right	Leaning to left to offset sensation of right-bank

Fig 9-6.

After a prolonged coordinated turn to the left you "feel" the wings are level (A). While rolling the wings level, you correctly feel that you are rolling into a right turn (B). However, once level, you feel the right wing is still low (C) so, in an attempt to reconcile the conflicting sensations, you lean to the left to what you perceive is the gravitational vertical.

Two potentially deadly illusions, as their names suggest, are the **graveyard spin** and **graveyard spiral**. These illusions can cause you to make inappropriate control movements based on false information. For example, if for whatever reason you find yourself in a prolonged spin[20] without the benefit of outside visual references to determine your aircraft's attitude (at night or in IMC), after about 15 to 20 seconds you will stop perceiving the spinning sensation (*see* Figure 9-7). The fluid in the semicircular canals has caught up to the speed of the canal walls, the sensors in the cupula have returned to their resting state, and no motion is perceived. When you attempt to recover from the spin you will experience a strong sensation of spinning in the opposite direction, even though the flight instruments indicate otherwise. If you respond to these erroneous feelings and ignore the instruments, you may attempt to recover from this falsely perceived spin and inadvertently re-enter a spin in the original direction.

A similar situation more likely to occur is when equilibrium is attained during a prolonged spiral dive.[21] In the USAF survey cited previously in this chapter, 31.7 percent of the 2,582 pilots experienced the graveyard spiral while flying their current aircraft type.[22] When you level the wings to recover from a prolonged spiral you will experience a strong sensation of entering a turn in the opposite direction. If you make control corrections based on these sensations instead of the information provided to you by your flight instruments, you could re-enter the original spiral dive. This illusion is likely to be fatal if adequate outside visual references are not made available in time.

This appears to be what happened to the pilot of a Beechcraft King Air B200 while flying in IMC on a winter evening in Colorado. Carrying members of the Oklahoma State University (OSU) basketball team to Stillwater, Oklahoma, the aircraft experienced an electrical failure shortly after reaching cruising altitude. This rendered the pilot's side flight instruments unusable except for the airspeed and turn-and-slip indicator. Not long after the failure, the B200 entered a descending turn to the right that was, according to the NTSB, "consistent with a graveyard spiral resulting from pilot spatial disorientation." The horizontal stabilizer was aerodynamically overloaded due to the pilot's pull-up maneuver, which led to an in-flight breakup near Strasburg, Colorado. All 10 people on board were killed (Report No: NTSB/AAR-03/01).

Fig 9-7.

In a prolonged spin the semicircular canals reach equilibrium and you will no longer perceive the spinning sensation (2). When you recover from the spin to wings-level you will experience a strong sensation of spinning in the opposite direction (3), even though the flight instruments indicate otherwise. If you ignore the instruments and try to correct for these erroneous feelings you may inadvertently re-enter a spin in the original direction (4).

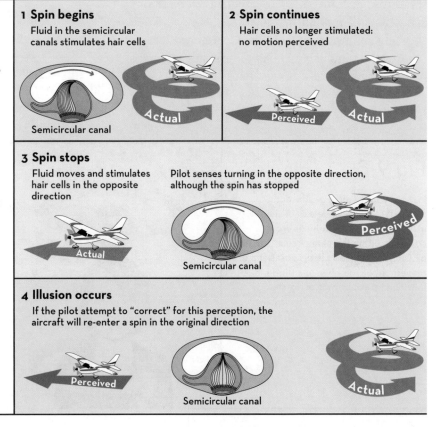

1 Spin begins
Fluid in the semicircular canals stimulates hair cells

Semicircular canal

Actual

2 Spin continues
Hair cells no longer stimulated: no motion perceived

Perceived   Actual

3 Spin stops
Fluid moves and stimulates hair cells in the opposite direction

Actual

Pilot senses turning in the opposite direction, although the spin has stopped

Semicircular canal

Perceived

4 Illusion occurs
If the pilot attempt to "correct" for this perception, the aircraft will re-enter a spin in the original direction

Perceived

Semicircular canal

Actual

The NTSB also concluded that the graveyard spiral was the likely cause of a 2015 fatal accident in East Patchogue, New York. The non-instrument-rated pilot encountered IMC and subsequently lost control of his Columbia LC41. He entered a descending right turn that continued until ground contact which, according to the NTSB, was "consistent with a somatogyral illusion known as the graveyard spiral" (NTSB Identification No: ERA14FA292).

Coriolis Illusion

One of the deadliest vestibular illusions is the **Coriolis illusion**. The USAF survey revealed that 60.8 percent of the pilots surveyed experienced the Coriolis illusion at least once while flying their current aircraft type and it was the second most common type of nonvisual SD after the leans.[23] After the semicircular canals have equilibrated during a prolonged turn, you might tilt your head to look for a chart or pick up a pencil off the floor (see Figure 9-8). This brings a second canal into the axis of rotation, causing its cupula to deflect, and moves the original canal out of the axis of rotation, causing its cupula to deflect in the opposite direction as its canal fluid begins to slow down. Because of the conflicting sensations of acceleration in one axis and deceleration in the other, this cross-coupling illusion produces very strong sensations of motion in the third. So powerful is this illusion that pilots who've experienced it have reported strong pitch and bank illusions, sensations of tumbling forward, and even nausea.

Accident investigators believe this is likely what happened to the pilot flying a U.S. Army Bell UH-1H Iroquois ("Huey") helicopter in IMC at night. It appears the copilot was experiencing SD during the MEDEVAC (medical evacuation) flight, so the aircraft commander decided to abort the mission. However, after his head was down to tune in a radio frequency, he too experienced SD, lost control of the aircraft, and crashed killing two and injuring two others on board. Investigators concluded the pilot lost control because he experienced the Coriolis illusion.[24]

We mentioned in Chapter 4 that the FAA provides physiology training to civilian pilots in Oklahoma City. One component of this training is familiarization with SD, including a practical demonstration of the Coriolis illusion in a Barany chair. A volunteer is securely strapped into the chair and asked to put her head down and close her eyes while the instructor turns the chair at a constant, relatively slow rate for at least 20 seconds. When the instructor stops the chair, the volunteer is asked to lift up her head and open her eyes. The effect on participants is disquieting: Their entire body moves as they try to stabilize themselves to a visual scene that is erratically rotating about them, and they feel as if they will topple off the chair. Some have even felt nauseous for several hours afterward.

Somatogravic Illusions

Illusions primarily involving the otolith bodies are sometimes referred to as **somatogravic illusions** (*soma* = body; *gravic* = gravity). These also often involve the somatosensory system, since once the linear acceleration detectors—the otolith membranes of

Fig 9-8.

Moving your head in a different plane of rotation while established in a prolonged turn induces cross-coupling within the semicircular canals causing strong (and false) sensations of movement or tumbling in a third plane in which no actual motion exists.

A

B

the saccule and utricle—equilibrate to the acceleration, the somatosensory senses alone are detected. These generally include the false climb illusion, the straight-climb-while-in-a-turn Illusion, the G-excess illusion, and the inversion illusion.

False Climb illusion

A serious hazard occurs after liftoff or during a go-around when the airplane is in the initial climb phase of flight, especially if that climb is made into IMC or in **dark-night conditions**. These conditions occur when there is minimum (or a complete absence of) celestial illumination from the moon or stars or the illumination is obscured by a broken or overcast sky condition, and when there is a lack of cultural (human-made) terrain lighting in the departure area off the end of the runway (as is often the case over water, for example). According to the Transportation Safety Board of Canada (TSB), at one time more than three-quarters of fatal night takeoff accidents in Canada occurred in dark-night conditions.[25] If you rely solely on external visual cues after takeoff on dark nights, you may fail to establish the required climb gradient to clear unseen rising terrain ahead, or you may experience a false sensation of a nose-up pitch attitude. This false climb illusion could in turn lead you to pitch the nose down, causing the airplane to descend into the ground or water.

Often called the *somatogravic illusion* by aviation physiologists, the false climb illusion arises from misinterpreted inputs from both the otolith bodies of the vestibular apparatus and the sensations provided by the somatosensory receptors when the aircraft is subject to rapid acceleration in the longitudinal (x) axis (+G_X, *see* Figure 8-1 in Chapter 8) when flying in impoverished visual conditions. As noted earlier, the plate-like membranes in the otoliths are unable to distinguish between straight-line accelerations and head-up or head-down tilt. Therefore, accelerating down the runway on takeoff, during a shallow climb after liftoff, or during a go-around has the same physiological effect as tilting your head up (*see* Figure 9-4). This illusion is further strengthened by your somatosensory receptor system since it cannot distinguish between gravitational and linear accelerations. These seat-of-the-pants sensations combine gravitational and linear accelerations into one resultant force, causing you to incorrectly interpret the result of the backward force of inertia and gravity as the gravitational vertical (*see* Figure 9-9).

Designers of full-motion visual simulators take advantage of this physiological trait to simulate acceleration; on takeoff the front of the device is tilted upward, tricking pilots into thinking they are accelerating along a level runway. If you are deceived by this illusion, you will correct for these false sensations by inadvertently placing the aircraft in a nose-down attitude, causing your aircraft to fly right into the ground or water! It should also be apparent that the more rapid the acceleration (as would be the case with high power/thrust aircraft), the more pronounced the illusion.

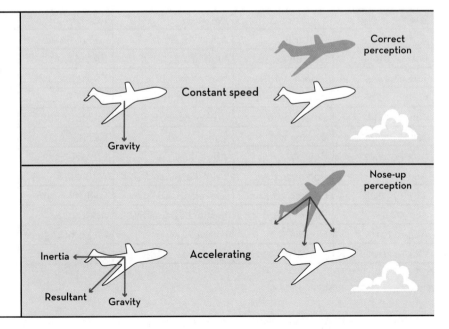

Fig 9-9.

The false climb (somatogravic) illusion.

As you read in the introduction to this chapter, this is what happened to the captain of a Gulf Air Airbus A320: The aircraft crashed into the Persian Gulf, killing all 143 people aboard after he experienced the somatogravic illusion during a go-around at Bahrain International Airport. It is also what happened to the captain of a Fairchild Metroliner III, operating on a scheduled commercial flight as Skylink 070 into Northwest Regional Airport in Terrace, British Columbia. According to the TSB, he experienced the somatogravic illusion while conducting a missed approach in IMC. In spite of verbal callouts from the FO that the aircraft was descending, the captain continued the descent and the aircraft crashed into the trees, killing all seven occupants (TSB Report No. 89H0007). It appears the captain of Armavia Airlines Flight 967, an Airbus A320 that recently crashed during a missed approach at night in IMC at Sochi International Airport in Russia, was also the victim of the false climb illusion. He initiated a go-around on short final and climbed above 1,600 feet, then pushed the nose down, causing the jet to descend at 4,300 fpm; the airplane crashed into the Black Sea killing all 113 people on board.[26]

More recently, in 2015, the flight crew of Avia Traffic Company Flight 768 averted a disaster when they evacuated six crew members and 153 passengers aboard their B-737 after the landing gear collapsed and the aircraft slid 1,600 feet down and off

Runway 12 at Osh International Airport, Kyrgyzstan. Because of poor visibility in fog they had to conduct a go-around on the previous approach, but while doing so the captain experienced the somatogravic illusion and pushed the nose down. Despite a GPWS aural warning, the aircraft struck the surface 740 feet beyond the runway's end with a force of +3.96 G at 178 knots, damaging the landing gear which was still halfway through its retraction cycle. Fortunately they were able to return to complete another approach, conduct a virtually wheels-up landing because of the damage previously done, and evacuate all aboard.[27, 28]

Although the danger of the false climb illusion has been known in the aviation community for well over half a century, this type of accident still occurs. And it appears its frequency is not abating. For example, Table 9-1 lists several relatively recent accidents that only occurred in Canada and the United States, where the somatogravic illusion during takeoff or a go-around was implicated in the accident. Notice that all of those listed occurred at night, with most in night visual meteorological conditions (NVMC).

Incidentally, the somatogravic illusion also works in reverse, as the crew of a Lockheed C-5 Galaxy discovered when the aircraft inadvertently entered a stall after the pilots probably corrected for a perceived nose-down attitude brought about from a rapid deceleration in level flight. Fortunately, they were able to safely recover.[29]

Table 9-1. Some recent U.S. and Canadian accidents during a takeoff or go-around attributed to the false climb (somatogravic) illusion.

Date	Aircraft	Location	Identification #	Weather	Certificate	Fatalities
Apr 28, 2017	Pilatus PC-12	Amarillo, TX	CEN17FA168	NIMC	ATP	3
Feb 1, 2016	Cessna 182	Mobile, AL	ERA16FA100	NIMC	ATP	2
Aug 10, 2015	Piper PA-28R	Marathon, FL	ERA15FA299	NVMC	PVT	1
Oct 12, 2014	Beechcraft 58	Palos Hills, IL	CEN15FA009	NIMC	PVT	3
Jun 13, 2014	Piper PA-46	White Plains, NY	ERA14FA288	NIMC	PVT	1
Jan 15, 2013	Cessna 208	Pellston, MI	CEN13FA135	NVMC	COM	1
Aug 24, 2012	Bell 407	Abingdon, VA	ERA12FA527	NVMC	ATP	1
Aug 27, 2011	Robinson R44	Saint-Ferdinand, PQ*	A11Q0168	NVMC	PVT	4
Jan 16, 2008	Beechcraft 58	Cleveland, OH	CHI08FA066	NVMC	ATP	1
Sep 30, 2005	Piper PA-31	Kashechewan, ON*	A05O0225	NVMC	ATP	0
Aug 8, 2003	Cessna 340	Bishop, CA	LAX03FA254	NVMC	COM	1
Oct 11, 2001	Fairchild SA226	Shamattawa, MB*	A01C0236	NVMC	ATP	2

*Canada
NIMC = night IMC; NVMC = night VMC
PVT = Private Pilot; COM = Commercial Pilot; ATP = Airline Transport Pilot

Straight-Climb-While-in-Turn Illusion

Other variations of the somatogravic illusion involve significant changes in aircraft load factor, or G-force (see Figure 8-1 in Chapter 8 for measurement of G-load along the three axes of x, y, and z). Primarily applicable to fighter and aerobatic pilots whose maneuvers regularly involve departure from normal +1 G flight, these illusions can trick any pilot—especially one struggling to recover from an inadvertent unusual attitude resulting from SD.

Positive vertical G_Z increase the strength of the gravitational acceleration that can lead to false sensations. For example, after 15 to 20 seconds in a coordinated turn at a constant bank angle, the speed of the fluid in the semicircular canals catches up to the speed of the canal walls; the tiny hairs are no longer deflected and you no longer "feel" like you are turning. In fact, it feels like you are flying in straight flight in a wings-level attitude. However, the somatosensory sense is still responsive to gravity and G accelerations.

Since the bank angle creates a resultant force that is greater than the +1 G of gravity, the somatosensory sense will create an illusion that the aircraft is pulling up into a climb—especially if the bank angle is steep (see Figure 9-10). This may cause you to lower the nose resulting in loss of altitude in the turn.

G-Excess Illusion

Positive vertical G_Z increase the strength of gravitational acceleration and provide more pull on the otolith organs, which intensifies any false sensations. For example, a 30 degree head tilt in a +1 G_Z environment (left diagram in Figure 9-11) exerts +0.5 G acceleration on the otolith membranes (+1 G × sin 30° = 0.5 G) and in a +2 G_Z environment (middle diagram) it exerts twice the acceleration (+1.0 G) on the otolith membranes (+2 G × sin 30° = +1.0 G). Therefore, positive 2 G_Z at the same head angle produces an illusion that the head is tilted back further than it is (right diagram).

Fig 9-10.

An illusion of a climb in wings-level straight flight after a prolonged coordinated level turn.

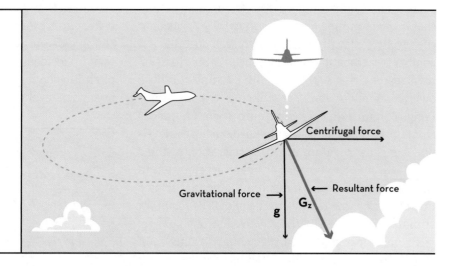

Fig 9-11.

An increase in positive acceleration (+G_Z) increases the backwards force on the otolith membranes creating the illusion of greater backward head tilt and steeper aircraft pitch attitude.

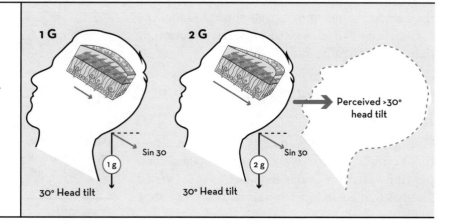

False sensations of pitch or bank can result when operating in a high +G_Z environment when head movement is initiated, or when your head is tilted backward or forward in relation to the direction of the applied +G_Z. This can happen, for example, in a tight turn while looking outside in the direction of the turn. Like other somatogravic-type illusions, the increased gravitational acceleration and greater pull on the otolith organs can lead to a **G-excess illusion**, which, if not recognized, will cause you to make inappropriate control responses. A Mooney M20K that crashed 19 seconds after takeoff at dusk in IMC was observed to level off over Runway 34 at Greater Binghamton Airport in New York, accelerate, and then climb up into an indefinite ceiling in fog. The NTSB determined the cause of this fatal accident was SD, likely involving a G-induced illusion (NTSB Identification No: NYC08FA039).

Inversion Illusion

Another variation of the somatogravic illusion occurs during an abrupt level-off from a steep climb that involves pulling negative vertical G (–G_Z) prior to the level-off. Usually restricted to high speed aerial combat or acrobatic flight maneuvers, this situation involves creating –G_Z by rapidly pushing the nose over and simultaneously creating positive G in the x (longitudinal) axis (+G_X; *see* Figure 8-1 in Chapter 8) from the rapidly increasing airspeed during the level-off. The centrifugal (or radial) acceleration in the z axis (–G_Z) and the tangential linear acceleration in the x axis (+G_X) creates a resultant force that rotates up and backwards relative to the pilot. The resultant stimulation on the otoliths creates a strong nose-up pitch illusion—so strong, in fact, that an illusion of flipping backward to an inverted position can result (*see* Figure 9-12).[30] Unfortunately, as is the case with the standard somatogravic (false climb) illusion, you may attempt to overcome this **inversion illusion** by pushing the airplane into a dive.

Oculogyral and Oculogravic Illusions

Vestibular and somatosensory illusions are sometimes complicated by the presence of certain accompanying vestibulo-ocular illusions, that is, visual illusions that are induced by vestibular activity. Most of these are classified as either oculogyral or oculogravic, depending on the type of illusion they are associated with; the oculogyral and oculogravic illusions being the visual (*oculo*=eye) components of the somatogyral and somatogravic illusions respectively.

The vestibular mechanisms associated with the somatogyral illusions are sometimes responsible for creating a visual reflex which makes objects "appear to rotate with the observer."[31] The changing force vectors responsible for somatogravic illusions can also cause apparent movement of objects in one's visual field.

Elevator Illusion

The **elevator illusion** is one such example: analogous to the initial acceleration involved in an up-moving elevator, in the absence of outside visual references a strong updraft or a sudden level-off from a descent increases the strength of the gravitational acceleration, stimulating the otolith organs. Because of inertia, the eyes automatically move downward creating the sensation that the nose of the aircraft has pitched up. If you correct for this by pitching the nose down while flying close to the ground, a controlled flight into terrain accident is possible. Of course, a nose-down pitch illusion is possible during a sudden downdraft or sudden level-off from a climb.

Fig 9-12.

The inversion illusion results from an abrupt level-off from a steep climb creating –G_Z and a rapid linear acceleration creating +G_X. This results in a strong nose-up pitch illusion and even the feeling of flipping upside down.

Nystagmus

If a person were suddenly stopped after being rotated on a piano stool for several seconds, an involuntary back-and-forth eye movement would occur. This visual form of disorientation, called **nystagmus**, can actually compound recovery from severe unusual attitudes such as spins. In normal circumstances, this automatic reflex contributes to the body's sense of balance. For example, upon moving the head to the left and then to the right, the eyes automatically move in opposite directions to provide a stabilized visual scene to the brain. Motion in the vestibular apparatus actually controls the eye muscles in this way. If it weren't for this automatic vestibulo-ocular reflex, a blurring of the visual scene would result during head movement in any of the three planes of movement.[32] During angular accelerations in flight, normal nystagmus involves involuntary eye movements opposite to the direction of motion followed by quick returns in the direction of motion. Since this reflex is proportional to the amount of cupulae deflection, nystagmus reduces to zero once a constant angular velocity is maintained. Unfortunately, during recovery from prolonged angular maneuvers that involve high rates of rotation, nystagmus can occur causing apparent back and forth movement of the visual scene that can last for several seconds after recovery. Therefore, this type of involuntary eye movement only serves to compound the difficulty of recovering from an unusual attitude.

Vertigo

Sometimes pilots use the term *vertigo* to describe SD, but its definition is actually much narrower in scope and, as a type of SD, refers to a spinning or twirling sensation either of yourself or your surroundings. It may also involve feelings of light-headedness or dizziness. One type of severe vertigo is the involuntary nystagmus that causes your visual scene to appear to move back and forth after recovery from prolonged angular maneuvers involving high rates of rotation. A person who experiences the Coriolis illusion will also suffer from the disorienting effects of nystagmus. Obviously, this phenomenon would make recovery from an unusual attitude even more difficult.

Classifying Spatial Disorientation

Aviation physiologists have identified three different types of SD. If you experience the first type—**Type I SD** (unrecognized)—you will be unaware of your disorientation and will base control of your aircraft on a false perception of your attitude. The somatogravic (false climb) illusion is an example of this, and an accident is likely if you fail to recognize it in time.

With **Type II SD** (recognized) you are aware that something is wrong and at first may suspect there is something wrong with your flight instruments. This is likely what happened to the pilot of the Cessna Citation which broke apart in flight near Cedar Fort, Utah, due to loss of control from SD while operating in IMC (*see* the beginning of this chapter). As the situation was developing, the pilot informed ATC that his flight management system had failed and shortly after he claimed he was "losing his instruments." Yet despite his claims, the NTSB investigators during post-accident examination and testing found nothing that would indicate any of the flight instruments had failed (NTSB Identification No: WPR16FA054).

When you recognize you are experiencing Type II SD you will likely experience **disorientation stress** as you fight your vestibular and/or somatosensory sensations in an attempt to trust and fly by the instruments—a process aviation physiologists call "establishing visual dominance."

Unfortunately, if you experience **Type III SD** (incapacitating), even though you are aware of your disorientation, you will likely be unable to properly take positive control of your aircraft.[33] Extreme aircraft attitudes, complicated by disorienting visual symptoms such as nystagmus, make it difficult, if not impossible, to recover from this type of SD.

An initial (and common) response to SD, unfortunately, can be **control reversal error (CRE)**, which involves making control inputs that that are exactly the opposite of what is required for desired flight parameters. The captain of Kenya Airways Flight 507, described previously, displayed CRE, likely because of the leans: the aircraft began a very slow roll to the right and as he took the controls he initially moved the control column further to the right. Realizing his mistake, he then moved it to left but then rolled the airplane back to the right, to the left, and back to the right again until it rolled over to more than 90 degrees. Due to Type II SD with resulting CRE it can be surmised the event progressed to Type III SD with resulting loss of aircraft and life.

Overcoming Spatial Disorientation

Pilots who have survived a serious disorientation episode have often reported that when they broke out of IMC into visual conditions, their SD *immediately* disappeared and they were able to correctly orient themselves using natural outside visual references. Therefore, you can avoid SD—or successfully defeat it if you experience it—by learning to rely on cockpit instrumentation designed to replicate the natural references of the outside world.

Trust Your Instruments

When properly scanned and interpreted, your aircraft's flight instruments give you an accurate depiction of the aircraft's orientation in space. Real-time information about altitude, airspeed, heading, rate of climb/descent, and rate of turn is provided to you by these instruments. Especially helpful is the attitude indicator that substitutes the natural horizon with an artificial one, providing you with a *direct* indication of the aircraft's pitch and bank attitude. Pilots who are proficient at using the flight instruments to fly their aircraft—and there are thousands of them who do so every day—have learned to trust what the instruments are telling them and to ignore their vestibular and somatosensory sensations.

Of course, to trust the flight instruments they must be trustworthy. It's important, therefore, to check them for proper operation and accuracy *before* you commit to the air. Not doing so could be disastrous, as the captain of a Cessna Citation II discovered shortly after takeoff from Mountain View Airport in Missouri. In a hurry not to miss his IFR departure clearance time, he rushed his departure procedures—the time from engine startup to takeoff was only about two minutes—and didn't allow adequate time for the gyros, which power the attitude and horizontal situation indicators, to spool up. The airplane crashed in IMC shortly after takeoff, killing all three people on board (NTSB Identification No: DCA83AA005).

Just because you've confirmed that the flight instruments are operating correctly before you launch doesn't mean they won't fail once you're airborne. Table 9-2 is a listing of only a few of several fatal SD accidents where some type of flight instrument failure,[34] or suspected failure, contributed to the SD experienced by pilots. In most cases other functioning secondary or back-up flight instruments were available to maintain control of the aircraft

This is what happened to the Beechcraft King Air B200 carrying members of OSU's basketball team (mentioned previously in this chapter); a complete captain's side instrument failure occurred. However, the airspeed and turn-and-slip indicator, along with four of the copilot's flight instruments, continued to function properly. An instrument failure also occurred in India's second-worst accident to date. Air India Flight 855, a Boeing B-747, crashed after takeoff killing all 213 people on board after the captain's atti-

Table 9-2. Sample listing of fatal airplane accidents where a flight instrument had failed or was suspected to have failed.

Date	Aircraft	Operator	Location	Fatalities
Jan 18, 2016	Cessna Citation	GA-Personal	Cedar Fort, UT	2
Jun 1, 2009	Airbus A330	Air France	Atlantic Ocean, east of Brazil	228
Feb 1, 2008	Cessna Citation	GA-Personal	West Gardiner, ME	2
Jan 27, 2001	King Air B200	Jet Express Services	Strasburg, CO	10
Dec 22, 1999	Boeing B-747	Korean Air	London Stansted Airport	4
Feb 6, 1996	Boeing B-757	Birgenair	Dominican Republic	189
Feb 15, 1992	DC-8	Air Transport International	Swanton, OH	4
Jul 31, 1989	Convair CV-580	Air Freight NZ	Auckland, NZ	3
May 30, 1984	Lockheed L-188	Zantop International Airlines	Chalkhill, PA	4
Jan 1, 1978	Boeing B-747	Air India	Mumbai Airport	213

tude director indicator failed, causing confusion and subsequent SD. According to the accident report, the crew of the Air India flight failed to gain control based on other available flight instruments and allowed the aircraft to roll over into a 108-degree left bank.[35]

Even though flight instruments for both the captain and FO's positions are powered by different sources, and basic standby instruments such as an attitude indicator, airspeed indicator (ASI), and altimeter are also powered by an independent source, it can sometimes be very challenging for crew members to distinguish between the failed flight instrument(s) and the reliable one(s). Tragic accidents have occurred because of blockages of pitot tubes and/or static vents that are used to provide reliable airspeed information to the crew.

For example, the crew of Birgenair Flight 301 lost control of their Boeing B-757 after departing Puerto Plata Airport in the Dominican Republic at night. The three pitot tubes used to measure airspeed were left uncovered for two days before the accident and investigators determined one was blocked (likely from a wasp nest) causing a spurious high reading on the captain's ASI. To counter the high indicated airspeed in the climb (350 knots) the autopilot/autothrottle, which was linked to the captain's air data computer, attempted to slow the airplane down by pitching the nose up and reducing thrust. The FO's ASI read only about 200 knots and decreasing, yet the airplane was simultaneously providing excessive speed warnings and stall stick shaker (slow speed/stall) warnings on the engine-indicating and crew-alerting system. The flight crew was very confused and by the time they figured it all out it was too late—all 189 people aboard died after they lost control of the airplane and it crashed into the ocean. According to the authorities, the crew failed to compare the three different sources of airspeed to determine that the captain's ASI was the culprit.[36]

A tragically similar accident occurred 13 years later in 2009. Pitot tubes on Air France Flight 447 became obstructed from ingested ice crystals while the Airbus A330 was cruising at FL360 over the Atlantic Ocean about 350 miles off Brazil's northeastern coast. This created intermittent and unreliable airspeed indications to the crew and automatic disconnection of the autopilot. Not only did the crew fail to properly diagnose the problem, the pilot flying (PF) experienced a **startle reflex** and overreacted to

the autopilot disconnect by pulling back on the side stick controller. This resulted in a stick shaker stall warning, which the PF responded to, but not to the degree necessary to ensure safe flight. A second stall warning appeared 40 seconds later, but the PF kept applying nose-up inputs on the side stick—likely because he thought they were in a high-speed situation—resulting in a stall from which the crew was unable to recover. The airplane hit the water at almost 11,000 fpm at a speed of only 107 knots. All 12 crew members and 216 passengers perished.[37]

Maintain Instrument Flying Proficiency

Maintaining proficiency in instrument flying techniques is a must if you plan to fly IFR. If you know an IFR flight is approaching, you can stay sharp by spending some time in the simulator or a flight training device (FTD), on a basic or advanced aviation training device (ATD), or even flying your own computer-based flight simulator. If it's been a while since you've received instruction in unusual attitude recovery using only the flight instruments, you should refresh those skills as well. Also, if your aircraft is equipped with a **glass cockpit**, make sure you have received proper training and are proficient using backup flight instrumentation if the electronic systems fail; a study by the NTSB in 2010 found that GA aircraft equipped with digital glass cockpits had a higher fatal accident rate than those with conventional electro-mechanical, or so-called *steam gauge*, flight instrumentation.[38]

Even though flight instrument failure is a relatively rare occurrence, as you have seen, an instrument failure can be catastrophic. That is why every pilot must be prepared for it and why you should maintain proficiency in partial panel flying, not just leaving mastery of it for your instrument proficiency checks. In the event of an instrument failure it's important to know how to cross-check, recognize, isolate, and ignore the failed flight instrument (or instrument cluster) and be proficient at flying with the remaining backup instruments. You should also be familiar with your aircraft's approved emergency and abnormal procedures checklist before you have to pull it out and use it.

When flying in impoverished outside visual references it's important to avoid large abrupt head movements, especially during prolonged turning maneuvers where the semicircular canals have equilibrated. It goes without saying that you should also avoid extreme pitch and bank attitudes; this will prevent tumbling not only of the instrument gyros but your inner-ear gyros as well. Avoiding excessive or unusual attitudes also reduces the possibility of SD symptoms that could arise when pulling positive vertical G_Z to recover from them.

Transition to Instruments Early

A study of 96 USAF F-15 pilots who experienced SD during flight operations in Desert Storm confirmed what other research has discovered: SD episodes often occur when a pilot transitions from using outside natural visual references (i.e., horizon, terrain) to flight instruments inside the flight deck, and vice versa.[39] Even pilots with significant experience in instrument flying are strongly conditioned to use outside visual references, in what is called an outside spatial strategy, to maintain spatial orientation. This is basically the only strategy humans use until they learn how to fly an aircraft (or simulator) by instruments or engage in playing certain types of video games.

When transitioning from outside references to a spatial representation of the outside world—i.e., artificial, human-made flight instruments—using an "inside spatial strategy," the transition is not instantaneous and SD may result as a pilot attempts to establish visual dominance when transitioning to them. SD can also result if the shift from an outside spatial strategy to an inside one is delayed until after entering IMC or dark-night conditions. The best strategy, therefore, is to shift to an inside spatial strategy before entering impoverished visual conditions. It should also be noted that you may be more susceptible to other types of illusions, such as the G-excess illusion, if you use an outside visual spatial strategy.[40]

Be Careful at Night

The risk of experiencing SD increases when you fly at night. For example, the odds of experiencing a fatal accident in a GA aircraft more than doubles when flying at night, and accidents in IMC at night are more than five times likely to be fatal compared to day accidents in VMC.[41] A U.S. Navy study of Class A **mishaps** between 1990 and 2000 found that 20 percent of the accidents were attributed to SD which accounted for 64 percent of all fatalities: half of

these occurred at night. Ten percent of all U.S. Navy mishaps between 2000 and 2007 involved SD which accounted for 40 percent of all fatalities: 72 percent occurred after dark.[42, 43]

During a 10-year period there were at least 66 SD accidents in VFR weather conditions involving U.S. GA aircraft: forty-five of them, or 68 percent, occurred at night.[44] A particular subtle threat is flying in good weather conditions on dark nights. Notice that all of the takeoff/go-around accidents listed in Table 9-1 occurred at night with most in VMC. Pilots often let their guard down, especially when flying in clear weather conditions at night. You may reason that flying at night is no different than flying in the daytime. If so, you would be mistaken. In fact, one pilot spoke almost those exact words to a friend on the ground before he died that very evening in a typical dark-night takeoff accident: it was a clear, dark, and moonless night at Grand Canyon National Park Airport in Arizona (NTSB Identification No: LAX96FA052). It may be true that flying at night is no different than flying during the day, except, as the saying goes, you can't see anything!

When flying VFR at night, supplement outside references with cockpit flight instruments to avoid not only vestibular and somatosensory illusions but also visual illusions (discussed in Chapter 12). You should continue to rely on the cockpit flight instruments until the outside references are distinguishable enough to maintain accurate orientation. You should also avoid flying at night if you are not proficient in instrument flying techniques or are not night-current.

Avoid VFR Flight into IMC

A non-instrument-rated private pilot was on a personal VFR cross-country flight when he encountered, and elected to continue flight into, IMC en route. Unfortunately, he and his passenger were killed after their airplane crashed into Lake Russell, near Lowndesville, South Carolina. Witnesses observed the Cessna 172 descending out of the "very low" overcast cloud layer (based at 100 to 200 feet above treetop level) in a 70- to 90-degree nose-down attitude before crashing into the lake. The NTSB determined the probable cause was the pilot's "inadequate preflight planning and improper decision to continue flight into deteriorating weather conditions, which resulted in spatial disorientation after entering instrument flight conditions" (NTSB Identification No: ERA09LA527).

A major cause of fatal SD accidents is attempting VFR flight into IMC. As was mentioned near the beginning of this chapter, those who attempt to fly in such conditions without the instrument flying skills required to do so have, on average, 178 seconds to live. Therefore, if you are a non-instrument-rated VFR pilot, or have no recent instrument experience, your only option is to completely avoid flying into IMC altogether. Sometimes this is not as easy as it sounds. Recent research indicates that even though the ability to accurately judge ceiling and visibility values from a moving airplane is a crucial component in avoiding these types of accidents, most pilots aren't very good at it. University of Illinois researchers recently had pilots fly a simulated VFR cross-country flight in weather conditions that had deteriorated to below-VFR minimums en route and found that most of them overestimated both visibility and ceiling values. They also discovered that those who diverted to avoid the simulated adverse weather were significantly more accurate in their estimates of flight visibility than those who continued to fly into it. They concluded that a major reason that pilots—especially those with fewer hours and less experience—continue flying into deteriorating weather is their inability to determine when they are in or nearing IMC.[45] To avoid flight into IMC, therefore, you need to hone your skill at accurately judging visibility values so you will better know if the weather is approaching IMC.

Better yet, you should establish your own personal weather minimums to guide you when the weather goes bad. Experienced VFR pilots know the value of establishing personal minimums and sticking to them even when the pressure to continue a flight becomes strong. Since VFR-into-IMC accidents have occurred in weather conditions that were higher than regulatory VFR weather minimums,[46, 47] it's crucial that you develop your own personal minimum ceiling and visibility values that are higher than basic minimums, and ensure that those are met before you depart or continue a flight. These should reflect your flight experience and comfort levels, and if you are a relatively new pilot, they most certainly should be conservative (i.e., considerably higher than regulatory minimums). In the words of one FAA official, personal weather minimums provide "a safety buffer between the demands of the situation and the extent of your skills."[48] Research supports their value as well. An extensive multi-national study of weather encounters found that pilots who reported flying into IMC had the most liberal personal weather minimums, while those who never flew into IMC had the most conservative ones.[49] However, establishing these minimums is of no value unless you resist pressure—both from yourself and from others—to continue flight when you encounter conditions below those minimums. In case you inadvertently find yourself in IMC, you should know how to conduct a 180-degree standard-rate turn using only the flight instruments. See the Helpful Resources at the end of this chapter for information designed to help you determine your own minimums and avoid inadvertent flight into IMC.

Obtain an Instrument Rating

If you are a non-instrument-rated pilot, why not gain some added insurance and versatility from your aircraft by obtaining an instrument rating? AOPA's statistics indicate that only 17 percent of accidents resulting from VFR flight into IMC involve instrument-rated pilots.[50] Not only are you more likely to use your IFR ticket in marginal weather, but if you inadvertently find yourself in the soup, you will have the skills necessary to get out of it and avoid becoming an accident statistic.

Get Help

To repeat, the key to beating SD is to fly the aircraft with reference to the flight instruments and ignore body sensations. However, if you still experience SD, especially the Type III incapacitation kind, and you are flying in a crewed flight deck, give the controls to the other pilot. It's seldom that you will both experience incapacitating SD at the same time. However, if your partner is also struggling with SD consider letting your third pilot, the autopilot, fly it. If you only fly with a crew of one, and your aircraft is autopilot-equipped, use it to level the wings and maintain altitude until the SD subsides. If you are a VFR pilot, and you inadvertently enter IMC, you should also know how to conduct an autopilot-assisted 180 degree turn to escape from the conditions.

Helpful Resources

The FAA's Civil Aerospace Medical Institute provides several free videos that graphically illustrate various aspects of spatial disorientation. Available in English and Japanese, *Spatial Disorientation Part 1: Vestibular Illusions* is available at www.faa.gov/pilots/training/airman_education/physiologyvideos/

The following short FAA videos are available at www.faa.gov/about/office_org/headquarters_offices/avs/offices/aam/cami/library/online_libraries/aerospace_medicine/sd/videos/

- *G-Excess Effect*
- *Grave Yard Spiral*
- *Inversion Illusion*
- *Otolith Illusions*
- *Pitch-Up Illusion*
- *Semi-Circular Illusion*

Spatial Disorientation: Confusion That Kills is an AOPA Air Safety Institute *Safety Advisor* that can assist you in managing the threat of spatial disorientation. (www.aopa.org/training-and-safety/air-safety-institute/safety-publications/safety-advisors)

Aeromedical Factors, Chapter 17 in the FAA's latest *Pilot's Handbook of Aeronautical Knowledge* (FAA-H-8083-25), provides an excellent overview of spatial disorientation. (www.faa.gov/regulations_policies/handbooks_manuals/aviation/phak/)

The Art of Aeronautical Decision-Making is an online FAA Safety Team tutorial that draws upon the collective wisdom and expertise of VFR pilots and instructors who have learned from the mistakes of others. It provides invaluable information to help you determine your own minimums and avoid inadvertent flight into IMC. (www.faasafety.gov/gslac/ALC/course_content.aspx?pf=1&preview=true&cID=28)

Endnotes

1. The term CAVOK (pronounced KAV-OH-KAY) is often used in Canada and international flight operations when the reported visibility at an airport is at least 6 statute miles (10 kilometers), there are no clouds below 5,000 AGL feet (1,500 meters) with no significant clouds such as towering cumulus and cumulonimbus, and no significant weather (i.e., no precipitation, obscurations and/or other weather phenomena).

2. Bahrain Civil Aviation Affairs, *Aircraft Accident Investigation Report, Gulf Air Flight GF-072, Airbus A320-212, REG. A40-EK on 23 August 2000 at Bahrain* (Kingdom of Bahrain: Bahrain Civil Aviation Affairs). Available at www.bea.aero/docspa/2000/a40-ek000823a/htm/a40-ek000823a.html.

3. Ibid.

4. Flight Safety Foundation, Aviation Safety Network, *Accident Description: Vladivostokavia Air, Tupolev-154, near Burdakovka, Russia, July 4, 2001.* Available at www.aviation-safety.net/database/record.php?id=20010704-0.

5. David Learmount, "Pilot Disorientation Accidents Have Become a Phenomenon," *Flight International* (January 29, 2010). Available at www.flightglobal.com/news/articles/pilot-disorientation-accidents-have-become-a-phenomenon-337743/.

6. Boeing Commercial Airplanes, *Statistical Summary of Commercial Jet Airplane Accidents: Worldwide Operations, 1959–2016* (Seattle, WA: Boeing, July 2017). The most recent summary can be found at www.boeing.com/resources/boeingdotcom/company/about_bca/pdf/statsum.pdf.

7. C.E. Davenport, "USAF Spatial Disorientation Experience: Air Force Safety Center Statistical Review," *Symposium on Recent Trends in Spatial Disorientation Research* (San Antonio, TX: Nov 15–17, 2000).

8. Terence J. Lyons, William Ercoline, Kevin O'Toole and Kevin Grayson, "Aircraft and Related Factors in Crashes Involving Spatial Disorientation: 15 Years of U.S. Air Force Data," *Aviation, Space, and Environmental Medicine* 77 (July 2006): 720–723.

9. William R. Kirkham, William E. Collins, Paula M. Grape, James M. Simpson and Terry F. Wallace, *Spatial Disorientation in General Aviation Accidents*, FAA-AM-78-13 (Oklahoma City, OK: FAA Civil Aeromedical Institute, March 1978).

10. William E. Collins and C.S. Dollar, *Fatal General Aviation Accidents Involving Spatial Disorientation: 1976–1992*, DOT/FAA/AM-96/21 (Washington, DC: FAA Civil Aeromedical Institute, August 1996).

11. AOPA Air Safety Institute, *Safety Advisor—Spatial Disorientation: Confusion That Kills*, Physiology No. 1 (Frederick, MD: AOPA ASI, August 2004).

12. Melchor J. Antunano, *Medical Facts for Pilots—Spatial Disorientation*, AM-400-03/1 (Oklahoma City, OK: FAA Civil Aerospace Medical Institute, 2003)

13. Ibid.

14. Leslie A. Bryan, Jesse W. Stonecipher and Karl Aron, "180-Degree Turn Experiment," *Aeronautics Bulletin* 52 (Urbana, IL: University of Illinois, September 1954).

15. David G. Newman, *An Overview of Spatial Disorientation as a Factor in Aviation Accidents and Incidents*, Report B2007/0063 (Canberra City, Australia: Australian Transport Safety Bureau, 2007). Available at www.atsb.gov.au/publications/2007/b20070063.aspx.

16. Roger S.J. Matthews, Fred Previc and Alex Bunting, "USAF Spatial Disorientation Survey," *RTO HFM Symposium on Spatial Disorientation in Military Vehicles: Causes, Consequences and Cures*, RTO-MP-086 (La Coruna, Spain: April 15–17, 2002).

17. Tim Jotischky, "The Tragedy of Flight KQ507," *The Telegraph* (March 18, 2012). Available at www.telegraph.co.uk/news/worldnews/africaandindianocean/kenya/9150349/The-tragedy-of-Flight-KQ507.html.

18. Flight Safety Foundation Aviation Safety Network, *Accident Description: Kenya Airways, B-737, 5.5 km SE of Douala Airport, Cameroon, May 5, 2007*. Available at www.aviation-safety.net/database/record.php?id=20070505-0.

19. Ronald F.K. Merryman and Anthony J. Cacioppo, "The Optokinetic Cervical Reflex in Pilots of High Performance Aircraft," *Aviation, Space, and Environmental Medicine* 68 (June 1997): 497–487.

20. A spin involves the airplane automatically rotating (simultaneous rolling, pitching, and yawing) about a vertical axis while the aircraft is stalled. Also called *autorotation*.

21. A spiral dive appears to resemble a spin only because the airplane is in a steep descending turn. However, unlike a spin, the airplane is not stalled and the airspeed and rate of descent are both high and rapidly increasing in a spiral. The recovery procedure for a spiral is completely different from a spin.

22. Matthews, Previc and Bunting, "USAF Spatial Disorientation Survey."

23. Ibid.

24. Vietnam Helicopter Pilots Association (VHPA), *UH-1H 66-17012, Incident number: 681215101ACD, Accident case number: 681215101*. Original source: Defense Intelligence Agency Helicopter Loss database, Army Aviation Safety Center database. Posted September 23, 2017, available at www.vhpa.org/KIA/incident/681215101ACD.HTM.

25. "Pitch Up, Pitch Down, Pitch Black," *Aviation Safety Reflexions* 4 (December 1993): 1–4.

26. Mark Lacagnina, "Into the Black Sea: A Go-Around Goes Awry in Sochi, Russia," *AeroSafety* World (October 2007): 44–49. Available at www.flightSafety.org/aerosafety-world/past-issues/.

27. The Boeing 737 Technical Site, *22 Nov 2015 - EX-37005 737-300 Landing Accident* (n.d.). Available at www.b737.org.uk/incident_ex37005.htm.

28. Qin Xie, "Passengers Hospitalised After a Plane Hit Ground so Hard That its Landing Gear Collapsed and The Left Wing Fell Off," *The Daily Mail* (November 24, 2015).

29. Fred H. Previc and William R. Ercoline, "Spatial Disorientation in Aviation: Historical Background, Concepts, and Terminology," Chapter 1, in *Spatial Disorientation* in Aviation, eds. Fred H. Previc and William R. Ercoline (Reston, VA: American Institute of Aeronautics & Astronautics, 2004): 1–36.

30. Bob Cheung, "Nonvisual Illusions in Flight," *Spatial Disorientation in Aviation*, eds. Fred H. Previc and William R. Ercoline (Reston, VA: American Institute of Aeronautics & Astronautics, 2004): 243–281.

31. A.J. Benson, "Spatial Disorientation—Common Illusions," *Aviation Medicine* (2nd ed.), eds. John Ernsting and Peter King (London: Butterworths, 1988): 297–317.

32. Ibid.

33. United States Department of the Army, *Aeromedical Training for Flight Personnel*, TC No. 3-04.93 (Washington, DC: August 31, 2009).

34. In some of these accidents, the pilot/flight crew reported a flight instrument anomaly but investigators were unable to ascertain with certainty if that was true or if the pilot had misread the instrument(s).

35. Flight Safety Foundation Aviation Safety Network, *Accident Description: Air India, B-747, Arabian Sea, off Bandra, January 1, 1978*. Available at www.aviation-safety.net/database/record.php?id=19780101-1.

36. Flight Safety Foundation Editorial Staff, "Erroneous Airspeed Indications Cited in Boeing 757 Control Loss," *Accident Prevention* 56 (October 1999).

37. Bureau d'Enquêtes et d'Analyses pour la Sécurité de l'Aviation Civile (BEA), *On The Accident on 1st June 2009 to the Airbus A330-203, Registered F-GZCP, Operated by Air France, Flight AF 447 Rio de Janeiro – Paris* (Paris, France: July 27, 2012).

38. National Transportation Safety Board, *Safety Study: Introduction of Glass Cockpit Avionics Into Light Aircraft*, NTSB/SS-01/10 (Washington, DC: March 9, 2010). Available at www.ntsb.gov/safety/safety-studies/Pages/SafetyStudies.aspx.

39. D.L. Collins and G. Harrison, "Spatial Disorientation Episodes Among F-15C Pilots During Operation Desert Storm," *Journal of Vestibular Research* 5 (November–December 1995): 405–410.

40. I am indebted to retired U.S. Naval Aerospace Physiologist Dr. Mike Prevost for his insights on this topic.

41. AOPA Air Safety Institute, *2008 Nall Report: Accident Trends and Factors for 2007* (Frederick, MD: 2009).

42. P. Wechgelaer, K. Johnson and T. Lett, "Spatial Disorientation in U.S. Naval Aviation 1990–2000," *Proceedings of Aerospace Medical Association Conference* (San Antonio, TX: May 2003): 145. Referenced in Randall Gibb, Bill Ercoline and Lauren Scharff, "Spatial Disorientation: Decades of Pilot Fatalities," *Aviation, Space, and Environmental Medicine* 82 (July 2011): 1–8.

43. Randall Gibb, Bill Ercoline and Lauren Scharff, "Spatial Disorientation: Decades of Pilot Fatalities," *Aviation, Space, and Environmental Medicine* 82 (July 2011): 1–8.

44. AOPA Air Safety Institute, *Safety Advisor—Spatial Disorientation: Confusion That Kills.*

45. Douglas Wiegmann and Juliana Goh, *Visual Flight Rules (VFR) Flight Into Adverse Weather: An Empirical Investigation of Factors Affecting Pilot Decision Making*, FAA Technical Report ARL- 00-15/FAA-00-8 (November 2000).

46. Transportation Safety Board of Canada, *Report of a Safety Study on VFR Flight Into Adverse Weather*, Report No. 90-SP002 (Hull, Quebec: November 13, 1990).

47. Federal Aviation Administration, "Night-Visual Flight Rules Visibility and Distance From Clouds Minimums: Final Rule," *Federal Register* 54.188 (September 29, 1989): 40324–40327.

48. Susan Parson, "Getting the Maximum from Personal Minimums," *FAA Aviation News* 45 (May/June 2006): 1–8.

49. David R. Hunter, Monica Martinussen, Mark Wiggins and David O'Hare, *VFR Into IMC—Who, What, When, Where, and Why Summary of Results from the International Weather Encounters Study.* Available at www.avhf.com/html/library/Tech_Reports/Aviation%20Weather%20Encounters%20-%20Summary.pdf.

50. AOPA Air Safety Institute, *Safety Advisor—Spatial Disorientation: Confusion That Kills.*

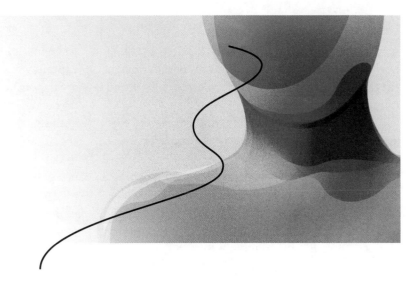

10

Why am I so tired?

Fatigue on the Flight Deck

He was a competent and experienced pilot. Following a 25-year career at Eastern Air Lines flying a variety of jet transports, including acting as captain on the McDonnell Douglas DC-9 and Boeing B-727, the nearly 21,000-hour ATP was now captain on the Douglas DC-8 flying for Connie Kalitta Services. He was well-regarded by his peers and described as "very conscientious," "a good pilot," "good at managing the crew," and displaying "good judgment when dealing with emergencies." His FO had a similar stellar background. Following a 23-year career at Eastern flying as FE, FO, and captain on variety of jet transport aircraft, the 15,000-hour ATP, now FO in the DC-8 flying for Kalitta, also received accolades from his colleagues and was considered a very "competent" and "excellent" pilot. The FE, who joined the two others on this flight from Norfolk, Virginia, to Guantanamo Bay, Cuba, was also experienced and described by his peers as "competent and conscientious," and that he did an effective job and spoke up when he observed an unusual or abnormal situation.

The involvement of such an experienced, qualified, and well-regarded crew only increased the level of bewilderment experienced by the NTSB personnel who investigated this accident. It was daylight and the weather was good, so ATC expected them to conduct a VFR approach. Leeward Point Field, the airport serving Guantanamo Bay, has only one runway, oriented east-west, so the crew of Flight 808 had a choice of landing in only one of two directions. Since Cuban airspace is about seven miles east of the threshold of Runway 28, it is typically the preferred runway because pilots can avoid Cuban airspace and fly a longer final approach

allowing them to more easily fly a stabilized approach to this 8,000-foot runway.

Runway 10, on the other hand, poses unique challenges to crews. Cuban airspace begins only three-quarters of a mile west of the runway threshold, and because aircraft are prohibited from flying into Cuban airspace, aircraft must fly a very close base leg at low altitude before turning onto final approach—not an easy task for any pilot, let alone one who has never flown into Guantanamo Bay (in fact, none of the crew members had ever landed a DC-8 at Leeward Point Field). There was even a warning in the VFR arrival/departure route chart that states: "Exercise EXTREME CAUTION when landing Runway 10 due to short final approach and prevailing crosswind."

During their initial contact with the Guantanamo radar controller at FL320 (or 32,000 feet), the FO requested Runway 28. However, the captain, who was the PF, changed his mind and stated to the other crewmembers, "...otta make that one zero approach just for the heck of it to see how it is. Why don't we do that, let's tell 'em we'll take [runway] one zero. If we miss we'll just come back around and land on two eight." After getting clearance from ATC, which included, "Cuban airspace begins three-quarters of a mile west of the runway. You are required to remain within this, within the airspace designated by a strobe light," the captain set up an approach from the south for a close right base for Runway 10. Neither the FO nor FE objected to this last-minute decision by the captain to attempt this difficult manual (hand-flying) approach and landing on Runway 10.

Initially the surface wind of 180 degrees at eight knots slightly favored Runway 10; but when they contacted the tower controller they were informed it was now at 220 degrees at seven knots, meaning a slight tailwind on landing and a tailwind on base leg. The controller offered them Runway 28, but the FO said they were going to try Runway 10 first. And they were again reminded to remain within the airspace designated by the strobe light. Unfortunately, the trainee controller who issued the clearances was unaware that the strobe was not operational that day.

It all began to snowball from there. As they were getting the airplane configured and slowed down for the landing, the captain was rightfully concerned about avoiding Cuban airspace. He could not see the strobe light and during the last minute of the flight had asked his crew where it was at least seven times. Investigators concluded that his fixation on locating the strobe light distracted him from focusing on hand-flying this very challenging visual approach to Runway 10. As it turned out, he ended up too close to the runway, he allowed the airspeed to drop seven knots below that required for the approach (despite warnings from the FE) and he initiated the turn to final from right base too late.

These factors, along with the tailwind, caused the airplane to overshoot the extended runway centerline. But instead of conducting a go-around, the captain, in an attempt to make it, steepened the angle of bank to beyond 50 degrees (increasing the load factor and raising the stall speed). The aircraft stick shaker activated seven seconds before impact and five seconds before the aircraft stalled, but the captain, in spite of urgings from the other crew members, failed to take appropriate stall-recovery action. Several witnesses observed the airplane trying to make the turn, with one reporting that it looked like the airplane's bank angle exceeded 60 degrees at 400 feet above ground level. He then saw the right wing stall and the aircraft roll over into 90 degrees of bank. The airplane burst into flames after crashing about a quarter-mile short of the runway threshold. Amazingly, all three crew members survived, but with serious injuries.

Investigators wondered why an experienced captain would attempt such a difficult approach into an airport he had never landed at before; why he was preoccupied with finding a non-operative strobe light at the expense of focusing his attention on conducting the approach; why he allowed the aircraft's airspeed to deteriorate; why, when it was clear the DC-8 was not going to make the turn, he failed to conduct a go-around but elected to steepen the bank even more; and why, after the stick shaker began to warn of an impending stall, he failed to initiate a normal approach-to-stall recovery procedure. They were also baffled by the behavior of the other crew members: why did they go along with the captain's decision to attempt such a difficult approach in the first place, and why weren't they more critical of his decision to conduct a steep descending turn at such a low altitude and airspeed?

The investigator's bewilderment began to clear up when they interviewed the crew members and examined their schedules. In his testimony before the NTSB's public hearing, the captain described his memory of the period before the accident occurred:

> All I can say is that I was—I felt *very lethargic or indifferent*. I remember making the turn from the base to the final, but I don't remember trying to look for the airport or adding power or decreasing power.
>
> On the final—I had mentioned...that I had heard Tom say something about he didn't like the looks of the approach. And looking at the voice recorder, it was along the lines of, are we going to make this?
>
> I remember looking over at him, and there again, *I remember—being very lethargic about it or indifferent*. I don't recall asking him or questioning anybody. I don't recall the engineer talking about the airspeeds at all. So it's very frustrating and disconcerting at night to try to lay there and think of how this—you know—*how you could be so lethargic when so many things, were going on,* but that's just the way it was.[1]

Investigators had surely heard such complaints from flight crews before, but this time, after they examined the crews' schedules, it all made sense. At the time of the accident, the flight crew had been on duty for 18 hours, and had flown about 9 hours.

Not the most ideal situation, but a common practice for nonscheduled cargo operations and within the regulations at the time. However, it was also discovered that before the accident, the captain had been awake for almost 24 hours, the FO 19 hours, and the FE 21 hours.

But it was even worse than that. The captain and FO started their four-day sequence together after a normal good night's rest, but under the schedule they were working the captain was awake for 17.5 hours after that, and was only able to get 5 hours of sleep during a daytime rest opportunity in a Dallas-Ft. Worth Airport hotel. He was awake after that for another 23.5 hours before the accident occurred. In other words, during the 46-hour period before the accident, he had only obtained 5 hours of sleep! The FO's experience was almost as bad. He was awake for 19 hours, after which he was able to get 8 hours of sleep during the same daytime rest opportunity and at the same hotel as the captain. He was then awake for 19 hours until the accident. Therefore, during the same 46-hour period he had only attained 8 hours of sleep! The FE, who joined them in Atlanta, was awake for only 9 hours and was able to get 6 hours of sleep during the same daytime rest opportunity at the same hotel as the captain and FO. However, he was awake after that for 21 hours before the accident occurred. Therefore, during the 36-hour period before the accident, he had obtained only 6 hours of sleep!

Investigators concluded that the entire crew suffered from cumulative sleep loss, they experienced extended (beyond normal) periods of continuous wakefulness, and their periods of daytime sleep were obtained in opposition to their body's normal circadian rhythms resulting in less sleep quality than they would normally have achieved if they had slept at night. Furthermore, the accident occurred late in the afternoon, during a window of physiological sleepiness and one of the two low periods in a person's circadian rhythm. Therefore, the NTSB concluded that the probable cause of the accident was the impaired judgment, decision making, and flying abilities of the captain and the other flight crew members that resulted from the effects of fatigue. Specifically, fatigue was responsible for the captain's failure to properly assess the conditions for landing and maintain vigilant situational awareness of the airplane while maneuvering onto final approach, prevent the loss of airspeed and avoid a stall while in the steep-banked turn and execute immediate action to recover from a stall (Report No: NTSB/AAR-94/04).

It may be hard to believe, but the 1993 Guantanamo Bay accident was the first time the NTSB cited fatigue as the probable cause of an aircraft accident.[2] It was cited as a contributing factor in several previous aircraft accidents, but not the direct cause of one. It's understandable that it took so long for them to do so because it was, and still is, extremely difficult to measure the role of fatigue in any given accident. Also, significant empirical research into fatigue didn't really begin until the mid-1950s;[3] therefore, it took time for this growing field to make somewhat accurate conclusions regarding the nature of the phenomenon and to make recommendations on how to best reduce its effects on human performance.

Fatigue in Aviation

Fatigue is a problem in all modes of transportation. For example, the National Highway Traffic Safety Administration (NHTSA) estimates that *drowsy driving* was responsible for 72,000 crashes, 44,000 injuries, and 800 deaths in 2013.[4] It is also responsible for 15 to 20 percent of accidents involving all modes of transportation—the largest identifiable and preventable cause of transportation accidents, surpassing alcohol and drug-related causes.[5] Despite its difficulty to measure, fatigue has been a concern in flying operations since at least as far back as Charles Lindbergh's historic non-stop solo flight from New York to Paris in 1927 in his modified Ryan monoplane dubbed the *Spirit of St. Louis*. He didn't have the best sleep the night before and he began to tire after only about 4 hours into this 33.5-hour flight. To "keep his mind clear" he descended to 10 feet above the water and opened his window. He later climbed back up a few hundred feet describing his battle with fatigue this way:

> My mind clicks on and off, as though attached to an electric switch with which some outside force is tampering. I try letting one eyelid close at a time when I prop the other open with my will. But the effort's too much. *Sleep is winning.* My whole body argues dully that nothing, nothing life can attain is quite so desirable as sleep. My mind is losing resolution and control.[6]

Today, common sense and regulations keep most pilots from attempting flight for such long durations. However, the advent of around-the-clock flight operations and the quest for maximum productivity, coupled with a general lack of appreciation and knowledge about human fatigue, have often pushed pilots to their limits. Regulations have also been wanting. For example, the captain of Kalitta Flight 808 was legally operating within the existing regulations at the time yet was on duty for 18 hours and awake for 23.5 hours when the accident occurred. After off-loading at Guantanamo, he and his crew were actually scheduled to ferry the DC-8 under Part 91 to Atlanta. That would have put their flight and duty time right at the legal limit (for overseas/international flights) of 12 hours and 24 hours, respectively. The captain would have been awake almost 30 hours when they arrived at Atlanta!

Fatigue accounts for about 4 to 8 percent of civil and military aviation mishaps,[7] most of which are incidents, not accidents. A third of all incidents and errors reported to the U.K. confidential human factors incident reporting program are fatigue-related, and in the U.S. it has been implicated in 21 percent of incidents reported to the NASA ASRS.[8]

Professional pilot surveys reveal high levels of concern about fatigue. For example, a survey of 1,424 pilots flying for 26 different U.S. regional air carriers found that 89 percent of them rated fatigue as a moderate or serious concern, 88 percent reported it was a common occurrence in regional flight operations, 92 percent reported that when fatigue occurs it represents a moderate or serious safety issue, and, astoundingly, 80 percent of the pilots acknowledged having nodded off during a flight at some time. In addition, 86 percent of those same pilots reported that they had received no training about fatigue from the companies for which they worked.[9]

A more recent study of airline pilots in eight European countries published by the European Cockpit Association found that more than 80 percent of pilots surveyed in Austria, Sweden, Germany, and Denmark had to cope with fatigue while flying and more than 50 percent of all pilots surveyed said fatigue impaired their performance while on flight duty. More than 70 percent of pilots in Sweden, Norway, and Denmark, and 40 percent in Germany, also admitted they made mistakes in flight because of fatigue.[10] Another recent survey, designed to measure the extent of fatigue in 456 Portuguese airline pilots, revealed that 89.3 percent suffered from fatigue during the previous two weeks of flying duty, and that 92.1 percent of long-haul pilots and 96.5 percent of medium/short-haul pilots reported mental fatigue was an issue during their recent flying. Just over 90 percent claimed they had made mistakes on the flight deck because of fatigue, while 67 percent felt so tired that they thought they shouldn't have been at the controls at all.[11]

The issue is so important that, with the exception of only a brief period (2013 to 2015), reducing fatigue–caused transportation accidents has been on the NTSB's *Most Wanted List of Transportation Safety Improvements* list since it was first introduced in 1990. In fact, for the 12 years between 2000 and 2012, the NTSB found that nearly 20 percent of 182 major transportation accident investigations (all aviation and all significant rail, road, marine, and pipeline accidents) identified fatigue as a probable cause, contributing factor, or a finding.[12]

Since the Kalitta Flight 808 accident, both the FAA and NTSB have encouraged significant research into the effects of fatigue on flight crew performance. In light of these findings, investigators now examine more closely factors such as the amount and quality of recent sleep obtained by crew members, how long they have been awake and on duty, circadian rhythm issues, sleep debt and restorative sleep opportunities, and the effects of operational workload in causing fatigue. As a result, investigators have cited fatigue as a probable cause or contributory factor in several major accidents since Guantanamo. Table 10-1 is a list of just some of these. What should be noted is that despite an industry awareness of the effects of fatigue, it continues to be a factor even today.

Table 10-1. A list of some fatal accidents since the Guantanamo Bay accident where fatigue has been cited as a probable cause or a contributing factor.

Date	Aircraft	Operator	Location	Fatalities
Aug 14, 2013	A300	UPS	Birmingham, AL	2
Jul 6, 2013	B-777	Asiana Airlines	San Francisco, CA	3
Feb 20, 2013	Beech Premier I	General Aviation, Part 91	Thomson, GA	5
May 22, 2010	B-737	Air India Express	Mangalore, India	158
Jul 31, 2008	Hawker Beechcraft 125	East Coast Jets	Owatonna, MN	8
Sep 16, 2007	MD-82	Go Airlines	Phuket Airport, Thailand	90
Mar 15, 2005	BN-2 Islander	Loganair	Machrihanish, U.K.	2
Oct 24, 2004	Learjet 35	Med Flight Air Ambulance	San Diego, CA	5
Oct 19, 2004	BAE-32	Corporate Airlines	Kirksville, MO	11
Oct 14, 2004	B-747	MK Airlines	Halifax, NS	7
Jan 17, 2004	Cessna 208	Georgian Express	Pelee Island, ON	10
Jan 4, 2002	CL604	Epps Air Service	Birmingham, U.K.	5
Dec 9, 1999	Cessna 525	College of the Ozarks	Branson, MO	6
Jun 1, 1999	MD-82	American Airlines	Little Rock, AK	11
Aug 6, 1997	B-747	Korean Air	Agana, Guam	228
Mar 2, 1996	Learjet	Madrid Táxi Aéreo	São Paulo, Brazil	9
Feb 16, 1995	DC-8	Air Transport International	Kansas City, MO	3
Dec 21, 1994	B-737	Air Algerie	Coventry, U.K.	5

The Effects of Fatigue

Fatigue can simply be defined as tiredness, whether physical, mental, or both. Other synonyms used to describe fatigue are sleepiness, weariness, lethargy, and exhaustion. However, a more descriptive and helpful definition of **fatigue** is one provided by the FAA:

> A physiological state of reduced mental or physical performance capability resulting from lack of sleep or increased physical activity that can reduce a flight crew member's alertness and ability to safely operate an aircraft or perform safety-related duties (14 CFR §117.3).

Notice in this definition the emphasis on the reduced performance ability of individuals when they are fatigued. As you saw at Guantanamo Bay, fatigue impaired the captain's performance to the point of causing an accident. The following discussion highlights only some of the human performance decrements discovered by academic research and aircraft accident analyses.

Information Processing

In Chapter 3 we introduced the field of cognitive psychology which postulates that, somewhat like a computer, humans process sensory information (inputs) received by their senses (eyes, ears, etc.) through various stages, or mental operations, such as perception, attention, memory, and decision making (*see* Figure 3-5 in Chapter 3). The end result of this processing is we execute a response (output) by doing something. In the flight environment, for example, we might pay *attention* to our navigation instruments and *perceive* we are off course, so we *respond* by moving the controls to a heading that should get the aircraft back on track. Or, our visual *sense* tells us we are getting close to the runway on final approach so, drawing from our *memory* of how this airplane is supposed to be configured for the expected runway environment, we make the *decision* to lower the flaps then *respond* by placing the flap selector switch to the extended position.

Using different kinds of tests designed to measure cognitive performance, including neuroimaging and techniques to measure metabolic rates and other physiological responses in the areas of the brain that are associated with different aspects of cognition, researchers have discovered that our overall mental processing abilities, as well as our performance, suffer when we are fatigued.[13] This includes what scientists call *cognitive slowing*, a reduction in the speed needed to process information that worsens as the time performing a task is prolonged. This overall cognitive impairment is evidenced in decrements in the various components of information processing, especially attention, memory, decision making and reaction times. We discuss these topics in greater detail in Chapters 14, 16, and 17, but for now we will only briefly describe how fatigue affects some of these areas.

Attention

Humans, in general, are notoriously bad at monitoring systems; it is just not in our nature to do so. Accordingly, accidents can happen when a pilot fails to pay attention to his or her environment. This usually involves long durations of simply watching for, and listening to, inputs from our environment. This sustained attention, or *vigilance*, generally degrades with time but is one of the components of mental performance that is particularly weakened when we are fatigued. This often manifests itself in "errors of omission (lapses) and commission (wrong responses)" and in our inability to pay attention to more than one stimulus at a time.[14] When we are tired we have the tendency to focus, or fixate, our attention on just one stimulus at the expense of others that may be more important. The captain of Flight 808 was so fixated on finding the strobe light (in spite of the fact that his FO assured him he was far enough away from Cuban airspace) that he neglected to pay attention to more important stimuli in his environment, like the aircraft's speed, its position relative to the runway, and the timing needed to complete a difficult turn to properly align with the extended centerline of Runway 10. This *tunnel vision* may also explain his non-response to the comment, "I don't know if we're going to make this," from one of his crew members.

Memory

Pilots are more prone to forgetting things when they are fatigued. An NTSB study of 37 flight-crew-caused major air carrier accidents found that compared to pilots who were awake for less than 12 hours, those awake for more than 12 hours made 40 percent more errors, committed more errors of omission by failing to act or, if they did act, by failing to do so in a timely manner, and made more procedural and tactical decision errors.[15] Memory deficits caused by fatigue often result in errors of omission. For example, in the accidents examined, the NTSB found that pilots omitted mandatory callouts (for altitude, speed, checklists, etc.), failed to verbalize checklist responses, inspect wings for ice contamination, consult pertinent charts, brief the missed approach, arm the speed brakes, extend the flaps, and remove an elevator control block.[16] This aligns with experimental data that indicate both short- and long-term memory are impaired by fatigue.[17]

Decision Making

"Fatigue Makes Cowards of Us All"
–George S. Patton, Jr., *War as I Knew It*

Results from accident analyses and empirical research also indicates that a pilot's decision-making ability is impaired when fatigued. For example, the same NTSB study of 37 major air carrier accidents found that flight crews who were awake for more than 12 hours made more tactical decision errors—such as making improper decisions and failing to change a course of action or heed warnings that suggest a change in a course of action is warranted—than did crewmembers who had been awake for less time. The most common decision error was failing to execute a missed approach or go-around when weather (e.g., thunderstorm, tailwind) or other conditions (e.g., unstabilized approach) dictated. Other examples included rejecting a takeoff above V_1, choosing not to order a second aircraft deicing, and deliberately flying below minimum descent altitude/decision height without obtaining adequate visual references.[18]

The topic of decision making is more fully explored in Chapter 17, but for now it is important to realize that since information that is perceived, attended to, and remembered is important in making critical decisions. Any deficiencies in these lower-order processes caused by fatigue will also affect the overall quality of decisions pilots make (*see* Figure 3-5 in Chapter 3). But fatigue affects many higher-level cognitive abilities also involved in decision making. For example, it impairs one's ability to "appreciate a difficult and rapidly changing situation; assess risk; anticipate the range of consequences; keep track of events-update the big picture; be innovative; develop, maintain, and revise plans; remember when events occurred; control mood and uninhibited behavior; show insight into one's own performance; communicate effectively; and avoid irrelevant distractions."[19] The captain of Flight 808 exhibited diminishing effectiveness in performing several of these cognitive tasks. Both his initial decision to hand-fly an extremely difficult visual approach involving a tight turn at low altitude in a large transport-category airplane and his continuation of the approach when circumstances indicated that a go-around should have been conducted, are indicative of his impaired risk assessment, his inability to "appreciate a difficult and rapidly changing situation" and abandon his plan to land on Runway 10, and his inability to avoid irrelevant distractions (the strobe light). He also displayed communication deficits as evidenced by missing and/or disregarding certain critical messages directed to him by his fellow crew members (e.g., airspeed).

Research has also discovered that emotions, or mood, are negatively affected by fatigue, maybe even more so than cognitive or psychomotor performance.[20] In general, moods tend to be more negative and worsen with increasing levels of fatigue.[21] If you have ever witnessed a toddler behave when he hasn't had his nap, you have seen the effects of fatigue on one's mood. Adults are better at controlling and hiding these feelings, but not necessarily when fatigued. In sleep-deprivation experiments researchers describe "irritability, impatience, childish humor, lack of regard for normal social conventions, and inappropriate interpersonal behaviors."[22] Though a written transcript misses the many nuances in verbal communication, perhaps you can still catch the captain's irritability in the following exchange as recorded on the cockpit voice recorder (CVR) after the stall stick shaker activated in the DC-8 at Guantanamo Bay.

CAM 3*	16:54:06	"Watch the, keep your airspeed up."
CAM	16:54:09	(sound similar to stall warning)
CAM ?	16:54:10	"(don't) stall warning."
CAM 1	16:54:11	"I got it."
CAM 2	16:54:12	"Stall warning."
CAM 3	16:54:12	"Stall warning."
CAM 1	16:54:13	"I got it. Back off."[23]

*CAM-1, -2, and -3 are the cockpit area microphone voices (or sound sources) of the captain, FO, and FE, respectively. CAM-? refers to an unidentified voice.

The captain also testified that he felt lethargic and "indifferent," and was baffled as to why he felt that way when so many things were going on in the cockpit. This lack of concern reveals a general lack of motivation and an I-don't-care attitude regarding the progress of the flight. In experimental settings, researchers have discovered that these traits evidenced in fatigued individuals also affect higher order cognitive processes such as judgment and decision making.[24] Perhaps General Patton, and later Vince Lombardi, the famous football coach who popularized the saying, were right: Fatigue *does* make cowards of us all.

Risk Taking

Emotional factors such as mood and diminished motivation are also involved in a fatigued person's tendency to underappreciate risk levels and take unnecessary risks. For example, normally rested participants in a card gambling task tend to shun exciting high-risk hands and choose more modest hands that result in better gambling outcomes. However, these same participants after two nights of sleep loss, shifted to making high-risk bets in spite of heavier losses involved in them.[25]

This inclination toward risk taking when fatigued likely occurs for several reasons. For example, if you are impaired by alcohol yet make the decision to drive while intoxicated, you are exhibiting a reduced capacity to judge the risks involved in engaging in such behavior. One reason for this is that you fail to grasp the extent of your own intoxication. Similarly, studies confirm that fatigued individuals are also poor judges of their own tiredness.[26] This may have occurred with the captain of Flight 808 at Guantanamo Bay: in his post-accident interview he stated that even though he would have rather gone to bed he "did not feel particularly fatigued."[27]

Using neuroimaging technology, researchers have also discovered that sleep-deprived individuals likely make more risky decisions and overestimate the likelihood of positive gains because of increased activity in the part of the brain that is associated with rewards. Similarly, when a tired person underestimates the consequences of losses, he or she may do so because there is less activation in the part of the brain that is associated with aversion, loss, and punishment.[28] Finally, a fatigued person may take risks because they suffer from reduced inhibitory control. That is, they are more prone to taking risks because they lack the ability to inhibit their emotional responses, an aspect that interacts with decision making.[29]

Some additional observations about the FO in the Guantanamo Bay accident: at the time of the accident he had been awake less than the captain (19 hours vs. 24 hours) but had only attained 8 hours of sleep for the same 46-hour period preceding the accident. The NTSB determined that all three crew members suffered from fatigue, yet the FO later stated that "as they approached the airport he felt fully alert and exhilarated, as though he were making an aircraft carrier landing."[30] It appears from this statement that he inaccurately assessed his own level of fatigue and was attracted to conducting the riskier approach to Runway 10—both factors that are in keeping with the findings of fatigue/risk research.

Reaction Time

Reaction time (RT) is slower when fatigued. In fact, several different RT tests are used in experimental settings to test for the effects of fatigue on various aspects of cognitive and psychomotor performance. In spite of several warnings from his fellow crew members ("Stall warning"), and in spite of being aware of the threat ("I got it...I got it. Back off"), the captain of Flight 808 reacted too slowly to the indications of the impending stall (stick shaker) and lost control of the airplane while the controls were still in his hands.

Being Tired is Like Being Drunk

Several researchers have noticed that the cognitive and emotional deficits measured in fatigued individuals are similar to those who are intoxicated by alcohol. Slowed thinking and RT, the inability to concentrate, attention and memory deficits, and impaired decision making, including the inability to recognize one's own fatigue levels and accurately assess risk, are common traits of both fatigue and alcohol intoxication. This has led researchers to find an equivalence between hours awake and blood alcohol concentration (BAC). Different estimates have been calculated depending on how and what performance metrics are measured. For example, one study found that being awake for 17 hours was the equivalent, in terms of cognitive psychomotor performance, of being impaired with a BAC of 0.05 percent[31] while another discovered equivalent performance at 28 hours of sleep deprivation and 0.10 percent BAC.[32] The U.S. National Sleep Foundation claims that being awake for 18 hours is comparable to having a BAC of 0.08 percent,[33] the legal limit for driving while under the influence of alcohol in most jurisdictions in the United States and Canada.

Of course numbers vary significantly between individuals, so a hard and fast rule using the above averages will not apply in all situations. However, regardless of what the actual numbers for any given individual may be, the comparison is worthwhile. Since most people are personally familiar with the effects of alcohol and know (at least after-the-fact) how they behave when intoxicated, and since research has determined that people underestimate their own fatigue levels, this comparison helps them to better appreciate the risks of their own diminished performance after an extended period without sleep. In other words, if you understand the reasons why you should avoid driving while drunk, maybe you will appreciate why you should avoid flying while fatigued.

Falling Asleep at the Controls

There comes a point when a person is so tired, that no matter how hard they fight it, the body wins and gets what it wants—sleep. This is obviously not good if your safety, and that of your passengers, depends on staying awake. If the ultimate risk of driving while fatigued is falling asleep at the wheel, the ultimate risk of flying while fatigued is falling asleep at the controls. In the 2012 European Cockpit Association study cited previously in this chapter, more than a third of all pilots surveyed reported they had inadvertently fallen asleep on the flight deck, with more than half of the pilots from Denmark, Norway, and Sweden reporting doing so. Forty-three percent of U.K. pilots reported involuntarily falling asleep with a third of them waking up only to see their fellow pilot also asleep![34]

Unfortunately, both pilots have been asleep at the controls at the same time in several incidents. Both pilots of a fully loaded Airbus A330 based in the United Kingdom recently fell asleep at the controls—they were only able to obtain five hours of sleep during the previous 36 hours before the incident.[35] You may also be familiar with two highly publicized incidents in the United States. In March, 2004, during a late-night flight in an Airbus A319, both pilots fell asleep about 45 minutes from their destination. This was the captain's third red-eye flight in a row. The air traffic controller tried several times to make contact but was unsuccessful. The crew missed their crossing restriction of FL190 and 250 knots at a certain fix; instead, the aircraft kept flying at FL350, traveling at over 500 knots. The captain finally woke up to hear frantic calls from ATC, so he woke up his FO and they landed without further incident at Denver International Airport (ASRS Report No: 611329).

In February 2008, a Mesa CRJ-200 operating as Go! Flight 1002 flew 26 NM past its destination after both the captain and FO fell asleep while cruising at FL210 on a flight from Honolulu to General Lyman Field in Hilo, Hawaii. ATC and other pilots in the area tried several times to make contact, but the CRJ continued on autopilot past its destination over the open ocean at FL210. The FO eventually awoke, and in turn woke up the captain. The flight arrived at Hilo without further incident (NTSB Identification No: SEA08IA080).

The Many Causes of Fatigue

Several factors contribute to high levels of fatigue, which generally fall into four categories: inadequate sleep, circadian rhythm disruption, high mental workload, and adverse environmental factors.

Inadequate Quantity of Sleep

As humans, we spend approximately a third of our lives asleep. Most adult humans need between about 7 to 9 hours of sleep at night every 24 hours to function normally during the remaining 15 to 17 hours of the day.[36] Most of us know how much sleep we need. If you are uncertain, keep a log; if you find you sleep longer on your days off, then add additional time to those days-on log numbers. Though there are several theories as to why we sleep, no one really knows for sure. The most common theory is we sleep so the body can rejuvenate and restore what it lost while it was awake. Scientists have discovered that several restorative functions, such as "muscle growth, tissue repair, protein synthesis, and growth hormone release occur mostly, or in some cases only, during sleep."[37] Regardless of the possible reasons, we know from our own experience what it's like when we don't get enough sleep: we progressively feel more sleepy during the day and, as we discussed previously, our mental performance suffers in a variety of ways, especially when operating sophisticated equipment such as an aircraft.

A distinction should be made between *physiological* sleepiness and *subjective* sleepiness: the latter being how sleepy you feel, the former being your actual physiological sleepiness based on a variety of measures. When you are deprived of food or water, the body sends signals to the brain that create the sensation of hunger or thirst that induces you to eat or drink. Similarly, when you are deprived of sleep, the body sends signals to the brain that create the physiological sensation of sleepiness (tiredness) that urges you to sleep. It was previously noted that tired people, unfortunately, are poor judges of their own tiredness. One of the reasons your subjective assessments of sleepiness are not always accurate is because it's easy to mask your true physiological sleepiness with social and other activities that energize you.[38]

Time Awake

Long flight duty hours can lead to fatigue, but the total time period since you woke up from your last sleep, or your **time awake** (before and during the duty period), can lead to even greater levels of fatigue.

We have already identified some of the performance issues regarding time awake, or time since awakening (TSA). For example, the NTSB study of 37 major air carrier accidents discovered that flight crews who had been awake for more than 12 hours made 40 percent more errors than crews who were awake for less than 12 hours.

Most countries today specify maximum duty time periods airline pilots must work each day that also allow for adequate rest (sleep) time between duty periods. However, following the rules doesn't guarantee a fatigue-free flight. It is physiologically normal to go to sleep at night and wake up in the morning; but if your duty day begins later in the day, you are already at a disadvantage in terms of time awake because you likely awakened several hours earlier. In fact, a 2014 study confirmed this problem by studying 40 commercial short-haul pilots during a total of 188 **flight duty periods (FDPs)**. Pilots whose duty period began later in the day (and whose duty time therefore ended later in the day) were more fatigued at the end of their duty period than pilots who started their duty periods earlier in the day. Even though these pilots obtained on average 1.1 hours more sleep the night before, they were awake 5.5 hours longer before commencing their duty period than those pilots who went to work earlier in the day.[39]

Sleep Debt

For millennia, humans generally went to bed after the sun set at night and awoke when it rose in the morning. Since the invention of electricity and artificial light it is now easier for humans to do other things after dark besides sleep. Entertainment, work, recreation, and social activities have taken place at night for so long now that we tend to minimize our need for sleep in favor of participating in other events. When this happens, we accrue a **sleep debt**. For example, if you normally obtain 8 hours of sleep per night but only sleep 6 hours, you have accrued a two-hour sleep debt. If this occurs for two nights, you have accrued an accumulated sleep debt of 4 hours. With a sleep debt you will experience an elevated sleep drive that makes you sleepy, reducing your alertness, and your body will naturally pay back that debt during your next sleep period by causing you sleep longer. Depending on the amount of sleep debt accrued, this will usually only take a couple of days until you are back in a fully rested state.

However, in the same way consuming alcohol can produce significant performance decrements, so can a sleep debt. For example, a two-hour reduction in one night of normal sleep time (two-hour sleep debt) is equivalent of drinking two to three beers, or a BAC of 0.045 percent. In terms of divided attention, vigilance, and memory, 4 hours of sleep loss during one night of sleep is the equivalent of drinking five to six beers, or a BAC of 0.095 percent.[40]

On August 14, 2013, the captain and FO—the only two occupants of this scheduled cargo flight, operating as UPS Flight 1354—died after their Airbus A300 crashed short of the threshold during a nonprecision approach to Runway 18 at Birmingham-Shuttlesworth International Airport in Birmingham, Alabama. The NTSB cited several reasons for the accident, but one of the contributing factors was fatigue experienced by both pilots. The FO, who was the PF, made several errors consistent with the effects of fatigue. Specifically, the FO did not clear the route discontinuity in the flight management computer (FMC), a routine procedure; she failed to recognize cues suggesting the approach was not set up properly; she did not adequately cross-check and monitor the approach (especially below 1,000 feet); and she missed critical verbal callouts. The NTSB evaluated her sleep history leading up to the accident and determined that due to a variety of factors—some within her control and others outside of it—the FO had experienced significant fatigue, including accumulating a severe nine-hour sleep debt during the two days leading up to the accident (Report No: NTSB/AAR-14/02). If the correlation between equivalent sleep loss and intoxication levels discussed in the previous paragraph is correct, her performance would have been the same as if she had consumed more than 10 beers or had a BAC of more than 0.19 percent.

Inadequate Quality of Sleep

The quantity of sleep obtained at night is important in determining the how we function during the day. But so too is its quality. Sleep is made up of two general types, both of which are important in obtaining adequate sleep: rapid eye movement (REM) sleep and non-REM sleep. In contrast to the popular notion that our brain and body simply shut down when we sleep, through a variety of techniques, including the use of electroencephalograms (EEG), scientists have discovered that a typical sleep period involves several cycles (approximately five or six) that alternate between relative inaction (non-REM) and significant activity (REM) throughout the night.

Each cycle lasts approximately 90 to 120 minutes and involves a sequential progression through Stages 1 to 4 (non-REM sleep) followed by REM sleep. During the first sleep cycle, when you begin to nod off, your body enters Stage 1 sleep for a few minutes, followed by Stage 2 sleep for another 10 to 25 minutes. The following are characteristics of these two stages, also known as **light sleep**:

- It is easier to awaken from noises or other factors.
- Your eyes may still move a bit.
- You may experience involuntary muscle twitching (called *hypnic jerks*).
- Heart rate, breathing rate, and other physiological functions slow down.
- Blood pressure and temperature drop.
- Brain activity begins to slow exhibiting low frequency *alpha* and *theta* waves.

After about 30 to 45 minutes you enter Stage 3 and 4 sleep. The following are characteristics of these stages, also known as **deep sleep**:

- It is harder to wake up.
- If woken, you will feel groggy for several minutes.
- Temperature, heart rate, breathing rate, and blood pressure are at their lowest levels.
- Brain activity at its lowest, exhibiting slow wave sleep consisting of very low frequency *delta* waves.

After approximately 20 to 40 minutes of deep sleep measurements of brain wave activity indicate a 5- to 10-minute ascent though the other non-REM stages to REM sleep.[41] This can be seen in Figure 10-1, a graph (called a *hypnogram*) of EEG readings representing the sleep cycles during a typical night's sleep. It is during REM sleep (darkened bars on graph) that most vivid dreaming and eye movements occur, the latter in response to the content of the dreams. The body also has a mechanism to temporarily relax arm- and leg- muscles so you presumably won't act out your dreams.[42]

The hypnogram also illustrates that most deep sleep (Stage 3 and 4) occurs in the first two to three cycles at the beginning of the sleep period and its duration shortens until there is very little, if any, near the end of the sleep period. In contrast, most REM sleep occurs in the latter cycles and its duration lengthens near the end of the sleep period. You can see from the graph that the last REM cycle occurs

Fig 10-1.

A hypnogram showing the cycles of non-REM and REM sleep throughout a typical night's sleep. Notice that most non-REM deep sleep (Stages 3 and 4) occurs near the first half of the sleep period while most REM sleep occurs during the latter half.

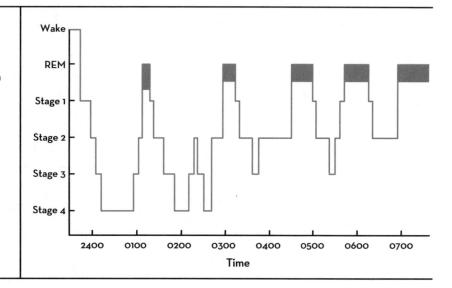

just before a person wakes up, which explains why people often say they just woke up from a dream.

For reasons not fully understood, deep sleep, REM sleep, and the cyclic nature of the entire sleep period are all essential elements in obtaining quality sleep. It appears to contribute to maximum body and brain recuperation, including processes mentioned previously such as tissue repair, muscle growth, and the release of certain hormones. The sleep cycle also likely contributes to other processes such as memory consolidation—the placing and strengthening of recent learning into long term memory storage.

If the normal cyclic progression of non-REM and REM sleep is interfered with, the quality of your sleep will suffer. This can be caused by several factors, including an environment not conducive to sleep (noise, light), a shortening of the sleep period (late to bed, early to rise), sleep disorders (insomnia, obstructive sleep apnea), various diseases, and stimulants (caffeine), drugs, and prescription and over-the-counter (OTC) medications.

Effects of Alcohol and Medication

Two common medications people use to try to facilitate sleep are alcohol and sleeping pills. Unfortunately, both can disrupt the normal cyclic sleep pattern. For example, even though alcohol may help sleep onset, as little as two or three beers or glasses of wine are enough to suppress almost all REM sleep during the first half of the sleep period, leading to **sleep fragmentation** in the latter half.[43] Sleep fragmentation involves waking up and going back to sleep several times during the sleep period. These awakenings may be few in number and long in duration (insomnia) or they may be of short duration and occur numerous times a night without you even knowing about them. This interrupts both non-REM and REM sleep, also reducing the overall quantity of sleep.

Many OTC or prescription sleep aids help sleep onset, but, unfortunately, they also hamper your quality of sleep. Like alcohol, prescription barbiturates, more commonly used in the past as sleep aids, suppress REM sleep and disrupt non-REM sleep, creating fragmented and poor quality sleep. Some sleep aids lose their effectiveness after several days of use and can actually cause insomnia (called *drug-dependent insomnia*). That is why doctors recommend you use the lowest dosage of any sleep aid and for as short a duration as possible. The FAA *Guide for Medical Examiners* states that "occasional or limited use of sleep aids, such as for circadian rhythm disruption in commercial air operations, is allowable for pilots. Daily/nightly use of sleep aids is not allowed regardless of the underlying cause or reason." When used, the *Guide* also requires minimum wait times before beginning flight duty status after taking certain prescription sleep aids. Wait times can be up to 72 hours after taking the last dose. The *Guide* further states that "all the currently available sleep aids, both prescription and over the counter, can cause impairment of mental processes and reaction times, even when the individual feels fully awake." It further states that medical conditions that "chronically interfere with sleep are disqualifying regardless of whether a sleep aid is used or not."[44]

Nonconsolidated Sleep

Another type of fragmented sleep, which is less restorative than continuous undisturbed sleep,[45] is **nonconsolidated sleep**. This occurs when pilots attempt to make up for sleep debt accrued during their regular sleeping periods by obtaining sleep during multiple short periods. In the summer of 2013, an Asiana Airlines Boeing B-777 collided with a seawall on short final while conducting a visual approach to Runway 28L at San Francisco International Airport in San Francisco, California. The NTSB discovered the sleep obtained by each pilot during the 24 hours preceding the accident occurred during multiple short sleep periods. Although the pilot monitoring and observer reported they had obtained enough total sleep, according to the NTSB their recent nonconsolidated sleep was fragmented, reducing its restorative value (Report No: NTSB/AAR-14/01).

Two pilots survived, but all five passengers died, after the captain of a Beech 390 Premier I attempted a go-around and crashed in a wooded area about a half-mile past the departure end of Runway 10 at Thomson-McDuffie County Airport in Thomson, Georgia. The NTSB determined that the ATP-rated pilot made two critical errors: he failed to follow airplane flight manual procedures for an antiskid failure and failed to immediately retract the lift dump after he elected to attempt a go-around while still on the runway. Contributing to the accident was his fatigue due to acute sleep loss and his ineffective use of time between flights to obtain sleep. The pilot woke up at 0230 hours on the day of the accident for a flight to John C. Tune Airport in Nashville, Tennessee, and had obtained only about 5.5 hours of sleep (he normally slept 8 hours per night). He tried to make up for his 2.5-hour sleep debt by sleeping in a chair in the pilot lounge at Nashville that morning. However, the accident investigation revealed that three outgoing calls were made during this four-hour sleep break. So not only did he experience insufficient sleep the night before, an early wake time, and a period of extended wakefulness, his cell phone activity disrupted his sleep break which would have "fragmented any sleep the pilot did obtain and degrade its restorative quality" (NTSB Identification No: ERA13MA139).

Sleep Disorders

A variety of sleep disorders, some recognized and some not by pilots who have them, contribute to fatigue by disrupting the normal sleep cycle and reducing overall sleep time. They have even contributed to aircraft accidents and incidents. For example, when both pilots inadvertently fell asleep while flying past their destination of Hilo, Hawaii, one of the reasons the captain was so fatigued and fell asleep at the controls of Go! Flight 1002 was he had an undiagnosed severe sleeping disorder, specifically obstructive sleep apnea.

Both flight crew and all six passengers died after Flight 81, a Hawker Beechcraft 125 operated by East Coast Jets, crashed while attempting a go around after landing on Runway 30 at Owatonna Degner Regional Airport, in Owatonna, Minnesota. According to NTSB investigators, the captain made the wrong decision: he attempted a go-around late in the landing roll with insufficient runway remaining. Contributing to the captain's degraded performance and decision-making abilities was, among other things, fatigue that resulted from significant acute sleep loss, an early start time, and a possible untreated sleep disorder. Though it could not be conclusively proven, investigators suspected the captain may have been suffering from an undiagnosed sleep disorder because of his excessive need for sleep. According to family and friends, he usually obtained between 8.5 to 12 hours of sleep a night, and normally took a daily afternoon nap of 2.5 to 3 hours, resulting in a total sleep time of about 11 to 15 hours per day. This high need for sleep is a major symptom of a sleep disorder (Report No: NTSB/AAR-11/01).

Sleep disorders can disrupt sleep to the point that its victims are tired throughout the day, even after a long night of sleep. Often the person is completely unaware that they are suffering from a sleep disorder. There are several sleep disorders, but two common ones are obstructive sleep apnea and periodic limb movement disorder.

Obstructive sleep apnea (OSA) occurs when your airway is blocked by relaxed throat muscles causing you to stop or pause your breathing (*a* = without; *pnea* = breathing). Usually after no more than 30 seconds (but could be as long as a couple of minutes!) the increase in carbon dioxide in the blood signals the brain to start breathing again which involves a brief awakening as you gasp (or snore) for air. Depending on the severity of the disorder, OSA episodes can occur a few times, or as many as 80 times per hour of sleep.[46] Besides contributing to long-term health problems (e.g., high blood pressure), experts believe that such fragmented sleep—which almost completely destroys deep sleep—accompanied by the oxygen starvation that occurs during each episode, is what causes excessive daytime sleepiness.[47]

Periodic limb movement disorder (PLMD) involves brief involuntary leg twitching or jerking that repeats periodically throughout the sleep period. Because it can cause up to several hundred mini-awakenings per night, PLMD, like OSA, leads to excessive sleepiness during the day. It is similar to restless leg syndrome (RLS), but isn't the same thing. Both lead to daytime fatigue, but PLMD occurs involuntary and unconsciously while sleeping; RLS is somewhat voluntary and occurs consciously while awake or when sleeping—in fact, it keeps a person awake when they're trying to sleep.

Most of us, at one time or another, have experienced a common sleep disorder—**insomnia** (*in* = without; *somnus* = sleep), the inability to fall asleep or stay asleep. Short-term (or acute) insomnia, often brought about by stress or troubling thoughts, disrupts sleep and leads to excessive daytime sleepiness. So too does longer-term (or chronic) insomnia, often caused by some physiological health condition, other sleep disorders, long-term stress, medications, or poor sleeping habits.

Circadian Rhythm Disruption

We mentioned previously that most adults need 7 to 9 hours of sleep per night. The key word is *night*. The human body is strongly predisposed to sleep at night, not during the day. This isn't just because our society primarily functions that way, nor is it because we have nothing better to do at night; it is because there is a mechanism within our brain, an internal **biological clock** if you will, with an internal timer/alarm system that tells the rest of body to do certain things at certain predictable times throughout the day. The fluctuations of these daily physiological functions are called **circadian rhythms** (*circa dies* = about a day) or *diurnal rhythms*.

There are actually several biological clocks in the body, including those that exist at the cellular level. What we call the biological clock is sometimes referred to by researchers as the *master clock* to distinguish it from these other clocks. It is believed to reside in the suprachiasmatic nucleus located in the hypothalamus, a part of the brain responsible for regulating many processes of the autonomic nervous system. The following are only a few of the physiological rhythms that automatically ebb and flow during a 24-hour day in response to the control of the biological clock:

- Sleep/wake cycle.
- Blood pressure.
- Heart rate.
- Respiratory rate.
- Core body temperature.
- Digestion.
- Hormone release (cortisol, insulin, melatonin, etc.).
- Cell metabolism.
- Immune system processes.

How do scientists know about the various rhythms controlled by this so-called biological clock? One way is by directly measuring several different physiological processes (e.g., heart rate, blood pressure, hormones, inner body temperature) of people who live in a controlled environment absent all time cues. That is, volunteers are asked to live their lives—eat, drink, sleep—for a period of days or even weeks in a soundproof room, with no natural light, clocks, and other cues that could reveal the actual time of day. What they have learned is that several of these internal physiological activities rise and fall according to a predictable schedule, independent of what the actual time of day it is in the environment.

Window of Circadian Low

One discovery is a fairly predictable and consistent rise and fall of core body temperature, as diagrammed in Figure 10-2. As you can see by the graph, core body temperature generally rises during the day and falls at night. Except for a slight drop in the late afternoon, core body temperature reaches its lowest between an average of about 0300 hours to 0500 hours (though the range is more likely between 0200 hours to 0600 hours to account for individual differences). This is often called the **window of circadian low (WOCL)**.

We previously made the distinction between subjective sleepiness (how tired you feel) and physiological sleepiness (how sleepy you actually are). Research has found that due to circadian factors such as reduced temperature and elevated melatonin, this early morning time-period corresponds to the time of maximum physiological sleepiness, or tiredness (your subjective sleepiness will likely also be very high as well). Not surprisingly, it is also the time of day when alertness and cognitive performance are also

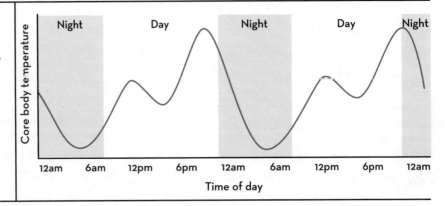

Fig 10-2.

With the exception of a slight dip in the late afternoon, core body temperature generally rises during the day and falls at night. The primary WOCL occurs between approximately 0300 hours and 0500 hours and a secondary WOCL between approximately 1500 hours and 1700 hours.

at their lowest. Though less in intensity, an increase in sleepiness and an associated drop in alertness and performance occurs in the later afternoon between approximately 1500 hours and 1700 hours during the secondary WOCL. This has often been described as the post-lunch dip.

For a normal night's sleep, physiological sleepiness begins when the core body temperature begins to drop and melatonin hormone levels rise and reaches its maximum when body temperature is at its lowest of the day and melatonin at its highest during the middle of the primary WOCL. Physiological sleepiness begins to wane, and the onset of wakefulness begins, when core temperature begins to rise and melatonin levels drop. Maximum wakefulness generally occurs when temperature is at its highest and melatonin levels at their lowest, generally later in the morning and in the early evening.

Studies have also found that the longest and best sleeps occur at night when timed according to the circadian drive to sleep (i.e., when temperature begins to drop and melatonin levels rise). If you delay the start of your normal sleep to later in the evening, your sleep will likely be shorter due to the onset of wakefulness that occurs according to the circadian schedule. Similarly, Stage 2 and REM sleep suffers if you force yourself to wake up too early during the WOCL in opposition to the biological drive to sleep.[48]

These findings have serious implications for operators of machines—trucks, buses, cars, and aircraft—that, as the NTSB cautions in its 2017–2018 *Most Wanted List*, "require complex human interaction and an operator's complete attention and proficient skill."[49] The percentage of fatigue-related automobile accidents illustrates that the stakes are high. For example, according to the NHTSA, drowsy-driving accidents occur most frequently between midnight and 0600 hours and in the late-afternoon corresponding to the primary and secondary WOCLs. Also, about half of the fatigue-related fatal aircraft accidents listed in Table 10-1 occurred during a time when the flight crews' biological drive to sleep would normally be present—between late evening and early morning. The fatal MD-82 accident in Little Rock, Arkansas, occurred two hours after the crew normally went to bed. The fatal Boeing B-747 accident in Guam that killed 228 people occurred almost four hours after the captain normally went to bed. The captain had been awake for 17 hours and the copilot

16 hours, in a fatal accident east of San Diego's Brown Field Municipal Airport when the crew of a Learjet 35 experienced controlled flight into terrain. The accident occurred about 4 hours after they normally went to bed (NTSB Identification No: LAX05FA015).

Several aircraft accidents have occurred during the primary WOCL, which generally ranges between about 0200 hours to 0600 hours. For example, at 0354 hours on October 14, 2004, a cargo-carrying B-747 attempted a takeoff on Runway 24 at Halifax International Airport in Nova Scotia, Canada. Unfortunately, the MK Airlines jumbo jet never made it and crashed about a half-mile beyond the end of the runway, killing all seven crew members. One of the pilots made a mistake in calculating the takeoff speeds and thrust settings—both values were too low to enable the aircraft to take off safely. The Transportation Safety Board of Canada (TSB) concluded that this error, and the crew's inability to detect it, was likely the result of fatigue. According to the TSB investigation, the pilots had been on duty for almost 19 hours and they were at their lowest levels of performance at the time of the accident, in part because they were at their expected lowest point in their circadian rhythms (TSB Report No: A04H0004).

It was previously noted that one of the factors that contributed to the fatal Airbus A300 accident in Birmingham, Alabama, was fatigue. The NTSB cited several fatigue-related factors, most attributed to the FO who was the PF at the time, but one factor was that the accident occurred about 0447 hours, a time of day associated with the WOCL. The NTSB concluded the FO was awake in opposition to her normal body clock and would have been more vulnerable to the negative effects of the fatigue that she was already experiencing (Report No: NTSB/AAR-14/02).

Finally, the pilots of Go! Flight 1002 fell asleep over Hawaii during the midmorning hours, a time of day normally associated with wakefulness and rising alertness. However, in addition to the captain's undiagnosed OSA, and significant sleep debts accrued by both pilots, one of the reasons they fell asleep at the controls was that they both reported for duty at 0540 hours and awoke at 0400 hours (captain) and slightly before 0500 hours (FO) each of the previous three days. These consecutive days of early-morning start times disrupted their sleep during their WOCL, reducing both the quantity and quality of their evening sleeps (NTSB Identification No: SEA08IA080).

Shift Work

The Mesa Go! pilots were operating in opposition to their normal circadian rhythms, but with the advent of 24/7 flight operations—especially overnight cargo delivery—many pilots must work all night. Abundant evidence indicates that shift work—working at times other than a typical daytime work schedule (night, partial night, early morning, or rotating shift schedules)—is hard on human health and well-being. Studies indicate that shift work significantly disrupts our normal circadian rhythms and may contribute to a variety of conditions such as gastrointestinal disorders (constipation, irritable bowel syndrome, ulcers), metabolic disorders (obesity, type 2 diabetes), cardiovascular disorders (heart disease, blood pressure), cancer (prostate, lung), women's reproductive function (premenstrual syndrome, preterm birth), and social problems with family and others who live in a normal day work/school schedule.[50]

A concern about shift work is the more immediate effect circadian disruption has on your physiological and mental well-being and your performance. Some researchers call these symptoms *shift-lag*, likening them to the symptoms of jet lag (discussed in the next section). These symptoms include "feelings of fatigue, sleepiness, insomnia, digestive troubles, irritability, poorer mental agility, and reduced performance efficiency." [51]

The problem with shift work is you are working against your normal circadian rhythms by attempting to be awake and alert when your body wants to sleep. There is evidence that some of the problems with shift work can be mitigated if there is a way to reset your internal biological clock. It was mentioned previously that in controlled settings, where there is an absence of all time cues and your circadian rhythms are allowed to free run, several internal physiological processes rise and fall according to the biological clock's schedule. What researchers have found is that when the clock is allowed to free run it is somewhat slower than the 24-hour day, exhibiting its daily up and down cycles in, on average, about 25 hours. This innate 25-hour circadian rhythm adjusts to 24-hours every day by synchronizing with environmental time cues such as light and darkness, eating meals at regular times, and social activities. The most effective synchronizer, or time cue (sometimes called a *zeitgeber*, a German word meaning *time giver*) is light. For example, you wake up earlier in the morning if

the curtains are left open allowing sunlight to enter your room. The reason for this is the light has a direct neural pathway to the internal clock in the suprachiasmatic nucleus (SCN) because, as its name suggests, it is located just above (*supra*) the location where the left and right optic nerves cross each other (*chiasm*, from Greek letter X, or *chi*). Thus, being exposed to daylight each day is enough to advance the circadian cycles from the inner biological 25-hour day and synchronize it to a 24-hour one.[52]

Since the internal clock is flexible enough to synchronize with the external clock, you are correct in concluding that if you can create an environment where you can live your life at night and sleep during the day, your biological clock will eventually synchronize with your outside world. However, this is easier to do in theory than in practice. First of all, you have to create an artificial environment that contains time cues (zeitgebers) that operate opposite than when they normally would. For example, to facilitate work at night and sleep during the day your environment must contain sufficient artificial light at night and be dark during the day. Assuming you can create such an environment, you also have to deal with social activities involving yourself, family, and friends that take place during the day. How do you do that? As soon as you walk outside into daylight your SCN will start to resynchronize its internal circadian rhythms back to their normal schedule. Also, even though there is flexibility in synchronizing the internal clock with the real clock, the process is not that fast—usually no more than about one hour per day.[53] So assuming you are able to achieve an ideal environment for resynchronization, it will take several days to totally adjust. Complicating matters is not all internal circadian rhythms synchronize at the same rate, and therefore, not at the same time.

What we have been describing is a person who moves to a full-time night schedule (the graveyard shift). Can you imagine how hard this is for someone who does this for only a short duration, or who changes from one shift schedule to another? In spite of the physiological discomfort, it's no wonder why most people revert to a normal diurnal schedule, both during and after shift work and on their days off; it's just too difficult to do otherwise.

Circadian Desynchronization (Jet Lag)

The circadian disruption involved in shift work is sometimes referred to as **circadian dysrhythmia**, a synonym for **jet lag**, the popular term used to describe circadian disruption problems created by the rapid crossing of multiple time zones. Before the advent of air transport, traveling east or west from one time zone to another was slow enough that people generally felt no ill-effects from moving from one time zone into another. The circadian rhythms synchronized with the external environment about as fast as, or faster, than people moved. However, with the advent of transmeridian flight—especially flights that crossed multiple time zones—people began to experience the negative effects of jet lag. You might arrive early in the morning (after sunrise) at a destination that promotes wakefulness, while your rhythms are aligned to induce sleep. Then throw in sunlight as a strong zeitgeber at your destination, and you have all the makings of a confused biological clock that is now not only out of sync with the new environment but its diverse physiological processes are out of sync with each other. The result is excessive sleepiness, fatigue or insomnia, disorientation, headaches, digestive problems, lightheadedness, and more.[54]

While just a one-hour time change when flying in either direction is enough to induce jet lag symptoms, it appears eastbound flights are generally more disruptive to our circadian rhythms than westbound. Flying west involves gaining time with the sun, extending your personal day; a situation the biological clock favors (remember its free run time is about a 25-hour day). Flying eastbound involves losing time, traveling the opposite direction of the sun and shortening the day. Some researchers estimate the internal clock can adjust up to about 1.5 hours either side of its free-run time of 25 hours. If this is true, its biological day can fall between approximately 23.5 and 26.5 hours without too much consequence. For example, your personal day is delayed by 5 hours on a westbound flight that crosses 5 time zones, creating a 29-hour biological day $(24+5=29)$. This *phase delay* creates a desynchronization of about 2.5 hours beyond its maximum range of 26.5 hours $(29-26.5=2.5)$. Crossing the same number time zones on an eastbound flight shortens your personal day by five hours creating a 19-hour biological day $(24-5=19)$. This *phase advance* creates a desynchronization of about 4.5 hours beyond its minimum range of 23.5 hours, $(23.5-19=4.5)$, an extra two hours compared to the same trip westbound.

A U.S.-registered Bombardier CL600 Challenger stalled and rolled immediately after takeoff from Runway 15 at Birmingham International Airport, Birmingham, U.K., killing all five people on board. The U.K. Air Accidents Investigation Branch (AAIB) determined that frost on the wings caused the loss of control. Investigators determined that the "judgement and concentration of both pilots may have been impaired by the combined effects of a non-prescription drug, jet-lag, and fatigue."[55] Even though other aircraft on the morning of the accident had been de-iced due to the moderate to severe icing conditions, and despite both crew members knowing about the frost because they had discussed it, neither requested deicing service. Investigators concluded the crew had disturbed and inadequate sleep for the two nights preceding the accident, and since the flight the previous day crossed five time zones, they may have been suffering from jet lag. Incidentally, it was partly as a result of this accident, in which the AAIB recommended the FAA delete all reference to "polished frost" within their regulations, that in 2010 the FAA did in fact remove the provision under 14 CFR §§ 91.527(a)(3), 125.221(a), and 135.227(a), that permitted pilots to takeoff with polished frost adhering to the wings or stabilizing- or control-surfaces.

There are a variety of ideas on how best to mitigate the effects of jet lag on pilot performance. Should you be a pilot who must deal with crossing multiple time zones for a living, the concluding section of this chapter will suggest some measures you can take to best manage this threat.

High Mental Workload

Flying takes mental work, another factor that leads to fatigue. Just as there are limits to how much physical workload the body can endure, so too are there limits to how much mental workload the mind can sustain before fatigue sets in. As discussed more fully in Chapter 14, the most mentally demanding phases of flight (i.e., those that involve numerous tasks and significant mental effort to accomplish correctly and precisely) are the vertical segments, especially the approach and landing. These challenging phases likely explain why these two phases are also the most risky, responsible for almost half of fatal commercial jet airplane accidents (*see* Chapter 1).

The type of fatigue you may experience after conducting a challenging approach and landing is **acute fatigue**, or *transient fatigue*, because it is relatively short-term and often dissipates after some rest or a single sleep period. However, if time-on-task is prolonged (i.e, you undergo lengthy periods of high mental workload without the opportunity to achieve adequate rest and/or sleep) you will also experience **cumulative fatigue**. Sometimes called *chronic fatigue*, cumulative fatigue is longer lasting and results from insufficient recovery from acute fatigue, the acumulation of several types of fatigue including sleep debt, poor quality sleep, or circadian dhysrythmia, and/or significant periods of high mental workload. An example of this latter factor is short-haul flight operations. Unlike long-haul pilots who fly one or two long-distance flights in a duty day, short-haul pilots fly several shorter segments involving approaches and landings at several different airports and quick turn-around times at each. Studies have found a linear relationship between the number of flight segments flown in a given time period and the reported fatigue levels reported by pilots: that is, pilots report greater fatigue levels after five short flights than after two longer ones.[56]

Adverse Environmental Factors

Do you remember your first flying lessons? I do. I remember the thrill, the challenge, and a certain amount of trepidation. But what I mostly remember is how tired I felt after each flight. It certainly had something to do with all the mental work involved in learning a new and very unfamiliar skill set, but it was also due to the elevated noise levels in the cockpit (physical fatigue). Environmental conditions such as noise, vibration, temperature, and humidity can all add to fatigue levels experienced by pilots. Discussed in Chapter 7, vibration and noise both cause an involuntary reflex action whereby different muscles respond by contraction. This in turn contributes to physical fatigue. Since atmospheric moisture content generally decreases as you ascend to higher altitudes, humidity levels on the flight decks of commercial jet airplanes at cruise altitudes are typically low. This in turn contributes to dehydration, another condition that contributes to fatigue. This and other fatigue factors are discussed more fully in the next chapter.

Fighting Fatigue

Some aircraft manufacturers have developed—and are developing—onboard technology that can detect when a flight crew member may be asleep at the controls. The system monitors commonly used switches—radio transmission switches, automatic flight mode control panel switches, FMCs, display select switches, and other similar airplane systems—to assess the level of crew interaction with them. If it fails to detect crew interaction with the systems appropriate for the phase of flight within a certain predictable time frame, it will present a visual advisory message via the engine-indicating and crew-alerting system. Should it not detect crew action after another short period, it will elevate to a caution level (amber, with aural) then eventually to a warning level (red, with aural) if still no action is detected. Such systems are considered passive in that they can't really warn a crew member until they may be fast asleep. Perhaps future crew-monitoring systems will morph into predictive fatigue monitoring whereby crews will be alerted to their fatigued condition before they fall asleep.

The proliferation of these systems will no doubt serve as a last line of defense in the fight against fatigue, but as a pilot you certainly don't want to wait for the machine to tell you that you are too tired to fly. You should always be proactive in combatting fatigue so you can perform your best during all phases of flight during the challenging task of flying an aircraft. As you have seen in this chapter, numerous factors contribute to pilot fatigue: sleep loss, impaired sleep quality, unpredictable and varying shift schedules, early-morning report times, limited opportunities for recovery sleep, less-than-optimal sleeping conditions, multiple flight segments, jet lag, and a fatigue-inducing environment that sometimes involves adverse noise, vibration, humidity, and temperatures. Countering some of these influences might seem formidable, but there are plenty of strategies you can use, both before and during flight, to reduce their impact.

Get a Good Night's Sleep

You owe it to your employer, your passengers, and yourself to show up to work fully rested. In fact, U.S. regulations require airline flight crews be **fit for duty** prior to commencing a flight (*see* the information box). This means being physiologically and mentally prepared and capable of performing assigned duties at the highest level of safety (14 CFR §117.3). The best way to do that is to get a good night's sleep. This is certainly easier to accomplish in your own bed, but it should also be your goal between duty periods at layover destinations. The new duty and rest rules implemented by the FAA in 2014 now require employers to provide a 10-hour rest period between FDPs with at least eight hours available for uninterrupted sleep. The old rule precluded a pilot from obtaining eight hours of uninterrupted sleep because it didn't account for the time it took to travel to and from the hotel and the going-to-sleep/waking-up time.

U.S. Flight Crew Member Duty and Rest Requirements: Part 117

On January 4, 2012, the FAA published a final rule, *Flightcrew Member Duty and Rest Requirements*, which created a new Part 117 regulation applicable to Part 121 passenger operations and certain Part 91 operations effective January 14, 2014. It also permitted Part 121 all-cargo operations to voluntarily opt into the Part 117 flight, duty, and rest regulations.

The FAA understands that no single element of the rule mitigates the risk of fatigue to an acceptable level; rather, they have adopted a systems approach, whereby the operator provides an environment that permits sufficient sleep and recovery periods and crew members accept responsibility for mitigating fatigue by taking advantage of that environment. The new rules address several components. Here are just a few of them:

1. **Fitness for duty.** The FAA expects pilots and airlines to take joint responsibility when considering if a pilot is fit for duty, including fatigue resulting from pre-duty activities such as commuting to work. At the beginning of each flight segment, a pilot is required to affirmatively state his or her fitness for duty. If a pilot reports he or she is fatigued and unfit for duty, the airline must remove that pilot from duty immediately.
2. **Fatigue education and training.** As part of their fatigue risk management plan, operators will every two years provide pilots, dispatchers, schedulers, and any person exercising operational control of flights, training on fatigue, the effects of fatigue on pilots, and fatigue countermeasures.
3. **Unaugmented/augmented operations.** The rule addresses circadian rhythms, the WOCL, total duty time, and number of flight segments conducted in a FDP for both augmented* and unaugmented flight operations. The maximum flight duty time (when the aircraft is moving under its own power) and FDP limit is reduced during nighttime hours to account for being awake during the WOCL (which is defined by the regulation as extending from 0200 hours to 0559 hours), when an FDP period consists of multiple flight segments in order to account for the additional time on task, and, if a flight crew member's circadian rhythm is not in sync with the theater in which he or she is operating (i.e., jet lag).
4. **Extensions of flight duty periods.** The rule imposes limits on, and distinguishes between, extended FDPs due to unforeseen operational circumstances that occur prior to takeoff and those that arise after takeoff.
5. **Consecutive night operations.** To reduce cumulative fatigue caused by repeatedly flying at night and during the WOCL, the rule requires a two-hour nighttime sleep opportunity. A split FDP involving a night flight (i.e., morning and evening flight with a break in duty between) requires a three-hour rest opportunity during the FDP. Limits are set for weekly and monthly flight times.
6. **Rest.** The rest period between FDPs is increased to 10 hours (with at least 8 hours available for uninterrupted sleep) from eight, and the length of continuous time off during a 7-day period is extended from 24 to 30 hours. Additional allowance is provided for those experiencing jet lag.

* An **augmented flight** contains more than the minimum number of flight crew members necessary to safely pilot an aircraft, and at least one onboard rest facility that allows flight crew members to work in shifts and sleep during the flight.

Sources:
1. Federal Aviation Administration, "Flightcrew Member Duty and Rest Requirements: Final Rule," *Federal Register* 77.2 (January 4, 2012): 330–403.
2. Federal Aviation Administration, *Fact Sheet—Pilot Fatigue Rule Comparison* (December 21, 2011). Available at www.faa.gov/news/fact_sheets/news_story.cfm?newsKey=12445.

Though not the ideal situation for obtaining the best sleep, do what you can to mimic your home location and routine when sleeping in a strange bed and location. Both at home and away, you should practice good "sleep hygiene" every night just before you go to bed: Avoid eating too much (especially foods that cause indigestion), avoid strenuous exercise (though it does help if done earlier), avoid stressful thoughts and conversations, and avoid screen time. Avoiding emails and social media—both of which may contain bothersome news—before bedtime helps you to avoid stress, a common cause of insomnia. Too much time looking at your personal electronic device also steals time away from sleeping, and more importantly, the light entering your eyes signals the SCN in the brain to reduce the production of melatonin—the exact opposite of what you need to help you fall asleep. The simple routine of reading a book (or, better yet, reading something boring like air regulations!) is often all that is needed to help you to sleep. If you are a light sleeper, consider using earplugs, but set multiple alarms and request a wake-up call just in case. Other ideas include keeping the room temperature lower (unless the cycling of the air conditioning proves too disruptive), using black-out eye shades to minimize light entering your eyes, and listening to relaxing music or using a portable sound machine to mask noises.

Even if you report for duty fully rested, it's still possible to accrue a sleep debt, especially toward the end of a multi-day trip. Fortunately, pay back for sleep debt is less than what you owe. For example, if you have six hours of accumulated sleep loss, it doesn't take an additional six hours of sleep in a night to make it up. However, if you need eight hours of sleep a night to function normally, and you sleep less than that for several nights in a row, it may take you few more nights of acquiring nine or more hours of sleep per night to pay back the debt and return to optimal performance.[57]

Manage Your Commute

It is common practice for airline pilots to live some distance from their **home base**, or *domicile*—the location of the airport from which they report to work—and commute from their home residence to their base by air travel. There are several good reasons for this: the cost of living may be expensive at their domicile; airlines may close or change domiciles, or

pilots are likely to pick different domiciles during their career; or, a domicile may lack the features that one considers necessary to support their family and/or quality of life (proximity of extended family and long-term friends). A consistent residence provides a degree of stability when a pilot changes from one domicile to another, when a pilot is furloughed, or when an airline merges with another.[58]

However, compared to residing close to your base, the stresses involved in commuting include ensuring you arrive for flight duty at your base in a timely manner, planning for potential delays, and adapting to sudden changes that are out of your control such as weather delays. Furthermore, commuting by air not only cuts into your day off at both ends of a multi-day trip, it also has the potential to produce significant levels of fatigue, either before you report for duty, or during the end of your first FDP, by lengthening your time awake on your first duty day.

To minimize commute-induced fatigue consider living closer to where you work. This may be feasible, especially if you can financially afford to and are willing to move again as your career situation changes and eventually stabilizes. You may still face some of the stresses of commuting by automobile to your domicile (or by airplane to a closer destination), but the fatigue induced by the commute itself will be less, the length of your first duty day will be less, the chance of accruing a cumulative sleep deficit will diminish, and you will have more time off—especially compared to day-long commutes to a domicile. If you are unable to reside closer to your home base, consider being flexible in how you schedule your commute. If you didn't get a good night's sleep, or if commuting might significantly extend your first duty day, it may be advantageous to leave earlier than normal and stay a night in a hotel near your domicile before a morning flight. This is certainly better than sleeping in an easy chair in a pilot's crew room.

Though it wasn't cited as a probable cause, and although the schedules of both pilot's on Colgan Air Flight 3407 that crashed near Buffalo, New York, in 2009 were within the flight and duty requirements at the time, NTSB investigators concluded that the performance of both pilots "was likely impaired because of fatigue" (Report No: NTSB/AAR-10/01). Neither pilot slept in a bed the night before the accident: both slept in the company crew room and their sleep was interrupted. The crew room was supposed to be a quiet area, and even though it had couches and recliners "it was not isolated and was subject to interruptions, sporadic noise and activity, lights, and other factors that prevent quality rest" (Report No: NTSB/AAR-10/01). It may cost you to stay at an airport hotel the night before a flight (though some operators may provide financial assistance), but it's worth it if you think you would otherwise be unable to arrive fit for duty.

Choose Flight Schedules Wisely

Airline seniority dictates the ability to pick and choose the most ideal flight schedules for your situation. However, whether you are a senior captain or junior FO, when bidding your trips you should try to use strategies that minimize fatigue. For example, some pilots like to bunch as many trips together as possible to maximize their days off. This works if you are assured you can obtain quality sleep and rest periods between flights. However, it can sometimes leave you exhausted near the end of your multi-day trips, especially if you have several early-morning flights. If you know you have consecutive flights with early-morning report times you should consider adjusting your sleeping schedule a few days beforehand by going to bed and waking up earlier than normal in preparation for such a schedule.

Take a Nap

Research has proven what most people already know: napping is an effective strategy for restoring alertness and improving performance. Naps are even more effective when you use them before you are drowsy to prevent future drowsiness.[59] Therefore, should the opportunity present itself, you should take a nap as a preventive measure if you are expecting a long day of work ahead. Research also indicates that if you are sleep-deprived (i.e., accruing a sleep debt from early-wake times, disrupted sleep, etc.), some sleep is better than no sleep, so take a nap if the opportunity presents itself.[60] Longer naps generally provide longer periods of improved alertness and performance than shorter ones, but you also need to consider the timing of the nap. For example, if you take a nap too close to your regular bedtime, it could interfere with your ability to fall asleep or sleep all night during your regular sleep period. Sometimes it is difficult to obtain a nap, especially during a circadian period of wakefulness when body temperature is at its highest;

however, you will usually have success if you take a nap during either of the two WOCLs. Studies have shown however, that **sleep inertia** usually lasts longer after waking up from a nap during a WOCL.[61] Sleep inertia, a period of impaired performance and reduced vigilance following awakening from a regular sleep episode or a nap, is a "transient physiological state characterized by confusion, disorientation, low arousal, and deficits in various types of cognitive and motor performance"[62] which usually lasts for up to 15 minutes, but may last longer than 30 minutes, especially after waking up from a long (deep) sleep or nap (more than 30 to 40 minutes) and during the primary and secondary WOCL.

It was mentioned earlier in this chapter that 80 percent of 1,424 regional airline pilots surveyed acknowledged having nodded off during a flight, which was not, and still is not, permitted under U.S. civilian air regulations. One possible answer to the problem of spontaneous unplanned napping is *controlled in-seat napping*. That is, to increase alertness and improve performance during the most challenging part of the flight—the approach and landing—a flight crew member takes a planned short nap during the cruise portion of flight and is awakened well before the top of descent. A major study used by some to support this practice was conducted by NASA in the 1990s. Twelve volunteer airline pilots were given the opportunity to have a 40-minute in-seat nap with a 20-minute post-nap recovery period (to recover from sleep inertia) while flying long-haul flights during the low-workload cruise portion of trans-Pacific flights on the flight decks of airliners operated by two major U.S. airlines. What they found was, compared to a control group of pilots who received no nap, crews who did nap (with an average length of 26 minutes) experienced greater alertness and performed better on all measures up to at least 90 minutes after taking the nap (which included the approach and landing phases of flight). Interestingly enough, they also found that almost half of the pilots in the no-rest control group spontaneously fell asleep![63]

This study involved B-747 aircraft that required three-person crews—not the traditional two that is common on most passenger jets today—and two pilots were awake and at their stations at all times. Such a study certainly reveals the benefits of an in-seat nap, but doesn't address the issue of overall safety should something serious occur while the napping crew member is still asleep or experiencing sleep inertia. Therefore, the FAA believes there is insufficient data about whether a controlled nap could safely be taken by a flight crew member during an unaugmented flight (i.e., the minimum number of flight crew members necessary—usually two—to safely pilot an aircraft). Even though it is not prepared at this time to allow the practice of controlled in-seat naps in unaugmented flights, several airlines in other countries do. For example, Air Canada's flight operations manual (FOM) sees strategic controlled naps as an "operational fatigue countermeasure that improves on-the-job performance and alertness when compared to non-countermeasure conditions."[64] Rules about controlled rests in Canada are found in CAR Part VII 720.23. Some of the rules are:

- Each rest period shall be limited to a maximum of 45 minutes to avoid sleep inertia when the flight crew member is awakened;
- Rest periods shall occur only during the cruise phase of the flight and shall be completed at least 30 minutes before the planned top of descent, workload permitting; and
- Unless required due to an abnormal or emergency situation, at least 15 minutes without any flight duties should be provided to the awakened flight crew member to allow sufficient time to become fully awake before resuming normal duties.

You may have heard about the FO of Air Canada Flight 878, a Boeing B-767 en route to Zürich, Switzerland at FL350 over the Atlantic Ocean at night. He pushed the nose down to avoid what he thought was an imminent collision with a U.S. Air Force Boeing C-17 and the captain responded by pulling the nose back up to maintain altitude; within five seconds the vertical acceleration forces went from −0.5 G_Z to +2.0 G_Z which resulted in injury to 14 passengers and 2 flight attendants. The FO had just woken up from a controlled rest only a couple of minutes prior to this and his captain had pointed out the location of the C-17, both outside and on the aircraft's navigation display. Initially he misidentified the planet Venus with the C-17 (hence the media reports that he tried to avoid a collision with the planet), but the captain corrected him and pointed out it was 1,000 feet below them (at FL340). The FO misperceived the location of the C-17 because, in essence, he was still asleep. According to Air Canada's FOM, he was only supposed to sleep a maximum of 40 minutes to avoid deep (slow-wave, *delta*) sleep and the severe sleep inertia associated with awakening from that; instead the captain let him sleep 75 minutes (at 0155 hours, also entering the primary WOCL). The captain was also supposed to allow at least 15 minutes after the FO awoke before allowing him to perform any flight duties to allow sufficient time for him to become fully awake; unfortunately he engaged the FO by getting him involved in the flight only one minute after waking.[65]

Avoid Alcohol and Drugs

The most common drug used to induce sleep is alcohol—after all, it is a depressant—yet the more you drink before going to bed, the more it interferes with your overall night's sleep, primarily because it reduces the total amount of REM sleep; an important component in healthy restorative sleep. You should also be very careful about using prescription and OTC medications, since many may be medically disqualifying for flight duty such as most allergy and cold medicines. Also, sedating OTC sleep aids are usually only effective for a few nights and leave you drowsy during the day. The *occasional* and *limited* use of sleep aids, such as for circadian rhythm disruption in commercial air operations, may be permitted under FAA medical guidelines (*see* caveats discussed previously in this chapter), but consult your local Aviation Medical Examiner before using. Alcohol and drugs are discussed in greater depth in the next chapter.

Maintain a Healthy Diet and Stay Active

Several studies have been undertaken to measure the effect of diet on fatigue. A variety of effects have been measured, but it really depends on what type of foods are used (high or low carbohydrate, protein, etc.), what fatigue effects are measured (light, deep, or REM sleep; nap length; sleep onset; sleep inertia; etc.) and when these effects are measured. Results depend on such a wide variety of factors that it is difficult to recommend dietary choices to enhance sleep. For example, it is generally believed that eating high-protein foods contributes to alertness while carbohydrates cause drowsiness. However, a major source of tryptophan, an essential amino acid that contributes to the development of sleep-inducing serotonin and melatonin, is found in most protein-based foods such as meat, poultry, seafood, nuts, seeds, and dairy products. Therefore, it is unwise to reduce your intake of protein in your diet.[66] You should also maintain normal blood sugar levels by not skipping meals, avoid going to bed with an empty stomach, and avoid eating a heavy or high-fat meal just before going to bed.

If you have a dog or a toddler I bet you have used this trick to help them sleep at night: keep them active during the day. Regular exercise not only improves overall health (discussed in next chapter), it improves both sleep quality and quantity. A recent U.S. study of more than 2,600 adults found that, compared to people with less physical activity, those who engaged in 150 minutes of moderate to vigorous activity a week experienced a 65 percent improvement in sleep quality and felt less sleepy during the day.[67] It helps you fall asleep faster, provides longer durations of deep sleep, and alleviates stress, a common cause of insomnia. Since exercise "increases physiological arousal and can help promote alertness in the short-term," you can also use it to enhance short-term alertness if you are sleepy. But, you should probably avoid strenuous exercise just before bedtime.[68]

Be Strategic with Caffeine

If you don't consume caffeine (coffee, tea, soft drinks, etc.), it is generally better to not start (this topic is further explored in the next chapter). However, if you do, use moderation and be strategic in your consumption. Studies have shown that caffeine improves alertness and performance for up to about five or six hours, especially for those who usually don't consume any caffeine or high doses of it. Habitually high consumption levels increase tolerance and reduce its effectiveness.[69] If your goal is to get a good night's sleep, you should avoid caffeine in the afternoon and evenings. However, if your goal is to stay awake, its use will help you. For example, if you are having difficulty staying alert near the end of a long flight, you should consume caffeine at least 20 minutes (it takes that long for it to be effective) before conducting the approach and landing. Keep in mind, however, that if you need to go to sleep within a few hours after landing, the caffeine will likely well keep you awake until its effects wear off several hours later.

Minimize Jet Lag

The first question you need to resolve before arriving at your destination after crossing multiple time zones is whether or not to let your body adapt to the new zone. Since their stay is generally longer and it is to their advantage to readjust to the new environment as quickly as possible, this is what passengers do. However, depending on how many time zones are crossed, it may take several days for your internal biological rhythms to resynchronize with the new external environment—generally about one day per time zone crossed. There are no hard and fast rules about what you should do, and it depends on a variety of factors, including the number of time zones crossed, but if the layover is less than 24 hours you should try to prevent your body from adjusting to the new time zone by tricking it into thinking it is still in your "home" time zone. It requires careful planning to prevent time cues (zeitgebers) from adjusting your body clock while you attempt to keep the same sleep/wake schedule as your home time zone. For example, if you travel eastbound and arrive at a destination while your body is ready to sleep, but dawn is breaking, or already has, you should avoid bright light (sunglasses perhaps), get to the hotel and use all your tricks to obtain a good sleep (e.g., keep the room dark and cool, use earplugs to dampen elevated daytime noise levels, notify room service not to disturb, etc.). It may be dark, or almost dark, when you awake so expose yourself to bright light (the strongest time cue), and continue to do so to decrease melatonin levels that signal to your brain that it is time to stay awake. Following the same meal schedule as you home time zone will also help minimize circadian disruption.

If you expect an extended layover of more than a couple of days, you should probably cooperate with your body's natural tendency to adjust to the new time zone. You can jump-start this process by adjusting your sleep/wake schedule a few days before departure to more closely match the destination time zone. If you arrive at your destination midmorning local time, but your body is ready to sleep, avoid taking a nap; instead, try to stay awake as long as you can so you can go to bed when everyone else does. Because of its effectiveness in resetting circadian rhythms, you should expose yourself to as much bright daylight as possible and you should eat meals in accordance with the new time zone (if it is lunch time in new location, eat lunch). Other ideas include resetting your watch to the destination time at the beginning of your flight to help you adjust more quickly to the time zone you will be visiting; staying active; using caffeine strategically to stay awake; and drinking plenty of water before, during, and after your flight, since flight deck humidity is low at cruise altitudes and dehydration exacerbates jet lag.[70]

As noted, research has shown that most people are not good judges of their own fatigue and have a tendency to underestimate, rather than overestimate, their degree of tiredness. If you have been awake longer than normal, have awakened earlier than usual, and/or have accrued a sleep debt, you will have a physiologically elevated drive for sleep. To paraphrase Charles Lindbergh, no matter how hard you fight it, sleep will win. Your job is to make sure you're not operating an aircraft when it does.

Helpful Resources

Fatigue Countermeasure Training, an online course developed by the FAA Safety Team, presents practical fatigue risk management tools to improve your health, get better sleep, and be safer on the job. Designed primarily for aviation maintenance crews, the principles apply to pilots and other aviators as well. One of the best parts is the informative and enjoyable 20-minute course introduction video, *Grounded*. This is not your typical FAA training video. (www.faaSafety.gov/gslac/ALC/CourseLanding.aspx?cID=174)

Fatigue in Aviation. A 16-minute award-winning video produced by the Airman Education Programs branch at the FAA CAMI that describes the symptoms of fatigue and suggested countermeasures to mitigate it. (www.faa.gov/pilots/training/airman_education/physiologyvideos/)

Fighting Fatigue. AOPA Air Safety Institute's *Safety Advisor* can assist you in understanding and reducing the threat of fatigue. Includes short videos. (www.aopa.org/training-and-safety/online-learning/safety-advisors-and-safety-briefs/fighting-fatigue)

Endnotes

1. National Transportation Safety Board, *Aircraft Accident Report: Uncontrolled Collision with Terrain, American International Airways Flight 808, Douglas DC-8-61, N814CK, U.S. Naval Air Station, Guantanamo Bay, Cuba, August 18, 1993*, NTSB/AAR-94/04 (Washington, DC: May 10, 1994).

2. Mark R. Rosekind, "Investigating and Managing Fatigue in Aviation: Lessons Learned," Presentation at *Bombardier Safety Standdown* (October 7, 2014).

3. Mark R. Rosekind, Philippa H. Gander, Kevin B. Gregory, Roy M. Smith, Donna L. Miller, Ray Oyung, Lissa L. Webbon and Julie M. Johnson, "Managing Fatigue in Operational Settings 1: Physiological Considerations and Countermeasures," *Behavioral Medicine* 21 (2010): 157–165.

4. Centers for Disease Control and Prevention, *Drowsy Driving: Asleep at the Wheel* (2017). Available at www.cdc.gov/features/dsdrowsydriving/index.html.

5. Torbjorn Akerstedt, "Consensus Statement: Fatigue and Accidents in Transport Operations," *Journal of Sleep Research* 9 (2000): 395.

6. Charles Lindbergh, *The Spirit of St. Louis* (New York: Charles Scribner's Sons, 1953): 233.

7. John A. Caldwell, "Fatigue in Aviation," *Travel Medicine and Infectious Disease* 3 (May 2005): 85–96.

8. Craig A. Jackson and Laurie Earl, "Prevalence of Fatigue Among Commercial Pilots," *Occupational Medicine* 56 (2006): 263–268.

9. Elizabeth L. Co, Kevin B. Gregory, Julie M. Johnson and Mark R. Rosekind, *Crew Factors in Flight Operations XI: A Survey of Fatigue Factors in Regional Airline Operations*, NASA Technical Memorandum 1999-208799 (Moffett Field, CA: NASA Ames Research Center, October 1999).

10. European Cockpit Association, *Pilot Fatigue: A Barometer* (Brussels, Belgium: 2012).

11. Cátia Reis, Catarina Mestre and Helena Canhão, "Prevalence of Fatigue in a Group of Airline Pilots," *Aviation, Space, and Environmental Medicine* 84 (August 2013): 828–833.

12. National Transportation Safety Board, "Reduce Fatigue-Related Accidents," *NTSB 2017–2018 Most Wanted List of Transportation Safety Improvements* (Washington, DC: 2017).

13. Nammi Goel, Hengyi Rao, Jeffrey S. Durmer and David F. Dinges, "Neurocognitive Consequences of Sleep Deprivation," *Seminars in Neurology* 29 (2009): 320–339.

14. Ibid., 323.

15. National Transportation Safety Board, *A Review of Flightcrew-Involved, Major Accidents of U.S. Air Carriers, 1978 through 1990*, Safety Study NTSB/SS-94/01 (Washington, DC: January 1994).

16. Ibid.

17. Goel, Rao, Durmer and Dinges, "Neurocognitive Consequences of Sleep Deprivation."

18. NTSB, *A Review of Flightcrew-Involved, Major Accidents of U.S. Air Carriers, 1978 through 1990*.

19. Yvonne Harrison and James A. Home, "The Impact of Sleep Deprivation on Decision Making: A Review," *Journal of Experimental Psychology: Applied* 6 (2000): 237.

20. June J. Pilcher and Allen I. Huffcutt, "Effects of Sleep Deprivation on Performance: A Meta-Analysis," *Sleep* 19 (1996): 318–326.

21. Rosekind, Gander, Gregory, Smith, Miller, Oyung, Webbon and Johnson, "Managing Fatigue in Operational Settings 1: Physiological Considerations and Countermeasures."

22. Harrison and Home, "The Impact of Sleep Deprivation on Decision Making: A Review," 239.

23. NTSB, *Aircraft Accident Report: Uncontrolled Collision with Terrain, American International Airways Flight 808*, 124.

24. William D.S. Killgore, "Effects of Sleep Deprivation on Cognition," *Progress in Brain Research* 185 (December 2010): 105–129.

25. Ibid.

26. William D. S. Killgore, "Sleep Deprivation and Behavioral Risk-Taking," Chapter 30, *Modulation of Sleep by Obesity, Diabetes, Age, and Diet*, ed. Ronald Ross Watson (New York: Elsevier 2014): 279–287.

27. NTSB, *Aircraft Accident Report: Uncontrolled Collision with Terrain, American International Airways Flight 808*. 14.

28. Killgore, "Effects of Sleep Deprivation on Cognition."

29. Ibid.

30. NTSB, *Aircraft Accident Report: Uncontrolled Collision with Terrain, American International Airways Flight 808*. 15.

31. Drew Dawson and Kathryn Reid, "Fatigue, Alcohol and Performance Impairment," *Nature* 388 (July–August 1997): 235.

32. A.M. Williamson and Anne-Marie Feyer, "Moderate Sleep Deprivation Produces Impairments in Cognitive and Motor Performance Equivalent to Legally Prescribed Levels of Alcohol Intoxication," *Occupational and Environmental Medicine* 57 (October 2000): 649–655.

33. National Sleep Foundation, *Detection and Prevention* (2018). Available at www.drowsydriving.org/about/detection-and-prevention/.

34. European Cockpit Association, *Pilot Fatigue: A Barometer.*

35. Rosa Silverman, "Airline Pilots Asleep in the Cockpit During Long-Haul Flight," *The Telegraph* (September 26, 2013).

36. National Sleep Foundation, *How Much Sleep Do We Really Need?* (2018). Available at www.sleepfoundation.org/articles/how-much-sleep-do-we-really-need/.

37. Division of Sleep Medicine at Harvard Medical School, *Why Do We Sleep, Anyway?* (December 18, 2007). Available at www.healthysleep.med.harvard.edu/healthy/matters/benefits-of-sleep/why-do-we-sleep.

38. Mark R. Rosekind, Philippa H. Gander, Linda J. Connell and Elizabeth L. Co, *Crew Factors in Flight Operations X: Alertness Management in Flight Operations Educational Module*, NASA Technical Memorandum NASA/TM-2001-211385 (Moffett Field, CA: NASA Ames Research Center, November 2001).

39. Martin Vejvoda, Eva-Maria Elmenhorst, Sibylle Pennig, Gernot Plath, Hartmut Maass, Kristjof Tritschler, Mathias Basner and Daniel Aeschbach, "Significance of Time Awake for Predicting Pilots' Fatigue on Short-Haul Flights: Implications for Flight Duty Time Regulations," *Journal of Sleep Research* 5 (October 2014):564–567.

40. Timothy Roehrs, Eleni Burduvali, Alicia Bonahoom, Christopher Drake, and Thomas Roth, "Ethanol and Sleep Loss: A 'Dose' Comparison of Impairing Effects," *Sleep* 26 (2003): 981–985.

41. Division of Sleep Medicine at Harvard Medical School, *Natural Patterns of Sleep* (December 18, 2007). Available at www.healthysleep.med.harvard.edu/healthy/science/what/sleep-patterns-rem-nrem.

42. Ibid.

43. Rosekind, Gander, Connell and Co, *Crew Factors in Flight Operations X: Alertness Management in Flight Operations Educational Module*.

44. Federal Aviation Administration, "Pharmaceuticals (Therapeutic Medications): Sleep Aids," *Guide for Aviation Medical Examiners* (April 12, 2016). Available at www.faa.gov/about/office_org/headquarters_offices/avs/offices/aam/ame/guide/pharm/sleepaids/.

45. Edward Stepanski, "The Effect of Sleep Fragmentation on Daytime Function," *Sleep* 25 (June 2002).

46. Rosekind, Gander, Connell and Co, *Crew Factors in Flight Operations X: Alertness Management in Flight Operations Educational Module*.

47. Ibid.

48. Giovanni Costa, "Shift Work and Health: Current Problems and Preventive Actions," *Safety and Health at Work* 1 (December 2010): 112–123.

49. National Transportation Safety Board, "Reduce Fatigue-Related Accidents."

50. Ibid.

51. Ibid., 113.

52. Rosekind, Gander, Connell and Co, *Crew Factors in Flight Operations X: Alertness Management in Flight Operations Educational Module*.

53. Giovanni Costa, "Shift Work and Health: Current Problems and Preventive Actions."

54. Federal Aviation Administration, *Circadian Rhythm Disruption and Flying*, AM-400-09/3 (Oklahoma City, OK: n.d.). Available at www.faa.gov/pilots/safety/pilotsafetybrochures/.

55. UK Air Accidents Investigation Branch, Report on the accident to Bombardier CL600-2B16 Series 604, N90AG at Birmingham International Airport 4 January 2002, AAR 5/2004 (Aldershot, UK: July 2004): 76.

56. David M. C. Powell, Mick B. Spencer, David Holland, Elizabeth Broadbent and Keith J. Petrie, "Pilot Fatigue in Short-Haul Operations: Effects of Number of Sectors, Duty Length, and Time of Day," *Aviation, Space, and Environmental Medicine* 78 (July 2007): 698–701.

57. Federal Aviation Administration, *Basics of Aviation Fatigue*, AC 120-100 (Washington, DC: June 7, 2010).

58. Committee on the Effects of Commuting on Pilot Fatigue, National Research Council, *The Effects of Commuting on Pilot Fatigue* (Washington, DC: National Academies Press, 2011).

59. Federal Motor Carrier Safety Administration (FMCSA), *CMV Driving Tips— Driver Fatigue* (March 31, 2015). Available at www.fmcsa.dot.gov/safety/driver-safety/cmv-driving-tips-driver-fatigue.

60. John A. Caldwell, Melissa M. Mallis, J. Lynn Caldwell, Michel A. Paul, James C. Miller and David F. Neri, "Fatigue Countermeasures in Aviation: Position Paper" *Aviation, Space, and Environmental Medicine* 80 (January 2009): 29–59.

61. Ibid.

62. Transportation Safety Board of Canada, *Aviation Investigation Report: Pitch Excursion, Air Canada, Boeing 767-333, C-GHLQ, North Atlantic Ocean, 55°00'N 029°00'W, 14 January 2011*, Report No. A11F0012 (Gatineau, Quebec: TSB, n.d.). 13.

63. Mark R. Rosekind, David F. Dinges, Linda J. Connell, Michael S. Rountree, Cheryl L. Spinweber and Kelly A. Gillen, *Crew Factors in Flight Operations IX: Effects of Planned Cockpit Rest on Crew Performance and Alertness on Long-Haul Operations*, NASA Technical Memorandum 108839 (Moffett Field, CA: NASA Ames Research Center, September 1994).

64. TSB, *Aviation Investigation Report: Pitch Excursion, Air Canada, Boeing 767–333.* 2.

65. Ibid.

66. Caldwell, Mallis, Caldwell, Paul, Miller and Neri, "Fatigue Countermeasures in Aviation: Position Paper."

67. Paul D Loprinzi and Bradley J. Cardinal, "Association Between Objectively-Measured Physical Activity and Sleep, NHANES 2005–2006," *Mental Health and Physical Activity* 4 (December 2011): 65–69.

68. Caldwell, Mallis, Caldwell, Paul, Miller and Neri, "Fatigue Countermeasures in Aviation: Position Paper." 43.

69. Ibid.

70. FAA, *Circadian Rhythm Disruption and Flying.*

11

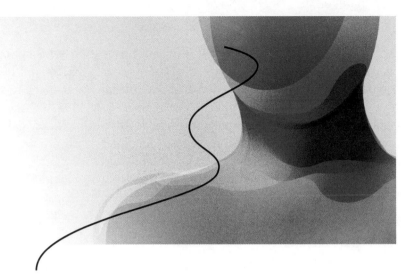

Am I fit to fly?
Health Maintenance and Lifestyle

It was their second flight of the day into Ennadai Lake, in Nunavut, Canada. The Douglas DC-3 was loaded with 6,600 pounds of building materials for the construction of a lodge. During the previous flight earlier that morning, the aircraft touched down near the beginning of the 2,700-foot-long ice strip, but the captain misjudged his VFR approach this second time around—ceiling and visibility at the time were about 1,500 to 2,000 feet AGL and 1.5 to 2.0 SM visibility in light snow—and the aircraft touched down almost halfway down the strip. A go-around was conducted and the landing gear was retracted; however, when the aircraft reached the end of the runway it entered a steep nose-up attitude then rolled to the left and descended into the ice killing both pilots aboard (TSB Report No: A00C0059).

While both pilots supervised the loading before departure, the captain expressed his concern to the FO that if the aircraft ran through an uncleared area off the ice strip after landing, it might nose-over. So he instructed the ground crew to load the materials in such a way that the CG was slightly aft. The section of the cabin the captain chose to load the 2x4 lumber did not have floor tie-downs, only wall attachments. Despite their suggestions to load it a different way, the ground crew complied with his instructions because, under the self-dispatch system used by the company, the captain was the final authority for load positioning. The Transportation Safety Board of Canada (TSB) discovered that the crew did not recalculate the weight and balance for this second flight of the morning and the CG was actually 32.3 inches aft of the aft limit for the airplane when they departed Points North Landing, Saskatchewan, for Ennadai Lake. They

concluded that elevator authority was marginal on the way to the lake, and was likely insufficient to prevent loss of control during the acceleration and configuration changes that occurred during the go-around. They also suggested that the load of 2x4s may have also shifted rearward (a large number were found at the back of airplane, aft of their original position), moving the CG even further backward, contributing to the fatal nose-up pitch.

TSB investigators wondered why the captain made the decision to load the aircraft in the configuration he did, and why such an experienced DC-3 pilot significantly misjudged his visual approach to the ice runway. Toxicological tests provided the possible answer. Elevated levels of CO were found in the blood of both crew members: the carboxyhemoglobin (COHb) level for the non-smoking FO was 8.7 percent, while the captain's—who smoked more than a pack of cigarettes a day—was 17.9 percent. If you remember from Chapter 4, hypemic hypoxia will result from breathing CO and that only 10 percent blood saturation puts a person at a physiological altitude of 7,000 feet. Even though basic physiological functions and the performance of psychomotor skills are usually not seriously affected with COHb levels below 20 percent, visual acuity and higher-level cognitive functioning are affected at levels between 10 and 20 percent (TSB Report No: A00C0059). Investigators discovered a leak in the heating system and that CO was entering the cabin heating system on the DC-3. They also concluded that it may not have been enough to significantly impair the FO, but when combined with the pre-existing levels of COHb from heavy smoking, the cabin CO may have been sufficient to impair the captain's judgment and decision making as well as his visual acuity, which could have affected his ability to conduct a visual approach in a "demanding landing environment with minimal visual cues" (TSB Report No: A00C0059).

Incapacitation

The concept of in-flight incapacitation—any physiological or psychological condition that adversely affects your ability to safely control an aircraft—was introduced in the earlier chapters of this book (*see* Chapters 3 and 4). Such impairment on the ground often results in limited consequences, but as seen in the DC-3 accident, when it occurs in the air it can often be fatal. Several adjectives are used to describe different types of incapacitation. Complete, or total, incapacitation occurs when the phenomenon or event renders a pilot unable to perform any in-flight duties, while partial incapacitation means he or she can perform some duties but performance is seriously degraded. The term **impairment** is sometimes used to describe partial incapacitation. Sudden incapacitation involves rapid onset of a condition or event, while subtle incapacitation results from slow or imperceptible onset that may be difficult for the victim and/or the second pilot to recognize.

Incidence of Incapacitation

In-flight physiological incapacitation can be caused by any number of factors such as hypoxia, smoke or fumes in the cabin, CO poisoning, trapped gas, spatial disorientation (SD), G-induced loss of consciousness (G-LOC), decompression sickness (DCS), food poisoning, illness, cardiovascular events, alcohol, drugs, medication, fatigue, falling asleep, and death. Fortunately, the incidence of these types of events and conditions is very low in the pilot population, and because airlines require two or more flight crew members—one of whom is present to take control should the other become incapacitated—the incidence of incapacitation accidents, let alone fatal accidents, is even lower.

A variety of studies have verified the low accident rate from incapacitation and impairment in multi-crew flight operations. A study of 1,800 Air France pilots and FEs discovered only 10 cases of in-flight incapacitation for the 20 years between 1968 and 1988. These were due to cardiac events, epileptic attacks, gastrointestinal bleeding, hypoglycemia, severe vertigo, hypoxia, and carbon dioxide intoxication (from dry ice cargo). None of these events resulted in an accident.[1]

Another study examined the incidence of in-flight medical incapacitations in U.S. airline pilots between 1993 through 1998. Of the 39 complete incapacitations (inability to perform any in-flight duties) and 11 impairments (degraded ability to perform in-flight duties), seven (15 percent) jeopardized the safety of flight; yet these only resulted in two non-fatal accidents in 54,295,899 airline flights during the six-year period. The investigators also determined that the rate of in-flight incapacitation and impairment was 0.04 and 0.01 per 100,000 hours, respectively. The most frequent categories were loss of consciousness (fainting, DCS), gastrointestinal (gall stones, trapped gas, food poisoning), neurological (seizures), cardiac (heart attack, abnormal heart beat, coronary spasm), urological (kidney stones), respiratory (fumes), fatigue, and vision (use of monovision contact lenses).[2]

Finally, using the results of 800 simulator exercises where pilots pretended to be incapacitated at a pre-determined point during a critical phase of flight, researchers discovered that the second pilot successfully took control in the majority of cases and only two incapacitation-related flights (0.25 percent, or 1 in 400) would have resulted in an accident.[3] Using this and other data, along with a variety of other assumptions and constraints, the probability of a single pilot in a crewed flight deck experiencing a medical incapacitation leading to a fatal accident is approximately one in one million (10^6) flight hours. Since a second pilot reduces the probability by a factor of 1,000 (the probability of both experiencing incapacitation at the same is significantly low), the overall probability of a fatal accident due to a medical incapacitation for two-pilot commercial airline operations is approximately one in one billion (10^9) flight hours.[4]

Since most GA flight operations rely on only one pilot, as you may have deduced, the incidence of in-flight incapacitation is greater for GA than for air carriers. However, its occurrence is still relatively low. A review of 2,696 fatal U.S. GA accident reports between 1990 and 1998 discovered that only 216, or 8 percent, mentioned some form of physical or physiological impairment or incapacitation.[5] A variety of factors led to pilot impairment or incapacitation in the GA accidents studied, including 4 percent from hypoxia and less than 2 percent from CO exposure and visual deficiencies, respectively. The majority of impairment or incapacitation events resulted from drugs (40.7 percent), alcohol (31.5 percent), and cardiovascular problems (12 percent). A recent study of 160,338 civilian aviation occurrences—8,302 accidents, 151,941 incidents, and 95 serious incidents—between 1975 and 2006 in Australia, found a total of 98 incapacitation events, 16 of which contributed to accidents, and 10 of which resulted in fatalities. The majority of medical and incapacitation events involved two-pilot airline operations. However, all 10 fatal accidents involved single-pilot flight operations.[6]

As you can see from the previous discussion, the term *incapacitation* is generally used to describe a physical or physiological condition that impairs a pilot's ability to perform his or her normal flight duties. However, incapacitation can also arise from psychological or cognitive factors—which can sometimes be induced by physiological impairment—such as perceptual misinterpretation (e.g., visual illusions, miscommunication), memory failure, attention deficiencies, or flawed decision making. Such factors, though, are usually identified directly as a cause or causal factor in an aircraft accident. Part III of this book address several of these cognitive causes of incapacitation.

Though incapacitation can occur in perfectly healthy individuals from such phenomena as hypoxia, SD, smoke in the cabin, and DCS, most incapacitation events relate to general health risks and health choices made by pilots. Of the 216 fatal GA accidents in which impairment or incapacitation was mentioned in the accident report, 84.2 percent involved drugs, alcohol, and cardiovascular problems—areas in which most people have at least some degree of control over. What is also certain—for both professional flight crews and GA pilots—is the probability of experiencing health problems increases with age. For example, of the 216 fatal GA accidents, pilots over 60 years of age suffered the highest percentage of impairment/incapacitation (19 percent) while the group of pilots younger than 26 years old experienced the lowest (7.9 percent).[7] Similarly, a study of pilots who were members of the Air Line Pilots Association (ALPA) found that the rate of loss of license due to cardiovascular disease was 0 per 1,000 pilots per year for pilots under 30 years of age and 27.33 per 1,000 pilots per year for pilots between 55 and 58 years of age. The study estimated the probability of experiencing serious in-flight incapacitation for ALPA-member pilots between the age of 55 and 59 at 1 per 3,500 pilots; for the group between 30 and 34 years of age, it was estimated at only 1 per 58,000 pilots.[8] Finally, a recent study of all 16,145 European professional pilots holding a valid European Union Aviation Safety Agency Class 1 medical certificate determined that the annual incapacitation rate was only 0.25 percent, but pilots in their 60s were five times more likely to experience in-flight incapacitation than those in their 40s.[9]

Generally, there are procedures to follow when situations arise—other than a pilot's own personal health problems—that could cause in-flight incapacitation. For example, there are procedures to help you recognize and remedy a cabin decompression that can lead to incapacitation from hypoxia, or impairment from DCS. There are also steps pilots can take to minimize the effect of SD and to recognize and respond to smoke in the cabin—both of which can cause impairment or incapacitation. However, there is no checklist to fix yourself should you experience a heart attack or some other health-related impairment while on duty on the flight deck. One of the ways in which the probability of this latter type of incapacitation can be minimized is through mandatory medical examinations for pilots.

Medical Certification

Medical certification of U.S. pilots officially began with the Air Commerce Act of 1926 which mandated that all pilots be medically qualified to fly.[10] Conditions that could cause sudden incapacitation or death, or could otherwise compromise aviation safety, are disqualifying for a medical certificate. With the exception of balloon and glider pilots, and certain pilots who qualify under the FAA's new **BasicMed**[11] program, medical certification is required in the United States to exercise the privileges of the following pilot certificates: ATP, commercial, private, recreational, flight instructor (when acting as pilot-in-command or as a required pilot flight crew member), flight engineer, flight navigator, and student certificate.

Medical Class

Table 11-1 lists the major pilot certificates, the type of medical certificate needed to exercise the privileges of the applicable pilot certificate, and the duration of the medical certificate. Regardless of the date of the medical examination, U.S. medical certificates expire at midnight on the last day of the month in which they are valid. When a higher-class medical certificate (e.g., first-class) expires, the pilot can still use it to exercise the privileges of a pilot certificate that requires a lower medical class (e.g., third-class), and can do so for the remainder of the lower medical class valid period. For example, after a first- or second-class medical expires, a pilot can still exercise the privileges of a private pilot for 60 calendar months (under age 40) or 24 calendar months (age 40 or older) after the month of the date of examination shown on the medical certificate. More detailed information can be found in 14 CFR §61.23.

Medical Standards

A medical examination—often called a *flight physical*—is conducted by an FAA Aviation Medical Examiner (AME), or Transport Canada-designated Civil Aviation Medical Examiner in Canada, who has a special interest in aviation safety and training in aviation medicine. The physician conducts a physical examination and evaluates your medical history to basically answer two questions:

1. Do you have any physical, psychological, or physiological conditions that would render you unable to safely fly an aircraft?
2. Is it probable that you will experience an in-flight incapacitation event during the valid period of your medical certification?

Part 67 specifies minimum standards required for the three medical classes in the U.S., including standards for vision; ear, nose and throat; mental; neurologic; cardiovascular; and general medical health. In addition, several medically disqualifying conditions for issue of a medical certificate are specifically spelled out in Part 67, including:

- Angina pectoris;
- Bipolar disorder;
- Cardiac valve replacement;
- Coronary heart disease that has required treatment or, if untreated, that has been symptomatic or clinically significant;
- Diabetes mellitus requiring insulin or other hypoglycemic medication;
- Disturbance of consciousness without satisfactory medical explanation of the cause;
- Epilepsy;
- Heart replacement;
- Myocardial infarction;
- Permanent cardiac pacemaker;
- Personality disorder that is severe enough to have repeatedly manifested itself by overt acts;
- Psychosis;
- Substance abuse and dependence; and
- Transient loss of control of nervous system function(s) without satisfactory medical explanation of cause.

Table 11-1. Major U.S. pilot certificate types, medical certificate required and medical certificate duration

Pilot certificate	Class of medical certificate required	Duration of medical certificate (in calendar months)	
		Under the age of 40	Age 40 or over
Airline Transport	First-class	12	6
Commercial	Second-class	12	12
Student, Private, Recreational, Sport,* Flight Instructor**	Third-class	60	24

When not using a U.S. driver's license as medical qualification
*** When acting as PIC*

Medical Waivers

Medical examiners can issue a medical certificate only if a candidate meets all the medical standards required for the class of medical certificate applied for. However, if you are denied certification because of a medically disqualifying condition, you have the right to be reconsidered by the FAA's Office of Aerospace Medicine through one of its regional flight surgeons. You may be granted an authorization for **special issuance** of a medical certificate with a specified validity period (that may be shorter than the normal medical valid period) provided you can demonstrate to the satisfaction of the FAA's Federal Air Surgeon by a special medical flight test, practical test, or another medical evaluation that the duties authorized by the class of medical certificate applied for can be performed without endangering public safety for the validity period of the authorization. However, depending on the type of condition you have, should you receive such an authorization the duration of such an issuance may be limited and you could be subject to periodic medical examinations to assure the FAA that your condition is nonprogressive (not getting worse).

Should you have a disqualifying medical condition that is static or nonprogressive, you may be granted a **statement of demonstrated ability (SODA)** by the FAA provided you can prove, through a special medical flight test or practical test, that you are capable of performing pilot duties without endangering public safety. SODAs are valid indefinitely unless subsequent medical examinations reveal the disqualifying medical condition has worsened.

To avoid health-related problems that could increase your odds of not just experiencing an in-flight incapacitation event but your career ending prematurely from a loss of medical certification, you must wisely and deliberately choose a healthy lifestyle that also contributes to living a long life. Therefore, the remainder of this chapter looks at those conditions and situations—often called **self-imposed stresses** because they are stresses you as a pilot can generally control—that arise from choices we make that could lead to physiological incapacitation. Such factors most often result from our choices and habits regarding what we eat, drink, inhale, or otherwise ingest into our bodies and our level of physical activity.

Tobacco

If you are a smoker, and desire to enjoy a long career as a pilot, do whatever you can to quit. Even though fewer Americans are smoking than ever before, it is still the number one leading preventable cause of death, claiming 480,000 lives in the U.S. and nearly six million deaths worldwide per year. Smoking harms almost every organ in the body, and besides contributing to the two highest overall causes of death in the U.S.—cardiovascular disease (heart attack, stroke) and cancer—it increases the risk of lung disease, emphysema, chronic bronchitis, diabetes, tuberculosis, eye disease, immune system problems, rheumatoid arthritis, and erectile dysfunction. Smokeless tobacco (chewing tobacco, snuff), though unburned, also contributes to several health problems, including mouth, esophageal and pancreatic cancer, various mouth diseases, increased risk of death from heart disease and stroke, and increased risk of early delivery and stillbirth when used during pregnancy. There is also an increased risk of becoming a cigarette smoker from using smokeless tobacco.[13]

The jury is still out on electronic cigarettes (e-cigs, vape pens). On the one hand, for smokers, they are generally less harmful than traditional nicotine-delivery devices, but they are still not safe for nonsmokers, especially youth and pregnant women. Inhaled aerosols can also contain several harmful cancer-causing chemicals. On the other hand, *vaping* may prove beneficial to existing cigarette smokers when used as a substitute for cigarettes and smokeless tobacco. Of course, all these products contain nicotine, a highly addictive drug that is not only difficult to quit using, but has its own harmful effects, especially on the developing adolescent brain, and pregnant women and the development of their unborn children.[14]

Besides the health effects, smoking obviously increases your risk of in-flight incapacitation from a cardiovascular event such as a heart attack or stroke. As you also learned in Chapter 4, CO from cigarette smoke significantly increases your physiological altitude putting you at greater risk of mental incapacitation from hypemic (or anemic) hypoxia when exposed to higher altitudes or higher levels of CO (as seen in the Ennadai Lake accident in Canada). All of this, plus an average of 13.2 (male) and 14.5 (female) years of potential life lost (YPLL) for adult smokers over non-smokers,[15] are good reasons to never start smoking, and to quit the habit if you still do.

Marijuana

If inhaling smoke from cigarettes is a threat to your health and career, so too is smoking marijuana. The U.S. Center for Disease Control and Prevention cites strong evidence that marijuana use may lead to addiction, breathing problems (including chronic bronchitis), short-term declines in memory, attention, and learning, and an increased risk of the following:

- low birth weight in babies;
- poisoning among children;
- psychosis or schizophrenia;
- some types of cancer;
- heart attack and stroke;
- decreased IQ, which can last a long time and may be permanent;
- lower academic and career success;
- lower income;
- poor school performance; and
- motor vehicle accidents.[16]

Of course, the pirmary active ingredient in the cannabis plant (marijuana) that produces the "high," tetrahydrocannabinol (or THC), can be taken in forms other than through smoking—vaping, eating, or absorbing through the skin—thereby reducing the serious health effects of inhaling smoke into your lungs.

In light of the fact that by 2019, 34 states and the District of Columbia, Guam, Puerto Rico, and the U.S. Virgin Islands had legalized marijuana for medical use, with 10 of those states and the District of Columbia legalizing it for recreational use, the U.S. National Academies of Sciences, Engineering, and Medicine conducted a comprehensive review of more than 10,700 high-quality primary research scientific reports and the most up-to-date systematic reviews to see what conclusions could be made regarding the health effects of using cannabis. They rated the evidence for outcomes based on five categories of certainty: conclusive, substantial, moderate, limited, and no/insufficient evidence. They found conclusive and substantial evidence that cannabis or cannabinoids are effective for treating chronic pain in adults and chemotherapy-induced nausea and vomiting,

and for reducing patient-reported multiple sclerosis spasticity symptoms. They found moderate evidence that cannabinoids help people with certain disorders/diseases to achieve better short-term sleep outcomes, and they found only limited evidence that cannabis helps in improving conditions associated with post-traumatic stress disorder, Tourette syndrome, and social anxiety disorders.[17] The extensive 487-page report determined, that despite marijuana's growing popularity for medical and recreational use and the changes in policy allowing its use in certain states, "conclusive evidence regarding the short- and long-term health effects (harms and benefits) of cannabis use remains elusive."[18]

Regardless of what you may think about the potential benefits or harm associated with using marijuana, it really doesn't matter. If you are a U.S.-certificated pilot you should completely abstain from using it: it is against federal law and you will likely lose your pilot certificate if you get caught. Marijuana, a psychoactive drug, is strictly illegal under federal law and deemed a Schedule I controlled substance (not legally available like Schedule II to IV drugs) by the U.S. Drug Enforcement Administration. That is, it has a high potential for abuse, there is no currently acceptable medical use in treatment, and there is a lack of accepted safety for its use under medical supervision.[19] The FAA—also a federal government organization—concurs with this position: regardless of whether a pilot has a prescription for it or not, or lives in a state where marijuana is approved for recreational use, they consider it an illicit drug.

In addition, federal drug testing rules require personnel who perform a safety-sensitive function—pilots, flight instructors, flight attendants, dispatchers, mechanics (14 CFR §120.105)—and who are employed by Part 121 air carriers, Part 135 commuter air carriers, on-demand air carriers, and commercial air tour operators to submit to drug and alcohol testing. This testing occurs prior to employment, during random checks, and when someone has reasonable suspicion you may be using. A urine sample is generally used to test for marijuana, amphetamines (methamphetamine, MDA), cocaine, opiates (codeine, morphine), and phencyclidine (PCP). Refusal to take a drug or alcohol test is grounds for denial of an application for, and suspension or revocation of, a pilot certificate (14 CFR §120.11).

On October 17, 2018, Canada became the second country in the world, after Uruguay, to legalize marijuana for recreational use. As of this writing, the situation is fluid and the impact of this new legislation for transportation workers, especially pilots, is not entirely clear. However, Air Canada, WestJet and Jazz are some of the air carriers that have recently updated their policy and, despite its legality in Canada, they have placed a total ban on its use—both on- and off-duty—for airline personnel in safety-critical areas (i.e., pilots, cabin crew, dispatchers, and maintenance staff).[20] Similar prohibitions by federal and/or provincial bodies, as well as rules enacted by private and commercial organizations, are currently being developed and it is likely that other air carriers will enact a similar ban on marijuana use. Canadian pilots should thoroughly understand any new rules that may affect their future flying career prospects should they choose to use marijuana.

In their 2014 safety study, the NTSB examined trends in the prevalence of OTC, prescription, and illicit drugs by toxicology testing 6,677 fatally injured pilots between 1990 and 2012. Even though the percentage of those pilots testing positive for marijuana was relatively low, it was the most commonly identified illicit drug found, and the proportion of pilots who tested positive for it doubled over the 23-year period. Using data from a variety of sources, including a study in which researchers concluded that compared to pilots who did not test positive for an illicit drug the probability of involvement is 10 times greater among pilots who did, the NTSB concluded there is evidence showing that "taking illicit drugs significantly elevates the risk of having an aviation accident."[21] The FAA Federal Air Surgeon recently summed it up succinctly when he stated that you should avoid marijuana if you want to fly: "If you are flying while under the influence of marijuana, you are flying impaired. If you are flying with marijuana or its metabolites detectable in your body, you are flying illegally."[22]

Alcohol

If the most commonly used illegal drug in the United States is marijuana, the most commonly used legal drug-of-choice for most Americans is alcohol. As much as alcohol provides benefit to its users (e.g., assists in relaxation, lowers stress, improves mood, and may bring certain health benefits), it also has a dark side. For example, alcohol is responsible for about 88,000 premature deaths annually in the U.S., including 10,500 road deaths and 20,000 cancer deaths (3.5 percent of all cancer deaths), the latter resulting in an average of approximately 18 YPLL per person.[23, 24, 25] Alcohol poisoning from binge drinking, defined as consuming 4 drinks (for women) or 5 drinks (for men) within 2 hours, kills about 2,200 people—primarily middle age men—per year.[26] In addition, alcohol is involved in about 40 percent of all violent crimes,[27] and about 18 million U.S. residents have alcohol use disorder (AUD), sometimes called alcohol abuse or alcoholism,[28] a disease characterized by "compulsive alcohol use, loss of control over alcohol intake, and a negative emotional state when not using."[29]

This data may not mean much to you, especially if you have not personally experienced the downside of alcohol use. However, even though this might be somewhat overstated, it is likely that there isn't a family in the U.S. and Canada that has not been impacted in some way or another by what the statistics don't tell you—the pain and distress that results from someone you know or love affected by the problems alcohol can bring.

Alcohol Regulations

Most pilots are familiar with federal regulations regarding alcohol and flying. No person may act, or attempt to act, as a crew member of a civil aircraft:

1. Within 8 hours after the consumption of any alcoholic beverage;
2. While under the influence of alcohol;
3. While using any drug that affects the person's faculties in any way contrary to safety; and
4. While having an alcohol concentration of 0.04 or greater in a blood or breath specimen.

14 CFR §91.17 further stipulates that a pilot is required to submit to an alcohol test (by providing a blood or breath specimen) if requested by a law enforcement officer authorized under state or local law to conduct the test and who has a reasonable suspicion that the pilot may have violated any of number 1, 2, or 4 above, or engaged in substantially similar conduct. Of course, if you fly for an air carrier, commuter air carrier, on-demand air

carrier, or commercial air tour operator, federal drug testing rules that apply to marijuana and other drugs equally apply to alcohol. Whether it is pre-employment, random, or reasonable-suspicion testing, you *must* submit to drug and alcohol testing. A breath and saliva specimen is usually used to test for alcohol.

Alcohol's Effect on Pilot Performance

There is good reason for all these rules: alcohol and flying, like driving, don't mix. The deleterious effects of alcohol intoxication on driving performance—currently responsible for almost one-third of all U.S. traffic deaths—have been well known for decades.[30] The effect on driving performance listed in Table 11-2 explains why.

However, it can be strongly argued that piloting a complex machine in all three-dimensions of space requires significantly greater levels of psychomotor, attentional, and cognitive skills to consistently achieve safe outcomes than driving an automobile. Therefore, it's reasonable to assume that such decrements in human performance while under the influence of alcohol will lead to a higher probability of experiencing an aircraft accident than an automobile accident.

Physiological Effects of Alcohol

The primary component of alcohol and the chemical compound responsible for alcohol intoxication—ethanol (C_2H_5OH)—consumed in drinks such as wine, beer, and liquor, is a psychoactive drug that alters several physiological and psychological functions. Keep in mind that just because it is used in drinks for recreational purposes, it is still a poison—it's also used as a solvent and as an additive to automotive gasoline. The U.S. National Institutes of Health defines a "standard" alcoholic drink (*see* Figure 11-1) as 0.6 fluid ounces (fl oz) of pure alcohol (ethanol), which is the generally (check the label) the equivalent of 12 oz of beer (5 percent alcohol content), 8 oz of malt liquor (7 percent alcohol content), 5 oz of wine (12 percent alcohol content), or 1.5 oz ("shot") of 80-proof (40 percent alcohol content) distilled spirits or liquor (e.g., gin, rum, vodka, whiskey).

Ethanol is rapidly absorbed from the stomach and intestine into the blood stream and then begins to affect every organ in your body. The level of alcoholic intoxication depends on a variety of individual factors such as how many drinks you've had, weight, sex (males generally tolerate more), diet, overall health, medications, genetics, and the

Table 11-2. Symptoms of alcohol and effects on driving performance at various BAC levels.[31]

BAC*	Typical effects	Predictable effects on driving
.02	• Some loss of judgment • Relaxation • Slight body warmth • Altered mood	• Decline in visual functions • Decline in ability to perform two tasks at the same time (divided attention)
.05	• Exaggerated behavior • May have loss of small-muscle control (e.g., eye focusing) • Impaired judgment • Usually good feeling • Lowered alertness • Release of inhibition	• Reduced coordination • Reduced ability to track moving objects • Difficulty steering • Reduced response to emergency driving situations
.08	• Muscle coordination becomes poor (e.g., balance, speech, vision, reaction time, and hearing) • Harder to detect danger • Impaired judgment, self-control, reasoning, and memory	• Reduced concentration • Short-term memory loss • Speed control • Reduced information processing capability (e.g., signal detection, visual search) • Impaired perception
.10	• Clear deterioration of reaction time and control • Slurred speech, poor coordination, and slowed thinking	• Reduced ability to maintain lane position and brake appropriately

*BAC is the percentage of ethanol concentration in a person's blood measured by the weight of alcohol in a given volume of blood. Legal intoxication for driving in most jurisdictions in the U.S. is .08 percent, or .08 grams (g) of alcohol per deciliter (100ml) of blood, or 210 liters of breath.

Fig 11-1.

Examples of one standard drink.

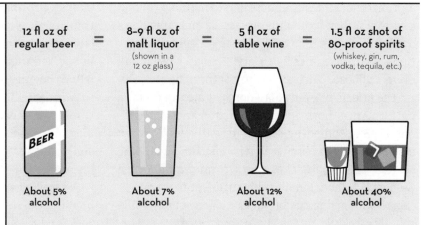

12 fl oz of regular beer	=	8–9 fl oz of malt liquor (shown in a 12 oz glass)	=	5 fl oz of table wine	=	1.5 fl oz shot of 80-proof spirits (whiskey, gin, rum, vodka, tequila, etc.)
About 5% alcohol		About 7% alcohol		About 12% alcohol		About 40% alcohol

The percent of "pure" alcohol, expressed here as alcohol by volume (alc/vol), varies by beverage.

amount of food in your stomach. However, alcohol is not metabolized—broken down and eliminated—as fast as it is absorbed. It is primarily metabolized by enzymes in the liver, but this organ is only able to do so at a certain rate. Depending on how much and how fast you drink, that means it can take only a short time (20 to 40 minutes) to get drunk but much longer (several hours) to get sober. The rate of alcohol metabolism is relatively constant at about one "standard" alcoholic drink per hour. So, depending on the factors mentioned, it will take at least four hours for your BAC to drop close to zero after drinking four beers. Drinking coffee, having a cold shower, breathing 100 percent oxygen, or other remedies will not speed up the process of alcohol elimination.

Alcohol is a central nervous system depressant, meaning that the functioning of virtually every system in your body, including sensation (vision, hearing, etc.), perception, thinking, motor functioning, emotion, and speech, is slowed down or sedated. In addition to the cognitive performance deficits (discussed below), three major physiological effects of alcohol on pilot performance are hypoxia, vision impairment, and increased susceptibility to SD.

Alcohol-Induced Hypoxia

As discussed in Chapter 4, alcohol interferes with the body's ability to utilize oxygen, contributing to histotoxic hypoxia. This in turn lowers the altitude at which a pilot will first experience hypoxia and it decreases the time of useful consciousness (effective performance time) at any given altitude after a rapid decompression. It is estimated that each ounce of alcohol consumed increases a person's physiological altitude by about 2,000 feet.[32]

Visual Problems and Susceptibility to Spatial Disorientation

Another physiological impairment is **positional alcohol nystagmus (PAN)**. As noted in Chapter 9, nystagmus is an involuntary rapid back-and-forth eye movement that creates similar apparent movement of the visual scene lasting for several seconds after recovery from significant angular accelerations. However, under the influence of alcohol it can also occur in straight and level unaccelerated flight. Alcohol diffuses into the semicircular canal membrane reducing the fluid's (endolymph) specific gravity which in turn increases the sensitivity, and therefore movement, of the hair cells (cupula) in the canals. This overexcites the normal vestibulo-ocular reflex (discussed in Chapter 9) leading to involuntary nystagmus even if little or no motion is present. This can occur with BAC as low as .03 percent, can extend for up to 72 hours after drinking,[33, 34] and is exacerbated if flying in a high-G environment. Because of greater sensitivity to slight movements in the semicircular canals, PAN increases susceptibility to dizziness and motion sickness and also increases the odds of experiencing SD and prolongs recovery from it should it occur.

Cognitive and Psychomotor Deficits

Besides its physiological impact, alcohol also affects virtually every cognitive process humans possess. Much like the effects of fatigue (discussed in the previous chapter), perception of one's surroundings is diminished, vigilance decreases, status monitoring suffers, forgetting increases, judgment, decision making and other higher level skills are impaired, and reaction times are increased. Emotions, mood, and the ability to accurately assess risk and one's own abilities are also affected—in a negative direction—when it comes to safety. That is why drunk drivers choose to drive; they're not thinking straight.

The effects of even small doses of alcohol on pilot performance, both in the simulator and in flight, have been studied by several researchers. Sixteen instrument-rated pilots each flew instrument landing system (ILS) approaches down to minimums in a Cessna 172 under simulated instrument flight conditions—with an instructor safety pilot on board—while sober and while under the influence of 0.04, 0.08, and 0.12 percent BAC. Besides discovering an inverse linear relationship between BAC and performance on localizer and glide path tracking and the frequency of major and minor errors—performance worsened with increasing levels of intoxication—the researchers discovered unacceptable levels of safety performance even at the minimum BAC allowed by regulations (< .04 percent).[35] Other studies have discovered performance decrements involving ATC vectoring, air traffic target detection and avoidance, descending, stick-and-rudder skills, tracking, coordination, reaction time, short-term memory, procedures, and judgment; and pilots even lost control of their aircraft at BAC levels between 0.01 and 0.03 percent, which is below the regulatory minimum of 0.04 percent![36]

Waiting "eight hours from bottle to throttle" may reduce your BAC to below 0.04 percent, but as the data reveal, you may be legal by following all the rules but you may not safe. Also, even when BAC returns to zero, your performance can suffer from a hangover (i.e., the effects *hang over*). Hangover symptoms include headache, dizziness, dry mouth, dehydration, stuffy nose, fatigue, upset stomach, irritability, impaired judgment, increased sensitivity to bright light, and visual and vestibular impairment. In some ways, a hangover is more dangerous than small amounts of alcohol because a pilot is usually more willing to fly with a hangover than with any alcohol in their system. Yet, even though blood-alcohol may have dropped to zero you can still be under its influence for another 48 to 72 hours after your last drink.[37]

Drunk Flying

With all the rules and regulations regarding alcohol consumption, and with all the evidence that even a small amount of alcohol is sufficient to impair a pilot's performance and endanger a flight, you would think pilots would know better than to drink and fly. However, that is not always the case. One of the most publicized incidents involved a Northwest Airlines (NWA) Boeing B-727 flying from Fargo, North Dakota, to Minneapolis-St. Paul International Airport. All three flight crew members lost their jobs and their pilot's licenses and served time in jail after being convicted for flying a commercial aircraft while intoxicated. They were tested for alcohol after the FAA received a tip that they had been seen drinking heavily the night before. BAC levels were 0.13, 0.06, and 0.08 percent for the captain, FO, and FE, respectively.[38]

Apparently the two required flight crew members of America West Airlines Flight 556 twelve years later had not heard about the NWA incident, or failed to heed its warning. Someone smelled alcohol on the captain's breath when they were getting ready to depart Miami International Airport. They had just pushed back from the gate when they were ordered back to the terminal. The captain blew 0.091 percent and the FO 0.084 percent on the breathalyzer test and they too lost their jobs and their licenses and served time in jail after being criminally convicted for flying an aircraft while drunk.[39]

In spite of examples like this, alcohol issues involving commercial airline pilots are relatively rare—less than 0.03 percent of mandatory alcohol testing violations involve commercial pilots.[40] Flying drunk is a bigger problem in GA operations. For example, a 30-year-old commercial pilot (who was also a certified flight instructor) and his two passengers died after the Cessna 172 he was piloting collided with rising terrain near North Bend, Washington. There were only a few low clouds, but the high overcast created a dark night. Radar tapes reveal that he was flying at about 1,500 feet MSL, but collided on the western face of the mountain at just under 2,000 feet MSL. Post-accident toxicology tests discovered the pilot's BAC was 0.154—almost twice the legal driving limit and four times the legal flying limit of 0.04 percent. The NTSB determined the probable cause of this accident was the flight instructor's physical impairment due to alcohol, which adversely affected his ability to operate the airplane and to maintain clearance from mountainous terrain while operating in dark-night conditions (NTSB Report No: WPR12FA105).

It was previously noted that only about 8 percent of U.S. GA accidents involved physical or physiological impairment or incapacitation; however, almost a third were the result of alcohol impairment.[41] A toxicological study of 1,587 fatally injured pilots in the five-year period between 1999 and 2003 found a slightly lower percentage (about 6.4 percent) of pilots who tested positive for ethanol.[42] Table 11-3 is a list of recent U.S. aircraft accidents where alcohol intoxication was a cited as a cause or contributing factor—all of them were Part 91 GA accidents.

The more alcohol you consume, the more likely you are to develop alcohol dependency or AUD, which is one of the 14 medically disqualifying conditions for issue of a medical certificate that is specifically spelled out in Part 67. That means if you are diagnosed with AUD you can no longer fly. However, since the 1970s airlines, in cooperation with the FAA, have developed programs that help airline pilots obtain treatment to help them kick the habit and eventually return to flight status. This program has recently been extended to GA pilots with all classes of medical certificates. The program involves several steps and progress is closely monitored. Minimum wait times and specific treatment milestones must be achieved before the FAA will authorize a special issuance medical certificate to pilots who are in satisfactory recovery. The good news is, the program works—it has an 85 percent success rate.[43]

If you don't drink alcohol, why start? If you do drink, and want to avoid losing your pilot certificate, losing your job, or developing an alcohol-related health problem, including developing dependency on the drug, you should avoid consuming too much alcohol by drinking only in moderation. Follow all the applicable rules, but keep in mind that they might not be enough. The fact that hangovers continue beyond the eight-hour rule, which is perhaps why other countries require a minimum wait time of 12 hours after the last drink, suggests it is wiser to go beyond the rules and play it safe (e.g., no drinking at all during layovers and/or waiting 24 hours after your last drink).

Medication

The use of illicit, prescription, and nonprescription drugs (OTC medications; medications you can purchase without a prescription) in the general population has grown significantly over the past several decades. This trend is also evident among pilots. For example, in the recent NTSB safety study cited earlier, toxicology testing of 6,677 fatally injured U.S. pilots between 1990 and 2012 revealed a significant increase in positive findings for drugs during the

Table 11-3. Sampling of recent NTSB Part 91 accidents where alcohol intoxication was cited as a cause or contributing factor.

Date	Aircraft	Location	Cause/contributing factor	Fatalities
Aug 16, 2018	C-152	Rhome, TX	Alcohol ingestion	1
May 4, 2017	Hy-Tek Hurricane	Redcrest, CA	Alcohol consumption and methamphetamine use	1
Jun 12, 2016	R44	Jonesboro, AR	Alcohol and diphenhydramine	1
May 18, 2016	C-P210	Sheridan Lake, CO	High levels of ingested alcohol	1
Oct 26, 2015	PA-31	Weston, FL	Alcohol consumption	1
Aug 8, 2015	Ultralight	Zeeland, MI	Alcohol consumption	1
July 4, 2015	7BCM	Portland, TX	Alcohol and drugs	2
Dec 1, 2014	PA-28	Sommerville, TN	Ethanol and chlordiazepoxide	1
Aug 28, 2014	C-150	Creedmoor, NC	Alcohol ingestion	0
Aug 10, 2014	PA-24	Big Lake, AK	Alcohol consumption	1
Jun 5, 2014	C-172	Laytonville, CA	Alcohol ingestion	1

23-year study period. Figure 11-2 indicates that the percentage of deceased accident pilots with at least one positive drug finding increased from 9.6 percent in 1990 to 39 percent in 2012; the percentage of pilots with more than one positive toxicology finding increased from 2 percent in 1990 to 20.5 percent in 2012; and the percentage of pilots with more than two positive toxicology findings increased from 0 percent in 1990 to 8.3 percent in 2012.[44] A separate study conducted by the FAA's Civil Aerospace Medical Institute Toxicology Lab in 2011 found that 42 percent (570) of 1,353 fatally injured pilots examined were tested positive for medications and 90 percent of them were flying under Part 91.[45]

Many pilots rely on OTC medications to relieve the symptoms of the various maladies they expe-rience. However, like prescription medications, many OTC medications have side effects when taken either alone or with other medications, and they can impair your ability to safely drive a car or fly an aircraft. The most commonly identified drug category in the NTSB safety study was sedating anti-histamines, with diphenhydramine (the active ingre-dient in Benadryl and similar products) as the most commonly identified sedating antihistamine overall and the single most commonly identified potentially impairing drug (see Figure 11-3).[46] Antihistamines in OTC medications treat such symptoms as allergies, influenza, colds, coughs, motion sickness, nausea, and itching. They are particularly sedating in OTC sleep aids.

Fig 11-2.

Percentage of fatally injured aircraft accident pilots with at least one, more than one, or more than two positive toxicology drug findings.

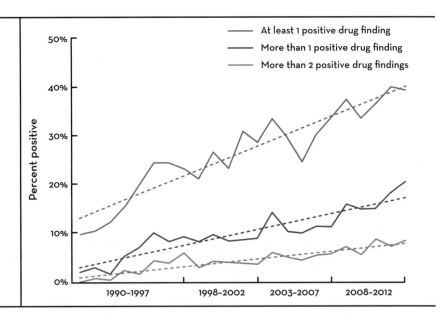

Fig 11-3.

Percentage of fatally injured aircraft accident pilots with positive toxicology findings for sedating antihistamines and diphenhydramine.

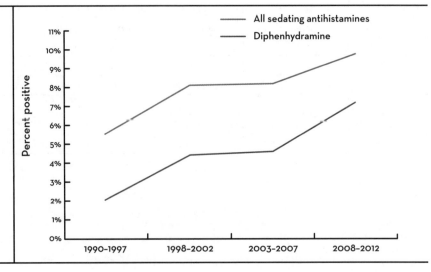

Despite the increased use of prescription and OTC medication, regulations prohibit pilots from operating an aircraft while using any drug that affects their faculties in any way contrary to safety (14 CFR §91.17). It appears from a small sampling of U.S. GA accidents over a recent two-year period that many pilots don't perceive drug use to be as big of a threat as it is (see Table 11-4). Note the prevalence of diphenhydramine and other sedating antihistamines.

Whether you are using a prescription drug or are considering taking OTC medication to relieve illness symptoms, one question you should ask yourself is, "Is the underlying condition I'm treating serious enough to prevent me from flying?" If it's bad enough for you to take medication for your symptoms, it's very likely the actual condition you are treating—headache, pain, sinus congestion, cold, flu, etc.—will impair your ability to fly safely.

A second question to ask is, "Does the medicine I'm taking have adverse side effects, impairing my ability to fly?" The FAA's *Guide for Aviation Medical Examiners* distinguishes between two categories of medications taken by aircrew: DNI (do not issue) medications that prevent an AME from issuing a pilot medical certificate, and DNF (do not fly) medications that can be used but not while flying. Though the FAA doesn't publish a list of approved medications for pilots, the most recent issue of the *Guide* will list both categories of medications.[47] Other aviation organizations also provide guidance (see the Helpful Resources at the end of this chapter).

You should also carefully read the U.S. Food and Drug Administration or Health Canada Drug Facts label affixed to the medication container. The top four areas on the label are the *active ingredient* (substance), its *uses* (symptoms the drug treats), *warnings* (when not to use, side effects, etc.), and *directions* (amount to take, how often, when to stop). The FAA says you should not fly if the label carries a precaution or warning that it may cause drowsiness, or if it advises you to be careful when driving a motor vehicle or operating machinery. This also applies even if the label states "until you know how the medication affects you" and even if you have used the medication before with no apparent adverse effects. These medications can cause impairment even when you feel alert and unimpaired; in other words, you will be "unaware of impair."[48]

The FAA also recommends you see an AME about the effect of taking single or multiple medications on performing flight duties. He or she can often make a better determination about the effects of certain drug combinations on your flying abilities and may also be able to recommend alternate medication that will keep you flying. Unless otherwise indicated, the FAA also recommends you wait at least five

Table 11-4. Some fatal GA accidents where a prescription or OTC medication was implicated in the cause of the accident.

Date	Aircraft	Location	Cause/contributing factor	Fatalities
Nov 18, 2015	AS350	Carlsbad, CA	Two psychoactive drugs	2
Oct 17, 2015	PA028R	Morongo Valley, CA	Impairing medications	2
Aug 1, 2015	AT-602	Wilmot, AR	Drug effects or cardiac event	1
July 4, 2015	7BCM	Portland, TX	Alcohol and drugs	2
Jun 22, 2015	T-MK1	Maricopa, CA	Butalbital and codeine	1
Dec 1, 2014	PA-28	Sommerville, TN	Ethanol and chlordiazepoxide	1
Oct 12, 2014	Savannah	Yerington, NV	Licit and illicit medications	1
Sep 28, 2014	Eagle Helicycle	Gallatin, TN	Sedating antihistamine	1
Sep 28, 2014	C-T33	Plano, IL	Diphenhydramine	1
Sep 1, 2014	C-180	North Hampton, NH	Sedating antihistamine	2
Aug 12, 2014	Bell 47	Mansfield, IL	Sedating medication	1
Jul 23, 2014	Bell 206	Wenatchee, WA	Sedating medication	1
Jun 23, 2014	Graszhopper	Ottawa, IL	Multiple sedating medications	1
Jun 7, 2014	Lancair	Duluth, MN	Diphenhydramine	1

times the half-life, or dosing interval, of the medication before resuming flying duties. For example, if a medication says to take it four times per day, the dosing interval would be every six hours. Therefore, the wait time after the last dose would be 30 hours (6 hours × 5 = 30 hours).[49]

Diet, Nutrition, and Exercise

We've all been told—likely since childhood—how important it is to eat right and exercise. But did you know how much of a difference heeding that advice can make in your life? Half of all adult Americans—about 117 million people—have one or more preventable, chronic disease such as type 2 diabetes, cardiovascular disease, or obesity that are related to poor quality eating patterns and physical inactivity.[50] For example, besides tobacco use, the two leading causes of death in developed countries—heart disease and cancer—are related to poor diet and physical inactivity. Fifty-seven percent of worldwide cardiovascular deaths are caused by physical inactivity and conditions arising primarily from poor eating habits—high blood pressure, high blood glucose, overweight and obesity, high cholesterol, and low fruit and vegetable intake. Similarly, up to 41 percent of certain cancers worldwide are caused by overweight and obesity and 14 percent of gastrointestinal cancers are caused by inadequate intake of fruits and vegetables.[51]

It is true that *we are what we eat*. The nutrients in the food we consume—protein, carbohydrates, fat, vitamins, minerals, and other elements—not only provide the fuel our bodies need to operate, but determine the strength and health of every cell in our body. If we are fueling our bodies with too much of the wrong foods (like sweets) and not enough of the right ones (like vegetables), our body's cells and its overall health will suffer and our day-to-day energy and performance will be impaired. It's like filling up with a lower-octane gasoline when the aircraft flight manual says to use a higher one—the aircraft won't perform as well and its vital systems will begin to prematurely fail.

If you want to know what you can do to increase your energy, improve your health, reduce your risk of chronic disease and increase your odds of living a longer life, you should follow the diet and activity recommendations published in the *Dietary Guidelines for Americans* (or *Canada's Food Guide*) and *Physical Activity Guidelines for Americans* (or *Canadian Physical Activity Guidelines*). The *Dietary Guidelines*, best distilled at *choosemyplate.gov*, provide three major recommendations that will improve your eating habits:[52]

- *All food and beverage choices matter—focus on variety, amount, and nutrition.* Choose nutrient-dense foods[53] and beverages that are from all the food groups—fruits, vegetables, grains, protein foods, and dairy (*see* Figure 11-4) and eat the right amount of calories based on your age, sex, height, weight, and physical activity level to assist you in maintaining an ideal body weight.

- *Choose an eating style low in saturated fat, sodium, and added sugars.* Use *Nutrition Facts* labels to determine the amounts of saturated fat, sodium, and added sugars in the foods and beverages you choose and reduce the amount you consume.

- *Make small changes to create a healthier eating style.* Improving eating habits is easier if you start with small shifts from less-healthy to healthier foods and portions. For example, make half your plate vegetables and fruit, make half your grains and fruit whole grains and whole fruit, vary your veggies and/or proteins, or drink a glass of water instead of a soda.

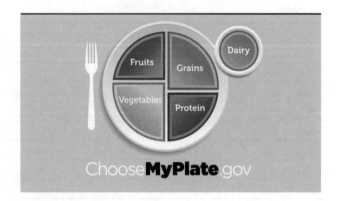

Fig 11-4.

The U.S. My Plate illustrates recommended relative amounts from the various food groups. Canada's Eat Well Plate is similar, except it adds symbols for water, milk alternatives, and oils and fats.

The *Physical Activity Guidelines for Americans* makes simple recommendations regarding physical activity for adults (18 to 64 years old):

- Avoid inactivity and do aerobic physical activity for at least 150 minutes each week at a moderate level (e.g., brisk walking, golfing, gardening) or 75 minutes each week at a vigorous level (e.g., lap swimming, jogging, very fast walk). Each activity should be for at least 10 minutes.
- Spread it out over at least three days a week (but 300 minutes spread over five days is better).
- Do muscle strengthening physical activity, like push-ups, sit-ups, and lifting weights, at least twice a week.[54]

Some activity is better than none, so if you are unable to meet these exercise targets, at least do something every day.

The body of scientific evidence regarding the effect of diet and exercise on health and longevity is robust. We know that developing consistent day-to-day healthy eating habits and making regular time to exercise is the key to good health and longevity. However, as a pilot you are at a distinct disadvantage when it comes to this. First, the job itself involves virtually no physical activity—in fact you're forced to remain seated for most of your duty time in an office we call the flight deck. Second, obtaining nutritious food away from home can often be a challenge, especially when you're on a multi-day trip.

The nature of the job means you will most likely get most of your exercise on your time off, although most hotels have small gyms so you may be able to get some in on layovers. They say the hardest part of exercise is just getting there (to the gym, pool, track, or wherever). Therefore, you should really try and find an activity that you enjoy doing; that will make it much easier to accomplish your exercise fitness goals. Besides choosing the healthiest choice of airline meals (though it is convention that you and your fellow pilot eat different meals in case of food poisoning from salmonella, etc.), or ordering special onboard meals in advance, the best way to obtain more control over your diet while on a multi-day trip is to bring your own healthy food and snacks with you.

Hypoglycemia

Related to the discussion of diet is **hypoglycemia** (*hypo* = low; *glycemia* = blood sugar). It is a condition of low blood sugar that is serious, especially should an episode occur during flight. Symptoms may include hunger, nausea, shaking of hands, sweating, dizziness, lightheadedness, weakness, difficult concentrating, anxiety, mental confusion, and even loss of consciousness. This condition is most commonly experienced by those diagnosed with diabetes, but can also occur in some who are not diabetic. The latter may be related to some underlying disease or it may be simply the result of going too long without food, a condition sometimes called *reactive hypoglycemia* because your body reacts to low blood sugar from not eating for a while. In either case, repeated episodes means you should be diagnosed properly by a medical expert and treated accordingly: the condition may be the precursor to developing diabetes.

Sometimes people will experience a mild form of hypoglycemia (reactive hypoglycemia) after several hours (usually within 4 hours) following a meal, especially if the meal consisted mostly of carbohydrates and/or sugary foods or drinks. The resulting "sugar crash" leads to the previously mentioned symptoms but usually at a lower intensity than a full hypoglycemia episode. Even so, it could be serious enough to affect your performance on the flight deck and you need to deal with the problem by eating something right away, preferably, and counterintuitively, something high in carbohydrates (fruit juice, candy, etc.) to get your blood sugar up quickly. However, to avoid another steep up-and-down spike in blood sugar, you should also follow with something from the other food groups (e.g., protein, grains, dairy) in addition to the carbs.

One way to keep your blood sugar at acceptable levels, and avoid this type of episode, is to never skip meals. For example, an ATP-certificated pilot skipped breakfast before he went flying, later admitting that he was "painfully hungry" before departure. He climbed to 12,500 feet and reported that he had problems opening the oxygen tank valve because his hands felt too weak. He also said he was confused about turning points, altitudes, and distances, and that he felt "woozy." As he approached his destination, he had difficulty determining pattern altitude, had trouble staying awake, and had difficulty pushing the throttle. His Beech Bonanza G35 landed hard and fast with the throttle still open, resulting in the nose gear collapsing and the airplane nosing over. He was rushed to the hospital after receiving serious injuries. The NTSB determined the probable cause of the accident was the pilot's failure to maintain directional control, in part because of his impairment from hypoglycemia and hypoxia (NTSB Identification No: SEA97LA159). In another accident, a Cessna 150 came to rest inverted after the pilot became dizzy and blacked out about 200 to 300 feet AGL on short final and, fortunately, received no injuries. His loss of consciousness—the cause of the accident—was later diagnosed as reactive hypoglycemia (NTSB Identification No: MIA90LA041).

Another way to reduce blood sugar fluctuations is to eat several healthy small meals or snacks throughout the day rather than the traditional "three squares"—a practice called grazing. Make sure to balance your intake from all food groups (protein, dairy, fruits, etc.) and avoid or limit food with saturated fats, sodium, and added sugars (including sugary drinks). You should also choose low glycemic index (GI) foods such as whole grain, high fiber foods, protein, and whole fruits and vegetables. Besides slowly digesting and reducing spikes in blood sugar, low GI foods lower cholesterol reducing the risk of developing heart disease and type 2 diabetes. They also tend to stave off hunger, prolonging a sense of fullness and reducing the tendency to overeat.[55]

Dehyrdation

It was noted that **dehydration** (de = loss of; hydrate = water) increases fatigue and lowers a pilot's tolerance to positive vertical G (see Chapter 8) and exacerbates jet lag (see Chapter 10). Approximately 50 to 60 percent of an adult's total body weight consists of water,[56] and if you lose more water than you take in—through perspiration, respiration, urination, and defecation—your health and performance will suffer. In fact, dehydration can kill you in just a few days if you don't get enough water into your system. Symptoms vary depending on the severity of dehydration, but can include thirst, headache, dark-colored urine, sleepiness, nausea, muscle cramps, dizziness, constipation, weakness, mental confusion, poor vison, seizures, kidney failure, and death.

Dehydration is caused by not consuming enough water. There are no set minimum recommendations for the amount we should consume—a lot depends on our weight, sex, activity level, and other factors. However, the Food and Nutrition Board of the U.S. Institute of Medicine reports that Canadian and American adult males between the age of 19 and 30 take in from the beverages they drink and the food they eat an average of approximately 3.9 quarts (3.7 liters) of water per day and females about 2.8 quarts (2.7 liters) per day. Since about 80 percent of our water usually comes from drinking, this translates to about 3.2 quarts (3.0 liters) and 2.3 quarts (2.2 liters) per day, for males and females, respectively.[57] These are average intakes and individual water needs will increase if exercising and or working outside in a hot environment.

Substances in some of the food and drinks we consume act as a **diuretic** (dia = through; uretic = urine); that is, they increase urination (diuresis). Alcohol and caffeine are two common diuretics. Since ethanol suppresses the production of the anti-diuretic hormone that helps the kidneys retain water, greater urination and subsequent dehydration will result during and after drinking alcohol. This is one of the many factors that contribute to a hangover. Therefore, if you drink alcohol you should also drink water along with it to reduce the effects of dehydration. The same thing for a hangover; even though drinking plenty of water during a hangover won't cure it, it will help reduce dehydration and its effects.

Caffeine, used by many as a wake-me-up in the morning and a pick-me-up throughout the day, is also a diuretic. In the last chapter we extolled its strategic use—only if you are already addicted to the substance—to increase alertness and performance, especially during the approach and landing at the end of a long flight. However, besides keeping you awake for several hours afterwards, caffeine causes increased urination and salt loss, which contributes to dehydration. Since the humidity in the cabins of commercial jets is low at normal cruise altitudes, it is important to drink plenty of fluids. However, don't be tempted to hydrate with just caffeinated beverages such as coffee, tea, or soft drinks. Since they are diuretics, you should drink water, or at least supplement your caffeine consumption with drinking water.

As with almost anything, you should consume only moderate amounts (or less) of caffeine. Generally 400 milligrams per day—the equivalent of about four regular cups of coffee—is the recommended upper limit of caffeine consumption for adults.[58] However, you may have a medical condition that is exacerbated by caffeine. For example, you should avoid it altogether of you have acid reflux disease, migraines, or high blood pressure, and if you are pregnant or breastfeeding. Besides diuresis and dehydration, you may experience other side effects if you consume too much caffeine, such as an elevated or irregular heart rate, high blood pressure, restlessness, nervousness, excitement, headache, irritability, insomnia, anxiety, and gastrointestinal problems. More reasons not to start consuming it if you don't already.

A handy acronym that you can use as a self-checklist before flight is IMSAFE. The poster produced by the Civil Aviation Authority of New Zealand (see Figure 11-5) nicely summarizes some of the major topics—with the exception of stress, discussed in Chapter 19—covered in this chapter. The FAA substitutes the "E" on the checklist with *Emotions*. However, most jurisdictions worldwide include emotions under *Stress* in the checklist.

Fig 11-5.

The IMSAFE checklist helps pilots to conduct a self-assessment of their condition before flight.[59]

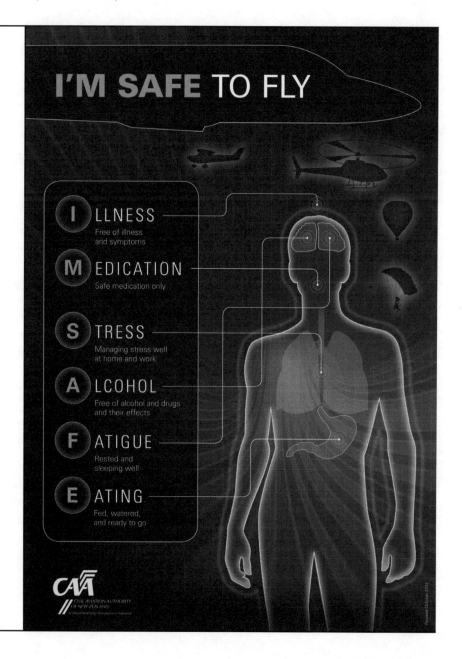

How we treat our bodies affects not only how we perform on the flight deck but our overall health. The detrimental effects of consuming various drugs—both legal and illegal—are well known. So too are the effects of poor eating habits and adopting a sedentary lifestyle. The good news is that most of these self-imposed stresses are completely controllable by the decisions you make. Armed with this knowledge, you have all you need to avoid jeopardizing your piloting career through loss of medical certification and the safety of yourself and your passengers from in-flight incapacitation.

This ends the second part (Chapters 4 to 11) of this book, which has focused primarily on the physiological aspects of pilot performance—the effects of high altitude and in-flight acceleration on our bodies; the limitations of vision, hearing and spatial orientation; the effects of fatigue on performance; and the impact a variety of self-imposed stresses have on our health and our performance. The next part, Chapters 12 to 18, examines some of the cognitive limitations and psychosocial influences that can contribute to errors made on the flight deck.

Helpful Resources

The Airman Education Programs branch at the FAA's Civil Aerospace Medical Institute has produced two helpful videos that are germane to this chapter: *Self-Imposed Stress and Aviation*, and *Fit for Flight*, both available at www.faa.gov/pilots/training/airman_education/physiologyvideos/.

Fitness to Fly: A Medical Guide for Pilots is a preventive maintenance handbook designed to help you maintain your fitness to fly and live a balanced lifestyle. A 22-page version of the book is available for download free from the International Federation of Air Line Pilots' Associations (IFALPA) at www.ifalpa.org/publications/library/fitness-to-fly--2684. The complete book is available for purchase at the ICAO website at store.icao.int/.

Aviation Medicals

Answers to questions about medical certification—obtaining a medical, disqualifying medicine or medical conditions, etc.—can be obtained from the following sources:

- AOPA: www.aopa.org/go-fly/medical-resources
- FAA: www.faa.gov/licenses_certificates/medical_certification/faq/
- Canada: www.tc.gc.ca/eng/civilaviation/opssvs/cam-menu.htm

Medication

Both AOPA and the Aviation Medical Advisory Service provide a list of FAA allowed/disallowed medications for pilots who hold FAA-issued medical certificates. (www.aopa.org/go-fly/medical-resources/medications-database; www.aviationmedicine.com/medication-database/)

Alcohol

Rethink Your Drinking is an informative web site created by the Ontario government that includes quizzes, videos and other resources to help you rethink the role of alcohol in your life. (www.rethinkyourdrinking.ca/information/)

Smoking

Want to quit smoking? Smoking cessation counselors are available to help at 1–800–QUITNOW or 1-877-44U-QUIT (National Cancer Institute) or via a live online chat line at livehelp.cancer.gov/app/chat/chat_launch. Canadians should go to Health Canada's interactive and very creative website at www.breakitoff.ca.

Endnotes

1. A. Martin-Saint-Laurent, J. Lavernhe, G. Casano and A. Simkoff, "Clinical Aspects of Inflight Incapacitations in Commercial Aviation," *Aviation, Space, and Environmental Medicine* 61 (March 1990): 256–260.

2. Charles A. DeJohn, Alex M. Wolbrink and Julie G. Larcher, *In-Flight Medical Incapacitation and Impairment of U.S. Airline Pilots: 1993 to 1998*, DOT/FAA/AM-04-16 (Oklahoma City, OK: FAA Office of Aerospace Medicine, October 2004).

3. P.J. Chapman, "The Consequences of In-Flight Incapacitation in Civil Aviation," *Aviation, Space, and Environmental Medicine* 55 (June 1984): 497–500.

4. International Civil Aviation Organization, *Manual of Civil Aviation Medicine*, 3rd ed., Doc 8984 (Montreal, Canada: ICAO, 2012).

5. Narinder Taneja and Douglas A. Wiegmann, "An Analysis of in-Flight Impairment and Incapacitation in Fatal General Aviation Accidents (1990–1998)," *Proceedings of the Human Factors and Ergonomics Society Annual Meeting* 46 (September 1, 2002): 155–159.

6. David G. Newman, *Pilot Incapacitation: Analysis of Medical Conditions Affecting Pilots Involved in Accidents and Incidents, 1 January 1975 to 31 March 2006*, Report B2006/0170 (Canberra, Australia: Australian Transport Safety Bureau, January 24, 2007). Available at www.atsb.gov.au/publications/2007/b20060170/.

7. Taneja and Wiegmann, "An Analysis of in-Flight Impairment and Incapacitation in Fatal General Aviation Accidents (1990–1998)."

8. L.L. Kulak, R.L. Wick and C.E. Billings, "Epidemiological Study of In-Flight Airline Pilot Incapacitation," *Aerospace Medicine* 42 (1971): 670–672; cited in DeJohn, Wolbrink and Larcher, *In-Flight Medical Incapacitation and Impairment of U.S. Airline Pilots: 1993 to 1998*.

9. Sally Evans and Sally-Ann Radcliffe, "The Annual Incapacitation Rate of Commercial Pilots," *Aviation, Space, and Environmental Medicine* 83 (January 2012): 42–49.

10. Federal Aviation Administration, *Aviation Medical Examiner (AME) Training: A Guide for Prospective FAA Aviation Medical Examiners* (September 20, 2017).

11. Federal Aviation Administration, *BasicMed* (January 19, 2018). Available at www.faa.gov/licenses_certificates/airmen_certification/basic_med/.

12. Center for Disease Control and Prevention, *Fast Facts: Diseases and Death* (2018). Available at www.cdc.gov/tobacco/data_statistics/fact_sheets/fast_facts/index.htm.

13. Center for Disease Control and Prevention, *Smokeless Tobacco: Health Effects* (2018). Available at www.cdc.gov/tobacco/data_statistics/fact_sheets/smokeless/health_effects/index.htm.

14. Center for Disease Control and Prevention, *Electronic Cigarettes* (2018). Available at www.cdc.gov/tobacco/basic_information/e-cigarettes/index.htm.

15. J.L. Fellows, A. Trosclair, E.K. Adams, C.C. Rivera, "Annual Smoking—Attributable Mortality, Years of Potential Life Lost, and Economic Costs—United States, 1995–1999," *Morbidity and Mortality Weekly Report* 51 (April 12, 2002): 300–303.

16. Center for Disease Control and Prevention, *Marijuana and Public Health* (2018). Available at www.cdc.gov/marijuana/index.htm.

17. National Academies of Sciences, Engineering, and Medicine (NASEM), *The Health Effects of Cannabis and Cannabinoids: The Current State of Evidence and Recommendations for Research* (Washington, DC: The National Academies Press 2017).

18. Ibid., 1.

19. Drug Enforcement Administration, *Drugs of Abuse: A DEA Resource Guide*, 2017 Edition (Washington, DC: 2017).

20. Bruce Campion-Smith, "Airlines Impose Cannabis Ban on Pilots and Cabin Crew," *The Toronto Star* (October 15, 2018).

21. National Transportation Safety Board, *Drug Use Trends in Aviation: Assessing the Risk of Pilot Impairment*, Safety Study NTSB/SS-14/01 (Washington, DC: September 9, 2014). 37.

22. Michael Berry, "Can You Fly While High?" *FAA Safety Briefing* (July/August 2017): 5.

23. Dafna Kanny, *The Surprising Link Between Alcohol and Cancer, Senior Scientist from CDC Division of Cancer Prevention and Control* [Blog post, April 14, 2014]. Available at blogs.cdc.gov/cancer/2014/04/14/the-surprising-link-between-alcohol-and-cancer/.

24. National Highway Traffic Safety Administration, *Traffic Safety Facts (2016 Data): Alcohol-Impaired Driving* (October 2017). Available at crashstats.nhtsa.dot.gov/Api/Public/ViewPublication/812450

25. D.E. Nelson, D.W. Jarman, J. Rehm, T.K. Greenfield, G. Rey, W.C. Kerr, P. Miller, K.D. Shield, Y. Ye and T.S. Naimi, "Alcohol-Attributable Cancer Deaths and Years of Potential Life Lost in the United States," *American Journal of Public Health* 103 (April 2013): 641–648.

26. Center for Disease Control and Prevention, *Alcohol Poisoning Deaths: A Deadly Consequence of Binge Drinking* (January 2015). Available at www.cdc.gov/vitalsigns/alcohol-poisoning-deaths/index.html.

27. National Council on Alcoholism and drug Dependence, *Alcohol, Drugs and Crime* (June 2015).

28. National Institute on Alcohol Abuse and Alcoholism, *Rethinking Drinking*, NIH Pub. No. 15-3770 (May 2016). Available at www.rethinkingdrinking.niaaa.nih.gov/.

29. National Institute on Alcohol Abuse and Alcoholism, *Alcohol Use Disorder* (n.d.). Available at www.niaaa.nih.gov/alcohol-health/overview-alcohol-consumption/alcohol-use-disorders.

30. Center for Disease Control and Prevention, *Impaired Driving: Get the Facts* (2017). Available at www.cdc.gov/motorvehiclesafety/impaired_driving/impaired-drv_factsheet.html.

31. Adapted from National Highway Traffic Safety Administration (NHTSA), *The ABCs of BAC: A Guide to Understanding Blood Alcohol Concentration and Alcohol Impairment*, DOT HS 809 844 (July 2016).

32. United States Department of the Army, *Aeromedical Training for Flight Personnel*, TC No. 3-04.93 (Washington, DC: August 31, 2009).

33. Jack G. Modell and James M. Mountz, "Drinking and Flying—The Problem of Alcohol Use by Pilots," *New England Journal of Medicine* 323 (1990): 455–461.

34. Naval Air Training Command, *Joint Aerospace Physiology Student Guide*, CNATRA P-204 (Rev. 03-02) (Corpus Christi, TX: March 2002).

35. Charles E. Billings, Robert L. Wick, Ralph J. Gerke and Robert C. Chase, *The Effects of Alcohol on Pilot Performance During Instrument Flight*, FAA-AM-72-41 (Washington, DC: FAA, January 1972).

36. Modell and Mountz, "Drinking and Flying—The Problem of Alcohol Use by Pilots."

37. Federal Aviation Administration, *Introduction to Aviation Physiology* (Oklahoma City, OK: FAA Civil Aerospace Medical Institute, n.d.).

38. "Airline Gives Ex-Drunken Pilot a Second Chance," *The New York Times* (October 14, 1993).

39. Sean Alfano, "Drunk Airline Pilots Face Prison," *CBS News* (July 21, 2005).

40. Guohua Li, Susan P. Baker, Yandong Qiang, George W. Rebok and Melissa L. McCarthy, "Alcohol Violations and Aviation Accidents: Findings from the U.S. Mandatory Alcohol Testing Program," *Aviation, Space, and Environmental Medicine* 78 (May 2007): 510–513.

41. Taneja and Wiegmann, "An Analysis of in-Flight Impairment and Incapacitation in Fatal General Aviation Accidents (1990–1998)."

42. Arvind K. Chaturvedi, Kristi J. Craft, Dennis V. Canfield and James E. Whinnery, "Toxicological Findings from 1587 Civil Aviation Accident Pilot Fatalities, 1999–2003," *Aviation, Space, and Environmental Medicine* 76 (December 2005): 1145–1150.

43. Michael Berry, "Course Correction" *FAA Safety Briefing* (September/October 2017): 5.

44. NTSB, *Drug Use Trends in Aviation: Assessing the Risk of Pilot Impairment.*

45. Federal Aviation Administration, "Pilots and Medication," *General Aviation Joint Steering Committee Safety Enhancement Topic Fact Sheet* (October 2018). Available at www.faa.gov/news/safety_briefing/archive/.

46. NTSB, *Drug Use Trends in Aviation: Assessing the Risk of Pilot Impairment.*

47. Federal Aviation Administration, 2018 *Guide for Aviation Medical Examiners* (Washington, DC: Office of Aerospace Medicine, September 2018). Available at www.faa.gov/about/office_org/headquarters_offices/avs/offices/aam/ame/guide/.

48. Ibid.

49. FAA, "Pilots and Medication."

50. U.S. Department of Health and Human Services (USHHS) and U.S. Department of Agriculture (USDA), *2015–2020 Dietary Guidelines for Americans*, 8th Edition (December 2015). vii. Available at http://health.gov/dietaryguidelines/2015/guidelines/).

51. World Health Organization, *Global Health Risks: Mortality and Burden of Disease Attributable to Selected Major Risks* (Geneva, Switzerland: 2009).

52. USHHS and USDA, *2015–2020 Dietary Guidelines for Americans.* Also see *ChooseMyplate.gov* at www.choosemyplate.gov/MyPlate.

53. Nutrient-dense foods contain essential vitamins and minerals, dietary fiber, and other naturally occurring substances that have not been "diluted" by the addition of calories from added solid fats, sugars, or refined starches, or by the solid fats naturally present in the food. USHHS and USDA, *2015–2020 Dietary Guidelines for Americans.* 12.

54. U.S. Department of Health and Human Services, 2008 *Physical Activity Guidelines for Americans* (Washington, DC: 2008).

55. University of Sydney GI Group, *About Glycemic Index* (Sydney, Australia: Boden Institute of Obesity, Nutrition, Exercise and Eating Disorders and Charles Perkins Centre, 2017). Available at www.glycemicindex.com/index.php.

56. Institute of Medicine (U.S.), *Dietary Reference Intakes: Water, Potassium, Sodium, Chloride, and Sulfate* (Washington, DC: National Academies Press 2005).

57. Ibid.

58. Mayo Clinic Staff, *Caffeine: How Much is Too Much?* (March 8, 2017). Available at www.mayoclinic.org/healthy-lifestyle/nutrition-and-healthy-eating/in-depth/caffeine/art-20045678.

59. Civil Aviation Authority of New Zealand (2012). Available at www.aviation.govt.nz/safety/publications/safety-posters/.

Part III
Psychological Aspects of
Flight Crew Performance

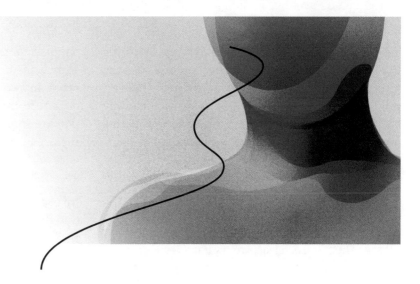

12

Seeing is deceiving.
Visual Perception

On September 10, 1999, a Eurocopter AS-350B helicopter crashed on the Juneau ice field near Juneau, Alaska, while conducting an on-demand sightseeing flight under Part 135. About two hours later, another Eurocopter helicopter crashed on the Juneau ice field while attempting a search and rescue mission for the first helicopter. Finally, a third helicopter crashed in the same area two hours later, in yet another attempt to rescue the stranded crew and passengers from the first two accidents. The commercial pilot in the third accident said the ceiling was at least 1,000 feet AGL and the visibility was more than 6 SM. The pilots of all three helicopters stated that just before impact, they thought they were at least 500 feet AGL.[1]

More recently, the NTSB issued Safety Alert SA-033 admonishing pilots to be careful not to land at the wrong airport after two experienced flight crews did just that: A Boeing B-747 Dreamlifter, destined for McConnell AFB in Wichita, Kansas, unintentionally landed on a 6,100-foot runway at Colonel James Jabara Airport, about eight miles north of McConnell; and a Southwest Airlines B-737 on approach to Branson Airport in Missouri mistakenly landed on a 3,738-foot runway at M. Graham Clark Downtown Airport, about five miles north of Branson. The crews of both aircraft were conducting visual approaches at night in VMC and all thought they saw the correct runway.

These occurrences illustrate the limitations of a major component of human information processing: visual perception. The experienced flight crews landing at the wrong airports in clear weather at night thought they were landing on the correct runway. The commercial helicopter pilots, flying in flat-light condi-

tions over a large featureless snow-covered ice field during the day, were confident they had plenty of altitude between their aircraft and terrain. What these pilots all had in common was they were deceived by their senses. But, unlike many other pilots who've been similarly duped, the passengers and crew members were able to walk away (although one passenger aboard the one of the helicopters suffered serious injuries).

Visual perception is one element in the cognitive approach to understanding human performance. Introduced in Chapter 3, this approach maintains that information processing begins with sensation—in this case, the receiving of sensory inputs (stimuli) by receptors located in our eyes. In Chapter 6, we discussed the physiological limitations of visual sensation, especially as it relates to avoiding a MAC and flying in the dark. The interpretation of these visual inputs is known as **visual perception**, which involves making *sense* of visual sensation. Any misinterpretation of visual inputs can reduce safety margins by adversely impacting higher level cognitive functioning such as problem solving, decision making, and response selection and execution (*see* Figure 3-5 in Chapter 3).

Psychologists have studied visual perception at great length and many insights have been gained. Some of the findings seem obvious while others do not; yet many questions remain unanswered. As briefly indicated in previous chapters, however, inadequate visual perception—especially in conditions of reduced visibility (e.g., flying in mist, haze or cloud, or during the hours of darkness)—has been the cause of many aircraft accidents. It explains why a pilot inadvertently landed his Cessna 172 on a 200-foot runway built for radio-controlled aircraft.[2] It also accounts for why a commercial jet unexpectedly crashed short of the runway when conducting a visual approach at night, when according to the crew members, everything outside looked normal.

Just as human visual *sensation* has its limitations, so too does visual *perception*. As you learned in Chapter 6, fatal MAC and CFIT accidents have resulted from pilots failing to detect important visual **sensory cues**. These cues, or clues, are characteristics in the environment that are received by our sensory receptors that aid us in accurately perceiving the outside world. In this chapter we will discuss how pilots, even though they may be successful at detecting visual cues, may incorrectly interpret them. The type of misinterpretation of the outside visual world that has the potential to be the most deadly is a *visual illusion*. Before discussing this specific topic let us look at some general problems associated with distance and depth perception.

Distance and Depth Perception

Various difficulties in flight have occurred due to improper distance and/or depth perception. Judgment of distance—from other aircraft, mountains, runways, etc.—is somewhat different from depth perception. Though both are related, depth perception involves three-dimensional (3D) vision. Three different kinds of cues contribute to our ability to perceive distance and depth: monocular cues, physiological cues, and motion cues.

Monocular Cues to Distance/Depth Perception

When both eyes are utilized, the distance between them contributes to depth perception. These are called "binocular cues" to depth perception and will be discussed in the next section. However, people with only one eye (monocular), or with only one eye open, can also judge distances fairly well. It would be logical to conclude that since the image on the retina is only two-dimensional, depth perception (3D vision) would be impossible in monocular conditions. However, the reason this is not the case is mainly

because of the physical characteristics of the visual stimuli themselves. Because these *object-centered* cues reside in two-dimensional images like a photograph or picture, **monocular cues** to distance/depth perception are sometimes called *pictorial cues*. The following represents a brief summary of the major monocular cues which have been identified by researchers and are applicable to visual perception in flight.

Interposition

Cue dominance studies have shown that **interposition** is likely the strongest distance/depth cue. We judge an object to be further away when it is blocked, or occluded, by another object. The object which interposes (overlays) the other is seen as being closer (*see* Figure 12-1).

Fig 12-1.

We know the United Airlines Boeing B-777 is further away from us than the Tarom B-737 because the latter is interposed between the B-777 and our eyes.

Relative Size

When we are familiar with the actual size of an object (e.g., airplane, automobile, adult human) we rightly interpret it as being further away when it casts a smaller image on our retinas. Similarly, if the object begins to subtend an increasingly larger visual angle—casting an increasingly larger image on our retinas—we interpret the object as moving closer, not expanding in actual size (*see* Figure 12-2). Therefore the **relative size** of an object is a cue to its distance. As will be discussed later in this chapter, problems can arise when we aren't aware of the actual size of an object (a runway for example).

Height in The Visual Field

Since the objects you see when looking straight out at the horizon (0 degrees) are usually further away than objects that you see when looking straight down toward your feet (90 degrees), an object's position relative to the horizon will also affect distance perception.[3] An object's **height in the visual field**, sometimes called *height in the plane*, influences our perception of its distance. An object seems further away the higher up it is in the visual field (or higher in the visual plane), compared to objects that are lower (*see* Figure 12-3).

Linear Perspective

Parallel lines created by railroad tracks or the edges of straight roads appear to converge to a single point with increasing distance. Pilots are quite familiar with this **linear perspective** distance cue. Because the far end of the runway in Figure 12-4 (top of figure) is the same size as the approach end (bottom of figure), the smaller relative size (discussed above) of the far end of the runway is a cue that it is further away. The image of the runway on the retina while on an approach to landing is not a rectangle (though every approved land aerodrome generally is) but a trapezoid.

Texture Gradient

This visual cue is really a combination of linear perspective and relative size. **Texture gradient** is a change in texture, such that distant objects appear smaller (relative size) and closer to each other (linear

Fig 12-2.

If both airplanes are the same actual size, the one on the right must be closer to you because it casts a larger image on your retina.

Fig 12-3.

Both airplanes are the same size and both cast the same-sized image on your retina; however, the airplane on the left appears to be further away because it is closer to the horizon.

Fig 12-4.

Parallel runway lines appear to converge with distance.

perspective). The textured elements in the rows of cotton in the top half of Figure 12-5 are finer (smaller, closer together, and denser) indicating the elements are farther way than those in the bottom half where they are appear coarser (larger, farther apart, and less dense).

Fig 12-5.

Elements in this picture of cotton rows appear smaller, closer together, and denser in the distance compared to the foreground.[4]

Aerial Perspective

Perceived distances of objects also depend upon the condition of the atmosphere. Distant objects are seen as more blurred and bluish in color due to the greater degree of light scattering from particulate matter in the air between the object and observer. Truer color and greater detail is seen when objects are closer due, in part, to reduced light scattering. The **aerial perspective** cue to distance perception can lead pilots to overestimate an object's distance on hazy days and underestimate it on exceptionally clear (usually dry as well) days.

Relative Brightness

The brightness of an object is also a cue to its distance. Darker objects are perceived as being smaller and further away while brighter objects are seen as larger and closer. It is likely that this **relative brightness** cue works similarly to that of aerial perspective because we perceive objects further away to be darker and smaller than objects which are closer to us.

Physiological Cues to Distance/Depth Perception

The previous collection of monocular cues are sometimes called pictorial cues to distance/depth perception because they depend entirely on stimuli that reside in the outside environment to judge distance/depth perception, not physiological factors. Physiological cues, such as accommodation, binocular convergence, and stereopsis, also contribute to our perception of distance/depth perception. These **binocular cues** depend on the use of both eyes to add additional information to our perception of distance and depth.

Accommodation

Within a certain range, additional cues to depth perception can come from the process of visual accommodation (focusing). Contraction of the ciliary muscles change the shape of the eye's lens indicating a focus on a close object, while relaxed muscles indicate focus on a distant object (*see* Figure 6-3 in Chapter 6). The visual system senses these physiological changes in accommodation as cues to an object's distance. Since the eyes' focal resting position is only about two feet to two yards away from the viewer (*see* empty-field myopia in Chapter 6), and no significant change in muscle tension occurs for focusing on objects beyond this distance, this cue to distance perception is useful only for objects within this small distance close to the viewer.

Binocular Convergence

A further physiological cue to depth perception is **binocular convergence**. Take a small object and hold it at arm's length directly in front of you. Bring the object closer to your nose as you stare directly at it. You will feel definite eye strain, and if someone were watching you they would see your eyes go cross-eyed. Focusing on an object that lies within about 20 feet away from the viewer requires an inward convergence of each eye. The closer the object is to the viewer, the greater degree of muscular effort is necessary to maintain focal tracking (*see* Figure 12-6). The visual system senses this eye-muscle strain and uses the information as another cue to an object's distance.

Retinal Disparity

A more important cue to depth perception which arises from binocular vision is known as *retinal disparity*. Take a small object and hold it directly in front of you. While staring at the object alternately

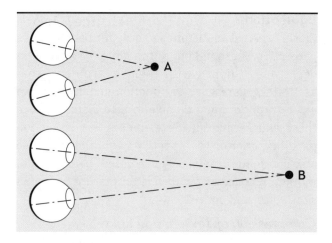

Fig 12-6.

Greater convergence is required to focus on close objects (A) than is required for distant objects (B).

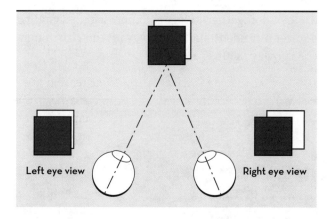

Left eye view   Right eye view

Fig 12-7.

Retinal disparity is another cue to distance perception. When looking at close objects the image the right and left eyes see are different.

Fig 12-8.

When traveling through space, stationary objects that appear to move by us quickly are closer, while those that appear to move more slowly are further away. The illustration represents the view out the window of a moving train or automobile (A) and the relative positions of objects after a short time period (B).

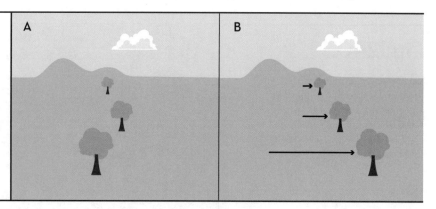

open your left eye (with the right eye closed) then your right eye (with the left eye closed). You will see it appear to move back and forth horizontally. Since the eyes are separated from each other (by approximately 2.5 inches) an object's image projected on each retina differs (see Figure 12-7). This difference increases the closer the object is to the viewer. The visual system senses these different images as cues to an object's distance and fuses the two disparate images together to form one 3D picture, a process called **stereopsis**. This cue to distance/depth perception is only valid for objects located within about 30 feet of the viewer.[5] Beyond that distance, the two images look essentially the same.

Motion Cues to Distance/Depth Perception

The motion of objects also contributes to distance and depth perception. Like most of the visual cues we have discussed, motion parallax and motion perspective operate at a relatively subconscious level and usually go unnoticed.

Motion Parallax

Motion parallax refers to the apparent motion of stationary objects as one moves past them. If you can explain to your five-year-old child why—as I unsuccessfully tried to do once—when traveling in the car the moon (or any other distant object for that matter) keeps moving with us while everything else moves past us, then you intuitively understand the concept of **motion parallax**. The *apparent* velocity of objects to a moving observer is such that objects quickly moving in direction opposite to you are perceived to be closer than objects moving slower or barely at all (see Figure 12-8).

Motion Perspective

While motion parallax describes the phenomena of apparent motion of objects moving past on either side of you as you move through space, **motion perspective** describes the phenomenon of an outward expanding visual field as you move directly toward an object and a contracting visual field as you move away from it. It is much like linear perspective in that the visual field seems to diverge as you move closer to it. Pilots use this cue when conducting approaches and landings. When describing this flow pattern, which pilots strongly rely upon in making safe approaches and landings, the "contours of the visual field appear to flow radially away from a focus that corresponds to the touchdown point, so that as objects move toward the edges of the field they seem to move faster and to get larger and their texture seems to coarsen" (*see* Figure 12-9).[6] This is how pilots bring an airplane to the desired flare-out point (or *aim point*). The desired spot (hopefully the runway landing zone) is the one that remains stationary on the windscreen, not the one that moves up, down, or to the side.

Egomotion

Closely related to distance and depth perception is perception of egomotion (self-motion). Though flight decks are equipped with flight instruments that accurately represent the direction and speed of an aircraft, pilots must be able to also visually judge these values using outside references. Besides motion parallax, motion perspective, and the distance and depth cues previously discussed, perception of motion in space also depends on texture compression, splay, and optic flow.

Compression of Texture and Splay

Equally spaced elements that are compressed (seen closer together) signal to the brain that not only are the elements further away (texture gradient cue to distance perception discussed previously), but the altitude of the viewer is lower. The equally spaced runway edge lights on the left runway in Figure 12-10 are closer together (texture compression), signaling a lower altitude than the runway on the right where the runway lights are less compressed.

Fig 12-9.

Motion perspective describes the outward expanding visual field from the runway landing flare-out point (aim point) as you move toward it.

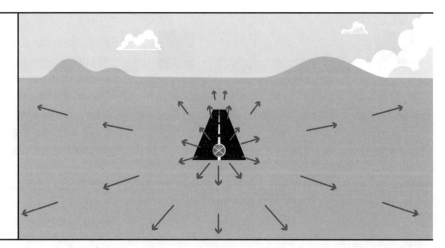

Fig 12-10.

Equally spaced runway edge lights are compressed in the left diagram signaling the aircraft is at a lower altitude than for the runway on the right, where the runway edge lights are less compressed.

The linear perspective cue involves parallel lines that appear to converge in the distance (*see* Figure 12-4). The angle of convergence of these lines is also a cue to altitude. For example, the convergence angle of the extended parallel runway edge lines—called the **splay**—of the two runways in Figure 12-10 differ. The larger angle of splay of the runway on the left is an additional cue that the aircraft and the pilot-viewer are at a lower altitude, while the smaller splay of the runway on the right indicates they are at a higher altitude. As will be discussed later in this chapter, problems can arise when pilots encounter runways that distort the normal texture compression/splay relationships; for example, runways that are sloped or those that have a different length-to-width ratio than pilots are accustomed to.

Optic Flow

As noted in Chapter 6, even though visual acuity—the ability to discriminate fine detail—is poor with ambient vision compared to foveal vision, this peripheral vision is crucial in determining our orientation in space. This also applies to motion perception. Similar to motion parallax and motion perspective, **optic flow** is the term used to describe both the direction and rate at which objects in our peripheral vision flow past us as we move through space. Pilots conducting a visual approach are influenced by the optic flow rate when judging their descent approach angle. As described previously, the flare-out point is the expansion point on the runway landing zone where there is no optic flow but all other elements in the visual scene radiate outward (backward, forward, and away to the side) from it (*see* Figure 12-9).

Global optic flow is a ratio of speed divided by altitude (flow rate=velocity/altitude).[7] For example, if you've ever experienced the difference between driving a sports car and a big semi-trailer truck at the same speed, then you understand this concept. The speed of the close-to-the-ground sports car seems much faster because of the increased optic flow in your peripheral vision. In fact, a car traveling 40 mph has a higher optic flow rate than a jet traveling 400 mph at 40,000 feet. Another question asked by my young son occurred while at FL390 on a vacation flight to Disneyland in California. As he was looking at the ground below through the window of the Boeing jet, he said, "I thought these big airplanes went really fast?" They do, but because of the airplane's high altitude,

he wasn't seeing it. This also explains why early B-747 pilots, sitting at almost twice the eye-to-wheel height (height of pilot's eyes above the apron) than they were accustomed to in the previous generation of narrow-bodied aircraft, tended to taxi too fast causing excess strain on the landing gear while turning. The optic flow of the apron's surface area moving past them in their visual field created the illusion that they were taxiing at the same speed they usually did. The same phenomenon occurs at night or in poor visibility, even with small airplanes with an eye-to-wheel height of only a few feet. As we will discuss later in the next section, optic flow (motion perspective) cues also create problems for pilots conducting visual approaches in black-hole conditions or toward runways with terrain that slopes up or down below the approach path.

Edge Rate

Another element similar to optic flow is **edge rate (ER)**. It is the rate at which the edges of textured elements, or discontinuities, flow past us as we move through space. Though similar to optic flow, ER is the ratio of velocity divided by the distance between edges and is independent of altitude. A high ER occurs when flying over finely textured elements (e.g., cities, or farmland with small fields) and produces a perception of increased speed; a low ER occurs when flying over coarsely textured elements (e.g., deserts, large bodies of water) and produces a perception of decreased speed. On a stretch of highway in Scotland where accidents were occurring because drivers were not slowing down sufficiently for an approaching traffic circle (roundabout), a clever experiment involved exponentially decreasing the spacing between markers on the side of the road hoping the finer edge rate would create an illusion of increasing speed as a driver approached the circle. The plan succeeded: drivers slowed down and the accident rate decreased.[8]

There has been some research into the possible speed and/or altitude illusions which pilots of low-flying aircraft (e.g., military nap-of-the-earth or other operations) might experience when edge rate varies. For example, the reduction of edge rate when flying from a finely textured surface (trees, shrubs, etc.) to a more coarsely textured surface (desert, water) could cause an illusion of increased height and therefore the pilot might erroneously descend to correct for this.

Geometric Illusions

A dramatic illustration of how our visual perception can deceive us is found in the phenomena of **visual illusions**. These create inaccurate perceptions of stimuli in the outside world. In other words, what you see is sometimes not what you get. Before examining the problem of visual illusions in the flight environment—especially during the approach and landing phases of flight—it is helpful to first examine **geometric illusions**, a fascinating topic studied for more than a century-and-a-half by physiologists, psychologists, artists, and even philosophers.

Geometric illusions—a class of optical illusions—involve the incorrect perception a variety of two-dimensional line drawings and geometric shapes. These simple illusions trick our visual system into incorrectly perceiving the size, shape, distance or direction of visual stimuli. You are probably familiar with some of these, including the horizontal-vertical line, Mueller-Lyer, and Ponzo illusions (see Figure 12-11).

For example, the vertical line in Figure 12-11A is the same length as the horizontal line, yet it appears longer. The same illusion is seen in the Gateway Arch in St. Louis, Missouri, where its height is the same as its width (630 feet), but still *looks* taller (see Figure 12-12). The illusion leads us to perceive a tree's length is greater when it is upright than after it has been felled.

Line AB in the Mueller-Lyer illusion (see Figure 12-11B) is the same length as line CD, yet it appears longer. This illusion even occurs even when there is no line (see Figure 12-13).

One of the many theories used to explain the Mueller-Lyer illusion suggests that our brain unconsciously perceives depth in these two-dimensional drawings, causing us to perceive the vertical line connected to the outward-pointed diagonal lines (right image in Figure 12-14) as the inside corner of a

Fig 12-11.

Common geometric illusions. The vertical line looks longer in the horizontal-vertical line illusion (A); line AB is the same length as CD, yet it looks longer in the Mueller-Lyer illusion (B); and the top horizontal line in Ponzo illusion (C) looks slightly longer than the bottom line.

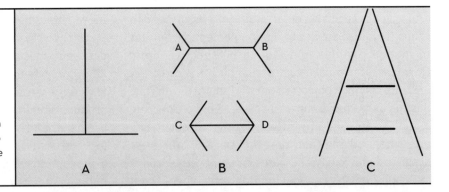

Fig 12-12.

The horizontal-vertical line illusion (see Figure 12-11A) is seen in the Gateway Arch monument where its height looks longer than its width, yet both are the same length.[9]

room or building, a common image in our 3D human-built environment. Using the monocular cues of linear perspective and relative size, our brain is fooled into thinking that the center vertical line in the right image must be longer than the center vertical line in the left image because its assumed distance is further away. If the brain perceives the center vertical line as the outside corner of a room or building, as in the left image in Figure 12-14, it is seen as closer and therefore, shorter.

The top horizontal line in the Ponzo illusion (*see* Figure 12-11C) is perceived to be somewhat longer than the lower horizontal line, even though they are the same length. Again, using the cue of linear perspective, the brain sees this 2D drawing as a 3D image with the top line being further away. Then, using the relative size cue, the brain interprets the top line that casts the same-size image on the retina as longer since it is perceived to be further away. There are variations to this illusion. In Figure 12-15, the circle and the square's horizontal line closest to the apex of the converging lines appear somewhat larger and longer, respectively.

Like the Ponzo illusion, there are other illusions where the stimulus being judged or estimated (the *focal stimuli*[10]) depends upon its context (the surrounding stimuli, or *background*). For example, the two orange circles in the Ebbinghaus illusion in Figure 12-16 are the same size, but the surrounding circles causes the left one to appear smaller than the right one.

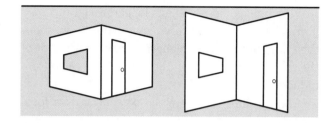

Fig 12-14.

One explanation for the disparity in vertical line length estimations in the Mueller-Lyer illusion is the center vertical line on the right is perceived as the inside corner of a building and further away from the viewer, creating the perception that it must be longer than the center vertical line on the left diagram.

Fig 12-15.

Variations of the Ponzo illusion. The circle on the top looks larger and somewhat distorted than the one on the bottom, while the top of the square looks expanded. These visual distortions likely occur because the brain perceives depth from the monocular cue of linear perspective.

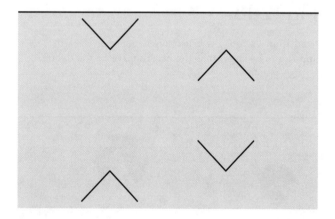

Fig 12-13.

The Mueller-Lyer illusion without vertical lines. Even though each distance is the same, the vertical distance between the apexes of the outward pointing diagonal lines (left) appears longer than the distance between the apexes of the inward pointing diagonal lines (right).

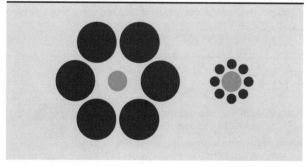

Fig 12-16.

The Ebbinghaus illusion. The background stimuli of small dots surrounding the orange circle on the right causes it to look bigger than the orange circle surrounded by large circles on the left.

Which diagonal red line is longer in Figure 12-17? If you guessed the left one, you would be wrong—they are both the same length. The arrangement of the background stimuli in the Sanders parallelogram induces this illusion.

Another illusion where the perception of a focal stimulus depends on its background stimuli is the irradiation illusion. Which square looks bigger in Figure 12-18, the white one on the left or the black one on the right? Of course, you can guess by now that they are both the same size, yet the white square surrounded by a black outline appears larger than the black square surrounded by white. This is the same as the relative brightness cue to distance perception discussed earlier in this chapter. The brightness contrast seems to induce the perception that the light of the left white square is irratiating out of the bigger black box in all directions and is therefore perceived to be bigger. As we will discuss in the next section on runway illusions, this phenomenon may be part of the reason why the intensity of runway

edge lights tends to influence a pilot's perception of their aircraft's distance from them.

It appears that the perceptual part of our brain—often called our "visual brain" by researchers because of the close connection between the eyes and the brain[12]—is strongly predisposed to see three dimensions in two-dimensional images. The role of various cues likely contributes to this. For example, in Figure 12-19A, a pink triangle appears to superimpose itself on top of three black circles and a black-lined triangle, and it also appears to be brighter than the surrounding visual field—even though a pink triangle isn't actually physically present! Our visual brain likely uses the monocular cue of interposition (occlusion) to create what are called *subjective* (or illusory) contours. An even stronger perception of depth occurs in the Illusory Pyramid illusion in Figure 12-19B. A 3D pyramid appears to overlay three black circles and the corner of a room, even though no such pyramid is there!

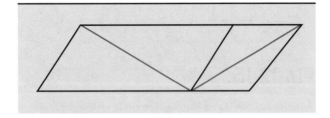

Fig 12-17.

Sanders parallelogram illusion. The red diagonal line on the left looks longer than the red diagonal line on the right, because of the context (surrounding stimuli) of the parallelogram.

Fig 12-18.

Irradiation illusion. The bright inner square on the left appears to be larger than the black square on the right.[11]

Fig 12-19.

Subjective (illusory) contours. A pink triangle appears to lie atop three black circles and a black triangle in the Kanizsa's triangle (A); and a pyramid appears to overlay three black circles and the corner of a room in the Illusory Pyramid illusion (B).[13]

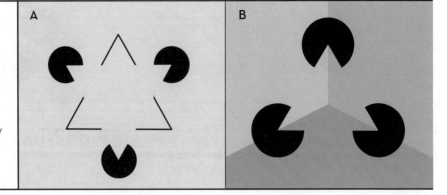

Experience and Expectancy in Visual Perception

The processes involved in visual perception are complex and still poorly understood. Our perception of the outside world depends on many factors, including the physical characteristics of the stimuli themselves and the physiological characteristics of our perceptual systems. But it also depends on the psychological characteristics of the perceiver, including our past experience and present expectancy. For example, what do you see in Figure 12-20? Do you see a Dalmatian sniffing the ground? If so, have you seen this picture before, or did the mention of a Dalmatian help you to see it? Either way, if you can see it now, you will always be able to in the future if you see it again: Your previous experience influences future perceptions.

Furthermore, sometimes we see what we expect to see. For example, what do you see in Figure 12-21? The face of an old man, or a naked woman? If you were previously exposed to A, then B, then C in Figure 12-22, you would likely see the old man; if you were previously exposed to D, then E, then F you would likely see the naked woman. Your previous experience influences perception, sometimes setting you up to see what you expect to see.

Expectancy, or the anticipation or motivation to perceive something you expect, is often helpful in flight operations. For example, when attempting to

Fig 12-20.

Can you see the Dalmatian?

Fig 12-21.

Do you see the face of an old man or a naked woman?[14]

Fig 12-22.

Previous perceptions influence future perceptions. If you previously saw A, then B, then C, you would likely see an old man's face in Figure 12-21; If you were previously exposed to D, then E, then F, you would likely see a naked woman sitting sideways in Figure 12-21.[15]

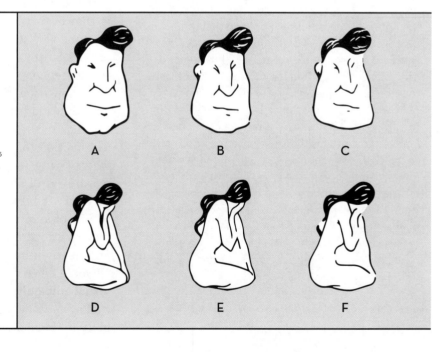

visually locate a geographical landmark or airport indicated at a certain location on a navigational chart, looking where you expect to see it is usually very efficient. Since you are at least eight times more likely to see another aircraft if air traffic control alerts you to its presence (e.g., "traffic, one o'clock, five miles, westbound, six thousand"), it is also effective to look where you expect the traffic to be.[16]

However, expectancy can also lead to errors. For example, most train engineers who inadvertently traveled through a red light signal (indicating they should stop) did so because they *expected* it to be green.[17] A military pilot accidently dropped a bomb on a buoy-laying ship after mistaking it for the actual target buoy during a training exercise in the Baltic Sea.[18] A terrible incident involved two U.S. Air Force F-15 pilots who shot down two of their own U.S. Army Black Hawk helicopters, killing all 26 people aboard both aircraft. A series of unfortunate circumstances led them to believe they were Iraqi Hind helicopters, so when they went in for a visual identification, they "saw" what they *expected* to see.[19] Another tragic accident claimed the lives of all 257 aboard Air New Zealand Flight 901, a McDonnell Douglas DC-10 when it inadvertently flew into Mount Erebus while on a sightseeing flight in the Antarctic. The flight crew believed they were elsewhere at time of accident, and not on a collision course with the volcano, in part, because the geographic features they saw outside conformed to what they *expected* to see.[20] This accident occurred in sector whiteout conditions, a threat discussed later in this chapter.

Visual Illusions in the Flight Environment

You may be wondering how the previous coverage of geometric illusions has anything to do with safely piloting an aircraft. The answer is that it has a great deal to do with it, because visual illusions are not confined to only simple two-dimensional line drawings; they are present in the real 3D world as well, including the three-dimensional working environment of those who fly aircraft. Therefore, if you can't completely trust your senses with simple line drawings, you also can't with more complex stimuli residing in the 3D world.

What all visual illusions have in common is their ability to trick you into seeing something that isn't there, or not seeing something that is. I have shared some ideas about how and why they may do this, and will share some more in the remainder of this chapter; but perception scientists are still not certain of the exact mechanisms involved. What we do know is that even the most experienced pilots are not immune to visual illusions. And even though they occur relatively infrequently in flight, when they do the consequences are often fatal. That's because by definition visual illusions *deceive* you into seeing the outside world incorrectly. We also know that visual illusions in the real world are more likely to occur in conditions of sparse visual stimuli. For example, when flying in poor visibility, at night, or over featureless or snow-covered terrain. These impoverished visual conditions limit the amount and quality of information needed for our visual brain to make an accurate assessment of the outside world and nearly mimics the two-dimensional world we explored when discussing geometric illusions. This **visual ambiguity** creates uncertainty for our perceptual system, increasing our visual brain's susceptibility to visual illusions.

Expectancy leads to overconfidence

I sighted the airport and was cleared for a visual approach to Runway 35...I had difficulty lining up with Runway 35 because the lighting seemed poor, but *having landed on Runway 35 the three previous times I flew the run, I was confident I had the runway*. On short final, I noticed that there was no edge lighting or VASI, and that the centerline lights were green. Although none of this seemed correct, *I was sure I had the runway*: I rationalized that the edge lights and VASI had been knocked out by lightning. Airport maintenance vehicles on the Tower frequency discussing lighting problems lent credence to my theory. It never occurred to me to check the directional gyro...until the nosewheel lowered and I saw the yellow painted centerline, I refused to let go of my belief that I was looking at Runway 35... After shutdown, I checked the airport diagram and determined that I had landed on taxiway Echo... In spite of the evidence—no edge lights, no VASI and green centerline lights—I refused to believe that it was not Runway 35.

Source: Office of the NASA Aviation Safety Reporting System, Callback (July 1991).

Approach and Landing Illusions

As noted in Chapter 1, almost one-half of the world's fatal commercial jet airplane accidents occur during the final approach and landing phases of flight. Because misinterpretation of outside visual cues has been responsible for several of these accidents, it is important that pilots fully understand the nature of **visual landing illusions**. These have led some pilots to unexpectedly crash short of the runway or land too hard on it; while others have landed long, running out of stopping distance. Some illusions during approach and landing are caused by certain atmospheric and runway lighting conditions; the majority, however, involve sloped runways, sloped terrain, runways with dimensions you are not used to, and approaches and landings on runways in the dark.

Sloping Runways

Pilots usually judge their approach angle by the familiar trapezoidal image the runway shape casts upon the retina (*see* Figure 12-23). Your visual brain unconsciously compares what you see in the outside landing environment with familiar patterns of linear perspective and runway splay (see earlier discussion) stored in your perceptual memory bank. However, runway slope can change these familiar images, leading to illusions. When flying on the correct approach angle to a sloped runway, depending on the direction of runway slope, a high-approach runway image or low-approach runway image is projected onto the retina of each eye.

For a variety of important reasons, it is usually not recommended to land on a downsloping runway. However, should there be need to, when you are on the correct approach angle to such a runway, the retinal image will be a low-approach shape, giving you the illusion you are too low. Figure 12-24 illustrates that in response to this false perception you will instinctively adjust your approach angle to visually acquire the normal approach image (or, normal linear perspective and splay) that you are accustomed to; the resulting high approach could lead to a go-around at best or a long landing and runway overrun at worst.

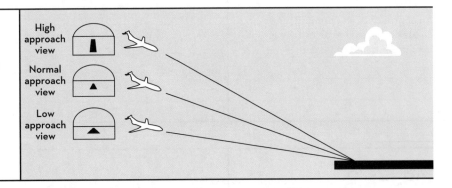

Fig 12-23.

Different runway approach views from the flight deck.

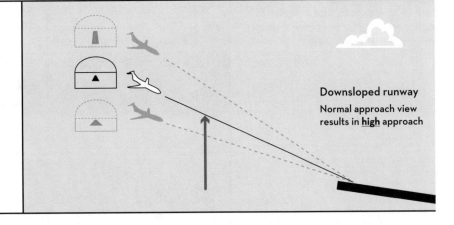

Fig 12-24.

An approach to a downsloped runway creates an illusion of being too low, resulting in a high approach.

Downsloped runway
Normal approach view results in **high** approach

The linear perspective and runway splay during a proper approach to an upsloped runway (see Figure 12-25) creates a high-approach image on your retina producing the illusion that you are too high, leading you to conduct a low approach.

This illusion is deadly; the resulting low approach could lead to a premature hard landing at best or a CFIT accident short of the runway at worst. Many pilots—novice and expert alike—have fallen prey to this illusion. This can happen during the day but is considerably strengthened at night, especially during dark-night conditions (i.e., moonless and/or an overcast sky conditions). For example, the experienced crew of a Canadian Airlines International Boeing B-767 was fooled by the upsloping runway at Halifax Stanfield International Airport in Nova Scotia during a nonprecision instrument approach to Runway 06 at night. The 0.77 percent upslope tricked both pilots into thinking their approach angle was too high, and in spite of mostly red precision approach path indicator lights indicating the jet was too low, they flew a low approach on short final that resulted in a premature hard landing and tail strike (TSB Report No: A96A0035).

These illusions are compounded when the runway is irregularly sloped. A visual loss of the runway end on an upsloping runway whose latter portion is level has led to blown tires because of needless braking or collision with trees from attempting an impossible go-around. For example, the unevenly sloped runway at Catalina Airport in Avalon, California, has contributed to several accidents and incidents. The first 2,000 feet of the 3,240-foot-long runway has a pronounced upslope gradient, and according to the U.S. Chart Supplement, pilots cannot see aircraft at opposite ends of the runway due to its gradient. The pilot of a Cessna 172 had trouble conducting a proper flare-out and ended up bouncing, porpoising, and losing directional control on Runway 22. He thought he was nearing the end of the runway, so he

Fig 12-25.

An approach to an upsloped runway creates an illusion of being too high, resulting in a low approach.

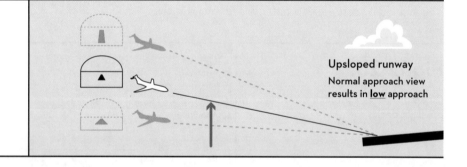

Upsloped runway
Normal approach view results in _low_ approach

Fig 12-26.

Effect of downsloping and upsloping terrain on approach. The influence of optic flow in a pilot's peripheral vision is dominant in these illusions.

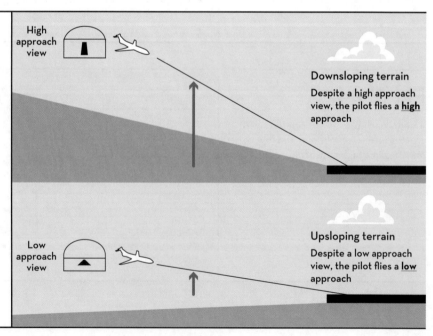

High approach view

Low approach view

Downsloping terrain
Despite a high approach view, the pilot flies a _high_ approach

Upsloping terrain
Despite a low approach view, the pilot flies a _low_ approach

intentionally turned left to avoid running off what he thought was the departure end. He collided with three parked aircraft, but luckily no one was hurt (NTSB Identification No: LAX96LA235).

Sloping Terrain

Sloping terrain underneath your landing approach path can also fool you into thinking you are too high or too low on the approach. For example, terrain below you that slopes down toward the threshold can create the illusion that you are too close to the terrain and therefore too low, leading to a high approach and possible long landing or go-around (*see* Figure 12-26 top). Even though the monocular cue of linear perspective, the motion cue of splay, and the resultant retinal image all indicate that your aircraft is on the correct approach angle, optic flow in your peripheral vision is dominant—generally during daylight conditions—and overrides the normal approach image on your retina. As already noted, optic flow is the rate at which objects in our peripheral vision flow past us as we move through space, and its value increases the faster the groundspeed and closer to the terrain we fly.

Terrain that slopes up toward the runway threshold potentially poses a greater hazard while conducting an approach (again, especially during the day when we can see the terrain below us). The significantly reduced optic flow in your peripheral vision creates the illusion that the aircraft is higher than it actually is, enticing you to fly lower than normal, which could result in a possible CFIT accident short of the runway (*see* Figure 12-26 bottom). This happened to a 1,380-hour instrument-rated pilot who allowed his airplane to impact terrain 30-feet short of the landing threshold for Runway 36 in Granbury, Texas. A contributing factor to the incident was the rising terrain on approach which had a 30 percent upslope to the runway threshold (NTSB Identification No: DFW07CA074).

Mountain pilots often have to contend with both upsloping landing strips and upsloping terrain at the same time. The combination of the high-approach retinal image from the upsloping runway and the reduced optic flow from the upsloping terrain below the flight path creates a very strong height illusion that can lead to a dangerously low approach. Both of these phenomena were operative in the Catalina Airport runway excursion accident previously cited. The airport sits atop a mountain with steeply upsloping terrain at each end of the runway; so not only is the first half of the runway sloped upward, but the terrain leading up to it is as well.

Runway Dimensions

As noted, the relative size cue to distance perception explains how an object of known size that casts a smaller image on your retina is rightly perceived as farther away, not contracted in size. Problems occur, however, when we think the size hasn't changed when in fact it has. For example, compared to larger North American-built automobiles, a greater proportion of smaller foreign-manufactured cars were rear-ended by other vehicles when they were first introduced to the U.S. and Canadian markets. Drivers incorrectly perceived the smaller (narrower) cars as larger ones that were farther away than in reality. As a result of this illusion, drivers who were accustomed to seeing only larger cars in front of them tended to apply their brakes too late, resulting in rear-end collisions.[21]

Because of this, a runway that has the same length-to-width (L/W) ratio (i.e., same proportions) of the runway a pilot is most accustomed to, could cause a visual illusion if it differs in size. For example, the larger runway in Figure 12-27 is 5,000 feet long by 200 feet wide, and the smaller runway 2,500 feet by 100 feet wide. Both have the same proportions (L/W = 25), making it difficult to tell them apart—especially when there is little or no surrounding context to provide cues to their actual size, such as in conditions of low-visibility or during the hours of darkness.

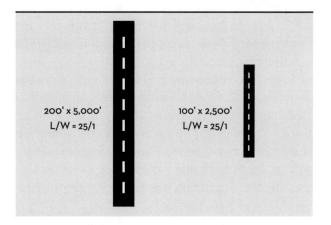

Fig 12-27.

Different-sized runways with same L/W ratio.

Pilots who experience an illusion because of this are said to suffer from a malady popularly known as the **home-drome syndrome**. Your home base aerodrome is so indelibly etched into your visual memory that it's easy to overestimate the distance of a runway that is smaller than the one you're accustomed to, or underestimate the distance of a runway larger than you're accustomed to, especially if you are a low-time pilot who lacks experience with different-sized runways.

Smaller-Than-Usual Runways

When approaching a runway that is smaller than what you are used to (the runway on the right in Figure 12-27), the relative size cue creates the illusion of increased distance between the runway and your aircraft. This illusion can lead to either a high approach or a low approach, depending on whether you perceive the runway as farther away horizontally or vertically. For example, if your visual brain interprets this illusion vertically, as an increase in altitude, you could be tempted to begin the approach prematurely and conduct a low approach; if it's perceived primarily as an increase in horizontal distance from the runway, you might commence the approach later than normal, which would put you too high on the approach.

The NTSB cited the visual illusion of a smaller and narrower runway as partially responsible for the low approach of a Piper Cheyenne on Runway 06 during civil twilight conditions at Chicago Executive Airport in Wheeling, Illinois. The PA-31T struck a 25-foot high unlighted utility pole 750 feet from the landing threshold and was able to land, but veered off the runway due to landing gear damage. Fortunately, the two commercial pilots aboard were uninjured (NTSB Identification No: CHI03IA108).

Regardless of how you might perceive this illusion of increased distance when conducting an approach to a runway that is smaller than you are used to, the illusion will alter your perception of when you should initiate the landing flare. The smaller runway will appear to be farther away in your visual field, so you are likely to initiate the flare later than usual, resulting in a hard landing.

Larger-Than-Usual Runways

Conversely, when approaching a runway that is larger than what you are familiar with (the runway on the left in Figure 12-27), the relative size cue

creates the illusion of decreased distance between your aircraft and the runway. Depending on whether your perceptual brain interprets this as vertical distance or horizontal distance, you might respond by conducting an approach that is either too high—resulting in a possible long landing or go-around—or too low—resulting in possible ground impact short of the runway. If you manage to overcome this illusion and make it safely to the runway threshold, the blossoming of the runway environment in your peripheral vision will often lead to a high flare-out and a possible stall over the runway. This is what happened to a pilot who landed hard and bounced several times before the propeller of his Cessna 172 struck the runway at Asheville Regional Airport in North Carolina. The pilot reported the runway was twice as long and twice as wide as his home runway, causing him to initiate the landing flare too high above it (NTSB Identification No: NYC07CA116).

The home-drome syndrome can also can create strong illusions when approaching runways with different L/W ratios than what you are accustomed to. For example, research in the 1980s confirmed that a low-approach illusion occurs when conducting an approach to a runway with a smaller L/W ratio (the runway on the left in Figure 12-28) than what you are used to, leading you to fly a high approach. The L/W ratio decreases with wider and/or shorter runways.[22] A more critical situation arises when the L/W ratio is greater than what you are used to. With a longer and/or narrower runway (the runway on the right in Figure 12-28), the illusion of being too high may induce you to fly an unsafe low approach, resulting in a premature hard landing or CFIT accident short of the runway.

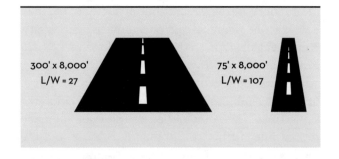

300' x 8,000'
L/W = 27

75' x 8,000'
L/W = 107

Fig 12-28.

Runways with different L/W ratios.

A student pilot flying a Piper PA-28 was killed when her aircraft struck the top of a moving semi-trailer truck as she conducted an approach to Runway 26L at the Sylvania Airport in Sturtevant, Wisconsin. Witnesses reported that the Cherokee approached the runway at a "very low angle" as it neared the four-lane highway that runs perpendicular to the final approach path. The pilot was used to landing at her home airport on runways that were 100 and 150 feet wide, which corresponded to L/W ratios of 32 and 28, respectively. The accident runway at this different airport was only 33 feet wide and had an L/W of 70—more than twice what she was used to. The NTSB cited this as a causal factor in the accident (NTSB Identification No: CHI98LA061).

Atmospheric Conditions

The aerial perspective cue to distance perception was introduced earlier: objects in the distance appear darker, bluer, and more blurred due to a greater degree of light scattering in the atmosphere from molecules and particulate matter between the object and observer, while closer objects appear brighter, with finer detail and truer color. Therefore, perceived distances of objects also depend on the opacity of the atmosphere. On exceptionally hazy days you might perceive an object—including a runway—as farther away than it really is. This could result in a higher or lower approach depending on how your visual brain perceives this illusion of distance: If interpreted as an increase in altitude, you might be tempted to begin the approach prematurely and conduct a low approach; if perceived primarily as an increase in horizontal distance from the runway, you might commence the approach later than normal, which would put you too high on the approach.

On unusually clear days, which often occur during cold dry winter conditions, the opposite eillusion can occur; objects appear closer than they actually are. If you perceive this as less horizontal distance between your aircraft and the runway, you could end up beginning your descent too far from the airport, resulting in a dangerously low approach. For example, a Canadian Armed Forces Lockheed C-130 Hercules crashed about 12 miles short of the runway at Alert airport, in Nunavut, Canada. The captain conducted a premature descent while on a visual approach at night, in part because the extremely clear air condi-

tions that night fooled him into thinking the aircraft was closer to the airport than it really was.[23]

Runway Lighting

The intensity of runway lights can affect your ability to conduct a successful approach at night. As noted, darker objects are perceived as smaller and further away while brighter objects are seen to be larger and closer. This relative brightness cue creates the illusion of being closer to runways with brighter-than-normal runway edge lights and farther away from runways with dimmer-than-normal runway lights. It was also noted previously that dark-night conditions contributed to the crew of a B-767 conducting a visual approach that was too low, resulting in a premature hard landing and tail strike at Halifax Stanfield International Airport. Another visual problem the same month at the same airport and runway, but 20 years later, vexed the crew of Air Canada Flight 624 while conducting a nonprecision approach at night in heavy snow. The Airbus A320 severed power lines and struck snow-covered ground about 740 feet before the runway threshold, destroying the aircraft and injuring 25 people. As one of several causes and contributing factors to the accident, the reduced brightness of the approach and runway lights was partly to blame for the flight crew's diminished ability to detect that the aircraft was further away from the runway than it should have been (TSB Report No: A15H0002).

As previously noted, these runway-distance illusions can lead to different responses depending on whether your perceptual brain interprets the distance illusion vertically or horizontally. For example, dimmer runway lights often lead to late flare-outs and hard landings, while brighter lights usually have the opposite effect.

Duck-Under Phenomenon

After conducting an approach to instrument landing minimums, some pilots have found themselves inadvertently descending below the glide path after transitioning to visual references. One possible explanation of this **duck-under phenomenon** is as follows: With good visibility and higher ceilings, you are accustomed to seeing the far end of the runway a certain distance up from the panel on the windscreen (*see* Figure 12-29 left). However, upon reaching decision altitude/height at instrument visibility minimums (usually 1/2 SM or **runway visual range** of 2,600 feet), the far end of the runway now appears to be lower on the windscreen (Figure 12-29 right), causing you to mistakenly believe the aircraft (and its nose) is higher than it should be. This could induce you to lower the nose, causing an excessively low approach and a possible hard landing short of the runway.

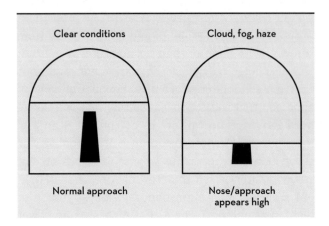

Fig 12-29.

Duck-under phenomenon.

The Black-Hole Approach

Undoubtedly, the most hazardous approach-and-landing illusion is the **black-hole approach illusion**. Black-hole conditions exist on dark nights (i.e., moonless and/or an overcast sky conditions) when there is unlighted terrain between the aircraft and the runway environment. These conditions have resulted in pilots conducting dangerously low approaches that for many have ended in a fatal CFIT accident short of the runway.

For example, the black-hole illusion, sometimes called the featureless terrain illusion, was a factor in a fatal accident involving a Rockwell Sabreliner 65 corporate jet on the approach to Kaunakakai Airport on the island of Molokai in Hawaii. The Sabreliner collided with mountainous terrain 3.3 NM from the airport, killing all six people aboard, after the crew terminated the instrument approach and attempted to fly a visual approach in VMC at night (NTSB Identification No: LAX00FA191). According to the NTSB, the black-hole illusion also claimed the lives of two passengers on board a Part 135 scheduled

passenger flight from St. Croix to the Cyril E. King Airport on St. Thomas, in the U.S. Virgin Islands. While the airline transport pilot was conducting a visual approach at night in VMC, the Cessna 402 crashed into the dark waters of the Caribbean Sea about three miles southwest of the airport (NTSB Identification No: MIA97FA082).

In relativity theory, a black hole is a region of space that has such a strong gravitational pull that nothing can escape its grasp. The same could be said about black-hole conditions on an approach to landing. If you are unprepared for it, you will be unable to keep your aircraft from being prematurely pulled toward the earth. Perception scientists don't know for certain what causes this illusion, and it is likely no one theory fully explains it. Boeing scientist Conrad Kraft and his colleagues conducted research on this phenomenon in the 1960s. Experienced Boeing instructor pilots (with more than 10,000 hours each) flew entirely visual approaches—with no altimeter or other glide path information available—to runways in black-hole conditions in a simulator. The result? Most of them flew excessively low approaches and crashed into the terrain short of the runway. The researchers explained that in the absence of lighted terrain between the aircraft and runway, pilots attempt to maintain a constant visual angle between the runway threshold and runway end lights (or the ground lights beyond).[24] Contrary to what you might think, a constant visual angle does not equal a constant approach angle. In fact, as Figure 12-30 illustrates, a constant approach angle results in an ever-increasing visual angle as you get closer to the runway. When you attempt to maintain a constant visual angle, the result is a curved flight path that extends below a safe approach angle (*see* Figure 12-31).

Some researchers claim the original Boeing conclusions are contradictory and that the mechanisms involved in visually landing an aircraft are still not fully understood.[25] Others have suggested that flight crews are enticed into flying a low approach because of the visual expansion of the runway environment that occurs when their vision transitions from near-focus (the flight deck instruments) to far-focus (the runway environment) when approaching the airport. This in turn causes an illusion of increased height, which results in a lower approach.[26] Of course, a critical visual cue pilots rely on for height perception while conducting approaches during the daylight—

optic flow—is completely absent in black-hole conditions. Without this relative motion of outside terrain features in your peripheral vision, it's virtually impossible to judge the aircraft's height above the ground. It is likely, therefore, that all of these factors play a role in deceiving pilots into thinking that they are too high when conducting approaches in black-hole conditions.

You should be aware that an upsloping runway only strengthens the black-hole approach illusion. As discussed earlier, an upsloping runway creates the illusion of being too high, causing you to fly a low approach. Add the tendency to descend below the glide path in black-hole conditions and premature flight into terrain short of the runway is likely. In one of Kraft's simulator experiments, 12 senior Boeing instructor pilots flew visual approaches in black-hole conditions to an upsloping runway environment without the aid of glide path information from an ILS or altimeter: eleven of them crashed short (by a few miles) of the runway![27] More recently, a Dassault DA-20 Falcon Jet was substantially damaged when it landed short of Runway 04 at the Blue Grass Airport in Lexington, Kentucky. The NTSB stated the dark-night conditions and uphill runway were factors that contributed to the captain misjudging the aircraft's distance and altitude to the runway (NTSB Identification No: NYC97LA165).

Unfortunately, awareness and experience with this particular illusion doesn't guarantee immunity from its effects. The flight crews in both the Hawaii and St.

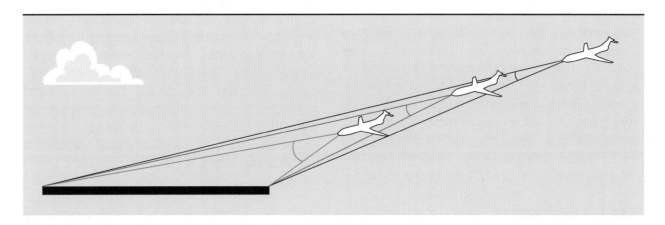

Fig 12-30.

Constant approach angle equals increasing visual angle.

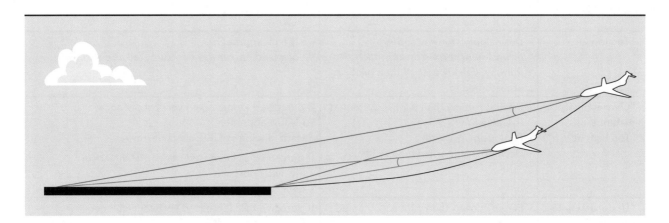

Fig 12-31.

Constant visual angle results in curved approach.

Thomas black-hole accidents were highly experienced pilots with more than 12,000 hours each. In another accident, a CFI, who knew the hazards of the black-hole approach and explained this phenomenon to his student while en route to the airport, still allowed the aircraft to strike the trees on final approach.[28]

Other Illusions in Flight

Most visual illusions occur during the approach and landing, and many of those occur during the hours of darkness when visual conditions are impoverished. However, your eyes can fool you during other phases of flight—day or night. The following are some of the more well-known that have played tricks on pilots.

Rain on Windscreen

Heavy rain on an aircraft's windscreen can create the illusion of increased height, which in turn could cause you to fly an excessively low approach. Much like the apparent bending of a pencil when placed in a glass of water, the presence of significant amounts of water on your aircraft's windows can produce a prism effect, causing the outside image to appear lower than it really is. The illusion is compounded by the darkening of the image due to the diffusion of light through the water.

This relative brightness cue only strengthens the false impression that you are farther away and higher than you really are. Transport Canada's AIM states that the downward bending can be as much as 5 degrees, causing an object (e.g., hilltop, runway) 1 NM away to appear as much as 500 feet lower than it really is.

Flat Light and Glassy Water

A condition similar to the black-hole phenomenon, but occurs during the day, is the phenomenon of **flat light**. Also known as *sector whiteout* or *partial whiteout*, flat light is not a zero-zero condition of snow and/or blowing snow (a condition that is usually just called "whiteout"); it is a situation where the aircraft is usually flying above snow-covered featureless terrain below an overcast cloud layer. The visibility could be unlimited; however, the scattering of light and lack of shadow drastically reduces contrast and depth/distance perception. Downhill skiers have experienced this when attempting to traverse snow-covered terrain. For pilots, both the en route and approach-to-landing phases of flight in such conditions are difficult if not impossible to fly without reference to instruments since, for all practical purposes, no outside visual references remain.

Table 12-1. Landing illusions and their potential consequences.

Illusion	Situation	Possible pilot response & consequences
"Too high"	• Black-hole conditions • Upsloping runway and/or upsloping terrain on approach • Runway with greater L/W than pilot accustomed to	• Fly low approach • Hard landing or CFIT short of runway
"Too low"	• Downsloping runway and/or downsloping terrain on approach • Runway with lower L/W than pilot accustomed to	• Fly high approach • Long landing, runway overrun, stall above runway
"Overestimate distance" (Too high or low*)	• Smaller runway than pilot accustomed to (same L/W) • Poor visibility (haze) • Dimmer-than-normal runway lights	If perceived as increased vertical distance: • Fly low approach • Hard landing or CFIT short of runway If perceived as increased horizontal distance: • Fly high approach • Long landing, runway overrun, stall above runway
"Underestimate distance" (Too high or low*)	• Larger runway than pilot accustomed to (same L/W) • Good visibility (clear) • Brighter-than-normal runway lights	If perceived as decreased vertical distance: • Fly high approach • Long landing, runway overrun, stall above runway If perceived as decreased horizontal distance: • Fly low approach • Hard landing or CFIT short of runway

*Depends if distance interpreted vertically or horizontally by subconscious visual perceptual "brain."

This phenomenon was one of the major contributors to New Zealand's worst aviation accident to date, an accident referred to earlier in this chapter in the discussion of expectancy: The 1979 crash of an Air New Zealand McDonnell Douglas DC-10 into Mount Erebus while on a sightseeing flight in the Antarctic. The crew was unaware the airplane was flying directly toward the rising terrain of the Mount Erebus volcano, in part because the snow-covered surface and overcast sky blended imperceptibly together in flat-light (sector whiteout) conditions.[29] More recently, a helicopter on a sightseeing flight crashed on the Herbert Glacier located on the Juneau Icefield in Alaska, killing the commercial pilot and six passengers. Three months later, as you read in the introduction to this chapter, three helicopters from the same charter company crashed within two miles of each other while flying over snow-covered featureless terrain: Overcast cloud and flat-light conditions prevailed and were cited by the NTSB as major causal factors.[30]

Reliance on aircraft flight instruments is the only way to accurately determine your aircraft's altitude and attitude in flat light conditions. Unfortunately, only one additional reference is added to your visual field during an approach and landing in these conditions: the runway. Certainly this is an improvement. However, as is the case with black-hole approaches,

depth perception while conducting an approach in this featureless terrain environment usually leads to an excessively low approach, increasing the chance of premature contact with the ground.

You should note that loss of depth perception can occur when conducting approaches over large bodies of water, especially calm **glassy water**; it's easy to descend into it unexpectantly. For example, a pilot was killed and the float-equipped Cessna 172 he was flying was destroyed when it impacted the water during a landing on Ash Lake near Orr, Minnesota. A pilot witness on the ground reported the airplane did not flare prior to impacting the water. The NTSB cited the visual illusion "caused by the glassy smooth water condition" as a factor in the accident (NTSB Identification No: CHI95FA307).

Various Night-Light Illusions

Autokinetic effect and flicker vertigo, two physiological illusions affecting visual perception, were discussed in Chapter 6. Many unusual attitudes have resulted at night from pilots who have experienced other visual illusions. For example, pilots have erroneously identified ground lights as stars, and stars as ground lights and have mistaken them for the actual horizon, a reference that is important in establishing an aircraft's attitude (*see* Figures 12-32 and 12-33).

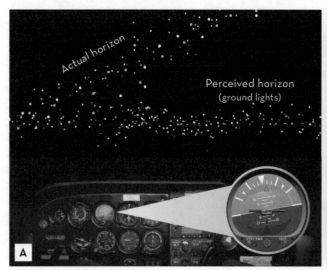
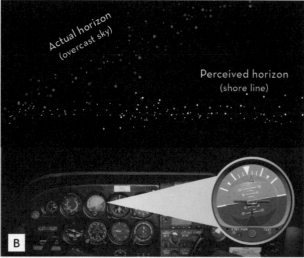

Fig 12-32.

The aircraft is aligned with a road (A) and the shoreline (B) instead of the horizon.

Fig 12-33.

At night, the horizon may be hard to discern due to dark terrain and misleading light patterns on the ground.

Illusions on the Apron

It was previously explained how reduced optic flow can create the illusion of reduced speed when taxiing on the apron at night, which in turn can cause pilots to taxi too fast. Other illusions also can confuse you during ground operations at the airport. Laterally blowing snow on the runway or airport apron can create the illusion of movement when the aircraft is stopped or the impression of being stationary when the aircraft is in fact moving. The movement of passenger loading bridges away from or toward an aircraft can also give you the illusion of aircraft movement, possibly leading to unnecessary braking action.

Overcoming Visual Perception Errors

Visual illusions are relatively rare events in flight, but as we've seen, when they do occur they can cause fatal accidents. They are not usually the result of simple physiological limitations inherent in the human eye (*see* Chapter 6 for a discussion of those)—the image on the retina doesn't lie, but our perceptual interpretation of it does. Perception psychologists call this the *indirect* view of perception: that is, it is not a "passive pickup of information from the world..." but "is highly active, constructing perceptions from hardly adequate information from

the senses."[31] For example, look at Figure 12-34—the lines of the classic Necker cube are received accurately by our visual sense, but our perception of them changes. Even though the lines are two-dimensional, our subconscious *visual brain* wants to see them as parts of a three-dimensional cube. One moment the top right 2D square looks like it might be the front of a 3D box, the next moment it appears to be the back of it. This is an example of an *ambiguous figure*, in which there isn't enough contextual information (stimuli) for us to accurately perceive its orientation. The figure, therefore, keeps reversing. It's almost like our visual brain makes two hypotheses (albeit unconsciously) as to which way the cube should be perceived, and since there isn't enough information, it alternates between both of them. When we rely solely on outside visual stimuli to fly our aircraft

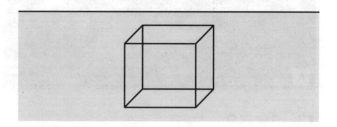

Fig 12-34.

Necker cube. An example of an ambiguous figure.

at night, in poor visibility, or both, we are flying in conditions of visual ambiguity and are therefore vulnerable to visual illusions.

Visual illusions are real and have tricked many pilots into seeing the outside world incorrectly. Under the right conditions they can be strong, persistent, and deadly. As a pilot, you should accept the fact that visual perception errors and illusions can and will occur. Being aware of their existence and knowing the situations in which you are most likely to encounter them are important first steps in overcoming them.

However, simple awareness isn't enough to fully protect you from being deceived. As noted earlier, the CFI in the tree-strike incident was fully aware of the black-hole approach illusion at the airport he and his student were approaching—that is why he elected to conduct the approach himself. He later reported it was ironic that he was consciously aware of the black-hole illusion and was even trying to correct for it right up to the moment he hit the trees on final approach to the runway! To effectively conquer visual illusions you must not only believe that they exist, but also understand that they can trick you into believing the outside world looks fine, and thus lead you to think that no apparent hazard is present—that is why they are called illusions. They are not the result of some personal defect or weakness; they are normal phenomena and none of us are immune. "Seeing is deceiving" is true for all pilots, not just inexperienced ones.

Besides awareness of visual perception limitations, you should also employ practical strategies designed to help you overcome them, especially in conditions of visual ambiguity—at night (in clear or not-so-clear weather), in poor visibility, and/or over featureless terrain.

Prepare Beforehand

Determine beforehand if a given airport is conducive to landing illusions by using all available resources—airport publications, notices to airmen, other pilots, airport operators—to ascertain the presence of irregular-shaped runways, sloping runways or terrain, or runways conducive to black-hole conditions at night.

If you suspect the possibility of a landing illusion, consider overflying the airport before conducting an approach to better familiarize yourself with it and the surrounding terrain, especially at night. Also, avoid long straight-in approaches (day or night), especially if you are unable to supplement outside natural visual cues with suitable altitude and glide path guidance information.

Be Careful During Ground Operations

Since optic flow is reduced when taxiing on the apron at night, it is easy to taxi too fast and miss an important sign or a taxiway marking, which could lead to a runway incursion. To avoid this, avoid staring straight ahead at the yellow taxiway line or green taxiway centerline lights, and occasionally look out the side window to see more-distant objects (light posts, buildings, etc.) to better judge your speed. Use an airport taxi diagram to help you successfully navigate and don't hesitate to request progressive taxi instructions if you are unfamiliar with the airport layout.

Get Familiar with Airport/Runway

If you are a low-time pilot, gaining experience during the day with a qualified instructor at airports with a variety of runway shapes and sizes can help if you later encounter these runways at night or during other impoverished visual conditions. The disproportionate rear-end accident rate for smaller cars when they were first introduced in North America eventually dropped off over time because drivers got used to varying-sized automobiles. The same learning occurs when you gain experience with different types of runways. Familiarity with sloped runways, sloped terrain, and runways with different dimensions creates a broader range of runway approach patterns available to you in your perceptual memory databank.

Sit in the Correct Location

We mentioned in Chapter 3 that there is an ideal seat adjustment that provides not only the best access to the flight controls, but also an optimum viewing angle for both cockpit instrumentation and the outside environment. Some aircraft manufacturers specify where the pilot's eyes need to be to obtain this optimal vision. It is called the design eye reference point (DERP)—also called the design eye position—and if your eyes are not positioned at this point in space, your ability to adequately see outside the flight deck will be hindered. If your seat is adjusted lower than the DERP while conducting an approach, your over-the-nose field of view below the horizon will be diminished and you might inadvertently lower the nose and descend below the glide path in an attempt to maintain sight of the runway environment. This happened to the captain of a scheduled Frontier Air flight into Moosonee, Ontario. His seat position resulted in his eyes being 4.7 inches lower than the DERP. The TSB report concluded the captain flying the Beechcraft C99 Airliner would not have been able to see anything below the horizon without lowering the nose of the aircraft. Unfortunately, in an attempt to maintain visual contact with the runway lights while conducting a visual approach at night, he pitched the nose too low, which resulted in an excessive descent rate of 1,200 fpm. The airplane crashed seven miles short of the runway, killing the FO and seriously injuring the captain and two passengers (Report No: A90H0002).

Most commercial transport aircraft are equipped with fixed eye level indicators located at eye level above the center glare shield that can be used to adjust the captain and FO seats for the proper DERP. It's usually just a matter of placing your head in the normal position while adjusting your seat until the appropriate-colored ball is superimposed directly over the other. Consult the aircraft flight manual if your aircraft is not fitted with such a device or contact the manufacturer for guidance. Failing that, if you want to find the ideal seat position on your own, the Transport Canada *AIM* suggests you adjust your seat so it is comfortable, allows unrestricted use of all flight controls through their full range of motion, provides an unobstructed view of all flight instruments and warning lights, and allows optimal out-of-the-cockpit visibility without being restricted by the nose of the aircraft.

Use Glide Path Instruments and Technologies

To ensure safe obstacle clearance while conducting an approach—especially at night or in poor visual conditions—use information from your aircraft's altitude and glide path instruments (ILS, global positioning system, distance measuring equipment (DME) readouts, altimeter) and from the airport's visual approach slope indicator systems.

If only DME is available, fly a 3-degree glide path by maintaining 300 feet above the runway threshold for each NM your aircraft is away from it. Multiplying your groundspeed by five also yields the descent rate needed to maintain a 3-degree glide path. For example, if you are approaching at a 120-knot ground speed, multiplying by five results in a 600 fpm descent rate needed to maintain an approximate 3-degree glide slope.

To avoid ducking under the glide path on a precision instrument approach, continue to supplement your outside visual references with ILS glide slope information down to the runway threshold crossing height (usually 50 feet).

Supplement Visual References in Flat Light or Heavy Rain

If you get caught in flat light or glassy water conditions, it's crucial to use your flight instruments to accurately confirm your aircraft's attitude and altitude until adequate outside visual references are clearly discernible. Conducting approaches in these conditions requires specialized training and extreme caution since you may be unable to acquire the visual references needed to maintain adequate terrain clearance.

To reduce the effect of a possible height illusion when flying in heavy rain, use other sources of glide path and altitude information to maintain acceptable terrain clearance—not just during the approach-to-landing phase of flight but also during the climb and en route portions.

Visual illusions have deceived pilots at all levels of experience since the dawn of flight, and they will deceive you too if you fail to learn all you can about them and take the steps necessary to effectively overcome with them. You can't completely trust your senses—sometimes they lie. Recognizing your limitations is half the battle in overcoming these illusions; knowing how to correct for them is the other half.

Helpful Resources

Spatial Disorientation—Visual Illusions (Part 2) is an informative 15-minute video, in English and Japanese, produced by the Airman Education Programs branch at the FAA's Civil Aerospace Medical Institute that focuses on visual illusions that can lead to spatial disorientation. (www.faa.gov/pilots/training/airman_education/physiologyvideos/)

Controlled Flight Into Terrain in Visual Conditions: Nighttime Visual Flight Operations Are Resulting in Avoidable Accidents is an NTSB Safety Alert (SA-013) that lists some notable accidents in which aircraft were flown into terrain in VFR weather conditions at night, and summarizes countermeasures you can take to prevent such an accident from happening to you. (www.ntsb.gov/safety/safety-alerts/pages/default.aspx)

Several articles on night flying are published in the FAA's magazine for GA safety, the *FAA Safety Briefing* (formally the *FAA Aviation News*). They can be found at www.faa.gov/news/safety_briefing/archive/

- *Good N.I.G.H.T.,* November/December 2015
- *[N]=Nightlights,* November/December 2015
- *[I]=Illusions,* November/December 2015
- *Shedding Light on Night Flight,* November/December 2008
- *N.I.G.H.T.,* November/December 2005
- *Be Aware of What Lurks in the Night,* November/December 2003

Chapter 12, "Night Operations," in the latest FAA *Helicopter Flying Handbook* (2019) provides excellent coverage of physiological and perceptual aspects of night flying, including practical suggestions on how to overcome these limitations when flying at night. (www.faa.gov/regulations_policies/handbooks_manuals/aviation/helicopter_flying_handbook/)

The AOPA Air Safety Institute provides several resources on night flying, including safety articles, briefings, advisors, quizzes and videos. (www.aopa.org/training-and-safety/technique/night-flying)

Weather to Fly—Rain on Windshield is short video produced Transport Canada that explains the effect of rain on the windshield of an aircraft. (www.youtube.com/watch?v=0HwsDtA6Kxw)

Flying in Flat Light and White Out Conditions, produced by the FAA, is available in HTML format at the FAASTeam Learning Center Library (www.faasafety.gov/gslac/ALC/libview_normal.aspx?id=6844). An informative FAA "Back to Basics" video by the same name is also available from YouTube. (www.youtube.com/watch?v=dptvV9u8nNQ)

Much of the latter half of this chapter is based on information found in Chapter 7, "Don't Be Caught in the Dark," and Chapter 8, "What You See Is Not Always What You Get," in *Managing Risk: Best Practices for Pilots* (by Dale Wilson and Gerald Binnema). These two chapters explore many of the challenges involved in night flying and the deceptive nature of visual landing illusions. (www.asa2fly.com/Managing-Risk-Best-Practices-for-Pilots-eBook-PD-P2031.aspx)

Endnotes

1. National Transportation Safety Board, *Safety Recommendation*, A-02-33 through -35 (Washington, DC: October 7, 2002).

2. J. Robert Dille, "Visual Illusions," *Aviation, Space, and Environmental Medicine* 58 (1987): 822.

3. George Mather, *Foundations of Sensation and Perception*, 2nd ed. (New York: Routledge, December 2015).

4. Cotton planted in the North Carolina coastal plain using strip-till methods, by Soil Science from Raleigh, October 2010 (https://commons.wikimedia.org/wiki/File:Cotton_Production_in_the_North_Carolina_Coastal_Plain.jpg) WC CC BY 2.0

5. Richard L. Gregory, *Eye and Brain: The Psychology of Seeing*, 5th ed. (Princeton, N.J.: Princeton University Press, 1997).

6. David Regan, Ken Beverly and Max Cyander, "The Visual Perception of Motion in Depth," *Scientific American* 241 (July 1979): 137.

7. Regan, Beverly and Cyander, "The Visual Perception of Motion in Depth."

8. Gordon G. Denton, "The Influence of Visual Pattern on Perceived Speed," *Perception* 9 (1980): 393–402.

9. Gateway Arch, St. Louis, Missouri, by Bev Sykes, April 2005 (https://commons.wikimedia.org/wiki/File:St_Louis_Gateway_Arch.jpg) WC CC BY 2.0

10. Stanley Coren and John Stern Girgus, *Seeing is Deceiving: The Psychology of Visual Illusions* (Hillsdale, NJ: Lawrence Erlbaum Associates, 1978): 164.

11. An optical illusion: the inner white square and the small black square are the same size, SVG version by Sopoforic. Original JPG version by Guam, July 2007 (https://commons.wikimedia.org/wiki/File:Black_and_white_squares.svg) WC CC BY-SA 3.0

12. Gregory, *Eye and Brain: The Psychology of Seeing.*

13. A. Kanizsa triangle, Fibonacci, March 2007 (https://commons.wikimedia.org/wiki/File:Kanizsa_triangle.svg) WC CC BY-SA 3.0

    B. Illusory Pyramid illusion, in Susana Martinez-Conde and Stephen L. Macknik, "Dark and Bright Corners of the Mind," *Scientific American Mind* 24.5 (November/December 2013): 20-22. Used with permission from original creators of Illusory Pyramid illusion, Pietro Guardini and Luciano Gamberini.

14. Adapted from Gerald H. Fisher, "Preparation of ambiguous materials," *Perception & Psychophysics*, 2.9 (1967): 421–422. Used with permission.

15. Ibid. Used with permission.

16. J.W. Andrews, "Modeling of Air-to-Air Visual Acquisition," *The Lincoln Laboratory Journal* 2 (Fall 1989): 475–480.

17. David Beaty, *The Naked Pilot* (London: Methuen 1991).

18. "Blinded Pilot Bombs Ship," *The Province* (Vancouver, BC, Canada: February 16, 1995).

19. United States General Accounting Office, *Operation Provide Comfort: Review of U.S. Air Force Investigation of Black Hawk Fratricide Incident*, Report to Congressional Requesters, Report No. GAO/OSI-98-4 (Washington, DC: November 1997).

20. P.T. Mahon, *Royal Commission to Inquire Into and Report Upon the Crash on Mount Erebus, Antarctica, of a DC-10 Aircraft Operated by Air New Zealand Limited* (Wellington, New Zealand: P.D. Hasselberg, Government Printer, 1981).

21. Ray E. Eberts and Allen G. MacMillan, "Misperception of Small Cars," *Trends in Ergonomics/Human Factors II*, eds. Ray E. Eberts and Cindelyn G. Eberts (New York: Elsevier, 1985): 33–39.

22. Henry W. Mertens and Mark F. Lewis, "Effect of Different Runway Sizes on Pilot Performance During Simulated Night Landing Approaches," *Aviation, Space, and Environmental Medicine* 53 (1982): 463–471.

23. Robert Mason Lee, *Death and Deliverance: The Haunting True Story of the Hercules Crash at the North Pole* (Toronto: Macfarlane Walter & Ross, 1992).

24. Conrad L. Kraft, "A Psychophysical Contribution to Air Safety: Simulator Studies of Visual Illusions in Night Visual Approaches," *Psychology: From Research to Practice*, eds. H.A. Pick, H.W. Leibowitz, J.E. Singer, A. Steinschneider and H.W. Stevenson (New York: Plenum Press, 1978): 363–385.

25. Martin F.J. Schwirzke and C. Thomas Bennett, "A Re-Analysis of the Causes of Boeing 727 'Black Hole Landing' Crashes," *Proceedings of the Sixth International Symposium on Aviation Psychology*, ed. R.S. Jensen (Columbus, OH: The Ohio State University, 1991): 572–576.

26. Stanley N. Roscoe, "When Day Is Done and Shadows Fall, We Miss the Airport Most of All," *Human Factors* 21 (1979): 721–731.

27. Kraft, "Psychophysical Contribution to Air Safety," 363–385.

28. Office of the NASA Aviation Safety Reporting System, "A Black Hole," *Callback* 161 (October 1992): 1.

29. Mahon, *Royal Commission to Inquire Into and Report Upon the Crash on Mount Erebus, Antarctica, of a DC-10 Aircraft Operated by Air New Zealand Limited*.

30. NTSB, *Safety Recommendation*, A-02-33 through -35.

31. Gregory, *Eye and Brain*, 8.

13

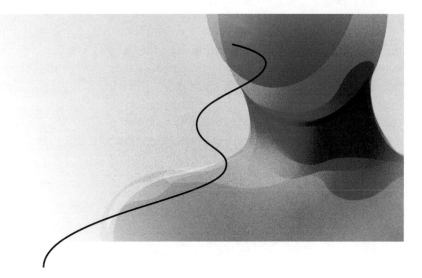

Did you say "gear up" or "cheer up"?

Auditory Perception

Imagine conducting a descent in IMC, when at approximately 1,000 feet above your assigned altitude, the aircraft breaks out of the clouds and you discover you're on a collision course with the ground only feet below you! This actually happened to the crew of a British Airways Boeing B-747 while conducting an approach to Runway 06 at Nairobi Airport in Kenya. At 10,000 feet MSL, ATC gave Flight 029 an altitude to descend to and the FO read back "cleared to five thousand feet." He then dialed 5,000 feet in the altitude selector/alerter on the autopilot while the captain commenced the descent. At approximately 6,000 feet MSL, while descending at more than 200 knots and at a rate of almost 1,800 fpm, the crew was astonished at what they saw after descending below the cloud deck: the ground was only 200 feet below them. Disaster was narrowly averted for the 299 souls on board after the crew immediately executed a go-around, the jumbo jet clearing the terrain by a mere 70 feet.[1]

This distressing incident reveals the limitations of a crucial component of human performance: auditory perception. Just as ambiguous visual stimuli can lead to visual illusions, deceiving a pilot into thinking everything outside looks fine (*see* Chapter 12), so too can ambiguous auditory stimuli lead to misinterpretation, leading a pilot into thinking accurate communication has taken place. The controller's clearance for Flight 029 was "descend seven five zero zero feet" (7,500 feet), but the captain and FO were convinced they had heard "five zero zero zero feet" (5,000 feet) and conducted their descent accordingly. Even though the clearance was issued in accordance with international procedures at the time, as you will

see later in this chapter, the nature of the clearance and the controller's wording contributed to the crew's misunderstanding.

Communication breakdown between controllers and pilots (extra-cockpit) and between flight crew members (intra-cockpit) has contributed to several fatal aircraft accidents. Extra-cockpit communication failures were involved in a 2009 midair collision involving a Piper PA-32R and Eurocopter AS350 over the Hudson River in New Jersey. The accident was caused, in part, by the failure of the controller to correct an incorrect readback of a frequency given to the airplane pilot. All nine people aboard both aircraft died in the crash (Report No: NTSB/AAR-10/05). Intra-cockpit communication failures were also implicated in two recent fatal accidents in the United States: a Boeing B-777 crash into a seawall at San Francisco Airport (Report No: NTSB/AAR-14/01), and an Airbus A300 CFIT accident on short final in Birmingham, Alabama. Unclear communications between flight crew members, and between dispatch and the flight crew, was cited by the NTSB as contributing factors to the Birmingham accident (Report No: NTSB/AAR-14/02).

Communication—the exchange of information between people—is primarily accomplished through spoken words, written words, and body language. Since verbal communication is the primary method of information transfer on the flight deck—though controller-pilot data link communication (CPDLC) systems are beginning to play a greater role—this chapter concerns itself with only this type.

Using Wicken's information processing model (*see* Figure 3-5 in Chapter 3) it is clear that distortions in the reception of auditory stimuli (auditory sensation; *see* Chapter 7) and the interpretation of those inputs (auditory perception) can reduce safety margins by adversely impacting higher level cognitive functions such as problem solving and decision making. Visual sensation is limited to stimuli within one's visual field of view, whereas the auditory sense is omnidirectional enabling voice messages and auditory warnings within hearing range to be detected. However, auditory inputs, such as verbal messages, are transient are transient and are subject to being forgotten, and, like visual stimuli, are subject to misinterpretation.

Evaluating 28,000 incident reports submitted by pilots and air traffic controllers during the first five years of the ASRS, NASA researchers found more than 70 percent involved problems with information transfer, primarily related to voice communications.[2] Using this data, NASA researchers in a subsequent study identified problems in voice communication between pilots and controllers that included incomplete and inaccurate content, ambiguous phraseology, absent communication (because of equipment failure or message not sent in first place), misperceived messages because of phonetic similarities, untimely message transmission, garbled phraseology, and recipients' failure to monitor the message.[3] It's not feasible to adequately explore the multifaceted and complex topic of human communication, let alone all the issues identified by the subsequent study (though we will revisit this topic again in Chapter 19). However, this chapter will highlight some important basic factors that contribute to auditory misunderstandings on the flight deck, as well as suggest mitigation strategies designed to overcome them.

Ambiguous Communication

A recent International Air Transport Association (IATA) *Phraseology Study* found the use of non-standard and/or ambiguous phraseology by ATC was the biggest communication issue for 2,070 airline pilots surveyed.[4] Ambiguous messages consist of words,

phrases, or sentences that have more than one meaning. For example:

- A flight attendant called the flight deck and told the captain to "turn around," so he turned the airplane back toward the departure airport because he "perceived her comment to mean that the flight was in jeopardy and the aircraft should be turned around and returned to [departure airport]." However, she had only wanted him to turn around, to see that the cabin door had opened and needed closing.[5]
- After being cleared to land on Runway 24, the pilot was asked by the tower controller, "Can you make Runway 15 Left?" The pilot said he could and lined the aircraft up on Runway 15L. However, the controller wanted to know if, *after landing on Runway 24*, he could make the first available left turn onto Runway 15L.[6]
- Noticing that the student had selected too much power just before landing, the instructor said "Back—on the power," but the student added even more power because he interpreted the message as "Back on—the power."[7]
- The captain said "Takeoff power," so the FO reduced the power setting. The captain said "Feather four," and the new copilot responded, "All at once, Sir?" The captain said "Feather one." "Which one?" said the copilot.[8]

Some common aviation phrases have double-meanings. For example, "contact approach" can be interpreted as a type of approach or a command to contact the approach controller. "Go ahead" can be interpreted as a request to speak or move the aircraft forward.

Numbers are a particularly vexing, especially those that sound the same as other words (called **homophones**), such as "two" ("to") and "four" ("for"). Ambiguous usage or interpretation of these four words—cited as the second biggest communication problem identified by pilots in IATA's *Phraseology Study*—was responsible for a fatal CFIT accident involving a Flying Tiger Line B-747 on final approach to Subang Airport in Kuala Lumpur, Malaysia. The crew misperceived ATC's clearance of "descend *two four zero zero*" (descend to 2,400 *feet*) as "*to four zero zero*" (descend to 400 *feet*).[9]

Since numbers can refer to a variety of completely different elements, such as runways, altitudes, headings, and airspeeds, even words that do not sound the same can be confusing. For example:

- After clearing a Learjet to "climb and maintain 14,000 feet," the controller issued instructions to "fly heading two zero zero." The pilot read it back as "two zero zero," then proceeded to climb to 20,000 feet (i.e., FL200 or "flight level two zero zero").[10]
- ATC instructed an airline flight crew to "maintain two three oh," meaning that they should maintain an airspeed of 230 knots. The captain responded "Roger, two three oh" and began to climb to 23,000 feet (ASRS Report No: 127825).

Non-Standard Phraseology

Ambiguity is reduced when pilots and controllers use standard words and phrases. For example, a controller instructing a pilot to change radio frequencies, said "Change one twenty five five." A pilot quoted in the *Phraseology Study* rightfully asks, "is that 120.55 or 125.5?"

Standards developed by the International Civil Aviation Organization (ICAO) are found in *Aeronautical Telecommunications* (Annex 10, Volume II) and the *Manual of Radiotelephony* (Doc 9432). Examples of standardization include the proper way to pronounce the English alphabet and numbers, common message transmission technique, the use and meaning of standard words and phrases, common ways for ATC to issue clearances, and distress and urgent communication procedures. For example, when similar-sounding letters could be misperceived (e.g., B, C, D, E, G, P, T) their full phonetic equivalents should be used (Bravo, Charlie, Delta, etc.). Since the spoken words "Five" and "Nine" sound similar, they should be pronounced as "FIFE" and "NIN-ER," respectively (the latter to also avoid confusion with the German word "Nein" which means "No").

Despite these radiotelephony (RTF) requirements, the use of non-standard phraseology was ranked as the number one complaint (along with ambiguous phraseology) by airline pilots in the *Phraseology Study*, with 44 percent of pilots experiencing non-standard phraseology at least once per flight. A variety of issues were identified—especially in the United States—including improper use of the phonetic alphabet (e.g., "Nectar" instead of "November") and using incomplete

call signs or call signs not in conformance with ICAO standards.[11]

"Zero, Zero, Zero"

Though they were cleared to "descend seven five zero zero zero feet" (7,500 feet), the captain and FO in the Nairobi near-CFIT incident discussed in the introduction, believed they had heard "five zero zero zero feet" (5,000 feet). To avoid this type of confusion, most jurisdictions now require altitudes (except flight levels) to include the words "hundred" or "thousand" as appropriate. For example, "7,500 feet" should be spoken as "seven thousand five hundred feet." Though this incident occurred more than 40 years ago, it points out a recurring problem that still exists today: pilots have difficulty interpreting messages with several "zeros" in them, especially with multiple instructions in one transmission. For example: "Altimeter three zero zero zero, cleared to flight level two zero zero, steer heading three five zero, maintain two zero zero knots." One can sympathize with this pilot's question: "Were we cleared to 10,000 feet 11 miles west of ARMEL, or 11,000 feet 10 miles, or 10,000 feet 10 miles, or 11,000 feet 11 miles?"[12]

Ten/Eleven

This pilot's confusion highlights another problem: the *ten/eleven* issue. An analysis of 191 ASRS reports, where crews overshot or undershot their assigned altitude by 1,000 feet, found that that the ten/eleven thousand foot pairing was by far the most common altitude combination at 38 percent of altitude busts; the next largest category accounted for less than 5 percent of the deviations.[13] The standard verbalization of 10,000 feet and 11,000 feet is "one zero thousand" and "one one thousand," respectively. However, misinterpretations still occur even when adhering to this standard phraseology. To increase clarity, U.S. controllers are now permitted to group digits: for example, "ten thousand" or "eleven thousand," for 10,000 feet and 11,000 feet, respectfully.[14]

The standard way to verbalize flight levels—pressure levels of 18,000 feet and above for most regions, using a standard altimeter pressure setting of 29.92 in Hg or 1013.25 hPa—is to pronounce the three digits separately (e.g., FL300 is verbalized "flight level three zero zero"). To reduce ambiguity and decrease the probability of flight level busts, controllers in the United Kingdom and some other European countries use "hundred" for flight levels that are whole hundreds (e.g., FL300 is verbalized "flight level three hundred" not "flight level three zero zero").[15]

Regional Differences

Unfortunately, these regional attempts to clarify altitude messages may result in pilots of international flights receiving altitude assignments in non-standard ways. Standard RTF is most effective if applied globally. While progress has been made in harmonization—for example, the United States now uses ICAO terminology "line up and wait" instead of "taxi to position and hold"—there are still differences:

- "Cleared direct" in most jurisdictions means fly direct to a fix/waypoint, while it may mean "fly the filed route" in others.[16]
- Aborting a landing is called a "go-around" in some locations and an "overshoot" in others (though in countries such as Canada it appears both terms are used).
- The rectangular flight pattern around an airport ("aerodrome" in many locales) is called a "traffic pattern" in some locations and a "circuit" in others.
- Two different terms are used to taxi an aircraft on the runway in the opposite direction from the landing/takeoff direction: "back-taxi" and "backtrack."

Call Signs

Mistaking an aircraft's call sign for another is another perennial problem in aviation communications.

Clearances meant for one aircraft but accepted by the pilot or crew of another have led to altitude and heading deviations, near midair collisions, and accidents. For example, both occupants of a Piper Seminole died after it collided with rising terrain at 5,500 feet near the Julian VOR in California. The pilot accepted and read back a descent clearance to 5,200 feet intended for another aircraft with a similar call sign (NTSB Identification No: LAX04FA205).

A variety of patterns contribute to similarity of call signs and/or flight numbers—the main reason for call-sign confusion: identical final digits (ACF, JCF; 523, 923); parallel digits (ABC, ADC; 712, 7012); anagrams (DEC, DCE; 1524, 1425); and block digits (ABC, ABD; 128, 128T).[17] Though shortening transmission times,

the practice of using abbreviated call signs in the presence of aircraft with similar call signs only exacerbates the call sign confusion problem.

Readback-Hearback

To confirm the proper understanding of an ATC clearance, pilots are required to read most of them back. Accidents can occur if a pilot incorrectly reads back a clearance and the controller doesn't catch it, known as the **readback-hearback problem**. For example, the B-747 pilots in both the CFIT accident in Kuala Lumpur and the near-CFIT accident in Nairobi inaccurately read back their altitude assignments and the controllers failed to recognize and correct their errors. A breakdown in this feedback loop (*see* Figure 13-1) often occurs when controllers are too busy to acknowledge the readback; unfortunately, pilots often interpret this silence as acceptance of their readback.

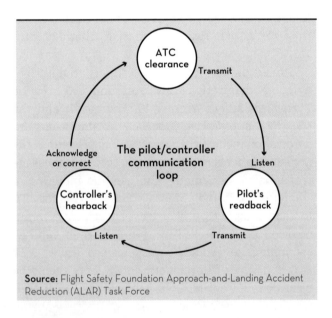

Source: Flight Safety Foundation Approach-and-Landing Accident Reduction (ALAR) Task Force

Fig 13-1.

Pilot/controller communication loop.[18]

Expectation Bias

As pilots sometimes see what they expect to see, they also hear what they expect to hear. For example, a wide body jet was cleared to FL230 on a heading of 340 degrees, and because their flight plan called for a final cruising altitude of FL340, the crew didn't fly the heading because they interpreted the instruction to mean "expect FL340" (ASRS Report No: 982516). A Cessna 210 pilot was told to expect a takeoff clearance before an incoming arrival. When told to "line up and wait" he misperceived this as a clearance to takeoff, which he did (ASRS Report No: 939023). Flight operations often involve routine tasks and clearances that are predictable, especially for scheduled airline operations; however, these expectations are what contribute to misperceptions when the unexpected occurs.

The nature of some ATC clearances may actually trigger an **expectation bias** on the part of pilots. For example, controllers will often issue a clearance for a pilot to *expect in the future*. The following is an all-too-common example. A loss of separation between a Learjet and a Piper Cheyenne occurred in New Mexico after the Learjet climbed to FL360. The pilot thought they had been given an unrestricted climb to FL360 but they were actually cleared to "climb to 17,000, expect FL360 ten minutes after departure." The pilot read back something to the effect of "roger, climbing to FL360," but the controller failed to catch the error (ASRS Report No: 876272).

English Language Proficiency

Successful communication requires a common language: for international flight operations that language is English. Communication errors are compounded when a non-native English-speaking pilot and/or controller are involved in the communication loop. The *Manual on the Implementation of ICAO Language Proficiency Requirements* points out that, in just three accidents, more than 800 people lost their lives, in part because of "insufficient English language proficiency on the part of the flight crew or a controller."[19]

English Accents and Pronunciation

Strong regional accents can be difficult to understand. A Challenger CL300 crew heard the following clearance from ATC: "descend to 310, eleven at TIRUL." Unsure of the clearance because of the controller's strong accent, they asked him to repeat it. After receiving the same instruction, they began a descent to 11,000 feet at TIRUL. Passing through FL300 the controller informed them their assigned altitude was FL310. The controller was attempting to say "descend to 310, *level* at TIRUL" (ASRS Report No: 1031335). Evidence suggests, however,

that once a pilot gains more experience with different dialects, comprehension is less of a problem during routine operations.[20]

Closely related to accents is pronunciation of navigation waypoints consisting of unique pronounceable five-letter name codes. Some non-native English-speaking controllers pronounce such fixes differently than native English-speakers, in part, because they have difficulty in pronouncing "English vowel-based words including the phonetic alphabet."[21]

Speech Rate

High speech rates by controllers, especially when giving multiple instructions in a single clearance, increases the probability of misinterpretation. This problem is exacerbated for non-native English-speaking pilots conversing with native English-speaking controllers, or native English-speaking pilots communicating with non-native English-speaking controllers. In one study, pilots reported that the "controller's speech rate was the biggest problem they experienced in communication."[22]

Code Switching

Sometimes multilingual pilots and/or controllers may switch back and forth between English and their mother tongue; or unilingual speakers may switch between different English dialects (e.g., aviation English and normal English). This **code switching** occurs for a variety of reasons, including the natural tendency to revert back to previously learned behavior when under stress.[23] Code switching may explain the otherwise confusing phraseology "We are now at takeoff," spoken by the Dutch FO of KLM Royal Dutch Airlines Flight 4805, a B-747, before it collided on the runway with a Pan American B-747 at Tenerife, on March 27, 1977. This accident remains the worst in aviation history, responsible for the deaths of 583 people aboard both airplanes. The controller interpreted "now at takeoff" to mean they were in position for takeoff; using a mixture of English and Dutch grammar, "now at takeoff" to the FO meant they were actually taking off.[24] (The lack of response by KLM 4805 to the controller's subsequent clearance "O.K....Stand by for takeoff, I will call you" only reinforced the belief in the controller's mind that the B-747 was waiting in position for departure; unfortunately, that transmission wasn't heard by the KLM crew because it was partially blocked, or *stepped on*, by a simultaneous Pan Am transmission.)

Mixed Languages

An extreme example of code switching is complete language switching. For example, both English and French are used in Québec and the National Capital Region of Canada to communicate with ATC. Pilots in these regions who initiate radio communication in the French language will receive communication from ATC in that language, while ATC will communicate in English to those who initially use English. When asked if there was a procedure or a common practice used by pilots or ATC that causes misunderstanding or errors, the most frequently mentioned concern of pilots in the *Phraseology Study* was "the use of mixed languages with international crews speaking English with ATC and the local crews speaking the country's language."[25]

The mix of languages poses at least two problems for unilingual English-speaking pilots. First, since they don't know when a conversation between ATC and another pilot speaking in a different language begins or ends, they often find themselves violating radio protocol by interrupting ongoing conversations.

Second, the use of different languages on the radio reduces situational awareness for pilots who only know one of the languages. Multiple parties communicating on a single radio frequency in the same language provide pilots with additional information they don't otherwise receive from only one-on-one communication with ATC. This **party-line information (PLI)** enhances a pilot's situational awareness by providing the location of other aircraft, weather phenomena that may affect their flight, runway information, and other activities in their vicinity. This loss of situational awareness was a major concern of native English-speaking pilots in the *Phraseology Study*. For GA pilots, PLI may be the only way to construct a comprehensive mental picture of the flight environment. As discussed in Chapter 6, it is difficult to detect the presence of another aircraft in your vicinity, especially small light-colored aircraft—even if directly in front of you—by reliance on human vision alone. Thus, understanding the intentions and locations of other aircraft is critical, and this information can sometimes only be gathered by listening carefully to radio transmissions.

PLI is reduced when two different languages are spoken or when two or more different radio frequencies are used (e.g., joint civilian-military airports with mix of VHF and UHF frequencies). Also, despite the benefits of communication between controllers and pilots through textual messages via CPDLC, greater reliance on it may degrade PLI available to pilots.

Basic Communication Models

Communication has been described from a variety of perspectives. Known as the Father of Information Theory, Claude Shannon postulated that basic communication consists of a sender (information source), a receiver (receiver and destination), a message, and noise (stimuli other than the message).[26] (*See* Figure 13-2.) There are several steps involved in sending and receiving a verbal message: the sender must think of what they want to say, encode it into a language the receiver will understand, then transmit it using speech; the receiver must first hear (or *sense*) the signal, recognize it as language, decode the language being used by the sender, then understand (or *perceive*) what it means. Communication is, of course, a two-way street so the process also applies as the receiver takes on the role of sender.

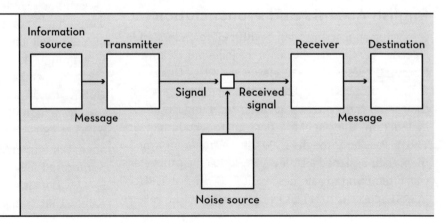

Fig 13-2.

Shannon model of communication. Information is transmitted by a sender via a message using signals (verbal language) to the receiver. Noise (non-message-related sounds) may affect the quality the message sensed by the receiver.

Generally, the higher the signal-to-noise ratio (SNR; *see* Chapter 7), the easier to detect and perceive the message. However, even with higher SNRs, ambiguity or imperfections at any point in the transmission process can lead to message misinterpretation.

Noam Chomsky, a major contributor to the psychological study of language (psycholinguistics), distinguished between the **deep structure** and **surface structure** of communication. The sender possesses the basic idea, or meaning, he or she wishes to communicate (deep structure) but the receiver only has access to the sequencing, or phonological arrangement of sounds and words (surface structure) used by the sender.[27] The receiver, therefore, can only infer the true meaning (deep structure) intended by the sender. The challenge for the sender is to effectively use what Chomsky describes as transformational grammar (syntax, phonetics, rules) to create the least ambiguous surface structure as possible. If this is not accomplished, the probability of misunderstanding increases. Figure 13-3 is a very simplified visual representation of these concepts.

Managing Auditory Perception Errors

"The great enemy of communication…is the illusion of it."

–William Hollingsworth Whyte, *Fortune*

Regardless of which model is used to explain verbal communication, they all assume there are numerous opportunities for error throughout the message transmission-reception process. Pilots should accept the fact that auditory perception and miscommunication errors can and will occur and they should practice countermeasures designed to minimize these errors on the flight deck. Several best practices designed to manage these errors are published in the FAA *AIM* Chapter 4, Section 2, "Radio Communications Phraseology and Techniques," ICAO's *Aeronautical Telecommunications* (Annex 10, Volume II) and *Manual of Radiotelephony* (Doc 9432), and Eurocontrol's *Air Ground Communications Briefing Note: 5—Radio Discipline*. Pilots and/or controllers should practice these, some of which are listed below:

- Incorporate the highest possible intelligibility in each transmission by enunciating each word clearly and distinctly at a constant volume and in a normal conversational tone, maintaining an even rate of speech not exceeding 100 words per minute (controllers should use a slower rate when a message needs to be written down by flight crews), and pausing slightly before and after numerals to reduce confusion.
- Use standard phraseology at all times. If unable due to unusual circumstances, make sure to clarify a received message if you are uncertain of its meaning.
- When using numbers, include key words describing what they refer to, such as altitude, flight level, heading, etc. (e.g., "*heading* two four zero," "climb to *flight level* two seven zero," "maintain 180 *knots*").
- To avoid call sign confusion, use the aircraft's full phonetic call sign. The controller in the Julian VOR in California CFIT accident didn't; he only used "four papa alpha" which were the same last three digits as the intended aircraft. Controllers should inform pilots of similar call signs operating on the same frequency.

Fig 13-3.

Chomsky's communication process. The receiver of a message only has access to surface structure used by the sender and must infer its true meaning.

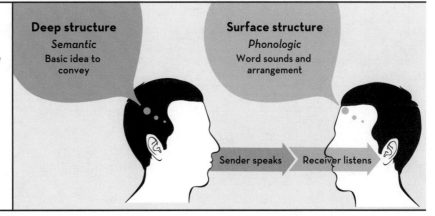

Deep structure
Semantic
Basic idea to convey

Surface structure
Phonologic
Word sounds and arrangement

Sender speaks   Receiver listens

- Employ effective listening strategies to avoid succumbing to expectation bias.
- Leverage PLI to increase your situational awareness by paying attention to conversations between ATC and other aircraft, especially in the vicinity of an airport.
- Even though radio communication with ATC is usually delegated to the PM, to increase situational awareness the PF should monitor the PM's communication with ATC.
- Read back ATC clearances and instructions in the same sequence as they are given. Always include full call signs when reading/hearing back clearances. If a readback is unacknowledged by ATC, ask for confirmation of acceptance. Using "Roger" in lieu of a full readback is unacceptable.
- Seek clarification if uncertain of a message's meaning, or a transmission is garbled, cutoff, or stepped on. Question an incorrect or inadequate clearance.

This chapter opened with a description of the brush with death the crew and passengers experienced aboard a B-747 while descending for Nairobi—all because the captain and FO misperceived a descent clearance to 7,500 feet as 5,000 feet. What I didn't tell you was the FE aboard actually heard the correct clearance of 7,500 feet. In fact, he thought the pilots in the seats in front of him also knew the correct clearance altitude, but because he was so busy with other duties, he never caught or corrected their misunderstanding until they were dangerously close to the ground.

Effective communication is crucial to flight safety. That's why we will revisit this multidimensional topic in Chapter 19 where, among other topics, we will explore how the participation of others on the flight deck can either help or hinder effective communication.

Helpful Resources

Radio Communications Phraseology and Techniques, an online course developed by the FAA Safety Team (FAASTeam)—based on a safety pamphlet of the same name (P-8740-47)—presents best practices for radio technique and communication with ATC. (www.faasafety.gov/gslac/ALC/libview_normal.aspx?id=17272)

Standard Phraseology, an article on Skybrary, an electronic repository of aviation safety knowledge, contains links to a number of articles, manuals, studies and other documents related to communication in the flight environment, including the IATA *Phraseology Study* referred to in this chapter and *Air Ground Communications Briefing Note: 5– Radio Discipline*, produced by Eurocontrol (the European Organization for the Safety of Air Navigation). (www.skybrary.aero/index.php/Standard_Phraseology)

The AOPA Air Safety Institute has several resources on communication, including safety articles, briefings, advisors, quizzes and videos. (www.aopa.org/training-and-safety/air-safety-institute/safety-spotlights/radio-communications-and-atc)

"Radio Communications Phraseology and Techniques" (Chapter 4, Section 2) in the FAA *AIM* is very helpful, especially for new pilots. So is the *Pilot/Controller Glossary*. (www.faa.gov/air_traffic/publications/#manuals)

ICAO's *Aeronautical Telecommunications* (Annex 10, Volume II) is available at: www.icao.int/Meetings/anconf12/Document%20Archive/AN10_V2_cons%5B1%5D.pdf

Endnotes

1. International Civil Aviation Organization, "British Airways, Boeing 747–136, G-AWNJ, Incident at Nairobi, Kenya, on 3 September 1974. Report No. 14/75, dated 20 October 1976, published by the Department of Trade and Industry, United Kingdom," *ICAO Circular, Aircraft Accident Digest* 21 (1977): 139–154.

2. Charles E. Billings and E.S. Cheaney, *Information Transfer Problems in the Aviation System*, NASA TP-1875 (Moffett Field, CA: NASA Ames Research Center, September 1981).

3. Ralph L Grayson and Charles E. Billings, "Information Transfer between Air Traffic Controllers and Aircraft: Communication Problems in Flight Operations," in NASA Technical Paper 1875, *Information Transfer Problems in the Aviation System* (Moffett Field, CA: NASA Ames Research Center, September 1981): 47–61.

4. Hanada Said, *Pilots & Air Traffic Controllers Phraseology Study* (Montréal, Québec: International Air Transport Association, 2011.)

5. Office of the NASA Aviation Safety Reporting System, "U-Turn? No, You Turn," *Callback* 295 (April 2004).

6. Office of the NASA Aviation Safety Reporting System, "Runway Confusion... by Request," *Callback* 289 (October 2003).

7. The CHIRP Charitable Trust, *Air Transport Feedback, U.K. Confidential Human Factors Incident Reports* 4 (Undated): 7. Available at www.chirp.co.uk/newsletters/air-transport?r=120.

8. Ibid.

9. Flight Safety Foundation, Aviation Safety Network, *Accident Description: Flying Tiger Line, Boeing 747-249F, N807FT, Kuala Lampur, February 19, 1989.* Available at www.aviation-safety.net/database/record.php?id=19890219-0.

10. Office of the NASA Aviation Safety Reporting System, "Heading for the Wrong Altitude," *Callback* 386 (March 2012).

11. Said, *Phraseology Study.*

12. Don George, "One Zero Ways to Bust an Altitude...Or Was That Eleven Ways?" *ASRS Direct Line* 2 (Fall 1991): 7–11.

13. Ibid.

14. Federal Aviation Administration, *Federal Aviation Administration Order JO 7110.65W, Air Traffic Control* (Washington, DC: December 10, 2015).

15. European Organisation for the Safety of Air Navigation (Eurocontrol), *European Action Plan for Air Ground Communications Safety*, Edition 1.0 (Brussels, Belgium: EUROCONTROL, May 2006).

16. O. Veronika Prinzo and Alan Campbell, *U.S. Airline Transport Pilot International Flight Language Experiences, Report 1: Background Information and General/Pre-Flight Preparation*, FAA Report DOT/FAA/AM-08/19 (Washington, DC: FAA, September 2008).

17. Eurocontrol, "Call-Sign Confusion," *Air-Ground Communication (AGC) Safety Letter* (August 2005).

18. Dale R. Wilson, "Failure to Communicate: Hearing—and Understanding—The Spoken Word is Crucial to Safe Flight," *AeroSafety World*, 11 (November 2016). Used by permission by the Flight Safety Foundation. Available at www.flightsafety.org/asw-article/failure-to-communicate/

19. ICAO, *Manual on the Implementation of ICAO Language Proficiency Requirements*, Doc 9835 (2004).

20. O. Veronika Prinzo, Alan Campbell, Alfred M. Hendrix and Ruby Hendrix, *United States Airline Transport Pilot International Flight Language Experiences Report 2: Word Meaning and Pronunciation*, FAA Report DOT/FAA/AM-10/7 (Washington, DC: FAA, April 2010).

21. Said, *Phraseology Study.*

22. O. Veronika Prinzo, Alan Campbell, Alfred M. Hendrix and Ruby Hendrix, *U.S. Airline Transport Pilot International Flight Language Experiences, Report 3: Language Experiences in Non-Native English-Speaking Airspace/Airports*, FAA Report DOT/FAA/AM-10/9 (Washington, DC: FAA, May 2010).

23. Lesya Y. Ganushchak and Niels O. Schiller, "Speaking One's Second Language Under Time Pressure: An ERP Study on Verbal Self-monitoring in German-Dutch Bilinguals," *Psychophysiology* 46.2 (2009): 410–419.

24. Steven Cushing, "Pilot-Air Traffic Control Communications: It's Not (Only) What You Say, It's How You Say It," *Flight Safety Digest* 14.7 (July 1995): 1–10.

25. Said, *Phraseology Study.*

26. Claude E. Shannon, "A Mathematical Theory of Communication," *The Bell System Technical Journal* 27 (October 1948): 623–656.

27. Noam Chomsky, *Aspects of the Theory of Syntax* (Cambridge, MA: The MIT Press, 1965).

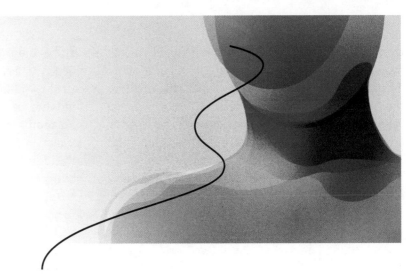

14

Why can't you just pay attention?

Attention, Vigilance, and Monitoring

In hindsight, we know it was just a light bulb. At the time, the crew of the Eastern Air Lines (EAL) Flight 401 thought it might be also. And like all good pilots, they wanted to make sure. During an evening approach into Miami International Airport, the green nose landing gear indicator light—signifying the nose gear is down and locked—failed to illuminate, even after the crew recycled the gear a second time. So they conducted a missed approach and, with ATC's permission, they held northwest of the airport at 2,000 feet while trying to troubleshoot the problem. To check if it was a burnt-out bulb the FO tried to remove and reinstall the light-bulb assembly, but was having difficulty. While the captain was trying to help him, the FE entered the forward electronics bay of the Lockheed L-1011 to check the status of the nose gear via another gear indicator. The FO had selected the autopilot to maintain 2,000 feet, but while they were preoccupied with troubleshooting the problem, someone (probably the captain) inadvertently bumped the flight controls. Now in the control wheel steering mode, the autopilot dutifully flew the TriStar in a gentle descent that, unfortunately, went unnoticed by the crew. It wasn't until seven seconds before impact that the FO first noticed something was amiss saying, "We did something to the altitude. We're still at two thousand, right?" Six radio altimeter beeps sounded in the cockpit two seconds before impact to warn the crew, but it was too late—the jumbo jet descended into the swamp of the Florida Everglades, killing 101 of the 176 people aboard. The NTSB determined the probable cause of the accident was the failure of the flight crew "to *monitor* the flight instruments during the final

four minutes of flight and failure to *detect* an unexpected descent soon enough to prevent impact with the ground. *Preoccupation* with a malfunction of the nose landing gear position indicating system *distracted the flight crew*'s attention from the instruments and allowed the descent to go unnoticed" (emphasis added) (Report No: NTSB-AAR-73-14).

The NTSB recently cited monitoring failures in three other air carrier accidents: The pilots of an Airbus A300 that crashed short of the runway in Birmingham, Alabama, failed to "monitor the aircraft's altitude during the approach" (Report No: NTSB/AAR-14/02), while the crews of an Asiana Airlines Boeing B-777 that crashed into a seawall at San Francisco, California (Report No: NTSB/AAR-14/01), and a Colgan Air Bombardier DHC-8 that crashed near Buffalo, New York (Report No: NTSB/AAR-10/01), both failed to "monitor airspeed."

Ineffective monitoring by flight crews is a leading cause of major airline accidents. For example, an NTSB study of 37 U.S. air carrier accidents between 1978 and 1990, in which the actions of the flight crew were cited as a causal or contributing factor, found that monitoring/challenging failures occurred in 31 of them (84 percent).[1] A follow-up study determined that failures in monitoring the aircraft's flight path were implicated in a further 17 major U.S. air carrier accidents between 1990 and 2013.[2] Flight path monitoring involves effectively scanning the "flight instruments and cockpit indications to derive information pertaining to aircraft energy state and trajectory." This includes the "attitude indicator, airspeed indicator, vertical speed indicator, altimeter, navigation instruments, and flight mode annunciations."[3] The study also found that the leading item not monitored in 25 major U.S. air carrier accidents that were responsible for the deaths of 894 people between December 1972 and July 2013 was the aircraft's airspeed. The leading item not monitored in 110 ASRS incident reports submitted by flight crews between 2000 and 2014 was the altimeter.

Incident data compiled by the Active Pilot Monitoring Working Group and published in the Flight Safety Foundation's (FSF) *A Practical Guide for Improving Flight Path Monitoring* (*Monitoring Guide* for short) also reveal the extent of the problem. The *Monitoring Guide* reports that the monitoring and cross-checking performance of 22 percent of flight crews was rated "poor" or "marginal" in more than 15,000 line operations safety audit (LOSA) observations in 70 LOSA projects worldwide, and that compared to the 78 percent of crews that were rated good/outstanding, these 22 percent had three times the number of mismanaged errors and two to three times the number of undesired aircraft states.[4, 5] Such monitoring errors have led to altitude, course, and airspeed deviations; runway incursions; LOC-I; CFIT; MAC; and other types of accidents. In one such accident, all six passengers, including U.S. Senator Paul Wellstone, and two crew members aboard a Raytheon (Beechcraft) King Air A100 were killed after the aircraft stalled and crashed during a VOR approach to Runway 27 at Eveleth-Virginia Municipal Airport in Minnesota. The NTSB concluded that the flight crew "failed to monitor the airplane's airspeed," allowing it to decrease to a dangerously low level, and failed to recognize that a stall was imminent, allowing the airplane to enter a stall from which they did not recover (Report No: NTSB/AAR-03/03).

Attention, Vigilance, and Monitoring

Using the language of the information processing approach to explain why pilots make errors, the pilots involved in monitoring accidents and incidents failed to pay **attention**; that is, they failed to detect and/or orient themselves to relevant sensory inputs needed to assure safe flight. More specifically, they failed to maintain *sustained attention*, referred to as **vigilance** using cognitive psychology's terminology, and **monitoring** in aviation parlance. In fact, the *Monitoring Guide's* definition of monitoring is virtually identical to vigilance: adequately watching, observing, keeping track of, or cross-checking.[6]

Unfortunately, research indicates that humans are not very good at paying attention, let alone doing so for extended periods. Pilots spend hours watching for abnormalities in flight instrument readings, changes in aircraft performance, systems anomalies, changing weather conditions, conflicting air traffic, and other tasks. Two major findings of vigilance research are: as far as detecting signals, human performance suffers—there is a vigilance decrement—even within the first half-hour of the watch; and the sustained attention needed for good vigilance/monitoring performance is very demanding of mental resources.[7] In other words, vigilance requires hard mental work, often leading to fatigue.[8]

The cognitive model of information processing asserts that humans possess a limited store of attentional resources (a commodity) needed to carry out the various mental operations involved in perception, memory recall and processing, decision making/response selection, and execution: The more attentional resources used by one mental operation, the less available for others (*see* the human information processing model in Figure 3-5, Chapter 3).

Furthermore, the amount of information that actually makes it to conscious perception, let alone higher levels of information processing, is severely limited. That is, there is a kind of *bottleneck* that hampers the flow of information. The major theories used to explain this bottleneck postulate that there is an attentional mechanism that filters out information that is not specifically attended to. One approach suggests this filter prevents all unattended information (stimuli) from moving from the short-term sensory storage stage of information processing to our conscious perception. According to this view, since humans can only attend to one thing at a time they are, in essence, single-channel processors.[9] This is represented in Figure 14-1 where only one sensory input from several actually makes it to conscious perception.

This is also illustrated in Figure 14-2. Each ball represents a single input from a single information channel, or **sensory modality**, or from two different modalities (e.g., an auditory input and a visual input), but an attentional mechanism (or gate) only allows one ball at a time to enter the pattern recognition, or perceptual, stage of information processing.

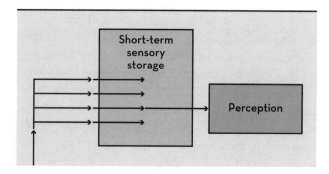

Fig 14-1.

Only one input from several senses makes it to the perception (interpretation) stage of information processing.

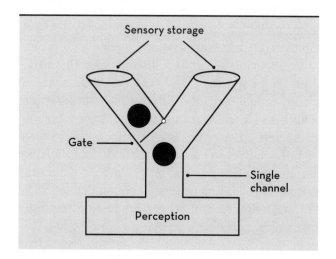

Fig 14-2.

Single channel processing. Information from only one channel at a time is allowed to enter conscious perception, after which an attentional mechanism (or gate) will allow inputs from other channels to enter.[10]

Another major theory suggests that the filter prevents most, but not all, unattended information from reaching our conscious perception (i.e., the bottleneck is slightly bigger, allowing more infor-

mation to flow though). Unattended information is not completely blocked off as Figures 14-1 and 14-2 suggest, but is attenuated (or weakened), and makes it through to our conscious perception only if the stimulus is relevant or salient—features that make it stand out from the attended information (e.g., larger, louder, brighter, etc.).[11] Pertinent, salient, or novel stimuli attract our involuntary attention, breaking through the filter, which in turn causes us to redirect our focus of attention (even if momentarily) to that new stimulus. An example of how unattended, but pertinent, information reaches our conscious perception is found in what is called the **cocktail party effect**. Even though you are concentrating on a conversation with someone in the noisy environment of a cocktail party (or other social gathering), when someone else across the room mentions your name it somehow makes it to your conscious perception. It turns out that our names and other pertinent words possess high levels of meaning for us and are more effective at attracting our attention. Two examples of relevant or salient stimuli on the flight deck are ATC radio calls that include our aircraft's call sign and flight deck warning signals (e.g., marker beacons, landing gear or altitude deviation horns, master caution lights, etc.).

Not explicit in the human information processing model in Figure 3-5 (*see* Chapter 3) are three general categories of attention: selective, focused, and divided.[12] Using the light beam of a flashlight as a metaphor, **selective attention** is the area attended to (the location where one points the beam at). For example, EAL Flight 401 descended into the Florida Everglades, in part, because the crew failed to select (attend to) a stimulus that was critical to their safety: the altimeter. Midair collisions (even in clear weather and good visibility) often occur because pilots fail to adequately select the outside environment as part of their attentional scan. **Focused attention** involves concentrating on a single stimulus in the environment to the exclusion of others (a narrow flashlight beam). The EAL crew members focused most of their attention on the landing gear light indicator at the expense of the altimeter. **Divided attention** is attending to two or more stimuli or tasks at once (a wide beam). If the EAL 401 crew had effectively divided their attention between the landing gear problem and the flight instruments (or assigned one crew member to *focus* their attention on one or the other), the accident would likely have not occurred.

Mental Workload

Unfortunately, divided attention is not as easy to accomplish or as effective as one might think. Dividing attention between two or more tasks involves mental work, and research indicates that, just as there are limits to how much physical workload the body can endure, so too are there limits to how much **mental workload** the mind can sustain before performance suffers. If the task demands are less than the pilot's attentional resources available, there is residual capacity available for an unexpected increase in mental workload; if task demands exceed the pilot's attentional resources, then task performance will suffer (*see* Figure 3-5 in Chapter 3).[13]

Attention Switching

People are often under the illusion that accomplishing two different tasks simultaneously is as effective as doing them separately, but it is not: Studies have shown that true multitasking is essentially a myth, and that one or the other task suffers because multiple tasks are not accomplished *simultaneously*, but *seqentially*, with an individual's attention switching rapidly back and forth between them. **Attention switching** takes time to select the information to attend to, process the information, encode the information into short-term memory, retrieve the information and act upon it.[14] Doing this multiple times exacts a cost, slowing down overall reaction time. Research indicates that reaction times involved in switching between tasks also increases as one approaches their senior years.[15] Overlearning a task through extensive training can make tasks—like the psychomotor skills involved in manually hand-flying an aircraft—more automatic, increasing a pilot's attentional capacity to accomplish other tasks. However, switching back and forth between two or more different tasks still slows performance, even for those who are highly trained, such as airline pilots and air traffic controllers.

Significant performance decrements also occur when performing two different tasks that draw upon the same regions of the brain using the same modality (e.g., simultaneously attempting two visual tasks or two auditory tasks). Research indicates that even though there is improvement, performance suffers even when executing two unrelated tasks that use two different modalities that draw from different regions of the brain (e.g., visually scanning flight instruments and listening to a radio broadcast).

Inattentional Blindness

The depletion of attentional resources when attempting to perform two or more tasks at once, or when there is too much information to process, causes stimuli in the environment to be unconsciously filtered. This prevents important information from making it to one's conscious attention for processing. Drawing attention away from one task to attend to another often leads to **inattentional blindness**, or "looking without seeing." For example, the attention of the EAL Flight 401 crew members was so fixated on the landing gear problem, that they did not perceive a half-second audio warning C-chord chime that indicated a 250-foot deviation from their selected altitude of 2,000 feet (Report No: NTSB-AAR-73-14). Studies have shown that automobile drivers using cell phones while driving fail to actually see up to 50 percent of the information in their environment, even when they are looking straight ahead out the window![16]

High Mental Workload

As you learned in the first chapter, the most demanding phases of routine flights are the vertical segments with approximately 61 percent of all fatal commercial airline turbojet accidents over a recent 10-year period occurring during takeoff, initial climb, final approach, and landing—phases which occupy only 6 percent of flight time. During these phases (*see* Figure 14-3) a significant number of monitoring and other critical tasks must be performed within relatively short-time periods: configuring the aircraft (landing gear, flaps, etc.), conducting altitude and heading changes, communicating with ATC and fellow crew members, conducting briefings, and making public address (PA) announcements. The *Monitoring Guide* reports that of the 188 Aviation Safety Action Program (ASAP) reports involving monitoring errors at one airline, 66 percent occurred during the vertical phases of flight (climb, descent, approach, and landing) and 22 percent occurred during taxi. Furthermore, researchers who evaluated the 110 ASRS incident reports submitted by flight crews between 2000 and 2014 (mentioned earlier in this chapter), found that 92 percent of flight path—altitude, heading, and/or airspeed—deviations resulted from ineffective monitoring during the vertical segments of flight. The two biggest tasks crews were accomplishing at the time of the deviation were programming the flight management system (FMS)

Fig 14-3.

The demands of the various tasks of each phase of flight and the relative pilot capabilities over the duration of the flight. Takeoff, initial climb, final approach, and landing account for 6 percent of total flight time, but have the greatest workload.

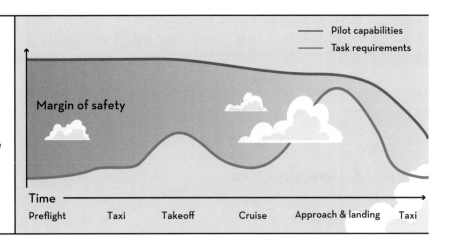

and communicating on the radio or PA system. This was followed by searching for traffic, dealing with abnormal situations, reading checklists, and reading charts/approach briefings.[17]

The crash of Delta Air Lines (DAL) Flight 1141 shortly after takeoff at Dallas-Fort Worth International Airport was mentioned in Chapter 2. The crew lost control of the airplane because they had neglected to extend the wing flaps for the takeoff position. Selecting takeoff flaps is accomplished during the TAXI checklist by the FO. According to the accident report, however, the FO was distracted and missed this item. When the aircraft was fourth in line for takeoff, the crew began to restart the number three engine (they had shut it down to conserve fuel as per company procedure when it became apparent there was going to be about a 25-minute delay before departure). There was another opportunity for the crew to check the flaps prior to taxiing to the runway, but something happened that they were not expecting: within 15 seconds of the number three engine start procedure, ATC cleared them to taxi onto Runway 18L and hold for takeoff, in effect putting them ahead in the cue making them first in line for takeoff. As the captain's attention was diverted to the visual task of taxiing past the three airplanes on the taxiway ahead, 39 seconds later they received their actual takeoff clearance. They had delayed completing the remainder of the TAXI checklist and the entire BEFORE TAKEOFF checklist until all three engines were running, so all of a sudden the FO and FE were extremely busy. In fact, it was virtually impossible for them to correctly accomplish all the items on the two checklists: the time between each checklist challenge and response was less than one second! The NTSB report states:

At this point, the CVR shows a distinct difference in the crew's conduct in the accomplishment of the checklists. Apparently, the second and first officer recognized the need for expeditious completion of the remaining checklist to prevent delay on the runway. Thus, where the checklists previously had been accomplished in an orderly/measured manner, the tone and behavior of the crewmembers clearly became rushed.

The report states that upon the FE's prompt of "FLAPS" on the checklist, the FO responded "FIFTEEN, FIFTEEN, GREEN LIGHT." This would be based on a visual check of the needle positions on the inboard and outboard flap position indicators and illumination of the green leading edge flaps and slats indicating light located on the center instrument panel. However, based on all the physical evidence, the NTSB concluded that the FO responded to the flap challenge in the taxi checklist "without looking at the status of the light and indicators" (Report No: NTSB/AAR-89/04). The other two crew members were so busy they missed the error. The task demands at this critical juncture in the flight exceeded the crew's attentional capacity, and as a result, of the 108 people aboard the Boeing B-727, 14 died and 26 were seriously injured.

American Airlines Flight 965 crashed into high terrain during an approach into Alfonso Bonilla Aragon International Airport, in Cali, Colombia, in part because the crew was rushed and mentally overloaded with tasks as a result of accepting a last-minute runway change (reprogramming the FMS, expediting descent, clarifying confusing communication with ATC, re-briefing approach charts for a different runway, etc.). At one point, they were so task-saturated that they failed to monitor the flight instruments which indicated the Boeing B-757 was turning toward the wrong waypoint. Almost a minute passed before they corrected for the course deviation; unfortunately, this caused their aircraft to driftsignificantly off course, which contributed to their collision with high terrain.[18]

Low Mental Workload

"Flying is 99 percent pure boredom and 1 percent sheer terror."

The positive aspect of this unsettling quote is that, fortunately, the increased reliability of modern aircraft means that abnormal events—systems' malfunctions and other anomalies—are relatively rare events. Unfortunately, humans are poor monitors for rare events. When automated systems precisely and reliably "fly the aircraft" within desired parameters day in and day out, pilots can easily become bored and their attention can drift away from their monitoring role, leaving both the controlling and monitoring functions entirely to the autopilot. We will discuss some of the challenging issues related to automation in the next chapter.

The nonlinear relationship between performance and task difficulty, and hence mental workload, was demonstrated more than a century ago in the Yerkes-Dodson curve (see Figure 14-4). Just as mental overload leads to diminished performance, so too does mental underload, with an optimal level of performance accomplished at moderate levels of workload.

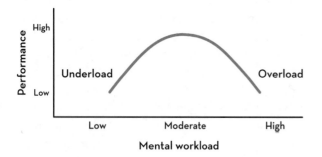

Fig 14-4.

Performance and mental workload (arousal). Performance is best at moderate levels of workload.

When in a low state of mental arousal, crews may be mentally unprepared for an unexpected event. In such circumstances, a startle reflex may be induced with an accompanying undesirable response. For example, an Airbus A340 encountered turbulence and exceeded the target airspeed, setting off the overspeed warning alarm. This surprised the PM who instinctively responded by pulling back on the side stick. The crew was so startled by the turbulence issue that they failed to monitor the flight instruments; it took them 90 seconds to realize that the PM had inadvertently disengaged the autopilot (the overspeed alarm masked the autopilot disconnect alarm) and had caused the aircraft to climb 3,000 feet above their assigned altitude of FL350.[19]

Situational Awareness

A closely related term often more widely used in aviation to describe certain aspects of attention is **situational awareness (SA)**. There are a variety of definitions for this term, but at its basic level it is simply the level of awareness or knowledge of your situation during flight operations. Even though SA involves attention and vigilance, the definitions of each are not synonymous. Information processing constructs such as attention, mental workload, memory, etc., can all influence your level of SA, but SA also encompasses higher-order thinking strategies such as anticipating changes, generating and evaluating options, and managing risk—all in the service of achieving optimal crew decision making (see Chapter 17). In other words, SA is an overall mindset that flight crews should attain and maintain in order to achieve safe flight operations.

A formal definition of SA, described 30 years ago by a leading researcher in this field, is still applicable today: It is the "perception of elements in the environment within a volume of time and space, the comprehension of their meaning, and the projection of their status in the near future."[20] According to this definition, SA encompasses several levels and elements.[21]

At its basic level—the first level—SA involves attending to relevant elements within your environment to attain awareness of the outside environment (e.g., terrain, airspace, airport, weather), the status of the aircraft and its flight condition (e.g., performance, energy state, systems, fuel), and your personal state of being (e.g., physiological, psychological, and psychosocial condition).

The second level of SA involves comprehending the current situation by understanding what those environmental elements mean in the context of your goals. For example, in Level 1 SA, you perceive another aircraft flying in your vicinity. In Level 2 SA, you need to know what the presence of that aircraft means. Is it on a collision course with your aircraft or not?

The third and final level of SA, the highest level, arises from an accurate perception of what has happened in the past and what is happening in the present to project what the near-future status of the flight, with all its elements, may entail. For example, you determine that a MAC will occur within a certain time frame if either your aircraft or the other aircraft does not change its heading.

Besides suggesting three levels of SA, the model also elaborates on several different SA elements a pilot must be aware of. Some of these were briefly noted previously, but the model articulates five, four of which are applicable to civilian flight operations:

- *Geographical SA*—the aircraft position relative to navigation waypoints; location of other aircraft in vicinity; terrain features (high terrain, sparsely settles area, open ocean); location of regulatory airspace, airways, and airports; taxiway and runway assignments, etc.
- *Spatial/temporal SA*—aircraft attitude, altitude, airspeed, heading, and course; projected flight path and time of landing; changes in flight plan route and/or clearances.
- *Environmental SA*—reported and forecast weather conditions at current location and destination (winds, visibility, ceiling, airframe icing, turbulence); runway conditions (length, crosswind, tailwind, contaminated runway).
- *Aircraft systems SA*—information from flight instrument and aircraft systems displays; configuration settings (flaps, gear); communication and navigation radio settings; automation modes; fuel status and projected fuel available.

Acquiring and maintaining SA can often be challenging in the complex and dynamic environment of flight, especially during non-normal situations. A variety of factors can lead to breakdowns in SA: high mental workload, forgetting, inadequate attention switching, distractions (*see* the next section), stress

(*see* Chapter 19), individual operator limitations, and other factors. When we talk about attention failures, therefore, it is not always because a pilot was inattentive, or that he or she was distracted. It could be because, for a variety of reasons, a pilot failed to appropriately distribute their SA resources by directing them to one or two types of SA to the detriment of others. The captain and other flight crew members in the EAL 401 CFIT accident in Florida failed to attain and maintain altitude and terrain awareness (spatial and geographical SA) and awareness of the aircraft's projected flight path (spatial SA); in part because it was dark and they were not monitoring the altimeter (aircraft systems SA) to make up for that deficiency, and because they were overemphasizing the use of other aspects of aircraft systems SA to troubleshoot the landing gear problem. Similarly, the captain in the Guantanamo Bay accident (discussed in Chapter 10) put too much emphasis on geographical SA (looking for the lighted beacon) and not enough effort on building his spatial SA (airspeed, flight path, and terrain avoidance).

It is important to attain and maintain SA of all the elements discussed. A pilot with a high level of SA will not only achieve maximum monitoring performance, but will also be aware of everything needed to know about their flight's status and its progress in order to anticipate and predict likely outcomes that will lead to the best possible decisions to achieve a safe and efficient flight. In other words, it involves flying ahead of the airplane, not behind it.

Distractions

As is true for monitoring behavior, SA is threatened by inattention, high workload, and **distraction**. A distraction is anything that draws your attention away from the task of flying your aircraft. Distractions are a major contributing factor in accidents involving all modes of transportation. For example, the U.S. Centers for Disease Control and Prevention (CDC) reported that 3,450 people died in 2016, and 391,000 in 2015 were injured, in motor vehicle accidents involving distracted drivers.[22] Distractions also contribute to aircraft occurrences. The Australian Transport Safety Bureau (ATSB) found that pilot distraction contributed to 260 aircraft incidents and 65 accidents between 1997 and 2004 in that country. These distractions resulted in a variety of deleterious outcomes, including collisions with other aircraft, terrain, powerlines, and buildings; altitude busts; controlled airspace violations; fuel starvation; hard landings; runway incursions and excursions; and wheels-up landings.[23]

Distractions were the number one cause of monitoring failures and subsequent flight path deviations in 41 percent of the 110 ASRS incident reports in the study cited earlier in this chapter. Other causes listed were automation reliance, fatigue, high workload, complacency, runway/arrival change, and rushing/time pressure.[24]

The CDC report found that motor vehicle drivers were distracted by a variety of stimuli and activities, including conversing with another occupant, using a cellular phone, adjusting controls and devices in the vehicle, heads-down activities, and daydreaming. It turns out that somewhat similar distractions afflict pilots. A study of NTSB-reported accidents attributed to crew error found that nearly half involved "lapses of attention associated with interruptions, distractions, or preoccupation with one task to the exclusion of another."[25] The study also evaluated 107 ASRS incident reports over an eight-year period and found that 90 percent of competing tasks that distracted or preoccupied pilots fell into four broad categories: communication, head-down work, searching for VFR traffic, and abnormal situations (see Figure 14-5).

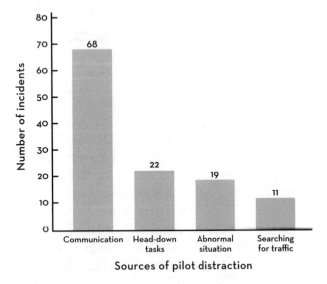

Fig 14-5.

Main sources of pilot distraction in 107 ASRS distraction incidents.[26]

More than half of the distractions were caused by communication, with about half of those resulting in altitude deviations or failure to make a crossing restriction. Normal operational conversations pertinent to the flight between the pilots, or a pilot and a flight attendant (FA), led to most of these deviations. The PM failed to catch errors caused by the PF in about one third of these distraction incidents, often because the PM was preoccupied with head-down activities such as paperwork or programming the FMS. Searching for VFR traffic and responding to abnormal situations, such as thunderstorms and systems anomalies, were competing activities that distracted pilots in the remainder of reports.

Even though the most demanding phases of routine flights are the vertical segments, an interesting study on the importance of checklist design and usage conducted in the 1990s found that, based on a review of NTSB accident reports and ASRS incident reports, flight crews are "most vulnerable to interruptions/distractions from the 'BEFORE START' phase through 'PUSH BACK,' 'START,' 'TAXI,' and 'BEFORE TAKEOFF' phases of operation." The study found that not only can this pre-departure phase of flight be the "most hurried," the events that take place "do not always occur in a logical sequence" and are often the least controllable by flight crew.[27] These interruptions and distractions can arise from maintenance personnel, baggage and fuel handlers, passengers, FAs, and ground handlers/push-back crews. Unfortunately, these interruptions can distract the crew from completing necessary duties including accurate checklist completion. In fact, some checklist items are dependent on some external activity being completed, such as closing the cargo door or finishing the refueling process.

Factors that led to the crash of DAL Flight 1141 shortly after takeoff were not only task overload experienced by the crew moments before takeoff, but included, according to the NTSB, "extensive non-duty related conversations and the *lengthy presence of the flight attendant in the cockpit*" which reduced their vigilance in ensuring that the aircraft was properly configured for takeoff (emphasis added) (Report No: NTSBAAR-89/04).

Distractions, by their very nature, are unexpected and involuntarily draw the crew's attention away from the primary task of monitoring the aircraft status. For example, I'm sure the flight crew of a Southwest Airlines (SWA) Boeing B-737 didn't think their use of the airplane's autobrake system would distract them from accomplishing the otherwise routine task of deploying the thrust reversers promptly after touchdown at Chicago Midway International Airport in Illinois. But, unfortunately, it did. Because they failed to use the available reverse thrust in a timely manner—thrust reverser deployment wasn't initiated until 15 seconds after touchdown—Flight 1248 ran off the departure end of Runway 31C and rolled through a blast fence, an airport perimeter fence, and then onto an adjacent roadway, where it struck an automobile, killing a child inside the vehicle, before coming to a stop. SWA was in the process of implementing the use of its new autobrake system on its fleet, and they had provided its pilots with a self-study training module on its usage, but this was the first time this crew had ever used the system. It was a challenging landing situation—the runway was contaminated with snow (with poor braking action reported for the latter half of the runway),[28] there was an 8 knot tailwind, and the usable runway distance was only 5,826 feet. Not being familiar with the performance of the autobrake system, the captain felt the airplane wasn't decelerating as it should have, so he reverted to manual braking. Unfortunately this diverted his attention from employing the reverse thrusters—a very important system, especially on contaminated runways—until it was too late (Report No: NTSB/AAR-07/06).

But pilots can also voluntarily distract themselves by redirecting their attention to something other than, or in addition to, the monitoring task. For example, in 2009, ATC lost radio contact with Northwest Airlines (NWA) Flight 188 an hour before it was scheduled to land at Minneapolis–St. Paul International Airport in Minnesota. Air route traffic control centers (ARTCCs) tried several means to establish communication with the NORDO (no radio communications) Airbus A320, including asking the airline's dispatch and other pilots nearby to make contact. Finally, 1 hour and 17 minutes after communications were lost, and more than 100 miles past their destination, a flight crew member transmitted to Minneapolis ARTCC, "we got distracted and we've overflown Minneapolis…and would like to make a one-eighty." It turns out the crew was completely unaware of the NORDO problem, in part, because they had inadvertently selected 132.125 MHz—a Canadian VHF radio communications frequency—instead of 132.17 MHz, the last one given by ATC and acknowledged by the crew.

So what were they doing during the time they were effectively NORDO for the U.S. controllers? Both pilots had their personal laptops out—which partially blocked their view of the primary flight and navigation displays—and the FO was tutoring the captain in the new flight schedule bidding process that resulted from the merger between NWA and DAL. According to the NTSB, the pilots allowed this conversation to "monopolize their attention" and, thus, lower their capacity to monitor their radio communications and detect the lack of contact by ATC. Understandably, both pilots heard radio chatter but did not hear a radio call for their unique and pertinent/salient call sign NWA188. According to the NTSB, they became "distracted" by a conversation, focusing their "attention" on non-operational issues which led to "reduced monitoring activities, loss of situational awareness, and lack of awareness of the passage of time" (NTSB Identification No: DCA10IA001).

The non-pertinent 3 minute and 11 second conversation between the flight crew members aboard Colgan Air Flight 3407, that crashed while on an instrument approach into Buffalo-Niagara International Airport, distracted them from performing critical tasks including significantly delaying checklist completion. The NTSB concluded that because of this conversation the flight crew members "squandered time and their attention, which were limited resources that should have been used for attending to operational tasks, monitoring, maintaining situational awareness, managing possible threats, and preventing potential errors" (Report No: NTSB/AAR-10/01).

Table 14-1. Example of accidents caused in part by distraction.

Date	Location	Synopsis	Distraction cause/factor	Deaths
May 31, 2014	Watkins, CO	A Cessna 150 stalled and crashed after the pilot lost control.	The pilot's LOC-I and subsequent aerodynamic stall due to spatial disorientation in night IMC. Contributing to the accident was the pilot's distraction due to his cell phone use while maneuvering at low-altitude (NTSB Identification No: CEN14FA265).	2
Oct 1, 2013	Wellton, AZ	An Air Tractor AT 402B descended into terrain in dark night conditions.	The pilot's distracted attention—he was reading a map in an effort to identify the correct field to spray—and failure to maintain sufficient altitude to clear terrain while maneuvering (NTSB Identification No: WPR14CA003).	0
Jul 5, 2013	Casa Grande, AZ	During a multi-engine checkride, a PA-44-180 landed with the landing gear retracted after completing an approach with a simulated single-engine failure.	The failure to extend the landing gear before landing because of the pilot and the flight examiners' distracted attention (by calls from other traffic) (NTSB Identification: WPR13CA316).	0
Jun 2, 2013	Bridgeport, CA	While on short final, a Cessna 182 struck the ground, bounced and impacted again in a nose low attitude. It flipped over and came to rest inverted just short of the runway.	The pilot's distracted attention—he was concerned about clearing a powerline—while on final approach which resulted in his failure to maintain adequate airspeed and subsequent loss of aircraft control (NTSB Identification No: WPR13CA257).	0
Aug 26, 2011	Mosby, MO	A Eurocopter AS350 emergency medical services (EMS) helicopter crashed after running out of fuel.	The failure to confirm that the helicopter had adequate fuel on board to complete the mission due to the pilot's distracted attention from personal texting on his cell phone during safety-critical ground and flight operations (Report No: NTSB/AAR-13/02).	4
Aug 8, 2009	Hoboken, NJ	A Eurocopter AS350 and a Piper PA-32R collided over the Hudson River.	In part, the controller's non-pertinent telephone conversation, which distracted him from his ATC duties (Report No: NTSB/AAR 10/05).	9
Aug 27, 2006	Lexington, KY	A Bombardier CL-600 was instructed to depart Runway 22 but instead attempted takeoff on Runway 26, which was only 3,500 feet long. It ran off the end of the runway and impacted the airport perimeter fence, trees, and terrain.	The flight crew's non-pertinent conversation during taxi, which resulted in a loss of positional awareness (Report No: NTSB/AAR-07/05).	49
Feb 16, 2005	Pueblo, CO	A Cessna Citation stalled and crashed on an ILS approach to Runway 26R.	The approach briefing conducted late in the approach was a distraction that impeded the flight crew's ability to monitor and maintain airspeed and manage the deice system (Report No: NTSB/AAR-07/02).	8

Improving Attention

Until recently, guidance for effective monitoring has been relatively sparse. However, in 2003, the FAA updated AC 120-71, *Standard Operating Procedures for Flight Deck Crewmembers*, renaming the term *pilot not flying* to *pilot monitoring* and further explaining the PM's role. It also added a new appendix which included suggestions for improving crew monitoring and cross-checking. It added even more helpful information in a new update in 2017 (*see* the Helpful Resources section at the end of this chapter). Furthermore, the FAA required U.S. air carriers by March 2019 to implement training on pilot monitoring into their existing training programs.[29] In consultation with industry, the U.K. Civil Aviation Authority also published in 2013 *Monitoring Matters: Guidance on the Development of Pilot Monitoring Skills*[30] and, as mentioned earlier in this chapter, the FSF in 2014 issued its *Monitoring Guide*. The guidelines and detailed strategies contained in these documents are best practices that should be included in SOPs, implemented in flight crew training programs, and adopted by individual pilots to improve monitoring performance on the flight deck. The following sections highlight a few general principles—some of which are further elaborated upon in these documents—that you should consider to improve your monitoring effectiveness.

Overlearn Tasks

Learning the skills necessary to successfully fly an aircraft during initial flight training seems overwhelming to a student pilot—the task demands often exceed the attentional resources they possess. With continued training, however, the same tasks become less demanding. That's because with repeated practice you learn these skills so well that accomplishing them becomes automatic. Just like riding a bicycle or driving a car, not only does it use a smaller amount of attentional resources, permitting significantly less mental effort to be expended to accomplish a task, but **automatic processing** provides more attentional resources to devote to other tasks. For example, the psychomotor skills involved in hand-flying an aircraft are so overlearned (or mastered) that pilots can not only perform them automatically without much conscious thought, they can successfully engage in other behaviors like adjusting the aircraft's configuration or communicating on the radio.

Therefore, you should strive to maintain **proficiency** in your flying ability—this will create more automatic processing for well-learned skills, providing more resources to attend to other tasks such as navigating in congested airspace or managing unexpected events such as distractions, systems anomalies, or emergencies. Unfortunately, since air carrier flight crews rely heavily on automated systems, they face the risk of losing proficiency, especially in hand-flying skills. In a 2013 *Safety Alert for Operators* (SAFO 13002) the FAA identified an increased frequency of manual handling errors in air carrier accidents, incidents, and normal flight operations, and recommended that flight crews hand-fly their aircraft more often to maintain proficiency. The topic of automation and how it can help—and sometimes hinder—pilot performance is discussed in the next chapter.

Use Other Sensory Modalities During High Workload Periods

Deliberately using more than one sensory modality during times of high mental workload provides a "redundancy gain" that minimizes inattentional blindness, improving attentional performance. For example, vocalizing a new altitude assignment issued by ATC, dialing it into the altitude selector, and then pointing to the new value in the selector uses at least three senses: vision, hearing, and touch. The *Monitoring Guide* recommends a *double point* procedure—idiomatically called *point-and-shoot*, where after one pilot points to a new entry, the other pilot verbally confirms the entry while also pointing to the correct display—for all changes in flight path.[31]

The Pilot Monitoring Should Effectively Monitor the Pilot Flying

Even though each pilot on the flight deck is supposed to monitor the status of the flight—including the actions of each other—there are specific roles for the PF and the PM that are clearly defined (*see* the information box on next page). However, research indicates that FOs are less likely to challenge deviations committed by captains than the other way around.[32] Regardless who is assigned the role of PM, it is part of their responsibility to monitor and challenge deviations committed by the PF. It helps if captains encourage this and airline policy supports it. For example, NASA research suggests that captains reinforce the importance of this behavior by telling FOs during the initial briefing something like: "I expect I will make errors on this flight—it is your job to catch them and point them out."[33]

Mentally Fly the Aircraft When the Other Pilot or Autopilot is Flying It

Periods of low task demands reduce mental workload and arousal which can lead to boredom and inattention, leaving you unprepared for unexpected changes. You can stay in the loop by mentally flying the aircraft when the aircraft is on autopilot or if you are designated as the PM.[34] An additional strategy is to develop the habit of making callouts of anticipated changes in altitude, flight mode annunciator, or other parameters just *before* they occur (not after) or before an associated aural alert annunciator is sounded (e.g., "1,000 to go" callout should be made just before the altitude alerter chimes).

Effectively Manage the Aircraft Flight Path During Critical Phases of Flight

The *Monitoring Guide* identifies critical phases of flight as high **areas of vulnerability**. These are predictable segments of flight that are particularly vulnerable to flight path deviations—segments where the flight path is changing—and where the severity of the consequences of deviating from flight path parameters is the greatest. High areas of vulnerability exist on the ground when taxiing in confined spaces, close to obstacles, and close to (or on) active runways; and in flight when flying at low altitude close to the surface and/or below the level of surrounding terrain, when initiating climbs and descents, when within 1,000 feet of level-offs, when turning, and when changing speed or configuration.[35]

Since there are more control inputs and parameters to monitor when the flight (and taxi) path is changing, and the risks are greater when flying closer to terrain, the *Monitoring Guide* recommends two overall strategies for pilots to employ during these high areas of vulnerability:

First, increase the **sampling rate** during the instrument scan. Sampling rate is the frequency with which a pilot directs his or her gaze and attention to the flight instruments and associated flight guidance automation indicators and, if operating in VMC, the external environment. The sampling rate must be high enough to notice an indication of a deviation quickly enough to prevent one from occurring or continuing.

Second, manage workload by shedding non-monitoring-related tasks; deferring them as much as possible to periods of low areas of vulnerability. Shedding non-priority tasks during high workload periods assures maximum attentional resources are available to accomplish the primary task of flying the aircraft, the first item listed in a commonly used task prioritization memory aid: *aviate, navigate, and communicate* (always fly the airplane first, then navigate—know where you are and where you're going—and communicate last). Also, scheduling non-monitoring tasks during periods of low mental workload flattens out task distribution (*see* Figure 14-3), freeing up attentional resources for higher workload periods. Listening to the automatic terminal information service broadcast, conducting the approach briefing, and entering the approach into the FMS before the top of descent from an approach are good examples of this.

Probably the highest area of vulnerability, and the most critical phase of flight, is the approach and landing. This phase requires your highest level of vigilance in order to accomplish safely, so you should do all you can to avoid any distractions—self-induced or otherwise—that would hinder that task. Athletes talk about how they need to stay "in the moment" to achieve their high levels of performance; pilots need to do so as well. Yes, good SA requires that you think ahead and be prepared for contingencies such as a go-around or missed approach, but flying a successful approach—especially in challenging conditions—demands all your resources, your skills, and the ability to stay focused. To facilitate real-time thinking during high-demand situations, some airline pilots say out loud "I, thou, here, and now" when they are having difficulty staying in the moment. While conducting an approach with only yourself and one other in a crewed flight deck, neither of you should be thinking about what just happened or what *will* happen, but should be focused on what is happening right now.

Minimize Interruptions and Distractions

You should treat interruptions and distractions as red warning flags.[36] Not only can they reduce the level of monitoring performance, but they also interfere with actions engaged in, or intended, before the distraction occurred. For example, pilots have forgotten to return to the same place on a checklist or have failed to initiate or complete a required checklist after being distracted. Some crews use novel *reminder cues* to ensure they return to the right place in the checklist, like putting the checklist in a conspicuous place for both crew members to see, fastening a paperclip on the last spot on the checklist, placing a clean Styrofoam cup over the thrust lever, etc.[37] An ATSB report on distractions suggests that if a checklist is interrupted pilots should consider returning to the beginning of the checklist to reduce the possibility of error.[38]

If a distraction cannot be avoided, assign one crew member to address it while the other continues the flight path monitoring function as the PF. If it involves an equipment malfunction or a non-normal situation, the roles of PF and PM should be clearly assigned by the captain so that the PF, in addition to conducting any needed concurrent tasks to assist with the abnormality, is primarily focused on monitoring and flying the aircraft.

Since head-down activities (reading charts and clearances, etc.) removes a crew member from monitoring the flight instruments and outside environment if in VMC, pilots should also defer these tasks to low-workload periods. If head-down work is unavoidable, it should be announced to the other crew member so he or she can direct their full attention to monitoring the flight path. Both pilots should never engage in head-down activity at once—there should always be one head up.

Manage the Unexpected, Don't Let It Manage You

Expect the unexpected in flight. Interruptions, distractions, and changes are bound to occur. Sometimes they're intentional (e.g., choosing a more favorable runway); sometimes they're not (e.g., diverting to another airport due to weather). Either way, it's important not to let them keep you from your primary job of flying the airplane and maintaining safe terrain clearance. The crew of American Airlines Flight 965 was given the choice of runways, but, according to the accident investigation report, the last-minute runway change significantly increased the flight crew's workload, causing them to rush their preparations for the approach. As you saw in the DAL Flight 1141 takeoff accident, the crew accepted an unexpected clearance for takeoff, which in hindsight, they shouldn't have.

Maintain a Sterile Flight Deck

In its report on EAL Flight 212, a McDonnell Douglas DC-9 that collided with terrain in the morning fog three miles short of the runway at Charlotte Douglas International Airport, the NTSB found that conversations not pertinent to the operation of the aircraft contributed to the accident. The crew talked about politics, used cars, and the location of a local theme park tower (Report No: NTSB-AAR-75-9). This accident which claimed the lives of 71 people, and many others like it, prompted the FAA to publish what is commonly known as the *sterile cockpit rule* in 1981. Required for Part 135 and 121 operations, this regulation (14 CFR §§135.100 and 121.542) prohibits crew members from engaging in nonessential activities (including extraneous conversations) that could distract them from completing the essen-tial duties required for the safe operation of their aircraft during the critical phases of flight. A **critical phase of flight** is one in which the level of risk is elevated—during periods of high workload when crew members are more likely to make mistakes and when the aircraft is operated closer to the ground. These include all ground operations—taxi, takeoff, and landing—and all other operations below 10,000 feet—climb, descent, and approach—except cruise flight. As the record clearly indicates, noncompliance with the sterile cockpit rule has contributed to several accidents. Therefore, you should comply with it. Doing so minimizes distractions, allows you and your fellow crew members to focus your attention on proper monitoring and aircraft control, and ensures the safest possible outcomes.

Helpful Resources

An *Awareness Test: How Many Basketball Passes Does the Team in White Make?* If you haven't already seen this one-minute video you should. It effectively demonstrates how difficult it is to successfully focus on more than one thing at a time. (www.youtube.com/watch?v=Ahg6qcgoay4)

These are three informative documents that provide several best practices that airline flight departments and flight crews should use to improve the effectiveness of flight crew monitoring:

- *Standard Operating Procedures and Pilot Monitoring Duties for Flight Deck Crewmembers* (FAA AC 120-71B). This recently updated Advisory Circular includes helpful chapters on checklist design and usage and on monitoring best practices. (www.faa.gov/regulations_policies/advisory_circulars/index.cfm/go/document.information/documentID/1030486)
- *Monitoring Matters: Guidance on the Development of Pilot Monitoring Skills*, published by the U.K. Civil Aviation Authority. (publicapps.caa.co.uk/modalapplication.aspx?appid=11&mode=detail&id=5447)
- *A Practical Guide for Improving Flight Path Monitoring: Final Report of the Active Pilot Monitoring Working Group*, published by the Flight Safety Foundation. (www.flightsafety.org/toolkits-resources/flight-path-monitoring/)

The elimination of distractions has been on the NTSB's *Most Wanted List of Transportation Safety Improvements* since 2013. More information can be found at the *Most Wanted List* webpage at www.ntsb.gov/safety/mwl/Pages/default.aspx

Airbus has produced several flight operations briefing notes applicable to all aspects of safe commercial airline flight operations. An excellent overview of situational awareness on the flight deck is their *Human Performance: Enhancing Situational Awareness*, available from Skybrary's online safety library. (www.skybrary.aero/index.php/Situational_Awareness).

Endnotes

1. National Transportation Safety Board, *A Review of Flightcrew-Involved, Major Accidents of U.S. Air Carriers, 1978 through 1990*, NTSB/SS-94/01 (Washington, DC: 1994).

2. Robert Sumwalt, David Cross and Dennis Lessard, "Examining How Breakdowns in Pilot Monitoring of the Aircraft Flight Path," *International Journal of Aviation, Aeronautics, and Aerospace* 2 (August 2015, Article 8): 1–25.

3. Ibid., 1.

4. An undesired aircraft state is safety-compromising position, condition, or attitude of the aircraft resulting from ineffective threat and/or error management by the flight crew.

5. Flight Safety Foundation, *A Practical Guide for Improving Flight Path Monitoring: Final Report of the Active Pilot Monitoring Working Group* (November 2014). Available at www.flightsafety.org/toolkits-resources/flight-path-monitoring/.

6. Ibid., 3.

7. Christopher D. Wickens, *Engineering Psychology and Human Performance*, 2nd ed. (New York: HarperCollins, 1992).

8. Joel S. Warm, Raja Parasuraman and Gerald Matthews, "Vigilance Requires Hard Mental Work and is Stressful," *Human Factors* 50 (June 1, 2008): 433–441.

9. Donald E. Broadbent, "A Mechanical Model for Human Attention and Immediate Memory," *Psychological Review* 64 (1957): 205–215.

10. Adapted from Figure 2 in Donald E. Broadbent, "A Mechanical Model for Human Attention and Immediate Memory," *Psychological Review* 64 (1957): 205–215. Publisher: American Psychological Association. Adapted with permission.

11. Anne M. Treisman, "Contextual Cues in Encoding Listening," *Quarterly Journal of Experimental Psychology* 12 (1960): 242–248

12. Wickens, *Engineering Psychology and Human Performance*.

13. Christopher D. Wickens, "Multiple Resources and Mental Workload," *Human Factors* 50 (June 2008): 449–455.

14. National Safety Council, *Understanding the Distracted Brain: Why Driving Using Hands-Free Cell Phones is Risky Behavior* White Paper (April 2012). Available at www.nsc.org/learn/NSC-Initiatives/Pages/distracted-driving-how-cell-phone-distracted-driving-affects-the-brain.aspx.

15. Christina Wasylyshyn, Paul Verhaeghen and Martin J. Sliwinski, "Aging and Task Switching: A Meta-Analysis," *Psychology and Aging*, 26 (March 2011): 15–20.

16. David L. Strayer, "Cell Phones and Driver Distraction," Presented at the *National Safety Council, Traffic Safety Coalition* (Washington DC: February 28, 2007).

17. Sumwalt, Cross and Lessard, *Breakdowns in Pilot Monitoring*, 9.

18. Aeronautica Civil of The Republic of Colombia, *Aircraft Accident Report: Controlled Flight into Terrain, American Airlines Flight 965, Boeing 757-223, N651AA, Near Cali, Colombia, December 20, 1995*, trans. Peter B. Ladkin (Santafe de Bogota D.C., Colombia: Aeronautica Civil of The Republic of Colombia, September 1996). Available in English at www.rvs.uni-bielefeld.de/publications/Incidents/DOCS/ComAndRep/Cali/calirep.html.

19. United Kingdom, Civil Aviation Authority. *Monitoring Matters: Guidance on the Development of Pilot Monitoring Skills*, 2nd ed., CAA Paper 2013/02 (April 2013): 19.

20. Mica R. Endsley, "Design and Evaluation for Situation Awareness Enhancement," In *Proceedings of the Human Factors Society 32nd Annual Meeting* (Santa Monica, CA: January 1988): 97–101

21. The following discussion of SA elements and levels elaborates upon and is adapted from Mica R. Endsley, "Situation Awareness in Aviation Systems," *Handbook of Aviation Human Factors*, eds. Daniel J. Garland, John A. Wise and V. David Hopkin (Mahwah, NJ: Lawrence Erlbaum Associates, 1999): 257–276.

22. Centers for Disease Control and Prevention, "Distracted Driving" (2019). Available at www.cdc.gov/motorvehiclesafety/distracted_driving/index.html.

23. Australian Transportation Safety Bureau, *Dangerous Distraction: An Examination of Accidents and Incidents Involving Pilot Distraction in Australia Between 1997 and 2004*, REPORT B2004/0324 (February 27, 2006).

24. Sumwalt, Cross and Lessard, *Breakdowns in Pilot Monitoring*, 10.

25. Key Dismukes, Grant Young and Robert Sumwalt, "Cockpit Interruptions and Distractions: Effective Management Requires a Careful Balancing Act," *ASRS Directline* 10 (December 1998): 4. Available at asrs.arc.nasa.gov/publications/directline.html.

26. Data from Key Dismukes, Grant Young and Robert Sumwalt, "Cockpit Interruptions and Distractions: Effective Management Requires a Careful Balancing Act," *ASRS Directline* 10 (December 1998): 9.

27. Federal Aviation Administration, *Human Performance Considerations in the Use and Design of Aircraft Checklists* (Washington, DC: January 1995): 16.

28. Braking action reports are generated by pilots who have used a runway and are provided to other arriving pilots by ATC. According to FAA Order 7110.65, "Air Traffic Control," braking action reports provided by controllers are to include a description of the braking action, using the terms *good, fair, poor,* or *nil,* and the type of airplane or vehicle from which the report was received.

29. Federal Aviation Administration, "Qualification, Service, and Use of Crewmembers and Aircraft Dispatchers: Final Rule," *Federal Register* 78.218 (November 12, 2013): 67800–67846.

30. U.K. CAA. *Monitoring Matters.*

31. FSF. *A Practical Guide*, 16.

32. Key Dismukes and B. Berman, *Checklists and Monitoring in the Cockpit: Why Crucial Defenses Sometimes Fail* NASA/TM—2010-216396 (Moffett Field, CA: NASA Ames Research Center, July 2010).

33. Ibid., 33.

34. U.K. CAA, *Monitoring Matters*, 33.

35. FSF, *A Practical Guide.*

36. Dismukes, Young and Sumwalt, "Cockpit Interruptions and Distractions."

37. FAA, *Human Performance Considerations*, 17.

38. ATSB, *Dangerous Distraction*, 46.

15

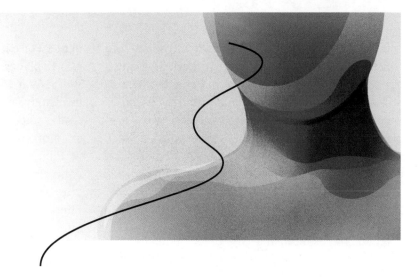

What's it doing now?
Flight Deck Design and Automation

It had to have been frightening. During an en route climb over Santa Maria, California, the crew of American Eagle Airlines Flight 3008 lost control of the aircraft in a **roll upset**. The autopilot unexpectedly disconnected while climbing through 11,500 feet MSL causing the Saab 340, with 25 passengers aboard, to enter a series of steep, uncontrolled pitch and bank attitudes that lasted for 50 seconds before the captain was able to finally regain control at 6,500 feet MSL. The autopilot was in the vertical speed mode set to maintain a selected rate of climb; however, the aircraft was picking up airframe ice more rapidly than the crew was aware of. Both factors caused the autopilot to increase the airplane's pitch attitude to maintain the selected rate of climb—leading to a reduction of airspeed—and to arrest a left-rolling tendency by applying opposite aileron. When the increasing control forces required to counter the left-rolling tendency exceeded the ability of the autopilot to do so, it disconnected, leading to the upset. Had a crew member been flying the airplane manually, they likely would have noticed the airspeed reduction and physically felt—through pressures exerted by the control column—the left rolling tendency that the autopilot was countering, but the autopilot's subtle corrections masked the severity of the asymmetrical icing situation. Fortunately, no one was injured during the +2.5 G_Z experienced on recovery, the airplane did not sustain any damage, and the flight crew was able to continue to their scheduled destination of Los Angeles International Airport.[1]

However, those aboard China Airlines Flight 140 weren't so lucky: All but 7 of the 271 aboard perished after the Airbus A300 stalled and crashed near the landing zone of Runway 34 at Nagoya Airport in Japan. At approximately 1,000 feet, while on an ILS approach, the FO accidentally activated the GO lever which commanded the flight director to conduct a go-around, triggering an increase in thrust and pitch attitude. The FO attempted to counter this by retarding the throttle and pushing the nose down to capture and maintain the glide path. The captain, seeing that this was not working, took control and called for a go-around. However, by this time the A300 was so badly out of trim—having reached its maximum nose-up trim—that the airplane's nose quickly and steeply pitched up and the crew was unable to arrest it in time to avoid an aerodynamic stall.[2] Several incidents involving pilots "fighting" the automatic flight control systems on the A300 aircraft (e.g., in Helsinki, Finland, and Moscow, Russia) preceded this tragic accident, prompting the manufacturer to issue a service bulletin (which later became an **airworthiness directive**) that allowed the flight crew to deactivate the autopilot when applying sufficient force on the control column in the landing and go-around modes. Unfortunately, China Airlines had not yet implemented the requirements of that bulletin.

The terrifying ride in the Saab 340 and the tragic accident of the Airbus A300 were both, in part, caused by advanced automated systems, one of the modern-day developments in flight deck capability that has generally increased the safety and efficiency of flight operations. By relieving flight crews of the need to continuously control the aircraft manually, automated systems reduce fatigue and enable pilots to allocate their limited attentional resources for other aspects of a flight. Unfortunately, as these two examples illustrate, technological advances in flight deck design have sometimes jeopardized, rather than enhanced, safety.

Flight Deck Design

If technology is defined as the practical application of scientific knowledge—usually involving inventing and making something—then the aircraft is indeed a technological marvel. From the early hot-air balloons floating aimlessly a few hundred feet off the ground at just a few miles per hour to supersonic passenger-carrying transports flying at 60,000 feet and more than twice the speed of sound (i.e., the Concorde), the technological progress in aviation has been nothing short of spectacular. So too has the progress of flight deck design and layout. The early round-dial, electro-mechanical-pneumatic, needle, ball and airspeed instruments have given way to intuitive controls, integrated electronic displays, and sophisticated automated flight capabilities that the earliest pioneers could not have imagined. To reiterate what was discussed in Chapter 1, the machine has indeed advanced more in a hundred years than the human brain has in a hundred thousand.

However, that doesn't mean its advance has been without problems. The misinterpretation of flight and navigation instruments and the improper use of flight deck controls have contributed to aircraft acci-dents. For example, it was noted in Chapter 3 that 400 airplanes were lost in a 22-month period during World War II because pilots confused the landing gear and flaps controls. The technology has significantly improved since then; however, even current state-of-the-art technology has its downside.

Flight deck design—especially the design of controls and displays—is a major factor in flight crew performance. Chapter 3 introduced the discipline of human factors (or ergonomics), defined for our purposes as the scientific study of the flight crew and the flight environment with the goal of optimizing the relationship between the two. Inherent in this definition is the idea that rather than design the human to fit the machine, the pilot's environment—especially the flight deck—should be designed to accommodate the limitations and capabilities of the human operator. This **human-centered design** contributes to reducing human error and maximizing human performance, safety, efficiency, and comfort. Accordingly, the first part of this chapter looks at the design of the pilot's workstation—primarily the displays and controls, the second part evaluates some of the issues pilots experience with the automated cockpit, and the third part concludes with suggestions on how to best manage that automation.

Human-Machine Interface

Flying an aircraft is an example of a **closed-loop feedback system** (*see* Figure 15-1). For each segment of flight, a certain aircraft state is desired in terms of vertical navigation (altitude or rate of altitude change), lateral navigation (heading and/or track),

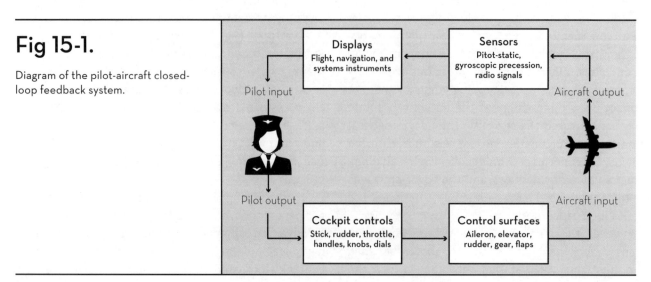

Fig 15-1.

Diagram of the pilot-aircraft closed-loop feedback system.

forward speed, etc. Any changes in these commanded "set point" values are communicated back to you, the pilot, via instrument displays located on the flight deck. Aircraft displays rely on sensors to accurately display various parameters regarding the aircraft's status. For example, a difference in static air pressure is measured in the altimeter to display altitude above MSL, the difference between static and dynamic air pressure in the pitot-static system is used to display airspeed on the airspeed indicator, gyroscopic precession in a traditional heading indicator displays a change in aircraft heading, gear position sensors are used to display extension or retraction status of the landing gear display, etc.

Your sensory modalities (primarily vision, but also hearing, touch, and smell) sense and perceive any change in the aircraft's set point status (attitude, altitude, speed, heading, power/thrust setting, etc.) primarily from information conveyed to you via the flight, navigation, and systems displays located on the flight deck. If any of the desired parameters are exceeded, you will respond by using the appropriate control (control column, side stick, throttle, gear handle, etc.) to bring the aircraft back to the desired set point value. For example, if the altimeter displays 100 feet above your desired altitude, you will push the control column (or side stick) forward, the elevator control surface will deflect, and the nose will pitch down. The change in static air pressure sensed by the static measuring system will indicate a change in altitude on the altimeter display indicating that you have reacquired the desired set point or need to make more control adjustments. This entire loop involves continuous feedback enabling continuous control to maintain a given set point.

The point of explaining this feedback loop is to illustrate the important role that flight deck displays and controls—the **human-machine interface**—play in helping you to accurately perceive and understand the aircraft's state and to provide control inputs to change it. For example, **displays** are used to communicate a representation of the state of the aircraft or outside world to you, the operator. However, if the information presented on them is inadequately illuminated, hard to read, cluttered, inaccurate, ambiguous, or difficult to interpret, then you will lack a full understanding of the true state of the aircraft and a proper basis from which to make appropriate control inputs. Similarly, the design of the **controls**

can help or hinder pilot performance. For example, a flap handle that makes the flaps go *down* when moved *up* could confuse a pilot not fully trained in that aircraft. Or, a change in control surface movement that is communicated to you through your tactile sense when holding a traditional control column (with cable- and hydraulic-powered flight controls) may be completely absent on newer side stick controls. In fact, most side-stick-equipped aircraft today provide little or no tactile feedback to the pilot flying (PF) from movements that occur from turbulence or from control inputs from the other pilot. Only recently have active side stick controls been introduced to commercial aviation. As opposed to passive controls, these mimic traditional direct-connect systems providing the PF an extra feedback channel that is absent in the passive side stick controls.

Since inadequately designed interfaces have contributed to errors made by pilots—and even accidents—the design and layout of flight deck displays and controls, much like that for automobile instrument panels, has constantly improved and evolved over the years to reduce the probability of interpretation and use errors made by pilots.

Interface Coding

Pilots of some early aircraft models had difficulty distinguishing between flap and landing gear controls because the switches for both were identical and located close together. One way to help reduce this, and other similar types of interface confusion, is to code displays and controls according to their function and how they are best understood by humans. The most common types of coding involve shape, color, and location.

Shape Coding

It was noted in Chapter 3 that engineering psychologists redesigned the shape of the landing gear and flap handles on the Boeing B-17s and other airplanes to reduce confusion. Psychologist Alphonse Chapanis placed the two controls further apart and attached a rubber tire to the end of the landing gear switch and a flap-shaped device on the flap actuation knob. This **shape coding** of the controls to look like the devices they control helped pilots to better distinguish between the two and the rate of inadvertent gear retractions was drastically reduced. Look-alike shapes are also used for other controls (*see* Figure 3-1 in Chapter 3) and on some displays (e.g., airplane symbol found on electronic-map displays).

Color Coding

It was also noted that **color coding** was implemented in the design of some controls to ease distinguishability for pilots (e.g., fuel mixture control knob is colored red to reflect red colored fuel that used to be common). But is has also been used in displays. For example, the airspeeds considered safe to operate, to be used with caution (and the aircraft only operated in smooth air), and should never be exceeded, are indicated by a green-colored arc, a yellow-colored arc, and a red-colored line (V_{NE}, never-exceed speed) on the airspeed indicator, respectively. These colors conform to **population stereotypes**, culturally agreed-upon understandings of what certain locations of switches, direction of switch movement, symbols, shapes, or colors mean. For example, in North America (and much of Western culture), a light switch is usually moved up to turn it on; a clockwise rotation of a knob usually increases its value (e.g., volume control, dimmer switch); and the colors green, yellow (or amber), and red mean safe or go, caution, and danger (or stop) respectively. However, except for red, which seems to indicate danger in most societies, pilots from other cultures may not have the same intuitive understanding (stereotype) of some of the colors used in Western flight decks and must learn what their meaning is.

One problem designers must overcome is to ensure there is enough contrast to make color-coded displays readable for all pilots in all lighting conditions (from bright sunlight to nighttime darkness). What Boeing discovered during extensive testing in the 1970s, when cathode ray tube displays first made their way into commercial airline flight decks, was that these lighting extremes meant that no more than six or seven different colors could be used on a display.[3]

Location Coding

The placing and arranging of displays and controls to best meet the processing needs of the human operator is known as **location coding**. Pilots are trained to scan their instruments, especially when relying on them during flight in IMC. However, proper inter-

pretation of the information needed from a variety of displays to perform a particular task takes more time and mental effort when they are not located in close proximity to each other.

Since the primary task of every pilot is to aviate, followed by navigate and communicate, the displays that a pilot views the most—the six major flight instruments—are placed directly in front of him or her (*see* Figure 15-2).

Fig 15-2.

The placement of the traditional six flight instruments is designed to aid in correctly interpreting the aircraft's flight status.

These are known as the primary flight instruments (PFI) and by regulation (14 CFR §23.1321) are located so a pilot, sitting at the normal reference point (*see* Chapters 3 and 12), doesn't have to move his or her head to see all of them. In fact, they are to fall within the **primary optimum field of view**, which is defined as 15 degrees above and below the normal line-of-sight (15 degrees below horizontal plane) and 15 degrees either side of the normal forward line-of-sight of the aircraft (*see* Figure 15-3).

The most important instrument—the attitude indicator—is directly in front of the pilot and close to the top of the instrument panel to also facilitate out-the-window viewing. The attitude indicator, sometimes called the artificial horizon, substitutes the natural horizon with an artificial one and is the only PFI that provides a *direct* indication of the aircraft's pitch and bank attitude. The attitude indicator is an

Fig 15-3.

A pilot's primary optimum vertical and horizontal field of view of the primary flight instruments.

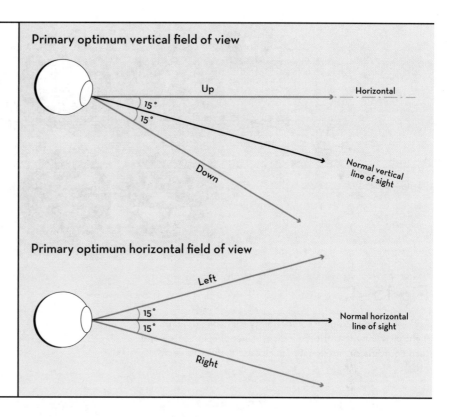

example of a **pictorial display**. In the belief that a picture is worth a thousand words, pictorial displays attempt to present the pilot with a realistic representative "picture" or a representation that "looks like" what it is supposed to represent—a principle of control/display design known as **pictorial realism**.[4] The attitude indicator represents the pitch and bank attitude of the aircraft in relation to the real-world horizon by depicting the position of a miniature symbolic airplane in relation to an artificial horizon separated by sky above (blue) and ground (sometimes with ground plane lines) below (brown). Pictorial displays involve fewer mental operations enabling faster and more accurate interpretation of the information presented.

Avoiding an aerodynamic stall and maintaining terrain clearance are two of the most crucial tasks in flight, so it makes sense that the aircraft's airspeed is displayed on the airspeed indicator immediately to the left of the attitude indicator and its altitude on the altimeter immediately to its right (*see* Figure 15-2). A changing (or steady) altitude is displayed on the vertical speed indicator immediately below the altimeter. The heading indicator is directly in front of the pilot below the attitude indicator, and the turn indicator, or turn coordinator (or turn-and-bank indicator), is to the left of the heading indicator.

The placement of these PFIs—commonly called the "six pack"—follow another principle of good display design known as the **proximity compatibility principle**. This means that when information from different displays need to be frequently compared to each other to gain a complete understanding of the aircraft's state (requiring close "mental" proximity), those displays should be physically located in close "physical" proximity to each other. This results in less time and effort needed to mentally integrate the information, thereby enhancing interpretation.[5] For example, the six pack communicates information regarding the three aspects of aircraft flight performance: lateral (turning), vertical (pitching), and longitudinal (forward movement) flight. Note in Figure 15-4 how the lateral flight instruments—attitude indicator, heading indicator, and turn coordinator—are located in close proximity to each other. Similarly, note in Figure 15-5 how the vertical flight instruments—attitude indicator, airspeed indicator, altimeter and vertical speed indicator—are located in close proximity to each other. Information for longitudinal flight is presented on the airspeed indicator which, since it is also related to pitch and is important even when looking out the window, is located in the top left section of the six instruments.

Fig 15-4.

Following the proximity compatibility principle, the lateral flight instruments—attitude indicator, heading indicator, and turn coordinator—are located in close proximity to each other.

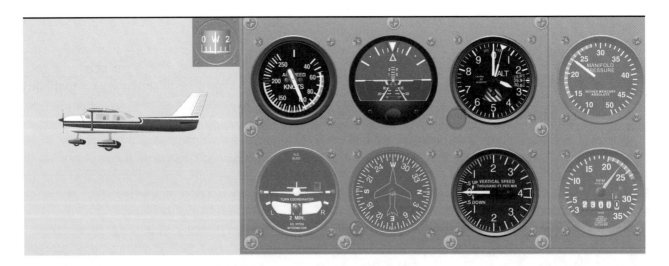

Fig 15-5.

Following the proximity compatibility principle, the vertical flight instruments—attitude indicator, airspeed indicator, altimeter, and vertical speed indicator—are located and grouped in close proximity to each other.

What is notable about the six-pack arrangement is that it has stood the test of time, because manufacturers not only use this same general arrangement for the newer electronic displays, but the exact location of most of these PFIs is prescribed and codified by regulation in 14 CFR §23.1321. Figure 15-6 shows the newer rectangular electronic flat-panel **primary flight display (PFD)** in the background with diagrams of the six traditional "round dial" displays superimposed over top to show how they are similarly arranged to the traditional six pack. Notice that the rectangular PFD—a pictorial display—is one large attitude indicator, with a horizon bar across the entire display. This is very helpful because, as previously mentioned, the pictorial nature of the attitude indicator enhances interpretation for pilots.

Another pictorial display is the navigation display (ND) found on many modern transport category aircraft and the **multi-function display (MFD)** found on newer general aviation aircraft. Notice how the plan (or bird's eye) view provided by the electronic display in Figure 15-7 enables instant and accurate perception of the location of water, terrain (and its elevation), airports, airways, and other airspace in relation to your aircraft (represented by the airplane symbol located in the lower middle of the display). This pictorial map is also an example of what is known as an **integrated display**, where related information, following the proximity compatibility principle, is presented together for easy comparison by the pilot. Where it used to take several separate instruments (usually round-dial) to display heading

(heading indicator), course (course deviation needle), distance (DME), location related to a fix (TO/FROM indicator), the pictorial MFD in map mode in Figure 15-7 visually integrates all these elements enabling a pilot to directly perceive and easily and quickly interpret the information.[6]

A major advantage of an integrated display is that it reduces attentional demands on the pilot, enabling his or her limited attentional resources to be used for other tasks. This explains why in experimental studies in simulators and in real flight, when compared to pilots who used separate displays, pilots who used integrated displays containing the same information performed significantly better at controlling attitude, altitude, and airspeed, even when these three parameters were not displayed on the integrated display itself![7]

Analog vs. Digital Displays

In Figure 15-6, the traditional round-dial analog altimeter and airspeed indicator are replaced by digital vertical-tape displays. In many ways, linear vertical tape displays of altitude and airspeed, with higher values depicted higher up on the tape and lower values shown lower down on the tape, better conform to the principle of pictorial realism than do traditional round-dial airspeed indicators and altimeters; neither speed or altitude are circular concepts—they are linear (horizontal for speed and vertical for altitude).[8] Before the advent of computerized displays it was impractical to include vertical

Fig 15-6.

A primary flight display (PFD) with round-dial display counterparts superimposed to show the similarity between the two types of displays.

tape displays for airspeed and altitude because the relatively large scales involved would require the displays to be excessively large or the scale markings would be so small as to make them unreadable. Even a tape display integrated into a computerized PFD is physically unable to show the entire range of speeds or altitudes, so when the values change, new values appear from the top or bottom of the display as necessary (see Figure 15-8). This leads to the distinction between digital and analog displays.

Digital displays present quantitative, discrete numeric information that is helpful in determining precise values, and usually involves less mental effort and fewer mental computations to interpret exact values. However, when numerical values are rapidly changing (e.g., airspeed, altitude), both the direction (increasing or decreasing) and rate of change is often very difficult for pilots to interpret.

Analog displays present qualitative, continuous information that represents the state of an aircraft attribute in symbolic or pictorial format, often with a moving indicator. The old-fashioned watch or clock with hour-, minute-, and second-hands that rotate clockwise around a face is a symbolic analog representation of how much time has passed or how much is left to go. For example, the minute-pointer positioned at 9 o'clock is three-quarters around the face which visually and instantly represents time as three-quarters through the hour with 15 minutes to go to the "top" of the hour.[9] These features of time

Fig 15-7.

Garmin G1000 multifunctional display (MFD).

Fig 15-8.

A primary flight display (PFD) with vertical tapes displaying airspeed (left; 120 knots), altitude (right; 5,000 feet), and vertical speed (right of altimeter tape; 200 feet per minute descent).

are easier to interpret than a digital display, which requires mental calculation for determining time passed or time-to-go. However, analog clocks are initially more difficult to learn how to read than digital ones and, because mental calculation is involved in combining the position of the small and large hands, are subject to greater interpretation errors when determining precise time.

The advantages and disadvantages of an analog clock are also true of the traditional round dial three-pointer analog altimeter (see Figure 15-9). When your goal is to fly level (a constant altitude), it is relatively easy with this type of altimeter—common to most aircraft since the early days of flight—to visually perceive how far off your aircraft is from your desired altitude.

Also, during a climb or descent, the moving pointers of a round-dial altimeter provide for relatively easy-interpretation of both the direction (clockwise rotation for increasing altitude, counterclockwise for decreasing altitude—conforming to a common population stereotype) and the approximate rate-of-change of altitude. The changing numeric values of a truly digital altimeter on the other hand (Figure 15-10 is a digital altimeter with a hundred-foot pointer), make it more difficult to perceive the direction and rate of altitude change, especially if the aircraft is gaining or losing altitude quickly.

However, in spite of its benefits, extensive research has concluded that the three-pointer altimeter, like the analog clock, is more susceptible to misinterpretation than a digital one. Unlike a digital altimeter, several mental steps are necessary to correctly determine an exact numerical altitude value from a three-point altimeter: you must attend to three different pointers (with three different lengths), you must understand what each pointer represents, and you must synthesize the three values to calculate an exact final number by mentally adding all three values.[11]

The most common error is misreading the altitude by 1,000 feet, usually over-reading it by 1,000 feet, leaving the false impression that the aircraft is higher than it really is. This could be catastrophic at night or when flying in IMC. We have known about this problem since the early days. A study of 270 errors involving reading and interpreting aircraft instruments conducted back in 1947 found that the single greatest type of instrument-reading error—at 15 percent of all errors reported—was misreading

Fig 15-9.

An analog three-pointer altimeter.

Fig 15-10.

A counter-drum-pointer altimeter that displays altitude digitally (on a background circular drum) and includes an analog hundred-foot pointer.

the three-point altimeter by 1,000 feet (13.5 percent) and by 10,000 feet (1.5 percent).[12] The study also found that the thousand-foot errors were more common at night and/or in IMC. Numerous studies since then have demonstrated that, compared to the counter-pointer-type altimeter that includes a digital component on the display (Figure 15-10), interpretation times are longest and altitude-reading errors are the most frequent when reading the simple analog three-pointer-only altimeter (Figure 15-9).[13] For example, Figure 15-11 indicates the number of errors 18 pilots made during a total of 1,080 readings from four common altimeter types—the counter-pointer (CP), counter-drum-pointer (CDP), drum-pointer (DP), and three-pointer (3P). The three-pointer altimeter, one of the most common altimeters still used today, is the clear loser when it comes to misinterpreting altitude.[14]

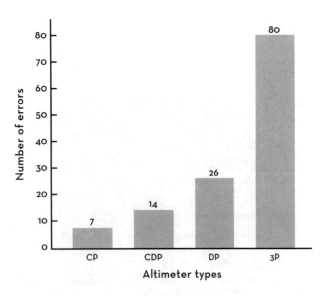

Fig 15-11.

Total number of errors made by 18 pilots on each of the four types of altimeters.

The pilot of a Schweizer SGS 2-33 ended up low on an approach to Runway 18 at Skyhaven Airport in Warrensburg, Missouri, because he misread the altimeter by 1,000 feet; he walked away, but the glider struck trees and a fence before contacting the ground (NTSB Identification No: MKC88LA117). Another glider pilot misread his altimeter by 1,000 feet which put him too high while in the traffic pattern. In the rush to lose altitude he misjudged

his flare and damaged his L-13 Blanik during a hard landing (NTSB Identification No: MIA87LA199).

A more serious accident involved National Airlines Flight 193 that descended into Escambia Bay about three miles short of Runway 25 at Pensacola Regional Airport in Florida. The aircraft was descending steeply (2,000 fpm) while the crew was conducting a nonprecision approach at night in IMC when the ground proximity warning system (GPWS) activated. The 100-decibel sound startled the crew and they thought it had to do with their steep descent rate, so when they looked at their counter-drum altimeters (with hundred-foot pointer) that each read 500 feet, both the captain and FO still "saw" it as reading 1,500 feet. Contributing to their misinterpretation was the fact the GPWS stopped warning them once the captain reduced the Boeing B-727's rate of descent. Of the 58 people aboard, three passengers drowned in the accident (Report No: NTSB/AAR-78-13).

Though less common, misinterpretation of the 10,000-foot pointer on the three-pointer altimeter has also led to accidents as well. For example, United Airlines Flight 389, a Boeing B-727, was cleared to descend to 6,000 feet MSL: however, the airplane, operating in a clean configuration (gear, flaps, and speed brakes retracted), continued its 2,000 fpm rate of descent at a normal cruise descent speed (about 200 knots) from FL350 past its 6,000-feet clearance limit right into the water of Lake Michigan, killing all souls aboard. There was no evidence of any systems or altimeter malfunctions and no concern was expressed to the approach controller during their last radio transmission which appeared to be completely routine and, unknown to the controller, occurred below their assigned altitude of 6,000 feet between about 500 to 2,000 feet above the water. Though they were unable to determine with certainty why the crew continued an uninterrupted descent into the lake, NTSB investigators concluded that the crew may have misread 6,000 feet as 16,000 feet, either because they were not paying attention or because of the known limitations in interpreting the three-pointer altimeter.[15]

Standardization

Shape, color, and location coding of controls and displays are all examples of flight deck **standardization**. Standardization in flight deck design involves making and arranging displays and controls that conform to a specified standard of design according to good human factors engineering principles, often as reflected in regulations and guidance material, such as 14 CFR §23.1321 and FAA ACs 23.1311-1C and 25-7D. This involves similarity of coding (color, shape, etc.), similarity of layout (the standard six pack), and similarity of operating principles (switch is selected up for ON, dial turned clockwise to increase, etc.).[16]

The safety benefits of providing agreed-upon standards for flight deck controls and displays has long been recognized by designers and safety engineers. Both mental effort and the probability of error increase when the displays and controls of different aircraft makes and models are designed differently or positioned in different locations in the cockpit. For example, a pilot's prior experience and learning may interfere with his or her performance when checking out in another aircraft if he or she is accustomed to a given control's location in a different one. This phenomenon is known as negative **transfer of training** (also called *transfer of learning*) where prior learning in one environment interferes with learning and performance in another. Two stark examples of how a lack of standardization in the design of landing gear controls and attitude indicator displays can lead to negative outcomes are discussed in the next two sections.

Inadvertent Landing Gear Retraction

Negative transfer of training was no doubt involved in numerous inadvertent landing gear retraction incidents in some of the early Beechcraft aircraft. Between 1975 and 1978, some Beech Bonanza (single-engine) and Baron (twin-engine) models were responsible for 61 percent of inadvertent gear retraction incidents when operating on the ground, yet these aircraft accounted for only 25 percent of the retractable-gear light airplane fleet in the United States. Why the disparity? It turns out that at least four design factors, including shape coding (the flap and landing gear switches on the early Bonanzas were not shape coded like other aircraft and were nearly identical in shape), contributed to transfer of training problems with pilots. The main problem, however, was that the gear control switch was closer to where the flap control was in other airplanes and the flap control switch was located closer to where the gear control was located in other airplanes. In

other words, these controls were positioned in non-standard locations. When pilots, who were used to flying other makes and models raised the flaps after landing, they inadvertently activated the landing gear and raised them instead. Here are some quotes from some of the reports:[17]

> "When I reached to retract the flaps, I hit the gear switch instead. I also own a PA-30 in which the switches are in reverse to the Beech."

> "I have thousands of hours in aircraft in which the flap switch is located where the gear switch is on the B-58 which was a contributing factor."

> "During rollout, at about 35/40 kts, pilot (me) retracted gear thinking it was the flap switch. Pilot used to flying Cessna 210 and flap switch is located where gear switch is located on Baron. Dumb pilot error."

> "Reached to retract flaps as for short-field procedures, however, flap switch on Baron is reversed with landing switch on Cessna and Queen Air, pilot retracted landing gear instead of flaps."

Flap device controls are now required to be placed to the right of the pedestal/powerplant throttle control centerline—and far enough away from the landing gear control to avoid confusion—and the landing gear control is to be located to the left of the throttle/pedestal centerline (14 CFR §23.777). However, these rules were put in place after the Bonanzas and Barons were type-certificated so they were exempt. When Beechcraft finally did change their design to conform to the rules, it was former Bonanza and Baron owners who had difficulties with the new locations of the gear and flap controls!

Inside-Out vs. Outside-In Attitude Indicators

Another principle of good display design is the **principle of the moving part**, a concept that states symbols on displays should move in the same direction as the part that they represent.[18] For example, if you roll the airplane to the right, the miniature airplane on the attitude indicator should bank to the right; if you pitch the nose up, the miniature airplane should move up. Since the earth's horizon is fixed and the aircraft moves in relation to it, it is logical and fits with our mental model that the airplane symbol should move, not the horizon. Simple enough, right? But, have you ever noticed what actually happens on the attitude indicator installed on the aircraft you fly? If you pilot an aircraft using a Western-type attitude indicator the miniature airplane does not move—the horizon bar does! The airplane symbol on the attitude indicator is fixed while the horizon moves, violating the principle of the moving part.

The violation of this principle in the Western-style attitude indicator—also known as the **inside-out attitude indicator**—points out the difficulty human-factors researchers sometimes have in designing displays that are most congruent with a pilot's mental model of the flight environment. Research clearly indicates that better performance and less confusion occurs when using an attitude indicator that displays a stationary horizon with a moving miniature airplane (as it is in the real world)—especially with flight-naïve participants (non-pilots)—also known as the **outside-in attitude indicator** and often used in airplanes from the former Soviet Union (*see* Figure 15-12). It comports with the idea that when a pilot moves a control column (or side stick) he or she is not moving a horizon that doesn't move, but an aircraft that does.[19]

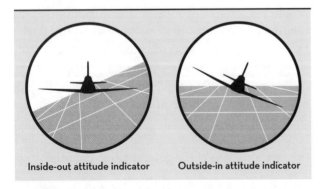

Inside-out attitude indicator   Outside-in attitude indicator

Fig 15-12.

Western-style inside-out attitude indicator with moving horizon (left) and outside-in attitude indicator with stationary horizon (right).

It turns out, much like the stationary airplane symbol on a moving background heading scale of a heading indicator, that many pilots prefer the stationary miniature airplane symbol of the inside-out attitude indicator. These pilots certainly know that it is their aircraft that is moving, not the stable outside world. However, their mental model of what should be displayed on an attitude indicator comports with what they see were they to look directly outside—a *moving* visual world in relation to their aircraft. In this sense the attitude indicator is mentally seen as a porthole in the nose of the aircraft—what you see through the porthole is what it looks like outside. In other words, the Western-style inside-out attitude indicator may violate the principle of the moving part but it conforms to a competing principle, the principle of pictorial realism.[20] And, even though the outside-in attitude indicator conforms to the principle of the moving part, it provides a bird's eye view of someone who might be outside and behind the aircraft, a view that violates the principle of pictorial realism for pilots sitting at their station inside their craft.

It is generally not too difficult for pilots to transition from one type of attitude indicator to another, provided they receive sufficient training and practice using the new one. However, as with other non-standard controls and displays that can interfere with performance in one environment because of previous learning in another, problems may arise should a pilot not acquire adequate experience with the different attitude indicator. It appears this may have been the case in a tragic accident involving Flight 821, an Aeroflot-Nord Airline flight in Perm, Russia, that killed all 88 people aboard. The crew of the B-737 was conducting an ILS approach in IMC at night to Runway 21 at Bolshoye Savino (now Perm International) Airport, when the aircraft rolled 360 degrees and collided with the ground approximately seven miles from the runway.

Several factors contributed to this accident, including a known throttle-stagger condition that required the flight crew to place the throttles up to 15 degrees apart from each other to obtain equal engine fan speeds. Unfortunately, as they leveled off at about 2,000 feet while on vectors for the approach, the FO who was the PF, synchronized the throttle controls, not engine thrust output. The autopilot counteracted the strong left-rolling tendency caused by the asymmetric thrust by adjusting the trim. However, when it reached the end of its trim limits, the autopilot disengaged and the airplane banked to the left. The FO had trouble controlling it, so he unexpectedly gave the controls to the captain who in turn experienced difficulty interpreting exactly what attitude the aircraft was in. According to Russian Air Accident Investigation Commission investigators, the primary cause of the accident was spatial disorientation caused by the captain's lack of proficiency and insufficient training in determining roll upset directions during his transition training in the Western-style (inside-out) attitude electronic attitude director indicator. He was accustomed to using Eastern-style (outside-in) attitude indicators on previous airplanes he had flown.[21, 22]

Control-Display Incompatibility

There is one more issue to discuss before moving to the topic of automation. Closely related to the principle of the moving part is control-display compatibility. Like the principle of the moving part, this principle states that control devices (knobs, handles, switches) and symbols on displays should move in the same direction as the part they are supposed to represent. For example, when you pull a handle up, its display pointer and the device it controls should move up; when you move an ON/OFF switch down, the system should turn off; and when you turn a dial clockwise, the intensity of the parameter being controlled should increase. This control-display compatibility principle is seen in typical flap and landing gear controls and displays: to move the flaps and landing gear down (extending them) the control handles and switches should also go down; when raising them up, the controls should move up. However, this isn't always so and **control-display incompatibility** has contributed to errors made by pilots. For example, to raise the landing gear or flaps on some aircraft, you must lower a handle; to read a traditional magnetic compass correctly, you must read it backwards; and to track a course on a VOR in reverse sensing mode, you must turn the opposite direction. Through training and experience, pilots learn to compensate for these contradictions; but such incompatible design pairings still contribute to error, especially when a pilot is under stress or busy with other tasks.

Automatic Flight Control Systems

A major addition to the flight deck human-machine interface are automated systems. Automation—the accomplishment of a task by a machine instead of a human[23]—has come a long way since Lawrence Sperry's "automatic pilot" was successfully demonstrated in a Curtiss C-2 biplane to a crowd of onlookers at the *Concours de la Sécurité en Aéroplane* (Airplane Safety Competition) in Paris on June 18, 1914. Taking advantage of his father's invention of the gyrocompass and stabilizers used for ships, the younger Sperry—nicknamed "Gyro"—invented a light-weight gyroscopic heading indicator and attitude indicator which, when coupled to hydraulically activated flight controls, enabled the airplane to maintain a constant heading and altitude without inputs from the pilot.[24]

Automatic flight control systems (AFCS), also called autopilot flight director systems or automatic flight guidance systems, are now standard equipment on most modern business and commercial transport category airplanes. They are part of the overall flight control and flight guidance system (FGS) that provides guidance for manual control (hand-flying) of flight and control using the AFCS to achieve a desired aircraft trajectory (altitude, airspeed, track, etc.). A typical FGS consists of several components, including an FGS computer, an air data computer, sensors, an attitude heading reference system, a flight management system (FMS), a crew interface system such as a control display unit (CDU), a flight director (FD), an AFCS, a mode control panel (MCP), a yaw damper, and electronic flight information system (EFIS) displays.

EFIS displays, often referred to as a glass cockpit, display flight, navigation, and engine information electronically usually using liquid crystal displays (LCDs). Older electromechanical instruments, sometimes pejoratively referred to as **steam gauges**, display information in separate individual displays, often round dial displays and often in analog format. EFIS software can integrate several sources of information and display them onto one screen, while older systems consist of several different fixed instruments/gauges that are independent of, and located separately from, each other. The MFD in Figure 15-7 and PFD in 15-8 are examples of EFIS displays. Figure 15-13 illustrates an example of combination ND/MFD common on most modern passenger jet aircraft. Another example is the engine-indicating and crew-alerting system (EICAS) display: this system replaces all analog gauges with integrated digital information that can be manipulated by the computer and pilot to display a variety of parameters.

The FGS receives inputs from a variety of sensors to determine the current, or measured, state of the aircraft and compares it to what the desired state should be. Besides measuring altitude, attitude, speed, track (course), heading, and other parameters, sensors detect geographic position information from the global positioning system (GPS), autonomous inertial navigation systems, and/or ground-based radio navigation signals, which in turn are used to navigate on selected tracks and airways to a programmed destination.

The flight crew provides short-term guidance inputs for selected targets (altitudes, airspeeds, flight paths, etc.) and modes using knobs, dials, and buttons on the autopilot MCP or flight control unit (FCU), and long-term (current and future flight legs) guidance via the FMS through the CDU (*see* Figure 15-14). The FGS issues guidance commands via the FD displayed on EFIS displays such as an ND, PFD, or MFD. When engaged, the autopilot responds to these commands by articulating control actuators at each control surface to achieve the desired results. Figure 15-15 provides a basic overview of a flight control/ flight guidance system.

If desired by the crew, the FD can command the autopilot—or "George" as it is affectionately known[27]— to fly the entire flight profile programmed into the FMS, or different segments of it, without the requirement for the pilot to physically manipulate the flight controls. For example, it can automatically control lateral navigation (LNAV), including flying headings, tracks, and airways. It can also automatically control vertical navigation (VNAV), including climbing and descending at desired speeds or pitch angles; levelling off and cruising at selected altitudes; conducting approaches to airports; and, for some aircraft flying an ILS approach to a qualified airport, landing on a runway in minimal visibility (autoland).

An AFCS also often includes stability augmentation systems that automatically dampen buffeting and oscillations. An example of such a system is a yaw damper, which automatically dampens yaw oscillations in the airplane's vertical (or normal) axis that could contribute to Dutch roll, especially on swept-wing airplanes.

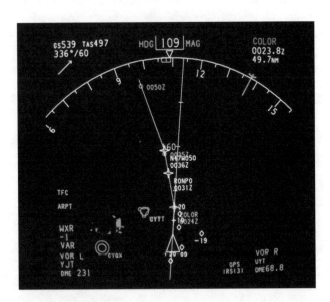

Fig 15-13.

Example a navigation/multifunction display (ND/MFD).[25]

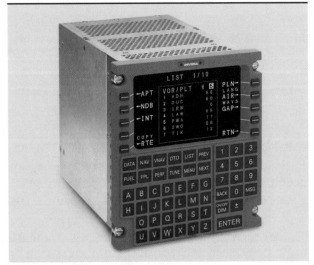

Fig 15-14.

A control display unit (CDU) from a Boeing B-737-300. The CDU is the interface the flight crew uses to program the flight management system (FMS).[26]

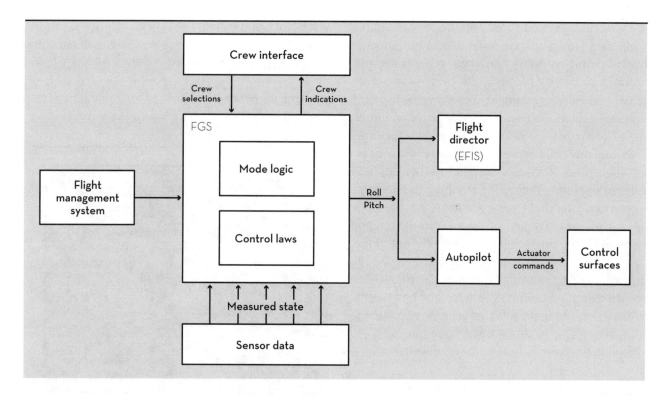

Fig 15-15.

Basic overview of a flight control/flight guidance system.

Benefits of Automation

Advances in computer processing and digital technology are no doubt responsible for the sophistication and increasing capabilities of today's flight decks, but the evolution from Sperry's early autopilot to the modern AFCS has been primarily influenced by the desire to increase safety and improve efficiency. What began as a desire to relieve flight crews of continuous physical manual control of the aircraft (reducing fatigue, especially for long-haul operations), enabling them to allocate limited attentional resources for other aspects of a flight, has matured into supplying them with greater geographic position awareness through location and terrain information displayed on MFDs and automatic advisories and warnings to assist in avoiding midair collisions through airborne collision avoidance systems, or collisions with terrain through terrain awareness and warning systems.

Most automated systems on modern transport category flight decks also provide **flight envelope protection**. Every aircraft has limitations in terms of airspeed, altitude, and load factor (or G-forces). Operations within these parameters define an aircraft's safe flight envelope. For most modern jets, autoflight systems are capable of preventing the aircraft from exceeding these limits even if a pilot inadvertently attempts to do so. The advent of electronic flight control via **fly-by-wire** technology makes such protection possible. The pilot's flight controls no longer have a direct mechanical connection to control surfaces (elevator, aileron, rudder, etc.); their movement is transmitted via electronic signals through wires to electronic devices and control actuators at each control surface. This technology enables FGS computers to automatically provide flight envelope protection, preventing the aircraft from flying too slow or fast, from flying too high, or from exceeding the aircraft's design limit load factor or other parameters. The two major manufacturers of transport category passenger jets—Boeing and Airbus—have slightly different philosophies and versions of flight envelope protection, but they are somewhat similar in scope. Airbus aircraft uses three levels (or Laws) of protection, depending on whether or not all the computers (and there are several) and components are fully and correctly functioning. For example, Normal Law operates when all electronic systems are active and fully operational, and provides in-flight envelope protection from excessive bank and pitch angles, airspeeds, angles of attack, and load factors.[28]

Automation and other technological advances on the flight deck have also increased efficiency and reduced operational costs by reducing the need for more than two flight crew members (at one time there were up to five, including a FE, navigator, and radio operator); producing more fuel-efficient climb, en route, and descent profiles; increasing engine life through full authority digital engine control systems and autothrottle/autothrust systems; and by adhering to more precise flight paths that achieve safer landing approaches and facilitate operations into airports located in terrain-challenging environments.

Automation: A Mixed Blessing

Despite its benefits, automation has sometimes proved a mixed blessing on the flight deck. As American Eagle Airlines Flight 3008 and China Airlines Flight 140 indicate (see this chapter's introduction), automation also has its downside: It appears that in an attempt to alleviate certain problems on the flight deck, it has created others. The following discussion highlights some of the problems flight crews have experienced with automation.

Dumb and Dutiful

Even though automated systems can reliably accomplish a variety of tasks, they are still machines. For example, if a pilot inadvertently enters incorrect information into the FMS, the machine usually won't know it—it is *dumb*. Even worse, it will also execute the erroneous commands programmed into the FMS—it is *dutiful*. For example, an Airbus A320 crashed into the side of La Bloss Mountain, about 10 NM from the runway at the Strasbourg-Entzheim airport in Strasbourg, France, killing all but seven of the 96 aboard. Instead of descending at approximately 800 fpm for the VOR-DME Runway 05 approach, accident investigators discovered the airplane descended at approximately 3,300 fpm—about four times the rate needed for the approach. Investigators concluded that the crew of Air Inter Flight 148 likely programmed the

wrong information into the FMS via the FCU interface and it dutifully did what it was told. Instead of selecting a –3.3 degree flight path angle (FPA) they likely inadvertently selected a vertical speed (VS) of 3,300 feet/min: the former depicted as "–3.3" on the FCU, and the latter displayed as "–33" (see Figure 15-16).

Fig 15-16.

A 3.3 degree glide slope is displayed as "-3.3" in the flight path angle (FPA) mode while a vertical descent rate of 3,300 feet per minute is displayed as "-33" in the vertical speed (VS) mode.

Mode Error and Finger Trouble

The crew in the A320 accident in Strasbourg likely committed two mode errors—first, they failed to select the correct mode in the FCU interface, and second, they failed to perceive the unsafe system state that this incorrect mode put the aircraft in. It was determined that the design of the interface—where the only difference between "-33" and "-3.3" is the decimal point—may have been a factor in these errors. **Finger trouble**—a descriptive term for manually inputting incorrect values—also occurs with less ambiguous displays. The drive to create crew interface designs that are elegant and simple, and that maximize the use of limited space, can actually facilitate the selection of the wrong dial or knob, or, as we have seen, the selection of the wrong value using the correct control.

An example of this is described in a recent FAA *Information for Operators* (InFO). InFO 16022 warns about inadvertent selection errors using concentrically centered knobs responsible for selecting more than one mode (bi- and multi-modal knobs). These are designed so a larger outer control knob changes cursor position and selects information category, operating/display mode, or large value changes, while the smaller inner knob selects subcategories of the position selected with the larger outer knob. Sometimes dials with completely different functions are located together; a change to one function might affect another totally unrelated function without being detected by the flight crew. For example, a pilot rotates the navigation course selection knob which results in an unintentional change to the barometric altitude setting! Other causes of unintentional selections include accidentally rotating two knobs at once as a result of finger positioning errors and/or finger slippage, and inadvertently selecting the wrong knob and subsequently failing to make appropriate corrections or failing to detect the inadvertent selection. Selecting an incorrect mode is a common issue for pilots: an international survey of 1,268 airline pilots found that 73 percent had on occasion, inadvertently selected the wrong mode.[29]

An example of finger trouble using different control knobs involved a tragic accident that claimed the lives of 92 of the 146 people aboard Indian Airlines Flight 605 that crashed short of Runway 09 at Bangalore International Airport, India. According to the accident report, the flight crew allowed the approach altitude and airspeed of the A320 to get dangerously low while on final approach which caused the automation to switch to stall angle of attack (AOA) protection mode, which resulted in an automatic go-around. Unfortunately, it was too late: it did not have enough airspeed or altitude to avoid striking the ground short of the runway. There were several factors that led to this accident, but one was the fact that the check pilot, who was the pilot monitoring for this flight, likely selected 700 feet using the altitude knob when he intended to select 700 fpm descent using the vertical speed knob. These two knobs are located close to each other on the FCU interface.[30]

Mode Confusion

Modern automation and flight management systems are complex and often difficult to understand. This is evidenced by how challenging it is for fully qualified and experienced flight crews to understand and operate them. For example, Boeing recently surveyed 966 captains and FOs who represented a broad spectrum of worldwide airline pilots and discovered that 62 percent did not feel comfortable with, or confident in, their ability to operate the FMS/autoflight system in their aircraft until after flying their current aircraft type on the line for a minimum of 3 to 12 months. Less than a quarter of the pilots felt comfortable in their ability to perform on their first line flight in their current aircraft type and 56 percent reported they had difficulty performing tasks with the FMS/automation in the first 6 months after their first line flight.[31]

The complexity of automated systems sometimes leads to **mode confusion**, a lack of understanding or awareness by flight crews of not only what particular mode the AFCS might be operating in, but in how such systems operate. We have already alluded to several possible modes the AFCS can operate in. For example, autoflight systems can maintain a desired airspeed (airspeed mode or flight level change [FLCH or FLC] mode), rate of descent or climb (vertical speed mode), pitch attitude relative to the horizon (pitch [PTCH] mode) or altitude (altitude select [ASEL] mode or altitude hold [altimeter HOLD] mode). These are just a few of the basic vertical navigation modes and do not include lateral navigation modes, or other complex modes associated with autothrottle/autothrust systems. In fact, a Boeing study identified up to 25 different vertical, lateral, and thrust modes for a typical transport category airplane.[32] A NASA study of this subject points out that this mode-rich environment often makes it difficult for pilots to keep track of them all.[33]

A classic example is the potential confusion between three related, but critically different modes: VNAV PATH (vertical flight path angle), VNAV SPD (airspeed), and VNAV ALT (altitude). Understanding these modes thoroughly and their differences is particularly important during area navigation arrivals and approach operations. For example, failure to recognize that the FD is in an FMS-generated VNAV SPD mode (airspeed hold) rather than VNAV PATH mode (vertical flight path angle) while flying below the FMS-generated path, can easily lead to a potential controlled flight into terrain situation; especially when the altitude window is set much lower while flying over mountainous terrain or set higher than the present altitude in preparation for a missed approach. Table 15-1 includes several of the modes (in abbreviated form) typical of modern automated flight systems.

Table 15-1. Sampling of abbreviated mode messages displayed on the flight mode annunciator (FMA). Listed alphabetically and updated to include modes found in a variety of modern automated flight systems from different aircraft manufacturers.[34]

Aircraft Flight Modes		
Autothrottle/ thrust modes	Vertical (pitch) modes	Lateral (roll) modes
ALPHA	altimeter SEL or ASEL	ATT
CLB	altimeter or altimeter HOLD	BC or B/C
DESCENT	APPR or APR	FMS
FLOOR	BC or B/C	1/2 BANK
FLX 42	CLB	GA
GA	DES	HDG
IDLE	FLC	HDG
HOLD	FPA	HOLD
N1	GA	HDG SEL
RTR	GS or G/S or GP	LNAV or LNV
SPD/MACH or SPEED	IAS	LOC
THR	PATH	NAV
THR REF	PITCH or PTCH or PIT	ROLL or ROL
TO/GA or TOGA or TO	SPD	ROLL HOLD
TOGA LK	TO	ROLLOUT
	VNAV or VNV	TO/GA or TOGA
	VPTH	TRK SEL
	VS or V/S	TRK HOLD or TRK
		VOR

Mode confusion refers to a variety of undesirable outcomes. At its basic level, it occurs when a pilot is ignorant or confused about what the cockpit automation is doing. More specifically, it occurs when the flight crew "believes the automation is in a mode different than the one it is actually in," or "does not fully understand the behavior of the automation in certain modes or how different modes interact" with each other.[35] Pilots often lack understanding of the system's "internal architecture and logic, and there-fore...lack understanding of what the machine is doing, and why, and of what it is going to do next."[36] This lack of understanding leads to an inaccurate mental model of what the automation is doing, which in turn could cause the crew to mismanage the aircraft's energy state and trajectory, leading to an unsafe condition.

Mode confusion has been a factor in several major airline incidents and accidents, including the previously discussed fatal crash of an A320 short of the runway at Bangalore International Airport. One of the reasons the flight crew of Indian Airlines Flight 605 failed to adequately monitor the A320's airspeed during final approach was because they were puzzled and preoccupied with attempting to figure out why the system had switched to the *idle—open descent* mode, instead of the *airspeed* mode.

More recently, mode confusion was involved in the crash of a Boeing B-777 into a seawall short of Runway 28L at San Francisco International Airport (*see* Chapter 10). Even though the ILS was inoperative, the weather and visibility were good so ATC cleared the crew of Asiana Airlines Flight 214 for a visual approach. However, rather than fly manually (hand-fly), the crew elected to use the automation to fly the approach. Since the jet was high on the approach, the PF selected the FLCH mode to increase the airplane's rate of descent; however, since the airplane was below a selected go-around altitude, that action inadvertently caused the autoflight system to initiate a climb. He then disconnected the autopilot, moved the thrust levers to idle, and pitched the airplane down, increasing the rate of descent. The accident report indicates he did not know (and observe) that manually moving the thrust levers to idle, while in the FLCH mode, caused the autothrottle system to switch to the HOLD mode and no longer controlled airspeed. The vertical speed of about 1,200 fpm caused the airplane to descend below the glide path with the precision approach path indicator displaying four red lights (meaning too low on the approach). About seven seconds before impact, the airspeed had deteriorated to 114 knots, a quadruple chime caution aural alert sounded, the master caution light illuminated, and an AIRSPEED LOW caution alert message was displayed on the EICAS indicating the airplane had decelerated to below the minimum required speed. The crew decided to conduct a go-around at an altitude of 90 feet. But it was too late; there wasn't enough airspeed and altitude to avoid striking the seawall short of the runway. Three of 307 people aboard died in the accident, but 49 were seriously injured and the airplane was destroyed by the impact forces and post-crash fire.

The NTSB concluded that the probable cause of this accident was the "flight crew's mismanagement of the airplane's descent during the visual approach, the pilot flying's unintended deactivation of automatic airspeed control, the flight crew's inadequate monitoring of airspeed, and the flight crew's delayed execution of a go-around after they became aware that the airplane was below acceptable glide path and airspeed tolerances." Investigators also concluded that the pilot's inadvertent deactivation of automatic airspeed control resulted from an *inaccurate understanding* of how the "autopilot and autothrottle systems interact to control airspeed" and a "*faulty mental model* of the airplane's automation logic." Furthermore, this mode confusion resulted from the *complexity* of the B-777 automatic flight control system and "inadequacies in related training and documentation" (Report No: NTSB-AAR-14/01).

Automation Surprise

The crew of American Eagle Airlines Flight 3008 was surprised when the autopilot of their Saab 340 disconnected resulting in a roll upset, and the crew of China Airlines Flight 140 was likely surprised also when the nose of their Airbus A300 pitched up so steeply and quickly that they couldn't avoid a stall (*see* this chapter's introduction). So too was the crew of Asiana Airlines Flight 214 when the autoflight system initiated a climb when they changed modes to the FLCH pitch mode to increase their B-777's rate of descent. **Automation surprise** is often the result of automation confusion. Automation complexity, coupled with an inadequate understanding of the system, leads to automation ignorance or confusion, which in turn leads to automation surprise—the reaction a flight crew member experiences when the automation does something different than what he or she expects it to do.

Several design features have been identified that increase the probability of mode confusion errors that can lead to automation surprise. Table 15-2 lists them.

Table 15-2. Software design features that increase the chance of mode errors.[37]

Design categories	Explanation
1. Interface interpretation errors	Computer interprets user inputs differently than the user does, usually because inputs are defined differently for different modes.
2. Inconsistent behavior	Depending on system status, selection of a mode sometimes results in different outcomes.
3. Indirect mode changes	Automation changes modes without any direct input from the flight crew.
4. Operator authority limits	Automation prevents activation of certain modes to protect aircraft from undesired aircraft state.
5. Unintended side effects	Selecting a mode may result in an additional (unintended) consequence.
6. Lack of appropriate feedback	Computer provides inadequate feedback regarding mode changes or aircraft status.

Each of these design limitations has no doubt led flight crews astray to one degree or another, but three categories have proven to be particularly vexing: inconsistent behavior (2 above), indirect mode changes (3), and lack of appropriate feedback (6).

Inconsistent Behavior

When a mode is selected, it is reasonable to expect the system to respond the same way in each instance. However, this is not always the case. When the autopilot activated the go-around mode, the FO of China Airlines Flight 140 that crashed at Nagoya Airport in Japan attempted to continue the approach by manually deflecting the control column. In most other aircraft, and in the A300 in all modes except the approach mode, this action would have disconnected the autopilot. However, he should have exited the go-around mode or disconnected the autopilot by other means, but he didn't. As a result, his struggle to keep the nose down, while the autopilot was attempting to pitch it up through trim inputs, put the airplane so far out of trim that it could no longer be controlled.

When a flight crew member pushes the TO/GA (takeoff/go-around) switch, it is also reasonable to expect the system to automatically activate a go-around (increase in thrust and pitch for climb). Though the final report had not been released at the time of this writing, it appears that this didn't happen when the captain of Flight 521, after landing at Dubai International Airport in the UAE, selected the TO/GA mode for the autothrottle. It was a particularly challenging landing—they experienced a tailwind and wind shear and the weight-on-wheels sensors indicated that the right main landing gear touched down at approximately 3,600 from the runway threshold followed three seconds later by the left main landing gear. Hearing the "LONG LANDING, LONG LANDING" aural warning from the runway awareness advisory system, and realizing they needed to conduct a go-around, the crew selected the TO/GA mode for the autothrottle and reduced the flap setting and raised the gear as if they were indeed conducting a go-around. However, they discovered the airspeed was decreasing and the thrust levers were still in the idle position. They then manually moved the levers to full thrust, but it was too late: the airspeed continued to bleed off and the B-777 rapidly sank back and impacted the runway coming to rest near its far end. Fortunately, none of the 300 people aboard died, and only one person received serious injuries in the accident. However, the airplane was completely destroyed by the impact forces and post-crash fire, and a firefighter from the airport rescue and firefighting services died while attempting to extinguish the fire.[38]

Indirect Mode Changes

Indirect mode changes—often called **mode reversions**—occur when the AFCS changes modes without any direct input from the flight crew. These mode changes can be expected (e.g., a mode changes from *armed* to *capture*) or unexpected depending on the pilots understanding of the automation and the level of feedback provided by the system (*see* the next section). For example, an unexpected and uncommanded (indirect) change in one mode (e.g., a vertical navigation mode) occurs after a crew member selects a change in another (e.g., a lateral navigation mode). Or, an uncommanded (indirect) mode change occurs to provide flight envelope protection, keeping the aircraft from exceeding its envelope limits (overspeed protection, stall alpha avoidance, etc.).

Crew members may possess an incorrect mental model of the aircraft's state if they are unaware of an indirect mode change, which could cause them to implement incorrect flight control commands. In an attempt to continue the approach and aid his ability to manually keep the nose down, the FO of

China Airlines Flight 140 manually reduced the thrust. However, the airspeed decreased, causing the AOA to increase to the point where an indirect activation of the stall alpha protection mode occurred; the increase in autothrust aggravated the situation by further pitching the nose up, due to underslung engines. As previously mentioned, by this time the airplane was so far out of trim (and unrecognized by the crew) that it could no longer be controlled.

We also mentioned previously that the flight crew of Indian Airlines Flight 605 failed to adequately monitor their A320's airspeed during final approach into Bangalore International Airport, in part because they were preoccupied with attempting to figure out why the system had switched to the *idle - open* descent mode instead of the *airspeed* mode. It appears likely that their inadvertent selection of a lower altitude—700 feet—instead of 700 fpm, caused the indirect mode change.

Lack of Appropriate Feedback

A design feature that might have reduced the confusion on the flight deck of China Airlines Flight 140 is better feedback designed to inform the crew of mode transitions—especially indirect ones. This is the recommendation made in a 2013 report by the Flight Deck Automation Working Group, a task group of the Performance-Based Aviation Rulemaking Committee and the Commercial Aviation Safety Team (CAST). The working group recommends that "equipment design should emphasize reducing the number and complexity of autoflight modes" and should "improve the feedback to pilots (e.g., on mode transitions)."[39]

Automation Complacency

The previous chapter began with a brief discussion of EAL Flight 401, where the flight crew allowed their Lockheed L-1011 to descend into the Florida Everglades killing 101 of the 176 people aboard. The FO had selected the autopilot to maintain 2,000 feet, but while they were preoccupied with troubleshooting a possible nose landing gear problem, someone had inadvertently bumped the flight controls causing the autopilot go into the control wheel steering mode. The crew didn't notice the gentle descent in the dark night, and the autopilot dutifully flew the TriStar into the terrain.

In another tragic accident, the flight crew of American Airlines (AA) Flight 965 was trying to set up for the approach to Runway 19 at Cali, Colombia (*see* Chapter 14). They accepted a last-minute runway change which dramatically increased their workload, and this—along with the communication misunderstandings between the captain and non-native English-speaking controller, inadequate communication between the two flight crew members, and misunderstanding of the FMS—all conspired to cause the Boeing B-757 to deviate from their expected course toward higher terrain. They inadvertently entered the wrong waypoint into the FMS and didn't realize the airplane had turned about 90 degrees off the assigned course until about a minute had passed. They managed to get the airplane turned around and back toward Cali; however, the GPWS alerted the pilots of rising terrain. They responded by adding full thrust and pitching the airplane into a steep climb attitude. Unfortunately it was too late; the airplane crashed into higher terrain, killing all but four passengers of the 164 people on board.[40]

These tragic accidents demonstrate another side effect of automation: the phenomenon commonly known as **automation complacency**. It appears the flight crews in both of these accidents were overly reliant on the automation to safely fly their airplanes: The captain of EAL Flight 401 delegated the job of flying the airplane entirely to the autopilot, while the crew of AA Flight 965 trusted the automated systems to keep them on course while they engaged in activity needed to prepare for the approach.

You were reminded in the previous chapter that flying can be 99 percent pure boredom and 1 percent sheer terror. The boredom comes because the autopilot does what you want it to do virtually every time, so with every flight your level of trust increases and you begin to relax your monitoring role—sometimes to the point of boredom. This low level of mental arousal (or "underload") reduces performance. The terror comes when something unexpected occurs and/or when you get behind the airplane after being overloaded with other tasks. In these situations,

flight crews certainly are not bored as they attempt to successfully accomplish multiple tasks; however, their performance in these high mental workload situations can suffer as much as it can in low mental workload situations (*see* Figure 14-4 in previous chapter). Because modern-day automation is highly reliable, it is tempting for flight crews to exhibit automation complacency by redirecting their attention away from their primary task of monitoring the aircraft's flight path and placing too much reliance on the automated systems to fly their aircraft.

Compounding the problem is an inconsistency about automation. One of the major goals of integrating automated systems into aircraft flight operations is to reduce the flight crew's workload. However, research has found that even though it does indeed reduce physical and mental workload, it usually only does so in low-workload periods such as during cruise flight. In high-workload periods, such as during an approach, it tends to increase overall workload—an **automation paradox**—especially if other circumstances (e.g., last-minute changes, systems anomalies) add to that workload.[41] In other words, the complex automation systems themselves often demand additional mental resources during otherwise high workload periods.

Automation complacency diminishes flight crew monitoring performance, leaving them unprepared when something goes wrong. As we have seen in this chapter, sometimes it is not always easy for pilots to understand what is going wrong, in part because the automation does not provide clear feedback about the status of the airplane and/or automation to them; in some cases, it actually hides it. For example, several in-flight loss of control accidents and incidents involving airframe icing have occurred because the autoflight system masked the presence of differential wing icing before suddenly disconnecting and hurling the aircraft into an abrupt roll. Table 15-3 lists some of the most notable airframe

Table 15-3. Partial list of U.S. airframe icing accidents involving roll upsets.

Date	Operator	Aircraft	Location	Fatalities
Jan 2, 2006	American Eagle Flight 3008	Saab SF340	Santa Maria, CA	0
Feb 16, 2005	Martinair	Cessna Citation 560	Pueblo, CO	8
Mar 19, 2001	Comair Flight 5054	Embraer EMB 120	West Palm Beach, FL	0
Jan 9, 1997	Comair Flight 3272	Embraer EMB 120	Monroe, MI	29
Oct 31, 1994	American Eagle Flight 4184	ATR-72	Roselawn, IN	68

icing accidents/incidents in the United States where flight crews lost control of the aircraft in a roll upset following an uncommanded autopilot disconnect in airframe icing conditions.

Another example of how overreliance on automation diminishes flight crew monitoring performance, leaving them vulnerable when something goes wrong, is China Airlines Flight 006. The Boeing B-747 was en route to Los Angeles International Airport when the number four (furthest right) engine lost thrust while cruising at FL410. The autopilot was maintaining altitude and wings-level while the crew was preoccupied with dealing with the engine malfunction. However, because of asymmetric thrust and gradually diminishing airspeed, the autopilot commanded a left-wing-down control wheel deflection to counteract the increasing asymmetric force resulting from the loss of thrust. The crew didn't seem to notice this; according to the NTSB, the autopilot effectively *masked* the approaching onset of the loss of control of the airplane. When it reached its limits, the airplane began to roll to the right. Seeing this, the captain disengaged the autopilot but it was too late: the B-747 yawed and rolled further to the right, nosed over, and entered an uncontrollable descent. It rolled over on its back while it continued rolling to the right and airspeeds dropped to a low of between 54 and 110 knots. At one point the airplane lost more than 20,000 feet in less than a minute. Fortunately, the captain was finally able to recover at about 9,500 feet and successfully land at San Francisco International Airport with only four passengers seriously injured. But not before the aircraft was subjected to positive vertical accelerations of up to +5.1 G_Z and high airspeeds that occurred during the upset and recovery maneuvers that damaged many components of the jumbo jet: bent wings, a broken left outboard aileron, separation of the landing gear uplock assemblies and an auxiliary power unit (APU) from their mounts, and separation of a large part of the left and right horizontal stabilizer (including the entire left outboard elevator). Information from the digital flight data recorder visually depicts the frightening uncontrolled descent in Figure 15-17.

The NTSB determined the probable cause of the accident was the captain's preoccupation with an in-flight malfunction and his failure to properly monitor the airplane's flight instruments which resulted in his losing control of the airplane.

Contributing to the accident was the captain's *overreliance on the autopilot* after the loss of thrust on the number four engine (Report No: NTSB/AAR-86/03).

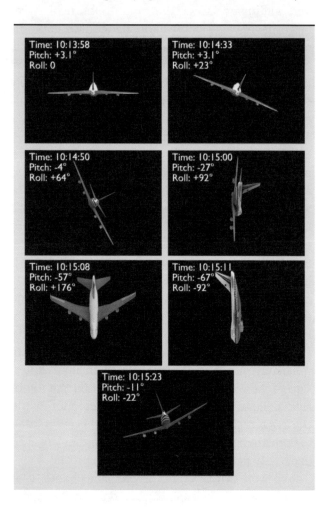

Fig 15-17.

Excerpts from computer animation, based on data from digital flight data recorder (DFDR), of uncontrolled descent of China Airlines Flight 006.[42]

Automation Addiction

Finally, overreliance on automation can also create dependency. Since airline pilots and other professional crews rely extensively on automation to fly their aircraft—the FAA estimates it is used 90 percent of the time in flight[43]—they become dependent, or addicted to its use, hampering their ability to safely fly without it. The loss of proficiency in manual flying skills, and diminished ability to fly without advanced avionics and automated systems, was documented in a recent study conducted by the Flight Safety

Foundation (FSF) involving 30 U.S. airline pilots. The performance of seventeen captains and 13 FOs (with an average experience level of 7.1 years flying narrow- and wide-body transport airplanes), who flew five basic maneuvers in a Level D simulator without using automation, was assessed using FAA performance standards for airline transport pilot certification. A maneuver score of 4.0 or higher (on a scale of 5) is required for airline standards, while a score of 3.0 and 2.0 indicates minor and major deviations from airline standards, respectively. Mean performance scores only ranged from a high of 3.2 for takeoffs and a low of 2.4 for holding maneuvers. The mean score for performing an ILS approach and missed approach was 2.9. A survey also asked the pilots to rate their basic instrument flying skills. Results indicate that the pilots rated their ability to conduct these maneuvers significantly higher than how they actually performed in the simulator.[44] This was attributed in part to "declines in the pilots' manual flight skills, coupled with the pilots' over-estimating their own manual proficiency."[45]

It appears the flight crew of Asiana Airlines Flight 214 was afflicted with **automation addiction** (dependency). As you recall, they were cleared for a visual approach at San Francisco International Airport, but elected to use the automation rather than hand-fly the approach. This was in keeping with Asiana's automation policy: it emphasized the full use of all automation to assist pilots during line operations. The NTSB accident report stated, however, that the PF "lacked critical manual flying skills" and had he "been provided with more opportunity to manually fly the 777 during training, he would most likely have better used pitch trim, recognized that the airspeed was decaying, and taken the appropriate corrective action of adding power" (Report No: NTSB/AAR-14/01).

In a follow-up to a previous 1996 report on modern flight deck systems, the Flight Deck Automation Working Group in 2013 analyzed 26 airline automation-related accidents and 20 major incidents that occurred since then and found that manual handling errors were identified as a factor in 60 percent of the accidents and 30 percent of the major incidents. Some of the results of these errors included incorrect upset recoveries, inappropriate control inputs, improper manual control handling after an autopilot or autothrottle/autothrust disconnect, lack of monitoring/maintaining energy/speed, and mismanagement of autothrottle/autothrust.[46]

Conventional wisdom suggests that the skills needed to manually fly an aircraft deteriorate over time. A study in 1971 found this to be only partially true. It discovered that basic psychomotor (hand-eye) skills needed to manually fly an aircraft, once thoroughly learned, were—much like the skills needed to ride a bicycle—remarkably resistant to significant decline. However, just as the 1971 research discovered, a 2014 NASA study found that the *cognitive skills* needed to successfully hand-fly an aircraft—such as recalling procedural steps, keeping track of which steps have been completed and which one's remain, visualizing the geographical position of the aircraft, performing mental calculations, and recognizing abnormal situations—do indeed degrade significantly over time.[47]

Unfortunately, to achieve the economic and safety benefits of automation, airline policies and operational requirements have historically discouraged pilots from practicing their hand-flying skills. Rather, with the exception of most takeoffs and landings, they have often been required "to fly the aircraft with the highest level of automation."[48] In recognition of this increase in manual flying errors, the FAA recently published *Safety Alert for Operators: Manual Flight Operations* (SAFO 13002) encouraging airlines and other operators to promote manual flight operations when appropriate. The SAFO reiterates that continuous use of autoflight systems does not reinforce a pilot's knowledge and skills in manual flight operations and could lead to degradation of a pilot's ability to quickly recover the aircraft from an undesired state. Taking this one step further, the Department of Transportation's Inspector General's Audit Report in 2016 recommended the FAA develop standards for air carriers to "determine whether pilots receive sufficient training opportunities to develop, maintain, and demonstrate manual flying skills."[49]

Managing Automated Systems

Flight deck design, advanced avionics, and sophisticated autoflight systems have continually improved over the past several decades. Besides reducing the workload and fatigue involved in physically hand-flying the aircraft, automation increases overall situational awareness by freeing up attentional resources to better manage all aspects of a flight. The ability to fly the aircraft more precisely during challenging flight segments (e.g., landing approaches), to create better positional awareness through advanced displays, and to provide flight envelope protection only adds to the safety benefits that automation provides.

However, for all its advantages, flight deck automation still has its limits. It has changed the role of the pilot from a direct manual controller of the aircraft to a systems' monitor and supervisor. Even when directly hand-flying, a layer of sophisticated automation—especially so in the new fly-by-wire systems—is interposed between the pilot and the aircraft, distancing him or her from the physical vehicle and its energy state.[50] Flight crews have sometimes called automation the "strong and silent partner" on the flight deck: Strong, because of the level of authority designers have granted it, and silent, because of the lack of acceptable feedback about the aircraft's state that flight crews would prefer to receive from it. As we have previously discussed, this latter characteristic makes it more difficult for pilots to accurately monitor the automated systems and to recover when the system fails.

Automation-induced errors have diminished as programming algorithms have improved and will continue to do so as automation design conforms more closely to the characteristics and thought patterns of the human operator. For example, even though mode status is almost always accurately displayed visually on EFIS displays, mode selection errors are still made by pilots. To help reduce these errors, flight crews have seen—and can expect to see in the future—greater use of auditory alerts and even artificial speech feedback whenever modes change (either manually or indirectly). Especially critical are timely alerts—often called "bark before bite" alerts—that warn pilots when the automation is compensating for some unusual condition and "controlling up to the limit of its authority for an extended period of time" (e.g., trimming for differential wing icing preceding imminent autopilot disconnect) without the flight crew's awareness of the hazard.[51]

However, no matter how many design improvements are made, pilots will always need to become effective managers of the automated systems on their aircraft. This will entail a thorough knowledge of not only how the autoflight system works, but also how and when to—and when not to—use it.

Understand How the Autoflight System Works

The CAST evaluated 480 ASRS automation-related incidents involving Part 121 air carriers between 2000 and 2006. They concluded that in almost all cases, the flight crew "did not comprehend what the automation was doing, or did not know how to manipulate the automation to eliminate the error."[52] A recent Boeing survey of 966 airline pilots (referenced earlier) found that only 23 percent felt comfortable operating the FMS on their first flight after training, only 15 percent felt comfortable after their initial operating experience, and the rest (62 percent) felt comfortable only *after* gaining line experience.[53] These results support the claim that autoflight systems are difficult to fully understand and suggest that airline training programs may not be as effective as they could be in helping pilots gain the understanding needed to effectively operate them. In fact, 42 percent of respondents reported their FMS training as "minimal with room for improvement" or "inadequately covers the operational use of the FMS."[54]

Even though this data is somewhat discouraging, there's no excuse for not learning all you can about how the AFCS works on the aircraft you fly. You should supplement any learning you acquire in the classroom and on the flight line with your own self-study. Answering these four fundamental questions—suggested by Airbus and a CAST report—will help you fully understand and effectively interact with the automation:

- How is the system designed?
- Why is the system designed that way?
- How does the system interact and communicate with the pilot?
- How does the pilot operate the system in normal and abnormal situations?[55]

It is especially important to understand, if applicable, the integrated nature of autopilot/flight director and autothrottle/autothrust modes on your aircraft. For example, just as manual deflection of the elevators and the use of thrust (or power) can control either airspeed, pitch attitude, or vertical speed when hand flying an airplane, the autopilot pitch modes and autothrottle/autothrust modes are paired in a coordinated way to achieve target values. You should be aware of how changes in either of these modes will affect the others and watch out for unexpected, though logical, indirect mode changes.

Follow Best Practice Procedures When Engaging the Autoflight System

Proven strategies to reduce errors when engaging and interacting with the autoflight modes have been adopted by several airlines. For example, before engaging the autopilot, or selecting an AFCS mode, use the "CAMI" or "VVM" procedure—both emphasizing the importance of pilot-to-pilot communication and verification of desired inputs.

The CAMI procedure is as follows:

- **C**onfirm airborne (or ground) CDU inputs to the FMS with the other pilot, ensuring the modes selected on the FCU are the correct ones for the intended flight path.
- **A**ctivate inputs.
- **M**onitor mode annunciations on the FMA, PFD, and ND/MFD to ensure the autoflight system performs as desired (i.e., correct modes armed or engaged and aircraft responding as desired).
- **I**ntervene if necessary.

The VVM procedure is similar: **V**erbalize, **V**erify, and **M**onitor.

Large pitch and/or bank attitude displacements required to achieve the intended flight path may result in the autopilot overshooting the intended vertical or lateral target, and/or surprise a pilot due to the resulting large pitch and/or roll and thrust changes. To avoid this, confirm the FD command bars do not display any large attitude displacements; if such displacements occur, disconnect, or do not engage, the autopilot and fly the aircraft manually to center the bars before engaging (or re-engaging) the autopilot.[56]

Be Prepared for Areas of High Vulnerability

In the previous chapter, several measures were suggested to implement during phases of flight that are considered high areas of vulnerability. These are predictable segments of flight that are particularly vulnerable to flight path deviations and when the severity of the consequences of deviating from flight path parameters is the greatest. These exist on the ground when taxiing in confined spaces, close to obstacles, and close to (or on) active runways, and in flight when flying at low altitude close to the surface and/or below the level of surrounding terrain, when initiating climbs and descents, when within 1,000 feet of level-offs, when turning, and when changing speed or configuration. Figure 15-18 illustrates high areas of vulnerability (in red) while airborne.

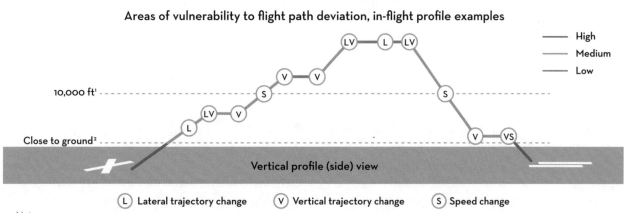

Areas of vulnerability to flight path deviation, in-flight profile examples

10,000 ft¹

Close to ground²

Vertical profile (side) view

ⓛ **High**
ⓜ **Medium**
ⓛ **Low**

Ⓛ Lateral trajectory change   Ⓥ Vertical trajectory change   Ⓢ Speed change

Notes:
1. 10,000 ft is used in the United States as the boundary altitude for sterile cockpit rules and for the 250 KIAS speed restriction (both required below 10,000 ft). For the purpose of the areas of vulnerability model, an altitude of other than 10,000 ft may be chosen, but it is suggested that this boundary match the use of sterile cockpit rules for your operator (or nation/state) for ease of operational applicability by flight crews
2. "Close to ground" may be defined by the operator, but it is suggested that this be an altitude no less than (a) 1,500 ft AGL or (b) the altitude of the surrounding terrain (if terrain threats exist within 5 NM [9 km] of the flight path), whichever is higher.

Source: Active Pilot Monitoring Working Group

Fig 15-18.

In-flight profile examples of areas of vulnerability for flight path deviations.[57]

If you know which segments are most vulnerable to flight path deviations during a typical flight you can strategically plan your activities and workload to accommodate that. For example, you could defer non-flight path-related activities to periods of low vulnerability and plan to increase your attention/monitoring tasks—by increasing your monitoring sampling rate (*see* Chapter 14)—during periods of high vulnerability. Conducting an approach briefing before the top-of-descent (e.g., during level flight at cruise altitude) is a good example of this.

Use Appropriate Levels of Automation

Flight crews can choose to use different levels of automation, depending what their needs are for a given situation. For example, you can elect to use the highest level of automation, allowing the autopilot fly the airplane by following the commands of the FD and preprogrammed FMS; or you can use the lowest level of automation by electing to hand-fly the aircraft using manual thrust control and raw data received directly from navigation aids (not from the FD or FMS). Then, of course, you can choose something in between.

The point is, sometimes you need to recognize what is the most appropriate level for a given situation and use it. For example, using the highest level of automation—autopilot, autothrottle, FMS—may be ideal for long-term navigation, but could become cumbersome, distracting you from adequately monitoring the aircraft's flight path in the short-term for last-minute changes to vertical or lateral navigation (e.g., in response to ATC requests). Such short-term changes should be made using the autopilot MCP/FCU. In certain circumstances, it may even be appropriate to revert to manual control with or without FD guidance and/or autothrottle.[58] Remember, when the automation isn't doing what it should, you should reduce the level of automation to the lowest needed for safe flight, all the way to manual flight if required, and then re-establish automation once the issue is addressed.

Practice Manual Flying

As you have already seen, when it comes to automation, too much of a good thing can be dangerous. One of the threats of continuous use of autoflight systems is the degradation of manual flying skills: You can become so dependent on George that when you must reduce the level of automation and revert to manually flying the aircraft, you—like the pilots in the FSF study referred to earlier in this chapter—may not perform that well. That is why the FAA's SAFO 13002, *Manual Flight Operations*, now recommends that airlines and other operators promote manual flight operations both during training (initial, upgrade, and recurrent) and when flying on the line, as appropriate. They specifically encourage the practice of hand-flying the airplane during low workload conditions, such as in cruise flight. However, the FAA has actually gone one step further than making recommendations: As part of the final rule, titled "Qualification, Service and Use of Crewmembers and Aircraft Dispatchers," U.S. airlines will be required by 2019 to train and evaluate their pilots on "their ability to manually fly a departure sequence and arrival into an airport" and to prevent and recover from an aircraft upset (e.g., stall) using manual handling skills.[59]

Don't be like the majority of automation-addicted pilots in the study previously cited in this chapter who tend to overestimate their own manual proficiency. Proficiency is a state of being highly skilled or competent. You need to be highly skilled in manual flight skills not only when the automation is functioning, but when it fails. This latter task is even more challenging because you may also have to rely on raw data or even backup flight instrumentation should the electronic systems fail.

Consider the Airbus Golden Rules

Finally, whether you are just beginning to fly automated aircraft or you are an experienced line pilot, you can benefit from knowing the Airbus "Operations Golden Rules" used to train pilots on modern automated aircraft. These golden rules are briefly explained and elaborated upon after the summary in the information box.

Source: Airbus, "Standard Operating Procedures, Operations Golden Rules," *Flight Operations Briefing Notes* (Blagnac, France: January 2004).

1. **Automated aircraft can be flown like any other aircraft.** No matter the degree of automation sophistication, you always have the authority to revert to hand-flying using the yoke/side stick, rudder, and throttles/thrust levers.

2. **Aviate (fly), navigate, communicate, and manage—in that order.** Whether using the automated systems or not, your number one priority—for both normal and non-normal/ emergency situations—is to maintain control of the aircraft. You can delegate the stick-and-rudder skills aspects of this to the autopilot, but be very careful—if you don't adequately monitor the system to ensure it is maintaining the desired vertical and lateral flight path, it could kill you. Knowing where you are, where the terrain is and where you should be going (navigate) is your next priority, followed by communicating with ATC. To close the loop, you must continue to manage the flight. Table 15-4 specifies the EFIS components designed to help achieve these priorities.

3. **One head up at all times.** There should be one pilot monitoring the status of the aircraft, using the PFD, ND, and EICAS/ECAM at all times. Only one pilot should have their head down (e.g., looking at approach charts, programming the FMS) at a time. It is also best practice to announce you are going "head-down."

4. **Cross check the accuracy of the FMS.** Even if you are relying primarily on GPS for navigation, it is always a good idea to check the accuracy of FMS navigation using raw data such as VOR and DME when within navigational aid coverage. For example, you can compare the bearing (track) and distance indicated on the appropriate FMS page with the DME distance indicated on the radio magnetic indicator, ND, or MFD as applicable.

5. **Know your FMA at all times.** The primary interfaces the crew uses to communicate with the aircraft systems are the FCU and CDU. The primary interfaces the aircraft systems uses to communicate with the crew are the PFD and ND/MFD. Of particular importance are the symbols on the speed and altitude scales, and the mode annunciations on the FMA on the PFD. Both pilots should at all times be aware of modes armed and engaged, target airspeeds and altitudes set, the response of the aircraft to these inputs, and mode transitions and reversions (i.e., indirect uncommanded transitions).

6. **When things don't go as expected—take over.** If, for whatever reason, the aircraft is not maintaining the desired airspeed or altitude, or is not following the desired vertical and lateral flight paths, and time does not permit analyzing the cause of this behavior, reduce the level of automation and hand-fly the aircraft if necessary.

Table 15-4. Glass-cockpit design supports the Golden Rules.

Golden rule	Display unit
Aviate (fly)	Primary flight display (PFD)
Navigate	Navigation/multifunction display (ND/MFD)
Communicate	Communication radio and/or datalink control and display unit or controller pilot data link communication
Manage	Flight management system (FMS), control display unit (CDU), electronic centralized aircraft monitor (ECAM), or engine-indicating and crew-alerting system (EICAS)

7. **Use the proper level of automation for the task.** The correct level of automation depends on the task to be performed, the flight phase, and the time available. The correct level of automation often is the one you feel the most comfortable with and depends on your knowledge and experience of the aircraft and systems, your skills, and your confidence. Reverting to hand-flying and manual thrust-control may be the correct level of automation for the prevailing conditions.

8. **Practice task sharing and back-up each other.** For all operations (normal, non-normal, or emergency conditions) the flight crew should share tasks, effectively cross-check, and backup each other during all ground and flight operations. This involves using effective monitoring strategies (*see* Chapter 14) and utilizing effective crew resource management (CRM) skills (*see* Chapter 19).

Over the years, pilots have often experienced a love-hate relationship with the machines they fly. Advances in flight deck control and display design, which have sought to accommodate the information processing needs of the human operator, have gradually improved this relationship and made flight operations safer. So too have advances in automation. Automated flight control systems bring several benefits to the task of flying, but as we have seen, placing too much reliance upon them creates its own set of problems that sometimes threatens the safety of flight. You should NEVER completely trust automation. For that matter, you should never completely trust yourself or the partner you share the flight deck with—double-check everything you both do with the automation and double-check the information you think it is telling you. You should never surrender your authority to a machine; it is a tool, an instrument of *your* will. *You* fly the aircraft—don't ever let it fly you. *You* are still the pilot-in-command and retain the right to use, or not use, the automated systems on your aircraft as you see fit. If it's not submitting to your will, disconnect the automation and *make* the aircraft do what *you* want it to do. As a grumpy old commander once said, "It is no sin if the aircraft is not doing what you want it to do, but it is if you continue to let it."

Helpful Resources

The free online FAA *Human Factors Awareness Course* has separate modules on displays (both visual and non-visual) and controls. (www.hf.faa.gov/webtraining/Intro/Intro1.htm)

A thorough exploration of the China Airlines A300 accident (discussed in this chapter's introduction), including an animation of the accident, can be found at the FAA's Lessons Learned library web site. (lessonslearned.faa.gov/ll_main.cfm?TabID=3&LLID=64&LLTypeID=0)

The FAA's 2013 SAFO 13002, *Manual Flight Operations*, encourages airlines and other operators to promote manual flight operations. (www.faa.gov/other_visit/aviation_industry/airline_operators/airline_safety/safo/all_safos/)

The Flight Safety Foundation's 2014 *A Practical Guide for Improving Flight Path Monitoring: Final Report of the Active Pilot Monitoring Working Group* is very helpful. (www.flightsafety.org/toolkits-resources/flight-path-monitoring/)

Endnotes

1. National Transportation Safety Board, *Safety Recommendation*, A-06-48 through -51 (Washington, DC: July 10, 2006).

2. Aircraft Accident Investigation Commission, Ministry of Transport of Japan, *Aircraft Accident Investigation Report 96-5: China Airlines, Airbus Industrie A300B4-622R, B1816, Nagoya Airport, April 26, 1994* (July 19, 1996).

3. Delmar M. Fadden, "Display Design," *Human Factors for Flight Deck Certification Personnel: Final Report, July 1993*, DOT/FAA/RD-93/5, eds. Kim Cardosi and M. Stephen Huntley (Cambridge, MA: U.S. DOT, Research and Special Programs Administration, John A. Volpe National Transportation Systems Center, May 1994): 243–268.

4. Stanley N. Roscoe, "Airborne Displays for Flight and Navigation," *Human Factors* 10 (August 1, 1968): 321–332.

5. Christpher D. Wickens, "Aviation Displays," *Principles and Practice of Aviation Psychology*, eds. Pamela S. Tsang and Michael A. Vidulich (Mahwah, NJ: Lawrence Erlbaum Associates, 2003).

6. Roscoe, "Airborne Displays for Flight and Navigation."

7. Ibid.

8. Wickens, "Aviation Displays."

9. David J. Osborne, *Ergonomics at Work* (New York: John Wiley & Sons, 1982).

10. Jack J. Shrager, *A Summary On Altitude Displays With An Annotated Bibliography*, Report No. FAA-R0-72-46 (National Aviation Facilities Experimental Center, Atlantic City, NJ: 1972).

11. Jiajie Zhang, Kathy A. Johnson, Jane T. Malin and Jack W. Smith, "Human-Centered Information Visualization," (2002). Available at www.semanticscholar.org/paper/Human-Centered-Information-Visualization-Zhang-Johnson/1452983a25d1ac559c91bf2698cd89925dc3967a.

12. Paul M. Fitts and R.E. Jones, *Psychological Aspects of Instrument Display I: Analysis of 270 "Pilot-Error" Experiences in Reading and Interpreting Aircraft Instruments*, Memorandum Report TSEAA-694-12A (Dayton, OH: USAF, October 1, 1947).

13. Shrager, *A Summary On Altitude Displays With An Annotated Bibliography*.

14. Data taken from Shrager, *A Summary On Altitude Displays With An Annotated Bibliography*. 30.

15. National Transportation Safety Board, *Aircraft Accident Report, United Air Lines, Inc., B-727, N7036U In Lake Michigan, August 16, 1965*, File 1-0030 (Washington, DC: December 19, 1967).

16. Richard Sulzer, *Transport Aircraft Cockpit Standardization (Federal Aviation Regulations Part 25)*, DOT/FAA/EM-81/11 (Atlantic City, NJ: FAA Technical Center, November 1981).

17. These quotes taken from Alan Diehl, "General Aviation Cockpit Design Features Related to Inadvertent Landing Gear Retraction Accidents," *Proceedings of the First Symposium on Aviation Psychology*, ed. Richard S. Jensen (Columbus, OH: The Ohio State University, April 21 and 22, 1981): 84–93.

18. Roscoe, "Airborne Displays for Flight and Navigation."

19. Ibid.

20. Wickens, "Aviation Displays."

21. Interstate Aviation Committee, *Air Accident Investigation Commission (AAIC) Aircraft Accident Final Report, Boeing 737-505, VP-BKO, Aeroflot-Nord Airline, Russia, near Bolshoye Savino Airport, Perm, 13 September 2008* (English translation). Available at www.aviation-safety.net/database/record.php?id=20080914-0.

22. Mark Lacagnina, "Misgauged Recovery," *AeroSafety World* (July 2010): 18–21.

23. Earl L. Wiener and Renwick E. Curry, *Flight Deck Automation: Promises and Problems,* NASA Technical Memorandum 81206 (Moffett Field, CA: NASA, June 1980): 13.

24. William Scheck, "Lawrence Sperry: Genius on Autopilot," *Aviation History Magazine* (November 15, 2017).

25. Navigation Display (ND) of the Boeing 747-400, by Saschaporsche, June 24, 2011 (https://commons.wikimedia.org/wiki/File:Navigation_Display_(ND)_on_Boeing_747-400.jpg) WC CC BY-SA 3.0

26. Federal Aviation Administration, *Instrument Flying Handbook*, FAA-H-8083-15B (Washington, DC: FAA, 2012).

27. The anthropomorphic title of "George" has often been used to describe the autopilot. The exact reason why is uncertain, but it has been suggested that the practice comes from the name of George DeBeeson who collaborated with Lawrence Sperry to patent the "Automatic Airplane Control" autopilot in 1931. *See* Tom Benenson, "Let 'George' Do It," *Flying* (September 3, 2009).

28. An fuller explanation of the Airbus A330 electrical flight control system (EFCS), including fly-by-wire and flight control laws, is found in: Australian Transport Safety Bureau, *Aviation Occurrence Investigation: In-flight upset 154 km west of Learmonth, WA, 7 October 2008, VH-QPA, Airbus A330-303*, ATSB TRANSPORT SAFETY REPORT AO-2008-070 (ATSB, Canberra, Australia, December 2011): 10–12.

29. Australian Bureau of Air Safety Investigation (BASI), *Advanced Technology Aircraft Safety Survey Report* (June 1998).

30. *Report on the Accident to Indian Airlines Airbus A320-231 Aircraft VT-EPN on 14th February, 1990 at Bangalore* (Government of India, Ministry of Civil Aviation). A better reference is lessonslearned.faa.gov/ll_main.cfm?TabID=1&LLID=71&faa_keyword=indian

31. Barbara Holder, *Airline Pilot Perceptions of Training Effectiveness* (Flight Deck Concept Center, Boeing Commercial Airplanes, 2012).

32. Daniel J. Boorman and Randall J. Mumaw, *A New Autoflight/FMS Interface: Guiding Design Principles* (Boeing Commercial Airplanes, 2004).

33. Charles E. Billings, *Human Centered Aviation Automation: Principles and Guidelines*, NASA Technical Memorandum 110381 (February 1996).

34. Ibid., 92.

35. Anjali Joshi, Steven P. Miller and Mats P.E. Heimdahl, *Mode Confusion Analysis of a Flight Guidance System Using Formal Methods* (22nd IEEE Digital Avionics Systems Conference, October 2003).

36. Billings, *Human Centered Aviation Automation*, 63.

37. Nancy Leveson, L. Denise Pinnel, Sean David Sandys, Shuichi Koga and Jon Damon Reese, "Analyzing Software Specifications for Mode Confusion Potential," *Proceedings of a Workshop on Human Error and System Development* (Glascow, 1997).

38. Air Accident Investigation Sector, *Accident—Preliminary Report—Runway Impact During Attempted Go-Around at Dubai International Airport, Boeing 777-31H, A6-EMW, August 3, 2016*, AAIS Case No: AIFN/0008/2016 (The United Arab Emirates: General Civil Aviation Authority, September 5, 2016).

39. Flight Deck Automation Working Group, *Operational Use of Flight Path Management Systems: Final Report of the Performance-Based Operations Aviation Rulemaking Committee/Commercial Aviation Safety Team Flight Deck Automation Working Group* (September 5, 2013): 7.

40. Aeronautica Civil of The Republic of Colombia, *Aircraft Accident Report: Controlled Flight Into Terrain, American Airlines Flight 965, Boeing 757-223, N651AA, Near Cali, Colombia, December 20, 1995* trans. Peter B. Ladkin (Santafe de Bogota D.C., Colombia: Aeronautica Civil of The Republic of Colombia, September 1996). Available in English at www.rvs.uni-bielefeld.de/publications/Incidents/DOCS/ComAndRep/Cali/calirep.html.

41. Earl L. Wiener, *Human Factors of Advanced Technology ("Glass Cockpit") Transport Aircraft*, NASA Contractor Report 177528 (Moffett Field, CA: NASA Ames Research Center, June 1989).

42. Anynobody, November 25, 2007 (https://commons.wikimedia.org/wiki/File:747-CA006-1.png) WC CC BY-SA 3.0

43. U.S. Department of Transportation, *Enhanced FAA Oversight Could Reduce Hazards Associated With Increased Use of Flight Deck Automation*, Office of Inspector General Audit Report Number AV-2016-013 (Washington, DC: FAA, January 7, 2016).

44. Michael W. Gillen, "Diminishing Skills?" *AeroSafety World* (July 2010): 30–34. Available at www.flightsafety.org/asw/email/asw_july10_notify.html.

45. U.S. Department of Transportation, *Enhanced FAA Oversight*, 10.

46. Flight Deck Automation Working Group, *Operational Use of Flight Path Management Systems*.

47. Stephen M. Casner, Richard W. Geven, Matthias P. Recker and Jonathan W. Schooler, "The Retention of Manual Flying Skills in the Automated Cockpit," *Human Factors* 56 (December 2014): 1506–1516.

48. U.S. Department of Transportation, *Enhanced FAA Oversight*, 12.

49. Ibid., 14.

50. Marianne Rudisill, *Crew/Automation Interaction in Space Transportation Systems: Lessons Learned from the Glass Cockpit*, NASA Technical Report (NASA Langley Research Center, Hampton, VA: Jan 1, 2000).

51. Federal Aviation Administration, *Approval of Flight Guidance Systems*, AC No. 25-1329-1C (Washington, DC: May 24, 2016).

52. Commercial Aviation Safety Team, *Mode Awareness and Energy State Management Aspects of Flight Deck Automation, Final Report*, Safety Enhancement 30 Revision-5 (August 2008): 3.

53. Holder, *Airline Pilot Perceptions of Training Effectiveness*, 1.

54. Ibid., 2.

55. Commercial Aviation Safety Team, *Mode Awareness*, 6.

56. Ibid.

57. Flight Safety Foundation, *A Practical Guide for Improving Flight Path Monitoring: Final Report of the Active Pilot Monitoring Working Group* (November 2014). Used by permission by the Flight Safety Foundation.

58. Commercial Aviation Safety Team, *Mode Awareness*, 5–6.

59. U.S. Department of Transportation, *Enhanced FAA Oversight*, 13.

16

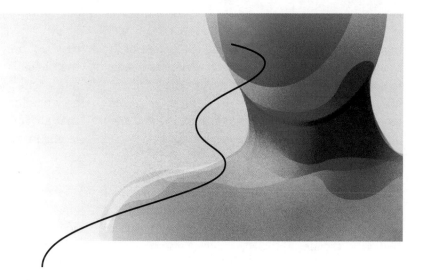

Don't forget to remember.

Memory

It was Christmas Day when the Pan American Clipper, a Boeing B-707, departed San Francisco. Flight 799 was loaded with cargo and mail for delivery to Cam Ranh Bay, Vietnam, via Tokyo, with a refueling stop and crew change at Anchorage International Airport in Alaska. The weather was below IFR landing minimums when they arrived, so they diverted to nearby Elmendorf AFB, also in Anchorage. The captain, FO, and FE drove from Anchorage, met the arriving crew at Elmendorf, and prepared for departure as the airplane was refueled.

However, the flight experienced several unanticipated delays before it was able to depart. A discrepancy in the computation of the mixed fuel density meant they had to add more fuel. They also had some difficulty getting the jet starter unit to provide power for the engine start. Originally cleared for Runway 05, the crew requested Runway 23 because of its greater useable length. However, they were unfamiliar with the airport and faced additional challenges as they taxied in the dark. The taxiways were covered in patchy ice and loose snow, the visibility was poor in ice crystals and fog, and a portion of the lights on one of the taxiways was unserviceable. Fortunately, the airport provided a "follow me" truck to guide the captain as he taxied to the runway.

They became quite occupied with a variety of duties once they got moving—the captain was trying to safely maneuver the heavy aircraft on the slippery taxiway, and the FO, in addition to completing his regular duties of accomplishing checklists and other matters, was busy handling numerous radio calls with various ATC facilities to coordinate their departure time. Since several international flights overfly or make refueling stops at Anchorage, the Oceanic Control Coordinator (OCC) at the Air Route Traffic Control Center needed to coordinate flights so departing aircraft wouldn't violate separation with en route aircraft flying over the Pacific Ocean. They assigned 20-minute block times for aircraft flying at the same flight level and issued "clearance void times" to departing aircraft. If an aircraft was unable to depart before that time, the crew needed to request another clearance void time from the OCC. Their void time had already been extended six times and if they didn't make their final void time of 0615 hours, ATC informed them they would be delayed another 45 minutes.

Finally, just 30 seconds shy of their clearance void time, they were cleared for takeoff. Nothing appeared out of the ordinary as they accelerated down the runway. However, as they lifted off after a V_R of 154 knots, the airplane became uncontrollable with the nose pitching up and down and the wings rolling left and right. Less than a minute after applying takeoff thrust, all three crew members lost their lives and the aircraft was destroyed as it crashed about 3,100 feet beyond the end of the runway.

The cause of this tragic accident? The crew forgot to extend the wing flaps for takeoff, and the takeoff warning system (TOWS) horn, designed to warn the crew of such an improper configuration, failed to activate. Trailing edge wing flaps, and in most modern transport category airplanes leading edge slats, are high lift devices that increase the coefficient of lift reducing the airspeed and takeoff distances needed to safely become airborne. The crew knew the critical importance of extending the flaps to the recommended setting—in this case 14 degrees—and they obviously thought they had been set since they had calculated their takeoff speeds (V_1, V_R, and V_2) based on that setting. In fact, the FO lowered the flaps before taxi during the initial reading of the taxi portion of the checklist, but the captain, for reasons which will be discussed shortly, raised them as they began to taxi. The FO even said, *"Okay, let's not forget them."* But they did forget, and the basic human factors question is, why?

It appears there were several reasons. The captain was preoccupied with carefully taxiing in less-than-ideal conditions and the FO was quite absorbed with coordinating departure times with ATC. Also, in the attempt to make their ATC void-time deadline they were rushed. And we all know it's easy to forget something when you're rushed. These factors, and more, were echoed in one of the findings in the NTSB accident report: "The crew was operating in a stressful environment created by lack of familiarity with the airport, adverse weather conditions, darkness, cumulative delays, and a self-imposed time envelope."[1]

But other matters beyond the crew's control also contributed to their forgetfulness. The reason the captain raised the wing flaps after the FO had extended them was to comply with the company's cold weather operating procedures. These stated that wing flaps should be left in the UP position until lined up for takeoff to reduce the chance of snow or ice being blown onto the flap mechanisms, which could adversely affect their operation (a wise and common practice, even today). However, there was no provision on the airline's before-takeoff checklist to remind the flight crew that the flaps should

be set: It only appeared once, on the taxi portion of the checklist. The NTSB cited this lack of critical reminder as one of the factors that contributed to the crew's failure to set the flaps and they recommended that air carriers review their flight deck checklists to ensure that they provided a means of reminding the crew, immediately prior to takeoff, that all items *critical for safe flight* had been accomplished.

Finally, the design of the TOWS, which alerted the crew if they forgot to properly set the flaps for takeoff, was such that the switch might not arm the system in very cold weather. Since engine pressure ratio (EPR) settings needed to achieve recommended takeoff thrust are typically lower in cold temperatures—it was 6°F (–14°C) at the time of the crash—the desired EPR on the B-707 could be reached before the thrust levers advanced to the 42 degree thrust-lever angle needed to actuate the TOWS. Boeing warned operators of this problem two years previously and recommended a modification that involved lowering the angle (to 25 degrees) at which the switch would activate should the aircraft be improperly configured. Unfortunately, the airline did not implement Service Bulletin 2384 for this airplane, nor was it required to do so by the FAA. In its report the NTSB, however, chastised Boeing for not making the bulletin more definitive, Pan American for not adequately evaluating the potential hazards involved in their operational environment (i.e., cold weather operations), and the FAA for not making the recommended change a higher priority at the time of initial service bulletin review.

Many improvements have been made since that terrible accident in 1968—regulations have been implemented, training has been enhanced, checklist procedures have been improved, and warning devices have been made more reliable. However, pilots still forget to select takeoff flaps before departure, as the accident list in Table 16-1 tragically shows.

Table 16-1. Partial list fatal accidents involving loss of control after takeoff due to improper flap configuration.

Date	Operator	Aircraft	Location	Fatalities
Aug 20, 2008	Spanair, Flight 5022	MD-82	Madrid, Spain	154
Sep 5, 2005	Mandala, Flight 091	B-737	Medan, Indonesia	149
Aug 31, 1999	LAPA, Flight 3142	B-737	Buenos Aires, Argentina	65
Aug 31, 1988	Delta, Flight 1141	B-727	Dallas-Fort Worth, TX	14
Aug 16, 1987	Northwest, Flight 255	DC-9	Romulus, MI	156
Nov 20, 1974	Lufthansa, Flight 540	B-747	Nairobi, Kenya	59

We forget things all the time: a phone number, a scheduled appointment, where we put our car keys. The consequences of such memory lapses, as they are often called, are usually not severe while moving about on terra firma; but, as we have seen, they can be deadly while navigating in the air. Fortunately, the aviation industry has long recognized the threat that memory failures play in causing aircraft accidents and has developed processes and procedures designed to reduce them.

However, the human condition hasn't changed, and memory failures still jeopardize safe flight operations. Recently, for example, an unattended crash fire rescue (CFR) vehicle rolled into a stationary Boeing B-757 at John Wayne/Orange County Airport in California; a near-midair collision (NMAC) occurred between a Bombardier CL-600 and an Embraer ERJ-145 regional jet at Chicago O'Hare International Airport; and a Beechcraft 35 received substantial damage during a landing on Runway 13R at King County International Airport (Boeing Field) near Seattle, Washington. The CFR vehicle driver forgot to set the parking brake, the Chicago tower controller cleared the ERJ for takeoff but forgot about the presence of the CL-600 on final approach, and the pilot of the Beechcraft forgot to lower the landing gear before landing (NTSB Identification No: LAX03LA167; OPS11IA552B; WPR13CA422).

But these examples barely scratch the surface: A cursory glance at ASRS incidents for a recent two-year period reveals a multitude of critical items that pilots failed to remember. The following are just a few:

- A crew on approach to Runway 28R at O'Hare International Airport executed a go-around after remembering at the outer marker that the runway was closed. The crew forgot to change the arrival data in the FMS (ASRS Report No: 1245537).
- A Bombardier CRJ-200 flight crew forgot to remove the standby pitot tube cover, while a Gulfstream G280 FO forgot to remove a static port cover. Both flights returned safely to their departure airports after the crews' realized their errors (ASRS Report No: 1336776; 1241462).

- The flight crews of an Embraer ERJ-175 and another regional jet both landed without a clearance because they forgot to switch over to tower frequency (ASRS Report No: 1296001; 1236264).
- An Embraer EMB-145 captain forgot to call for the delayed engine start checklist. After being cleared for takeoff the crew discovered they had forgotten to start engine number one (ASRS Report No: 1394157).
- The propeller of a Piper PA-28 struck a tow bar during taxi because the flight instructor forgot to remove it, and a Grumman American AA-5B pilot forgot to remove the tow bar from the aircraft but was able to depart with it still attached (ASRS Report No: 1276043; 1305020)!
- A Cessna 402 pilot forgot to turn the alternators ON after engine start and, when nearing his destination, the aircraft lost all electrical power from the depleted batteries (ASRS Report No: 1263158).
- A Cirrus SR22 pilot forgot to reinstall both fuel caps after refueling and flew for about an hour before he was notified that someone found one of the caps on the apron (ASRS Report No: 1288561).
- A Mooney M20 pilot, a Cessna 310 pilot, a Lake Amphibian pilot, and an experienced pilot and his flight instructor in their Piper PA-44 Seminole, all forgot to extend the landing gear resulting in a gear-up landing. A Beechcraft BE-76 pilot also forgot to remember this critical task but was able to execute a go-around at the last second, but the propeller still hit the runway (ASRS Report No: 1390174; 1280039; 1300812; 1255934; 1297315).
- An air carrier crew forgot to retract the landing gear on a go-around at Newark Liberty Airport, and an Airbus A320 crew did the same after departing Phoenix Sky Harbor Airport, resulting in the aircraft exceeding the safe gear retraction speed (ASRS Report No: 1332015; 1230642).
- The FO of a McDonnell Douglas MD-11 forgot that he was hand-flying the airplane and wondered why it started to turn and didn't level off on its own (ASRS Report No: 1272134).

One of the most effective ways to guard against memory lapses, especially when you need to accomplish lengthy procedures, is to use checklists. But what if you forget to use the checklist, as the crew members in the following incidents recently did?

- An MD-11 flight crew averted a catastrophe by conducting a rejected takeoff on Runway 25R at Los Angeles International Airport when the TOWS sounded; they failed to properly configure the flaps because they forgot to accomplish items on the before-takeoff checklist (ASRS Report No: 1306536).
- After a short taxi and an immediate takeoff clearance, a Boeing B-737 flight crew, also departing out of Los Angeles, discovered they forgot to complete the before-takeoff checklist resulting in incorrect settings for the start switches and transponder and flight attendants not being properly seated when the takeoff was commenced (ASRS Report No: 1304044).
- A CRJ-900 captain forgot to finish the shutdown checklist and left the APU running; it wasn't until he was on his way to his hotel in the shuttle van that he realized his mistake (ASRS Report No: 1368646)!

Air traffic controllers also forget things. The worst runway incursion accident on U.S. soil occurred when a B-737, after landing on Runway 24L, collided with a Metroliner SA-227 at Los Angeles International Airport in February 1991. The controller cleared USAir Flight 1493 to land but forgot that she had also cleared SkyWest Flight 5569 to taxi to position and hold on the runway. The USAir crew reported that they never saw the Metro until their landing lights illuminated it after the nose wheel touched down on the runway during the landing rollout. Both aircraft were destroyed by the impact and post-crash fire and 34 people—all 12 occupants on the Metro and two crew members and ten passengers on the B-737—died in the accident (Report No: NTSB/AAR-91/08).

A study of controller errors and deviations at the busiest control towers in the U.S., published a decade after this accident, found that the number one cause of operational errors in 251 reports analyzed was that the controller forgot something: an aircraft they had cleared for takeoff, landing, to position and hold,

or to cross a runway; a vehicle on a runway; or the fact that a runway was closed.[2]

The prevalence of these types of incidents involving pilots and controllers (not to mention aviation maintenance technicians) illustrates the limitations of another crucial component of human cognitive performance: memory. Information received by our senses, which is attended to and successfully identified during the perceptual stage of information processing, moves into our memory system so it can be used later (*see* Figure 3-5 in Chapter 3). Memory is the process by which information is stored in our brain and many mental operations—such as perception, attention, problem solving, and decision making—are dependent upon it. For example, short-term memory is needed to remember radio frequencies, ATC-assigned altitudes and headings, and minimum altitudes for instrument approaches. Long-term memory is relied upon to visually recognize previously learned geographical landmarks, including airports, and to remember how aircraft systems work, the details of a weather forecast, and the actions to take in an emergency.

Storage Box Model of Memory

The storage-box model of memory, sometimes called the Atkinson-Shiffrin model after the researchers who proposed it in the 1960s, was one of the first comprehensive models of memory that is still used today. It postulates three basic types of memory using storage boxes as an analogy: short-term sensory information storage (or *sensory memory*), where inputs from our senses are momentarily available for possible processing in short-term memory; short-term memory (more commonly called *working memory*), where attended information is stored, elaborated upon and available for retrieval for a longer, yet still relatively short period of time; and long-term memory, where well-learned information is stored for an indefinite period.[3] Some have likened the transient information stored in short-term memory to the random-access memory (RAM) found on a computer, while information stored in long-term memory is analogous to the information stored on its hard disk drive. Figure 16-1 is a simple visual representation of the storage box model of memory.

Fig 16-1.

Storage box model of memory. Sensory information that is attended to reaches short-term (working) memory; coded items make it to long-term memory for later retrieval.

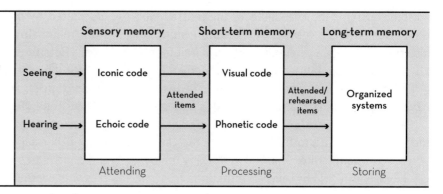

Sensory Memory

At any given moment, when we are awake at least, our senses receive vast amounts of stimuli (inputs or information) from the outside world. Our eyes detect a variety of colors and intensities of light. Our ears hear sounds of varying pitch and volume. We may smell different odors though our nose, feel different textures with our hands, and sense different tastes from receptors in our tongue. For items to remain in memory, an internal mental representation of the external sensory stimuli must be created, or *encoded*, for processing. Each sensory modality encodes information in its own way. For example, visual information is encoded as a mental picture, or icon, in the *iconic* image store. Auditory information is encoded acoustically—that is, verbally, by the sounds of the words—in what researchers call the *echoic* store.

Even though short-term sensory storage (STSS), or **sensory memory** "holds virtually all the information impinging on a particular sense organ,"[4] it can do so for only a few seconds—unless it is attended to and transferred into short-term working memory. This transfer process is facilitated in part when items in sensory memory match previously learned patterns in long-term memory; a process called pattern recognition. Results of experiments indicate that visual sensory information in the visual STSS (*iconic* store) lasts for only about one-half second to 1 second, whereas auditory sensory information in the acoustic STSS (*echoic* store) lasts up to maybe 1 to 2 seconds.

Working Memory

Sensory information that is attended to is transferred into **working memory** (*see* Figure 16-1), also called short-term memory (STM) because retention of stored items is limited to a maximum of about 15–20 seconds (if no rehearsal takes place). As its name implies, working memory is the mechanism whereby

we consciously process information from both our environment (received in the STSS) and from information retrieved from long-term memory to perform cognitive activities, or **mental operations**, such as attending, thinking, reasoning, problem solving, and decision making. Working memory is not just a memory storage system, but an attentional system as well.[5] One of the reasons working memory is so important is that it is where information is manipulated. For example, when you make calculations on the fly, such as estimating the rate of descent needed to reach a desired altitude by a certain time or fix, calculating your ETA at your destination, or mentally comparing ceiling and visibility values of possible alternate airports that you just received from an in-flight briefing from the flight service specialist over the radio, you are using your working memory.

According to one of the world's leading researchers in this field, working memory is not, like the original box-model of memory suggests, a single unitary storehouse of temporary information: It entails multiple components, including a separate storage for verbal information (called the *phonological loop*), visual and spatial information (called the *visual-spatial sketchpad*), and events (the *episodic buffer*)—all controlled and manipulated by a *central executive* that interfaces with attention and coordinates the flow of information between the three STM storage systems and long-term memory.[6]

Evidence for these three distinct storage systems comes from numerous studies, including research indicating that performance suffers when a person simultaneously performs two tasks using the same sensory modality (e.g., two auditory tasks, or two visual tasks) yet is not significantly impacted when performing two tasks using two different modalities (e.g., an auditory task and a visual task). This multiple component model of STM proposes that the episodic buffer is indispensable for the central executive: Not only is it a memory store for events, but also the mechanism whereby short-term inputs from all the sensory modalities are manipulated and integrated into a whole. It is also believed to be involved in various types of encoding into long-term memory.[7]

Virtually all mental operations depend on working memory processing to function. Nevertheless, our ability to remember items stored in working memory is adversely affected by several limitations.

Rehearsal

Auditory, or articulatory, rehearsal involves vocal or mental (subvocal) repetition of an auditory input in the *phonological loop* (sometimes called the articulatory loop). Visual information is also maintained in working memory via the visual-spatial sketchpad by attending to or manipulating a visual image or spatial location in the mind. Maintenance rehearsal involves inserting the information back into working memory (through the phonological/articulatory loop) using simple rote techniques, such as repeating (out loud or in thought) a decision altitude (DA) several times while conducting an ILS approach, or repeating a transponder code or ILS frequency while dialing it into the appropriate avionics device. Have you ever looked up a phone number and by the time you reach for the phone to dial it you've forgotten it? This is an example of how information—especially meaningless information—can decay if not rehearsed. It is the reason why radio advertisers repeat their 1-800 number so many times during one commercial: they know about the transience of information held in working memory. Elaborative rehearsal, on the other hand, involves relating the new information to previously learned material. This type of rehearsal is generally more effective in storing information into long-term memory.

Interference

Unrehearsed information in working memory decays quite quickly, but interference from both new and previously learned information can also interfere with remembering new information held in working memory. **Retroactive interference** occurs when new information/activity interferes with the recall of previously stored information in long-term memory or material to be remembered (MTBR) in working memory. For example, when trying to dial a new phone number, you forget it because you were distracted by an interruption that prevented you from rehearsing it in the phonological/articulatory loop. Pilots face challenges with this type of interference when trying to remember ATC instructions or clearances. For example, you receive a heading and altitude clearance by a controller, after which you are immediately questioned by the captain about some other aspect of the flight status unrelated to the controller's clearance. If this distraction occupies your working memory long enough, the original ATC instruction will drop out of the loop and you will forget it.

Proactive interference occurs when previously learned information/activity interferes with the recall of new information in working memory. For example, when trying to dial a new phone number, a previously learned number similar to the new one may interfere with your ability to remember it. Or, when a student pilot is first learning a new psychomotor skill (e.g., taxiing an airplane using rudder inputs) a previously learned psychomotor skill may interfere causing her or him to make the wrong response (e.g., taxiing an airplane using aileron inputs). This latter example, where the previous learning of steering an automobile interferes with steering an airplane, is also an example of negative transfer of training/learning (*see* the discussion in previous chapter).

Proactive interference also occurs with ATC clearances. For example, if you receive a clearance for one thing (e.g., a speed to climb at and an altitude to climb to) and only a couple of seconds later receive an additional clearance (e.g., a heading to fly), the first clearance may interfere with the recall of the second—especially if similar numbers are involved (*see* Chapter 13 for examples). In a study of controller-pilot communications, researchers found that proactive interference is reduced if the time between two distinct ATC clearances is at least 10 seconds.[8]

Researchers have also discovered that interference is usually worse if the MTBR and the interfering information/activity is from the same sensory modality. For example, spatial and visual information/activity interferes with spatial/visual recall more than with verbal recall; and verbal information/activity interferes with verbal recall more than with spatial/visual recall.[9] This partly explains the phenomenon noted previously—that performance is significantly degraded when you try to perform two concurrent tasks using the same sensory modality compared to doing the tasks alone or with another task that uses a different modality (e.g., an auditory task and a visual task). It is believed that rather than drawing upon one undifferentiated pool and competing for the same limited resource, there are several distinct resource pools each corresponding to a particular modality. For example, research seems to indicate that there is one pool for visual/spatial information and another for processing verbal/phonetic information.[10] Somewhat analogous to the ability to walk and read a newspaper at the same time, this multiple resource theory explains why a pilot can engage in two (or more) different modal tasks simultaneously such as talking to ATC and looking for aircraft traffic at the same time.

Confusion

Related to interference is confusion. Similar items held in working memory simultaneously can be confused with each other. For example, controllers experience confusion when managing two or more aircraft from different airlines with the same call number (e.g., UAL 123, DAL 123) or from the same airline with similar call signs (e.g., UAL 123, UAL 213), the latter being usually more problematic than the former.[11] A study of 386 ASRS reports during a five-year period found that aircraft with similar call signs were the biggest factor in miscommunications between pilots and ATC contributing to 54 percent of incidents involving pilots accepting clearances intended for other aircraft, 21 percent of loss-of-separation incidents and 43 percent of NMACs.[12] This problem is compounded at busy airports that have high-traffic volumes and a higher proportion of **stepped-on transmissions** (two talking on the same frequency at once). Chapter 13 probed more deeply into some of these confusions.

Capacity

As noted, there is also a limit to how much information can be held in working memory at one time. As its title indicates, George Miller's classic paper, *The Magical Number Seven, Plus or Minus Two: Some Limits on Our Capacity for Processing Information*, published more than 60 years ago, suggested the limit is about five to nine items.[13] It is generally agreed that Miller's numbers are somewhat optimistic for most people and that it may be closer to only about four or five items. But it depends on the nature of the MTBR (digits,

letters, words, etc.). For example, four five-letter words (for a total of 20 letters—considerably more single items than what can normally be remembered in working memory) can be recalled from working memory because the letters are recoded into meaningful wholes (i.e., words), or patterns, stored in long-term memory. Each unrelated letter taken alone is considered a *chunk* of information, but so too are five related letters grouped into a word. Therefore, more information can be recalled if grouped together into higher-information chunks. For example, you would have difficulty remembering all 15 letters if they were read to you as follows, with a slight pause at each hyphen: DF-WSF-OJF-KL-AXM-IA. But if you chunked them into meaningful wholes, like DFW-SFO-JFK-LAX-MIA, you would have less difficulty.

Chunking even works for spatial/visual information. When asked to remember the locations of the pieces placed on a chess board, researchers found there was no difference in recall performance between novice and expert chess players when the pieces were arranged randomly. However, when the pieces were arranged according to the recognized patterns of normal game-piece movement, the experts had superior memory, presumably because of chunking into familiar patterns stored in long-term memory.[14]

Pilots face working memory capacity challenges when ATC includes too much information in a clearance. For example, it is recommended that controllers give pilots no more than three pieces of information in a single clearance. The reason is that several studies indicate that pilots inaccurately remember the details of longer and more complex clearances, often requiring the controller to repeat them. For example, multiple instructions given by a controller in the same transmission are involved in almost half of all altitude deviations; clearances containing five or more pieces of information account for about a quarter of readback errors; and almost two-thirds of pilots who had difficulty remembering ATC ground instructions said that controllers speak too rapidly and their transmissions contain too much information.[15] For these reasons, it is also recommended that controllers speak slowly and distinctly, especially when conversing with foreign pilots, whose native language is not English.

Long-Term Memory

Our knowledge of people's faces, names, and personal characteristics, our understanding of concepts and facts, our comprehension of spatial locations, and details of events that we have experienced—virtually everything we have learned, including the stick-and-rudder skills needed to fly an aircraft—resides in what is called our **long-term memory (LTM)**. When you memorize something, you are putting it into LTM. The quantity of information and the length of time it resides in LTM is theoretically unlimited. But people do forget things stored in LTM.

Figure 16-2 illustrates LTM is generally divided into two types: explicit and implicit. Explicit memory (also called declarative memory because the memories can be verbalized, or *declared*) involves conscious recall of facts, concepts and ideas (**semantic memory**) and events and experiences that have occurred in your life (**episodic memory**). There are various categories of implicit (*non-declarative*) memory, but the one most applicable to flight operations involves using previously learned psychomotor skills to do things such as hand-fly an aircraft (called **procedural memory**). Because these motor skills are so well-learned, this type of memory—sometimes called *muscle memory*—doesn't involve much, if any, conscious thought. Explicit memory is mostly about knowing *what* while implicit memory is about knowing *how*. Completing checklists may involve a combination of explicit and implicit LTM since this involves frequent repetition of procedures and motor actions (setting flaps, checking gauges etc.).

Encoding

Information in working memory is transferred into LTM storage if it is consciously attended to and encoded (*see* Figure 16-1). Information is encoded several ways: visual or spatial information in the visual-spatial sketchpad is encoded as an image or location, and auditory information is encoded acoustically, or *phonetically*, by the sounds the words make. In sensory memory we referred to these as *iconic* and *echoic* encoding, respectively (*see* the sensory memory in Figure 16-1).

One way of transferring information from working memory to LTM is by rehearsing it—the more something is rehearsed, or repeated, the greater the chance it will enter LTM. The example of repeating a phone number in order to remember it until we dialed it on the telephone was previously used. This rehearsal is a type of acoustic (or phonetic) coding that occurs in the phonological/articulatory loop. This loop gets its name from the idea that storage of transient phonologic information (e.g., sounds of speech) involves repeating it over and over (in a loop) to keep it from dropping out of working memory. An interesting aspect of written language is even though you might think it would normally be coded visually as an image in the visual-spatial sketchpad, it is often converted into phonetic coding while reading. When reading, have you ever found yourself vocalizing (mentally, not out loud) and maybe even moving your lips slightly? This subvocalization, sometimes called *implicit speech* or an *inner voice*, involves speaking to yourself—inside your head—and involves switching visual images on the printed page into auditory inputs in the phonological loop.

Of course, as also discussed, elaborative rehearsal is more effective than maintenance rehearsal since the MTBR is linked in some way to previously learned material stored in LTM. Information stored in LTM, however, is mostly coded semantically, or in accordance with its meaning. Somewhat like elaborative rehearsal, semantic coding involves organizing the MTBR into logical categories and integrating the information into previously learned mental frameworks or *schemas*. Temporal encoding, involving storing information in the chronological order in which events occurred, is another way in which information is encoded in LTM.

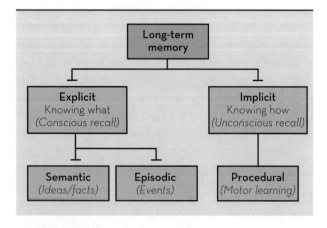

Fig 16-2.

Two basic types of long-term memory: memory for knowing what (explicit) and for knowing how (implicit or procedural).

Forgetting

Forgetting information stored in LTM can occur from interference. As we discussed in the section on working memory, retroactive interference occurs when new activity hinders our ability to recall previously acquired information, while proactive interference occurs when previous information/activity hampers our ability to recall new information.

However, many researchers believe that we primarily forget information in LTM, not because of interference, nor because the information has necessarily disappeared, but because the information is difficult to retrieve. One of the main reasons for this difficulty is the lack of appropriate **memory retrieval cues**. Without any conscious effort on our part, these contextual features—both external (environmental) and internal (physiological or psychological) conditions—were also stored in our LTM at the same time the MTBR was first encoded and stored in our LTM.[16, 17] Memory is significantly improved when the context at the time of retrieval is the same as when it was encoded and stored into LTM. These contextual cues aid our recall of the information. Examples of retrieval cues include better recall of what took place on a particular camping trip when we actually re-visit the same campsite; remembering a thought or a mood when listening to a particular piece of music; or remembering why you left the room only after returning to it and doing what you were doing before you left. This latter type of memory failure, sometimes called a **loss-of-activation error**, is resolved because the retrieval cues (returning to room and re-engaging in the previous activity) are *reactivated*, thereby aiding your recollection.

Prospective Memory

To reduce the chance of snow or ice being blown onto the flaps during taxi, the conscientious crew of Pan Am Flight 799 departing Elmendorf AFB postponed setting them until after they had finished taxiing. Unfortunately, as discussed in the introduction to this chapter, even though the FO said "Okay, let's not forget them," they did. Flight crews often forget to recall or do an intended action in the future. Unlike **retrospective memory**, which involves recollecting past information (whether it be semantic, episodic, or procedural), **prospective memory** involves remembering to perform an intended action in the future. It

appears that most memory failures on the flight deck are prospective, not retrospective. For example, in a random sample of 1,299 ASRS reports, 75 described memory failures made by pilots. However, only one of the 75 involved a retrospective memory failure—the rest were prospective memory failures.[18] It has been suggested that the reason for this difference lies in the fact that "airline training, operating procedures, cockpit design, and cockpit documents help support retrospective memory,"[19] and that declarative (explicit) information is often available outside of one's memory in documents such as approach charts and other publications. Prospective memory incidents in the study included such failures as forgetting to level off at the correct altitude, change to tower frequency to obtain a landing clearance, and set the altimeter to or from the standard altimeter setting (29.92 inches of mercury) when flying through FL180. Several other examples of prospective memory failures, such as forgetting to change data in the FMS, remove tow bars and fuel caps, and retract the landing gear, were also included in a list of ASRS incidents mentioned near the beginning of this chapter.

Were you ever convinced that you said or did something, only to find that you hadn't? After discovering you didn't actually perform the action, you wondered if maybe your memory was playing a trick on you. The term *reality monitoring*, which involves the ability (or inability) to distinguish between real and imagined events, is sometimes used to describe the confusion between what we thought of doing and what we in fact actually did. You certainly thought about doing it, and formulated an intention to, but were interrupted, or distracted, from actually accomplishing it; then later, when you recalled the memory, your brain made the assumption that you had, in fact, completed it.

This false memory phenomena may also play a role in prospective memory failures. For example, the crew of NWA Flight 255, a McDonnell Douglas DC-9 that crashed 14 seconds after liftoff from Runway 03C at Detroit's Metropolitan Wayne County Airport, forgot to set the flaps and slats for takeoff, resulting in the deaths of two people on the ground and all but one passenger of the 155 people aboard. The accident report indicates the flight crew neither called for nor accomplished the taxi checklist, which ultimately was the probable cause of the accident (this checklist calls for the captain and FO to set and visually and orally verify that the flaps and slats were positioned correctly). Because there was a last-minute runway change from Runway 21 to 03C, the attention of the FO during the time when the taxi checklist would normally have been completed (and flaps set for takeoff) was diverted to listening to an updated automatic terminal information service then determining performance parameters for the new runway to ensure they could use Runway 03C for takeoff, the shortest of the three available runways. The NTSB suggests he may have also intentionally delayed setting the flaps in case his performance calculations revealed the need for a different flap setting for the new runway. Either way, the NTSB investigators concluded that by the time the airplane reached a point during the taxi where the taxi checklist would have normally been completed, the flight crew members believed that they had indeed completed the taxi checklist. These interruptions right at the time they would have usually accomplished the checklist, and several more after the captain missed the proper turnoff for taxiway Charlie, may have contributed to the false memory that they had accomplished what they had only intended (Report No: NTSB/AAR-88/05).

Forgetfulness on the Flight Deck

Though memory failures have led to serious incidents such as forgetting to set the altimeter or dial in the appropriate communications frequency, they have also been prominent in several, and sometimes fatal, air carrier and GA accidents. Recent examples include pilots forgetting to: remove control locks, leading to loss of control on or after takeoff;[20] change fuel tanks, resulting in fuel starvation (NTSB Identification No: CEN16LA196); extend the landing gear, causing substantial damage to aircraft (NTSB Identification No: WPR13CA422); and, as seen in the Pan Am B-707 accident in Anchorage, properly configure flaps, resulting in LOC after takeoff. The unfortunate scenario of forgetting to lower the landing gear has spawned an adage, mentioned in Chapter 9, designed to impress upon pilots the seriousness of memory problems in flight: "There are two types of pilots—those who've landed with the gear up, and those who will." A variety of factors contribute to memory failures on the flight deck,

but four situations stand out in increasing a pilot's vulnerability to them: deferred checklist items, distractions, time pressure, and stress.

Deferred Tasks

Prior to departure from Denver, as the preflight checklists were being accomplished, it was noted that the plane was not fueled yet. The crew continued [deferred the item for later completion] in accomplishing the rest of the checklist and related preflight duties. Approximately ten minutes after takeoff the second officer noted that the plane was not fueled. The flight returned to Denver for additional fuel... (ASRS Report No: 2855)

Checklists are designed to ensure critical items are not forgotten. However, operational pressures often preclude accomplishing a checklist item in its normal sequence. For example, Pan Am's procedure in cold weather operations was to configure flaps just prior to departure, forcing the crew of Flight 799 to defer that item to a later time. Even though the crew fully intended to do so, their prospective memory failed them and they forgot.

There are a variety of reasons why it is especially difficult to remember to perform a deferred task. First, as previously noted, it is difficult to hold something in working memory for any appreciable length of time—it requires significant brain processing power to keep the task-to-be-remembered "active" in working memory. Second, the time at which a deferred task (such as extending the flaps, switching to the tower controller frequency, etc.) must be recalled often occurs when the crew is performing other demanding cognitive tasks, preventing them from rehearsing the information held in working memory. Finally, the absence of a retrieval cue, such as the words "flaps set" on the before-takeoff checklist (which was absent in the Elmendorf accident), eliminates a redundancy designed to trigger the recall of performing the deferred task.

Distractions

The problem of flight crew distraction was discussed at length in Chapter 14. Cited in that chapter was a study of 110 ASRS incident reports submitted by flight crews between 2000 and 2014 that found distractions were the number one cause of monitoring failures and subsequent flight path deviations. Distractions not only redirect our attention away from what we were doing, but they also prevent us from rehearsing MTBR in working memory, often causing us to completely forget what we were doing, or planning to do, before the distraction occurred.

In several ASRS incidents so far mentioned in this chapter, the pilots forgot critical items because they were distracted. For example, the CRJ-900 captain who left the APU running after deplaning forgot to finish the shutdown checklist because he was distracted by passengers; the Embraer EMB-145 pilots who forgot to start engine number one before being cleared for takeoff were distracted by the failure of their Jeppesen computer application; the flight crew of an Embraer ERJ-175 that landed without a clearance because they forgot to switch over to the tower frequency did so because they were distracted by several events, including a wake vortex encounter; and the Lake Amphibian pilot who forgot to extend the landing gear before landing was distracted by a malfunctioning airspeed indicator (ASRS Report No: 1368646; 1394157; 1236264; 1300812).

Time Pressure

On-time departure and arrival performance is a major goal of every airline and pilot. The consequences of not meeting schedule are inconvenience to passengers—especially if they miss connecting flights as a result of a delay—and additional costs to an airline. On-time performance is also published by government agencies, such as the U.S. Bureau of Transportation Statistics and other organizations, serving to remind airlines and their customers the degree to which they are succeeding on this metric. It is understandable, then, that flight crews often feel pressure to meet schedule. In fact, pilots often take pride in their ability expedite their duties in the most efficient manner possible to minimize delays—it's a big part of their job.

However, time pressures have contributed to accidents and incidents. According to the NTSB, one of the reasons the crew of Pan Am Flight 799 in Anchorage forgot to set the flaps for departure was because they rushed to meet a self-imposed time envelope to make their clearance void time for departure at Elmendorf. In Chapter 14, we also discussed how the flight crew of DAL Flight 1141, a Boeing B-727 that crashed after takeoff at Dallas-Fort Worth International Airport,

imposed significant time pressure on themselves by accepting an unexpected clearance to taxi to position on Runway 18L, even though they were still fourth in line and were just starting the number three engine. As a result, they forgot to extend the flaps and slats for takeoff, resulting in the deaths of 12 passengers and two flight attendants (Report No: NTSB/AAR-89/04).

In a study of 125 ASRS incident reports involving time-related problems, researchers identified what they called the *hurry-up syndrome* defined as any situation where a pilot's human performance is degraded by a "perceived or actual need to hurry or rush tasks or duties for any reason."[21] Such flight crew performance degradation resulted in the breaking of regulations, deviations from ATC clearances, runway incursions, deviations from company procedures, heading/track deviations, fuel errors, paperwork errors, and more. The study found that 38 percent of these incidents involved errors of omission where the pilot failed to carry out a required task. Errors of omission are often caused by forgetfulness. A variety of reasons for these time pressures were cited in the study, including "the need of a company agent or ground personnel to open a gate for another aircraft, pressure from ATC to expedite taxi for takeoff or to meet a restriction in clearance time, the pressure to keep on schedule when delays have occurred due to maintenance or weather, or the inclination to hurry to avoid exceeding duty time regulations."[22]

Task Overload and Stress

Just as time pressure can create high mental workload leading to memory failures, so too can high stress levels. The effects of excess stress on pilot performance is further explored in Chapter 19. For now, however, it is important to realize that nonnormal or emergency events on the flight deck can create significant levels of situational acute (short-term) stress, which in turn can impair a variety of cognitive abilities including memory retrieval. For example, the crew of United Airlines Flight 553 found themselves 700 feet above the outer marker on a nonprecision approach to Runway 31L at Chicago Midway International Airport. To reach their minimum descent altitude (MDA) of 1,040 feet MSL, they activated the spoilers and descended at a rate of more than 1,500 fpm. However, upon leveling off, the B-737 decelerated, stalled, and crashed in a residential neighborhood, causing the deaths of 40 passengers, three crew members and two people in a house. It appears the crew forgot they had extended the spoilers and failed to retract them or compensate for them by adding more thrust. The NTSB concluded that the "rush of cockpit activities" during the final descent created an "error-provoking environment that set the stage for the crew's failure to notice that the spoilers were still extended at level-off and to arrest the rapid deterioration of airspeed that followed" (Report No: NTSB-AAR-73-16).

The attentional demands placed on the crew of DAL Flight 1141, by the sheer number of checklist items they needed to accomplish, exceeded the attentional resources they had available to them and they forgot to extend the flaps and slats for takeoff. It is reasonable to assume that, after they accepted the unanticipated to-position-and-hold clearance, the crew experienced significant levels of situational stress, which contributed to the failure to remember to set the flaps/slats for departure, especially when they were subsequently cleared for takeoff only 39 seconds later (Report No: NTSB/AAR-89/04).

NASA researchers studied 12 major airline accidents that involved hull loss or loss of life and that were deemed to involve significant levels of acute situational stress on the part of the flight crew after the onset of non-normal/emergency events that preceded the accident. They found that more than two-thirds of 212 flight crew errors identified were errors of omission, many of which were prospective memory failures.[23]

American Airlines Flight 965 (see Chapters 14 and 15) crashed into high terrain during an approach into Alfonso Bonilla Aragon International Airport in Cali, Colombia, in part because the crew was mentally overloaded with tasks—reprogramming the FMS, re-briefing approach charts for a different runway, etc.—as a result of accepting a last-minute runway change. At one point, they were so task-saturated that they failed to monitor the flight instruments that indicated the B-757 was turning toward the wrong waypoint. The official report indicates the captain appeared to be under "considerable stress" which compromised his ability to perform and maintain good situation awareness.[24] The FO responded to a GPWS warning by initiating a proper GPWS escape maneuver (nose-up pitch and full thrust) to avoid contact with terrain, but in the extreme stress of this highly challenging situation, neither pilot remembered to stow (retract) the speed brakes (spoilers) that were previously extended to expedite the descent. According to investigators, had they done so, the aircraft likely would have cleared the trees at the top of the ridge.[25]

Improving Your Memory

As we turn to the topic of how you can reduce memory failures on the flight deck, I am reminded (no pun intended) of an experience that, despite all the information presented in this chapter to the contrary, demonstrates just how resilient human memory really is. One of my former students (who was a flight instructor at the time) asked me if I would like to fly with him in his Cessna 152. It was during a period when I hadn't been an active pilot for quite a while, and it had been close to 25 years since I had flown that particular model. However, as I walked out to the airplane I asked my young instructor-pilot if my recollection of various airspeeds was correct and sure enough they were. I accurately recalled the best rate of climb (V_Y), angle of climb (V_X), best engine-out glide, and approach speeds. In addition, when I got my hands on the controls it was just like riding a bicycle—I still remembered how to fly. I conducted two steep turns and lost 100 feet of altitude on the first one (just like I used to!) and performed a stall and recovery. But the best part were my two landings—though I wasn't current, nor proficient, I greased them both on the runway. Not only did I remember facts and figures stored in my long term explicit/declarative memory, but previously learned psychomotor skills stored in my long term implicit procedural memory as well.

This story illustrates just how dependent we are on LTM to pilot an aircraft, and how overlearning tasks as a strategy to improve attention, as suggested in Chapter 14, effectively and permanently consolidates information into LTM making such tasks almost automatic. There are numerous other ways to strengthen the learning of information and its retrieval from LTM.

Utilize Chunking

It was mentioned previously that chunking, or grouping, bits of information into meaningful wholes enhances learning and memory. Relating information together and organizing it through chunking is a form of semantic encoding which provides for deeper processing and easier recall. The reduced number of high-information items in working memory from chunking also leads to more effective rehearsal, which is another way to transfer information into LTM. There is some evidence that grouping four-digit transponder codes into two separate chunks helps pilots remember them. For example, the code 4173, usually heard as four separate digits ("four one seven three") when presented by ATC or repeated by the pilot, is easier to recall when stated as 41 73 ("forty-one seventy-three").[26]

Try Using Mnemonics

Deeper processing and easier recall is also associated with **mnemonics**. The word *mnemonic* derives from the ancient Greek word μνημον (mnēmon), meaning mindful, or having to do with remembering. When learning new material, use a mnemonic if at all possible. It facilitates learning by organizing the information into previously learned categories or mental schemas, arranging it into high-information chunks, or associating it with visual images stored in LTM. One type of mnemonic commonly used by pilots is the acronym. For example, when trying to remember what additional aircraft equipment is required under 14 CFR §91.205 for VFR at night, pilots have used FLAPS: **F**uses, **L**anding light (if operated for hire), **A**nti-collision lights, **P**osition lights and **S**ource of electricity. When recalling the acceleration errors of a compass they use ANDS: **A**ccelerate **N**orth, **D**ecelerate **S**outh. ARROW, GRABCARD, and AVIATES are other popular acronyms.

A rhyme or story is another mnemonic device. For example, pilots have used the following to remember the lights on a visual approach slope indicating system:

> "Red over white, you're right.
> Red over red, you're dead.
> White over white, you're high as a kite,
> And nothing more needs to be said."

Another mnemonic takes advantage of the power of mental images. One example involves associating a list of items to be learned with a specific well-known location (like your home)—hence it is called the *method of loci* (location). Mentally place each item to be remembered in a well-known location that you can visualize with your mind's eye, such as the front porch, the hallway you usually walk into, the kitchen table, etc. Associating each item to be remembered to specific spatial locations stored in LTM is an effective way of encoding the material and aiding memory recall.

You can also associate new material with other images. The more novel, unusual, or bizarre, the better. If you have trouble remembering names, you might try to link some characteristic of that person with an image. For example, if the person's name is Neil, you might visualize them *kneeling* before a King. Or if it is Lewis, think of the Lewis, of Lewis and Clark fame, hiking and paddling their way to the U.S. Pacific Northwest. There are other mnemonic systems, some which have been used for centuries— like the complicated *number-consonant* system—that may be helpful depending on what type of material you want to learn.

Grouping material into higher-information chunks and using mnemonics are ways in which material can be more easily stored in and recalled from LTM. But they also, along with the following strategies, assist you in recalling items stored in working memory.

Use Checklists

Cognitive scientist Donald Norman observes that humans rely on knowledge "in the world" in addition to knowledge "in the head" to ease the burden of remembering things.[27] For example, if we want to remember to return a library book, we may put the book by our front door where we are sure to see it before we leave the house. Or, we use memory aids such as alarm clocks, to-do lists, and pocket calendars. We do the same in aviation. For example, after the loss of a Boeing B-17 Flying Fortress shortly after takeoff from Wright Field in 1935—because all three crew members forgot to remove the elevator/rudder control lock before flight—we learned that memory alone cannot be relied upon to recall all the knowledge needed to safely fly an aircraft. It was after this accident that the U.S. Army Air Corps began to supplement knowledge in the head with knowledge in the world by requiring the use of **checklists** for every flight. In fact, during WWII, the B-17 aircraft flight manual stated that the aircraft was too complex for even experienced pilots to operate by reliance on memory alone, and that it was "absolutely essential that the cockpit checklist be used properly by pilot and co-pilot at all times."[28] Compliance with these "new" checklists worked: U.S. Army pilots went on to log more than 100,000 hours without a fatal accident.[29]

Using or not using a checklist is analogous to the distinction often made between *recognition* and *recall* memory. For example, recognition memory involves choosing options from a list (e.g., true/false or multiple-choice questions on a test) while recall memory involves direct information retrieval from LTM (e.g., essay questions on a test). The former requires less cognitive effort so it is easier for pilots to choose from a list of alternatives on a checklist to solve a problem than to recall from memory an exact procedure to follow.

Today's sophisticated flight decks are significantly more complex than the cockpits of old, requiring both captain and FO to accomplish numerous tasks—involving both recall and recognition memory—in order to safely accomplish each phase of flight. Along with read-and-do and challenge-and-response checklists, airline and other professional pilots conduct memorized procedural **flows** during virtually every phase of flight. Flows consist of a logical, organized sequence of actions accomplished by both the captain and the FO to configure the controls and systems for the next phase of fight, or next step within a phase of fight. These memorized tasks often (but not always) follow a linear or geographic (left-to-right, bottom-to-top, etc.) flow pattern. Some GA pilots use flows while others prefer to rely on mnemonics and other strategies that are somewhat similar to flows in that they follow a memorized orderly sequence.

Read-and-do checklists are used to ensure items are accomplished in the proper sequence (e.g., engine start and shutdown procedures) and procedural flows are, in turn, generally followed up with the appropriate challenge-and-response checklist to make sure designated flow items and other items are completed. Checklists help support prospective memory by helping you to "remember to remember" to perform the required actions needed to achieve safe flight operations. Operational considerations sometimes make it difficult to consistently use a checklist; but from our discussion on memory, it should be clear that checklists should always be used.

A disadvantage of most paper checklists is that there is no placeholder feature to return to an item when you are distracted from completing the checklist or if an item must be deferred (e.g., for fueling). You either must keep your thumb on the spot on the checklist or rely on your short-term working memory to not forget the item when the time comes—a difficult task, as we have already seen. One possible answer to this problem is electronic checklists (ECLs). There are various levels of ECL sophistication, but the best ones automatically integrate with aircraft sensors that detect if an item has actually been accomplished or not. For example, critical items on the Boeing B-777 ECL will not turn green unless the sensors detect that the "switch/item is in the proper position for that phase of flight."[30] Most of these advanced ECLs will notify crews if a critical item hasn't been accomplished and some will prevent them from continuing with the checklist until the item is.[31]

Of course, the time-tested way of easing the burden of remembering to remember is to transfer knowledge to the world by writing down MTBR such as ATC clearances, frequencies, and other important information. Another way is to transfer it to onboard electronic reminder systems. For example, Boeing recently developed a flight crew reminder function for its B-777 and B-787 airplanes. Much like the reminder programs on personal electronic devices, this function allows you to pre-program reminder cues that automatically alert you and your fellow crew member—both visually and aurally—when certain events have been achieved or when certain actions need to be performed. Examples of event alerts include passing a certain waypoint, reaching a certain altitude, or when a change in the ETA to a specific location occurs. Examples of crew-action reminder alerts include when to initiate a certain checklist, when to climb to the final cruise altitude as per previous ATC instructions, or when to call a resting crew member to the flight deck during augmented flight operations.[32]

Verbalize the Important Stuff

It was suggested in Chapter 14 that during periods of high mental workload attention can be improved if you use more than one sensory modality (e.g., sight, hearing, etc.). Verbalizing MTBR also reduces the chance of forgetting something. Airline SOPs recognize this by requiring crew members to conduct verbal briefings and to use standard verbal callouts. In addition to improving attention, monitoring performance, communication, and flight crew coordination, conducting out-loud briefings (for critical portions of flight such as takeoff and approach) and using standard callouts (for performance parameters, changes in aircraft configuration and altitudes, navigation deviations, and FMS autopilot mode changes, etc.) involve actively rehearsing MTBR which keeps crucial information in one's working memory. Verbalizing also allows fellow crew members to confirm or disconfirm the accuracy of the information. Most airline SOPs specifically spell out the types of calls to be made by both the PF and PM for various parameters. For example, when reaching 100 feet above DA/MDA on an instrument approach, a standard callout for the PM might be, "One hundred to go," to which the PF would respond by saying "approaching minimums." Verbal callouts like these force both pilots to look up these critical altitudes on the approach chart, think about them, and rehearse them in their minds, thereby facilitating memory recall.

Manage Interruptions and Distractions

You were urged in Chapter 14 to also treat interruptions, distractions, and any non-routine situations that draw your attention away from completing routine flight deck duties, as red warning flags with potentially dangerous repercussions. This also applies to deferred checklist items. As was noted, it is extremely difficult to remember to perform a deferred task. In fact, recent research indicates it is even harder for less experienced pilots and pilots who are older, and also more difficult under conditions of high mental workload and when the cues associated with remembering the task are less salient.[33]

Currently there is no set policy or procedure for creating a new reminder cue once the chain of activity in a checklist has been broken from distraction. Therefore, if your aircraft is not equipped with electronic "smart" checklists that prevent you from jumping ahead of a checklist item, or an electronic flight-crew reminder function, then you must create your own reminder cues to alert you to return to the deferred item. This may involve such strategies as placing the checklist in a conspicuous place for both crew members to see, fastening a paperclip or some sticky note on the last spot on the checklist, or placing a Styrofoam cup over the thrust lever.[34] When facing a possible prospective memory breakdown in a crewed flight deck you can designate one pilot to be the a memory cue "detector" so there is no question as to who is responsible for detecting the cue and ensuring the action is eventually carried out.

The importance of complying with the sterile flight deck rule was also discussed in Chapter 14. This regulation prohibits you from engaging in nonessential activities (including extraneous conversations) that could distract you from completing the essential duties required for the safe operation of your aircraft during the critical phases of flight—all ground operations and in-flight operations below 10,000 feet MSL, except cruise flight. Complying with this reduces the possibility of self-distraction allowing you and your fellow crew member to not only focus your attention on proper monitoring and aircraft control but also to reduce the likelihood of forgetting something.

Avoid the Rush

Throughout this book, you've seen examples of how unanticipated events can create time pressures that result in performance decrements. For example, a last-minute runway change significantly increased workload for the crews of American Airlines Flight 965 (this chapter and Chapter 15) and Air Inter Flight 148 (see Chapter 15), causing them to rush their preparations for the approach. You also saw the effect of time pressures on the crews of Pan American Flight 799 and DAL Flight 1141, where both crews forgot to properly set the flaps for takeoff.

If you are behind schedule, avoid the temptation to rush. When you are faced with an unexpected event that will cause you to rush, make a realistic assessment of your ability to accomplish the tasks needed to achieve a safe outcome within the limited time frame given you; if you don't think you can, then buy more time (e.g., slow down, request a hold, conduct a go-around, or request an alternate clearance). This will increase your ability to conduct checklists properly and not forget anything. Like most pilots, it's difficult to admit—to others and yourself—when you might be getting behind the airplane. When things begin to snowball, rather than trying to save face and risk getting in deeper, admit you're having trouble and consider a Plan B. Often that's the first step in avoiding an accident.

Effectively Manage Situational Stress

You've also seen throughout this book that excess stress impedes memory recall. A non-normal or emergency situation is a stressful event. This can range from an alternator failure which usually poses no serious threat to an airliner, to an in-flight fire which may require an immediate landing in order to avoid a catastrophe. Though it may be stressful in these situations, it is important to focus your energy on resolving the problem, not on the consequences should you be unable to. Much like the stress induced by a job interview or checkride, it is counterproductive to direct your energy toward thinking about the consequences of failure. Such thinking sets up a vicious cycle which increases the likelihood that you will indeed fail. You will need all your mental resources to focus on successfully assessing and resolving the problem. Fortunately, there are checklists for most emergency and abnormal situations, usually available in the *Quick Reference Handbook* along with the EICAS or ECAM, if so equipped. Some emergencies may also require the crew to accomplish memorized **immediate action items** followed by the appropriate checklist. Many emergency and non-normal procedures' checklists are read-and-do checklists requiring you to follow the proper sequence of outlined items in the checklist.

Forgetting is seen as a failure of memory, but, unfortunately, it is also a normal aspect of human behavior. For the most part, the consequences of forgetting are not serious when it occurs on the ground; given enough time and the use of a variety of retrieval strategies, we usually remember what it is we were supposed to do or say. In flight, however, we don't often have that luxury. As a pilot, therefore, it is important that you are aware that it is normal to suffer from this limitation in human information processing and you should take active measures to combat it. Fortunately, there exist several strategies designed to facilitate memory on the flight deck such as conducting flows, using checklists, following SOPs, conducting briefings, using callouts, and complying with the sterile cockpit rule. All you have to do is use them.

Helpful Resources

Checklist Memory Items (Research Project EASA.2013.01). This relatively short research report, sponsored by the European Aviation Safety Agency, contains a concise summary of memory and the role of checklists in aviation. (www.easa.europa.eu/document-library/ research-projects/easa20131)

The Flight Safety Foundation (FSF) has produced several helpful *Briefing Notes* as part of their Approach and Landing Accident Reduction (ALAR) Tool Kit project. The following apply to this and other chapters in this book and are available from Skybrary, a reference for aviation safety knowledge developed by the FSF and other partners at: www.skybrary.aero/ index.php/Flight_Safety_Foundation_ALAR_Toolkit.

- *FSF ALAR Briefing Note 1.4—Standard Calls*
- *FSF ALAR Briefing Note 1.5—Normal Checklists*
- *FSF ALAR Briefing Note 1.6—Approach Briefing*
- *FSF ALAR Briefing Note 2.4—Interruptions/Distractions*

Endnotes

1. National Transportation Safety Board, *Aircraft Accident Report: Pan American World Airways, Inc., Boeing 707-321C, N799PA, Elmendorf Air Force Base, Anchorage, Alaska, December 26, 1968*, File 1-0045 (Washington, DC: November 19, 1969).

2. Kim Cardosi and Alan Yost, *Controller and Pilot Error in Airport Operations: A Review of Previous Research and Analysis of Safety Data*, Final Report, DOT/FAA/AR-00/51 (Cambridge, MA: U.S. Department of Transportation, John A. Volpe National Transportation Systems Center, January 2001).

3. Richard C. Atkinson and Richard M. Shiffrin, "Human Memory: A Proposed System and its Control Processes," *The Psychology of Learning and Motivation: Advances in Research and Theory* (Vol. 2), eds. Kenneth W. Spence and Janet Taylor Spence (New York: Academic Press, 1968): 89–195.

4. Geoffrey R. Loftus and Elizabeth F. Loftus, *Human Memory: The Processing of Information* (New York: Lawrence Erlbaum Associates, 1976): 8.

5. Alan Baddeley, "Working Memory," *Science* 255 (January 1992): 556–559.

6. Alan Baddeley, "Working Memory: Theories, Models, and Controversies," *Annual Review of Psychology* 63 (January 2012): 1–29.

7. Ibid.

8. Geoffrey R. Loftus, Veronica J. Dark and Dianne Williams, "Short-Term Memory Factors in Ground Controller/Pilot Communication," *Human Factors* 21 (April 1, 1979): 169–181.

9. Christopher D. Wickens, *Engineering Psychology and Human Performance*, 2nd ed. (New York: HarperCollins, 1992).

10. Ibid.

11. Randall S. Bone, William J. Penhallegon, Leslie M. Benson and Gregory L. Orrell, *Evaluation of Pilot and Air Traffic Controller Use of Third Party Call Sign in Voice Communications with Pilot Utilization of Cockpit Display of Traffic Information*, Mitre Technical Report, MTR130347R1 (McLean, VA: The MITRE Corporation, July 2013).

12. Kim Cardosi, Paul Falzarano and Sherwin Han, *Pilot-Controller Communication Errors: An Analysis of Aviation Safety Reporting System (ASRS) Reports*, Final Report, DOT/FAA/AR-98/17 (Cambridge, MA: U.S. Department of Transportation, John A. Volpe National Transportation Systems Center, August 1998).

13. George A. Miller, "The Magical Number Seven, Plus or Minus Two: Some Limits on Our Capacity for Processing Information," *Psychological Review* 63.2 (March 1956): 81–97.

14. William G. Chase and Herbert A. Simon, "The Mind's Eye in Chess," in *Visual Information Processing*, ed. W. G. Chase (New York: Academic Press, February 1973): 251–281.

15. Kim M. Cardosi, *Human Factors for Air Traffic Control Specialists: A User's Manual for Your Brain*, DOT/FAA/AR-99/39 (Cambridge, MA: U.S. Department of Transportation, John A. Volpe National Transportation Systems Center, November 1999).

16. Endel Tulving, "Cue-Dependent Forgetting," *American Scientist* 62 (January–February 1974): 74–82.

17. Saul McLeod, *Forgetting* (2008). Available at www.simplypsychology.org/forgetting.html.

18. Jessica Lang Nowinski, Jon B. Holbrook and R. Key Dismukes, "Human Memory and Cockpit Operations: An ASRS Study," in *Proceedings of the 12th International Symposium on Aviation Psychology* (Dayton, OH: The Wright State University, 2003): 888–893.

19. Ibid., 892.

20. Four such events occurred in the United States in a recent two-year period alone (NTSB Identification No: ERA14MA271; ERA13CA350; ERA13FA372; GAA15CA088), prompting the NTSB to issue a *Safety Alert* (SA-048) in December 2015, urging pilots to use checklists during their aircraft preflight inspections.

21. Jeanne McElhatton and Charles Drew, "Hurry-Up Syndrome," *ASRS Directline*, 5 (March 1994): 19.

22. Ibid.

23. R. Key Dismukes, Timothy E. Goldsmith and Janeen A. Kochan, *Effects of Acute Stress on Aircrew Performance: Literature Review and Analysis of Operational Aspects*, NASA/TM—2015–218930 (Moffett Field, CA: NASA Ames Research Center, August 2015).

24. Aeronautica Civil of The Republic of Colombia, *Aircraft Accident Report: Controlled Flight Into Terrain, American Airlines Flight 965, Boeing 757-223, N651AA, Near Cali, Colombia, December 20, 1995*, trans. Peter B. Ladkin (Santafe de Bogota D.C., Colombia: Aeronautica Civil of The Republic of Colombia, September 1996): 45.

25. Ibid.

26. Loftus, Dark and Williams, "Short-Term Memory Factors."

27. Donald A. Norman, *The Design of Everyday Things* (New York: Doubleday, 1988).

28. Timothy P. Schultz, "Where Did Checklists Come From?" *The Combat Edge* (March/April 2012): 12–13.

29. Fred George, "Checklists and Callouts: Keep It Simple, Avoid Distraction, Prevent Ineptitude," *Business & Commercial Aviation* (April 30, 2015).

30. Patrick R. Veillette, "Give E-Checklists an A+," *Business & Commercial Aviation* (January 2012): 39.

31. Paul L. Myers III, "Commercial Aircraft Electronic Checklists: Benefits and Challenges (Literature Review)," *International Journal of Aviation, Aeronautics, and Aerospace* 3 (February 2016).

32. Brad Cornell and Gordon Sandell, "New Flight Crew Reminder Function," *Boeing Aero* 51 (Quarter 3, 2013): 17–20.

33. Kathleen D. Van Benthem, Chris M. Herdman, Rani G. Tolton and Jo-Anne LeFevre, "Prospective Memory Failures in Aviation: Effects of Cue Salience, Workload, and Individual Differences," *Aerospace Medicine and Human Performance* 86 (April 2015): 366–373.

34. Federal Aviation Administration, *Human Performance Considerations in the Use and Design of Aircraft Checklists* (Washington, DC: January 1995).

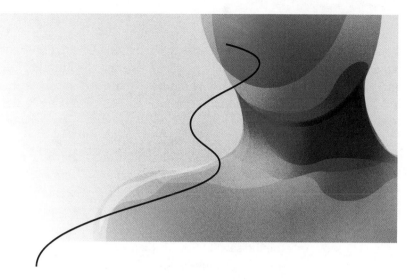

17

Decisions, decisions, decisions.

Decision Making

Who Killed Jessica? That was the question stamped on the cover of *Time* magazine, along with a picture of seven-year-old Jessica Dubroff wearing a baseball cap proclaiming *Women Fly*.[1] It was the second day of a record-setting coast-to-coast, eight-day trip from Half Moon Bay, California, to Falmouth, Massachusetts, and back again, by the youngest "pilot" ever. Of course, Jessica wasn't the pilot—she couldn't obtain a student pilot certificate until she was at least 16 years old, but at the time she could receive flight instruction as a pilot-trainee. Her flight instructor who occupied the right seat of the Cessna 177 Cardinal, who had almost 1,500 hours of total flight time, was the PIC.

They had planned to depart Cheyenne Airport, Wyoming, on a VFR flight to Lincoln, Nebraska—the first scheduled fuel stop of the day's intended flights—no later than 0615 hours mountain daylight time (MDT) to beat a cold front that was forecast to pass though Cheyenne that morning. However, because of media events the previous evening and at least three media interviews that morning, they got off to a late start arriving at the airport between 0715 and 0730 MDT. Between about 0801 and 0807 hours, the PIC received a weather briefing provided by the Casper automated flight service station (FSS) that indicated the cold front was just beginning to pass over Cheyenne and that there was a line of thunderstorms with tops above 30,000 feet with icing and IFR conditions just southwest of the airport moving from south to north. The ceiling at Cheyenne at the time of the briefing was 2,600 feet AGL and the visibility was more than 10 SM, but the weather was deteriorating rapidly. Eyewitnesses reported that the weather conditions at the time of the accident were windy, with moderate to heavy mixed precipitation (rain, snow, and sleet), thunder, and lightning. The NTSB concluded that the accident sequence took place near the edge of a thunderstorm.

At 0816 hours an airline transport-rated pilot departed from Runway 30 in a Cessna 414 and reported to the tower, who in turn relayed to the Cessna 177 pilot, that he experienced moderate low-level wind shear with airspeed fluctuations of plus or minus 15 knots. Just before takeoff, the tower visibility lowered to 2.75 SM, so the Cardinal pilot requested and received a special VFR (SVFR) clearance and was cleared for takeoff at 0821 MDT.[2]

Witnesses observed the airplane depart Runway 30 in a northwesterly direction and then execute a gradual right turn to an easterly heading. They observed the airplane was at a low altitude and airspeed, a high pitch attitude, and that the wings were wobbling. As it was rolling out of the right turn, at about 400 feet AGL, they saw the airplane rapidly descend in a near-vertical flight path and impact the ground approximately 4,000 feet north of the departure end of Runway 30 in a residential neighborhood. All three on board—Jessica, her flight instructor, and her father in the back seat—died instantly in the crash. The NTSB determined the probable cause of the accident was the PIC's "*improper decision* to take off into deteriorating weather conditions (including turbulence, gusty winds, and an advancing thunderstorm and associated precipitation)...resulting in a stall caused by failure to maintain airspeed" (emphasis added) (Report No: NTSB/AAR-97/02).

In retrospect, it's obvious he made the wrong decision—he should not have departed, especially on a VFR flight in IFR weather and into an approaching thunderstorm. Not only was the poor and rapidly deteriorating weather confirmed by others—the FSS specialist, the tower controller, and a pilot report from a Cessna 414—but he saw it with his own eyes. Yet, he still chose to depart. As pilots, we scratch our heads and ask why would he make such a decision? Our natural inclination is to assign blame: "I guess he was just a poor pilot," or "he must have lacked common sense," or "maybe he was deficient in moral character."

The problem, however, is we *know* what happened—after the NTSB took almost 11 months to determine for us—but the pilot didn't, at least not until it was too late. Do you think that if he was able to predict the future, and knew what we know now, he would have departed? You see, because we know the outcome, we suffer from one of several powerful, yet often unconscious, biases: the **hindsight bias**. It's the I-knew-it-all-along effect. Or, as the Old Italian proverb notes, "After the ship has sunk, everyone knows how she might have been saved." What appears obvious to us after the fact—in hindsight—did not appear obvious to the pilot before the fact. The hindsight bias causes us to believe the cause of the crash is so blatantly obvious that we rush to judge the pilot and conclude that we would *never* do what that pilot did. Psychologists call it the **fundamental attribution error**: the tendency to blame internal characteristics in others for their attitudes, behavior, or failures while blaming situational circumstances to excuse our own.[3] A major problem is we stop digging deeper to determine the factors that may have contributed to the pilot's erroneous decision. Worse yet, we may actually make ourselves more vulnerable to just such an accident because hindsight bias distorts our perceptions leading us to overestimate our own wisdom—we acquire a type of *cognitive conceit*—thereby precluding us from truly learning from the mistakes of others.

The question is, would it really be that easy for you to make the decision to abort the flight if you were in his shoes? He knew all about the weather situation. He knew about the incoming cold front and how important it was to get out of Cheyenne before it arrived—that is why he insisted that they depart by 0615 hours. The prospect of waiting until it passed was not acceptable because they would have had to wait several hours for the weather to improve, delaying their flight significantly. He was wise to make the decision to depart early, and had done everything he could to do so. However, media demands and other issues delayed him more than he had wanted.

The NTSB also concluded the pilot asked for and received a satisfactory weather briefing. But there were some elements in the briefing that may have confirmed his belief (*confirmation bias*, to be discussed later) that if he could depart quickly he would leave his weather problems behind. For example, in response to the FSS specialist's statement that Grand Island and Sidney were clear and that it was "good out there," the pilot responded that he could see the sun shining to the east. The specialist also mentioned thunderstorms were forecast for Lincoln and Grand Island in the afternoon and then said, "if you can venture out of there and go get east it look (sic)," and "stay south." The transcript is somewhat incomplete, but the implication is that the weather would be suitable if he were to depart to the east and stay south. At least it appears that is how the pilot interpreted it when he responded, "yea it looks pretty good actually."

The weather deteriorated during the 15 minutes between briefing and takeoff. However, the pilot may have thought it was still acceptable since only a few minutes before his departure he had witnessed a light twin successfully depart from Runway 30. When the tower informed him that the tower visibility had dropped to 2.75 SM, it was only one quarter-mile short of the 3 SM required for VFR flight, so asking for a SVFR clearance wasn't unreasonable—it was certainly higher than the required minimum of 1 SM for SVFR. In fact, the automated surface observation system (ASOS) observations indicated 10 SM visibility and light rain a few minutes before his briefing, 5 SM visibility and moderate rain 5 minutes before takeoff, and 5 SM visibility and back to light rain at the time of the accident. Thunderstorms were first reported only in this last ASOS report.

Other factors seemed to gang up on the pilot. First, it appears he had limited experience conducting takeoffs in high density altitude (DA) conditions— the DA was 6,670 feet MSL at the time of the accident—and the NTSB concluded that this may have contributed to the reduction of airspeed that led to the stall. Second, the mixture control knob was in the full rich (forward) position at the accident site, which likely means he did not lean the mixture which would also diminish engine performance (although it could have moved to the full forward position from impact forces). Third, the airplane was 96 pounds overweight at takeoff. Investigators concluded that the high DA and overweight condition decreased the airplane's best rate-of-climb to no more than 387 fpm, compared to 685 at sea level. Fourth, the NTSB determined that the combination of bank angle immediately after takeoff, rain on the wings, and overloaded condition increased the stall speed by almost 10 percent. Fifth, what was initially a crosswind during the takeoff roll and initial airborne phase became a tailwind after the airplane began its right turn.

The NTSB concluded that since the pilot was most likely looking outside the airplane during the VFR departure, he may not have been adequately monitoring the airspeed indicator or he may have had difficulty monitoring it because of airspeed fluctuations (remember there was wind shear reported), and he may have misperceived the increased ground speed from the tailwind as an increase in airspeed (a common illusion pilots face when turning downwind). If this is so, he may have misjudged the margin of safety above the airplane's stall speed and increased the airplane's pitch angle to compensate for the decreased climb rate because he erroneously thought his airspeed, not his ground speed, was increasing.

It appears from the accident report that other people subtlety, yet strongly, influenced his decision to depart. To break the record they had to complete the trip before Jessica reached her eighth birthday on May 5. The itinerary was tight and there were activities planned—including media interview appointments—and people to see at destinations along the way. The trip had made national news and it is apparent there was a lot riding on it. The NTSB said as much when it identified the pilot's desire to adhere to an overly ambitious itinerary, in part, because of media commitments, as a contributing factor in his decision to takeoff.

Finally, he was tired. The NTSB discovered that the pilot accumulated a significant sleep debt (see Chapter 10) and received only 6.5, 6.75, and 5.5 hours of sleep each night during the three days prior to the start of the trip, compared to the 8.5 to 9 hours of sleep that he typically received per night on weekends. Furthermore, he told others he was tired (he told a witness in Rock Springs, Wyoming, he was tired, and after arriving in Cheyenne he telephoned his wife and said that he was "really tired"); others said he looked tired (the airport manager at Rock Springs said that the pilot was "noticeably exhausted," and the Cheyenne radio station director said all three looked tired); and he committed several errors before departure that are consistent with a lack of alertness (e.g., he started the airplane engine while the nosewheel was still chocked, read back a radio frequency incorrectly, and used incorrect phraseology by requesting a special IFR clearance instead of a special VFR clearance).

You learned in Chapter 10 that people tend to underestimate their own level of tiredness. According to the NTSB accident report, the fact that he self-reported being tired "probably reflected a high level of fatigue" (Report No: NTSB/AAR-97/02). From our discussions on fatigue, you also learned that fatigue leads to a variety of cognitive deficits including forgetfulness, reduced attention, slowed reaction time, errors in judgment, increased risk taking, and reduced decision-making ability. It appears that these factors impaired the pilot's judgment leading to his decision to depart Cheyenne on that fateful day.

Unfortunately, despite all these limitations and pressures—imposed by others and by himself—the pilot still made the decision to depart Cheyenne. Whether he did so by active deliberation or by passive default (maintaining the status quo by just going along with his previous decision to depart), this is what killed him and his two passengers.

Do you still think it would be easy for you *not* to takeoff knowing now what it might have been like to be in his shoes? Was it really an obvious clear-cut case of poor decision making? We will never really know what was going on inside the pilot's head, but as you may discern from this discussion which began with an explanation of hindsight bias, numerous factors influence our decision making, many of which we are barely—if at all—conscious of.

Pilot Decision Making and Aircraft Accidents

"Good judgment is the result of experience, and experience the result of bad judgment."

—Unknown

Decision errors afflict pilots at all levels of certification and are responsible for a significant percentage of airline and GA aircraft accidents, as borne out by numerous safety studies.

Airline/Commercial Flight Operations

A study of 37 major U.S. airline accidents that occurred between 1978 and 1990, where the actions of the flight crew were a causal or contributing factor to the accident, found that tactical decision errors (improper decision, failing to change course of action or heed warnings that suggest a change in a course of action was warranted, etc.) were the third leading type of flight crew error, accounting for 51 (or 17 percent) of the 302 total flight-crew errors identified. As noted in Chapter 10, the most common tactical decisional error was failing to execute a missed approach or go-around when weather or other conditions required it. Other examples included failure to conduct a rejected takeoff (RTO) above V_1, failure to order a second deicing of the aircraft, and flying below minimum descent altitude/decision height (MDA/DH) without adequate outside visual references. The study also discovered that tactical decision errors were the number one error type committed by captains, as opposed to the FOs.[4] Other studies have confirmed the prominent role decision errors play in aircraft accidents:

- An analysis of 119 U.S. aircrew-related Part 121 and 135 scheduled air carrier accidents, that occurred during a seven-year period between 1990 and 1996 inclusive, found that 29 percent of them were associated with decision errors made by flight crews.[5]
- The Flight Safety Foundation (FSF) conducted a study of 76 worldwide fatal approach and landing accidents and serious incidents involving large jet and turboprop aircraft that occurred between 1984 and 1997, and found the most frequent causal factor (74 percent) was deficient flight crew decision making (i.e., professional judgment/airmanship).[6] Examples included failure to execute a missed approach when conditions required it, ignoring GPWS alerts, and deciding to execute a nonprecision approach in demanding conditions when a precision approach was available.
- Flawed pilot decision making was the second leading cause (behind inattentiveness) of pilot-error-induced air-taxi accidents in the U.S. between 1983 and 2002. Some of these flawed decisions involved flying the aircraft with a known defect, flying low, or flying into adverse weather. Some also involved decisions related to gear problems, engine power loss, or engine shutdown.[7]

General Aviation Flight Operations

Back in 1988, errors of judgment and decision making contributed to 66 percent of GA accidents.[8] It appears this percentage hasn't significantly changed since then: a more recent study of 2,801 U.S. GA accidents that occurred between 2008 and 2010 found the pilot's actions, decision making, or cockpit management was the cause of 70 percent of fatal, and 59 percent of non-fatal, airplane accidents.[9]

The Bureau of Air Safety Investigation found more than 70 percent of fatal aircraft accidents in Australia during a three-year period were caused by pilot factors, the most common involving poor judgment and decision making.[10] The study found this factor also involved poor in-flight planning and operating an aircraft beyond the pilot's experience or ability. Examples of this included flying into adverse weather, continuing a flight with known low fuel on board, and engaging in unauthorized low flying.

Finally, a comprehensive 2013 study evaluated 29,081 Part 121, 135 scheduled, 135 nonscheduled, and 91 accidents and found the percentage of accidents caused by decision errors made by the pilots/flight crews was 13, 24, 30, and 27 percent, respectively. More accidents are caused by skill-based errors (23, 56, 53, and 67 percent, for Part 121, 135 scheduled, 135 nonscheduled, and 91, respectively) but the study revealed that those involving decision errors were more likely to be fatal.[11]

Even though the numbers above vary from study to study (e.g., different time spans, different definitions of what constitutes decision-making errors, etc.), it is clear that faulty pilot decision making contributes to a significant proportion of fatal and non-fatal accidents.

Types of Decision-Making Errors

Several different types of decision-making errors manifest themselves on the flight deck. Examples include:

- Continuing flight into adverse weather (gusty winds or strong crosswinds, downdrafts, airframe icing conditions, wind shear, etc.);
- attempting VFR flight into IMC;
- choosing an inappropriate takeoff or landing runway/site;
- failing to refuel or attempting flight with known low fuel on board;
- failing to abort a takeoff or conducting an RTO after V_1; and
- failing to conduct a missed approach or go-around.

A distinction should be made between decision *errors* and decision *violations*. The former are unintentional errors or mistakes (the pilot may not know better) while the latter are decisions that intention-

---

Two Troubling Decision Errors That Afflict Airline and GA Pilots

Failure to go-around. Statistics indicate that approximately 65 percent of all worldwide commercial jet airplane accidents and about half of all fatal accidents, occur during the final approach and landing phases of flight—segments that account for only about 4 percent of flight time.[1] In addition, about a third of all worldwide major and substantial-damage transport-category turbojet and turboprop aircraft accidents are runway-related accidents with 97 percent of them classified as runway excursions (a veer-off the side, or an overrun off the end, of the runway). In its recent go-around decision-making study, the FSF concluded that the number one risk factor in runway excursions (RE) and approach and landing accidents is the failure of the flight crews to conduct a go-around. The study claims that 83 percent of REs "could have been avoided with a decision to go around," and that "about half of *all* accidents could be prevented with a decision to go around."[2] The study confirms what has long been known about pilot behavior: *they are reluctant to conduct a go-around when it is needed*—only 3 percent of unstable approaches, a major contributor to REs, result in pilots complying with their airline's go-around policy.[3]

Attempted VFR-into-IMC. Why does a qualified pilot flying a perfectly good twin-engine Cessna crash into a wooded swamp in Florida, killing himself and his two passengers? Or a high-time commercial helicopter pilot lose control of his aircraft while maneuvering during a search and rescue flight near Talkeetna, Alaska, killing himself and his two passengers? The NTSB says that these two accidents, which occurred within six weeks of each other in 2013, occurred because of the pilots' decisions to continue VFR flight into deteriorating weather and IMC (NTSB Identification No: ERA13FA133; Report No. NTSB/AAR-14/03). These types of accidents occur less than twice a month within the United States and Canada—a big improvement since the 1980s when they averaged more than twice a week.[4] In spite of improvements over the years, attempted VFR flight into IMC still remains the number one cause of fatal GA weather-related accidents. Unfortunately, compared to a fatality rate of about only 19 percent for other GA accidents, almost 90 percent of these accidents result in fatalities. That's because pilots who attempt VFR flight into IMC either fly under CFIT or experience spatial disorientation resulting in LOC-I and uncontrolled flight into terrain. The NTSB recently published a *Safety Alert* warning GA pilots of the dangers of flying in conditions of reduced visual references,[5] and they also added "hazardous weather in GA operations" to their *Most Wanted List of Safety Improvements*.[6]

Sources:

1. Boeing Commercial Airplanes, *Statistical Summary of Commercial Jet Airplane Accidents: Worldwide Operations*, 1959–2016 (Seattle, WA: July 2017).
2. Flight Safety Foundation, *Reducing the Risk of Runway Incursions* (Alexandria, VA: May 2009).
3. Tzvetomir Blajev and William Curtis, *Go-Around Decision-Making and Execution Project, Final Report* (Alexandria, VA: Flight Safety Foundation, March 2017).
4. Dale R. Wilson and Teresa A. Sloan, "VFR Flight into IMC: Reducing the Hazard," *Journal of Aviation/Aerospace Education & Research*, 13 (Fall 2003): 29–42.
5. National Transportation Safety Board, *NTSB Safety Alert: Reduced Visual References Require Vigilance*, SA-020 (Washington, DC: March 2013).
6. National Transportation Safety Board, *General Aviation: Identify and Communicate Hazardous Weather* (Washington, DC: 2014).

ally involve noncompliance with regulations, rules, and procedures that are designed to ensure safe flight operations (the pilot knows better but makes the decision anyway). Pilots usually commit a violation because they believe it will better facilitate the accomplishment of the flight, even if they know it might involve an elevated level of risk. Violations are also known as *willful noncompliance*. Some of the decision errors discussed above involve willful noncompliance. Other examples include flying an aircraft with a known defect, flying too low or below the minimum safe/regulatory altitude, or descending below the MDA or DH without obtaining adequate visual references.

Two particularly vexing decision errors that pilots continue to make are failing to conduct a missed approach/go-around when runway, weather, or other conditions would require it, and attempting VFR flight into IMC; the former of particular concern to airline operations, the latter primarily involving GA flight operations (*see* the information box on the previous page for more information).

Decision-Making Models

Decisions come in all forms. Pilots face numerous routine decisions, such as choosing how much fuel to carry, determining the best time for departure, figuring out what altitude to fly at to avoid turbulence, and deciding whether to visit the restroom before boarding the aircraft (this last one is always a good idea). However, sometimes pilots need to make non-routine decisions, such as deciding if they should delay or divert a flight because of weather, diagnosing a systems malfunction, or responding to an emergency. Different approaches and theories are used to describe the various aspects of decision making. These models usually fall under two broad types: normative vs. descriptive models, and compensatory vs. non-compensatory models.

Normative vs. Descriptive Models

Normative decision-making models describe how decisions should be made to arrive at the best possible choice, while descriptive models attempt to explain how humans actually do make decisions. A **normative decision-making model** is a rational, logical, analytical, and sometimes even mathemat-

ical or statistical approach for obtaining optimal decision-making outcomes. A normative approach to decision making will lead to the best possible decision and can be used in a wide variety of decision-making tasks. For example, a person deciding which home or automobile to purchase could list the attributes deemed important for each alternative, assign numerical weights to each attribute (depending on their relative importance), rank each, then tally and compare the totals to arrive at the best decision. To a certain extent this approach is reflected in the FAA's definition of aeronautical decision-making (ADM)—a "systematic approach to the mental process used by pilots to consistently determine the best course of action in response to a given set of circumstances."[12]

However, on several dimensions, ADM is not the same as choosing what car to purchase. For one, flying involves significant risk—a wrong decision in flight could lead to the deaths of everyone aboard. Secondly, evaluating large quantities of information often takes considerable time—a strategy that works well when purchasing a home or a car, but a luxury pilots in flight simply do not have. In addition, the flying environment is dynamic, meaning conditions are constantly changing, which further complicates pilot decision making.[13] For example, a thunderstorm is reported moving near the destination airport but the FSS specialist doesn't know exactly when it will be clear of the area and therefore when it would be safe to land. Should you divert to another airport or continue? Where should you divert to? What are the consequences of diverting? At what point must you make this decision before fuel and aircraft range concerns become an issue?

Research indicates, however, that there is a large discrepancy between how humans *should* decide (normative) and how they actually *do* decide. **Descriptive decision-making models** try to capture how humans actually make decisions. Whether because of the limitations of human information processing or because of the fact that most decisions don't require complex analysis of large amounts of information, or both, researchers have found that people often do not use a normative approach to decision making, but instead prefer to use shortcuts or basic rules of thumb. They may not always lead to the most optimal decision, but often to a decision that is good enough.[14]

Compensatory vs. Non-Compensatory Models

Another approach makes a distinction between compensatory and non-compensatory strategies. Decision making involves choosing one or more alternatives from among several. Some alternatives possess a mixture of desirable and less desirable attributes. A person who chooses an option with a less desirable trait because another desirable trait compensates for it, is adopting a compensatory approach to decision making. For example, if a systems malfunction requires a diversion to a suitable alternate airport—either airport A or airport B—the flight crew must consider several variables. There may be adequate repair facilities and personnel at both airports. However, airport A is 20 minutes further away than airport B but has more comfortable passenger facilities and better connecting flights than airport B. If the crew chooses airport A because of these latter attributes, then they have decided that those attributes are desirable enough to compensate for the increased time and fuel used to get there.

On the other hand, a non-compensatory approach to decision making is made if an alternative is unacceptable because one or more of its attributes doesn't meet some minimum criterion, even though it may possess other attractive characteristics. For example, if neither airport A or B has a runway with sufficient length for a landing or takeoff, then it doesn't matter how desirable their other attributes are: they cannot compensate for this one critical attribute and the crew will need to look for another airport.

Information Processing and Decision Making

Decision making is an especially complex component of human information processing. However, it essentially involves assessing or diagnosing a situation and then choosing a course of action. A *good* decision involves accurately assessing the situation, making a choice that will lead to an optimal (or at least satisfactory) outcome, and responding by effectively executing that decision. However, it can readily be seen in the information processing model (*see* Figure 3-5 in Chapter 3) that any distortions upstream in the model—such as errors in sensation, perception, attention and working/long-term memory—will adversely affect downstream cognitive processes such as decision making, and response selection and execution.

For example, an engine of a twin-engine turboprop airplane fails while climbing out from an airport. In order to reduce drag and obtain the maximum climb performance using the one remaining engine, the flight crew must accurately assess the situation by using their perception, attention, and memory to correctly identify the failed engine (e.g., "identify dead engine, verify dead engine," etc.), then choose and implement the correct actions by feathering the propeller (pitch angle increased and propeller stopped to reduce drag) and securing the dead engine. If the crew incorrectly assesses the situation, and chooses the wrong engine, a catastrophe such as that involving TransAsia Airways Flight 235 that crashed three miles east of Runway 10 at Taipei's Songshan Airport could occur. The picture taken from a dashboard camera video of the left wing clipping a taxi and a highway overpass just before crashing into a river is chilling. About a minute after takeoff, an uncommanded autofeather occurred on the number 2 engine of the Regional Air Transport ATR-72; however, the captain reduced power and shut down the number 1 (operative) engine, leaving them with no thrust at all. The aircraft stalled, killing 43 of the 58 people aboard. The captain chose to reduce power and shut down the left engine because he failed to accurately assess the situation, or as the official accident report noted, he "failed to perform the documented failure identification procedure before executing any actions."[15]

Figure 17-1 is an adaptation of a decision-making model that describes in more detail the decision-making component in Figure 3-5 in Chapter 3. The diagram is an attempt to simplify the understanding of the various mechanisms involved in this higher-level component of human information processing. As previously mentioned, decision making generally involves two aspects, or steps: situation assessment (or diagnosis) and choosing a course of action. The need for a choice is often triggered by stimuli indicating a change in the environment. For example, the crew may see a landing gear indicator light that fails to illuminate, or hear a pilot report indicating deteriorating destination airport weather, or smell smoke fumes indicating a possible fire on board.

Fig 17-1.

Decision making involves situation assessment (diagnosis) and choice, as well as other mental processes.[16]

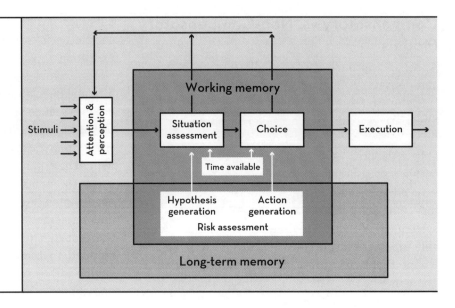

Relying on information learned and stored in LTM, flight crew members will formulate, using their working memories, a hypothesis of what the true state of affairs is and will direct their attention to other sources of environmental stimuli to confirm or disconfirm the veracity of their hunches or educated guesses. For example, to confirm the hypothesis that the landing gear is likely working even though one of its indicator lights isn't, they will check to see if the landing gear light bulb is burnt-out. Or, to test their hypothesis that the weather conditions are unsatisfactory for landing, they may contact an ATC or an FSS specialist to obtain up-to-the-minute destination weather information. Or, to ascertain if the smoke smell originates from incoming contaminated bleed air in the air-conditioning system or from electrical wiring, they may sample information from engine, hydraulic, pneumatic, and electrical gauges, or consult the emergency and abnormal checklist (or *Quick Reference Handbook*). Should it be determined that it is an electrical fire, knowledge stored in their LTM indicating that "where there's smoke there's fire" will inform them that the threat level is elevated, and a decision may need to be implemented quickly.

It should be pointed out that in the dynamic environment of the flight deck, decision making (i.e., situation assessment and choice) also requires an assessment of risk and an estimation of time available to make a choice and implement it. For example, if the landing gear has truly malfunctioned, then there are choices that could mitigate the severity of consequences of landing with a collapsed or collapsing gear. Should the crew jettison fuel to make the aircraft lighter? Should they land on a different runway? Does the airport have aircraft rescue and firefighting services? If not, is there another suitable airport nearby? Or, what are the options if the destination airport weather is unsuitable for a landing? The amount of fuel remaining will limit the range of options. Finally, if the source of the smoke fumes is unknown, what is the level of risk of continuing to the destination or diverting and landing at the nearest suitable airport?

Finally, after assessing the situation, a pilot must choose and implement the best choice from a generated list of possible alternatives. Pilots will use information stored in their LTM to select the best option (using compensatory or non-compensatory criteria as discussed previously), guidance provided in airline-published procedures (e.g., checklists), or a combination of both.

Decision Making in the Face of Uncertainty

Decisions may involve certain or uncertain situation assessment, risk assessment, choice selection, and outcomes. For example, many day-to-day operational decisions involve a high degree of certainty: advancing the throttle levers will increase thrust and airspeed; pushing the control column forward will pitch the nose down, also increasing airspeed; extending the flaps will facilitate a slower approach speed; etc. However, like some of the scenarios previously mentioned (e.g., deteriorating airport weather, fumes in the cabin), there is a degree of uncertainty in the accuracy of the diagnosis, risk assessment, and the consequences of the choice(s) decided upon. For example, how certain is a safe outcome should the pilot decide to land on a contaminated runway (e.g., water, snow, ice) after receiving a braking action report of "medium" from ATC? Or, what is the likely outcome if the pilot elects to continue a flight into gradually deteriorating weather? Or, how sure is the captain that the fire is fully extinguished after they have followed all the steps in the *engine fire in flight* checklist?

To better understand the types of decisions pilots make, it is helpful to consider the distinctions between skill-, rule-, and knowledge-based behaviors,[17] all of which are involved in performing the task of piloting an aircraft. Skill-based behaviors involve highly practiced manual/physical motor skills that occur almost automatically and usually at an unconscious level. These well-learned behaviors are utilized when you automatically reduce the power before descending or make minor stick-and-rudder control inputs to remain within altitude and heading parameters when flying manually (hand-flying).

More germane to the discussion of decision making are rule-based behaviors. These are predetermined actions that apply to specific situations. Using an "if X, then Y" formula (e.g., *if* the cabin depressurizes, *then* descend to 10,000 feet or minimum safe altitude), this framework assists crews in both diagnosing a situation and choosing a course of action. Many of these responses are learned during initial and recurrent flight training and are often recalled from memory with the aid of checklists or adherence to SOPs. For example, if the left alternator light illuminates, the crew carries out the steps prescribed in the *illumination of alternator light* checklist and the problem is dealt with. Or, *if* the crosswind for the intended runway exceeds a particular crosswind value, *then* in compliance with the published SOPs the crew chooses a different runway (or airport) where a safe landing can occur. If-then formulations make decisions easier for the crew and significantly reduce uncertainty.

Initial and recurrent pilot training, along with airline flight deck operating practices, have evolved to the point where they are very successful in aiding most pilot decisions at the skill- and rule-based levels. However, pilots occasionally encounter novel situations in which they have not been trained or for which no predetermined response has yet been formulated. These knowledge-based behaviors can present a greater challenge to flight crews because they must rely primarily on their own experience and previously learned knowledge to solve a novel problem. This is further exacerbated if sufficient cues in the environment are lacking to make an accurate assessment of the situation. Uncertainty in relation to situation assessment and choice is reduced if a problem is *well-structured*, or well defined. In this case the flight crew may be able to apply a previously formulated response such as is found in a checklist—as for rule-based decisions—or they may be able to arrive at an optimal decision relying solely on knowledge stored in their LTM.

However, if an unanticipated *ill-structured* problem occurs in flight for which no predetermined solution has been formulated, the crew can only rely on the experience and knowledge stored in their LTM. Fortunately, such novel situations are rare in flight, but the consequences can be catastrophic if the crew is unable to accurately diagnose and resolve the situation. The crew of Flight 232, a United Airlines DC-10 that crash-landed in Sioux City, Iowa, faced just such a situation.

They heard a loud explosion in the tail section and felt the airframe vibrate and shudder. At first they had no idea what had happened, but reasoned that it was very likely an engine problem (i.e., they formulated a hypothesis). To further diagnose this problem, they searched for more information by directing their attention to the engine instruments and confirmed that the number two tail-mounted engine had failed. They completed the engine shutdown checklist (*if-then*, rule-based) procedure for the number two engine. At that time the FE discovered the airplane's hydraulic pressure and quantity gauges indicated zero. The aircraft was descending in a right turn and the FO informed the captain that he could not control the airplane. The captain took control and confirmed that it did not respond to flight control inputs. He then reduced thrust on the number one engine to see what the airplane would do (hypothesis testing), and it began to roll left to a wings-level attitude. The FE and a United Airlines check pilot riding as a passenger conducted visual inspections of the wings and empennage and confirmed that the controls were not working properly and there was damage to the tail surfaces. At this point, despite the fact the FO wouldn't let go of the controls, the realization that they likely had no hydraulic power informed their decision-making process and they moved from diagnosis mode into choice mode. They deployed the air driven generator, which powers the number one auxiliary hydraulic pump, but it did not restore hydraulic power. The only thing they could do to effect any semblance of control was to apply differential thrust from the remaining two engines to achieve partial control of this wide-body jet with 296 souls on board.

In hindsight, we now know what happened. Accident investigators discovered that the catastrophic separation, fragmentation, and forceful discharge of uncontained stage one fan rotor assembly parts from the number two engine severed the three hydraulic systems that powered the airplane's flight controls, rendering them useless. Fortunately, the crew was able to maneuver the airplane to Runway 22 at Sioux City; however, the minimal control provided by the use of differential thrust precluded the crew from preventing the airplane from hitting hard on the runway and cartwheeling onto the side of the runway and rolling inverted. Several people died in the crash, but 185 survived (Report No: NTSB/AAR-90/06).

This was an ill-structured knowledge-based problem: There was no if-then checklist to act as a countermeasure for this situation—the manufacturer, the FAA, and the airline thought the odds of something like this occurring were so remote that they didn't develop one. Using good CRM skills, they utilized all resources available to them—including the services of an off-duty captain who eventually ended up in charge of manually operating the thrust levers—and together, they drew upon their deeply ingrained knowledge of how airplanes fly, stored in their LTM, to regain a degree of control using differential thrust.

More recently, as noted in Chapter 2, the crew of US Airways Flight 1549 lost thrust in both engines two minutes after departing Runway 04 at LaGuardia Airport after encountering a flock of Canada geese at only 2,800 feet AGL. In one way, their decision making was simplified for them: Because of insufficient thrust, they had no other choice but to land the Airbus A320 somewhere within gliding distance.

They even had an if-then dual-engine failure checklist, which they followed. However, rather than a well-defined, rule-based problem, it turned out to be an ill-defined knowledge-based problem for the crew. The captain, who was the PF, had to rely on his previously learned psychomotor skills stored in his implicit memory (or procedural memory; see Chapter 16) to hand-fly the airplane, judge its gliding distance using external visual motion cues, and choose the most suitable landing spot. He thought of turning back to LaGuardia, but he wasn't sure of the outcome. He reasoned that it would have been catastrophic it they didn't make it to the field, with the airplane likely crashing into buildings near the highly populated area of Manhattan. ATC offered Teterboro Airport as an option and the crew initially accepted that option. However, they quickly realized that even though the airport was located in the general direction the aircraft was heading (i.e., they didn't have to turn as much as they would have had to for LaGuardia), it was even further away than LaGuardia. And again, what would be the consequences had they failed to make that airport? That area too was heavily populated. They finally elected to perform a water landing on the Hudson River. According to Captain Sullenberger, it was "long enough, smooth enough, and wide enough."[18] Less than three minutes after the Airbus engines ingested the birds, the captain landed the airplane on the water and the passengers began evacuating. If you saw the news, or watched the movie, you know that all on board were saved—truly a miracle on the Hudson.

In its accident report, published some 16 months after the accident, the NTSB investigators came to the conclusion (i.e., they made their decision) that the captain had made the right decision to ditch on the Hudson River rather than attempt to land at an airport. His choice "provided the highest probability that the accident would be survivable." Furthermore, the Board concluded that even though there were two possible checklists the crew could have used—the ditching checklist and the dual-engine failure checklist—the crew's choice of the latter was the best choice for the situation. However, even the use of that checklist was problematic—not only could they not complete all three pages of this checklist (they simply did not have enough time), they really couldn't get much further than item number 2 on the first page since the next item required an engine relight speed of 300 knots, a speed which they were unable to attain given their low altitude and airspeed. According to the accident report, Airbus had designed the checklist for a dual-engine failure that would occur above 20,000 feet and had not considered developing one for use at a low altitude. Despite this, the captain wisely completed another item on the checklist, and started the APU which, according to the NTSB, improved the outcome of the ditching.

Despite the availability of if-then checklists for the situation, which would at face value suggest a simple rule-based procedure was required, the crew faced an ill-structured knowledge- and skill-based situation that was ripe with uncertainty. However, their knowledge, skills, and experience, along with their professionalism and "excellent crew resource management during the accident sequence contributed to their ability to maintain control of the airplane, configure it to the extent possible under the circumstances, and fly an approach that increased the survivability of the impact" (Report No: NTSB/AAR-10/03).

Heuristics and Biases

The distinction was made earlier between normative and descriptive decision-making models, the former describing how decisions should be made, the latter explaining how humans actually do decide. A normative approach is a rational, logical, and analytical process designed to achieve the most optimal decision. Depending on the nature of the decision-making task, mathematical and probabilistic reasoning may be used to determine a decision's maximum value (the sum of the outcomes multiplied by their probabilities). This is an optimum approach to making the best possible decisions, especially for those that require the processing of substantial amounts of information.

A significant body of research, however, indicates there is large discrepancy between how humans *should* decide (normative) and how they actually *do* decide (descriptive). Two main reasons for this are: most decisions don't require complex analysis of large amounts of information; and logical, mathematical, and probabilistic reasoning is simply too hard to do—limitations inherent in the human cognitive system, especially limitations in attention and working memory (*see* Chapters 14 and 16), preclude us from regularly engaging in this type of thinking. Rather

than engaging in normative strategies to make decisions, we usually use basic rules of thumb, or **heuristics**, when making evaluative judgments and choices. These shortcuts may not always lead to the best decision, but to a decision that is often good enough, or suffices; a process which economist and cognitive psychologist Herbert Simon coined **satisficing**, where the search for alternatives is stopped when an option is found that *satisfies* the decision maker's most important criteria.[19] Most of the time the use of heuristics and satisficing serves us well; it simplifies our decision making by reducing the amount of information we need to process, making decision making quicker and easier. However, overreliance on heuristics can not only stop short our evaluation of alternatives, but also lead to **decision-making biases**—distortions, or errors, in our thinking and judgment. Obviously, this less-than-optimal decision making could lead to trouble on the flight deck.

Availability Heuristic

Several heuristics and biases have been identified. The **availability heuristic** is used when we estimate the frequency or probability of something "by the ease with which instances or associations could be brought to mind."[20] We tend to overestimate the frequency of items or information that are easily recalled from our memories—especially those that are recent, familiar, or vivid—and underestimate the frequency of those that are not. For example, you may overestimate the frequency of earthquakes if you recently lived through one. Or, since most of us are quite familiar with information and items reported by the media—which powerfully informs our perceptions about the state of the world, with reports of child abductions, airplane accidents, and shark attacks—you may believe that such events are more frequent than they really are. Did you know that you are actually 30 times more likely to be killed by a falling coconut than from a shark attack, 60 times more likely to die by falling out of bed than by being attacked by a dog, or more likely to be killed by hot water than an airplane crash?

The availability heuristic may have been involved in the LOC-I and crash of an Air Illinois Hawker Siddeley HS-748 as it approached Southern Illinois Airport in IMC at night, killing all 10 people aboard. Shortly after takeoff from Springfield, Illinois, Flight 710 lost power from the left DC generator. However, instead of shutting down the left generator, the FO erroneously shut down the right generator and, unfortunately, the crew was unable to get it back on line. The NTSB accident report notes that the maintenance records and flight log contained "numerous write-ups describing problems with the right generator" in the days leading up to the accident and states that the FO had assumed, as heard on the cockpit voice recorder, that the "problem was on the right side." His familiarity with recent difficulties with the generator possibly triggered the availability heuristic causing him to incorrectly identify the right generator as the problem. Rather than turn back, they attempted to fly the remaining 39 minutes to their destination and lost all electrical power (Report No: NTSB/AAR-85/03).

The availability heuristic may have also been involved in a captain's decision to execute the airline's wind shear/microburst escape procedure rather than the aircraft in-flight upset/stall procedure. An American Airlines Airbus A300 experienced LOC-I following a stall while flying in IMC near West Palm Beach, Florida. Fortunately, the crew was able to recover and land with only one seriously injured passenger. The NTSB determined the probable cause was the flight crew's failure to maintain adequate airspeed during a level off from their descent—which led to an inadvertent stall—and their subsequent failure to use proper stall recovery techniques. When the right wing dropped, the captain initially called for pitching the aircraft "20 degrees up, 20 degrees up, firewall" which only aggravated the stall recovery. The captain commanded his FO (who was the PF at the time) to execute the wind shear/microburst escape procedure, because, as they later testified, they thought it was a microburst (NTSB Identification No: DCA97MA049).

What would cause the crew to misdiagnose a stall for a microburst? It turns out their flight was delayed in a hold to avoid adverse convective weather at their destination airport of Miami. First, they received an updated aircraft communications addressing and reporting system report that tornadoes were observed in the Miami area. Second, they observed on their onboard weather radar a very distinctive thunderstorm cell 10 miles ahead of them. Third, they had illuminated the fasten seat belts signs because of turbulence and instructed the passengers to remain in their seats. Fourth, they felt the turbu-

lence begin to increase in intensity to continuous moderate turbulence. And finally, just before the upset they heard wind-rumbling noises with the FO testifying he felt a "sudden push of wind apparently from our right to left" just before the event.[21] In other words, the *familiarity* of these *recent* and *vivid* weather events led the crew to believe they were experiencing a wind shear event, not a pre-stall buffet or full stall.

Illusory Correlations

Recent and familiar experiences may lead to you to make **illusory correlations**. That is, you may believe a relationship exists between two variables when none exists. For example, you went flying after receiving a weather briefing forecasting poor weather, but found the weather was just fine. If this occurs several times within a relatively short time span, the availability heuristic may lead you to believe the FSS specialist was deliberately painting a pessimistic weather picture just to be on the safe side. Unfortunately, this illusory correlation between poor-weather weather briefings and actual good weather may cause you to disbelieve future briefings, tempting you to fly in hazardous weather. Or, flying in the inclement weather, you may overestimate the probability of successful flight through it because of another illusory correlation: you remember when you personally flew this same route several times before, in the same weather conditions, and made it safely through.

Gambler's Fallacy

People often make errors when judging the probabilities of random chance events. Even though each flip of a coin is independent of previous flips, many of us believe that if the coin comes up heads 11 times in a row, it is more likely that it will come up tails on the 12th flip. However, each toss of the coin is independent of the others and the chances of throwing heads or tails on any particular throw will always be 50-50. We tend to see chance as self-correcting and therefore after a run of bad luck we think that good luck is sure to follow. For a VFR pilot who has been delayed several times due to poor weather, the **gambler's fallacy** could lead to trouble. It might seem logical that after several days of poor weather, better conditions are bound to follow. This type of reasoning could lead to a decision to fly in weather which would normally be considered unacceptable.

Anchoring and Adjustment

In situations where judgments need to be revised (*adjusted*) from initial data (the *anchor*), results obtained vary according to the value of the initial information. For example, higher answers were obtained for participants who were given five seconds to guess the product of $8 \times 7 \times 6 \times 5 \times 4 \times 3 \times 2 \times 1$ (*high anchor* condition, median 2,250) and lower values were obtained for participants to guess the product of $1 \times 2 \times 3 \times 4 \times 5 \times 6 \times 7 \times 8$ (*low anchor* condition, median 512). We tend to make adjustments that are biased toward the initial values. We also tend to make insufficient adjustments—the true product is 40,320.[22] Researchers even found that anchoring affected the severity of sentences recommended by mock jurors: presenting them with a list of possible verdicts ordered from the harshest to the most lenient led to harsher sentences than if the order was reversed![23]

The **anchoring and adjustment heuristic** has been suspected in contributing to pilots' decisions to continue VFR flight into IMC. For example, when obtaining updated weather information that describes more serious conditions than originally forecast (the anchor), pilots may make insufficient adjustments to their judgment of weather severity and elect to continue on to their destination in the face of deteriorating weather. A study in New Zealand recently confirmed this suspicion when they asked 196 private, commercial, and airline pilots to estimate weather conditions (as replicated on a flight computer screen) after being exposed to either low ceiling and visibility (low-anchor) weather conditions or higher ceiling and visibility (high-anchor) weather conditions. They confirmed that pilots who were previously exposed to better weather conditions (high-anchor) had significantly higher estimates of subsequent ceiling and visibility values than those who were first exposed to poorer weather conditions. The high-anchor participants were also significantly more likely to assess the new weather conditions as safe than those who were first exposed to the low-anchor weather.[24]

Framing Bias

Choice preferences are influenced by the framing of a decision problem. For example, let's say you are given a choice between A and B below. What would you choose?

A. A sure win of 85 dollars.
B. An 85 percent chance to win 100 dollars.

Now, what would you choose if your choice is between the following?

C. A sure loss of 85 dollars.
D. An 85 percent chance to lose 100 dollars.

In the first example, you are most likely to choose option A, preferring the certain gain over the chance of a possible greater gain. In the second example, however, you are most likely to choose option D, preferring the chance of a loss over a certain smaller loss.

When researchers asked participants to choose between two programs designed to ameliorate the effects of a deadly disease that is expected to kill 600 people, most people chose A:

A. If program A is chosen, 200 people will be saved.
B. If program B is chosen, there is a ⅓ probability that 600 people will be saved (and a ⅔ probability that no one will be saved).

However, when the problem was re-formulated, so that when program C is chosen, 400 people will die, and when program D is chosen, there is a ⅓ probability that nobody will die (and a ⅔ probability that 600 people will die), most people chose program D.[25] Both choice scenarios are identical, yet participants respond differently depending on how the choice is framed. When the decision is framed in terms of gains (i.e., lives saved), people are *risk averse* and more likely to choose a certain gain over the chance of an even greater gain. When framed in terms of losses (i.e., lives lost), people are *risk seeking* since they are more likely to avoid choosing the certain loss in favor of only the chance of an even greater loss.

Simply presenting identical information in two different ways—either positive or negative—is enough to bias decisions one way or another. For example, when treatment for lung cancer is framed in terms of survival rates versus the corresponding mortality rates, a change in preference for one treatment over another occurs.[26] As Daniel Kahneman, one of the leading researchers in this field, has observed, we avoid losses: "10% mortality is more frightening than 90% survival."[27] The **framing bias** parallels the old question, "Is the glass half empty or half full?"

Empirical evidence indicates that the framing bias may be involved in pilots' decisions to continue flight into deteriorating weather. Researchers presented pilots on a computer-simulated VFR cross-country flight—with marginal weather forecast at their destination—with the decision to continue flight or divert to another airport framed in terms of either losses or gains. The study found that participants were more likely to continue VFR flight into adverse weather when the decision was framed in terms of the losses associated with diverting.[28] In deciding whether to continue VFR flight into deteriorating adverse weather you're likely to avoid the certain losses associated with turning back/diverting (e.g., passenger displeasure, family disappointment, missed meetings/connections, employer displeasure, revenue loss, etc.) and risk only the possibility of the greater loss of an accident should you continue. If you frame the problem in terms of choices between two positive outcomes, however, you will tend to be risk averse. That is, you are more likely to choose a certain gain in favor of only the chance of a gain. For example, if you frame the decision in terms of the certain preservation of life you will gain if you turn back/divert, with only the possibility of making it through the poor weather, you're likely to choose the former. So, be careful how you formulate your go/no-go decision. It could mean the difference between life and death.

Escalation Bias

When there is too much invested to quit in terms of time, energy, and other resources, we are often reluctant to abandon a given course of action even when it is a failing one. For example, you continue to wait on the telephone for someone to answer while you're on hold for an inordinately long time—but you've waited too long to hang up now! Or, you sit through an entire movie even when you determined early on that it was a bad choice—you paid for your ticket so you can't waste it. One thing after another has broken down on your 20-year-old car—you've spent $2,000 on repair bills this past year alone, but if you sell it you will lose everything you put into it so you keep it, even though you'll probably sink more money into it later (sometimes referred to as the *sunk cost effect*).

On one occasion, a student of mine was driving in the country late one night, and his gas gauge indicated near empty. He was in the middle of nowhere and didn't know if he would find a gas station before

he ran out of fuel. If he turned back he felt confident he would make it to a station he had passed 10 minutes earlier, but he struggled with the decision because turning back would mean all of the resources (in terms of time and energy) that he had invested would be lost. (He probably also struggled with how to frame this problem: he knew the *certain loss* if he turned back, while if he kept going there was a chance he would make it and only a chance he would run out of gas.)

This sunk cost effect—also known as the **escalation bias**, or entrapment bias—may make it difficult for you to turn back in the face of poor weather and is one of many complex and usually unconscious psychological factors that influence decisions to press on into deteriorating weather, a condition commonly known among pilots as *get-home-itis*. In fact, researchers have discovered that unlike other types of accidents, those involving VFR flight into IMC tend to occur closer to the intended destination airport.[29] It appears that most of these accidents also occur on the last leg of a return trip because the desire to get home overrides the ability to make a sound go/no-go decision. We have a name for it in aviation: the **last-leg syndrome**. This parallels the finding that escalation/entrapment is stronger the closer one is to reaching their goal, or the observation that most risky bets (long shot bets) at the track are made during the last race of the day.[30, 31]

Just as we pilots find it difficult to conduct a go-around when the situation indicates that we should (*see* "Failure to go-around" in the information box earlier in this chapter) because of the investment of time, energy, and resources, we also find it difficult to turn around in the face of deteriorating weather. It is especially difficult if it has been a long trip that has required many unplanned stops because of marginal weather and your destination is only a short distance away ("I've made it this far—I can't turn back now!"). Therefore, you are dealing not only with a weather trap, but a psychological trap as well. Research indicates that this is even stronger for those situations where the status quo can be passively maintained by not actively making a decision: it's easiest to simply keep the airplane going in its original direction.[32] The status quo is maintained and no decision is required; it was already made before takeoff. In his book, provocatively titled *The Naked Pilot*, airline pilot-writer-psychologist David Beaty summarizes the problem by stating that a pilot, like an animal, "prefers to follow his nose, look at the goal and go where he is looking. The nearer the goal, the stronger the pull. The nearer the airport, the more hypnotic the drive to continue."[33]

Confirmation Bias

"I don't like clouds. There are mountains in them."

—Winston Churchill

The phenomenon of **confirmation bias** describes our tendency to look for information which confirms, rather than disconfirms, our beliefs. An early example demonstrates this phenomenon. Participants were asked to discover a simple rule the experimenter had in his mind. He then gave them three numbers ("2, 4, 6") that conformed to the rule. They in turn were to give him three other numbers and he informed them if those numbers conformed or didn't conform to the rule. After they were sure of the rule they were to stop. Out of the 29 people who were confident they had figured out the rule only six actually had it correct. The reason? Most of them gave examples that confirmed the rule (like "8, 10, 12" or "21, 23, 25", etc.) rather than disconfirm it (like "12, 10, 8"). The rule was simply *three numbers in increasing order of magnitude* (i.e., "1, 2, 3" or "2, 10, 13" etc.).[34]

The tendency to look for evidence that confirms our hunches, rather than evidence that discredits them, can get us into trouble in flight. For example, I remember a student who insisted so much on finding a particular feature indicated on his VFR navigation chart that he eventually found it—never mind that it was actually 10 miles from where he thought he was! Good navigation involves looking for features that not only confirm your position but also disconfirm your hunches. If the information from the outside visual environment and/or the inside navigation instrumentation doesn't disconfirm your hunch, then your aircraft is probably located where you think it is. That is the problem with confirmation bias—once we have found the evidence we think confirms our understanding of the situation, we stop our search for alternative evidence that may very well prove us wrong.

The tragic accident involving Jessica Dubroff was highlighted in the introduction to this chapter. Going over some of the transcript, we also noted that there were some elements in the preflight weather briefing that seemingly confirmed the pilot's belief that it might be safe for him to depart, and his words indicate that he may have latched on to that. Confirmation bias has also been implicated in numerous other accidents and incidents, including three mentioned in previous chapters:

- Comair Flight 5191, a Bombardier Challenger CL-600 Regional Jet (CRJ), ran off the end of the runway during takeoff at Blue Grass Airport in Lexington, Kentucky, impacting the airport perimeter fence, trees, and terrain, killing 49 of the 50 people aboard. The crew mistakenly attempted a takeoff on Runway 26 (which was of insufficient length for departure) instead of Runway 22. Several cues were available that were not consistent with a taxi onto Runway 22, including a runway holding position sign for Runway 26, a 75-foot painted width of Runway 26 (versus the 150-foot width of Runway 22), the absence of runway edge lights and precision runway markings (such as threshold markings and touchdown zone markings) on Runway 26, and a painted Runway "26" number on the runway. The NTSB concluded that both pilots failed to recognize that they were initiating a takeoff on the wrong runway because they did not evaluate evidence that would *contradict the airplane's position* on the airport surface at the time and they were likely influenced by confirmation bias (Report No: NTSB/AAR-07/05).

- On January 12, 2014, during a night visual approach in VMC, Southwest Airlines Flight 4013, a Boeing B-737, was cleared to land on Runway 14 at Branson Airport (KBBG) in Branson, Missouri, but the crew mistakenly landed six miles north on Runway 12 at M. Graham Clark Downtown Airport. The NTSB report indicates that the flight crew looked outside and *confirmed* they saw what they thought were the lights for KBBG; however, once they had what they believed to be KBBG in sight, they did not reference onboard navigation guidance. Had they done so, the information provided to them would have *disconfirmed* their belief they were approaching KBBG (NTSB Identification No: DCA14IA037).

- The same type of mishap occurred almost two months earlier. On November 21, 2013, in night VMC, a Boeing B-747 Dreamlifter, destined for McConnell AFB in Wichita, Kansas, mistakenly landed on a 6,100-foot runway at Colonel James Jabara Airport about 8 miles north of McConnell. They were cleared for the RNAV GPS 19L approach at McConnell AFB but once they saw what they thought were the lights for the airport, they completed the flight by visual reference only (NTSB Identification No: DCA14IA016).

Deciding-becomes-believing

Compounding the problem of confirmation bias is the *deciding-becomes-believing effect*, or the **choice-supportive bias**. Research shows that once we've made a decision we tend to increase our belief in the superiority of the chosen option and our belief in the inferiority of the option(s) we didn't choose. For example, gamblers feel more optimistic about their chosen bet after they decide than before they do.[35] After you've made the decision to continue to your destination in poor weather (rather than divert to a more suitable airport), you increase your belief that it was a much better choice than the other option.

It's possible we do this to reduce the stress associated with making the decision—decision making in and of itself can be stressful—but it is also likely that we do this to alleviate any threat we may feel to our self-esteem if we have made the wrong decision. The latter involves the subconscious desire to avoid what is commonly called *buyer's remorse*. This may partly explain why pilots are reluctant to conduct a go-around: the decision to land has been made and we avoid the mental discomfort caused by conflicting ideas, or **cognitive dissonance**, associated with changing our minds. Evidence indicates this bias also strengthens as we get older.[36] The bottom line is that once we've made up our minds, we're often quite resistant to changing it. This is obviously good if the decision is a correct one, but what if it isn't?

Belief Perseverance

"It ain't what you don't know that gets you into trouble. It's what you know for sure that just ain't so."

—Unknown (often misattributed to Mark Twain)

A closely related phenomenon is **belief perseverance**. This occurs when we think our beliefs are true even in the face of evidence that discredits them. Studies have been conducted where participants, after developing their own explanation as to why a given assertion (belief) might be true, continue to believe it is so even after the experimenter later provides clear evidence refuting that claim.[37] As one researcher noted, "Once subjects have made a first pass at a problem, the initial judgment may prove remarkably resistant to further information, alternative modes of reasoning, and even logical or evidential challenges."[38] This can be a problem for pilots if they think their decision or belief is the right one, even in the face of evidence proving otherwise. For example, a Gulfstream Aerospace G-IV traveled off the end of the 6,000-foot long runway at Teterboro Airport in New Jersey at a speed of about 40 to 50 knots and then, fortunately, came to rest 100 feet into an engineered materials arresting system. Despite evidence that they needed to change their persistent belief that they could land safely—they conducted an unstable approach at an excessively high airspeed (15 knots above V_{REF}) and eventually touched down with only 2,250 feet of runway remaining—both crew members later stated that they *continued to believe* the airplane would stop on the remaining runway (NTSB Identification No: ERA11IA006).

Optimistic Bias

Overwhelming evidence indicates that humans are often unrealistically optimistic:

- Rutgers University students were asked to rate the probability of experiencing such events as obtaining a good job after graduation, owning their own home, and living a long life. Almost all of them indicated they had a greater chance than their classmates. Most also believed they had a lower chance than their peers of experiencing such negative events as being fired from a job, developing a drinking problem, and experiencing a heart attack.[39] Since it is logically impossible for the majority of students in a given group to have a greater (or lesser) chance of experiencing a positive (or negative) event than the median of the group, some type of **optimistic bias** is assumed to be at work.

- Most people believe they are at less risk than others in developing health-related problems such as influenza,[40] mental breakdown,[41] or AIDS.[42]
- Most cigarette smokers see themselves as having less risk of developing smoking-related health problems than the average smoker.[43]

When it comes to gauging the risk of a transportation accident, most people also believe they are less likely than others to be involved in an automobile accident[44, 45] and most GA pilots rate their chances of having an aircraft accident as below average.[46] Using actual accident probabilities, one study asked GA pilots to rate their chances of being involved in an aircraft accident—over 95 percent of respondents indicated probabilities that were substantially lower than actual objective values.[47] Finally, in a study published by myself and a colleague, 160 VFR pilots were asked "In comparison to other pilots with similar flight background and experience as yourself, what do you feel are your chances of experiencing an accident due to inadvertent flight into instrument meteorological conditions (i.e., cloud or fog)?" Results indicated a significant majority of them believe they were less likely than pilots just like them to experience a VFR-into-IMC accident.[48]

The FAA determined the trait of unrealistic optimism has contributed to numerous aircraft accidents, especially in GA. In response, they sponsored research and published training manuals to improve ADM. An important aspect of this training is helping pilots recognize the presence of possible hazardous attitudes, one of which is the attitude of **invulnerability**—the attitude that an accident might happen to the other person, but it won't happen to me.[49] This type of wishful thinking is the same as the optimistic bias we have been discussing and could lead a pilot to take unnecessary risks in flight.

Ability Bias

Most people are not only unrealistically optimistic—especially when it comes to their likelihood of experiencing an accident—they also believe they are superior to others when it comes to personal virtues, skills, and abilities. The following highlights only some of the evidence for the **ability bias**:

- In a College Board survey of one million students, most rated themselves as above average in athletic and leadership ability. When judging their ability to get along with others, not one student rated themselves below average, and 60 percent and 25 percent of respondents put themselves in the top tenth and first percentile respectively![50] Again, since it is logically impossible for most of the students in a given group to be "above average," some type of ability bias is assumed to be at work.
- Most college students identify such positive personal traits as responsibility, resourcefulness, self-discipline, loyalty, friendliness, and kindness as more applicable to them than the average college student.[51]
- Most Americans believe they are more intelligent than their fellow citizens.[52]
- In Sweden and the United States, automobile drivers believe they drive better and are less risky than their fellow drivers: 93 percent of U.S. drivers rated themselves "more skillful," and 88 percent rated themselves as "safer," than the median driver.[53]

Pilots are no different than the rest of the population. For example, studies of GA pilots reveal that most believe they are safer, are much less likely to take risks in flying, and possess greater flying skill than their peers.[54, 55] In the study conducted by myself and my colleague, VFR pilots were also asked "How would you rate your ability to successfully fly out of instrument meteorological conditions should inadvertent flight into cloud or fog occur?" Results indicate a significant majority of them believe they were better than other pilots at avoiding IMC and successfully flying out of it.[56] This most closely aligns with the hazardous attitude of **macho**—the "I can do it" attitude described in the FAA's ADM training literature. It appears, therefore, that most of us tend to believe that we have a lower than average chance of experiencing an aircraft accident (optimistic bias), and believe we possess greater than average piloting ability which will help us to avoid such an accident (ability bias).

Overconfidence

"When anyone asks me how I can best describe my experience in nearly forty years at sea, I merely say, uneventful. Of course there have been winter gales, and storms and fog and the like, but in all my experience, I have never been in any accident of any sort worth speaking about...I never saw a wreck and never have been wrecked, nor have I been in any predicament that threatened to end in disaster of any sort."

The above words were spoken in 1907, by E. J. Smith, the captain of the RMS Titanic.[57] One consequence of the optimistic and ability biases is the **overconfidence bias**. Researchers have discovered that people are often more confident in the accuracy and assessment of their beliefs, decisions, and abilities than is warranted. For example, when people are asked to indicate their confidence levels to answers they give to various questions, they are almost always more confident of the correctness of their answers than they are actually correct.[58]

Unfortunately, overconfidence (including ability bias) has been implicated several aircraft accidents:

- A Cessna 170 pilot lost directional control and nosed over when attempting to land on a rough field. The NTSB cited *overconfidence* in his own ability and his aircraft's ability as contributing factors to the accident (NTSB Identification No: MKC87LA014).
- Both occupants aboard a Cessna 206 died after the aircraft impacted rising terrain 31 miles from their destination. Nearby witnesses reported seeing the aircraft flying between 100 and 300 feet AGL just below an overcast ceiling with only 1 SM ground visibility. The VFR pilot received two weather briefings and was aware of the low ceilings. When the briefer mentioned ceilings as low as 500 feet AGL, the pilot responded, "...five hundred up there doesn't bother me because...I'm real familiar with the area." The NTSB cited the pilot's *overconfidence* in his own abilities as a contributing factor (NTSB Identification No: CHI93FA024).

- The flight crew of GP Express Airlines Flight 861 lost positional awareness while conducting an instrument approach at Anniston Metropolitan Airport in Anniston, Alabama. The Beechcraft C99 crashed under CFIT killing three people aboard (including the captain) and seriously injuring the rest of the occupants. The NTSB stated the FO's *overconfidence* in his abilities was evident several times during the flight (Report No: NTSB/AAR-93/03).
- A helicopter pilot died when the Bell 206 he was piloting descended at a high rate of speed into the waters of San Francisco Bay after he flew into adverse weather in visual conditions at night. The NTSB report indicates the pilot failed to obtain a weather briefing, intentionally flew into the known poor weather conditions, and was *overconfident* in his own ability to safely fly in adverse weather conditions (NTSB Identification No: LAX89LA073).

In the years before seat-belt legislation, many motorists refused to wear them despite extensive educational campaigns to do otherwise. After years of driving accident-free, many people—especially more experienced drivers—didn't feel the need to wear them. Their experience with numerous safe outcomes reinforced their more risky behavior.[59] The same phenomenon occurs with pilots. For example, as a VFR pilot gains more and more exposure flying in marginal weather he or she attains fairly high levels of confidence in their ability to continue that behavior and feels more confident to fly in even worse (or sometimes even illegal) weather conditions. This may account, in part, for the historically high VFR flight into IMC accident rate among commercial pilots flying in places such as Northern Canada and Alaska. Two NTSB studies, one published in 1980 and the other 15 years later, confirmed that fatal VFR flight into IMC accidents were the leading safety problems for air taxi operations and commuter airlines in Alaska. There were 48 VFR flight into IMC accidents during a five-year period that were responsible for 47 percent and 67 percent of Alaska's fatal air taxi and commuter accidents respectively. Figure 17-2 clearly illustrates the disparity between the VFR-into-IMC accident rates in Alaska and the rest of the United States.[60]

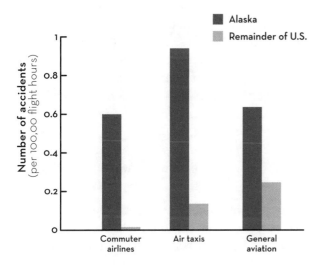

Fig 17-2.

VFR flight into IMC accident rates for Alaska commuter, air taxi, and GA compared to the remainder of the United States for five-year period from 1989 through 1993.[61]

The 1980 study reported the prevalence of a "mindset of risk-acceptance and a willingness to take risks," a condition commonly called *bush syndrome*. The 1995 follow-up study concluded that the situation hadn't really changed and inadvertent *and intentional* operation of VFR flights in IMC were still accepted and VFR flights in IMC were not an unusual occurrence.[62]

Confidence in the cockpit is essential. Aircrew are trained to the highest standards and they should know what they're doing and have a high degree of confidence in their abilities. However, overconfidence can lead to cognitive conceit that can, in critical flight situations, prevent us from making decisions that would lead to the best outcomes.

> "Carelessness and overconfidence are usually more dangerous than deliberately accepted risks."
>
> —Wilbur Wright

Biases Contribute to Good Health?

Many of these biases, including optimistic, ability, choice-supportive, and overconfidence biases, are part of a family of what have historically been called **self-serving biases**. These biases serve to protect our egos by painting an overly positive view of ourselves.

Interestingly, these biases may actually be an essential part of good health. A number of studies indicate that compared to mildly to moderately depressed people, so-called "normal" people are more optimistic yet less realistic about life.[63] Also, the field of health psychology indicates that there is a link between a positive, optimistic approach to life and reduced susceptibility to physical illness. So, paradoxically, even though these biases may be unrealistic and often unjustified, they seem to be very good for both our mental and physical well-being. However, the downside of these biases is an attitude of invulnerability could develop (it-won't-happen-to-me effect).

Summary of Heuristics and Biases

It's apparent that the abandonment of simple heuristics and the adoption of a normative approach to decision making would reduce errors and yield more optimal results; however, normal everyday human decision making involves the use of heuristics and biases. As we discussed at the beginning of this section, one reason for this is that a normative approach, which often requires logical and complex analytical—and sometimes mathematical and statistical—reasoning is unnecessary for most decisions, even those made on the flight deck. Another reason is that time constraints for in-flight decisions often preclude reliance on a time-consuming normative approach. Finally, for most of us such thinking is simply too hard to do. Limitations in LTM recall and working memory make it difficult to use normative procedures, especially if we are under stress.[64]

Heuristics, for the most part, produce satisfactory decisions that can be made relatively quickly with the least amount of cognitive effort. Also, as previously discussed, because most decisions don't require perfection, we tend to stop our search for alternatives when we've found one that satisfies some minimum acceptable criteria (i.e., *satisficing*). However, depending on the nature of the decision, satisficing on the flight deck may lead to inadequate decisions, or decisions that may even jeopardize safety.

Fatigue and Decision Making

We explored the effects of fatigue on flight crew performance in Chapter 10, noting that fatigue negatively affects a variety of cognitive abilities including perception, attention, memory retrieval, and decision making. It can lead to channelized attention causing pilots to miss important cues or to become fixated on a course of action or a desired outcome. It also reduces working memory capacity and interferes with memory retrieval including remembering whether required tasks have been completed. These limitations also make it difficult for pilots to remember, generate, or entertain hypotheses and alternatives needed for effective situation assessment and decision making.

These limitations appeared to be involved in the decision making of the captain of American Airlines Flight 1420, a McDonnell Douglas MD-82 that collided with a fence, localizer antenna array, and an approach lighting system and then traveled over a rock embankment after running off the end of Runway 04R, the 7,200-foot runway at Little Rock National Airport in Little Rock, Arkansas. This RE claimed the lives of the captain and 10 passengers, and seriously injured the FO, the flight attendants, and 105 passengers. The captain decided to continue the night approach and landing in spite of the presence of a severe thunderstorm at the airport—which was producing heavy rain, significant wind shear, and turbulence on final approach—and a wet runway with a five-knot tailwind, which exceeded the maximum crosswind limitation for the wet runway, and a RVR of 1,600 feet (below the 2,400 feet RVR authorized for the instrument landing system approach to Runway 04R).

Besides making what the NTSB concluded was the wrong decision to continue the approach and landing, the crew's performance was degraded, as evidenced by their operational errors on a number of tasks:

- They failed to complete the second half of the before-landing checklist;
- the captain did not realize that he hadn't called for the flaps and commanded the 40 degrees final landing flap configuration only after being queried by the first officer;
- neither pilot armed the spoilers, nor did they verify if the autospoilers had automatically deployed after landing;
- the captain failed to manually extend the spoilers after touchdown when they did not deploy (as a result, the wings continued to

support most of the airplane's weight, contributing to poor braking action);
- the captain elected to use manual braking (which contributed to the overrun) and neither pilot considered the use of automatic braking in light of the deteriorating weather conditions (which would have provided more effective braking); and
- the captain used reverse thrust that exceeded engine pressure ratios values (this contributed to poor directional control).

The NTSB concluded from their investigation that these operational errors, the flight crew's extended continuous hours of wakefulness, and the time at which the accident occurred were consistent with the development of fatigue. They also concluded that the crew's performance was affected by the stress of the adverse threatening weather and their efforts to expedite the landing before conditions got worse. The probable causes of the accident were the flight crew's failure to discontinue the approach when severe thunderstorms and their associated hazards to flight operations had moved into the airport area, and the crew's failure to ensure that the spoilers had extended after touchdown. The number one contributing factor to flight crew's impaired decision making, however, was their impaired performance resulting from fatigue and the situational stress associated with the intent to land under the circumstances (Report No: NTSB/AAR-01/02).

Making Better Decisions

"The heart is deceitful above all things...Who can understand it fully and know its secret motives?"

—Jeremiah 17:9

It appears the old prophet Jeremiah, speaking to his people more than 2,500 years ago, was right. Despite more than a century of using the scientific method to understand human thought and behavior, a full understanding is currently beyond our grasp. However, what we know so far indicates that human thinking and decision making is predisposed to error and bias. It doesn't help that most of these errors usually occur at an unconscious level, making identifying our own decision-making flaws even more difficult. We are very effective at deceiving ourselves.

In spite of this rather pessimistic appraisal of human decision making, you should not be discouraged: the vast majority of our decisions result in their desired outcomes and pilots make thousands of decisions that result in their passengers arriving safely at their destinations every day. It is for those very few poor decisions—the types we've been discussing in this chapter—that we need to especially guard against. Fortunately, there are plenty of behaviors you can practice that will assist you in making the best possible decisions while piloting your aircraft.

Increase Your Expertise and Maintain Proficiency

As a pilot, there is no substitute for knowledge and experience. We previously described the *Miracle on the Hudson*. Yes, it was considered a miracle by most, but it would not have occurred had it not been for the crew's knowledge, skill, and experience. If you remember, after losing power in both engines, the crew had no choice but to rely on that knowledge and experience to safely land their Airbus A320 in a manner and location that would minimize the threat to people in the airplane and on the ground. The crew decided that the best choice of action under the circumstances was a water landing on the Hudson River, all done in less than three minutes, because of the crew's professionalism and use of good CRM skills, and because of their knowledge and experience. Captain Sullenberger acknowledged as much when he told a news reporter, "In many ways, as it turned out, my entire life up to that moment has been a preparation to handle that particular moment."[65]

One of the reasons experts in a specific domain are at an advantage when it comes to decision making is because they are able to draw upon more semantic (facts, concepts and ideas) and episodic (experiences) memories to facilitate better decisions. In the previous chapter, for example, we mentioned how there is no difference in memory recall performance between novice and expert chess players when chess pieces are arranged randomly on the board; but when the pieces are arranged according to the recognized patterns the experts possess vastly superior memory. Pilots with significant levels of experience are also at a distinct advantage when it comes to decision making. This is especially so in novel situations because of the vast storehouse of experiences in their LTM that increases their ability to recognize

and match similar patterns in their environment and enables them to almost immediately assess the true state of a situation. These types of decisions—known as **recognition-primed decisions**[66]—are arrived at relatively quickly, do not require comparing short or long lists of options (compensatory decision making), and involve less cognitive effort to generate hypotheses when assessing a situation.

You may not have logged 20,000 hours of experience as Captain Sully has, but you can do much to increase your level of expertise. Some of the accidents you have read about in this book have involved the crew's improper response to aircraft emergencies. It is imperative, therefore, that you thoroughly learn everything you can about how the systems on your aircraft work, how to troubleshoot anomalies and failures, the checklist rationale, and procedures for such emergencies and emergency drills. Doing so will store and/or consolidate this domain-specific knowledge in your LTM making it more readily available if and when you need it. If you are rusty, get back in the books to maintain your proficiency. Hitting the books will also better prepare you to make enlightened decisions that will assist you in avoiding or extricating yourself from other emergencies or threats such as engine failures on takeoff, loss of cabin pressurization, midair collisions, runway incursions, thunderstorm encounters and low-level wind shear, airframe icing, spatial disorientation and visual illusions. Many of these topics are thoroughly covered in a book I cowrote with Gerald Binnema, *Managing Risk: Best Practices for Pilots*, published by Aviation Supplies and Academics, Inc.

Comply with SOPs

SOPs are written and tested procedures that are applied uniformly and consistently to all aspects of flight operations, including normal, non-normal (abnormal), and emergency operations.[67] Good SOPs contain best practices—the collective wisdom drawn from airlines, manufacturers, regulatory bodies, and others—designed to ensure safe operations for every aspect and phase of flight. Many major accidents, and some of the accidents highlighted in this book, would likely not have occurred if the flight crews adhered to the SOPs published by their respective organizations. Others would likely have been avoided if the organizations themselves had incorporated some of the industry best practices into their SOPs. For example, the NTSB noted that at the time of the American Airlines RE accident in Little Rock, Arkansas, the airline provided their flight crews with only general advisory information on severe weather avoidance, not specific operational guidance that would include decision aids and flow charts in quick reference checklists from which flight crews could more easily make "go" or "no-go" decisions concerning operations near hazardous weather.

After the accident, American Airlines amended their SOPs to do just that. They strengthened their guidance for handling wind shear warnings by *requiring* pilots to execute a go-around or wind shear escape maneuver should they receive a microburst alert. They prohibited takeoffs and landings when thunderstorms are near the airport, unless the runway and flight path are clear of thunderstorm hazards. They provided more explicit guidance about wind and gust limits for landings, expanded the quick reference crosswind table, strengthened guidance for landing on slippery runways during crosswinds, and, most importantly, implemented a no-fault go-around policy that recognizes a successful approach can end in a missed approach (Report No: NTSB/AAR-01/02).

Good SOPs not only take the guesswork out of safety decision making—by providing expert guidance that supports decisions that lead to the safest possible outcomes—but they relieve the burden on the pilot when faced with making such decisions. If you fly for an organization that doesn't use SOPs, or if you are a private pilot that flies for pleasure, consider emulating SOPs by establishing your own personal standards and procedures, including weather minimums. Contact a flight instructor or the FAA (or Transport Canada) and either will be glad to assist you in developing your own personal SOPs, including personal weather minimums.

Improve Your Situation Assessment

If an unexpected problem arises in flight, take the time necessary to accurately assess the situation (assuming, of course, that a split-second decision is not required). As you have seen in this chapter, pilots have shut down the wrong engine or generator because they were too quick to rush to judgment. Flight instructors used to tell their students to "wind the clock" when something goes wrong. They didn't really mean that this is what you should do; they wanted to emphasize that you need to avoid

the hazardous attitude of **impulsivity** by not doing anything that would make matters worse before taking the time to accurately troubleshoot the problem. The harmless winding of the clock meets an impulsive person's need to do something.

Your first instinct during (and after) the situation assessment stage of decision making should be to see if there is a checklist or SOP to aid you. As we previously mentioned, most rule-based and some knowledge-based problems are often resolved this way. If the problem proves to be an ill-structured knowledge-based problem, that is where your depth-of-knowledge and proficiency come in. Of course, if you fly on a crewed flight deck you should fully utilize your CRM skills to resolve the issue. The other crew member can help you fly the aircraft, generate alternative hypotheses to help you assess the situation, and help you choose the best alternative. Even if you are in a single-pilot operation you can still use most of the CRM principles and skills—through what is called **single-pilot resource management (SRM)**—to help you make the best decision (*see* the next section on CRM and SRM).

Practice CRM and SRM Skills

CRM, and its single-pilot corollary SRM, involve effectively using all available resources—people, information, and equipment—to achieve safe and efficient flight operations. The FAA defines SRM more specifically as is the art of managing all onboard and outside resources available to a pilot before and during a flight to help ensure a safe and successful outcome. Airlines and other professional flight organizations using aircraft requiring two or more pilots provide CRM training for both initial and recurrent training, which is often reinforced through annual **line-oriented flight training** scenarios in the simulator. Such realistic training will help you improve your interpersonal, communication, and decision-making skills, assist you in managing stress, help you apply the principles of leadership and followership, and teach you how to work together with others as team.[68] Since poor CRM skills have been implicated in numerous airline incidents and accidents, including more than 70 percent of approach-and-landing incidents or accidents,[69] it would be wise to learn and practice the principles in your everyday flying. *See* Chapter 19 for a complete discussion of this topic.

Manage Stress

Practicing CRM skills will also assist you in effectively managing stress. Like fatigue (*see* Chapter 10), excess situational stress causes perceptual and attentional narrowing, impedes memory recall, and interferes with optimal situation assessment and decision making (*see* Chapter 19 for more information about stress). To minimize the effects of stress when faced with a non-normal or emergency situation, it is important to develop strategies to manage it. On an individual level, you should devote your energy to solving whatever the problem is that you are facing. This will help you stay focused on finding an acceptable solution and avoid dwelling on possible negative consequences. It will also help you avoid one of the other hazardous attitudes identified in the FAA's aeronautical decision-making literature, the attitude of **resignation**; the propensity to give up when under stress. By the way, research indicates there are at least five of these attitudes that could impair your decision making on the flight deck (*see* Figure 17-3).

The Five Hazardous Attitudes	Antidote
Anti-authority: "Don't tell me." This attitude is found in people who do not like anyone telling them what to do. In a sense, they are saying "No one can tell me what to do." They may be resentful of having someone tell them what to do or may regard rules, regulations, and procedures as silly or unnecessary. However, it is always your prerogative to question authority if you feel it is in error.	**Follow the rules. They are usually right.**
Impulsivity: "Do it quickly." This is the attitude of people who frequently feel the need to do something, anything, immediately. They do not stop to think about what they are about to do, they do not select the best alternative, and they do the first thing that comes to mind.	**Not so fast. Think first.**
Invulnerability: "It won't happen to me." Many people falsely believe that accidents happen to others, but never to them. They know accidents can happen, and they know that anyone can be affected. However, they never really feel or believe that they will be personally involved. Pilots who think this way are more likely to take chances and increase risk.	**It could happen to me.**
Macho: "I can do it." Pilots who are always trying to prove that they are better than anyone else think, "I can do it—I'll show them." Pilots with this type of attitude will try to prove themselves by taking risks in order to impress others. While this pattern is thought to be a male characteristic, women are equally susceptible.	**Taking chances is foolish.**
Resignation: "What's the use?" Pilots who think, "What's the use?" do not see themselves as being able to make a great deal of difference in what happens to them. When things go well, the pilot is apt to think that it is good luck. When things go badly, the pilot may feel that someone is out to get them or attribute it to bad luck. The pilot will leave the action to others, for better or worse. Sometimes, such pilots will even go along with unreasonable requests just to be a "nice guy."	**I'm not helpless. I can make a difference.**

Fig 17-3.

The five hazardous attitudes identified through past and contemporary study.

Fortunately, there are checklists and SOPs for almost every situation. If you are faced with a novel problem, you will fall back on your knowledge and training to help you optimize your decision. Even if you're a single-pilot operation, you're not alone—good CRM/SRM practice involves using all available resources, including other people. You can leverage the brains of your fellow crew members, ATC, company dispatch or maintenance, FSS specialists, and others. Having a second crew member on the flight deck can help reduce overall stress and work-load since they can assist in flying the airplane and troubleshooting any problems that may arise.

Minimize Bias

We can't completely de-bias ourselves, but recognizing we are prone to faulty decision making is half the battle in combatting it. Such conscious aware-ness of our unconscious biases is often enough to mitigate them. The other half of the battle is to question our own judgment until we are certain we have arrived at the correct decision. Biases such as confirmation, optimistic, ability, and overconfidence can be overcome by considering why your preferred choice might be wrong. Play the devil's advocate and consider the opposite of what you may be thinking. Solicit more information, including the opinion of others (if available). Don't just go with first idea that comes to your mind, but take the time to look for other alternatives and/or information that might disconfirm your original hypothesis. You may find that evaluating disconfirming information leads to affirming your original choice, but you may also find the original choice a poor one that should be replaced by a better one.

Also, when faced with the choice of canceling a flight or diverting to another more suitable airport, be careful how you formulate your go/no-go deci-sion. Avoid framing it in terms of the certain loss of diverting (e.g., passenger inconvenience, missed appointments) over only a chance of a loss were you to continue to your original destination (i.e., an accident). Rather, frame the decision in terms of the certain gain of landing safely if you divert over only a chance of a gain should you try to make it to your destination.

"Learning to fly takes hours, learning when not to fly takes years."

To close this chapter, we'll revisit the fatal decision-making scenario discussed previously: a GA pilot continuing VFR flight into IMC. In this chapter, we have often cited this scenario to illustrate some of the complexities involved in decision making. This scenario is an example of continuation bias, also known as a **plan continuation error**, the decision to stick to your plan to continue a course of action even though the evidence suggests you shouldn't. Whether it's the reluctance of pilots to divert to another airport or to conduct a go-around during a poorly executed approach, several possible reasons have been suggested in this chapter as to why pilots refuse to adjust their plan in the face of conditions that indicate they should and decide instead to continue with their original plan.

The marginal VFR weather is below your personal weather minimums and as such you wouldn't normally fly in it. But you've been delayed several days due to weather and because you're so close to home—only 20 miles (last-leg syndrome)—you take what you perceive as an acceptable risk and fly in it anyway (escalation bias). There are plenty of wonderful reasons for getting home—a return to your job, your family, and your own bed (with your spouse in it with you). Almost without conscious awareness, you begin to reframe your situation to make it easier to continue home (framing bias), but from the comfort of your chair as you're reading this paragraph, you can clearly see how biased it is to narrow the choice down to only these two options: the benefits of arriving home and the losses of turning around and waiting (risk-seeking frame). Instead, you need to think of the possible losses of continuing (an accident) and the benefits of diverting (staying alive). But that is not easy; it's been a long trip with many unplanned stops because of poor weather and it's hard to cut your losses. You think to yourself, "My destina-tion is only a short distance away. I've made it this far—I'm almost home!" Instead, you need to think of how many people have pushed the weather and didn't make it, and remember what you've learned in this chapter. Don't be the animal that prefers to follow its nose. Heed the words of W.C. Fields, who once said, "If at first you don't succeed try, try again. Then quit. No use being a damn fool about it."

Helpful Resources

If you want a fuller understanding of decision making—including heuristics and biases—*Thinking, Fast and Slow*, written by the renowned psychologist and Nobel Prize winner Daniel Kahneman, is a must read. This thought-provoking book, which has won many awards including the National Academy of Sciences Best Book Award in 2012, will challenge and enlighten you about the complexities and often irrational nature of human thinking.

The free online FAA *Human Factors Awareness Course* has a separate module on decision making, including heuristics and biases. (www.hf.faa.gov/Webtraining/Cognition/Cognition1.htm)

The Art of Aeronautical Decision-Making is an online FAA Safety Team tutorial that draws upon the collective wisdom and expertise of VFR pilots and instructors who have learned from the mistakes of others. It provides invaluable information to help you determine your own minimums and avoid inadvertent flight into IMC. (www.faasafety.gov/gslac/ALC/course_content.aspx?pf=1&preview=true&cID=28)

Do The Right Thing: Decision Making for Pilots is an online interactive course available from the AOPA Air Safety Institute that uses decision-making scenarios and other information to help you evaluate risk and determine your own personal weather minimums. (www.aopa.org/training-and-safety/online-learning/online-courses/do-the-right-thing)

Endnotes

1. "Who Killed Jessica? Her Shocking Death Raises Questions About How Far We Push Our Kids", *Time* 147 (April 22, 1996).

2. 14 CFR §91.157 allows pilots of fixed-wing aircraft to conduct special VFR flight operations below 10,000 feet MSL in controlled airspace at an airport in weather conditions that are less than VFR (1,000 feet AGL ceiling and 3 SM visibility) if the visibility is at least 1 SM, the aircraft can remain clear of clouds, and they have received an ATC clearance authorizing it.

3. Edward E. Jones and Victor A. Harris, "The Attribution of Attitudes," *Journal of Experimental Social Psychology* 3 (January 1967): 1–24

4. National Transportation Safety Board, *A Review of Flightcrew-Involved, Major Accidents of U.S. Air Carriers, 1978 through 1990*, Safety Study NTSB/SS-94/01 (Washington, DC: January 1994).

5. Douglas A. Wiegmann and Scott A. Shappell, *A Human Error Analysis of Commercial Aviation Accidents Using the Human Factors Analysis and Classification System (HFACS)*, DOT/FAA/AM-01/3 (February 2001).

6. Ratan Khatwa and Robert Helmrich, "Killers in Aviation: FSF Task Force Presents Facts about Approach-and-Landing and Controlled-Flight-into-Terrain Accidents," *Flight Safety Digest* 17 & 18 (Nov-Dec 1998/Jan–Feb 1999): 5.

7. Guohua Li, Jurek G. Grabowski, Susan P. Baker and George W. Rebok, "Pilot Error in Air Carrier Accidents: Does Age Matter?" *Aviation, Space, and Environmental Medicine* 77 (July 2006): 737–741.

8. Julie Anne Yates Hegwood, "Application of Modified Feggetter Model to Identification of Selected Human Factors in 1988 General Aviation Accidents", *71st Annual Meeting of the Transportation Research Board* (Washington, DC: 1992).

9. United States Government Accountability Office, *General Aviation Safety: Additional FAA Efforts Could Help Identify and Mitigate Safety Risks*, Report to Congressional Committees, Report No. GAO-13-36 (Washington, DC: U.S. GAO, October 2012).

10. Bureau of Air Safety Investigation, *Human Factors in Fatal Aircraft Accidents* (Canberra, Australia: BASI, April 1996).

11. Sharon Monica Jones, Joni K. Evans, Mary S. Reveley, Colleen A. Withrow, Ersin Ancel and Lawrence Barr, *Identification of Crew-Systems Interactions and Decision Related Trends*, NASA/TM–2013-218000 (Washington, DC: NASA, May 2013).

12. Federal Aviation Administration, "Aeronautical Decision-Making" (Chapter 2), in *Pilot's Handbook of Aeronautical Knowledge*, FAA-H-8083-25 (Oklahoma City, OK: 2016): 2-1.

13. Judith Orasanu and Terry Connolly, "The Reinvention of Decision-Making," *Decision-Making in Action: Models and Methods*, eds. Gary A. Klein, Judith Orasanu, Roberta Calderwood and Caroline E. Zsambok. (Norwood, NJ: Ablex Publishing, 1993): 3-20.

14. Herbert A. Simon, "Rational Choice and the Structure of the Environment," *Psychological Review* 63 (March 1956): 129–138.

15. Aviation Safety Council of Taiwan, *Aviation Occurrence Report: 4 February, 2015, TransAsia Airways Flight GE235, ATR72-212A, Loss of Control and Crashed into Keelung River, Three Nautical Miles East of Songshan Airport*, ASC-AOR-16-06-001 (Sindian City, Taiwan: July 2016).

16. Adapted after Christopher D. Wickens and John M. Flach, "Information Processing," Chapter 5, in *Human Factors in Aviation*, eds. Earl L. Wiener and David C. Nagel (San Diego: Academic Press, 1988): 111–155. Used with permission.

17. Jens Rasmussen, "Skills, Rules, and Knowledge: Signals, Signs, and Symbols, and Other Distinctions in Human Performance Models," *IEEE Transactions on Systems, Man, and Cybernetics* 13 (May–June 1983): 257–266.

18. Eric Auxier, "Keep Calm and Fly the Plane: Lessons from US Airways 1549," *Airways* (September 19, 2016). Available at airwaysmag.com/capnaux/lessons-from-us-airways-1549/.

19. Simon, "Rational Choice and the Structure of the Environment."

20. Amos Tversky and Daniel Kahneman, "Availability: A Heuristic for Judging Frequency and Probability," *Cognitive Psychology* 5 (1973): 207–232.

21. National Transportation Safety Board, Aviation Accident Report, Near West Palm Beach, FL, *United States, May 12, 1997: Attachment 7 Flight Crew Statements; and, Operations Group Chairman's Factual Report*, Identification Number DCA97MA049 (May 21, 1997 & August 12, 1998).

22. Amos Tversky and Daniel Kahneman, "Judgment Under Uncertainty: Heuristics and Biases," *Science* 185 (1974): 1124–1131.

23. Jeff Greenberg, Kipling D. Williams, and Mark K. O'Brien, "Considering the Harshest Verdict First: Biasing Effects on Mock Juror Verdicts," *Personality and Social Psychology Bulletin* 12 (March 1, 1986): 41–50.

24. Stephen Walmsley and Andrew Gilbey, "Cognitive Biases in Visual Pilots' Weather-Related Decision-making," *Applied Cognitive Psychology* 30 (April 8, 2016): 523–543.

25. Daniel Kahneman and Amos Tversky, "The Framing of Decisions and The Psychology of Choice," *Science* 211 (January 30, 1981): 453–458.

26. Barbara J. McNeil, Stephen G. Pauker, Harold C. Sox and Amos Tversky, "On the Elicitation of Preferences for Alternative Therapies," *New England Journal of Medicine* 306 (May 27, 1982): 1259–1262.

27. Daniel Kahneman, "Judgment and Decision-making: A Personal View," *Psychological Science* 2 (May 1991): 142–145.

28. David O'Hare and Tracy Smitheram, "'Pressing On' Into Deteriorating Weather Conditions: An Application of Behavioral Decision Theory to Pilot Decision-making," *The International Journal of Aviation Psychology* 5 (1995): 351-370.

29. David O'Hare and Douglas A. Wiegmann, *Continued VFR Flight Into IMC: Situational Awareness or Risky Decision-making?* Final Report (April 17, 2003).

30. Jeffrey Z. Rubin and Joel Brockner, "Factors Affecting Entrapment in Waiting Situations: The Rosencrantz and Guildenstern Effect," *Journal of Personality and Social Psychology* 31 (June 1975): 1054–1063.

31. William H. McGlothlin, "Stability of Choices Among Uncertain Alternatives," *American Journal of Psychology* 69 (December 1956): 604–615.

32. Joel Brockner, Myril C. Shaw and Jeffrey Z. Rubin, "Factors Affecting Withdrawal From an Escalating Conflict: Quitting Before It's Too Late," *Journal of Experimental Social Psychology* 15 (September 1979): 492–503.

33. David Beaty, *The Naked Pilot: The Human Factor in Aircraft Accidents* (Shrewsbury, England: Airlife Publishing, 1995).

34. Peter C. Wason, "On the Failure to Eliminate Hypotheses in a Conceptual Task," *Quarterly Journal of Experimental Psychology* 12 (July 1960): 129–140.

35. Robert E. Knox and James A. Inkster, "Postdecision Dissonance at Post-Time," *Journal of Personality and Social Psychology* 8 (May 1968): 319–323.

36. Mara Mather and Marcia K. Johnson, "Choice-Supportive Source Monitoring: Do Our Decisions Seem Better to Us As We Age?" *Psychology and Aging* 15 (Dec 2000): 596–606.

37. Craig A. Anderson, Mark Lepper and Lee Ross, "Perseverance of Social Theories: The Role of Explanation in the Persistence of Discredited Information, *Journal of Personality and Social Psychology* 39 (December 1980): 1037–1049.

38. Richard E. Nisbett and Lee Ross, *Human Inference: Strategies and Shortcomings of Social Judgment* (Englewood Cliffs, NJ: Prentice-Hall, 1980): 41.

39. Neil D. Weinstein, "Unrealistic Optimism About Future Life Events," *Journal of Personality and Social Psychology* 39 (November 1980): 806–820.

40. Laurie Larwood, "Swine Flu: A Field Study of Self-Serving Biases," *Journal of Applied Social Psychology* 8 (September 1978): 283–289.

41. Linda S. Perloff and Barbara K. Fetzer, "Self-Other Judgments and Perceived Vulnerability to Victimization," *Journal of Personality and Social Psychology* 50 (March 1986): 502-510.

42. Vera Hoorens and Bram P. Buunk, "Social Comparison of Health Risks: Locus of Control, the Person-Positivity Bias, and Unrealistic Optimism," *Journal of Applied Social Psychology* 23 (February 1993): 291–302.

43. Frank P. McKenna, David M. Warburton and M. Winwood, "Exploring the Limits of Optimism: The Case of Smokers' Decision-making," *British Journal of Psychology* 84 (1993): 389–394.

44. Frank P. McKenna, "It Won't Happen To Me: Unrealistic Optimism or Illusion of Control?" *British Journal of Psychology* 84 (1993): 39–50.

45. Leon S. Robertson, "Car Crashes: Perceived Vulnerability and Willingness to Pay for Crash Protection," *Journal of Community Health* 3 (Winter 1977): 136–141.

46. Harvey Wichman and James Ball, "Locus of Control, Self-Serving Biases, and Attitudes Towards Safety in General Aviation Pilots," *Aviation, Space, and Environmental Medicine* 54 (June 1983): 507–510.

47. David O'Hare, "Pilots' Perception of Risks and Hazards in General Aviation," *Aviation, Space, and Environmental Medicine* 61 (July 1990): 599–603.

48. Dale R. Wilson and Marte Fallshore, "Optimistic and Ability Biases in Pilots' Decisions and Perceptions of Risk Regarding VFR Flight into IMC," *Proceedings of the 11th International Symposium on Aviation Psychology* (Columbus, OH: March 2001).

49. Federal Aviation Administration, *Aeronautical Decision-Making*, AC 60-22 (Washington, DC: December 13, 1991).

50. David Dunning, Judith A. Meyerowitz and Amy D. Holzberg, "Ambiguity and Self-Evaluation: The Role of Idiosyncratic Trait Definitions in Self-Serving Assessments of Ability," *Journal of Personality and Social Psychology* 57 (December 1989): 1082–1090.

51. Mark D. Alicke, "Global Self-Evaluation as Determined by the Desirability and Control Ability of Trait Adjectives," *Journal of Personality and Social Psychology* 49 (1985): 1621–1630.

52. Ruth C. Wylie, *The Self-Concept. Vol. 2: Theory and Research on Selected Topics* (Lincoln, NB: University of Nebraska Press, 1979).

53. Ola Svenson, "Are We All Less Risky and More Skillful Than Our Fellow Drivers?" *Acta Psychologica* 47 (1981): 143–148.

54. Wichman and Ball, "Locus of Control, Self-Serving Biases, and Attitudes."

55. O'Hare, "Pilots' Perception of Risks and Hazards."

56. Wilson and Fallshore, "Optimistic and Ability Biases in Pilots' Decisions."

57. Daniel Allen Butler, *Unsinkable: The Full Story of the RMS Titanic* (London: Frontline Books, 2011): 48.

58. J. Frank Yates, *Judgment and Decision Making* (Englewood Cliffs, NJ: Prentice-Hall, 1990).

59. Paul Slovic, "Only New Laws Will Spur Seat-Belt Use," *Wall Street Journal* (January 30, 1985): 26.

60. National Transportation Safety Board, *Safety Study: Aviation Safety in Alaska*, NTSB/SS-95/03 (Washington, DC: November 1995)

61. National Transportation Safety Board, *Safety Study: Aviation Safety in Alaska*, NTSB/SS-95/03 (Washington, DC: November 1995).

62. Ibid.

63. Shelley E. Taylor and Jonathon D. Brown, "Illusion and Well-Being: A Social Psychological Perspective on Mental Health," *Psychological Bulletin* 103 (March 1988): 193–210.

64. Alan F. Stokes, Kenneth L. Kemper and Roger Marsh, *Time-Stressed Flight Decision Making: A Study of Expert and Novice Aviators*, Technical Report (Savoy, Illinois: Aviation Research Laboratory Institute of Aviation, December 1992).

65. David K. Li, "Sully: My Whole Life Was For This," *New York Post* (February 9, 2009).

66. Gary A. Klein, "A Recognition Primed Decision (RPD) Model of Rapid Decision Making," *Decision Making in Action: Models and Methods*, eds. Gary A. Klein, Judith Orasanu, Roberta Calderwood and Caroline E. Zsambok. (Norwood, NJ: Ablex Publishing, 1993): 138–147.

67. Federal Aviation Administration, "Standard Operating Procedures and Pilot Monitoring Duties for Flight Deck Crewmembers," Advisory Circular 120-71B (Washington, DC: January 10, 2017).

68. Richard S. Jensen, *Aeronautical Decision-making—Cockpit Resource Management*, DOT/FAA/PM-86/46 (Washington, DC: FAA, January 1989).

69. Airbus Customer Services, CRM *Aspects in Incident/Accidents*, Flight Operations Briefing Notes SEQ 02, REV 03 (June 2004).

18

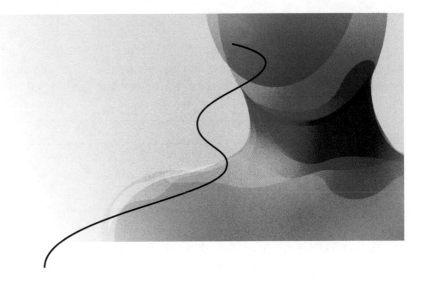

Who's flying my airplane anyway?
Social Influence

Wapiti Flight 402 was on a scheduled IFR flight at night from Edmonton to High Prairie, Alberta, but the pilot should never have departed. The forecast and actual weather were IFR ceilings and visibility in snow and fog with moderate to heavy icing in cloud and precipitation, yet there was no approved instrument approach procedure (IAP) published for High Prairie Airport—operations required VMC. In addition, there was no working autopilot on the fully loaded ten-seat Piper PA-31 Navajo Chieftain to assist the pilot, and only one of the NDB receivers was serviceable (both were required according to the company's operating certificate). This would normally have been a two-pilot operation, but the co-pilot had been bumped to make room for an extra passenger. With needed fuel reserves, the takeoff weight at Edmonton was 7,400 pounds, about 400 pounds above the maximum certificated takeoff weight (MCTOW).

When reflecting on the flight several years later, the pilot—Erik Vogel—stated, "I had no less than five adequate reasons to cancel or postpone my flight, but I chose to go—it was Friday night and all my passengers wanted to go home as well."[1] His plan was to fly to his destination on an IFR flight plan then cancel IFR and descend below the minimum obstruction clearance altitude (MOCA) of 5,600 feet MSL and level off at 2,800 feet MSL (about 800 feet above field elevation). Unfortunately, he misjudged when to begin his descent and began too early; the aircraft struck tree-covered terrain 50 feet below the crest of a 2,900-foot hill 20 miles east-southeast of High Prairie Airport. Though Erik and three passengers survived, the six remaining passengers unfortunately perished. Among the dead was the passenger who replaced the bumped co-pilot: the leader of the Province of Alberta's New Democratic Party, Grant Notley.

The distinction between errors and violations was made in Chapter 2—the former involving unintentional mistakes (the pilot may not know better), the latter intentional noncompliance with regulations, rules, and procedures designed to ensure safe flight operations (the pilot knows better but makes the decision anyway). Mr. Vogel's actions that night involved errors, but mostly violations. He knew he was operating over the MCTOW; he knew he shouldn't have conducted the flight with inoperable equipment; he knew it was against the regulations to descend below the MOCA of 5,600 feet, let alone the minimum enroute IFR altitude of 7,000 feet, without first establishing that VFR weather conditions existed; and he knew it was illegal to conduct an unpublished instrument approach into an airport not authorized for one.

So what caused him to go against his better judgment and knowingly conduct a flight in such conditions? In a letter to the editor of Transport Canada's *Aviation Safety Letter* several years after the accident, Mr. Vogel essentially asks himself the same question: "I was attempting an unpublished nonprecision IFR approach and busted my own minimums. It was an action I was unable to explain properly, either to myself or to the subsequent trials and inquiries."[2]

The last chapter pointed out the problem of hindsight bias—our after-the-fact knowledge of the cause of an accident that leads us to attribute the pilot's decision to some sort of character flaw or lack of training, that further leads us to not only stop digging deeper to determine all the factors that may have contributed to the pilot's poor decision(s), but prevents us from truly learning from the accident. Keep this in mind when I tell you that on one level it is clear the pilot was guilty of willful noncompliance—he deliberately refused to comply with established rules and regulations designed to make flying safer—yet on another level he was not. He *was complying* with exactly what he thought the company expected of him: dispatch bumped the co-pilot and expected him to conduct a single-pilot operation, the company refused to let him land en route to refuel, they expected him to fly with a non-functioning autopilot and an unserviceable NDB receiver, and they expected him to fly an unauthorized IAP into High Prairie. In fact, the accident report indicated that this illegal procedure had been demonstrated by the senior company pilot on an earlier occasion and that "operational flying procedures of this kind were not uncommon in the company."[3]

The accident occurred during a downturn in the economy and pilot jobs were scarce. The major airlines weren't hiring so the small airlines and charter operations weren't either. Yet 33 pilots had either quit or were fired at the company during the previous year: according to Mr. Vogel, "almost all for refusing flights."[4] A few days before the accident, the pilot conducted—against his better judgment—a medical evacuation (MEDEVAC) flight as the sole pilot when weather conditions required two. He also had been criticized by the chief pilot for taking too much time at the weather office. This, along with a variety of other organizational factors, including several confrontations with management on the day of the accident about other matters relating to flight operations, contributed to Mr. Vogel's belief that he had no choice but to fly—if he refused he would lose his job. He said that "to this day, I still cannot believe how I allowed myself to deteriorate to such a level that I was incapable of flying safely. It cost six passengers their lives and ended my career. This was a decision I must still live with."[5]

A few years earlier, Downeast Airlines Flight 46 crashed a mile short of Runway 03 at Knox County Regional Airport in Rockland, Maine, while on a nonprecision instrument approach at night in fog, killing all but one of the 18 people aboard. The NTSB concluded that the de Havilland DHC-6 Twin Otter crashed because the flight crew descended below the minimum descent altitude of 440 feet without establishing visual contact with the runway environment. They were unable to determine exactly why they did this, but they uncovered several management practices and unwritten policies that were contrary to Part 135 safe operating procedures which had a direct, or at least a strong indirect, influence on the events surrounding this accident. Fourteen former Downeast pilots testified that some of these practices and policies included the following (Report No: NTSB/AAR-80-5):

- Establishing "company minimums" between 200 to 350 feet, which is below the legal FAA minimums for the Knox County Regional Airport;
- using unapproved instrument approaches;
- directing pilots to make repeated instrument approaches and to "get lower" during adverse weather conditions;
- offering to pay fines of pilots who received violations and suggesting that FAA enforcement actions were unlikely;
- pressuring pilots to not carry extra fuel, especially IFR-reserve requirements;
- pressuring pilots into flying over MCTOW, repeatedly permitting ground personnel to overload aircraft and providing pilots with knowingly inaccurate baggage weights and counts;
- ridiculing pilots in front of others and suggesting that pilots who were unable to land when others had were less skilled or were cowardly;
- pressuring pilots into flying aircraft with known mechanical defects contrary to Part 135 requirements (e.g., single-pilot IFR with inoperative autopilot);
- threatening a pilot for canceling a revenue flight because of a mechanical defect;
- firing a pilot for canceling a revenue flight which in his judgment could not be conducted safely because of weather conditions; and
- firing a pilot for deicing an aircraft without prior approval.

According to former company pilots, relatives, and a close friend, captain James Merryman—who recently, and perhaps even reluctantly, had become the chief pilot for the company—was not an assertive person and he felt that he had been subjected to constant pressure and criticism from the company president. As a result, he not only feared for his job, but he suffered from health problems—loss of appetite, exhaustion, preoccupation, chest pains, and breathing difficulties—arising from what the NTSB concluded was job-related stress. In the end, the NTSB concluded that *inordinate management pressures*, including the pressure to complete the flight even if it meant a descent to a lower altitude than approved minimums, was a major factor in the accident (Report No: NTSB/AAR-80-5).

To captain Merryman's family, Erik Vogel, and other pilots who have found (or who may find) themselves caught between a similar rock and a hard place, this chapter is for you.

Social Influence—Subtle and Not-So-Subtle

Did you ever do something uncomfortable at the bequest of others, only to regret it later? I did. When I was a child, I wanted so desperately to be able to play with a group of older boys in the neighborhood, but they usually just ignored me. One day they took an interest in me and asked me to play "Cowboys and Indians" (an ethnocentric, racist game really, but back then we honestly didn't know any better). I was one of the Indians, but to prove my worth I had to stand completely still about 10 yards distant while the "leader" threw a homemade spear at me three times. It's just a homemade spear, right? What are the chances it will hit me? Besides, even if it does, what real damage can it do? Well, I very courageously didn't move, but I was hit just under the eye on the third throw and I was rushed to the hospital to get stitches—while the others all fled in hiding (the cowards). Pretty dumb, huh? Hopefully you never went along with the gang to the point where you did something like that...but maybe you did.

"But," you may say, "that's the kind of behavior you can expect from a child and surely succumbing to peer pressure like that doesn't happen as an adult." Well, it does. And to pilots too. When I was all grown up and working as a flight instructor, I was the PIC

in a small airplane with an experienced airline pilot in the right seat, who also happened to be my boss. We were departing from a non-towered airport that had no automated surface weather observing system broadcast capability, so I was left to guess what the wind speed and crosswind component was by looking only at the wind sock. It looked somewhat questionable to me, but I heard no objections from my more experienced pilot-boss in the right seat beside me. Besides, we had students back at our home airport waiting for us for a planned weekend field trip, and I, and I'm sure my boss, didn't want to let them down. I used aileron and rudder to help keep the airplane straight as I applied power but found that as the airplane accelerated down the runway, even with almost full application of rudder to maintain directional control, I was having trouble keeping it straight in the crosswind. I began to think that maybe I was taking off in a wind that exceeded the airplane's capability. I had only a couple of seconds to make the decision to abort. I heard no words of objection from the more experienced pilot beside me I so I assumed that he expected me to continue the takeoff. I did not reject the takeoff and had to apply slight braking on the rudder to keep the airplane from departing from straight flight. In retrospect, I made several errors in my thinking: even though his feet and hands were not at the controls, I erroneously thought my co-pilot's greater level of experience would enable him to judge if the crosswind was acceptable or not; I assumed he wanted us to go, despite the crosswind (we were running late and people were waiting for us); and I didn't want to disappoint him, so I was willing to accept an elevated level of risk.

In hindsight I likely experienced, to some degree perhaps, what another junior pilot did a few years earlier, only flying a bigger airplane with 79 souls aboard. However, he wasn't so lucky. Immediately after rotation and liftoff from Runway 36 at Washington National Airport in Washington D.C., the Boeing B-737 experienced difficulty climbing, struck a bridge, and then crashed into the ice-covered Potomac River. Seventy-four occupants aboard and four people on the bridge died in the accident on that snowy winter day.

The one-hour fifteen-minute airport closure for snow removal significantly delayed all flights out of Washington, including Air Florida Flight 90 ("Palm 90"). Heavy snow was still falling when it reopened, and after the aircraft was deiced the crew finally got their pushback clearance. However, because the tug wasn't equipped with tire chains, it couldn't push them back in the snow, ice, and slush. The crew thought they would help the tug operator by deploying reverse thrusters (witnesses said for about 30 to 90 seconds); however, a significant amount of snow and ice was observed blowing around the aircraft from the engines. They eventually used another tug equipped with chains to successfully push them out.

Snow continued to accumulate during the taxi and the CVR conversations revealed the crew was concerned about taking off in such poor weather conditions; they were also puzzled about some anomalous engine readings as they were taxiing to the runway. During the early part of the takeoff roll the FO, who was the PF, commented "God, look at that thing! That don't seem right, does it?" A few seconds later he remarked, "...that's not right...," to which the captain responded, "Yes it is, there is eighty." The FO again reiterated, "Naw, I don't think that's right." The NTSB concluded that the FO was referring to one or more of the following conditions: (1) the general slow acceleration of the airplane, (2) the lower than normal engine noise, and (3) the position of the engine thrust levers, which would have been set significantly less forward than for a normal takeoff using normal takeoff thrust settings. Fifteen seconds later, and still on the takeoff roll, the FO commented, "...maybe it is," but then, two seconds later, after the captain called, "Hundred and twenty," the first officer said, "I don't know."[6]

The aircraft stall warning stick shaker activated and the aircraft experienced a stall buffet almost immediately after liftoff and continued until it impacted the bridge and river. The captain said "Forward, forward...Come on, forward, forward, just barely climb." Just before impact, the FO said "Larry, we're going down, Larry," to which the captain responded, "I know it" (Report No: NTSB/AAR-82-8).

The crew saw the correct takeoff thrust setting for the airport conditions and takeoff weight, an engine pressure ratio (EPR) value of 2.04. However, the accident investigation revealed that the engine inlet pressure probes on both engines were blocked with ice—likely from the inappropriate use of reverse thrusters to assist in the pushback—causing the EPR gauges to overread. Therefore, the thrust actually produced by each engine during the takeoff was

only the equivalent of an EPR of 1.70, or 3,750 pounds of thrust per engine less than that which would be produced at the actual takeoff EPR of 2.04. As a result, the aircraft accelerated slower than normal requiring nearly 5,400 feet of runway—about 2,000 feet more than normal—to reach liftoff speed. Unfortunately, the crew failed to add maximum thrust once they realized they were in trouble; had they done so they likely would have overcome the adverse effects of the late liftoff and the airframe snow and ice contamination, enabling the aircraft to successfully climb out from the airport environment. The NTSB determined that the probable cause of the accident was the flight crew's failure to use engine anti-ice during ground operation and takeoff, their decision to take off with snow/ice on the wings, and the captain's failure to reject the takeoff during the early stages when his attention was called to anomalous engine instrument readings (Report No: NTSB/AAR-82-8).

The Influence of Others on the Flight Deck

It is the latter portion of the probable cause statement that has bearing on this chapter—the captain's failure to reject the takeoff during the early stages when his attention was called to anomalous engine instrument readings. The FO felt there was something wrong and he expressed his concern at least four times during the takeoff roll, yet the captain basically said or did nothing (it is believed that when the captain did say something, "Yes it is, there is eighty," he was referring to the airspeed indicator). **Social influence**—the actual or perceived influence exerted by other people to feel, think, or behave in a certain manner—can be blatant and obvious, or it can be subtle and veiled. Like Erik Vogel, James Merryman, and myself, the FO in the Palm 90 accident deferred to a higher authority—in this case his captain—and continued with the flight. However, unlike Erik Vogel and James Merryman, who both felt compelled to go against their better judgment because of direct and obvious pressure to do so, including the perceived threat of job loss, the FO in the Air Florida accident and I weren't coerced into obedience from what someone else may have said or done—we actually interpreted lack of action and verbal silence from the higher authority sitting next to us as pressure to continue what we were doing!

These examples tell us what social psychologists have been telling us for years: We as humans are profoundly influenced by others, even when we think we're not. Without us even being aware of it, other people can influence us to the point that *they* are the ones making our decisions for us—with the result that we are no longer flying the aircraft, but they are. As we discussed in the previous chapter, it's difficult for even the experts to understand all the factors involved in the complex process of decision making. It is even more difficult to ascertain the exact role that other people might play in pilots' decisions to continue on a course of action in the face of evidence that suggests it might not be wise. Most of what we know comes from anecdotal evidence gathered from accident reports, only a few of which are shared with you in this chapter, but very little data have been collected in the form of statistical analysis or from empirical studies. However, some of the data we do have is shared in the rest of this chapter.

VFR-into-IMC

As mentioned in previous chapters, a particularly vexing type of accident, primarily involving GA pilots but also others, involves attempting VFR flight into IMC. It is the number one cause of fatal GA spatial-disorientation accidents in the United States, with a lethality rate of more than 80 percent for fixed-wing aircraft (compared to 20 percent or less for all GA accidents).[7, 8, 9] As identified in Chapter 1, these accidents involve VFR pilots either departing into existing adverse weather or more typically continuing VFR flight into gradually deteriorating weather then inadvertently flying into IMC and losing their outside visual references. If they are VFR-only pilots, or pilots with inadequate instrument flying skills, they either fly under CFIT or experience SD and lose control of their aircraft. The latter results in uncontrolled flight into terrain (UFIT) or in-flight structural failure due to the pilot overstressing the aircraft while recovering from an unusual attitude.

Germaine to the issues discussed in this chapter is a major finding from a comprehensive review of 409 U.S. GA airplane VFR-into-IMC accidents during an eight-year period—a significantly higher proportion of these types of accidents carry passengers on board.[10] For example, a non-instrument-rated private pilot and his five passengers all died after the Piper PA-34 Seneca II they were in struck two high-tension power lines about 200 feet AGL near Huntington Tri-State Airport in Huntington, West Virginia. The purpose of the flight was to look at airplanes for sale in Raleigh-Durham, North Carolina, and in Clearwater, Florida. The NTSB determined the probable cause was the pilot's decision to continue VFR flight in IMC despite his lack of an instrument rating and proficiency in instrument flying, which resulted in SD and impact with terrain (NTSB Identification No: ERA09FA145).

In another tragic accident, after departing Santa Monica Municipal Airport the non-instrument-rated private pilot experienced SD and lost control of his Beech A36 Bonanza. The airplane stalled, entered a spin, and crashed into a three-story apartment building in the Fairfax District of Los Angeles, California. The pilot, his three passengers, and one person in the apartment building were killed and seven others on the ground were seriously injured. The purpose of the flight was to drop off his niece in Las Vegas and continue on to Sun Valley, where he was going to show his property to the other two passengers. Before the flight, he and his passengers had been at the airport for at least eight hours waiting for weather conditions to clear. The accident investigators concluded that the pilot's *self-induced pressure to complete the flight* was a factor in the accident (NTSB Identification No: LAX03FA182). Although the pressure was, according to the NTSB "self-induced," it is unlikely the pilot would have felt compelled to attempt the flight in adverse weather if he did not have passengers aboard.

Commercial pilots aren't immune from this threat either. For example, it was noted in the previous chapter that a study revealed almost half of all Alaskan fatal air taxi accidents and two-thirds of fatal commuter accidents were the result of attempted VFR flight into IMC. In another study, 50 percent of Alaska commuter and air taxi pilots surveyed by the NTSB stated that they had flown in IMC on a VFR flight, and 84 percent reported that they had inadvertently entered IMC on a VFR flight—both *in response to operational pressures*. These pressures were not just self-induced—they included demands from managers, passengers, other pilots, and even the U.S. Postal Service.[11]

Emergency Medical Services Operations

Another area where it is evident that external pressures from others influence pilots' decisions to embark on, or continue, a flight in adverse circumstances is emergency medical services (EMS) aircraft accidents. More than 80 percent of U.S. EMS (or air ambulance) operations consist of helicopters and provide an important service for on-scene responses to accidents and transportation services for patients and medical teams.[12] However, although this sector's safety record has been improving, these types of operations involve significant levels of risk and the accident record reflects that. In response to the increased number of accidents in the mid-1980s, the NTSB published a safety study that determined the "accident rate for EMS helicopters involved in patient transports is approximately twice the rate experienced by Part 135 nonscheduled helicopter air taxis and one-and-a-half times the rate for all turbine-powered helicopters."[13] A more recent FAA review of U.S. helicopter EMS (HEMS) accidents that occurred over a seven-year period found that three factors were involved in 85 percent of the accidents: CFIT, inadvertent entry into IMC during night operations, and lack of operational control.[14]

The 1988 NTSB study, and a subsequent 2006 study, discovered that pilots often continue VFR flight into reduced visibility and/or IMC because their judgment and decision-making ability is impaired by self-imposed and externally imposed pressures to complete an EMS flight.[15, 16] These pressures primarily arise from factors somewhat unique to EMS helicopter operations: the influence of the mission itself, program competition, and EMS program management.

The Mission

Saving lives is often its own reward for EMS pilots, but a study conducted by the Air Medical Physician Association concluded that time pressures related to the patient's condition—including rapid mission preparation—and the flight to the patient pick-up location were frequent issues in EMS aircraft accidents. They discovered that the patient's condition was cited in 44 percent of the EMS accident or incident reports as a contributor to time pressure leading to inaccurate or hurried preflight planning.[17]

The Competition

Other people who can significantly impact decision making in EMS operations are the pilot's customers and competitors. For example, during poor weather conditions EMS dispatchers calling various HEMS operators in sequence until one agrees to take a flight assignment—a practice known as *helicopter shopping*—has led HEMS pilots and operators to accept flights that would normally have been declined had they been aware of all of the facts surrounding the assignment.[18] This practice was involved in a fatal HEMS accident in Newberry, South Carolina, when a single-engine Bell 407 crashed at night in fog 10 minutes after picking up an injured passenger. The pilot, flight nurse, flight paramedic, and patient were all killed in the crash. What the pilot didn't know was that three other HEMS operators declined the flight because of the weather, and one even had to turn back because of fog (NTSB Identification No: CHI04MA182).

Program Management

The helicopter shopping phenomenon is only one of several ways in which the actions of management and customers can negatively influence pilot behavior in EMS operations. The NTSB also determined that a major factor in the Newberry accident was inadequate weather and dispatch information relayed by management to the pilot. The 2006 NTSB study identified lack of management controls in many EMS accidents, including a lack of consistent, comprehensive flight dispatch procedures and aviation flight risk evaluation programs for EMS operations. For example, an EMS helicopter crashed into mountainous terrain about 27 NM southwest of Battle Mountain, Nevada, in poor weather conditions at night. The pilot chose to take a direct route over a remote area of rugged mountainous terrain with little lighting instead of a slightly longer route that followed an interstate highway that would have avoided the highest terrain. The NTSB concluded that if a risk management program had been in place the dark night conditions and the mountainous route might have raised the risk-rating for the mission, which may have led the pilot to take measures to lower the risk, such as taking a less mountainous route (NTSB Identification No: SEA04MA167).[19]

Social Psychology

We have been talking about how other people influence the decision making of pilots. As mentioned in Chapter 3, social psychology can be defined as the scientific study of how people's thoughts and behaviors are influenced by others. The discipline looks at a variety of issues such as social influence, group behavior, social thinking, attitudes, persuasion, interpersonal relationships, prejudice and discrimination, stereotyping, liking and aggression, and conflict. An area of considerable concern to pilots and other personnel concerned with flight safety has to do with how other people—either individually or collectively as a group—can negatively influence our thoughts, feelings and behaviors on the flight deck. This sub-discipline of social psychology—commonly known as social influence—studies how the actual or perceived presence and/or the behavior of others can lead us to conform, comply, and obey, even when it might not be the safest thing to do. Before we explore these topics, we need to first make some general observations about groups.

Groups

Several studies have found that an individual's feelings, beliefs, and behavior are influenced by simply being in the presence of other people. People usually find less satisfaction and participate less the larger the size of the group. People also tend to conform to group expectations the larger a group's size. These expectations are often referred to as **norms**—the unwritten rules of expected (or what is considered *normal*) behavior dictated by the majority of the group. To varying degrees, people feel pressure to conform to group norms. For pilots, this can be a good thing if an organization's culture is permeated with norms that encourage safe flight operating practices. An organizational culture, or corporate culture, consists of a variety of components including an organization's shared beliefs, values, written and unwritten rules (norms), and behavioral practices that make up its social and working environment. A corporate culture consisting of norms that discourage safe flight operating practices can lead to what many call *an accident waiting to happen*. For example the NTSB found marked differences between Downeast Airline's written policies and their verbal and unwritten policies (norms) that were contrary to Part 135 safe operating procedures.

Roles consist of a set of socially defined norms that define how people in a given social situation should behave. Roles are generally classified as assigned or emergent. The captain has an assigned role to play by the airline industry and the airline they work for: she or he is the captain, the leader, the PIC, etc. The FO also has a subordinate, but important assigned role: the follower, the monitor, the supporter, etc. Sometimes a role materializes to meet the needs of a given situation. For example, a check pilot riding as a passenger aboard United Airlines Flight 232 fulfilled an emergent role of manually controlling the thrust levers to maintain a degree of control of the DC-10 that crash-landed in Sioux City, Iowa (*see* the previous chapter).

Status is the prestige bestowed by the group on its members. A pilot's status is even evident by the insignia on the shoulder epaulets and blazer arms of his or her uniform—four stripes for captain and three for the FO. **Group cohesiveness** is the extent to which individual group members are bonded together with each other. Cohesive groups tend to perform better as a team and it has been suggested that the structure of airline flight crew schedules, where pilots rarely fly together—especially at bigger airlines—do not promote cohesive flight crew pairings. However, individual members of highly cohesive groups also tend to experience greater pressure to conform to the wishes of the group.

Group Decision Making

At least two flight crew members are required to operate a scheduled commercial airline flight. This regulatory requirement eases the manual and mental workload involved in flying the airplane, provides an additional crew member should one of the pilots become physically, physiologically, or psychologically incapacitated, and an extra crew member to assist with troubleshooting and handling non-normal or emergency events. Another "brain" on the flight deck to assist the captain when making assessments and decisions—especially with ill-defined problems that may present themselves to the crew (*see* the previous chapter)—is an enormous benefit in flight operations. Theoretically, two people on the flight deck should provide optimal assessments compared to one individual acting alone because of the increase in both the quality and quantity of information and experiences available stored in the long-term memory of each person. Two heads should also be better than one when generating needed alternatives for optimal decision making. Evidence indicates, however, that not all group-involved decision making yields the best results. Just as individual decision making is subject to bias, so too is group decision making.

Group Polarization

Researchers have discovered that after a group discusses an issue, individual group members sometimes tend to shift their position to a more extreme version of the position they initially held. For example, if a person initially leans toward caution, during group discussion they may shift their viewpoint further to the cautious side—a **conservative shift**. If, however, their initial predisposition is to favor risk, they may shift their viewpoint towards higher levels of risk—a **risky shift**. Polarization of an entire group occurs when the group makes decisions which shift conservative or risky, an obvious bias in group decision making. Individual polarization also creates a problem if it results in significant differences of opinion between members within a group, such as could occur on a crewed flight deck. Fortunately, polarization is reduced if information is clear and unambiguous. Therefore, crew members who face a puzzling problem on the flight deck should do all they can to accurately diagnose the situation before making a decision on a course of action.

In a tragic accident that killed all 160 people on board, the captain and FO didn't properly diagnose their situation so they both disagreed as to what the problem was on their McDonnel Douglas MD-82. West Caribbean Airways Flight 708 was flying in level cruise at FL330 near convective activity—with its associate turbulence and icing conditions—so the captain called for the engine and wing anti-ice systems to be turned on. What the captain didn't realize, however, was that with anti-ice on, which results in a reduction of thrust, the airplane at that altitude was now above its two-engine operation cruise altitude capability. As a result, the airspeed gradually dropped and the autopilot slowly pitched the nose up to maintain altitude. The captain seemed fixated on the lower EPR readings, so he began a descent to FL310, but before the aircraft got there it

entered a stall which it remained in until it crashed near the town of Machiques in Venezuela.

Rather than push forward on the controls, the captain kept pulling back which only deepened the stall. Because of his possible *channeling of attention* he erroneously concluded that the engines of the MD-82 had momentarily flamed out, so in response he kept trying to pitch the nose up to regain altitude. The FO on the other hand had done a better job of assessing the situation and told the captain at least twice that they were in a stall. The captain maintained his version of the situation and the rest is history. This polarization of assessments between the two pilots occurred primarily because they failed to engage in any reasonable form of troubleshooting (barely any conversation, let alone reference to checklists) which the accident report cites as the crew's inefficient and ineffective exchange of ideas during the emergency. Had they done so, the captain may have stopped fixating his attention and changed his mind. The accident report also cites FO's unassertive communication and action on the flight deck.[20] The problem of unassertive FOs will be discussed more thoroughly in the next chapter.

Bystander Effect and Social Loafing

Bystander apathy, or **bystander effect**, is a disconcerting phenomenon that occurs in situations where a crowd is present and a stranger needs some sort of assistance (e.g., due to a crime or medical emergency) but doesn't receive any. In fact, studies have found that the higher the number of bystanders observing the situation the less likely anyone will offer it. Recently, an assault victim outside a neighborhood 7-Eleven store in Chicago fell onto the street after being knocked unconscious by his assailant. Store video footage shows a group of bystanders near the victim who then just walked away. A minute later he was run over by a taxi and later died at a hospital.[21]

It is human nature for us to judge the bystanders as uncaring and assert that we would never do what they did, but as we discussed in the previous chapter we may be guilty of the fundamental attribution error, minimizing the role of situational factors and attributing flaws in their character for their inaction. Numerous experimental studies into bystander effect indicate that lone bystanders are more likely to help a victim and that as the number of onlookers increases the less likely a single individual will notice the incident (especially in a large crowd), interpret the incident as an emergency requiring assistance (especially in an ambiguous situation), or assume responsibility to render assistance.[22] When bystanders attempt to interpret a situation, they often look to other bystanders, and if they don't appear to be concerned or aren't providing assistance, the individual may not interpret the situation as an emergency. The reluctance to assume responsibility to help someone is caused by a number of factors, one of which is **diffusion of responsibility**, the phenomenon of diffusing (or dividing) responsibility for actions and consequences amongst the group, minimizing one's own individual share of responsibility.

Diffusion of responsibility is also evident in **social loafing**. Have you ever played the tug-of-war game where two teams pull at opposite ends of a rope to pull the rope a certain distance? If so, did you pull as hard when your team consisted of many members compared to when the team consisted of only two or three people? Studies conducted more than 100 years ago suggest that you likely did not. A variety of empirical studies since then have confirmed that group members often expend less individual effort to accomplish a goal than they would if they were acting alone. Somewhat related to bystander effect, the diffusion of responsibility involved in social loafing is obviously undesirable in work settings since employers expect maximum input and performance from their employees. It is especially intolerable in safety-critical professions such as aviation. Fortunately, social loafing and diffusion of responsibility are less of a problem in small cohesive, or highly valued, groups[23]—such as the two-person group on the flight deck—because individual group members are well aware of how crucial their individual behavior is in obtaining optimal group-goal outcomes (i.e., safe and efficient flight).

However, as flight deck membership expands, as is the case with a four-pilot long-range international flight deck crew, these phenomena start to have more of an effect. When the majority are inclined to deviate from certain details of SOPs, such as wearing the oxygen mask when the other pilot leaves the flight deck or carrying on a conversation during a period when the sterile cockpit rule is in effect, or if the majority simply doesn't seem interested in conducting a thorough briefing or debriefing, the minority pilot finds him or herself under a significant amount of social pressure to go along with the perceived wishes of the group. A friend of mine who flies long range wide-body airplanes for a large international carrier once told me "I try to hold myself to the highest standards regardless of the behavior of the rest of the pilots I fly with, but sometimes you either have to let some things go unchallenged and pick your battles, or you risk being labeled as being 'too anal' or too much of a 'company man' and consequently have a breakdown in CRM as the crew becomes less cohesive for the rest of the trip."

Groupthink

Diffusion of responsibility may be partly responsible for another bias in group decision making known as **groupthink**, the phenomenon that occurs during a group decision-making task whereby individuals in the group tend to agree with the group consensus—or their perception of the consensus—in spite of their own personal reservations about the group's decision. This occurs primarily because their desire to maintain harmonious relationships within the group overrides their concern for achieving an optimal group decision-making outcome. This type of thinking—which leads to poorer decisions than if made by individuals alone—has been blamed for several flawed group decisions including U.S. officials ignoring the warnings of the impending Japanese attack on Pearl Harbor and the decision to attempt to overthrow Cuba's Fidel Castro in the Bay of Pigs Invasion fiasco.

Groupthink is strongest within cohesive groups. It was mentioned previously that cohesive groups generally tend to perform better as a team, but its members also tend to experience greater pressure to conform to the group's wishes. It was also noted that, theoretically, two heads on the flight deck are better than one. Groupthink, however, shows us that the opposite can also be true: "None of us is as dumb as all of us."[24]

Groupthink is cited as responsible for flawed decisions that contributed to two NASA space-mission disasters: the breakup of space shuttle Challenger after liftoff in 1986 and the disintegration of space shuttle Columbia during re-entry in 2003. On the morning of January 28, 1986, the Challenger broke apart 73 seconds after liftoff from Cape Canaveral, Florida, killing all seven astronauts aboard. The investigation discovered that the cause of the explosion was the failure of an O-ring in the right solid rocket booster to properly seal because of cold air temperatures. However, they also concluded the cause was due to the flawed decision to launch in the first place.

There was concern about conducting the operation at colder-than-previous launch temperatures, so at a teleconference meeting the evening before the launch NASA asked the contractor that made the O-rings, Morton Thiokol, to provide their input into the situation. At first, the company advised delaying the launch due to forecast temperatures below 53°F (it was about 36°F), but after considerable discussion they reversed their position and recommended that they could go ahead with it. When the explosion occurred, one of the Thiokol engineers said, "we all knew exactly what happened."[25]

Table 18-1 summarizes the eight main symptoms of groupthink, as developed by Irving Janis, the leading researcher into this phenomenon. Not all eight need to be present but the greater the number of symptoms involved in a group decision the greater the likelihood the group will suffer from the negative effects of groupthink.

It appears that at least five of these symptoms were present in the meetings and deliberations before the ill-fated decision to launch the space shuttle Challenger:

- *Illusion of invulnerability.* Prior success of the Apollo program and NASA's stellar reputation of successfully solving almost any engineering problem caused them to be overly optimistic about their own abilities, creating the illusion of invulnerability that led them to treat the O-ring temperature problem as an acceptable risk. Morton Thiokol's liaison for the Solid Rocket Booster project at Kennedy Space Center warned that "I wouldn't want to have to be the person to stand up in front of board of inquiry and say that I went ahead and told them to go ahead and fly this thing outside what the motor was qualified to."[27] In spite of this pre-accident warning it appears they still felt they were invulnerable.

Table 18-1. Symptoms and characteristics of groupthink.[26]

Groupthink syndrome	
Symptoms	**Description**
Overestimation of group	
Illusion of invulnerability	Members believe the team is invulnerable which breeds unrealistic optimism and the propensity to take greater risks.
Belief in inherent morality of group	Unquestioned belief the in group's morality leads them to ignore the ethical consequences of their decision .
Closed-mindedness	
Collective rationalizations	Rationalizations, or explanations, are created that minimize or discount the credibility of information or warnings that challenge the group's beliefs.
Stereotypes of out-groups	A sense of superiority leads the group to minimize the credibility of outside groups who oppose them.
Pressures toward uniformity	
Self-censorship	Members keep silent about doubts to avoid deviating from what they think is the group consensus.
Illusion of unanimity	Self-censorship and silence from other group members creates an illusion that the group is in agreement even though they are not.
Direct pressure on dissenters	Censorship of members who express opposition to ideas or the illusions of group.
Self-appointed mindguards	Some members shield the group from adverse information or warnings.

- *Collective rationalizations.* Thiokol warned NASA about the O-ring problem and advised delaying the launch. But NASA personnel questioned the seriousness of Thiokol's warning suggesting that they reconsider their data and conclusions. They did, and reversed their original decision "all due to pressure and rationalization from NASA."[28]
- *Illusion of unanimity.* Thiokol's decision reversal was made by only three managers and a manager/engineer—the rest of the Thiokol engineers were excluded since it was "time to make a management decision." The result was a poll of only a few people who were mostly in favor of reversing the original recommendation to scrub the launch. Thiokol's ambivalence about the seriousness of the O-ring problem wasn't even communicated to senior-level decision-makers at NASA.
- *Direct pressure on dissenters.* After Thiokol initially recommend that NASA scrub the launch, NASA personnel at Marshall Space Flight Center (MSFC) rejected their rationale and one official told them he "was appalled" at their recommendation. Another official at MSFC said, "My God, Thiokol, when do you want me to launch, next April?" The only engineer in the four-person group at Thiokol who reversed their original decision was asked by the Senior Vice President to "take off his engineering hat and put on his management hat."[29] This all had the effect of silencing the dissenters.
- *Self-appointed mindguards.* Thiokol's chief expert on O-rings, who would have presented a conflicting viewpoint, was left out of the decision-making process, and senior-level decision-makers at NASA were never informed about Thiokol's concern about the negative effect of cold temperatures on the O-rings.

The decision to accept an elevated level of risk in the Challenger launch (and 17 years later in the Columbia mission) had its roots in organizational and political pressures "to meet an increasingly ambitious launch schedule."[30] As we've seen in several aircraft accident examples in this and previous chapters, the pressure to meet a flight schedule is a powerful influence on a pilot's decision to continue a flight even if she or he has misgivings about the safety of doing so. Whether the pressure is exerted by managers, by a group, or by others (including yourself), the result is the temptation to accept—either consciously or unconsciously—an elevated level of risk to continue the mission.

Conformity and Obedience

A major symptom of groupthink is conformity to the consensus of the group. **Conformity** is a "change in behavior or beliefs as a result of real or imagined group pressure."[31] The latter part of the definition acknowledges that sometimes an individual doesn't have to be in the presence of the group, or that group pressure may not actually exist in reality even if an individual thinks it does. Sometimes when the NTSB cites a pilot's "self-induced pressure" to complete a flight it may be in response to real or imagined pressure from others.

Psychologists generally distinguish between two types of conformity: compliance and acceptance. Compliance involves outwardly conforming to the values, beliefs or norms of the group while privately disagreeing with them. Acceptance involves conforming to them and inwardly agreeing to them and internalizing them as one's own.[32] A type of compliance that involves complying with requests or orders from an authority figure (or more than one such person) is **obedience to authority**.

Sherif's Autokinetic Effect Experiments

The autokinetic effect was discussed in Chapter 6. In a completely dark environment, a small stationary light will actually appear to move about a person's field of view when stared at directly. In a landmark experiment conducted by social psychologist Muzafer Sherif in the 1930s, participants sitting in a dark room were asked to verbally estimate how far a small light moved. Of course, the participants didn't know the light was completely stationary. While not in the presence of others, each participant's verbal distance estimates varied widely; however, when tested in groups of two or three, each person eventually adjusted their answers until all participants had virtually the same distance estimates!

Fig 18-1.

Sherif's Autokenetic Experiment.
Participants' estimates of how far a stationary light moved varied when tested individually, but converged to the same answer by day 4 in the presence of others.[34]

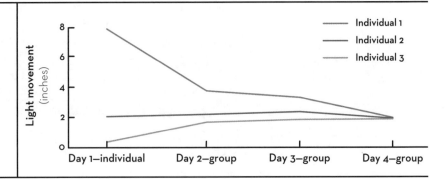

Figure 18-1 represents the results of one group tested over four days. Tested alone (day 1) the three participant's estimates varied significantly from each other, but when tested together (day 2, 3, and 4) each person adjusted their estimates with their verbal answers converging together until by day 4 they were virtually the same. The people in these studies appear to have completely accepted, or internalized, the group norms, since when they were later tested individually, they tended to use the new group norm instead of their previous individual estimates. Sherif concluded that when people lack information they tend look to others for correct information. So when others verbally share their belief (how far the light moved) in an ambiguous situation such as this, individuals abandon their own distance estimate norms and adopt the group norm.[33] This type of acceptance conformity is often called **informational conformity** since those who conform do so primarily because they are seeking information in order that they can be correct in their understanding of the situation.

The Asch Conformity Experiments

Another important study that provided significant insight into the phenomenon of conformity was the Asch conformity experiments (after the psychologist Solomon Asch). One of these involved eight male participants who compared a card with three lines of different lengths with another card that had a single line with the same length as of one of the three lines. Their job was to match the correct-length line (A, B, or C) with the reference line (*see* Figure 18-2). This matching task wasn't difficult: when individual subjects were tested alone the error rate was less than 1 percent.

However, of the eight participants, only one was the real subject of the experiment—but he didn't know it. The other seven were confederates (accom-

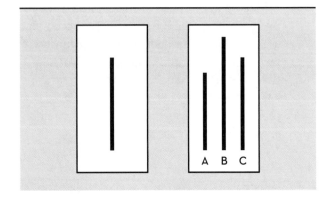

Fig 18-2.

An example of one of several pairs of cards used in Solomon Asch's experiments. Participants were asked to compare a reference line (on the left card) to the three lines (on the right card). Clearly line C is the same length as the reference line.[35]

plices) in the experiment and the subject was led to believe that they were all participants like himself. He would walk into the room, and because the confederates arrived early, the subject would always end up seated in the last (or near-last) chair. As the experimenter showed the cards to the group, each participant in sequence would verbally answer with the true subject of the experiment answering last (or second-to-last). This proved to be fine for the first two trials—everybody easily identified the correct-length line—but on the third and several subsequent trials all the confederates deliberately (in coordination with the experimenter beforehand) gave the same wrong answer. This put the true subject in a difficult situation, and as Asch states, "Two alternatives were open to the subject: he could act independently, repudiating the majority, or he could go along with the majority, repudiating the evidence of his senses."[36]

Of the 18 trials, the confederates gave the same wrong answer in 12 of them. You might think that hardly anyone conformed to the group. However, in these 12 critical trials more than one-third of the subjects went along with the group and verbalized the obviously incorrect answers! Post-experiment interviews with subjects suggest that most who conformed to the group did so because of their desire to be accepted by the other group members. In contrast to informational conformity demonstrated in Sherif's autokinetic effect experiments, where participants conformed to group norms because they were seeking information in an ambiguous situation and inwardly internalized them as their own, this type of peer pressure is often called **normative conformity** since most participants privately disagreed with the group but conformed anyway because of their desire to be accepted by the other group members.

Encouragingly, only a very small percentage of the subjects conformed to the crowd all the time, and about a quarter of the subjects never conformed at all to the majority of the group. In other versions of the experiment a second subject, or another confederate, broke with the group by verbally providing the correct answer—conformity decreased substantially in this situation, pointing to the power that just one other person can have to break the influence of a group.

Milgram's Shocking Experiments

In the Sherif and Asch experiments researchers wanted to determine the degree to which individuals would conform to group norms. There were no explicit directives to the participants from the experimenters or confederates to conform to the group, yet a significant number of people still did. Motivated by a desire to try and understand why people in Nazi Germany obeyed their superiors in carrying out the extermination of millions of Jews in the holocaust, and especially the claim by Adolph Eichmann and others at their criminal trials that they were "only following orders," Stanley Milgram at Yale University wanted to discover the degree to which everyday ordinary people would inflict pain on others when commanded to do so by an authority figure.

Participants were told that they were studying the effects of punishment on learning. One participant, with his arms wired up to an electric shock generator, is responsible to learn and remember specific word pairs (the *learner*); the other participant sitting in an adjacent room (the *teacher*) is to administer increasing levels of electric shock to the learner for every incorrect answer given in the paired-word memory task. The voltage switches on the shock generator range from 15 to 450 volts. As the task proceeds, the learner fails to remember some word pairs and the teacher administers a dose of shock by toggling one of the switches on the shock generator. The dosage increases with subsequent incorrect answers. However, the setting is not all that it appears; the learner does not actually receive the shocks—he is a confederate of the experiment—but the unsuspecting subject (the teacher) certainly believes he does, especially when pre-recorded protests, howls, and screams are heard from the learner as the shock levels progressively increase. Whenever the subject questions the experimenter (the "authority figure" in a lab coat) about what is happening to the learner the experimenter responds with pre-rehearsed injunctions to continue, such as "The experiment requires that you continue," or "You have no other choice; you must go on." Milgram wanted to measure the degree to which people would obey an authority figure. What he found was 25 out of 40 subjects (63 percent), despite their protests, obeyed to the end administering what they thought was the full 450 volts to their victims.[37]

These were not evil or sadistic people. If you watch the films they made of the experiment, most participants are clearly bothered by what they are doing to the other person (the twitching, the rubbing of their foreheads, the nervous laughter, and the emotion-laden protests). Nevertheless, despite their conscience, they felt they had to obey the authority figure. They were regular law-abiding folk like you and me. Once again, like the phenomena of social loafing and groupthink, diffusion of responsibility seems to also play a role in a person's propensity to obey authority. Milgram suggested that people are more willing to engage in cruel acts if the authority figure they are obeying takes responsibility for their actions, as was the case in this experiment. You can imagine the emotional stress this experiment had on the participants in the study. While Milgram discovered that a high majority indicated they weren't significantly affected by their participation in the study, his methodology would never be acceptable under today's American Psychological Association ethical- and code-of-conduct guidelines.

Obedience and Conformity in Aviation

"Never fly in the same cockpit with someone braver than you."

—Richard Herman Jr.

As a pilot, you may not think you are susceptible to obedience and conformity when it comes to flight activities. But experimental studies, accident examples, and my own personal experiences shared in this chapter—and perhaps your own experiences also—suggest otherwise. Believe it or not, sometimes normal pilots like you and me let other people—customers, passengers, supervisors, dispatchers—influence us to a point that they're making our decisions for us and, in effect they are flying our aircraft instead of us.

Sometimes We Let Passengers and Customers Fly Our Aircraft

All members of the Youngstown State University football team are required to use emergency exits and slides to evacuate a chartered McDonnell Douglas DC-9 which had just landed off the side of Runway 24 at Erie International Airport in Pennsylvania. Against his better judgment the pilot, in his effort to meet the schedule of his customers, knowingly continued an approach in questionable weather (ceiling 100 feet, visibility one-half SM). The NTSB concluded the flight crew's deficient performance was partly due to the *encouragement of the company dispatcher to attempt the approach, as well as the subtle pressure exerted on them by the business manager who occupied the jumpseat* (emphasis added) (Report No: NTSB/AAR-86/02/SUM).

You're the pilot of a MEDEVAC flight that will arrive after dark, but you and your aircraft are not qualified for such a mission at night. The doctor has determined that a woman seriously injured in an accident at a remote fishing camp requires immediate evacuation. You're the only pilot available. The woman needs help. What do you do? It's not so easy, is it? A commercial helicopter pilot in Quebec, who was considered to be professional and competent and who had taken two courses in risk management even though there was no requirement to do so by Transport Canada, faced just such a situation. He decided to go, ended up in poor weather, lost control, and crashed. All aboard died, including the woman he was trying to save.[38]

Sometimes We Let Our Boss and Others in Authority Fly Our Aircraft

Even though neither were actually on board, the pilots involved in the Wapiti and Downeast Airlines accidents effectively let their bosses fly their airplanes. Though not the captain's direct boss, the VIP aboard a Polish Air Force Tupolev Tu-154 passenger jet might as well have been—his name was Lech Kaczynski, the President of Poland. The captain went against his better judgment and attempted a difficult approach in inadequate weather (visibility had deteriorated to less than one-quarter SM in fog) knowing there was a high probability he would need to conduct a go-around. It was during the missed approach, after descending below the approved decision altitude, that the airplane hit trees at such a force that part of a wing separated in flight causing the airplane to strike the ground in an inverted position. All four flight crew members, four flight attendants, and 88 passengers on board—including the President and other high-ranking officials, instantly died in this horrible crash near the city of Smolensk, Russia, in April of 2010.

Once again, it appears there was significant indirect pressure to complete the flight. Besides the subtle pressure of the presence of the Commander-in-Chief of the Polish Air Force, who entered the flight deck two minutes before the airplane crashed, the captain's words "I'm not sure, but if we don't land here, he'll give me trouble," referring to the President, reveals the pressure he likely felt as he continued to conduct the approach in the face of several warnings the weather was too low to land.[39] The captain was also likely thinking about a previous flight with the President when he was the co-pilot. On that flight his captain "defied President Lech Kaczynski's order to make a risky landing in Georgia's capital" and had to divert elsewhere.[40] Because the President was inconvenienced—he and his entourage were forced to drive all day to his destination—he never allowed that captain to be involved in any of his flights again. He later publicly stated that "if someone decides to become a pilot, he cannot be fearful."[41]

Sometimes We Let Friends and Fellow Pilots Fly Our Aircraft

In the previous chapter, I related a story of a student of mine who was driving in the middle of nowhere late one night when he noticed his gas gauge indicated near-empty. Knowing there was a late-night gas station about 10 minutes behind him, he struggled with the decision to turn back because of all the wasted time and resources expended if he did so. What I didn't tell you was he also had his girlfriend in the car with him. He told me it would have been much easier to turn around had she not been with him.

Also briefly noted in the last chapter was the fatal crash into a wooded swamp in Florida that killed a low-time (392 hours) non-instrument-rated private pilot and his two passengers. The flight was returning from the Bahamas to Florida when they encountered IFR weather conditions—a front was passing over Florida at the time. The pilot decided to fly low and "scud run" to a nearby destination. The last three minutes of radar data showed the airplane maneuvering at an altitude between 100 and 200 feet MSL with the final radar target indicating a left circuit at 200 feet, about an eighth of a mile southwest of the accident site. Besides his "personal pressure to get home," the NTSB concluded that his high-time (4,515 hours) commercial-rated passenger likely advised the pilot-in-command to continue VFR flight in the face of IMC, and unfortunately, he complied (NTSB Identification No: ERA13FA133).

Sometimes, other pilots don't even have to be on the flight deck. Simply knowing that other pilots "made it" has a strong influence on our decision to continue. According to NTSB accident reports, the pilots of the Air Florida B-737, as well as the Delta Air Lines L-1011, that flew through a microburst and crashed short of the runway at Dallas-Fort Worth International Airport (see Chapter 14), were influenced to continue their departure and landing, respectively, by their knowledge that previous airplanes only minutes before them were successful in making it. The NTSB said as much in their investigation of an accident involving a DC-9 that collided with trees and a private residence during an attempted missed approach from an instrument landing system approach at Charlotte Douglas International Airport, in North Carolina. The crew conducted the missed approach because they encountered microburst-induced wind shear that was produced by a rapidly developing thunderstorm located at the approach end of Runway 18R.

Both crew members were well aware of thunderstorm activity in the area: the CVR records them talking about the heavy rain they were encountering; their airborne weather radar indicated a cell south of the airport with a red center and yellow edges indicating heavy and moderate precipitation, respectively; the controller advised them there was rain south of the field; and both crew members discussed the possibility of a missed approach because of wind shear. As they got closer, they could see the thunderstorm ahead of them and the controller issued a couple of wind shear alerts as they were approaching minimums. Three minutes before the accident, the controller cleared them to land, informing them that the aircraft ahead of them reported "a smooth ride all the way down the final." The captain thanked the controller for the PIREP "from that guy in front of us." A minute later, the controller told a departing USAir B-737 that another departing flight just ahead of them also reported a "smooth ride on departure." Though not included in the probable cause statement, the NTSB stated that "The flight crew's decision to continue the approach into an area of adverse weather may have been influenced by weather information from the crews of preceding flights that had flown the flight path to runway 18R previously" (Report No: NTSB/AAR-95/03). Thirty-seven passengers died and the rest aboard USAir Flight 1016 were injured.

By the way, this type of social influence can also lead to safer outcomes. Apparently, there was a long line of passenger jets waiting patiently for departure during winter operations at a major U.S. airport. When the pilot of one particular airplane finally reached the front of the line and received his takeoff clearance he was heard telling the tower that as much as he wanted to he couldn't accept the clearance and instead requested permission to taxi back to get deiced a second time. Do you know what happened? One by one, all the others waiting in line behind him requested the same thing. That was good, but what would have happened had the first pilot not aborted his departure?

Managing Social Pressure

Do you see how strong an influence other people can have on our lives? Aristotle was correct when he wrote in the fourth century BCE that man is, by nature, a social animal. We are social beings who live in a social environment where social norms and expectations are imposed on us. While social influence is often necessary to protect and help us (think rules of the road, saying please and thank you, etc.), it can also negatively influence our behavior. Pilots have long lived with the downside of social pressure. For example, did you know that 31 of the first 40 U.S. Air Mail Service pilots "were killed in action" trying to meet and conform to the expectations imposed on them from the authority figures in government and industry?[42] As we've seen in this and previous chapters, pressures from self, passengers, and company officials are also a major psychological cause of VFR flight into IMC accidents.[43] So, how do you avoid succumbing to negative pressure on the flight deck? Mostly, it involves awareness of social influence, knowledge of proper flight operations and assertiveness in the face of negative pressure.

Be Aware of Social Influence

Like a fish in its natural habitat, we swim in a sea of social relationships and influence; and like the fish who is the last one to discover he's in water, we are seldom aware of the degree to which social influence impacts our lives. Therefore, the first defense in guarding against negative influence from others is to simply be aware of its reality in the first place. Reading this chapter has certainly helped you do just that. When you encounter a situation that involves a conflict between what others may expect of you and what is safe, this knowledge will help you to better recognize it and act accordingly.

Maintain Expert Knowledge of Proper Flight Operations

One reason we tend to imitate others is because we lack information as to how things are supposed to be done (informational conformity). Imitating others is a major way to learn something. It begins at an early age—even before we are old enough to talk—and continues throughout our lifetimes, especially when we are in a new unfamiliar situation, like our first job at an airline. Other pilots, more experienced than ourselves, possess information and expertise that serves as a source of our learning. That is the major reason we are hired on as FOs first, and not as captains. We still have much to learn; so we do as other pilots do, we imitate them. But the problem arises when they do something you think they are not supposed to do. Notice how I said *you think*. As a new-hire pilot you may be uncertain about your assessment and, since you likely lack confidence and feel somewhat inferior to your more-seasoned captain, you begin to doubt yourself.

Part of the remedy for lack of confidence, doubt, and intimidation is to know everything you possibly can about the aircraft you fly and the company's SOPs developed to assist you in conducting flight operations in the safest manner possible. Doing this during your initial and recurrent training, as well as in between these evaluations, will increase your confidence to speak up when something doesn't look right or when another crew member appears to be doing something that doesn't conform to SOPs.

Be Assertive

A crew of two is a group, and the dynamics of group interaction play a strong role in decision making. Sometimes there are disagreements between you and your fellow crew member so it is important that you both communicate until you are on the same and correct page—especially when diagnosing an ambiguous situation that may present itself on the flight deck. The crew of West Caribbean Airways Flight 708 each possessed a different mental model of what state the MD-82 was actually in and the FO, who had the correct understanding, failed to change the captain's mind. They were both cited for failure to communicate and to at least refer to checklists to make ambiguous information less ambiguous. The report said had they done this the captain may have "changed his mind" about the true state of the aircraft.

Cordial and harmonious relationships on the flight deck are essential for smooth flight operations; yet if you see something you don't like, or are not sure of, it's important to speak up even if it turns out you misinterpreted the situation. Like the FO in the West Caribbean Airways MD-82 should have done, if safety requires it you should avoid a "go along to get along" attitude and exercise more assertive behavior. Make your concerns known in a straightforward and even forceful, yet respectful, manner if necessary. The next chapter looks at using the various practices associated with CRM, including the importance of assertiveness, as a strategy to achieve safe outcomes in flight.

Helpful Resources

The free online FAA *Human Factors Awareness Course* has a separate module on team/group performance. (www.hf.faa.gov/Webtraining/Cognition/Cognition1.htm)

Short videos showing actual subjects participating in the Asch conformity experiments (www.youtube.com/watch?v=NyDDyT1lDhA) and Stanley Milgram's shocking obedience to authority experiments (www.youtube.com/watch?v=yr5cjyokVUs) are available on YouTube.

The old television show *Candid Camera* captures unwitting participants in a conformity experiment using an elevator. Very amusing, if it wasn't so real. (www.youtube.com/watch?v=BgRoiTWkBHU)

More unwitting participants are caught on camera in a recent social conformity experiment demonstrated in a five-minute video from the *National Geographic Brain Games*' television show. It takes place in an eye doctor's waiting room and is a real eye opener. (www.youtube.com/watch?v=o8BkzvP19v4)

In 1964, Catherine "Kitty" Genovese was brutally beaten, stabbed, and killed in in Queens, New York, while perhaps as many as 38 people heard her screams or saw something from their windows but did next to nothing about it, including calling the police. *The Bystander Effect: The Death of Kitty Genovese* is a seven-minute video introducing the bystander effect and diffusion of responsibility highlighting some of the work of two pioneers in this area, John Darlye and Bibb Latane. (www.youtube.com/watch?v=BdpdUbW8vbw)

Endnotes

1. "CFIT—The Pilot's Viewpoint," *Aviation Safety Letter*, Issue 1/96 (Ottawa: Transport Canada 1996): 1–2.

2. Ibid.

3. "Major Accident Report: Piper Navajo PA-31 Chieftain, High Prairie, Alberta, 19 October 1984," *Aviation Safety Letter*, Issue 4/90 (Ottawa: Transport Canada 1990): 4–6.

4. Carol Shaben, *Into the Abyss: An Extraordinary True Story* (NY: Grand Central Publishing 2012).

5. "CFIT—The Pilot's Viewpoint."

6. Federal Aviation Administration, "Air Florida Flight 90, Boeing Model 737-200, N62AF, Accident Overview," *Lessons Learned from Civil Aviation Accidents*. Available at lessonslearned.faa.gov/ll_main.cfm?TabID=1&LLID=2.

7. AOPA Air Safety Institute, *Safety Advisor—Spatial Disorientation: Confusion That Kills*, Physiology No. 1 (Frederick, MD: August 2004).

8. AOPA Air Safety Institute, *VFR Into IMC Accidents: 2012* (Frederick, MD). Available at www.aopa.org/asf/ntsb/vfrintoimc.cfm?window=3.

9. AOPA Air Safety Institute, *2010 Nall Report: General Aviation Accident Trends and Factors for 2009* (Frederick, MD: 2011).

10. Juliana Goh and Douglas Wiegmann, "Visual Flight Rules (VFR) Flight into Instrument Meteorological Conditions (IMC): A Review of the Accident Data," *11th International Symposium on Aviation Psychology*, ed. Richard Jensen (Columbus, OH: The Ohio State University 2001).

11. National Transportation Safety Board, *Safety Study: Aviation Safety in Alaska*, NTSB/SS-95/03 (Washington, DC: 1995).

12. United States Government Accountability Office, *Aviation Safety: Improved Data Collection Needed for Effective Oversight of Air Ambulance Industry. Report to the Chairman, Subcommittee on Aviation, Committee on Transportation and Infrastructure, House of Representatives*, Report No. GAO-07-353 (Washington, DC: February 2007).

13. National Transportation Safety Board, *Safety Study: Commercial Emergency Medical Service Helicopter Operations*, NTSB/SS-88/01 (Washington DC: January 28, 1988).

14. Matthew J. Rigsby, *U.S. Civil Helicopter Emergency Medical Services Accident Data Analysis, the FAA Perspective* (Washington DC: FAA, September 2005).

15. NTSB, *Safety Study: Commercial Emergency Medical Service Helicopter Operations*.

16. National Transportation Safety Board, *Special Investigation Report on Emergency Medical Services Operations*, NTSB/SIR-06/01 (Washington DC: January 25, 2006).

17. Ira J. Blumen and the UCAN Safety Committee, *A Safety Review and Risk Assessment in Air Medical Transport: Supplement to the Air Medical Physician Handbook* (Salt Lake City, UT: November 2002).

18. U.S. GAO, *Aviation Safety: Improved Data Collection*.

19. NTSB, *Special Investigation Report on Emergency Medical Services Operations*.

20. Civil Aviation Accident Investigation Board, "English Translation of Main Text of Venezuelan Accident Report," *Informe Final, West Caribbean Airways DC-9-82 (MD-82) Matricula HK4374X Machiques, Venezuela, 16 De Agosto de 2005*, JIAAC-9-058-2005 (Gobierno Bolivariano de Venezuela: August 2010).

21. Sebastian Murdock, "A Chicago Assault Victim Might Still Be Alive If Bystanders Had Cared Enough to Help," *Huffington Post* (April 21, 2016).

22. David G. Meyers, *Social Psychology*, 4th ed. (New York: McGraw Hill, 1993).

23. Steven J. Karau and Kipling D. Williams, "Social Loafing: A Meta-Analytic Review and Theoretical Integration," *Journal of Personality and Social Psychology* 65 (October 1993): 681–706.

24. A saying commonly now used at NASA and cited by astronaut Mark Kelly in "Lessons from NASA and the Dangers of 'Groupthink' in Technology Rollouts," published at Concert Technologies. Available at www.concerttech.com/avoid-technology-rollout-groupthink/.

25. Howard Berkes, *Remembering Roger Boisjoly: He Tried to Stop Shuttle Challenger Launch*, interview for National Public Radio (February 6, 2012).

26. Data for this table is from Irving L. Janis, *Groupthink: Psychological Studies of Policy Decisions and Fiascoes* (Boston: Houghton Mifflin 1983).

27. William P. Rogers, *Report to the President by the Presidential Commission on the Space Shuttle Challenger Accident* (Washington, DC: June 6, 1986).

28. Robert D. Dimitroff, Lu Ann Schmidt and Timothy D. Bond, "Organizational Behavior and Disaster: A Study of Conflict at NASA," *Project Management Journal*, 36 (June 2005): 28–38.

29. Rogers, *Report to the President*.

30. Dimitroff, Schmidt and Bond, "Organizational Behavior and Disaster: A Study of Conflict."

31. Charles A. Kiesler and Sara B. Kiesler, *Conformity* (Reading, MA: Addison-Wesley, 1969).

32. Meyers, *Social Psychology*.

33. Muzafer Sherif, "A Study of Some Social Factors in Perception," Chapter 3, in *Archives of Psychology* 27 (1935): 23–46.

34. Data from Muzafer Sherif, "A Study of Some Social Factors in Perception," Chapter 3, in *Archives of Psychology* 27 (1935): 23–46.

35. Fred the Oyster, November 5, 2014 (https://commons.wikimedia.org/wiki/File:Asch_experiment.svg) WC CC BY-SA 4.0

36. Solomon E. Asch, "Opinions and Social Pressure," *Scientific American* 193 (November 1955): 31–35.

37. Stanley Milgram, *Obedience to Authority: An Experimental View* (New York: Harper & Row, 1974).

38. "Systemic Deficiencies," *Aviation Safety Reflexions* 14 (June 1996): 5–8.

39. Ellen Barry, "Report on Polish Crash Finds Pilot Error, but Says Powerful Passengers Share Some Blame," *The New York Times* (January 12, 2011). Available at www.nytimes.com/2011/01/13/world/europe/13crash.html.

40. Ibid.

41. Ibid.

42. Charles Perrow, *Normal Accidents: Living with High Risk Technologies* (New York: Basic Books, 1984).

43. R.G. Mortimer and J.S. Hanson, *Aviation Safety Research: Literature Review of Sources of Aviation Accident and Incident Data and Selected Factors Contributing to Accidents*, Volume 1 (Springfield, VA: National Technical Information Service, 1993).

Part IV
Risk Management

19

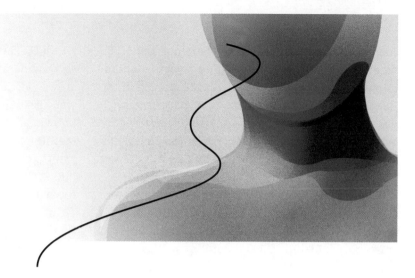

Working together.

Crew Resource Management

It was early evening when they arrived. United Airlines Flight 173 was a scheduled passenger flight from John F. Kennedy International Airport to Portland International Airport, with an intermediate stop at Denver. The McDonnell Douglas DC-8 was descending through 10,000 feet MSL on vectors for a visual approach to Runway 28L at Portland when the captain reported seeing the airport in sight. At 8,000 feet, the captain, who was the PM, lowered the flaps and landing gear. That's when he and the other crew members heard and felt a loud "thump, thump," felt a strong vibration, and saw and felt the airplane yaw. The green light of the nose landing gear position indicating system illuminated but the others did not.

The captain rightfully rejected their landing, and with the assistance of ATC conducted a vector-assisted hold at 5,000 feet southeast of the field while the crew worked at troubleshooting the problem. The NTSB investigation concluded that the right main landing gear retract cylinder assembly, which prevents the landing gear from free-falling when the gear is extended, had failed due to corrosion causing the right gear to free-fall. This sudden drop of the right main landing gear disabled the microswitch that completes an electrical circuit to the gear position indicator lights in the cockpit. After consulting with company dispatch and maintenance personnel, as well as conducting other important landing gear checks, the crew eventually came to the correct conclusion that all three gear were fully extended, but it took them considerable time to determine this and to prepare the flight attendants for a possible difficult landing and evacuation in case they weren't. Unfortunately, they squandered

a full hour doing this; with the DC-8 configured with the landing gear down and flaps extended 15 degrees it burned considerable fuel and the engines began to flame out from fuel exhaustion. All four engines eventually quit and a couple of minutes later the DC-8 crashed six miles southeast of the airport. The aircraft was destroyed and of the 189 people aboard, 8 passengers, the FE, and a flight attendant (FA) were killed (Report No: NTSB-AAR-79-7).

How could a perfectly qualified flight crew of three, good weather, and an airplane capable of landing safely end in a fatal accident? The NTSB determined that the probable cause of the accident was the failure of the captain to properly monitor and respond to aircraft's low fuel state and to properly respond to the crew members' advisories regarding the fuel state. Contributing to the accident was the failure of the FO and FE to either fully comprehend the criticality of the fuel state or to successfully communicate their concern to the captain. The report further concluded that this accident exemplified a recurring problem in commercial aviation—a breakdown in cockpit management and teamwork during a situation involving malfunctions of aircraft systems in flight. It further concluded that even though "the captain may exert subtle pressure on his crew to conform to his way of thinking" and possibly "force another crew member to yield his right to express and opinion," the FO and FE have a responsibility to ensure they effectively communicate their concerns to the captain. Therefore, the NTSB recommended that commercial air carrier operators ensure that their flight crews are trained in the "principles of *flight deck resource management*, with particular emphasis on the merits of *participative management for captains* and *assertiveness training for other cockpit crew members*" (emphasis added) (Report No: NTSB-AAR-79-7).

The NTSB's recommendations emanating from this accident, along with others preceding it, were major catalysts for the implementation of CRM training for airline flight operations. Worldwide, between 1968 and 1976, more than 60 major airline accidents were caused in part by inadequate CRM in flight.[1] Accident analyses also indicated that 66 percent of air carrier, 79 percent of commuter, and 88 percent of GA accidents were not the result of technical breakdowns or adverse weather, but flight crew failures in interpersonal communications, decision making, and leadership. The industry was anxious to reduce these types of errors made by those responsible for the safety of their passengers.[2]

In June of 1979—only six months after the Portland accident—NASA sponsored the first industry workshop on *Resource Management on the Flight Deck* in San Francisco, California. This seminal three-day event, involving dozens of experts in government, academia, and the airline industry, explored such topics as social psychology, crew selection, interpersonal skills training, communication, assertiveness, stress management, line-oriented flight training, and command/leadership training.[3] It was at this workshop that the term *cockpit resource management* was coined to describe the set of attitudes and behaviors required of flight crews to reduce errors on the flight deck.[4] The name was later changed to *crew resource management* in the late-1980s to better reflect the need to include not only flight crew members in the front of the airplane but cabin crew in the back.

United Airlines (UAL), the operator of the DC-8 that ran out of fuel outside Portland, was the first in the United States to implement an extensive CRM training program for its pilots: it was called *command leadership resource management*. The self-study and pilot group-seminars involved the use of case studies and personal questionnaires to help participants identify their own communication, behavioral, and leadership styles when working together as a team on the flight deck.[5]

All U.S. air carriers since 1998 have been required to provide approved CRM training to their flight crews (14 CFR §121.404). In 1999, the requirement was also extended to FAs and dispatchers; the latter known as *dispatch resource management*, or DRM.[6] Maintenance personnel are also trained in CRM principles called *maintenance resource management*, or MRM.[7] CRM has continued to grow and evolve, and so too has its influence. Over the years virtually every airline in the world has developed CRM training for their flight crews, cabin crews, and other safety-critical personnel.

In 1990 the FAA issued Special Federal Aviation Regulation No. 58, "Advanced Qualification Program" (AQP), which allows for an alternate method of qualifying, training, certifying, and otherwise ensuring competency of flight crew members, FAs, dispatchers, other operations personnel, instructors, and evaluators who are required to be trained or qualified under Part 121 and 135. In addition to traditional competency training, AQP provides ground instruction in CRM that is reinforced and practiced though in-flight training scenarios (in a simulator or flight training device) during line-oriented simulations (LOS). One type of LOS is line-oriented flight training (LOFT). Rather than emphasizing traditional maneuver-based training, LOFT simulates real-time gate-to-gate line flights in which crew members, after being presented with a non-normal or emergency situation somewhere along the flight, are evaluated on both their technical and CRM skills. Another type of LOS is special purpose operational training that consists of full or partial flight segments designed to address specific training objectives of the flight department.[8]

Defining CRM

A variety of definitions of CRM exist. The most descriptive definition is the one provided in the FAA's AC 120-35D, and only slightly modified for clarity: CRM is the effective use of all available resources—people, information, and equipment—to achieve safe and efficient flight operations.[9] The definition indicates that CRM practices are first designed to reduce flight crew error and enhance safety. A side benefit is it enhances efficiency. Since the goal of every airline is to make a profit, and part of that is attaining on-time performance with as little disruption to the schedule as possible, the teamwork and other skills involved in CRM also enhances the efficiency of flight operations—but never at the expense of its number one goal, safe flight operations. The definition also stresses the importance of leveraging *all* available resources to achieve the safety and efficiency goals inherent in every flight operation.

While CRM is primarily applicable to multi-crew operations, an offshoot of CRM specifically tailored to single-pilot operations—known as *single-pilot resource management* (SRM)—is the art of managing all onboard and outside resources available to a pilot before and during a flight to help ensure a safe and successful outcome.[10] SRM is an important strategy to improve pilot performance, but because most of the concepts involved in SRM are included in CRM, the focus of this chapter is primarily on CRM practices that are applicable to crewed flight decks.

CRM Elements

Consider the Portland accident. The day's flights were uneventful until the captain lowered the landing gear. Besides your technical understanding of how the landing gear works, if you were the FO, what non-technical skills would you need to effectively assist in managing the situation? It's an abnormal event, possibly an emergency—that will likely create a considerable amount of situational stress. Therefore, stress management techniques will be important. Since there is a lot going on—assessing the gear situation, flying the airplane in a hold, preparing the FAs for a possible emergency landing—you will need crew coordination and other skills to effectively work together as a team to appropriately divide the workload between you and your fellow crew members. You must possess problem-solving and decision-making skills so you can work together at arriving at the best solution for the situation you now find yourself in. You will also need highly developed communication skills to effectively communicate with your fellow flight crew members, FAs, and ATC, as well as maintenance personnel through the aircraft communications addressing and reporting system. As time progresses, you become increasingly concerned about the remaining fuel on board. You must communicate that to the captain. If he possesses good leadership and communication skills he will listen to you and respond accordingly. However, if he doesn't appear to be as concerned as

you think he should, you need to be willing and able to shift your communication strategies into high gear and assertively state your concern in a direct and forthright manner until he gets it. This may likely produce conflict (and more personal stress), but you need to persist in your communication strategies while simultaneously using conflict resolution skills.

Even though CRM has gone through several iterations over the years, the following non-technical skills are the foundational skills still needed to achieve safe and efficient flight operations: situational awareness, task management, crew coordination, teamwork, communication, assertiveness, problem solving and decision making, stress management, leadership, and conflict resolution. Some of these topics have been explored in previous chapters; the others, most of which generally fall under the following categories, are discussed in the remainder of this chapter:

1. Communication.
2. Teamwork.
3. Decision making.
4. Stress management.

Communication

"The single biggest problem in communication is the illusion that it has taken place."

—George Bernard Shaw

This is at least the third time the topic of communication has been addressed in this book. That's because it's such an important component of flight safety (not to mention life in general). Whereas the mechanics of hearing and sound, and the basic structure of verbal communication were addressed in Chapters 7 and 13, respectively, this section focuses on the higher-level thinking and approaches needed to consistently and effectively communicate on the flight deck. There are five important aspects of effective communication: inquiry, listening, advocacy, conflict resolution, and critique.[11]

Inquiry

If something doesn't appear right on the flight deck the first thing to do is seek information. You can look more carefully at the flight or system's instruments, or consult manuals, but often it involves seeking clarification from your fellow crew member(s). It is important to ask questions, even if you may feel a little awkward doing so. If you are a new FO you may feel unsure about yourself and doubt the depth of your knowledge and abilities, causing you to feel uncomfortable speaking up. However, if you heed the advice given in the last chapter to learn everything you can about the aircraft you fly and the company's SOPs which tell you how to fly it, you will feel less intimidated. Inquiry is also used to clarify understanding throughout a conversation.

Listening

People prefer listening to themselves, not others. Have you ever tried to have a conversation with someone who isn't really listening to you? They may *pre-plan*: they are so focused on formulating what they want to tell you that they don't actually hear what you are saying. Or they take a *detour*: they wait until you mention a key word that provides them opportunity to take the conversation in a different direction—theirs. Or they may like to *debate*: for whatever reason it seems they like to always play the devil's advocate and argue the opposite to what you are saying. Finally, they may *tune out*: they make no pretense of listening to you and just stop listening to you altogether. True listening is active; it involves paying close attention, looking directly at the other person (not always easy to do on the flight deck), avoiding distractions, asking questions for clarification (more inquiry), and sometimes paraphrasing what the other person is saying to make sure you have properly understood them.[12]

Advocacy

After making inquiries and listening to input from others, you may find you have a different understanding of the situation than the other person does so you need to advocate for your position. Advocacy involves stating what you know or believe in a direct and forthright manner. The NTSB concluded that both the FO and FE in the Portland accident either failed to fully comprehend the criticality of the fuel state, or if they did comprehend it, they failed to successfully s their concern to the captain. Four years later, the FO in the Air Florida Flight 90 accident noticed something wasn't right with the engine pressure ratio and other engine instruments during the takeoff roll at Washington National Airport (*see* Chapter 18) and in his own way attempted to inquire of the captain: "...look at that thing! That don't seem right, does it?...That's not right...Naw, I don't think that's right." He barely inquired and certainly didn't effectively advocate for what he believed.

Chapters 10 and 17 discussed some of the results of an NTSB study of 37 major U.S. airline accidents where the actions of the flight crew were a causal or contributing factor to the accident. An intriguing finding was that the captain was the PF in more than 80 percent of the 37 accidents.[13] Assuming that captains and FOs equally shared PF duty periods, a common practice in the airlines, what does this tell to you? It suggests that FOs are less likely to tell captains about their errors and mistakes than captains are in telling their FOs.

Assertive Communication

There are several reasons FOs may be reluctant to fully advocate their position to their captain. It could be because of their own inexperience and insecurities as discussed previously, but it could also be their own personal orientation toward two important dimensions: task orientation and relationship orientation. The relationship-task grid in Figure 19-1 depicts an important concept. If you take a course in CRM you will likely complete an extensive survey that helps you determine where your behavior falls on this matrix.

- *Nurturing*—High relationship/Low task. If your orientation is primarily in the top-left quadrant you have a high concern for attaining and maintaining good relationships and a friendly atmosphere on the flight deck. The adjectives to the right of the dashed line describe desirable characteristics for good interpersonal communication. However, since you are low on task orientation, if you are overly nurturing you are in danger of violating your own rights by letting others get their way, which could lead to less safe outcomes.
- *Aggressive*—Low relationship/High task. The aggressive orientation is the basically the opposite of nurturing. If your orientation is primarily in the bottom-right quadrant you have a high concern for accomplishing the task with minimal concern for the thoughts and feelings of others. The adjectives above the dashed line describe desirable characteristics for command performance. However, since you are low on relationship orientation,

Behavioral dimensions

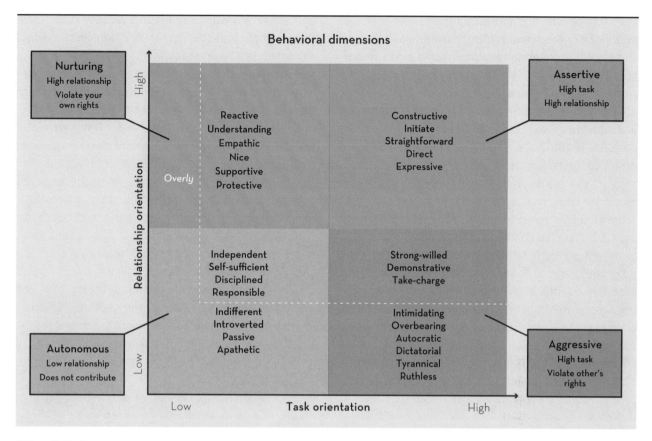

Fig 19-1.

The relationship-task grid. Wherever your tendencies may fall on the grid, you should aim to change your behaviors to align with the top-right assertive quadrant where you display a high concern for both good relationships with team members and a high desire to accomplish the tasks needed for safe flight operations.

the adjectives below the dashed line indicate you are overly aggressive and are in danger of violating the rights of others. This in turn tends to stifle input from others which could lead to less safe outcomes. This basically describes the stereotypical autocratic captain who says to his or her FO, "Gear up. Flaps up. Shut up." This type of captain views the FO and others as extensions of his or her brain, not as a collection of other brains that could help him or her out.

- *Autonomous*—Low relationship/Low task. If your orientation is primarily in the bottom-left quadrant you have a low concern for attaining and maintaining good relationships and a low concern for accomplishing a task. The adjectives above and to the right of the dashed line are desirable; but, if you are

overly autonomous and/or possess the characteristics described below the dashed line, you are essentially checked out and not contributing to the overall performance of the team, which could lead to less safe outcomes.

- *Assertive*—High relationship/High task. If your orientation is primarily in the top-right quadrant you have a high concern for both task accomplishment and maintaining good relationships and a friendly atmosphere on the flight deck. All the characteristics in this quadrant are desirable on the flight deck.

It is not necessarily detrimental if your tendencies fall outside the assertive quadrant—with perhaps the exception of the autonomous quadrant. There may be times when you will need to shift your orientation in one direction or the other. An emergency may require quick action and accomplishing the proper task will take priority over maintaining harmonious relationships. Or, a crewmate may need some extra understanding so a shift to a nurturing orientation may be needed. However, when it comes to flight safety, a high task orientation is always primary. What good is it to have great relationships in the cockpit if the airplane is going down in flames because the team didn't focus on accomplishing the fire checklist? It appears that most professional pilots recognize this since one study found that about 90 percent of them scored high on task orientation, while only 50 percent scored high on relationship orientation.[14]

Wherever your tendencies may fall on the grid, you should aim to change your behaviors toward the assertive quadrant where you display a high concern for accomplishing the tasks needed for safe flight operations but also maintaining cordial relationships and a friendly, relaxed, and supportive tone on the flight deck and aircraft cabin. This assertive orientation enables you to practice a critical tenet of effective communication: advocating your position by clearly stating what you know or believe in a direct and forthright manner.

Unassertive FOs

One of the roles of the second-in-command is to take control of the airplane in case the captain becomes incapacitated. However, a simulator study conducted by United Airlines had captains, who were designated the PF, feign subtle incapacitation while conducting an approach. In approximately 25 percent of the trials the aircraft hit the ground—either because the FOs failed to notice the incapacitation or failed to take over the controls. For the FOs who did recognize the incapacitation, it took anywhere from 30 seconds to 4 minutes to recognize the captain was incapacitated and to correct the situation.[15]

It is essential that the FO assertively communicate his or her concerns to the captain in a forthright manner. The main reason for such an emphasis is because accidents have occurred because subordinate crew members were too intimidated to do so. For example, when faced with a flap asymmetry (0 degrees right flap, 15 degrees left flap), an aural stall warning, and stick shaker activation on final approach, the captain of Empire Airlines 8284 took control from the FO at about 700 feet AGL and tried to salvage an extremely unstable approach instead of conducting a missed approach, as was dictated by the SOPs. Unfortunately, his actions only made things worse and the Avions de Transport Regional Aerospatiale ATR-42 stalled and crashed just short of the runway at Lubbock Preston Smith International Airport in Lubbock, Texas. The aircraft was substantially damaged, but fortunately both crew members—the only occupants aboard the cargo flight—were able to escape the burning aircraft before it was engulfed in smoke and fire (Report No: NTSB/AAR-11/02).

According to the company's procedures, a go-around is required when the stick shaker activates (indicating an imminent stall) and the PF (in this case the FO) should call out "go-around" and initiate the procedure. The FO was aware of this policy but rather than complying with the SOPs and directly asserting her concern about the unstabilized approach, she instead asked the captain, "Should I go around?" During a post-accident interview the FO indicated that asking this question was her way of saying that she wanted to go around "without stepping on toes."[16]

Her response is typical of an *indirect* style of communication, which FOs are often guilty of using. This type of polite, careful, don't-rock-the-boat communication is much like the nurturing style in the relationship-task grid (Figure 19-1). A person's true feelings and ideas are often hidden when using this style of communication—something not conducive to safe flight operations. A direct style, on the other hand, clearly states what your concern or intention is, getting straight to the issue at hand.

Flight Deck Authority Gradient

The captain of Flight 8284 had 20 years' experience flying for the airline, had just under 14,000 total flight hours (2,052 hours of which were in the ATR-42) and had extensive experience flying in icing conditions. The FO, with just over four month's flying for the airline, had about 2,100 total flight hours (130 hours of which were as second-in-command in the ATR-42) and very limited experience flying in icing conditions. The NTSB concluded that the large disparity between the captain's and the FO's total flying experience, their experience in the ATR-42, and their experience in icing conditions likely created a steep authority gradient in the cockpit that contributed to her failure to assert herself to the captain and initiate a go-around maneuver when she recognized the unstabilized approach (Report No: NTSB/AAR-11/02).

Sometimes unassertiveness arises out of the authority structure on the flight deck. The **flight deck authority gradient**, also known as the trans-cockpit authority gradient, describes the actual and/or perceived difference in authority between the captain and his or her subordinates. Your knowledge, ability, years and type of flying experience, proficiency, rank, age, sex, reputation, persona, and other factors influence how others perceive your authority.[17] There *should be* some authority gradient between the captain and the FO; after all, the captain usually possesses more experience than his or her FO. This is represented by Figure 19-2A. However, the NTSB concluded that there was a steep authority gradient between the captain and FO in the ATR-42 accident. This is represented by Figure 19-2B. In this case, the captain's actual authority was significantly greater than the FO's (the captain had seven times the flight time and had 16 times the hours in type than the FO), but because the FO likely lacked confidence in her own abilities and training, her perception of the captain's authority was greater than it should have been and the perception of her own authority was likely lower than it should have been as well. The captain may have had the same perception of her authority (and/or his), since he failed to act appropriately to her question to conduct a go-around and in accordance with SOPs. Either way, a steep gradient means an unjustifiably small perception of one crew member and/or an inappropriately large perception of the other.

A steep authority gradient can also be seen in the relationship-task grid in Figure 19-1. A steep gradient produced by an over-nurturing FO (top-left quadrant) and an overly aggressive captain (bottom-right quadrant) is one of the worse-case-scenarios. An aggressive captain violates the rights of the FO and a nurturing FO violates his or her own rights by letting their opinions be minimized. The NTSB further concluded in the Empire Airline's accident that the captain's quick dismissal of the FO's go-around inquiry likely discouraged her from voicing her continued concerns and challenging the captain's decision to continue the unstabilized approach (Report No: NTSB/AAR-11/02). As we have seen, this lack of assertiveness can and does lead to accidents.

There are other gradients that in some cases can be just as threatening to safety. A flat gradient (Figure 19-2C) exists when two pilots with the same level of actual and/or perceived authority are flying together. Speaking from personal experience, there's nothing worse than two flight instructors flying in the same airplane—each thinks they know better than the other! In this case it is important that both pilots fully understand who is the PIC and who is the FO, assisting the PIC to the best of her or his ability, thus enhancing the safety of the flight rather than hampering it. Rarely will you see a negative gradient on the flight deck (Figure 19-2D), but situations such as airline mergers and other instances of highly experienced pilots being hired into a strict seniority-based system (thus resulting in low seniority relative to their overall experience level) have led to such crew pairings. It can be a problem, especially if the negative direction is steep: when the FO possess signifi-

Fig 19-2.

Flight deck authority gradient (AG) examples.

A   **Normal AG**

B   **Steep AG**
"Gear up, flaps up, shut up."

C   **Flat AG**
"My airplane."
"No, my airplane."

D   **Negative AG**
"This captain's an idiot, but I have to listen to him."

cantly greater experience, wisdom, and authority than the captain. In this case it is also important that the FO serve as FO-follower to the best of his or her ability, rendering assistance when required.

Conflict Resolution

We not only like to hear ourselves talk, but we often hold doggedly to our positions. Therefore, whenever people are advocating their positions, there's bound to be conflict. You should not seek to avoid conflict; it often brings about a deeper understanding of things which can lead to better overall solutions and safer outcomes. It was mentioned in the previous chapter that differences of opinion between group members is reduced if information is clear and unambiguous. Therefore, when conflict arises from polarization of positions on the flight deck, it is important that all crew members spend the time necessary to obtain an accurate and reliable diagnosis about a given situation. To facilitate optimum problem solving and decision making, and to minimize bruising the egos of your fellow crew members, you should not focus the discussion on *who* is right but *what* is right.

Critique

At the beginning of every trip the captain should conduct a pre-departure briefing for all crew members (pilots and FAs) addressing not only important operational factors, but crew coordination and communication issues. The captain sets the tone for the flight in this briefing. That tone should be one of complete open communication. Every crew member should be encouraged to communicate any concerns they may have to the captain, especially if something doesn't seem right. These briefings are most effective when conducted in a conversational and deliberate manner, with plenty of opportunity for two-way communication between the captain and the rest of the crew. Distractions should be minimized whenever possible during the briefing (gate agent interruptions, passenger boarding, fuelers, etc.). Time permitting, the information should not be treated as a series of bullet items to be covered, but rather incorporated into a genuine conversation to establish human rapport between the captain and his or her crew with whom, oftentimes, the captain has never flown with before.

In the same way, after a flight the captain should conduct a constructive debriefing with the appropriate crew members (flight and/or cabin crew) that involves giving and receiving feedback about activities they performed and the processes used, especially if they encountered an unusual, non-normal, or emergency situation. It is often difficult to provide a critique and even more difficult to receive one. However, we learn how we can do better when we receive feedback from others on our team.

Chapter 13 highlighted how difficult it is sometimes to effectively get our message across. It was noted that more than 70 percent of 28,000 incident reports submitted by pilots and air traffic controllers to the NASA ASRS involved problems with voice communications. But take heart, research also indicates that when faced with a non-normal or emergency situation on the flight deck, crews who communicate more—make more statements, inquiries, commands, and acknowledgements—perform better and the outcomes are more positive than those who don't.[18]

Teamwork

The task of flying a modern passenger jet is no solo task; it takes at least two on the flight deck and several more in the cabin to carry out all the tasks necessary to achieve safe and efficient flight, especially during non-routine situations. Teamwork, therefore, is essential. A variety of models propose several different components required to achieve effective team performance. For the purpose of aircrew performance we can narrow them down to just a few: commitment to achieving a common purpose, expertise of complementary roles, effective communication, leadership, and a supportive corporate culture.

Common Purpose

A basic definition of a team is a group of two or more people working together to achieve a common goal. The purpose of each flight is not a mystery for flight and cabin crew: it is to transport themselves and their passengers to their destination as safely and efficiently as possible. However, crews need to be flexible if challenges arise that might threaten accomplishment of that goal. For example, adverse weather or other factors may require a landing at an alternate destination. Numerous tasks and several decisions must be accomplished, especially by flight crews, in order to redirect the flight to another location.

Role Expertise

An aircrew consists of individuals who each play a different, yet complementary role—captain, FO, sometimes FE, FA—that enables accomplishment of tasks that cannot be completed by one individual alone. These team members possess significant expertise arising from extensive initial and recurrent training in their specified roles, from their experience on the line, and from their understanding of and compliance with company SOPs. When everyone is carrying out their duties to the standard that is expected of them team performance is elevated.

Communication

Most of what has been said about communication was discussed previously in this chapter. Fostering open communication and using effective communication strategies are critical components in developing a well-functioning aircrew team. Without communication, accomplishing anything as a team would be impossible. It is, if you like, the grease that keeps the wheels turning. Also, as discussed, direct, assertive and frequent communication results in better crew performance and outcomes.

Leadership

The captain is the PIC and is directly responsible for, and is the final authority as to, the operation of the aircraft (14 CFR §91.3), including the safety of passengers, crew members, cargo, and the airplane (§121.535). As such, he or she is the leader of the flight. To effectively lead, a captain must have the trust and respect of his or her followers. Good leadership engenders good followership; but good followership also begets good leadership. However, even though the primary role of the FO, as a follower, is to support and assist the captain in the safe operation of the flight, he or she also acts as a leader (when acting as the PF or when the captain is absent the flight deck) and must possess the qualities of a good leader. The FO is expected to exercise an appropriate degree of assertiveness and be an active participant in the decision-making process. He or she is also expected to state an opinion and possess the skills needed to question a captain's decision while still demonstrating respect for the captain's overall command authority.[19]

So what are the traits of a good leaders and followers? It turns out that even though the role of each differs, the traits that make them both effective are similar, and in many cases, identical. Several personal virtues that describe a person—like honesty, integrity, sincerity—and the behaviors a person displays have been suggested as desirable traits of a good team member. However, the most essential traits can be summarized in the six leadership/followership skills outlined in Table 19-1. All crew members should strive to practice good leadership/followership skills and if you feel you do not possess some of these, you need to work at adding them to your repertoire.

Table 19-1. Traits of effective leaders and followers.[20]

Trait	Behavior
Envisions	Creates and articulates a clear plan or picture of a future desired state. This facilitates completion of the team's common goal(s).
Models	Exhibits behavior that is consistent with the industry's highest technical and ethical standards. It involves "do as I do," not just "do as I say." A good role-model on the flight deck gains the respect of others and motivates them to follow.
Receptive	Encourages, pays attention to, and conveys understanding of another's ideas, comments, or questions. As an essential element of effective communication, receptivity shows respect for fellow team members, their expertise, and their ideas.
Influences	Obtains commitment from others to ideas or actions using effective interpersonal skills, styles, and methods. A major skill is tactfulness, which involves courtesy, respect, and rapport.
Initiates	Begins an action without external direction to accomplish necessary tasks. Often seen as the job of the captain, an FO displays initiative when he or sees a need and offers to help (calls the flight service specialist for weather, reminds the captain about something he or she forgot to do, etc.).
Adaptive	Adjusts to changing environments, ambiguity, and abnormal situations. Highly adaptive aircrews expect the unexpected (e.g., air traffic delays, changing weather) and are able to quickly shift priorities and accomplish the tasks needed accommodate such changes.

Supportive Culture

Some experts in the field of team formation believe that teams must to go through several stages of development—a process that takes time—before they are able to achieve peak performance. One theory states that teams must go through *forming*, *storming*, and *norming* before they can achieve maximum *performing*. When team members first meet, they are polite and cordial and are excited and possibly anxious to work together (forming). But as they work together, differences of opinion and different styles conflict, causing a degree of friction and frustration between members (storming). As the group gets to know each other better, and their individual styles, members are more accepting of each other's peculiarities and they begin to work together as a team (norming). Finally, once the group has gone through the previous three processes their focus on achieving a common goal produces results (performing).[21]

Think about this model in the context of a typical flight sequence at a large air carrier. The aircrew, who have seldom (if ever) flown together, arrive at the airport about the same time and within only about an hour they are working together as a team at 40,000 feet. How do they do that? If the model above is correct, not very well. Fortunately, besides possessing extensive experience in one's role, crew members also receive considerable support from their organization in team performance skills. Airlines and other professional flight organizations provide their aircrew initial and recurrent training in developing leadership, communication, and teamwork skills. Effective team performance is also supported by providing quality SOPs, which spell out how the captain, FO, and FAs are to conduct virtually every facet of their assigned roles. When crew members arrive for duty, they already know the group's goals, who the main leader is, how they should interact with each other, and what they need to do to effectively accomplish their goals. All crew members feel safe to share any concerns they may have about the flight, knowing they will be listened to and respected—even if their concerns prove to be unfounded. That's because the captain, ideally, has set the tone by fostering a relaxed, open, friendly, and supportive atmosphere on the flight deck. The positive atmosphere—often interspersed with ample doses of humor—makes it easier for them to do their jobs and helps alleviate stress, especially should they need to contend with anything unexpected like a non-normal or emergency situation.

It was noted in the previous chapter that cohesive groups generally tend to perform better as a team, yet it has been argued that typical airline crew trips do not promote cohesiveness. If anything, cohesiveness, if it occurs at all, develops only near the end of a trip together. However, it is also true that individual members in cohesive groups tend to be more susceptible to conforming to the group's wishes (or perceived wishes). The NTSB concluded that the captain's decision to unnecessarily conduct a challenging approach to Runway 10 at Guantanamo Bay, Cuba, was inappropriate. If you remember the details (*see* Chapter 10), the captain chose to conduct a visual approach to Runway 10 despite it requiring a close base leg to avoid Cuban airspace. The captain overshot the final approach, steepened the turn onto final, and the DC-8 stalled. Since the captain and FO had flown eight separate flights together during the two days before the accident, the cohesiveness of the team was likely higher than most. Yet neither the FO nor FE objected to the captain's last-minute decision to attempt this difficult approach, and when they were concerned about its success their communications were subtle and not assertive (Report No: NTSB/AAR-94/04). So it appears the airlines may have it right: the lack of time available to form cohesive teams on the flight deck and cabin may not be as big of a threat that some have conjectured, while longer trips that contribute to cohesive teams may possibly, at least in some instances, elevate the risks.

Decision Making

The topic of decision making was explored in Chapter 17. As previously noted, on a crewed flight deck the captain is the final authority as to the operation of the aircraft, including all decisions needed to safely complete a flight. Just like a ship deck, there is no democracy on the flight deck. However, most captains today, in part because of CRM training, understand that their subordinates are a valuable resource in accomplishing the goal of safe and efficient flight operations. Most captains also know what was pointed out in the previous chapter: their followers are not just physical extensions of their own brain but additional brains that can assist in a variety of tasks including situation assessment, problem solving, and decision making—especially when faced with an abnormal or emergency situation or when a problem is ill-defined.

As discussed in the previous chapter, group decision making, like individual decision making, may be subject to bias. This is something to be aware of on the flight deck. For example, many FOs (and FEs) have "gone along to get along" when captains have made less than optimal choices. However, CRM skills are designed to effectively combat bias and assist the captain in arriving at the best possible decisions. Besides simply recognizing that the "group" may be subject to faulty decision making, we need to question the veracity of our own judgments and decisions by seeking more information until we are confident that we have arrived at the best choice. That is where leveraging the brains of your fellow crew member(s) and others comes in. Besides helping you fly the airplane or sharing other tasks, your fellow crew member(s) can help clarify a problem, assist in assessing a situation, and generate more ideas and alternative hypotheses to help you make the best possible choice. The result of this can sometimes lead to **synergy** (*syn*=together; *ergy*=work), an outcome that produces a higher level of group performance than the sum of the individual performance of its members.[22] With regard to problem solving and decision making—especially involving ill-defined problems or other challenging situations—a decision involving crew input is sometimes better than the best decision achieved by any individual crew member alone, including the captain.

In the NTSB study of 37 major U.S. airline accidents where the actions of the flight crew were a causal or contributing factor to the accident, it was found that even though tactical decision errors were the third leading type of flight crew error overall, they were the number one error-type committed by captains.[23] Combining this with the fact that captains were the PF in more than 80 percent of the accidents logically leads to the conclusion that FOs find it more difficult to be assertive with their captains than the other way around. The problem of unassertive FOs, along with the seemingly safer flying record with FOs at the controls, has led some to suggest that airlines re-think how they run things on the flight deck and that perhaps captains should fly less and manage more.[24]

Stress

Investigators in the Portland crash pointed to a recurring problem in commercial aviation: a breakdown in cockpit management and teamwork during situations involving malfunctions of aircraft systems in flight. Both common sense and research point to an obvious causal factor in these breakdowns: the stress induced by the emergency or threatening event. High levels of stress—especially stress that borders on, or grows into, anxiety—significantly impairs human performance that leads to perceptual (both visual and auditory), attentional, and cognitive narrowing, which in turn impairs problem-solving and decision-making skills. It also reduces verbal communication, an important practice for optimal team performance. Table 19-2 lists only some of the effects of excess stress on a pilot's cognitive and social performance.

Table 19-2. Effects of excess stress on human performance.[25,26,27,28,29]

Function	Performance impact
Perception	Perceptual narrowing, reduced ability to visually perceive details, increased attentional blindness, impaired auditory perception.
Attention	Reduced ability to effectively manage attention, greater likelihood of distraction by salient or threatening stimuli, difficulty switching attention, limited ability to fully process information.
Memory	Working memory capacity impaired; long-term memory retrieval hampered; difficulty performing normal calculations; difficulty understanding, interpreting, and assessing a situation; impaired prospective memory (remembering to perform an intended action).
Decision making/ problem solving	Incomplete situation assessment, less systematic and more hurried, fewer alternative choices considered.
Team performance	Reduced team performance, reduced communication and less information sharing, disregarding social and interpersonal cues, confusion of roles and responsibilities.

What is Stress?

Stress has historically been defined as the body's response to any stressor, or demand, placed upon it. **Stressors** include any environmental/physical, physiological, psychological/cognitive, or social demand placed upon your body and/or mind. A list of some of these stressors, or demands, that may impact pilot performance are included in Table 19-3. Notice that some positive circumstances (marriage, new job) are also considered stressors.

Table 19-3. Stressors, or demands, placed on an individual usually originate from one or more of four areas: environmental/physical, physiological, psychological/cognitive or social.

Types of Stressors	
Environmental/ Physical	Excess noise, vibration, temperature and humidity extremes, acceleration, systems malfunction, and adverse weather.
Physiological	Fatigue, hypoglycemia, hypoxia, trapped gas, DCS, spatial disorientation, poor physical fitness, smoking, OTC medication, alcohol, drugs, dehydration, and illness.
Psychological/ cognitive	Excess mental workload, ill-defined problem in flight, non-normal event or in-flight emergency, decision making under uncertainty, and emotional extremes.
Social	Marriage, new baby, financial difficulties, marital conflict, separation/divorce, child issues, moving, changing domiciles, family crisis, death in the family, job interviews, expectations at work, difficult relationships at work, job promotion, job demotion, performing in a team, and long absences from home.

Fight or Flight

Canadian researcher Hans Selye was one of the first to describe the body's response to stressors. Subjecting lab mice to different stressors, he observed a variety of physiological and behavioral responses which he termed the *general adaptation syndrome*. This involved three responses: alarm reaction, resistance, and exhaustion.

The first response to a stressor is the *alarm reaction* stage where the pituitary gland produces elevated levels of adrenaline, noradrenaline, cortisol, and other hormones to respond to the threat. This results in pupil dilation, a faster heart and breathing rate, greater perspiration, more acute vision and hearing, and other physiological responses often described as the *fight or flight response*. The body shifts into high gear to either fight the threat or run away from it (e.g., like early man being attacked by a wild animal).

As your body continues to resist the threat, stress hormone secretion is reduced, and blood pressure, sugar levels, and other elements are increased to repair the body and maintain its energy to continue to meet the threat during the *resistance* stage. If this period is sustained for too long the body's hormonal and other physiological and mental resources are depleted leading to the *exhaustion* stage where symptoms such as fatigue, irritability, depression, illness, and disease (e.g., cardiovascular, digestive system problems) may be experienced. However, if the resistance stage is of short duration and the stressor has been removed or adequately managed, the body returns to its normal functioning—called the *recovery* stage—and the deleterious effects of the exhaustion stage are avoided.

The work of psychologists Robert Yerkes and John Dodson on the relationship between performance and arousal, which predates Selye's work, is also related to stress. Their research involved administering varying levels of shock to mice as they completed tasks in a maze. At low levels of electric shock, and therefore, according the researchers low levels of arousal, the mice did not perform well; however, as shock levels increased arousal presumably increased and the mice performed better until they performed their best at moderate levels of shock. At higher levels of shock their performance suffered, and all they wanted to do was run away from the testing apparatus altogether (the *flight* response).[30] The original research used the somewhat vague term "arousal" to describe the response the mice made to the electric shocks, so it is not surprising that researchers since Selye's work have substituted "stress" for arousal on the abscissa (horizontal x axis) on the classic inverted "U-shaped" Yerkes-Dodson curve (*see* Figure 19-3). And why not? Certainly an uncomfortable electric shock is considered a stressor—and the higher the level of shock the greater the intensity of the stressor.

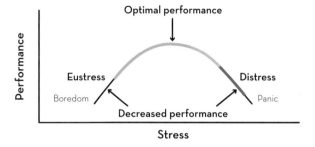

Fig 19-3.

Yerkes-Dodson curve modified with colored arcs to show relationship between stress and performance. Performance is best at moderate levels of stress (top of green arc).[31]

Figure 19-3 indicates that performance increases, to a point, with increasing levels of stress. Therefore, some degree of stress is actually desirable to obtain optimal performance. This is analogous to the nervous energy a pilot has when they are preparing for departure. This arousal (or stress) actually helps a pilot perform better. Selye called this *eustress* (*eu* = good) to indicate favorable stress (the green arc on the curve). However, if you experience excessive stress, or anxiety, your performance suffers. Selye called this *distress* (*dys* = bad) to indicate harmful stress (the red arc on the curve). As an interesting aside, the term distress in aviation is used to describe a situation when your flight is in serious and/or imminent danger and you require immediate assistance. The international radiotelephony signal "Mayday" is used to declare a distress situation.[32]

The phrase "mental workload" has also been used to substitute for arousal on the abscissa on the Yerkes-Dodson curve (*see* Figure 14-4 in Chapter 14). As task demands increase, mental workload increases to meet the demands of the task until at moderate levels of workload performance peaks. Beyond that, however, task requirements prove to be too demanding resulting in mental overload and diminished performance.

Short-term and Long-term Stress

Acute stress, also known as **situational stress**, is relatively short-term and results from demands placed on the body by the immediate task at hand. This is the type of stress that pilots are likely to experience during an emergency situation that poses a threat on the flight deck (*see* psychological/cognitive stressors in Table 19-3). As the degree of uncertainty regarding the outcome of a threatening situation increases, and as a person's perceived ability to successfully manage it decreases, he or she views the situation as a threat which leads to anxiety that can in turn impair performance in ways indicated in Table 19-2.[33] It's analogous to **checkride-itis**, the phenomenon of an otherwise competent pilot performing poorly and failing a checkride not because they're incapable of successfully demonstrating the skills necessary to pass it, but because they are too anxious about failing (also known as *test anxiety*).

Chronic **life stress** is long-term stress that results from ongoing demands placed upon body. Difficult life circumstances, such as those listed in social stressors in Table 19-3—marital conflict, moving, family crisis, work issues, prolonged absences from home, etc.—can lead to physical, physiological, and psychological symptoms such as "muscle tension, worry or preoccupation, disrupted sleep/fatigue, change in appetite...withdrawal, irritability, or difficulty concentrating."[34]

Situational Stress and Flight Operations

As is the case with fatigue (*see* Chapter 10), it's not always easy for investigators to determine a direct and indisputable causal link between acute situational stress, pilot performance, and aircraft accidents. However, various lines of research do point to such links. For example, as noted in Chapter 16, a recent NASA study on acute stress and threat-induced anxiety on the flight deck examined 12 major airline hull-loss/loss-of-life accidents (mostly in the United States) where errors of highly experienced flight crews made on the flight deck were very likely related to the highly stressful situation they faced (i.e., systems malfunction, airplane upset from unexpected autopilot disconnect, fire, thunderstorm on landing, etc.). A total of 212 errors were made that were likely caused by threat-induced anxiety. What they found supports the research on acute stress conducted in controlled laboratory settings. Of the eight different categories of error they discovered, the most common type was inadequate comprehension, interpretation, and/or assessment of the situation (24 percent of errors). This involved failing to assess, comprehend, consider relevant aspects of, recognize the gravity of, integrate, or interpret in a timely manner the situation that they faced. They also misinterpreted the aircraft state and were slow to assess and respond to the situation.

The NASA scientists maintain that this data is congruent with the findings that people's attentional abilities are diminished in conditions of high stress. Unfortunately, at a time when greater-than-normal mental resources are required to successfully manage the threat, there's a tendency to "fixate on one threatening aspect to the neglect of other relevant aspects...making them more distractible." In addition, during a stressful situation such as an in-flight emergency, demands on working memory are significantly increased as the flight crew must rapidly switch from one task to another to successfully resolve it. Several lines of research indicate, however, that threat-induced situational stress diminishes working memory, "leaving less capacity for managing tasks" making it more difficult to "keep track of multiple pieces of information and to integrate that information into a coherent mental model." The study also found that more than two-thirds of the 212 flight crew errors identified were "errors of omission," many of which were prospective memory failures—the inability to remember to accomplish an intended action. The NASA study also reviewed several research studies that indicate excess situational stress also impairs other tasks that rely heavily on attention and working memory, such as reasoning, problem solving, decision making, communication, crew coordination, and teamwork.[35]

Acute situational stress has been implicated in several major aircraft accidents. For example, according to investigators, the captain of American Airlines Flight 965, a Boeing B-757 that collided into mountainous terrain near Cali, Colombia (see Chapters 14, 15, and 16), appeared to have been under "considerable stress." While conducting an unexpected GPWS escape maneuver to avoid colliding with high terrain, both pilots forgot to retract the speed brakes (spoilers) that were previously extended to expedite the descent. Had they done so, the aircraft "may well have cleared the trees at the top of the ridge."[36]

The NTSB concluded that the stress imposed upon the flight crew of a Pan American Clipper by their attempts to meet an air traffic control deadline was also a contributing factor in their failure to

remember to extend the flaps for takeoff (see Chapter 16). This resulted in the Boeing B-707 crashing a half-mile beyond the end of Runway 23 during takeoff from Elmendorf Air Force Base in Alaska.

A Cessna C-208 Caravan stalled after attempting to takeoff from Pelee Island, Ontario, Canada, killing all 10 people on board. The Transportation Safety Board (TSB) of Canada concluded that the pilot's lack of appreciation for the hazardous effects of airframe icing and flying overweight—it was loaded 15 percent over its maximum certificated takeoff weight—was inconsistent with his previous practices. According to everyone the TSB spoke to, the captain had a good reputation for being "conscientious and professional in his work." However, the Board determined that the "short turnaround time, the large passenger load, the adverse weather conditions, the lack of de-icing equipment, and the need to complete the flight may have acted as stressors," and that his decision to depart was likely adversely affected by a combination of stress and fatigue (TSB Report No: A04H0001).

The NTSB determined the probable causes of the American Airlines Flight 1420 runway excursion accident at Little Rock National Airport in Little Rock, Arkansas (see Chapter 17), were the flight crew's failure to discontinue the approach when severe thunderstorms and their associated hazards to flight operations had moved into the airport area and their failure to ensure that the spoilers had extended after touchdown (Report No: NTSB/AAR-01/02). Both pilots were well aware of the severe thunderstorms moving toward the airport from the west but thought their flight would arrive before the adverse weather did. Instead, the thunderstorms beat them to the airport. The FO said, "it's going right over the...field," and the captain exclaimed, "we're goin' right into this," but they continued the approach anyway. Two minutes before touchdown, ATC relayed the current weather conditions to the crew: wind 330 degrees at 32 to 45 knots, RVR visibility 1,600 feet. The wind exceeded the authorized crosswind for landing and the RVR was below the authorized visibility for the approach. The captain stated "this is a can of worms," but he still continued the approach. In a post-accident interview the FO indicated that, "there was no discussion of delaying or diverting the landing" because of the weather (Report No: NTSB/AAR-01/02).

Investigators concluded that both the adverse weather conditions and the efforts to expedite their landing were "stresses" to the flight crew. The report suggests that because of these stresses, the crew selectively focused on only a subset of cues in the environment, their situation assessment was incomplete, their ability to evaluate an alternative course of action was impaired, and their decision making was therefore degraded. They concluded that the crew's intention to expedite the landing, despite the weather situation, diverted their attention away from other required activities during the final minutes of the flight which contributed to their degraded performance, including forgetting to deploy the spoilers—the single most important factor in their inability to stop the airplane within the available runway length (Report No: NTSB/AAR-01/02).

Life Stress and Flight Operations

If it's not easy for investigators to conclusively determine a direct causal link between acute situational stress, pilot performance, and aircraft accidents, it's even more difficult to do with chronic life stress. How do you measure its effect on flight crew performance, let alone find conclusive evidence that it caused an aircraft accident? A recent research review exploring the relationship between life stress, pilot performance, and aircraft accidents was conducted by NASA. Even though the study arrived at no definitive answers, it did find support for possible links between life stress and accidents from flight crew surveys, correlational studies, and laboratory research.

Several surveys and questionnaires administered to civilian and military pilots indicate that pilots with a high degree of chronic life stress report that it affects their performance on the flight deck. For example, a stress questionnaire designed to measure self-reported home and job stressors and their effects on flying performance was administered to U.S. Coast Guard helicopter pilots. Measures of stress included numerous questions about home- and job-related stressors such as those listed in *Social stressors* in Table 19-3. The study found that as home stress increased, so did job stress; and, when home stress contributed to job stress (i.e., spilled over into their work), pilots reported their own flying performance was adversely affected by it. Worry at work, not listening as intently, feeling slowed down, and not being "ahead of the game" in flight were directly related to the level of home-induced stress at work. The stressed pilots also reported other effects, including reduced smoothness and accuracy of landings, degraded airmanship, and reduced ability to divide attention. The two most commons ways home stress affected their work were rumination (worry) about the home-stressor and fatigue.[37]

In another survey of 442 British Airline Pilots Association pilots, 13.1 percent said they experienced recurring stressful thoughts during periods of low workload in flight, 8.4 percent reported decreased concentration, and 7.2 percent reported becoming detached from some of the tasks at hand.[38]

Though few in number, correlation studies provide some evidence that life stress may be linked to aircraft accidents. For example, a survey of 8,819 Canadian fixed- and rotary-wing pilots, ranging in certification from private to ATP, were asked about several different life events and experiences, including if they had had an accident within the previous 10 years. Direct correlations between accident experience and other variables, including stress-related factors, were found; the most common being preoccupation with marital separation or divorce and concern about business decisions.[39] Other studies together have found common traits that appear to be correlated with the likelihood of experiencing an accident. The five items most likely to have a causal relationship is a pilot who:

1. recently became engaged;
2. made recent decisions regarding the future;
3. has difficulty with interpersonal relationships;
4. recently experienced the death of a family member or close friend; and
5. recently had trouble with superiors, peers, or subordinates.[40]

Just like situational stress, research also indicates that chronic life stress does affect human cognitive performance. For example, using different techniques and measures, a variety of studies have found those who experience significant life stress events experience more intrusive thoughts, which in turn reduces their performance on working-memory tasks. This is especially true for those tasks that require greater demands on memory. Deliberately trying to suppress intrusive thoughts also interferes with memory capacity, thereby decreasing overall cognitive performance. One study had participants deliberately worry about something important to them while trying to conduct a memory task. They found that this affected the central executive components of their working memory, the most important part of memory needed for higher-level functions such as problem solving and decision making. The NASA report suggests that worrying-pilots may experience performance impairment, especially during low workload periods when such thoughts more easily intrude.

Similar findings for the effect of life stress events have been found in attention and overall information processing abilities. For example, participants were each given a total "stress score" after answering several questions about non-work stressful feelings and stressful events (major decisions regarding job or career, separation or divorce, bereavement, unemployment, etc.). They were then asked to perform different playing-card sorting tasks that varied in difficulty. Predictably, the time to solve these tasks (reaction time) increased as difficulty level increased. However, those with high stress scores took longer to solve these tasks than those who had lower scores. The authors concluded that stress levels have a significant effect on a person's information processing ability.[41]

As previously noted, establishing the link between an aircraft accident and chronic life stress of the pilot is more difficult than it is for situational stress. However, it has been implicated in several accidents. For example, in addition to a noisy cockpit with no crew intercom system and a navigation radio incapable of picking up aural station identifiers, some significant stress-inducing life events in the lives of both pilots were cited as contributing factors in a fatal crash of a Beech B99 near Shenandoah Valley Regional Airport, in Weyers Cave, Virginia, that killed everyone on board (*see* Chapter 7). Radio calls indicated the crew of Henson Airlines Flight 1517 was confused as to their exact location (they were in IMC) before the aircraft impacted terrain in controlled flight at 2,300 feet MSL on a magnetic course of 045 degrees. As noted in Chapter 7, it appears their confusion was the result of following the 045 degree radial off the Montebello VOR instead of the 045 degree inbound course on the Shenandoah ILS.

The accident report noted that both crew members were also experiencing personal events that are known to induce stress. The captain announced his engagement to be married two days before the acci-

dent and he had a job interview with a major airline the day after. Five days before the accident, the FO, whose mother had died of cancer at age 47, reported to her doctor that she felt she had symptoms of possible breast cancer. The NTSB concluded that these stress-inducing events were partially responsible for the crew's substandard performance (Report No: NTSB/AAR-86-07).

Stress and Fatigue

The detrimental effects of fatigue on human performance were thoroughly discussed in Chapter 10. Ample evidence confirms that significant levels of fatigue, no matter what its source, negatively impacts perception, memory, attention, problem solving, and decision making. These factors, along with reduced risk perception and a greater inclination to take risks when fatigued, support the conclusion that being fatigued is like being drunk. Several studies have discovered that a major symptom of significant life stress is interrupted sleep and overall sleep-loss, both major contributors to fatigue. Therefore, chronic life stress can also lead to fatigue which can in turn can increase the probability of performance impairment and an aircraft accident.[42]

Managing Stress

Just as excess strain and stress on an aircraft's airframe (e.g., from turbulence and G-force) can lead to "stress" fractures and ultimately structural failure, so too can stress on a pilot cause his or her performance to fail. This is true to a point, but using this mechanical analogy to describe human stress leads to a somewhat mechanical view of it—too much stress and something breaks, often at predictable levels. However, research indicates that different people respond differently to the same stressors: The performance of one person may be significantly impaired by stress while another's isn't. And at different times, or under different circumstances, the same person may respond to the same stressor(s) differently.

Stress was earlier defined as the body's response to any stressor, or demand, placed upon it. It would be more accurate to say *perceived* demand. Unlike the mice in earlier experiments whose stress-response was viewed deterministically, according to more recent stress models both the perception you have about the threat-level of a particular stressor (or demand) and the perception you have of your ability to meet that demand impact the level of stress you will actually experience. This is visualized by the flow diagram in Figure 19-4.

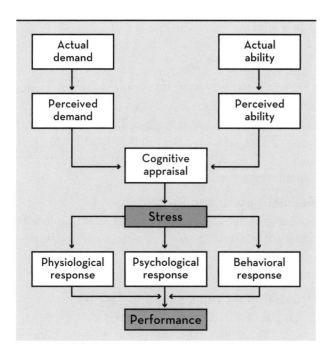

Fig 19-4.

Your level of stress and the physiological, psychological, and behavioral responses to it are in large part determined by the perceived demand and your perceived ability to meet it.[44]

Whether it occurs quickly and reflexively as would be the case when a car suddenly pulls out in front of you, or it transpires slowly and with thoughtful deliberation as might occur if a caution light goes on in the cockpit, when a stressor presents itself we make a cognitive appraisal of both its degree of threat and our ability to handle it.[43] Such an appraisal is based on a host of factors including our past experiences, temperament, emotions, knowledge, and training. If we clearly recognize the nature of a stressor and determine that it could be a threat (e.g., alternator light illuminates) but also remember we are trained to successfully manage it and have support in doing so from checklists, SOPs, etc., then we are likely to assess it as more of a *challenge* than a *threat* and our body will respond as it should, as illustrated in the green arc (eustress) of the modified Yerkes-Dodson curve. If, however, we fail to understand what the light means and we erroneously think it is more

sinister than it really is and we are at a loss of what to do, then we will appraise the encounter as stressful and our physiological, psychological, and behavioral responses will be negatively affected. This cognitive appraisal occurs for short-term situational demands (e.g., in-flight emergency) and for chronic long-term personal or job-related stressors.

The good news, therefore, is you don't have to be a passive victim of stress. When you encounter a challenging situation that at first may seem overwhelming—which often occurs when a solution doesn't immediately present itself—you can seek to make a more accurate cognitive appraisal of the actual threat level and your actual ability to handle the stressor. If you are the type of person who tends to overestimate the threat a given stressor poses and underestimate your own ability to successfully manage it, such a re-appraisal will often be enough to reduce the stress and the deleterious effects it has on your cognitive abilities while managing it. This is especially true in cases of situational stress while piloting an aircraft.

Were you aware that you have already received stress inoculation training? The initial and recurrent simulator and flight training you received in handling non-normal and emergency situations increases your proficiency and confidence in your ability to handle the stress associated with these situations and your cognitive stress appraisals become more positive.[45] Your actual ability is also higher than you may think because of the support provided to you from information in the aircraft flight manual, SOPs, and checklists—especially the aircraft's approved emergency and abnormal procedures checklist, often called the *Quick Reference Handbook*.

When faced with an abnormal or emergency situation, always keep in mind that you have two things to manage: the situation and your stress. The latter is important because you know that excess stress can interfere with your ability to successfully manage the situation, thereby contributing to a self-fulfilling prophecy should you fail to manage stress. To increase your odds of succeeding, make a realistic appraisal of the actual situation and your own actual abilities, avoid unnecessarily focusing on the consequences of what could happen should you fail to manage the situation, and direct all your energy to solving the problem at hand.

As with situational stress, the key to reducing the negative effects of chronic life stress is to gain a degree of control over it, not by avoiding it, but by taking steps to effectively manage it. According to Selye, the absence of stress is death; so even though you might not be able to eliminate all the negative stress from your life, you can certainly do all you can to bring it down to acceptable levels. Volumes have been written on how to manage life stress, but for our purposes it's sufficient to consider the methods for managing it suggested in the FAA's publication *Aeronautical Decision Making—Cockpit Resource Management*, which are moderation, rest and relaxation, exercise, humor, communication, religious faith and practice, and professional counseling and therapy.[46]

Moderation

Engaging in behaviors that promote good health and avoiding those that diminish it are excellent tactics for reducing overall stress. Chapter 11 provides strategies for reducing so-called self-imposed stress, those stressors that you can control. One recommendation from that chapter is to reduce the amount, and be careful about the type, of substances you put into your body—food, alcohol, caffeine, etc. A balanced diet is an important part of this.

Rest and Relaxation

Part of taking care of yourself is moderation when it comes to work: it's easy for pilots to work too much. It's important to reduce your fatigue levels and practice good sleeping habits (*see* Chapter 10 for strategies). Take frequent short breaks and even short naps between flights if you can. Practice relaxation techniques such as deep breathing, yoga, and meditation. Take all the time-off owed to you by your employer, including taking a vacation (or two) with your family. A more balanced work-life schedule helps reduce fatigue and stress.

Exercise

The importance of regular exercise to prevent health problems and possible loss of medical (both a cause of stress) was mentioned in Chapter 11. Besides distracting your attention away from stressful thoughts, exercise is an effective stress reliever. It produces endorphins, your body's natural feel-good drug, improving your mood and helping you to relax. As long as it is not too close to bedtime, exercise also helps your sleep.

Humor

Laughter is good medicine, so bring humor into the conversation—it almost always helps you and those around you to relax, reducing stress to more manageable levels.

Communication

If you are facing a difficult relationship at home or at work, talk to the person. Don't let the friction build. Be assertive—high task, yet high concern for maintaining a good relationship—by telling them how you feel and that you want the relationship to work. It is also good therapy to share your feelings with trusted friend, spouse, or family member.

Religious Faith and Practice

Numerous scientific studies indicate that people who adhere to religious or spiritual beliefs and practices—such as prayer and meditation—to help them cope with the stresses of life report lower levels of stress.

Professional Counseling and Therapy

If the stress of life is too much, and you are beginning to experience the symptoms of depression—persistent sadness, feelings of hopelessness and worthlessness, fatigue, insomnia, difficulty concentrating, forgetfulness, weight loss or gain, thoughts of death and suicide—you should seek professional help. Depression is treatable with an 80 to 90 percent recovery rate.[47] Talk to an aviation medical examiner (AME), and keep in mind that you will need to remove yourself from flying duties. A diagnosis of depression is by no means the end of your flying career. "In fact," as the Director of the AOPA's Medical Certification Section says, "there are relatively few circumstances involving a diagnosis of depression that would result in permanent denial of medical certification."[48] And, according to an experienced AME whose article appears on the FAA web site, "the FAA is willing to return virtually all clinically depressed pilots back to flying after successful treatment."[49] Several U.S. airlines have reporting and monitoring programs that provide a pilot with a path to report their condition, be treated for it, and return to the flight deck once the FAA has determined—through a rigorous evaluation—it is safe to do so.[50] The same process occurs for GA pilots—progress is monitored, then minimum wait times (at least 60 days after discontinuing medication) must be achieved before the FAA will authorize a special issuance medical certificate to pilots who have been treated for depression.

In addition to airline reporting and monitoring programs, the Air Line Pilots Association has recently implemented confidential, nonjudgmental, pilot peer-support hotlines for its members who may be dealing with "work- and nonwork-related issues of a personal or emotional nature." Trained pilot volunteers are also available to help pilots "better cope with the events that could otherwise threaten their medical certificates and careers." As of this writing, several of these peer-to-peer programs have been implemented, such as the Pilot Assistance Network at Delta Air Lines, the Pilot Assistance Telephone Hotline at FedEx Express, and the Support Outreach Assistance Resources peer support program at United Airlines.[51]

Does CRM Work?

The world's airlines boast the lowest accident rate in history, thanks in large part to the implementation of CRM into their training programs. Various studies have shown that crews trained in CRM concepts benefit from such training. For example, air medical crews who received CRM, communication, and team building training scored significantly better on measures of crew interaction and communication in everyday and developing situations than those who did not.[52] In an analysis of 16 CRM empirical studies to gauge the effectiveness of CRM training, investigators found a strong positive effect from CRM training on participants' attitudes and behaviors and a medium positive effect on their knowledge.[53] Finally, NASA and FAA assessments have also shown that CRM-trained crews operate more effectively as teams and cope more effectively with non-routine situations.[54] Scientists would say that it is difficult, if not impossible, to conclusively prove a direct cause-and-effect link between the use of CRM and the prevention of accidents. How can you prove a causal relationship between any variable and a negative event? But don't tell that to Captain Al Haynes or other pilots who've had somewhat similar experiences like him.

About an hour after departing Denver's Stapleton International Airport, United Airlines Flight 232, en route to Chicago, cruising comfortably at FL300, experienced an uncontained engine failure of the number two (center tail-mounted) engine. Some of the decision-making aspects of this accident were introduced in Chapter 17, but the majority of crew and passengers wouldn't have lived it if wasn't for CRM. The debris from the engine fragments penetrated the horizontal stabilizer and severed all three hydraulic lines rendering the three hydraulic-powered flight control systems of the McDonnell Douglas DC-10 inoperative. The airplane began a descending turn to the right. The captain reduced thrust on the left (number one) engine and the wings leveled—that was the only way they could regain some semblance of control over the wide-body jet with almost 300 people on board. The airplane had no back-up system to compensate for a total hydraulic failure and the crew had no procedure to aid them in getting the airplane safely on the ground—the manufacturer, the FAA, and UAL considered the probability of such a situation occurring so remote that they had no technology or procedure to counter it. However, it turns out the airplane was marginally flyable using asymmetrical thrust from the number one and three engines.

An FA informed the captain that a company DC-10 training check pilot was seated in a first class passenger seat and had volunteered his assistance. Captain Haynes immediately invited him to the flight deck and assigned Captain Dennis "Denny" Fitch the job of manipulating the throttles to control pitch and roll using engine power to counter the jumbo jet's up-and-down phugoid motion and its tendency to turn right. With the captain and FO freed from the job of flying the airplane, they could both get down to business to figure this problem out and resolve it to the best of their ability. As briefly described in Chapter 17, there were a myriad of things they had to do. They had already shut down the number two engine, tried other possibilities for getting hydraulic power, and had figured out how to maintain some degree of aircraft control. But they needed to continue diagnosing the problem, double-check aircraft systems, get advice from UAL maintenance, communicate with ATC, determine where to land, jettison fuel, and prepare the FAs and passengers for the emergency landing.

As also described in Chapter 17, this was an ill-defined problem involving a high degree of uncertainty, risk, and stress. Using data from simulator flights during the subsequent accident investigation the NTSB determined that a safe landing was virtually impossible. However, the crew was trained in command leadership resource (CLR) management, UAL's version of CRM. The captain encouraged complete, open and frequent communication—at its peak there was one communication per second[55] —while the cognitive workload and stress for all crew members was at the distress end of the Yerkes-Dodson curve. The NTSB stated that under the circumstances, the flight crew's performance was highly commendable and greatly exceeded reasonable expectations, and that the interaction of all the flight crew members, including the check pilot, was testimony to the value of the CRM training they received at UAL (Report No: NTSB/AAR-90/06). In Captain Hayne's own words, "It was a team effort"[56] and "if I hadn't used CLR, if we had not let everybody put their input in, it's a cinch we wouldn't have made it."[57]

Unfortunately, the landing at Sioux Gateway Airport in Sioux City, Iowa, didn't go as they had hoped. Because the right wing had dropped when they were about 100 feet above the runway, the airplane hit hard, rolled, and cartwheeled to an inverted position and was destroyed by impact forces and fire. One hundred eleven people died in the crash. However, if it wasn't for the actions of the crew, including their adherence to principles taught them in their CRM training, the other 185 people aboard would have perished with them.

Twenty years after the Sioux City accident, an ill-defined problem presented itself to the flight crew of US Airways Flight 1549. As you also recall from Chapter 17, the Airbus A320 lost thrust in both engines after encountering a flock of geese during the climb-out from New York's LaGuardia Airport. These two pilots had lots to do as well: diagnose the degree of thrust loss, follow checklists, improvise when checklists proved unsatisfactory, fly a 75-ton airplane as you would a glider including judging gliding distance, choose a location to land, communicate with ATC, advise FAs—all in less than three minutes!

The airplane landed on the Hudson River and all five crew members and 145 passengers aboard were saved. Captain Sullenberger said he thought that the crew coordination was "amazingly good" considering how suddenly the event occurred, how severe it was, and what little time they had. He also credited the company CRM training for providing him and his FO with the skills and tools that they needed to build a team quickly and open lines of communication, share common goals, and work together. The NTSB concluded the flight crew's excellent CRM during the accident sequence contributed to their ability to maintain control of the airplane, configure it to the extent possible under the circumstances, and fly an approach that increased the survivability of the impact (Report No: NTSB/AAR-10/03).

The previous 18 chapters of this book described many of the human factor issues that contribute to increased risk levels on the flight deck. The emphasis in this chapter has been on how to best manage those risks by employing the principles of CRM on the flight deck. Besides receiving training in CRM, the crew of US Airways Flight 1549 also received training in threat and error management (TEM), principles that are now incorporated into most CRM curricula. TEM—discussed in our next and final chapter—and CRM are tools to help you and your team attain the best possible performance on the flight deck. Practicing the principles and skills taught in both of these risk-management approaches during every flight will not only maximize your performance during routine flight operations, but will also prepare you to better manage any non-normal or emergency situation that you may face.

Helpful Resources

The free online FAA *Human Factors Awareness Course* has a separate module (its last) on "Team Performance," which also includes information on the history and fundamental concepts of CRM. (www.hf.faa.gov/Webtraining/Cognition/Cognition1.htm)

The FAA has also produced three videos related to topics covered in this chapter, as well as other parts of this book:

- *The History of Crew Resource Management*, summarizes the history of CRM and some of the concepts introduced in this chapter. (www.faa.gov/tv/?mediaId=447)
- *Stress in The Aviation Environment*. This 20-minute video explores the topic of stress and provides keen insight into acute and chronic stress. (www.faa.gov/tv/?mediaId=450)
- *Self-Imposed Stress*, recommended in Chapter 11, this video examines self-imposed stresses and offers advice on how to reduce their effects on performance. (www.faa.gov/pilots/training/airman_education/physiologyvideos/)

Brief helpful reenactments and/or animations of the following accidents are available on the FAA's Lessons Learned website: lessonslearned.faa.gov/

- Eastern Air Lines Flight 401 (near Miami, FL) lessonslearned.faa.gov/ll_main.cfm?TabID=1&LLID=8
- United Airlines Flight 173 (Portland, OR) lessonslearned.faa.gov/ll_main.cfm?TabID=1&LLID=42
- Air Florida Flight 90 (Washington, DC) lessonslearned.faa.gov/ll_main.cfm?TabID=3&LLID=2&LLTypeID=0

Endnotes

1. John K. Lauber, "Resource Management on the Flight Deck: Background and Statement of the Problem," *Resource Management on the Flight Deck: Proceedings of a NASA/Industry Workshop Held at San Francisco, California June 26–28, 1979*, eds. George E. Cooper, Maurice D. White and John K. Lauber (Moffett Field, CA: NASA Ames Research Center, March 1980): 3–16.

2. George E. Cooper, Maurice D. White and John K. Lauber eds., *Resource Management on the Flight Deck: Proceedings of a NASA/Industry Workshop Held at San Francisco, California June 26–28, 1979* (Moffett Field, CA: NASA Ames Research Center, March 1980).

3. Ibid.

4. Robert L. Helmreich, Ashleigh C. Merritt and John A. Wilhelm, "The Evolution of Crew Resource Management Training in Commercial Aviation," *International Journal of Aviation Psychology* 9 (1999): 19–32.

5. United Airlines, *Command/Leadership/Resource Management: Seminar Materials* (Austin, TX: Scientific Methods, Inc., 1981).

6. Federal Aviation Administration, *Dispatch Resource Management Training*, AC 120-32A (Washington, DC: November 21, 2005).

7. Federal Aviation Administration, *Maintenance Human Factors Training*, AC 120-72A (Washington, DC: April 11, 2017).

8. Federal Aviation Administration, *Flightcrew Member Line Operational Simulations: Line-Oriented Flight Training, Special Purpose Operational Training, Line Operational Evaluation*, AC 120-35D (Washington, DC: March 13, 2015).

9. Ibid., 2.

10. Federal Aviation Administration, *Single-Pilot Crew Resource Management*, General Aviation Joint Steering Committee Safety Enhancement Topic (Washington, DC: March 2015).

11. Richard S. Jensen, *Aeronautical Decision Making—Cockpit Resource Management*, DOT/FAA/PM-86/46 (Washington, DC: Federal Aviation Administration, January 1989).

12. Ibid.

13. National Transportation Safety Board, *A Review of Flightcrew-Involved, Major Accidents of U.S. Air Carriers, 1978 through 1990*, Safety Study NTSB/SS-94/01 (Washington, DC: January 1994).

14. Jensen, *Aeronautical Decision Making—Cockpit Resource Management*.

15. C.R. Harper, G.J. Kidera and J.F. Cullen, "Study of Simulated Airline Pilot Incapacitation: Phase II. Subtle or Partial Loss of Function," *Aerospace Medicine* 42 (September 1971): 946–948.

16. National Transportation Safety Board, *Aircraft Accident Report: Crash During Approach to Landing, Empire Airlines Flight 8284, Avions de Transport Régional Aerospatiale Alenia ATR 42-320, N902FX, Lubbock, Texas, January 27, 2009*, NTSB/AAR-11/02 (Washington, DC: April 26, 2011).

17. Antonio I. Cortés, "Flight Crew Leadership", Paper presented at 4th *Bombardier-Learjet Safety Standdown, European Business Aviation Convention and Exhibition* (Geneva, Switzerland: May 2010).

18. H. Clayton Foushee and Karen L. Manos, "Information Transfer Within the Cockpit: Problems in Intracockpit Communications," *Information Transfer Problems in the Aviation System*, NASA Technical Paper 1875, eds. Charles E. Billings and E.S. Cheaney (Moffett Field, CA: NASA Ames Research Center, September 1981): 63–71.

19. Federal Aviation Administration, *Flight Crewmember Mentoring, Leadership and Professional Development Aviation Rulemaking Committee* (MLPARC) Report (November 2, 2010).

20. Joseph H. Dunlap and Susan J. Mangold, *Leadership/Followership Recurrent Training: Student Manual* (Washington, DC: Office of the Chief Scientific and Technical Advisor for Human Factors to the Federal Aviation Administration, February 1998).

21. Bruce W. Tuckman, "Developmental Sequence in Small Groups," *Psychological Bulletin* 63 (1965): 384–399.

22. Jensen, *Aeronautical Decision Making—Cockpit Resource Management*.

23. National Transportation Safety Board, *A Review of Flightcrew-Involved, Major Accidents of U.S. Air Carriers, 1978 through 1990*.

24. Stuart D.H. Beveridge, Simon T. Henderson, Wayne L. Martin and Joleah B. Lamb, "Command and Control: The Influence of Flight Crew Role Assignment on Flight Safety in Air Transport Operations," *Aviation Psychology and Applied Human Factors* 8 (January 2018): 1–10. A short review article, written by Eric Dolan, is available at www.psypost.org/2018/06/airline-captains-supervising-less-flying-according-new-aviation-research-51381.

25. M. Lojowska, T. Gladwin, E. Hermans and K. Roelofs, "Freezing Promotes Perception of Coarse Visual Features," *Journal of Experimental Psychology: General* 144 (2015): 1080–1088.

26. Ashley Ebersole, *Stress as a Moderator of Visual Perception: Do Elevated Stress Levels Interfere with Visual Cognition?* Masters Theses 2439 (2016). Available at thekeep.eiu.edu/theses/2439.

27. Robert Hoskin, Mike D. Hunter and Peter W.R. Woodruff, "The Effect of Psychological Stress and Expectation on Auditory Perception: A Signal Detection Analysis," *British Journal of Psychology* 105 (2014): 524–546.

28. Sabrina Kuhlmann, Marcel Piel and Oliver T. Wolf, "Impaired Memory Retrieval after Psychosocial Stress in Healthy Young Men," *The Journal of Neuroscience* 25 (March 16, 2005): 2977–2982.

29. R. Key Dismukes, Timothy E. Goldsmith and Janeen A. Kochan, *Effects of Acute Stress on Aircrew Performance: Literature Review and Analysis of Operational Aspects*, NASA/TM—2015–218930 (Moffett Field, CA: NASA Ames Research Center, August 2015).

30. Robert M. Yerkes and John D. Dodson, "The Relation of Strength of Stimulus to Rapidity of Habit-Formation," *Journal of Comparative Neurology and Psychology* 18 (November 1908): 459–482.

31. Hebbian version of the Yerkes Dodson curve, by Yerkes and Dodson, Hebbian, n.d. (https://commons.wikimedia.org/wiki/File:HebbianYerkesDodson.svg) WC CC0 1.0 Public Domain

32. Federal Aviation Administration, *Pilot/Controller Glossary* (Washington, DC: January 30, 2020).

33. Dismukes, Goldsmith and Kochan, *Effects of Acute Stress on Aircrew Performance*.

34. James A. Young, *The Effects of Life-Stress on Pilot Performance*, NASA/TM–2008-215375 (Moffett Field, CA: NASA Ames Research Center, December 2008): 1.

35. Dismukes, Goldsmith and Kochan, *Effects of Acute Stress on Aircrew Performance*.

36. Aeronautica Civil of The Republic of Colombia, *Aircraft Accident Report: Controlled Flight into Terrain, American Airlines Flight 965, Boeing 757-223, N651AA, Near Cali, Colombia, December 20, 1995*, trans. Peter B. Ladkin (Santafe de Bogota D.C., Colombia: Aeronautica Civil of The Republic of Colombia, September 1996): 45.

37. Edna R. Fiedler, Pam Della Rocco, David J. Schroeder and Kiet T. Nguyen, *Aviators' Home-Based Stress to Work Stress and Self-Perceived Performance*, Final Report, DOT/FAA/AM-00/32 (Oklahoma City, OK: FAA Civil Aeromedical Institute, October 2000).

38. Reported in Young, *The Effects of Life-Stress on Pilot Performance*.

39. Peter H. Platenius and Gerald J. Wilde, "Personal Characteristics Related to Accident Histories of Canadian Pilots," *Aviation, Space, and Environmental Medicine* 60 (January 1989): 42–45.

40. Young, *The Effects of Life-Stress on Pilot Performance*.

41. Mike Kolich and Durhane Wong-Reiger, "Emotional Stress and Information Processing Ability in the Context of Accident Causation," *International Journal of Industrial Ergonomics* 24 (October 1999): 591–602.

42. Young, *The Effects of Life-Stress on Pilot Performance*.

43. Richard S. Lazarus and Susan Folkman, *Stress, Appraisal, and Coping* (New York: Springer Publishing Company, 1984).

44. Information for this flow diagram comes from the ideas presented in Richard S. Lazarus and Susan Folkman, *Stress, Appraisal, and Coping* (New York: Springer Publishing Company, 1984).

45. Mark A. Staal, Stress, *Cognition, and Human Performance: A Literature Review and Conceptual Framework*, NASA/TM—2004–212824 (Moffett Field, CA: NASA Ames Research Center, August 2004).

46. Jensen, *Aeronautical Decision Making—Cockpit Resource Management*.

47. Glenn R. Stout, Jr., *Just for the Health of Pilots* (n.d.). Available at www.faa.gov/licenses_certificates/medical_certification/hop/media/depression.pdf.

48. Gary Crump, *Mental Health as an Aviation Safety Consideration* (Frederick, MD: Aircraft Owners and Pilots Association, June 1, 2017). Available at pilot-protection-services.AOPA.org/news/2017/june/01/mental-health-as-an-aviation-safety-consideration.

49. Stout, Jr., *Just for the Health of Pilots*.

50. Federal Aviation Administration, *Fact Sheet—Pilot Mental Fitness* (June 9, 2016).

51. John Taylor, "Pilot Peer Support: Addressing Member Health, Wellness with a New Resource," *Air Line Pilot Magazine* (August 2018).

52. John Fisher, Ed Phillips and Jeff Mather, "Does Crew Resource Management Training Work?" *Air Medical Journal* 19 (October–December 2000): 137–139.

53. Paul O'Connor, Justin Campbell, Jennifer Newon, John Melton, Edwardo Salas and Katherine A. Wilson, "Crew Resource Management Training Effectiveness: A Meta-Analysis and Some Critical Needs," *International Journal of Aviation Psychology*, 18 (October 2008): 353–368.

54. Federal Aviation Administration, *Crew Resource Management Training*, AC 120-51E (Washington, DC: January 22, 2004).

55. American Psychological Association, *Safer Air Travel through Crew Resource Management* (Washington, DC: February 2014).

56. Matt Breen, *United Flight 232 Captain Al Haynes Gives Final Speech 27-Years after Sioux City*, Archive Story (Quincy, IL: WGEM, Nov 16, 2016).

57. Al Haynes, *The Crash of United Flight 232*, Transcript of speech given at NASA's Dryden Flight Research Facility, Edwards, CA, May 24, 1991 (Edwards, CA: NASA, May 24, 1991).

20

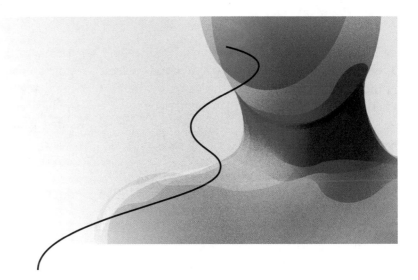

Managing the risks.
Threat and Error Management

"But a line pilot is wary all of the time...To be continuously aware you must know what to be wary of. Learning the nature and potentialities of the countless hazards is like walking near quicksand."

—Ernest K. Gann, *Fate is the Hunter*

If you have read this far, it should be clear to you that when it comes to flying, stuff happens. Murphy's Law—*what can go wrong will go wrong*—is only supplanted by that of his wife's: *Murphy was an optimist*. Flying involves risks. Whether these risks arise from the machines we've created that carry us into the skies, from the environment that we coax them to fly through, or from the everyday human errors that affect our ability to safely fly them, most aviation safety experts agree: Threats to safe flight are ubiquitous and, even when we do our best to avoid them, errors are inevitable.

An effective approach to risk management that freely acknowledges that threats to safe flight are ever-present and errors made by pilots are inescapable—but that also prescribes effective strategies to manage them—is **threat and error management (TEM)**. Initially developed in the 1990s by researchers at the University of Texas at Austin with funding from the FAA, and working in cooperation with Delta Air Lines (DAL) and Continental Airlines, TEM is a broad model that was initially developed as a systematic observation tool in line operations safety audits (LOSA).

LOSAs involve highly trained expert observers who collect safety-related data while riding in the aircraft jump seat during regularly scheduled airline flights. These observers record and code *threats* to safety that flight crews may face and the *errors* that they may make, and more importantly, how they manage them. In order to obtain cooperation from pilots and their unions, the data collected during these observations are de-identified (sanitized of all references that could associate it with the crew being observed), thus guaranteeing a strictly no-jeopardy observation of the crew. Similar to a patient's annual physical examination, a LOSA provides a diagnostic snapshot of the overall strengths and weaknesses of an airline's flight operations, which in turn is used to improve their training and safety guidance. LOSA, and its use of the TEM approach in identifying threats and errors, has expanded its reach into several major airlines the world over and, since the beginning of the new millennium, has been embraced as a successful risk reduction strategy by the International Civil Aviation Organization.[1]

TEM can also be used as a reporting tool for incidents and an analysis tool for accidents and incidents; but it has also proved effective as a training tool to help pilots successfully manage risk. As mentioned in the previous chapter, CRM has gone through several iterations over the years. Since the major reason for developing CRM programs in the first place was to help flight crews effectively manage risks on the flight deck,[2] TEM has been incorporated into many of today's CRM training programs. In fact, many would say that TEM is the term for latest generation CRM, and has essentially supplanted the term CRM. Several of the basic concepts of TEM were mentioned in Chapter 2. The remainder of this chapter will expound on some of these and introduce others that make up the TEM approach to increasing safe flight operations.

Threats Pilots Face

As noted, TEM involves managing threats that pilots may encounter and errors they may make. A **threat** is any condition, event, or error outside of the influence of the flight crew that increases the operational complexity of a flight, often leads to pilot error, and requires attention and management if safety margins are to be maintained.[3] A more familiar word for threat is hazard; both essentially mean the same.

Arising from numerous sources, threats in airline operations are divided into two basic categories: those that come from the environment (aircraft system malfunctions, adverse weather, high terrain close to airport) and those that originate from within the airline itself (maintenance error, uninformed dispatch, inadequate SOPs, etc.). Some threats are expected (forecast wind shear, an approaching thunderstorm, etc.), while others are not (aircraft system malfunction). Fleshing out these threats in greater

detail, we discover that they originate primarily from four sources that generally align with the FAA's familiar PAVE model (*see* Chapter 2): the *aircraft*, the *environment*, other people's actions (*external pressures*), and the physiological or psychological condition of the *pilot* (not their actions). Table 20-1 lists several examples of threats pilots may face.

Aircraft Threats

A common aircraft threat is an unexpected system malfunction. Both Eastern Air Lines (EAL) Flight 401 (*see* Chapter 14) and United Airlines (UAL) Flight 173 (*see* Chapter 19) experienced landing gear indicator malfunctions while on approach to Miami and Portland airports, respectively.

Environmental Threats

A persistent environmental threat that requires crew vigilance to properly manage is adverse weather. American Airlines Flight 1420 overran the runway during an attempted landing during a thunderstorm in poor visibility and adverse winds at Little Rock National Airport (*see* Chapters 17 and 19). Airframe icing is another environmental threat. An NTSB

Table 20-1. Types and examples of threats pilots may encounter.

Threat types	Examples
Aircraft	• Design deficiencies (displays, controls, lighting, etc.) • Automation complexity (confusing modes, dumb/dutiful) • Systems malfunctions (engine, electrical components, fire) • Minimum equipment list (MEL) items • Aircraft model differences, limitations, airworthiness
Environment	• Atmospheric environment—night, flat light, adverse weather (low-level wind shear, low ceilings/visibility, thunderstorms, airframe icing, IMC, crosswinds) • Cabin environment—temperature, humidity, vibration, lighting, high altitude • Airspace and airport environment—complex airspace, inoperative navigation aids, air traffic congestion, airport layout, runway contamination • Terrain—high terrain near airport, open ocean • Time pressure—delays, connecting flights
Other people	• Errors of, or distractions by, others—cabin crew, ground/ramp crew, dispatch, weather briefer, maintenance technicians, passengers (unruly, drunk, sick, dead, security threat), supervisor, training department • Operational/supervisory pressure • Inadequate training, SOP, checklist and flight manual information errors • ATC issues—radio congestion, fast clearances, confusing clearances, language difficulties, call sign confusion, speed requests, last-minute runway changes
Pilot condition	• Adverse physiological condition—spatial disorientation, hypoxia, illness, OTC medication effects, fatigue, sleep disturbance, jet lag, motion sickness • Adverse mental condition—visual illusions, automation complacency, mental overload, mental fatigue, forgetful, hazardous attitudes, stress

safety study found that at least 583 airframe icing accidents over a 19-year period in the United States were responsible for more than 800 deaths.[4]

People Threats

Other external threats come from the actions (or inaction) of people other than the flight crew. Several accidents have resulted from real or perceived pressures from passengers and supervisors on pilots to continue a flight. The pilots of Wapiti Flight 402 and Downeast Airlines Flight 46, both felt pressure from management to complete their flights—both aircraft crashed after descending below minimum authorized altitudes during instrument approaches at night in IMC (see Chapter 18).

Passengers can exert subtle pressure on pilots to continue in the face of adverse weather as indicated by the fact that GA pilots have a greater chance of experiencing a VFR-into-IMC accident if they have passengers on board (see Chapter 18). Other people threats include errors and distractions caused by others. Recent accidents in Watkins, Colorado, Mosby, Missouri, and Hoboken, New Jersey, were caused in part by the pilots' distraction while talking or texting with other people on their cellphones (see Table 14-1 in Chapter 14).

Pilot Condition Threats

Since a pilot's physiological or psychological condition[5] may be outside of their influence (circadian dysrhythmia, spatial disorientation, visual illusions, forgetful, illness) or not outside their influence (OTC medication, fatigue from poor sleep habits, alcohol use, automation complacency, hazardous attitudes), this threat category is somewhat difficult to classify. Is a pilot's condition considered a threat or an error? Since errors involve actions or inaction (see the next section), and since an adverse physiological or psychological state/condition can lead to errors, for the purposes of this discussion it will be considered a threat to safe flight.

Of course, the more threats a pilot faces at once the greater the overall threat to safe flight. For example, a New Mexico State Police (NMSP) Agusta Westland AW109 helicopter impacted terrain following VFR flight into IMC near Santa Fe, New Mexico. Two environmental threats (darkness of night and IMC), three pilot condition threats (fatigue, situational stress, and self-induced pressure), and several threats from other people significantly increased the overall threat level. According to the NTSB, the threats by others involved:

- An organizational culture that prioritized mission execution over aviation safety;
- deficiencies in the NMSP aviation section's safety-related policies, including lack of a requirement for a risk assessment at any point during the mission;
- inadequate pilot staffing; and
- a lack of an effective fatigue managment program for pilots (Report No: NTSB/AAR-11/04).

Errors Pilots Make

In the TEM framework a threat is any condition, event, or error outside of the influence of the pilot that jeopardizes safety, while an error is any action or inaction on the part of the flight crew that leads to a deviation from crew or organizational intentions and that can lead to an undesired aircraft state, increasing the probability of an accident or incident. These errors of commission and omission, as they are sometimes called, could be an incorrect action or any action that was needed but wasn't executed (or executed too late) by the flight crew.

Even though the goal of every pilot is to avoid committing errors, the TEM approach openly acknowledges that despite our best attempts we pilots—even those of us with several years of experience—are naturally prone to various slips, lapses, and mistakes (see Chapter 2) that we call errors.

Different types of error were discussed in Chapter 2 (perceptual, skill-based, decision errors, etc.), but within the TEM framework they can generally be categorized into three broad categories: handling and proficiency errors, procedural errors, and ineffective resource management.

Handling and Proficiency Errors

These include manual (hand-flying) skill errors, poor technique, improper systems or radio operation (finger trouble), and errors such as instrument misinterpretation and failure to see and avoid another aircraft on a potential collision course with yours. For example, the Airbus A320 that collided with terrain short of the runway at Bangalore International Airport in India did so in part because the pilot monitoring most likely selected 700 feet using the "altitude" knob, when he intended to select 700 feet per minute descent using the "vertical speed" knob (see Chapter 15). More recently, the PF of Asiana Airlines Flight 214, the Boeing B-777 that crashed into the seawall short of Runway 28L at San Francisco International Airport, "lacked critical manual flying skills" and if he had more experience hand-flying the B-777 he would most likely have taken the appropriate corrective action needed to avert the dangerously low approach (Report No: NTSB/AAR-14/01).

Procedural Errors

These occur when you fail to operate the aircraft according to the manufacturer's instructions found in the *aircraft flight manual* or the company SOPs, fail to use the checklist properly, or unintentionally deviate from regulatory procedures. For example, not following the checklist due to distraction or forgetfulness is responsible for many tragic takeoff stall accidents (see Table 16-1 in Chapter 16).

Ineffective Resource Management

Unsuccessful communication, failure to manage distractions, and failure to manage stress, are all examples of errors due to ineffective resource management skills. Common to both single-pilot operations (SRM) and multi-pilot flight decks (CRM), inadequate resource management is responsible for several aircraft accidents, including UAL Flight 173 in Portland, Oregon, and Air Florida Flight 90 in Washington, D.C. (see Chapters 18 and 19).

Violations

A distinction should be made between errors, which are unintentional mistakes, and violations, which are willful actions that do not comply with regulations, rules and procedures designed to ensure safe flight operations. Often called *willful noncompliance*, violations are generally of two kinds: routine violations that represent a somewhat habitual "bending of the rules" by a pilot, and which may be tolerated or possibly even encouraged by the company (e.g., Wapiti Flight 402 and Downeast Airlines Flight 46; see Chapter 18), and exceptional (rare) violations which are not typical of a pilot's behavior and are not condoned by the company.

Despite being known by his peers as a "conscientious and competent pilot" who "flew by the book,"

the experienced 24,000-hour captain of an Air Ontario Fokker F-28, that crashed a half-mile beyond the end of the runway at Dryden Municipal Airport in Ontario after an attempted departure with snow and ice on the wings, went against his better judgment by deliberately violating several rules required by his airline to ensure safe flight operations. As indicated in Chapter 2, these included conducting hot fueling operations with passengers aboard, failing to deice the airplane while snow was falling and ice was accumulating on the wings, and making the decision to depart in such conditions. However, as also discussed in Chapter 2, strong situational factors—mostly involving constraints placed upon the captain by the company itself—put significant pressure on the crew to violate company procedures. They were unexpectedly dispatched with 10 additional passengers, which meant they now had to make a stop in Dryden for refueling before continuing to their destination of Winnipeg, Manitoba. However, since ground-start equipment was unavailable at Dryden, they had to leave an engine running for hot refueling because they were dispatched with an unserviceable auxiliary power unit—shutting them both down would have stranded crew and passengers at Dryden. Finally, since company policy prohibited ground deicing procedures with one or more engines operating, the crew chose not to get the wings deiced before takeoff.

Unless required for an emergency distress situation (in which case a pilot may deviate from any regulation to meet that emergency; see 14 CFR §91.3), violating rules and procedures, no matter how infrequent, is unacceptable in flying operations: they are there for a reason—adhering to them contributes to safer flight operations. However, in certain circumstances, such as those present in the Wapiti, Downeast, and Air Ontario accidents, the pressure on pilots from their organization and other people, including passengers, to cut corners can be significant.

Undesirable Aircraft States

When unsuccessfully managed, threats can lead to errors or violations that can further lead to an undesired aircraft state (UAS)—an aircraft condition, attitude, or position that compromises safety and, if not properly managed, can lead to an accident or incident. Most pilots are trained in how to recognize and correct for a UAS; however, sometimes they are unaware of it in the first place (or become aware too late). For example, several inadvertent roll upsets and aerodynamic stall/spin accidents have occurred because pilots were unaware of the UAS created by significant ice accumulation on the airframe—sometimes as a result of the autopilot masking such a condition (*see* Chapter 15). An unwanted aircraft state can occur in four areas: configuration, handling, approach and landing, and ground operations.

Configuration States

Aircraft configuration generally refers to the position of lift devices and landing gear, but this category also includes any undesired powerplant, systems, instrument, or automation settings. The crew of the MD-82 that ran off the end of the runway at Little Rock National Airport in Arkansas was unaware that their flaps were not properly configured and their spoilers were not armed for landing until it was too late (*see* Chapters 17 and 19). The crew of Helios Airways Flight 522 was not aware that the cabin pressurization mode selector was in the MAN position instead of the AUTO setting, causing a UAS when the aircraft climbed into hypoxic altitudes, debilitating everyone aboard (*see* Chapter 4).

Aircraft Handing States

A UAS can also be caused by aircraft handling errors from abrupt or excessive bank or pitch control, lateral or vertical flight path deviations, airspeed deviations, or penetrating adverse weather or unauthorized airspace. A Boeing B-757 entered a UAS by significantly deviating both laterally and vertically from an appropriate trajectory when the crew allowed it to fly off course toward higher terrain during a steep descent into Alfonso Bonilla Aragon International Airport, in Cali, Colombia (*see* Chapters 14, 15, 16, and 19).

Penetration of adverse weather, a recurring theme highlighted throughout this book, is another type of undesired aircraft handling state. For example, many low-level wind shear accidents have occurred because pilots have attempted an approach into convective thunderstorm activity. Jessica Dubroff, her father, and her pilot-instructor died after their Cessna Cardinal was flown into deteriorating weather conditions, including turbulence, gusty winds, and an advancing thunderstorm with associated precipitation (*see* Chapter 17). Another undesired handling state occurs when an aircraft without airframe icing protection systems (IPS) enters icing conditions. The 583 airframe icing accidents responsible for 800 deaths over a 19-year period in the United States were mostly GA aircraft that were not equipped with IPS.

A UAS resulting from improper handling, if not adequately corrected for, can result in an **airplane upset**, a condition whereby an airplane unintentionally exceeds parameters normally considered safe. Often called an unusual attitude that can sometimes lead to LOC-I, an airplane upset involves a pitch attitude greater than 25 degrees nose-up or 10 degrees nose-down (pitch upset), a bank angle greater than 45 degrees (roll upset), and/or inappropriate airspeeds (too fast or slow) for the conditions. A variety of factors can cause an upset—which can involve an aerodynamic stall or spin—including wake turbulence, airframe icing, severe weather, microbursts, wind shear, and/or inadvertent or unanticipated autopilot disconnect. This latter factor, coupled with the crew's failure to monitor airspeed, caused a harrowing series of steep uncontrolled nose-down pitch and bank attitudes for the 25 passengers on board a Saab 340 that lasted for almost a minute before the captain was finally able to regain control of the aircraft (*see* Chapter 15).

Approach and Landing States

A UAS can arise from a poorly executed approach and landing. Examples include an unstable approach resulting from airspeed deviations and vertical and lateral approach course deviations, and hard, short or long landings. For example, most runway excursions occur during landing, primarily because of unstable approaches (*see* Chapter 1). Conducting a steep turn at a low speed onto final approach at 400 feet AGL in a McDonnell Douglas DC-8, as occurred in Guantanamo Bay, Cuba, certainly qualifies as an undesirable approach and landing state (*see* Chapter 10). So too does flying a slightly low approach, as occurred with a Canadian Airlines International Boeing B-767 that landed short and hard after the crew succumbed to a landing illusion by the upsloping runway at Halifax Stanfield International Airport in Nova Scotia during a nonprecision instrument approach to Runway 06 at night (*see* Chapter 12).

Ground Operation States

An undesired ground operation state can occur when an aircraft is improperly handled during taxi, or is at or proceeding to a wrong location on the airport, such as the wrong runway, taxiway, ramp, hold spot, or gate location. A Cessna 441 Conquest II pilot mistakenly believed he had back-taxied into position on Runway 31 in accordance with his ATC clearance at St. Louis Lambert International Airport in Bridgeton, Missouri. However, it was a dark night and he inadvertently taxied into position on Runway 30R. He and the only other occupant of the Conquest were killed when it was struck by a departing Trans World Airlines (TWA) McDonnell Douglas DC-9 (*see* Chapter 6).

Results of a UAS

A UAS does not have to lead to an accident, but if left unmanaged a collision with terrain or another object will result.

Colliding into Terrain

One possible outcome of a UAS is collision with terrain. For example, LOC-I caused by a variety of physiological threats (hypoxia, spatial disorientation), environmental threats (airframe icing, microburst, IMC), or flight crew errors (failing to monitor airspeed or airframe ice accretion) can lead to uncontrolled flight into terrain.

CFIT, where the aircraft is under positive control but the pilot is unaware of its impending collision with nearby terrain, is the result of a lack of lateral and/or vertical positional awareness and is caused by a variety of environmental threats (VFR flight in the dark or into IMC), pilot physiological and mental condition (hypoxia, black-hole illusion), or pilot errors (automation complacency). For example, all 92 people aboard TWA Flight 514 died after the Boeing B-727 impacted higher terrain in controlled flight about 25 miles short of Runway 12 at Dulles International Airport in Washington, D.C. It appears the crew faced several threats: they had to divert from their original destination of Washington National to Dulles, which meant they had to conduct an approach at an airport and runway they hadn't originally prepared for; they were conducting a nonprecision VOR/DME approach (approaches with no glide slope guidance are inherently more risky); the approach chart did not adequately specify the minimum safe altitude for the approach, and according to the NTSB, could have misled the crew into believing that 1,800 feet was a safe altitude while still 40 miles from the airport; they thought that they were under radar surveillance (they were not); and the crew had a misunderstanding of what the controller meant when he said "cleared for the approach." Since they probably believed that there was no altitude restriction, except for the 1,800-foot minimum altitude at the final approach fix (FAF), they thought that they could descend to it immediately. The major error resulting from this was their early descent below 3,400 feet, rather than waiting until reaching the Round Hill fix further along the approach where the profile view (but not the plan view) of the approach chart showed that descent below 3,400 feet was appropriate (Report No: NTSB-AAR-75-16).

Following this accident, several major safety initiatives were implemented: the FAA required the installation of ground proximity warning systems (GPWS) on all U.S. large turbojet and turboprop airliners, the NASA ASRS program was created, and the FAA created a new publication called the *Pilot/Controller Glossary* to promote a common understanding of the terms used in the ATC system.

Colliding into Other Aircraft

Collisions with other aircraft in flight can result from environmental threats (glare from the sun), threats from other people's actions (a distracting passenger), or from pilot errors (failure to conduct an adequate visual scan for traffic). Collisions with other aircraft, vehicles, or pedestrians on the ground can arise from environmental threats (night, poor visibility, poor lighting), other people's actions (incorrect ATC clearance or incorrect readback/hearback), or errors on the part of the pilot (not studying the airport diagram, failing to ask ATC to clarify a misunderstood taxi clearance).

Event Cascade

A UAS can result directly from a threat (such as an unexpected strong downdraft from a microburst) or from a pilot error (poor airspeed monitoring). However, as you have seen in several accidents throughout the chapters in this book, a UAS is often caused by a combination of both (*see* Figure 20-1). For example, a short runway is contaminated by snow and ice (threat) but the pilot chooses to attempt a landing on it anyway (error).

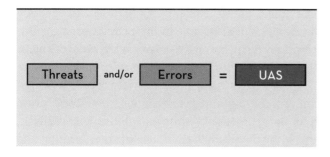

Fig 20-1.

A UAS can result from a threat or an error, or both.

Generally, however, a UAS results from a domino effect, also called an **event cascade** (*see* Figure 20-2), that occurs when a threat—often unanticipated—presents itself to the crew that in turn precipitates an error, or several errors, that subsequently leads to a UAS. For example, the crews of EAL Flight 401 in Miami and UAL 173 in Portland were both faced with a landing gear indicator problem (a threat). In response, the flight crews committed several errors: the pilots of Flight 401 failed to assign a crew member to fly the airplane and to monitor altitude, and the FO and FE of Flight 173 failed to effectively communicate the fuel status to the captain and the captain focused too much on passenger readiness. Unfortunately, these UASs evolved into full-blown accidents because both crews failed to manage the threats they encountered—itself an error.

Countermeasures

In an ideal world, pilots would avoid threats and errors altogether. But as should be clearly evident from the information presented throughout this book, encountering them in the real world is often part and parcel of everyday flying. Remember the old saying, "just because you're not paranoid, it doesn't mean they're not out to get you!" It's important, therefore, that you learn as much as you can about the threats you may encounter in flight, the errors you are prone to make, and the strategies needed to either avoid them or minimize (or mitigate) their effects.

The most important weapons against threats and errors are **countermeasures**. Using a metaphor from military and cybersecurity operations, a countermeasure in flight operations is any measure or action taken to counter a threat or error. Countermeasures—the most important component of a TEM approach to managing risk in flight operations—can be either passive or active. Examples of *passive* countermeasures that aircraft manufacturers use to help pilots avoid a UAS—often viewed as a last line of defense against threats and errors—include alarms and onboard warning systems, such as terrain awareness warning systems (TAWS or enhanced GPWS), airborne collision avoidance systems (ACAS or TCAS), and other devices. These countermeasures, however, are not enough; the primary countermeasures needed to ensure acceptable levels of safety are *active* countermeasures in the form of prescribed flight crew behaviors and practices.

Fig 20-2.

The precipitating event in a UAS is often a threat which in turn spawns flight crew errors as they attempt to manage the threat.

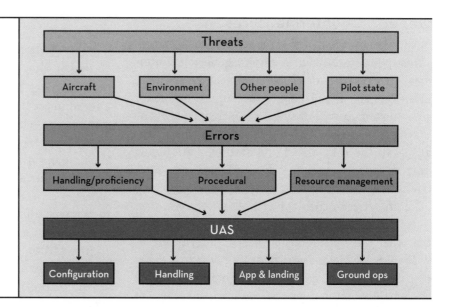

Threat- and Error-Specific Countermeasures

Defending yourself against threats and errors often involves using countermeasures that are applicable to the type of threat you may encounter or the kind of errors you may make. For example, specialized knowledge and behaviors are essential when attempting to manage the threats associated with flying in IMC, at high altitudes, at lower altitudes in the mountains, or during the darkness of night. Threat-specific countermeasures are also necessary to avoid a midair collision, a runway excursion or incursion, or an encounter with different types of weather phenomena. Many of the strategies needed to combat these types of threats are systematically presented in *Managing Risk: Best Practices for Pilots*, which I cowrote with Gerald Binnema (*see* the Helpful Resources section at the end of this chapter for more information).

Domain-specific knowledge of the human factor issues discussed in this book, and the strategies outlined in each chapter, are also effective in targeting specific threats you may encounter and errors you may make. For example, to avoid succumbing to the black-hole illusion during a visual approach in dark-night conditions, supplement your outside visual references with glide slope information from the ILS; to remember a clearance, write it down; to reduce confirmation bias when making a decision, consider the opposite of what you may be thinking or ask others for their input.

Generic Countermeasures

In addition to threat- and error-specific countermeasures, pilots also need to employ generic countermeasures that are applicable to almost every flight. These one-size-fits-all countermeasures are good for covering a multitude of sins. Good drivers do this by practicing defensive driving techniques: they visually scan the road ahead and around them (using mirrors) for the presence of other vehicles and pedestrians, they provide a safety buffer by leaving plenty of room between their car and other vehicles, they refrain from texting, and they attempt to follow all the other rules of the road. Using countermeasures in flight is like defensive driving for pilots.[6]

Fortunately, today's pilots don't have to reinvent the wheel when it comes to countermeasures. For example, quality training, education, and life-long learning have always been important generic countermeasures pilots use to manage the risks of flight. So too is maintaining flight proficiency, a strong defense in fighting against a variety of errors—especially handling and proficiency errors. Conducting adequate preflight planning before every flight, including obtaining a thorough weather briefing and checking all applicable NOTAMs, has long been an effective countermeasure against adverse weather threats and other hazards.

Several generic countermeasures that have developed and evolved over the years—often at the expense of lives lost in accidents—have been codified as best practice countermeasures into SOPs used by most of today's airlines. A **best practice** is an industry-recognized procedure or set of behaviors that operational experience and research have proven to result in the best possible outcome for a given task. These procedures, though generally standardized throughout the airline industry, are not static, but gradually evolve and improve as new information is discovered or new technologies are implemented.

The airlines boast an enviable safety record, carrying millions of passengers safely to their destinations each year, in large part because of the efficacy of the countermeasures pilots use to detect, avoid, or mitigate the threats they face—and avoid, detect, and correct and mitigate the errors that they make. It's true the airlines possess safety advantages that other aviation sectors—especially single-pilot GA operations—do not. For example, they are required by regulation to use safety management systems that usually include a variety of other organizational tools, such as LOSA and flight operational quality assurance, to help flight crews achieve a high level of safety. Besides using some of the most sophisticated aircraft in the business, they also usually employ the most experienced and best-trained pilots, using at least two of them to pilot every flight. Despite this, the airlines have long recognized the fact that pilots still make mistakes—sometimes they have difficulty focusing on the task at hand, they get distracted, they forget things, they execute the wrong actions, or they execute the correct actions too late.

In addition to obtaining quality training and education, maintaining proficiency, and conducting adequate preflight planning before every flight, there are at least a dozen other generic best practice countermeasures that airline and other professional crews use to help them effectively manage threats and errors on the flight deck. The remainder of this chapter focuses on several of these. If you do not fly on a crewed flight deck and only partake in single-pilot operations, don't think that the following countermeasures aren't applicable to you—each one can be used, at least to some extent, to help you combat the threats and errors that you may experience in flight while flying as the sole pilot.

Standard Operating Procedures

As explained in Chapter 17, SOPs are written procedures that are applied uniformly and consistently for every aspect and phase of flight, including normal, non-normal, and emergency operations. SOPs incorporate the collective wisdom of lessons learned from a multitude of aircraft accidents and incidents and provide expert guidance that supports flight crew actions that lead to the safest possible outcomes. Many aircraft accidents over the years could have been averted if the flight crews involved would have simply adhered to the published SOPs. Compliance with SOPs is essential in coordinating the actions of airline flight crews, especially since individual pilots seldom fly with each other. If you are involved in single-pilot GA operations and do not use SOPs, you should consult a flight training provider, the FAA, or Transport Canada to help you develop SOPs applicable to the aircraft you fly.

Flows and Checklists

Flows were discussed in the chapter about memory (*see* Chapter 16). Airline pilots conduct memorized procedural flows to help streamline the accomplishment of flight deck tasks involved in normal, non-normal, and emergency operations. For example, during normal operations FOs and captains are each responsible for executing at least a dozen different memorized flows that are unique to their roles as captain and FO (e.g., before start, after start, before takeoff, after takeoff, climb, descent, approach, landing, after landing, etc.). These flows usually involve following a logical, linear, or geographic (left-to-right, bottom-to-top, etc.) pattern that helps you properly complete the tasks required for the different segments of flight.

Of course, a flow is of no use if you forget to use it, or if you forget to accomplish an item on it. A powerful countermeasure used in almost all flight operations is checklist usage. Observing strict checklist discipline is an effective countermeasure against forgetfulness and is added protection to ensure designated flow items and other critical actions have been completed correctly. Written read-and-do checklists are used to ensure items are accomplished in the proper sequence while challenge-and-response checklists are often used to make sure specified flow items and other tasks have been completed.

As with flows, checklists are also useless if you forget to use them in the first place, or if you fail to actually check and confirm that the action has been accomplished. As noted in Chapter 14, this happened in the DAL crash shortly after takeoff from Runway 18L at Dallas-Fort Worth International Airport. The NTSB concluded that though the FO said "FIFTEEN, FIFTEEN, GREEN LIGHT" in response to the "FLAPS" challenge item on the checklist, he did not actually look at the status of the light and indicators.

Since maintaining strict checklist discipline involves work, pilots—especially GA pilots—are sometimes tempted to not use them, especially during high workload situations. However, if you get into the habit of always using them, they will become easier to use consistently and you will consistently reap their benefits.

Monitoring and Cross-Checking

Numerous accidents have occurred because pilots failed to adequately monitor the status of their aircraft. As noted in Chapter 14, 84 percent of U.S. air carrier accidents in which the actions of the flight crew were cited as a causal or contributing factor, involved monitoring/challenging failures. A major countermeasure, therefore, is maintaining vigilance in monitoring the status of the flight. At the very least there should always be one pilot designated as the *pilot monitoring*, who is actively and constantly visually scanning the instruments and cross-checking for deviations from the crew's intentions. This should also preclude both pilots from having both heads down at once. As discussed in Chapter 14, this type of sustained attention involves work and can be tiring, especially during periods of high mental workload. Some of the following countermeasures are also designed to enhance attention, vigilance, and monitoring.

Verbalized Procedures

A countermeasure designed to improve pilot performance is verbalization. As noted in Chapter 16, airline crews conduct verbal departure and approach briefings as well as verbal callouts for critical parameters (speeds, altitudes, flight path deviations, configuration changes, etc.). Verbalizing provides what is known as a **redundancy gain** by using an additional sensory modality—besides vision—to help you better focus on the task at hand, which in turn contributes to improved monitoring and decreases the chance of forgetting something. It also allows your fellow crew member to confirm or disconfirm the accuracy of the information. Most airline SOPs specifically spell out the types of calls to be made by both the PF and PM for various parameters. For example, when passing through 1,000 feet above your assigned altitude while on a descent, the PM calls out "one thousand to go." As explained in Chapter 16, verbal callouts increase monitoring performance by helping you both to pay closer attention to the aircraft's performance and state.

Workload Management

Another countermeasure against poor monitoring performance is effective workload management. This involves balancing workload distribution not only between you and your fellow crew member, but between different workload-dependent flight segments. For example, as noted in Chapter 14, the task requirements for a typical flight are usually lowest during cruise flight, and highest during takeoff, approach, and landing. These latter phases of flight were identified as high areas of vulnerability that are particularly vulnerable to flight path deviations and where the severity of the consequences of deviating from flight path parameters is the greatest (see Chapters 14 and 15). In addition to increasing the sampling rate during your instrument scan during periods of high workload, you should also shed non-priority tasks and focus on the primary task of flying the aircraft. One way to do this is to defer non-monitoring tasks to periods of low areas of vulnerability. For example, conducting the approach briefing and entering the approach parameters into the flight management system before reaching the top of descent.

Distraction Management

A major cause of errors are distractions. Not only do they draw your attention away from monitoring, they also cause you to forget what you were doing or were intending to do, such as accomplishing an item on a checklist. Therefore, distraction management is a major countermeasure against poor monitoring and forgetting. Chapters 14 and 16 offer several suggestions on how to combat distractions, including using reminder cues to get you back on track after a distraction, returning to the beginning of the checklist after a distraction, delegating one crew member to manage an extended distraction, and complying with the sterile cockpit rule.

The importance of complying with the sterile cockpit rule has been noted several times in this book. As you recall, the regulation prohibits airline crew members from engaging in any duties that could distract them from completing the essential duties required for the safe operation of their aircraft during the critical phases of flight—all ground operations and all other operations below 10,000 feet except cruise flight (14 CFR §§121.542 and 135.100). Examples of prohibited activities include: engaging in nonessential conversations within the flight deck, with the company (such as obtaining flight time data), and between the cabin and flight deck; passenger announcements pointing out sights of interest; filling out company payroll and related records; eating meals; and reading publications not related to the safety of the flight. In addition, during all phases of flight (not just the critical phases) the use of personal wireless communication devices or laptop computers is prohibited unless needed for the safe operation of the aircraft, for an emergency, or for approved employment-related communications.

Noncompliance with this rule has been implicated in several major incidents and fatal accidents, including a Northwest Airlines flight whose crew failed to communicate with ATC for more than an hour and flew past its destination of Minneapolis by 100 miles (see Chapter 14); a wrong runway departure of a CRJ-100 from Blue Grass airport in Kentucky, killing 49 people (see Chapter 17); the loss of 13 people aboard a Corporate Airlines BAE Jetstream 32 that crashed on final approach in Kirksville, Missouri (Report No: NTSB/AAR-06/01); the crash of a Hawker Beechcraft 125 during an attempted go-around in

Owatonna, Minnesota, that killed all eight occupants (*see* Chapter 10); LOC-I of a Bombardier CRJ-200 near Jefferson City, Missouri that killed the FO and captain (Report No: NTSB/AAR-07/01); and LOC-I of a Bombardier Q400 on an approach into Buffalo, New York, that claimed the lives all 49 people aboard and one person on the ground (*see* Chapters 10 and 14).

Though not required for most Part 91 operations, if you are a GA pilot you should avoid extraneous conversations and all non-essential activities that might cause distraction during taxi, takeoff, approach, landing, and any flight in the vicinity of an airport. You should also brief your passengers that, unless it is necessary for safety, they should avoid conversations with you during these critical phases of flight.

Automation Management

The mismanagement of automated flight control systems (AFCS) has also contributed to accidents—not just in airline operations, but more recently, with the introduction of sophisticated avionics and automated systems into small aircraft cockpits, in GA operations as well. The complications they can present—such as mode confusion, automation complacency, and the diminution of hand-flying skills—were thoroughly discussed in Chapter 15. So too were the countermeasures needed to help you fly the machine by not letting it fly you.

Since even experienced airline flight crews can be intimidated by the complexity of glass cockpits and advanced avionics, successful automation management requires that you thoroughly know how they work, including the integration of the autopilot, flight director, and autothrottle systems into the overall AFCS. Only then will you be able to know how to effectively use them and avoid confusion when the system changes modes or does something that would ordinarily surprise a less-informed pilot.

Other suggestions for effectively managing the automation include following best practices when programming or making changes to the system, such as using the CAMI procedure (confirm, activate, monitor, and intervene) before engaging the autopilot (*see* Chapter 15) and practicing the point and shoot procedure with one pilot pointing to the new entry and the other pilot verbally confirming the input while also pointing to the correct display (*see* Chapter 14).

The final skill needed to effectively manage the automation is to know when not to use it. It can become a distraction during last-minute or short-term changes to vertical or lateral navigation, especially during periods of high areas of vulnerability. Reduce the level of automation and hand-fly the aircraft if necessary.

Stabilized Approaches

Since most fatal accidents occur during the approach-and-landing phase of flight, and most of those are the result of unstabilized approaches, a major countermeasure used by professional pilots is to fly only stabilized approaches and to conduct a go-around if unable to do so. An unstabilized approach (too high, low, fast, or slow) significantly adds to your workload, decreasing your odds of a successful landing. Combined with other required tasks—such as configuring the aircraft, completing checklists, and communicating with ATC, to name a few—flying an unstabilized approach demands more attention than you may be able to give and could lead to a critical or fatal error. According to AC 120-71, *Standard Operating Procedures and Pilot Monitoring Duties for Flight Deck Crewmembers*, a stabilized approach involves flying a relatively constant approach angle and rate of descent (normally no greater than 1,000 fpm) down to the flare-out point within the touchdown zone of the runway. An accurate track and glide path angle should be flown from the glide path intercept point, or by the FAF inbound, with no more than *normal* bracketing corrections needed to maintain them both. Unless otherwise specified in the SOP for your operation, the approach should be stabilized by no lower than 1,000 feet height above touchdown (HAT) in IMC or 500 feet HAT in VMC, the airplane should be in the landing configuration, airspeed and power changes should be within the normal range as per your aircraft operating manual, and all checklists and most callouts should be completed. Even though you may be tempted to try and salvage an unstablized approach, you should execute a missed approach if these parameters cannot be met. Making it a habit to stabilize the approach earlier, rather than later, gives you the ability to focus on the task at hand and increases the likelihood of a successful landing.

Crew Resource Management

As noted in the previous chapter, CRM acts as an effective countermeasure against a variety of threats and errors. Of course, combining TEM principles with a traditional CRM approach increases its effectiveness even more. Airlines expect flight crew members to exercise such CRM skills as working together as a team, employing effective decision making and communication strategies, applying assertiveness skills when necessary, and managing stress. If you fly a single-pilot operation, you can still borrow from airline CRM efforts by using SRM skills such as aeronautical decision making, automation management, risk management, task management, and situational awareness to manage all available resources—from inside the cockpit or from without—to achieve safe flight.

You have reached the end of this book. It is appropriate, therefore, to reflect on what it means to be an aviator. Like many of us at first, you may have embraced aviation because of the thrill, the freedom, the excitement, and maybe even the prestige. But along the way, also like most of us, the thrill begins to abate and you discover that flying safely and accurately involves work. In exchange, however, your attitude begins to change and though the initial source of your excitement may diminish, a deeper wisdom and satisfaction matures as you fully learn what it means to master your craft. Though it is an immense challenge and a great honor to be entrusted with the responsibility of transporting people and goods to their destinations and to do so safely, day in and day out, there is also great reward.

You fully recognize that the rather trite and overused saying—*just because you're not paranoid doesn't mean they're not out to get you*—is 100 percent true. Your learning from books, from your own experiences, and the experiences of those who have gone before you, has shaped your entire approach to the challenge of flying. You are more skeptical than you were before, and you agree with one of the greats—Ernest K. Gann—that a pilot is continuously *wary* all the time. You no longer unreservedly trust anyone, including yourself, but double-check everything. You know how important it is to not let down your guard by acknowledging another worn-out-but-true adage: *if something can go wrong it will*. Whether that something—threat or error—resides within yourself, the airplane, the environment, or in other people, you know that to die of natural causes—and not in an aircraft accident—you must be thoroughly prepared for them by fully understanding them and being vigilant in consistently practicing the countermeasures needed to defeat them.

Helpful Resources

A thorough coverage of ten major threats to safe flight and best practice countermeasures to combat them are presented in *Managing Risk: Best Practices for Pilots*. Topics include runway incursions, midair collisions, airframe icing, VFR flight into IMC, low-level wind shear, high altitude flight, flying at night, visual illusions, spatial disorientation, and CFIT. (www.asa2fly.com/Managing-Risk-Best-Practices-for-Pilots-P2030.aspx)

The seminal work on TEM is James Ray Kinect's 2005 dissertation for his doctoral degree earned at the University of Texas at Austin, titled *Line Operations Safety Audit: A Cockpit Observation Methodology for Monitoring Commercial Airline Safety Performance*. (repositories.lib.utexas.edu/handle/2152/1967) Dr. Klinect also co-authored a helpful article on TEM, titled *Defensive Flying for Pilots: An Introduction to Threat and Error Management*. (www.skybrary.aero/bookshelf/books/1982.pdf)

A description of the TEM model upon which LOSA is based upon is found in Appendix 1 of the FAA's *Line Operations Safety Audits* advisory circular (AC 120-90). (www.faa.gov/airports/resources/advisory_circulars/index.cfm/go/document.information/documentNumber/120-90)

Endnotes

1. Federal Aviation Administration, *Line Operations Safety Assessments* (LOSA): History (August 26, 2014). Available at www.faa.gov/about/initiatives/maintenance_hf/losa/history/.

2. Robert L. Helmreich, Ashleigh C. Merritt and John A. Wilhelm, "The Evolution of Crew Resource Management Training in Commercial Aviation," *International Journal of Aviation Psychology* 9 (February 1999): 19–32.

3. The definitions and explanations of TEM terms and concepts in this chapter are primarily from the FAA's Advisory Circular 120-90, *Line Operations Safety Audit*, and have, in some instances, been slightly changed and expanded upon to provide a better understanding for the reader.

4. K.R. Petty and C.D.J. Floyd, "A Statistical Review of Aviation Airframe Icing Accidents in the United States," *The 11th Conference on Aviation, Range, and Aerospace* (Hyannis, MA: October 4–8, 2004).

5. I am grateful to Douglas Weigman and Scott Shappel for this distinction in their HFACS model in *A Human Error Approach to Aviation Accident Analysis: The Human Factors Analysis and Classification System (HFACS)* (Burlington, VT: Ashgate, 2003).

6. Ashleigh Merritt and James Klinect, *Defensive Flying for Pilots: An Introduction to Threat and Error Management* (December 12, 2006).

Appendices

Appendix A: Abbreviations and Acronyms Used in This Book

A

AA	American Airlines
AAIB	Air Accidents Investigation Branch (U.K.)
AC	Advisory Circular
ACAS	airborne collision avoidance system
ADM	aeronautical decision-making
AFB	Air Force Base
AFCS	automatic flight control system
AFM	aircraft flight manual
AGL	above ground level
AGSM	anti-G straining maneuver
AI	artificial intelligence
AIM	*Aeronautical Information Manual*
A-LOC	almost loss of consciousness
ALPA	Air Line Pilots Association
AME	aviation medical examiner (FAA)
ANR	active noise reduction
AOPA	Aircraft Owners and Pilots Association
APU	auxiliary power unit
AQP	advanced qualification program
ARC	abnormal runway contact
ARTCC	air route traffic control center
ASAP	aviation safety action program
ASEL	altitude select mode
ASI	airspeed indicator
ASOS	automated surface observation system
ASRS	Aviation Safety Reporting System (NASA)
ATC	air traffic control
ATIS	automatic terminal information service
ATP	airline transport pilot
ATSB	Australian Transport Safety Bureau
AUD	alcohol use disorder
Auto-GCAS	automatic ground collision avoidance system

B

BAC	blood alcohol concentration
BPR	bypass ratio

C

C	Celsius
CAME	civil aviation medical examiner (Canada)
CAMI	Civil Aerospace Medical Institute (FAA)
CAMI	confirm, activate, monitor, intervene
CARs	Canadian Aviation Regulations
CAST	Commercial Aviation Safety Team
CAVOK	ceiling and visibility OK
CDP	counter-drum-pointer altimeter
CDU	control display unit
CFI	certified flight instructor (U.S.)
CFIT	controlled flight into terrain
CFR	crash fire rescue
CFR	Code of Federal Regulations (U.S.)
CG	center of gravity
CHL	conductive hearing loss
CICTT	CAST/ICAO Common Taxonomy Team
CO	carbon monoxide
CO_2	carbon dioxide
COHb	carboxyhemoglobin
CP	counter-pointer altimeter
CPDLC	controller-pilot data link communication
CRE	control reversal error
CRM	crew resource management
CTOL	collision with obstacles during takeoff or landing
CVR	cockpit voice recorder

D

DA	decision altitude
DA	density altitude
DAL	Delta Air Lines
dB	decibel
DCS	decompression sickness
DEP	design eye position
DERP	design eye reference point
DFDR	digital flight data recorder
DH	decision height

DME	distance measuring equipment
DNF	do not fly medications
DNI	do not issue (a medical certificate)
DP	drum-pointer altimeter
DRM	dispatch resource management

E

E-AB	experimental-amateur built
EAL	Eastern Air Lines
ECAM	electronic centralized aircraft monitoring
ECL	electronic checklist
ECS	environmental control system
EEG	electroencephalogram
EFB	electronic flight bag
EFIS	electronic flight information system
EICAS	engine-indicating and crew-alerting system
EMAS	engineered materials arresting system
EMS	emergency medical services
EPR	engine pressure ratio
EPT	effective performance time
ER	edge rate
ERA	engineering reliability analysis
ETA	estimated time of arrival

F

F	Fahrenheit
FA	flight attendant
FAA	Federal Aviation Administration
FADEC	full authority digital engine control system
FAF	final approach fix
FARs	Federal Aviation Regulations (U.S.)
FCU	flight control unit
FD	flight director
FDP	flight duty period
FDR	flight data recorder
FE	flight engineer
FGS	flight guidance system
5M	man, machine, media, mission, management
FL	flight level
FLC or FLCH	flight level change mode
FMA	flight mode annunciator
FMC	flight management computer
FMS	flight management system
FO	first officer
FOM	flight operations manual
FOQA	flight operational quality assurance
fpm	feet per minute
FSDO	Flight Standards District Office (FAA)
FSF	Flight Safety Foundation
FSS	flight service station
FTD	flight training device

G

g	acceleration produced by gravity
G	acceleration produced by aircraft maneuvering
GA	general aviation
GAO	Government Accountability Office (U.S.)
GI	gastrointestinal
GI	glycemic index
G-LOC	G-induced loss of consciousness
GPS	global positioning system
GPWS	ground proximity warning system
G_X	longitudinal acceleration
G_Y	lateral acceleration
G_Z	vertical acceleration
$+G_Z$	positive vertical acceleration
$-G_Z$	negative vertical acceleration

H

HAT	height above touchdown
Hb	hemoglobin
HbO_2	oxyhemoglobin
HEMS	helicopter emergency medical service
HFACS	human factors analysis and classification system
Hg	mercury
HOLD	altitude hold mode
hPa	hectopascal
HRA	human reliability assessment
Hz	Hertz

I

IAP	instrument approach procedure
IAS	indicated airspeed
IATA	International Air Transport Association
ICAO	International Civil Aviation Organization
ICE	airframe icing
IFR	instrument flight rules
ILS	instrument landing system
IMC	instrument meteorological conditions
InFO	Information for Operators (FAA)
in Hg	inches of mercury
IPS	icing protection system
ISA	international standard atmosphere

K

KLM	Royal Dutch Airlines
km	kilometer

L

LASIK	laser-assisted in situ keratomileusis
LNAV	lateral navigation
LOC-G	loss of control on the ground

LOC-I	loss of aircraft control in flight	OSHA	Occupational Safety and Health Administration (U.S.)
LOE	Letter of Evidence	OTC	over-the-counter medications
LOFT	line-oriented flight training	O_2	oxygen
LOS	line-oriented simulations		
LOSA	line operations safety audit	**P**	
LTM	long-term memory	PA	public address system
L/W	length-to-width ratio	PAN	positional alcohol nystagmus
		PAPI	precision approach path indicator
M		PAVE	pilot, aircraft, environment, external pressures (FAA)
MAC	midair collision	PED	personal electronic device
mb	millibar	PF	pilot flying
MCP	mode control panel	PFD	primary flight display
MCTOW	maximum certified takeoff weight	PFI	primary flight instruments
MDA	minimum descent altitude	pH	potential of hydrogen
MEDEVAC	medical evacuation	PIC	pilot in command
MEL	minimum equipment list	PIREP	pilot (weather) report
MFD	multi-function display	PLI	party-line information
MHz	megahertz	PLMD	periodic limb movement disorder
mm	millimeter	PM	pilot monitoring
MOCA	minimum obstruction clearance altitude	PRICE	pressure, regulator, indicator, connections, emergency
MRM	maintenance resource management	PRK	photorefractive keratectomy
MSL	mean sea level	PROTE	portable reduced oxygen training enclosure
MTBR	material to be remembered	PSI	pounds per square inch
		PTCH	pitch mode
N			
n	load factor	**R**	
NASA	National Aeronautics and Space Administration	RE	runway excursion
ND	navigation display	REL	recommended (noise level) exposure limit
NDB	nondirectional beacon	REM	rapid eye movement sleep
NHTSA	U.S. National Highway Traffic Safety Administration	RI	runway incursion
		RNAV	area navigation
NIHL	noise-induced hearing loss	RPM	revolutions per minute
NIL	noise immission level	RT	reaction time
NIMC	night instrument meteorological conditions	RTF	radiotelephony
NIOSH	U.S. National Institute for Occupational Safety and Health	RTO	rejected takeoff
		RVR	runway visual range
nm	nanometer		
NM	nautical mile	**S**	
NMAC	near midair collision	SA	situational awareness
NORDO	no radio	SAFO	Safety Alert for Operators (FAA)
NOTAM	notices to airmen	SCF-NP	system/component failure—non-powerplant
NRR	noise reduction rating		
N_2	nitrogen	SCF-PP	system/component failure—powerplant
NTSB	National Transportation Safety Board (U.S.)	SCN	suprachiasmatic nucleus
NVFR	night visual flight rules	SD	spatial disorientation
NVMC	night visual meteorological conditions	SHELL	software, hardware, environment, liveware others, liveware crew
NWA	Northwest Airlines		
		SM	statute miles
O		SMS	safety management systems
OCC	Oceanic Control Coordinator		
OSA	obstructive sleep apnea		

SNR	signal-to-noise ratio
SODA	statement of demonstrated ability
SOP	standard operating procedures
SRM	single-pilot resource management
STM	short-term memory
STSS	short-term sensory storage (memory)
SVFR	special VFR
SVS	synthetic vision system
SWA	Southwest Airlines

T

TAS	true airspeed
TAWS	terrain awareness and warning system
TEM	threat and error management
3P	three-pointer altimeter
TO/GA	takeoff/go-around
TOWS	takeoff warning system
TSA	time since awakening
TSB	Transportation Safety Board of Canada
TUC	time of useful consciousness
TWA	Trans World Airlines

U

UAL	United Airlines
UAS	undesired aircraft state
UIMC	unintended flight into IMC
UNICOM	universal communications

UNK	unknown or undetermined
UPS	United Parcel Service
USAF	U.S. Air Force
USOS	runway undershoot/overshoot

V

VFR	visual flight rules
VHF	very high frequency
VMC	visual meteorological conditions
VNAV	vertical navigation
VOR	VHF omnidirectional range
V_1	takeoff decision speed
V_2	takeoff safety speed
V_{NE}	never exceed speed
V_R	takeoff rotation speed
V_{REF}	reference landing speed
V_X	best angle of climb speed
VVM	verbalize, verify, monitor
V_Y	best rate of climb speed
VS	vertical speed mode

W

WOCL	window of circadian low

Y

YPLL	years of potential life lost

Appendix B: Aviation Occurrence Categories

Two reports published in 1997—the *White House Commission on Aviation Safety and Security and the National Civil Aviation Review Commission*—challenged the government and aviation industry to reduce the U.S. commercial aviation accident rate by 80 percent over 10 years. In response, the FAA and industry collaborated to form the Commercial Aviation Safety Team (CAST). The goal of this task force, consisting of a variety of stakeholders including the FAA, NASA, pilot and air-traffic-controller unions, and airport, aerospace, and airline associations, is to reduce the commercial aviation fatality risk by 50 percent from 2010 to 2025.[1]

In 1999, the CAST joined with the International Civil Aviation Organization (ICAO) to form the CAST/ICAO Common Taxonomy Team (CICTT) that consists of members from industry and government in several countries, including the United States, Canada, United Kingdom, the European Union, France, Italy, and the Netherlands.[2]

The goal of aircraft accident investigation is to determine probable cause, or causal factors, so that those in government and industry may take informed measures to reduce future accidents. Since different organizations and countries use different terms and definitions to describe the same event, a major goal of the CICTT is to develop standardized definitions and taxonomies (i.e., classifications) of aircraft occurrences (accidents and incidents). Worldwide adoption of these definitions and terms better aids investigators in precisely determining the causal factors of aircraft accidents and incidents, which in turn leads to better strategies to prevent them.

The following is an abridged list of aviation accident and incident categories, or defining events, derived from the CICTT's *Aviation Occurrence Categories: Definitions and Usage Notes (Revised December 2017 (4.7))*. Consult this document for more detailed descriptions.[3]

Occurrence category	Acronym	Description	Examples
Abnormal runway contact	ARC	Any landing or takeoff involving abnormal runway or landing surface contact.	Hard, off-center, nose-wheel first, or gear-up landing. Tail or wingtip strike.
Abrupt maneuver	AMAN	The intentional abrupt maneuvering of the aircraft by the flight crew.	Abrupt avoidance of collision with terrain, obstacle, weather, or other aircraft.
Aerodrome	ADRM	Occurrences involving aerodrome (airport) design, service, or functionality issues.	Poor airport lighting or signage. Inadequate snow removal.
Airprox/TCAS alert/loss of separation/ NMAC	MAC	Air proximity issues, loss of separation or near collisions or collisions between aircraft in flight.	Two aircraft get too close to each other or collide in flight. TCAS/ACAS alerts.

Continued...

Occurrence category	Acronym	Description	Examples
ATM/CNS	ATM	Occurrences involving ATC/air traffic management (ATM) or communication, navigation, surveillance (CNS) service issues.	NAVAID outage or errors. Controller error or ATC radar/computer failure.
Bird	BIRD	Occurrences involving collisions/near collisions with bird(s).	Collision with bird(s) in any phase of flight.
Cabin safety events	CABIN	Miscellaneous occurrences in the passenger cabin of transport category aircraft.	Supplemental oxygen problems. Missing or malfunctioning cabin emergency equipment.
Collision with obstacle(s) during takeoff and landing	CTOL	Collision with obstacle(s) during takeoff or landing while airborne. Crew aware of obstacle.	Contact with trees, wall, snowdrift, structure power cable, offshore platform.
Controlled flight into, or toward, terrain	CFIT	In-flight collision or near collision with terrain, water, or obstacle without crew awareness of impending collision.	Visual landing illusion causing premature surface contact. Crew not monitoring altitude in IMC or at night.
Evacuation	EVAC	Occurrence involving problems with evacuation or injury during an evacuation.	Unnecessary evacuation or injury during evacuation.
External load related occurrences	EXTL	Occurrences during or because of external load or external cargo operations.	External load or load-lift equipment contacts surface, becomes entangled in helicopter rotor, or injures ground crew.
Fire/smoke (non-impact)	F-NI	Fire or smoke in or on the aircraft—in flight or on the ground—that is not the result of impact.	Engine fire. Fire or smoke from component failure or malfunctions in the cockpit, cabin, or cargo area.
Fire/smoke (post-impact)	F-POST	Fire/Smoke resulting from impact.	Post-impact/accident fire.
Fuel related	FUEL	One or more powerplants experienced reduced or no power output due to fuel exhaustion, starvation, mismanagement, contamination, or wrong fuel, or carburetor and/or induction icing.	Pilot allowed fuel tank to run dry. Insufficient fuel quantity or incorrect fuel type. Water or other contaminants entered fuel system.
Glider towing related events	GTOW	Premature, inadvertent, or non-release during towing; entangling with towing, cable, loss of control; or impact into towing aircraft/winch.	Loss of control because of entering towing aircraft's wake turbulence. Airspeed out of limits during tow.
Ground collision	GCOL	Collision while taxiing to or from a runway in use.	Collision with aircraft, obstacle, building, person, etc., while on surface other than an active runway.
Ground handling	RAMP	Occurrences during, or as a result of, ground handling operations.	Occurrence caused by jet blast, prop/rotor downwash, or improperly secured door. Events involving boarding, loading, deplaning, or pushback/towing.
Icing	ICE	Accumulation of snow, ice, freezing rain, or frost on aircraft surfaces that adversely affects aircraft control or performance.	Accumulation of ice—on ground or in flight—on windscreen, sensors, antennae, wings, and engine intakes.
Loss of control —ground	LOC-G	Loss of aircraft control while the aircraft is on the ground.	Contaminated runway (snow, ice, etc.) leads to loss of control while taxiing.
Loss of control—in flight	LOC-I	Loss of aircraft control while, or deviation from intended flight path, in flight.	Stall. Loss of control from configuration issues. Pilot-induced or pilot-assisted oscillations.

Occurrence category	Acronym	Description	Examples
Loss of lifting conditions en route	LOLI	Landing en route due to loss of lifting conditions (applicable only to aircraft that rely on static lift, e.g., gliders, balloons, airships).	Loss of updrafts to maintain altitude for glider. Motorglider engine unable to re-start.
Low altitude operations	LALT	Collision or near collision with obstacles or terrain while intentionally operating near the surface (excludes takeoff or landing phases).	Buzzing neighbor's house. Crop duster hits low wires. Flying too low in mountain canyon in attempt to maintain VFR.
Medical	MED	Occurrences involving illnesses of persons on board an aircraft.	Pilot experiences hypoxia or falls ill in flight. Passenger's illness preoccupies crew.
Navigation errors	NAV	Occurrences involving the incorrect navigation of aircraft on the ground or in the air.	Incorrect inputs into FMS. Airspace incursion. Altitude bust. Landing on wrong runway or airport.
Other	OTHR	Any occurrence not covered under another category.	
Runway excursion	RE	A veer off or overrun off the runway surface.	Landing fast or long resulting in runway overrun. Departing with excessive crosswind causing veer off side of runway.
Runway incursion	RI	Any occurrence at an aerodrome involving the incorrect presence of an aircraft, vehicle, or person on the protected area of a surface designated for the landing and takeoff of aircraft.	Aircraft departing while other aircraft is crossing from a landing. Aircraft landing when another aircraft is on runway waiting for departure clearance.
Security related	SEC	Criminal/security acts which result in accidents or incidents (per Annex 13 to the Convention on International Civil Aviation). Technically not classified as an accident.	Hijacking, sabotage, bomb on board, flight control interference, suicide, etc.
System or component failure or malfunction (non-powerplant)	SCF-NP	Failure or malfunction of an aircraft system or component other than the powerplant.	Improper maintenance of component. Failure in software or database. Flap failure. Runaway trim.
System or component failure or malfunction (powerplant)	SCF-PP	Failure or malfunction of an aircraft system or component related to the powerplant.	Failure of engine, propeller system, powerplant controls including resulting from improper maintenance.
Turbulence encounter	TURB	In-flight turbulence encounter.	Turbulence from clear air, mountain wave, mechanical, and/or wake vortices.
Undershoot or overshoot	USOS	A touchdown off the runway/helipad/helideck surface.	Landing short of runway. Black-hole and other illusions can also cause this.
Unintended flight in IMC	UIMC	Unintended flight in IMC.	Inadvertent VFR flight into IMC by VFR-only pilot leading to CFIT or LOC-I.
Unknown or undetermined	UNK	Insufficient information exists to categorize the occurrence.	Missing aircraft.
Wildlife	WILD	Collision with, risk of collision, or evasive action taken by an aircraft to avoid wildlife on the movement area of an aerodrome.	Encounter with wildlife on a runway or taxiway. Gear collapses as result of evasive action taken to avoid contact with a deer on runway.
Wind shear or thunderstorm	WSTRW	Flight into wind shear or thunderstorm.	Microburst causes aircraft to collide with surface. Loss of airspeed results in LOC-I.

Occurrence Category by Group

Occurrence category	Acronym
Airborne	
Abrupt maneuver	AMAN
Airprox/TCAS alert/loss of separation/NMAC	MAC
Controlled flight into or toward terrain	CFIT
Fuel related	FUEL
Glider towing related events	GTOW
Loss of control–in flight	LOC-I
Loss of lifting conditions en route	LOLI
Low altitude operations	LALT
Navigation errors	NAV
Unintended flight in IMC	UIMC
Aircraft	
Fire/smoke (non-impact)	F-NI
System/component failure or malfunction (non-powerplant)	SCF-NP
System/component failure or malfunction (powerplant)	SCF-PP
Ground Operations	
Evacuation	EVAC
Fire/smoke (post-impact)	F-POST
Ground collision	GCOL
Ground handling	RAMP
Loss of control—ground	LOC-G
Navigation errors	NAV
Runway excursion	RE
Runway incursion	RI
Wildlife	WILD
Miscellaneous	
Bird	BIRD
Cabin safety events	CABIN
External load related occurrences	EXTL
Medical	MED
Other	OTHR
Security related	SEC
Unknown or undetermined	UNK
Non-Aircraft-Related	
Aerodrome	ADRM
ATM/CNS	ATM
Takeoff and Landing	
Abnormal runway contact	ARC
Collision with obstacle(s) during takeoff and landing	CTOL
Undershoot/overshoot	USOS

Weather	
Icing	ICE
Turbulence encounter	TURB
Wind shear or thunderstorm	WSTRW

1. The Commercial Aviation Safety Team, *History* (2017). Available at www.cast-safety.org/apex/f?p=102:1:10847808259073::NO::P1_X:history.

2. The CAST/ICAO Common Taxonomy Team, *About CICTT* (2014). Available at www.intlaviationstandards.org/apex/f?p=240:1:2202876 027673::NO::P1_X:.

3. Available at www.enac.gov.it/sites/default/files/allegati/2018-Lug/CICTT%20Occ.%20Cat.%20%28v%204.7%20-%20Dec%20 2017%29.pdf.

Appendix C: Glossary

Ability bias. The belief that you are better than most people when it comes to personal virtues, skills, and abilities. (Chapter 17) *See* **optimistic bias**, **invulnerability**, **impulsivity**, **macho**, and **resignation**.

Acceleration. The rate of change (over time) of velocity. Velocity refers to both the magnitude (speed) and direction of a moving object. (Chapter 8)

Accommodation. The process of the eyes' focusing. (Chapter 6). It is also a binocular cue to depth perception. (Chapter 12). *See* **binocular cues**.

Active noise reduction (ANR). Also known as *active noise control* or *noise cancellation*, ANR systems used in aircraft and crew headsets reduce noise caused by the aircraft engines and airframe by transmitting sound waves of the same frequency and amplitude of the unwanted noise, but 180-degrees out of phase (antiphase), thereby cancelling the noise waves. (Chapter 7)

Acute fatigue. Short-term transient fatigue that often dissipates after some rest or a single sleep period. (Chapter 10) *See* **cumulative fatigue**.

Aerial perspective. A monocular cue to distance perception. Distant objects are seen as more blurred and bluish in color due to the greater degree of light scattering from particulate matter, while truer color and greater detail is seen when objects are closer due to reduced light scattering. This cue can lead pilots to overestimate an object's distance on hazy days and underestimate it on exceptionally clear (usually dry as well) days. (Chapter 12)

Airborne collision avoidance system (ACAS). ACAS interrogates ATC transponders of nearby aircraft and displays potential collision threats by providing traffic advisories (TAs) to assist pilots in visually acquiring the intruding aircraft and, when another aircraft gets too close, resolution advisories (RAs) in the form of voice commands and visual guidance displayed on the vertical speed indicator and primary flight display (PFD) to indicate the desired vertical speed to be flown to help the crew avert a midair collision. Traffic-alert and collision avoidance system (TCAS) is one type of ACAS. (Chapters 1, 15, and 20)

Air carrier. In the U.S., a commercial aviation operator that has been certificated under Part 121 or 135 to carry passengers or cargo for hire. (Chapter 1)

Aircraft accident. An occurrence associated with the operation of an aircraft which takes place between the time any person boards the aircraft with the intention of flight and all such persons have disembarked, and in which any person suffers death or serious injury, or in which the aircraft receives substantial damage (49 CFR §830.2). (Chapter 1)

Aircraft incident. An occurrence other than an accident, associated with the operation of an aircraft, which affects or could affect the safety of operations (49 CFR §830.2). (Chapter 1)

Airplane upset. An event in which an airplane unintentionally exceeds parameters normally considered safe in flight. Often called an *unusual attitude* that sometimes leads to loss of control in flight (LOC-I), an airplane upset involves a pitch attitude greater than 25 degrees nose up or 10 degrees nose down (pitch upset), a bank angle greater than 45 degrees (roll upset), and/or airspeeds inappropriate for the conditions. A variety of factors can cause an upset—which can involve a stall or spin—including wake turbulence, airframe icing, severe weather, microbursts, wind shear, and/or inadvertent/unanticipated autopilot-disconnect. (Chapters 15 and 20) *See* **loss of control in flight**.

Airworthiness Directive (AD). A legally enforceable regulation issued by the regulator (FAA, TC, etc.) to correct an unsafe condition in an aircraft product (i.e., an aircraft, engine, propeller, or appliance). (Chapter 15)

Almost loss of consciousness (A-LOC). The experience of near loss of consciousness, primarily involving the cognitive deficits (e.g., confusion, stupor, memory loss, amnesia, etc.) usually associated with the relative incapacitation stage of G-LOC, but of somewhat lesser intensity and which does not involve complete loss of consciousness (G-LOC). (Chapter 8)

Alternobaric vertigo. *See* **pressure vertigo**.

Altitude decompression sickness (DCS). At low ambient pressures associated with flight at or above 18,000 to 25,000 feet in an unpressurized cabin, or after a sudden decompression in a pressurized cabin, nitrogen in solution in the body evolves into gaseous form leading to a variety of deleterious symptoms such as the bends (limbs, joints, muscles), the chokes (lungs), the staggers (neurological and visual), and the creeps (skin). (Chapter 5) *See* **bends**, **chokes**, **staggers**, and **creeps**.

Altitude dysbarism. A term sometimes used to describe the various ills which are experienced at high altitudes that involve *trapped* and/or *evolved* gases in the body, but not hypoxia. (Chapter 5)

Ambient vision. Peripheral vision, which is good at detecting motion and determining orientation in space, but not good at seeing fine detail or stationary targets. (Chapter 6) *See* **foveal vision**.

Analog displays. Analog displays present qualitative, continuous information that represents the state of an aircraft attribute in symbolic or pictorial format. Compared to digital displays, direction, and rate of change are relatively easy to ascertain in analog displays, but precise numeric values are not. (Chapter 15)

Anchoring and adjustment heuristic. In situations where judgments need to be revised (adjusted) from initial data (the anchor), people tend to make insufficient judgments depending on the value of the initial information. (Chapter 17)

Anthropometry. Study of the measurement of the size and shape of the human body. (Chapter 3)

Anti-G straining maneuver (AGSM). A maneuver that involves simultaneous muscle tensing in the arms, legs, buttocks, and abdomen, with cyclic breathing at regular intervals to raise tolerance thresholds while pulling +G_z. (Chapter 8)

Areas of vulnerability. Predictable segments of flight that are particularly vulnerable to flight path deviations and when the severity of the consequences of deviating from flight path parameters is the greatest. For example, taxiing close to obstacles or active runways, flying at low altitude close to the surface and/or below the level of surrounding terrain, initiating climbs and descents, within 1,000 feet of level-offs, turning, and changing speed or configuration. (Chapters 14, 15, and 20)

Armstrong line. The altitude of approximately 63,000 feet MSL at which the atmospheric pressure is so low that bodily fluids change from a liquid to gaseous state—i.e., blood boils. (Chapter 4)

Astigmatism. Blurred vision from uneven focusing due to irregularly shaped cornea or lens. (Chapter 6)

Attention. The process of detecting, and orientating toward, sensory inputs. (Chapter 14) *See* **vigilance** and **monitoring**.

Attention switching. Switching attention back and forth from one stimulus to another. This sequential (serial) switching is what is often erroneously called *multitasking*, the so-called ability to do several parallel tasks simultaneously. Pilots flying, navigating, and communicating at the same time, and air traffic controllers communicating with several aircraft at a time, are very good at attention switching because of their extensive training. (Chapter 14)

Attenuate. To reduce the intensity of, or weaken, a sound (noise) or signal (speech). (Chapter 7)

Auditory fatigue. Temporary decline in hearing ability due to prolonged exposure to noise. If high noise levels are avoided to allow the auditory receptors to recover then permanent hearing loss can usually be avoided. (Chapter 7)

Augmented flight. An unaugmented flight contains the minimum number of flight crew members necessary to safely pilot an aircraft. An augmented flight crew has more than the minimum number of flight crew members required by the airplane type certificate to operate the aircraft to allow a flight crew member to be replaced by another qualified flight crew member for in-flight rest. (Chapter 10)

Autokinetic effect. In a very dark environment a small stationary light appears to move about a person's field of view when stared at directly. (Chapter 6)

Automatic flight control system (AFCS). Also called the *autopilot flight director system* (AFDS) or *automatic flight guidance system* (AFGS), the AFCS is part of flight control and flight guidance system (FGS) that provides visual guidance for manual control (hand-flying) of flight and direct control using computers or other means to achieve a desired aircraft trajectory (altitude, airspeed, track, etc.). (Chapter 15)

Automatic processing. Skills that are overlearned, such as stick-and-rudder psychomotor skills, become so automatic that they can be accomplished using minimal attentional resources freeing up more resources to devote to other tasks. (Chapter 14)

Automation addiction. Pilots become so dependent on the automation that they are unable to fly effectively without it, such as when they need to manually fly (hand-fly) the aircraft. (Chapter 15)

Automation complacency. The tendency for flight crews to reduce their monitoring responsibilities because of their overreliance on the automation to fly their aircraft. (Chapter 15)

Automation paradox. Designed to reduce flight crew workload, the extra effort in managing automated flight systems can sometimes increase it. (Chapter 15)

Automation surprise. The reaction a flight crew member experiences when the automation responds differently to what he or she expects it to. (Chapter 15)

Availability heuristic. Tendency to estimate the frequency of something based on how easy the phenomenon can be recalled from memory. Recent, familiar or vivid information or events are more easily remembered and hence their frequency or probability is often overestimated. (Chapter 17)

Aviation Safety Action Program (ASAP). In partnership with the FAA, an ASAP is a program at participating airlines that encourages employees to voluntary report safety critical information that may be critical to identifying potential precursors to accidents. These safety issues are resolved through corrective action rather than through punishment or discipline.

Aviator's breathing oxygen. Oxygen that is purer and drier than other types of oxygen (e.g., medical, industrial oxygen) and which meets the standards required for flying at high altitudes. (Chapter 4)

Barany chair. Named after Hungarian physiologist Robert Barany, an early researcher into the vestibular system who won the Nobel Prize in medicine in 1914 for his work in vestibular orientation, the Barany chair is similar to a swivel office chair, but with foot rests in addition to arm rests, and is used to demonstrate a variety of disorientation scenarios to blindfolded subjects. (Chapter 9)

Barodontalgia. Tooth pain during ascent from trapped gas in a tooth, usually caused by imperfect dental work, such as a loose filling or an improperly filled root canal. (Chapter 5)

Barosinusitis. Sinus pain brought on by a sinus blockage. (Chapter 5)

Barotitis media. Pain and possible ear damage occurs when trapped air in the middle ear cannot escape and the pressure cannot be equalized with that of the outside ambient pressure in the outer ear. (Chapter 5)

BasicMed. A program approved in 2016 that relieves student, recreational, and private pilots from holding an FAA medical certificate, provided they possess a U.S. driver's license, obtain a physical exam from a state-licensed physician using the Comprehensive Medical Examination Checklist, complete a BasicMed medical education course, and possessed an FAA medical after July 14, 2006. Aircraft restrictions—maximum certificate takeoff weight 6,000 pounds, certified to carry no more

than 6 occupants—and operating requirements (operates in the U.S. below 18,000 feet MSL at speeds not exceeding 250 knots with no more than 5 passengers) apply. (Chapter 11)

Belief perseverance. Maintaining trust in the truthfulness of our beliefs even in the face of evidence that discredits them. (Chapter 17)

Bends. The most common Type I DCS symptom—joint pain—which results from nitrogen bubbling into the joints and muscles. (Chapter 5) *See* **chokes**, **creeps**, and **staggers**.

Best practice. Industry-recognized procedures or set of behaviors that experience and research has proven to result in the best possible outcome for a given task. (Chapter 20)

Binocular convergence. A binocular cue to distance perception. The eye-muscle strain that results from both eyes converging when focusing on closer objects communicates distance information to the brain. (Chapter 12) *See* **binocular cues**.

Binocular cues. Physiological depth perception cues, such as accommodation, binocular convergence and retinal disparity that arise from viewing an object with two eyes. (Chapter 12)

Biodynamics. The study of the body's response to dynamic (acceleration/deceleration) forces imposed upon it. (Chapter 8)

Biological clock. Internal mechanism that regulates the ebb and flow of many bodily functions throughout the day. (Chapter 10)

Black-hole approach illusion. Sometimes called the *featureless terrain illusion*. In black-hole conditions on dark nights (moonless and/or an overcast sky conditions) with no ground lighting between the aircraft and the runway threshold, a pilot who is relying solely on outside visual cues for guidance will likely fly an approach that is too low resulting in a CFIT accident short of the runway. (Chapter 12) *See* **dark-night conditions**.

Blackout. The complete loss of vision, while still remaining conscious, that occurs when exposed to positive vertical Gs ("gees") of approximately $+3.5\ G_Z$ to $+4.5\ G_Z$ when not using countermeasures such as a G-suit or anti-G straining maneuvers. These values depend on the G-onset rate and individual tolerance. (Chapter 8) *See* **grayout** and **G-induced loss of consciousness (G-LOC)**.

Blossom effect. When looking at another aircraft on a collision course with yours its apparent size looks very small until it is very close when it quickly gets bigger (blossoms) in size, perhaps even too late to take effective evasive action. (Chapter 6)

Boyle's Law. At a constant temperature, the volume of a gas is inversely proportional to the pressure exerted on it. (Chapter 4) *See* **Dalton's Law**, **Fick's Law**, **Graham's Law** and **Henry's Law**.

Bystander effect. Also known as *bystander apathy*. Individuals are less likely to render assistance to a victim when other onlookers are present. As the number of onlookers increases the less likely a single individual will notice the incident, interpret the incident as an emergency requiring assistance, or assume responsibility to render assistance. (Chapter 18)

Cabin altitude. The actual air pressure inside the cabin of an airplane, whether pressurized or unpressurized, expressed as an equivalent altitude above mean sea level. (Chapter 4)

Central vision blindness. Since the foveal cones are shut down when using pure night vision (scotopic vision), the absence of rods in the fovea results in the inability to see a dim light source when staring directly at it. (Chapter 6)

Checklist. A formal list used to identify, schedule, compare, or verify a group of elements or actions. A checklist is used as a visual and/or oral aid that enables the user to enhance short-term human memory. Read-and-do checklists are used to ensure items are accomplished in the proper sequence while challenge-response checklists are used to confirm items have already been accomplished. (Chapter 16)

Checkride-itis. The phenomenon of an otherwise competent pilot performing poorly and failing a checkride (practical flight test) not because they're incapable of successfully demonstrating the skills necessary to pass it, but because they are too anxious about failing. (Chapter 19)

Choice-supportive bias. Also known as *deciding-becomes-believing*. After we have made a decision we have tendency to increase our belief in the superiority of the chosen option and our belief in the inferiority of the option(s) we didn't choose. (Chapter 17)

Chokes. A Type II DCS symptom that involves breathing difficulty and pain as a result of nitrogen bubbling in the lungs. (Chapter 5) *See* **bends**, **creeps**, and **staggers**.

Chunking. Grouping information into larger or higher-information chunks to increase the amount of information that can be stored in working memory at any one time. (Chapter 16)

Circadian dysrhythmia. *See* **jet lag**.

Circadian rhythms. Up and down fluctuations of daily physiological functions—such as sleep/wake cycle, blood pressure, temperature, hormone release, and digestion—controlled by an internal body clock. (Chapter 10)

Closed-loop feedback system. A system that involves continuous feedback to enable continuous control inputs to maintain a desired state. (Chapter 15)

Cocktail party effect. The breaking through of unattended salient, pertinent, or novel stimuli into your conscious perception, as might occur when your attention is directed at the person you are talking to at a cocktail party (or other social gathering) and you perceive your name being spoken by someone else in another group that you are not paying attention to. (Chapter 14)

Code switching. During a conversation multilingual pilots and/or controllers switch back and forth between English and their mother tongue, or unilingual speakers switch between different English dialects. (Chapter 13)

Cognitive dissonance. Mental discomfort caused by evidence that contradicts what you think or believe about something. (Chapter 17)

Cognitive psychology. The scientific study of human thought and behavior. (Chapter 3)

Color coding. Use of color to distinguish controls or displays (or their individual elements) from others. For example, the airspeed indicator contains colored lines and arcs to indicate critical speeds such as stall speed, flap operating speed range, maximum structural cruising speed and never exceed speed. (Chapter 15)

Color vision deficiency. Sometimes called *color blindness*, color vision deficiency is the Inability to distinguish between certain colors due to a deficiency of photopigments in retinal cones or the absence of certain types of cones altogether. (Chapter 6)

Communication. The transfer of information between people using speech, written words, body language, or other means. (Chapter 7)

Compensatory stage of hypoxia. In this stage of hypoxia (generally between 10,000 and 15,000 feet MSL) the body tries to *compensate* for reduced oxygen by significantly increasing the rate and depth of breathing, and by increasing the pulse rate, blood circulation rate, and cardiac output. Flight at these altitudes can only be accomplished for short durations without experiencing the incapacitating symptoms of hypoxia. (Chapter 4) *See* **indifferent stage of hypoxia**, **disturbance stage of hypoxia,** and **critical stage of hypoxia**.

Cones. Receptors in retina of eye that convert incoming light energy into neural impulses during day (photopic) vision. (Chapter 6) *See* **rods**.

Confirmation bias. The tendency to look for information that confirms, rather than disconfirms, our beliefs. Unfortunately, ambiguous information may be interpreted as confirming our beliefs, stopping any search for alternative evidence that might disconfirm the accuracy of our hunches or conclusions. (Chapter 17)

Conformity. Changing your beliefs or behavior to comply with real or imagined group pressure. (Chapter 18)

Conservative shift. The tendency of an individual's viewpoints and opinions to shift towards greater caution and conservatism while participating in a group than when acting alone—especially if that person's views and opinions leaned toward caution before interaction and discussion with the group took place. Group decision making leans towards greater caution than that of its individual members if most of the group members' viewpoints and opinions were somewhat cautious before group interaction and discussion took place. (Chapter 18) *See* **risky shift**.

Control-display incompatibility. Occurs when control devices (knobs, handles, switches) and symbols on displays do not move in the same direction as the part they are supposed to represent. (Chapter 15)

Controlled flight into terrain (CFIT). A mechanically normally functioning aircraft, under the control of a fully qualified pilot or flight crew, is inadvertently flown into the ground, water, or an obstacle. (Chapters 1 and 20). *See* **loss of control in flight** and **uncontrolled flight into terrain**.

Controller-pilot data link communication (CPDLC). A system air traffic controllers and pilots use to communicate with each other that involves sending and receiving clearances and other information via written words presented on a visual display, reducing congestion on a single voice-communication frequency. (Chapter 13)

Control reversal error. Control inputs that that are exactly the opposite of what is required for desired flight parameters. A phenomenon of spatial disorientation. (Chapter 9)

Controls. Control column (or side-stick control), handles, levers, dials, and knobs used by the pilot to change various aspects of an aircraft's state (pitch, bank, altitude, speed, power setting, configuration, etc.). (Chapter 15)

Coriolis illusion. A powerful illusion brought about by movement in two or more axes—such as when moving your head to pick up a pencil while in a steady turn—which causes cupulae deflection in opposite directions producing sensations of motion in a third axis. (Chapter 9)

Corporate culture. A variety of components including an organization's shared beliefs, values, written and unwritten rules (norms) and behavioral practices that make up its social and working environment. (Chapters 2 and 18)

Countermeasure. Any measure or action taken to counter a threat or error. (Chapter 20)

Creeps. A Type I DCS symptom that involves prickling, tingling, itching and other manifestations resulting from nitrogen bubbling near the nerves of the skin. (Chapter 5) *See* **bends**, **chokes**, and **staggers**.

Crewed flight deck. An aircraft that legally requires two or more pilots to operate. (Chapter 3) *See* **flight crew**.

Crew resource management (CRM). The effective use of all available resources—people, information, and equipment—to achieve safe and efficient flight operations. (Chapters 2 and 19) *See* **single-pilot resource management**.

Critical phase of flight. All ground operations involving taxi, takeoff and landing, and all other flight operations conducted below 10,000 feet, except cruise flight. (Chapter 14) *See* **sterile cockpit rule**.

Critical stage of hypoxia. Above 20,000 feet unconsciousness can occur from hypoxia in about three to 10 minutes from circulatory or central nervous system failure or cardiovascular collapse. (Chapter 4) *See* **indifferent stage of hypoxia**, **compensatory stage of hypoxia**, and **disturbance stage of hypoxia**.

Cumulative fatigue. Longer lasting than acute fatigue, cumulative, or chronic, fatigue results from insufficient recovery from acute fatigue, sleep debt, poor quality sleep, circadian dhysrythmia, and/or significant periods of high mental workload. (Chapter 10) *See* **acute fatigue**.

Dalton's Law. The total pressure of a mixture of gases is equal to the sum of the partial pressures of each individual gas ($P_{total} = P_1 + P_2 + P_3...$). (Chapter 4) *See* **Boyle's Law, Fick's Law, Graham's Law,** and **Henry's Law**.

Dark adaptation. The process of changing from cone vision during daylight to rod vision at night. The process takes a minimum of 30 minutes in a darkened environment. (Chapter 6)

Dark-focus. *See* **empty-field myopia**.

Dark-night conditions. Generally, no ground lights and a lack of moonlight or starlight to illuminate the surface. Specifically, a lack of cultural (human-made) terrain lighting and minimum (or a complete absence of) celestial illumination from the moon or stars or illumination that is obscured by a broken or overcast sky condition. (Chapter 9) *See* **black-hole approach illusion**.

Decision errors. Errors in determining, choosing and executing the correct course of action by incorrectly arriving at a correct solution to a problem, making the wrong choice, or by incorrectly following standard procedures (SOPs, checklists). (Chapters 2 and 17)

Decision-making biases. Distortions, or errors, in thinking, judgment, and decision making. (Chapter 17)

Decompression sickness (DCS). *See* **altitude decompression sickness**.

Deep sleep. The deepest stages (Stage 3 and 4) of non-REM (rapid eye movement) sleep that follows Stage 1 and 2 light sleep. Many physiological functions and brain wave activity are at their lowest. (Chapter 10) *See* **light sleep**.

Deep structure. Term used to describe the basic idea, or meaning, a sender desires to communicate. (Chapter 13) *See* **surface structure**.

Defenses-in-depth. Multiple safeguards, or barriers, used to guard against an accident or incident. If one or even a few fail, others will be able to stop the hazard from causing an accident or incident. These defenses typically include training, regulations, rules, procedures, and technology. (Chapter 2)

Defining event. According to the NTSB, the one event—the defining event—that describes the type or category of accident that occurred. Examples include loss of control in flight, controlled flight into terrain, midair collision, runway incursion, etc. (Chapter 1)

Dehydration. Excessive loss of water from the body, resulting in a variety of undesirable symptoms, including headache, weakness, fatigue, lightheadedness, nausea, confusion, seizures, kidney failure, and even death. (Chapter 11)

Denitrogenation. Prebreathing oxygen (preoxygenation) for no less than 30 minutes immediately before a flight to reduce the amount of nitrogen stored in the body's tissues and fluids, thereby raising DCS altitude thresholds. (Chapter 5)

Descriptive decision-making models. Decision-making models that describe how humans actually make decisions, as opposed to how they should. Humans generally prefer to use shortcuts—basic rules of thumb, or heuristics—when making evaluative judgments and choices. (Chapter 17) *See* **heuristics** and **normative decision-making models**.

Design eye position. *See* **design eye reference point**.

Design eye reference point (DERP). A single reference point in space selected by the aircraft designer where the midpoint between the pilot's eyes is assumed to be located when the pilot is properly seated at the pilot's station. Also known as the *design eye position* (DEP), the seat adjustment that places a pilots eyes at the DERP provides not only the best access to the flight controls, but also an optimum viewing angle for both cockpit instrumentation and the outside environment. (Chapters 3, 12, and 18) *See* **primary optimum field of view**.

Diffusion of responsibility. The tendency to divide (diffuse) responsibility for actions and consequences amongst the group, minimizing one's own individual share of responsibility. (Chapter 18)

Digital displays. Digital displays present quantitative numeric information which, compared to analog displays, usually takes less mental effort to interpret exact values. However, direction and rate of change are usually more difficult to interpret on digital displays. (Chapter 15)

Disorientation stress. The experience of a pilot who is aware he or she is experiencing spatial disorientation (SD) and is trying to put their complete trust in instrument flying—a process called *establishing visual dominance*—to recover from the SD. (Chapter 9)

Displays. Flight, navigation and aircraft systems' instruments that convey information to the pilot about the state of the aircraft or outside world. (Chapter 15)

Distraction. Any interruption that draws a pilot's attention away from tasks involved in flying the aircraft. (Chapter 14)

Disturbance stage of hypoxia. Between 15,000 and 20,000 feet MSL the physiological mechanisms designed to compensate for oxygen deficiency are insufficient—even for relatively short durations—to prevent the onset of hypoxia and its negative symptoms. (Chapter 4) *See* **indifferent stage of hypoxia**, **compensatory stage of hypoxia,** and **critical stage of hypoxia**.

Diuretic. Any substance that increases urination (diuresis), such as alcohol and caffeine. (Chapter 11)

Divided attention. Attending to two or more stimuli or tasks at once. This is analogous to a wide light beam of a flashlight. (Chapter 14) *See* **focused attention** and **selective attention**.

Duck-under phenomenon. Tendency to descend below the glide path after transitioning to visual references. (Chapter 12)

Ear block. *See* **barotitis media**.

Edge rate. The rate at which the edges of textured elements, or discontinuities, flow past us as we move through space which is dependent on speed and distance between edges (not altitude). A high edge rate occurs when flying over finely textured elements (e.g., cities or farmland with small fields) and produces a perception of increased speed; a low edge rate occurs when flying over coarsely textured elements (e.g., deserts, large bodies of water, etc.) and produces a perception of decreased speed. (Chapter 12) *See* **motion parallax**, **motion perspective** and **optic flow**.

Effective performance time (EPT). Traditionally known as *time of useful consciousness*. EPT is the time of available useful consciousness before you succumb to the deleterious effects of hypoxia rendering you incapable of making and executing the decisions needed to combat it. (Chapter 4)

Electronic flight bag (EFB). An electronic information management device that helps flight crews perform flight management tasks more easily and efficiently with less paper. EFB applications generally replace conventional paper products and tools, traditionally carried in the pilot's flight bag. (Chapter 1)

Elevator illusion. A false sense of pitching up brought about by a strong updraft, or a sudden level-off from a descent, that increases the strength of the gravitational acceleration, stimulating the otolith organs and causing the eyes to reflexively move down. (Chapter 9)

Empty-field myopia. Sometimes called *empty-sky myopia*, *night myopia*, or *dark focus*, empty-field myopia is a nearsightedness that occurs in empty-field conditions, such as in the dark, in poor visibility, or at high altitude where terrain and cloud features are absent. (Chapter 6)

Engineered materials arresting system (EMAS). Lightweight crushable concrete or other materials placed at the end of a runway to stop an aircraft that may overrun it. The aircraft tires sink into the material and the aircraft is decelerated as it rolls through it. (Chapter 2)

Engineering reliability analysis (ERA). A formal process to test, quantify and predict the reliability, or dependability, of an aircraft airframe, powerplant, or component. (Chapter 2)

Episodic memory. Recall of life-events from long-term memory. It is a type of explicit or declarative memory because the memories of the events can be verbalized (declared). (Chapter 16) *See* **semantic memory** and **procedural memory**.

Ergonomics. *See* **human factors**.

Error. Failure to perform the correct action, or the act of performing the wrong action. In the context of aviation, flight crew error is more specifically defined as any action or inaction that leads to a deviation from crew or organizational intentions or expectations. (Chapters 2 and 20) *See* **unsafe acts** and **violation**.

Escalation bias. The reluctance to abandon a given course of action when there is too much invested to quit in terms of time, energy, and other resources—even if it's a failing one. (Chapter 17)

Euphoria. A feeling of well-being and confidence. One of the most hazardous symptoms of hypoxia besides unconsciousness. (Chapter 4)

Event cascade. A domino effect where a threat contributes to the commission of an error, or errors, during a pilot's attempt to manage the threat. (Chapter 20)

Expectancy. The anticipation or motivation to perceive (e.g., see or hear) something you expect. For a pilot, this can be helpful, but sometimes harmful. (Chapter 12)

Expectation bias. Previous knowledge creates an expectation that influences future perception of an event or stimuli, leading to sometimes seeing or hearing what you *expect* to see or hear, not what is actually seen or heard. (Chapter 13)

Extra-cockpit communication. Flight crew communication with other people outside the flight deck (e.g., controllers, cabin crew, maintenance personnel, etc.), as opposed to intra-cockpit communication between flight crew members. (Chapters 2, 7, and 13)

False climb illusion. A false sense of pitching-up during straight-line acceleration during a takeoff or go-around that can lead you to pitch the nose down, causing the airplane to descend into the ground or water. It occurs because the otolith bodies and the somatosensory system cannot distinguish between head-back tilt and linear acceleration. (Chapter 9) *See* **somatogravic illusions**.

Farsightedness. Blurred vision for close objects and clear vision for distant objects results when an image is focused behind the retina. (Chapter 6)

Fatigue. A physiological state of reduced mental or physical performance capability resulting from lack of sleep or increased physical activity that can reduce a flight crew member's alertness and ability to safely operate an aircraft or perform safety-related duties. (Chapter 10)

Fick's Law. Molecules of high-concentration passively move to areas of low-concentration. (Chapter 4) *See* **Boyle's Law**, **Dalton's Law**, **Graham's Law**, and **Henry's Law**.

Field of view. Vertical and horizontal range (in degrees) of vision. (Chapter 6)

Finger trouble. Informal term referring to inputting incorrect values in radios, instruments, computers and other devices on the flight deck. (Chapter 15)

Fit for duty. Being physiologically and mentally prepared and capable of performing assigned duties at the highest degree of safety. This includes arriving for work properly rested. (Chapter 10)

5M model. A systems error-model used to describe the various components—man, machine, medium, mission, and management—that could be involved in errors committed by flight crew members, who are only one component of the overall system. (Chapter 2)

Flat light. Also known as *sector whiteout* or *partial whiteout*. Flat light is a condition that causes pilots to lose their visual depth-of-field and contrast. It usually occurs when the aircraft is flying above snow-covered featureless terrain below an overcast cloud layer. The visibility could be unlimited, but the scattering of light and lack of shadow drastically reduces contrast and depth/distance perception. (Chapter 12)

Flicker vertigo. Aircraft strobe and beacon lights, along with sunlight passing through an airplane's propeller or a helicopter's rotor blades can create a flicker, or strobe-light, effect at low RPM and can create symptoms from nausea to headaches to unconsciousness. (Chapter 6)

Flight crew. Minimum required number of crew members—pilot, flight engineer, or flight navigator—required for, and assigned to duty in, an aircraft during flight time. Most new commercial jet transport airplanes require a minimum of two pilots to act as flight crew members during flight: the captain and first officer. (Chapter 3) *See* **crewed flight deck**.

Flight deck authority gradient. The actual and/or perceived difference in authority between the captain and his or her subordinates. Problems in crew communication and performance can arise when the gradient is too steep, too flat, or negative. (Chapter 19)

Flight duty period (FDP). A period that begins when a flight crew member is required to report for duty with the intention of conducting a flight, a series of flights, or positioning or ferrying flights, and ends when the aircraft is parked after the last flight and there is no intention for further aircraft movement by the same flight crew member. (Chapter 10)

Flight envelope protection. The capability in many modern automated flight control systems to prevent an aircraft from exceeding its design limit envelope, preventing it from flying too slow or fast, from flying too high, or from exceeding its design limit load factor and other parameters. (Chapter 15)

Flight environment. In most systems error-models the flight environment consists of all components—the physical, operational, and social environments—other than the flight crew. (Chapter 3)

Flight operational quality assurance (FOQA). A voluntary safety program designed to improve commercial aviation safety through the proactive use of de-identified aggregate information provided in flight data recorders (FDRs) and/or quick access recorder (QARs). Operators use these data to identify and correct deficiencies in all areas of flight operations to reduce or eliminate risks, and minimize deviations from regulations. (Chapter 1)

Flows. Logical, organized sequence of actions accomplished by both captain and FO to configure controls and systems for the next phase of flight, or next step within a phase of fight. These memorized tasks often (but not always) follow a linear, or geographic (left-to-right, bottom-to-top, etc.), flow pattern that is usually followed up by a corresponding checklist. (Chapters 16 and 20)

Fly-by-wire. Rather than providing a direct linkage (cable, hydraulic push-pull rods, etc.) from the control column to the flight controls (elevator, aileron, rudder), fly-by-wire systems convert control movements into electric signals, which in turn are sent via electrical wires to control actuators that activate the controls. (Chapter 15)

Focused attention. Concentrating on a single stimulus in the environment to the exclusion of others. (Chapter 14) *See* **selective attention** and **divided attention**.

Foveal vision. Foveal (focal, or central) vision is used when staring directly at an object and yields the greatest visual acuity (only in daylight). (Chapter 6) *See* **ambient vision**.

Framing bias. Choice preferences vary depending how a situation is framed. When decisions are framed as a choice between gains, people tend to be *risk averse*, choosing a certain gain over the chance of an even a greater gain. When the same decisions are framed as a choice between losses, people tend to be *risk seeking*, avoiding a certain loss in preference for a chance of an even greater loss. (Chapter 17)

Fundamental attribution error. The tendency to blame internal traits or character flaws in others for their attitudes, behavior, or failures, while blaming situational circumstances for our own. (Chapter 17)

Gambler's fallacy. The tendency to see chance as self-correcting. Therefore, after a run of bad luck we think that good luck is sure to follow. (Chapter 17)

General aviation (GA). All civilian flight operations other than scheduled commercial air carrier passenger and cargo service, consisting of piston- and turbine-powered (single- and multi-engine) airplanes, rotorcraft (helicopters), balloons, airships, and gliders. (Chapter 1)

Geometric illusions. The incorrect perception of two-dimensional line drawings and geometric shapes. (Chapter 12)

G-excess illusion. A type of somatogravic illusion—involving the otolith bodies and the somatosensory system—that creates false sensations resulting from head movement while engaged in high positive vertical G_Z flight operations. (Chapter 9)

G-induced loss of consciousness (G-LOC). The complete loss of consciousness that occurs when exposed to positive vertical G_Z of approximately +4.5 G_Z to +5.5 G_Z when not using countermeasures such as a G-suit or anti-G straining maneuvers. These values depend on the G-onset rate and individual tolerance. (Chapter 8) *See* **grayout** and **blackout**.

Glass cockpit. Instead of electro-mechanical flight instruments, consisting mostly of separate analog dials and gyroscopic instruments, a glass cockpit is equipped with electronic flight displays consisting of cathode ray tubes or flat-plate screens that integrate information from several sources into one or two displays. (Chapters 9 and 15)

Glassy water. A very smooth mirror-like water surface makes it difficult for a pilot to accurately judge their aircraft's altitude above it. (Chapter 12)

Graham's Law. A gas under high pressure will flow toward low pressure. (Chapter 4) *See* **Boyle's Law, Dalton's Law, Fick's Law,** and **Henry's Law**.

Graveyard spin. When recovering from a prolonged spin in IMC or at night, in which the cupulae of the semicircular canals have equilibrated, a strong sensation of entering a spin in the opposite direction is experienced. If you respond incorrectly you may inadvertently re-enter a spin in the original direction. (Chapter 9)

Graveyard spiral. When recovering from a prolonged spiral dive in IMC or at night, in which the cupulae of the semicircular canals have equilibrated, a strong sensation of entering a spiral in the opposite direction is experienced. If you respond incorrectly you may inadvertently re-enter a spiral dive in the original direction. (Chapter 9)

Grayout. Visual dimming and blurring, reduced color vision, and a loss of peripheral vision (tunnel vision) that occurs when exposed to positive vertical G_Z ("gees") of approximately +3 G_Z to +4 G_Z when not using countermeasures such as a G-suit or anti-G straining maneuvers. These values depend on the G-onset rate and individual tolerance. (Chapter 8) *See* **blackout** and **G-induced loss of consciousness**.

Ground proximity warning system (GPWS). *See* **terrain awareness and warning system**.

Group cohesiveness. The extent to which individual group members are bonded together with each other. Cohesive groups perform better as a team, but individual members may be more susceptible to group conformity. (Chapter 18)

Groupthink. Flawed group decision making that results from individual group members who, in their desire for harmony, tend to agree with the group consensus—or their perception of the consensus—in spite of their own personal reservations about the group's decision. (Chapter 18)

Head tilt reflex. *See* **optokinetic cervical reflex**.

Height in the visual field. Sometimes called *height in the plane*. A monocular cue to distance perception where objects near the horizon appear further away than they actually are. (Chapter 12)

Hemoglobin (Hb). Iron-rich protein in the red blood cells that transports oxygen to the body's cells. (Chapter 4)

Henry's Law. The amount of gas dissolved in solution is directly proportional to the pressure of the gas over the solution. Used to describe behavior of evolved gases in decompression sickness. (Chapter 5) *See* **Boyle's Law, Dalton's Law, Fick's Law,** and **Graham's Law**.

Heuristics. Simple rules of thumb, or shortcuts, used to make decision making quicker and easier that usually result in adequate, but not always optimal, outcomes. (Chapter 17)

Hindsight bias. The reason(s) for a certain outcome after an event takes place (e.g., an aircraft accident) seems obvious and predictable; but it is only because of our after-the-fact knowledge of the outcome that made us come to that conclusion. Also known as the *I-knew-it-all-along effect,* when we read the conclusions of an accident report, the hindsight bias causes us to believe that the cause is so blatantly obvious that we rush to judge the pilot and conclude that we would never make the same mistake. (Chapter 17)

Histotoxic hypoxia. Any situation that interferes with the normal utilization of oxygen in the body's cells. Alcohol and other drugs can bring about this condition. (Chapter 4) *See* **hypoxia, hypemic hypoxia, hypoxic hypoxia,** and **stagnant hypoxia**.

Home base. Also called the *domicile*. Home base is the location designated by a certificate holder where a flight crew member normally begins and ends his or her duty periods. (Chapter 10)

Home-drome syndrome. More common for low-time pilots who lack experience with different-sized runways, this syndrome involves unconsciously comparing any new runway to the one that is indelibly etched in your visual memory—the home aerodrome (airport)—sometimes resulting in distance and altitude misjudgments when approaching and landing on a runway you are unaccustomed to. (Chapter 12)

Homophones. Words that have same pronunciation, but different meanings, such as *two* and *to*, or *four* and *for*. (Chapter 13)

Human-centered design. The use of human factor's principles and knowledge in the design of systems to best meet the physical, physiological and psychological needs of the human user or operator. (Chapter 15)

Human factors. Also called *ergonomics*. Human factors is a multidisciplinary field that seeks to optimize the effectiveness of human-machine systems through design that accommodates the limitations and capabilities of the human operator, thereby reducing human error and maximizing human performance, safety, efficiency, and comfort. Human factors for pilots can be simply defined as the scientific study of the flight crew and the flight environment with the goal of optimizing the relationship between the two. (Chapter 3)

Human factors analysis and classification system (HFACS). A comprehensive human error framework, or taxonomy, that draws on some of James Reason's research on human error and which is used to assist safety investigators to systematically examine underlying human causal factors to improve aviation accident investigations. (Chapter 2)

Human-machine interface. The place where information about the aircraft's state is perceived by the pilot (i.e., the displays) and where outputs from the pilot (i.e., the controls) are used to change the state of the system. (Chapter 15)

Human reliability assessment (HRA). A formal process using a variety of methods to test, quantify, and predict the reliability, or dependability, of the human operator of a system. (Chapter 2)

Hypemic hypoxia. Any condition that interferes with the oxygen-carrying capacity of the blood. (Chapter 4) *See* **hypoxia**, **hypoxic hypoxia**, **histotoxic hypoxia**, and **stagnant hypoxia**.

Hyperventilation. Overbreathing resulting from anxiety or fear, or when flying above 10,000 feet MSL in an unpressurized aircraft, leads to the expulsion of excess carbon dioxide upsetting the acid-alkaline balance in the blood. (Chapter 4)

Hypoglycemia. A condition of low blood sugar that may result in deleterious symptoms such as nausea, shaking of hands, sweating, dizziness, lightheadedness, weakness, difficult concentrating, anxiety, mental confusion and even loss of consciousness. (Chapters 8 and 11)

Hypoxia. A state of oxygen deficiency in the blood, tissues, and cells sufficient to cause impairment of physiological and physical body functions and mental performance. (Chapter 4) *See* **hypoxic hypoxia**, **hypemic hypoxia**, **stagnant hypoxia**, and **histotoxic hypoxia**.

Hypoxic hypoxia. Any condition that interrupts the flow and quantity of oxygen to the lungs. Often called *altitude hypoxia* by aviators because flying at high altitudes causes this type of hypoxia. (Chapter 4) *See* **hypoxia**, **hypemic hypoxia**, **stagnant hypoxia**, and **histotoxic hypoxia**.

Illusory correlations. Assuming two or more different variables are related to each other when they are not. (Chapter 17)

Immediate action items. Actions that must be taken in response to a non-routine event so quickly that reference to a checklist is not practical because of a potential loss of aircraft control, incapacitation of a crew member, or damage to or loss of an aircraft component or system, which would make continued safe flight improbable. (Chapter 16)

Impairment. Any physiological or psychological condition that degrades a flight crew member's ability to perform his or her normal flight duties. Also called *partial incapacitation*. (Chapter 11) *See* **incapacitation**.

Impulsivity. One of five "hazardous attitudes" identified in the FAA's aeronautical decision-making literature, which is an inclination to act on impulse rather than thought, resulting in the tendency to do something quickly rather than methodically. The antidote for such thinking is "Not so fast, think first." (Chapter 17) *See* **ability bias**, **optimistic bias**, **invulnerability**, **macho**, and **resignation**.

Inattentional blindness. The inability to perceive conspicuous stimuli in our environment when focused on other stimuli despite the fact that they register on our sensory receptors. (Chapter 14)

Incapacitation. Any physiological or psychological condition that renders a flight crew member partially or completely incapable of performing his or her normal flight duties, including the ability to safely control the aircraft. Sudden incapacitation involves a rapid onset of the condition, while subtle incapacitation results from slow or imperceptible onset that may be difficult for the victim and/or the second pilot to recognize. (Chapter 4) *See* **impairment**.

Indifferent stage of hypoxia. With the exception of decreased night vision at or above 5,000 feet, and mild hypoxia for long-duration flights at or near 10,000 feet, the body is relatively *indifferent* to the effects of reduced partial pressure of oxygen in this stage (from sea level to 10,000 feet MSL). (Chapter 4) *See* **compensatory stage of hypoxia, disturbance stage of hypoxia,** and **critical stage of hypoxia.**

Informational conformity. The tendency to conform to group norms and expectations and internalize them as his or her own, because a person lacks information and desires to be correct in their understanding. (Chapter 18) *See* **conformity** and **normative conformity.**

Information processing. The framework used by cognitive psychology that postulates that, somewhat like a computer, inputs (information or stimuli) from the environment are received by the senses and processed before a response (output) is made. (Chapter 3)

Inside-out attitude indicator. Western-style attitude indicator that displays a moving horizon and stationary miniature airplane. Though it violates the principle of the moving part, it comports with most pilots' mental models of what they see looking directly outside—a moving visual world in relation to their aircraft. (Chapter 15) *See* **principle of the moving part** and **outside-in attitude indicator.**

Insomnia. The inability to fall asleep and/or stay asleep. (Chapter 10)

Instrument flight rules (IFR). Regulations which allow flight in weather conditions that are below VFR regulatory weather minima. (Chapter 4) *See* **instrument meteorological conditions** and **visual flight rules.**

Instrument meteorological conditions (IMC). Weather conditions that are below VFR regulatory weather minima. (Chapter 1) *See* **visual flight rules** and **visual meteorological conditions.**

Integrated display. A single display that portrays several related components in close proximity to each other to allow for easy comparison and direct perception by the pilot. (Chapter 15) *See* **proximity compatibility principle.**

Interposition. Likely the most dominant monocular cue to distance perception. An object is perceived as further away than another object that overlays or blocks it. (Chapter 12)

Intra-cockpit communication. Communication between flight crew members on the flight deck, as opposed to extra-cockpit communication with other people outside the flight deck (e.g., controllers, cabin crew, maintenance personnel, etc.). (Chapters 2, 7, and 13)

Inversion illusion. Resulting from an abrupt level-off from a steep climb creating $-G_z$ and a rapid linear acceleration creating $+G_x$, the inversion illusion involves a strong nose-up pitch illusion and possibly the feeling of flipping upside down. (Chapter 9)

Invulnerability. One of five "hazardous attitudes" identified in the FAA's aeronautical decision-making literature, which is the belief that a bad event (accident) may happen to the other person, but not oneself. The antidote for such thinking is "It could happen to me." (Chapter 17) *See* **ability bias, optimistic bias, impulsivity, macho,** and **resignation.**

Jet lag. Circadian disruption created by rapidly crossing multiple time zones. (Chapter 10)

Lapse. A properly formulated action unintentionally not executed because the person forgot to. *See* **mistake** and **slip.** (Chapter 2)

Last-leg syndrome. The desire to get home impairs a pilot's ability to make a sound go/no-go decision during the last leg of a trip. (Chapter 17)

Leans. The most common vestibular illusion. Involves the sensation that you are still turning (or the wing is low) after leveling the wings from a prolonged turn. To reconcile conflicting sensations one will lean in the direction of the original turn. (Chapter 9)

Lethality rate. The percentage of a given type of accident that result in fatalities. (Chapter 1)

Life stress. Chronic long-term stress that results from ongoing demands placed upon body. (Chapter 19)

Light sleep. The beginning stages (Stage 1 and 2) of non-REM (rapid eye movement) sleep that lasts for 30 to 45 minutes. Physiological functions and brain wave activity begin to slow down. (Chapter 10) *See* **deep sleep.**

Linear perspective. A monocular cue to distance perception. Parallel lines appear to converge to a single point with increasing distance. (Chapter 12) *See* **splay.**

Line operations safety audit (LOSA). A formal process conducted under strict no-jeopardy conditions that involves the use of highly trained expert observers who collect safety-related data on environmental conditions, operational complexity, and flight crew performance while riding in the jumpseat during regularly scheduled airline flights. The data collected are used to gauge the strengths and weaknesses of an airline's flight operations with the goal of implementing improvement strategies to increase safety. (Chapters 1 and 20)

Line-oriented flight training (LOFT). Initial or recurrent airline pilot simulator training, involving a full flight crew complement, that, rather than emphasizing traditional maneuver-based training, represents actual realistic daily gate-to-gate flight operations; however, non-normal or emergency situations are introduced and the flight crew is evaluated on both their technical and CRM skills. (Chapter 19)

Location coding. The placing and arranging of displays and controls to best meet the processing needs of the human operator. (Chapter 15)

Long-term memory (LTM). Well-learned information is stored for an indefinite period of time in LTM. (Chapter 16)

Loss-of-activation error. Forgetting an intended behavior and remembering it only after reactivating the memory retrieval cue(s) present at the time of its original formulation by re-engaging in the activity (e.g., returning to your desk after forgetting why you got up in the first place). (Chapter 16) *See* **memory retrieval cues**.

Loss of control in flight (LOC-I). Unintended departure of an aircraft from controlled flight (e.g., stall, spin). (Chapter 1) *See* **airplane upset**.

Macho. One of five "hazardous attitudes" identified in the FAA's aeronautical decision-making literature, which is the belief that one is superior in their abilities—"I can do it." The antidote for such thinking is "Taking chances is foolish." (Chapter 17) *See* **ability bias**, **optimistic bias**, **impulsivity**, **invulnerability**, and **resignation**.

Masked. Masked speech is speech that is covered and prevented from being heard because of other noise sources. (Chapter 7) *See* **signal-to-noise ratio**.

Memory retrieval cues. External (environmental) and internal (physiological or psychological) contextual features that are unconsciously stored in long-term memory at the same time the material to be remembered is encoded and stored in long-term memory. (Chapter 16) *See* **loss-of-activation error**.

Mental operations. Performing cognitive activities such as attending, retrieving memories, calculating, reasoning, making inferences, problem solving and decision making. (Chapter 16)

Mental workload. Analogous to physical workload, mental (or cognitive) workload is the amount of effort exerted when performing mental operations (i.e., attending, remembering, problem solving, decision making, etc.) to meet the demands of a given task or tasks. Performance suffers if cognitive task demands are too high or too low. (Chapter 14)

Mesopic vision. Both rods and cones are activated simultaneously in relatively dim lighting conditions. (Chapter 6) *See* **photopic vision** and **scotopic vision**.

Midair collision (MAC). An event where two aircraft come into contact with each other while in flight. (Chapters 1 and 6)

Mishap. A U.S. military term for an occurrence (an incident or accident). Mishaps are generally classified into four categories, ranging from Class A (the most serious involving a fatality or permanent total disability and/or significant property damage) to Class D (the least serious involving minor injury and/or minimal property damage). (Chapter 9)

Mistake. Unintentional formulation of a faulty assessment or an incorrect action needed for the situation. *See* **lapse** and **slip**. (Chapter 2)

Mnemonic. A device, such as an acronym, rhyme, story, or other trick designed to help you remember something. (Chapter 16)

Mode confusion. Failure to understand which mode the automated flight control system (AFCS) is operating in. (Chapter 15)

Mode reversion. A mode change executed by the AFCS without any direct input from the flight crew. These automatic/uncommanded (indirect) mode changes can be expected, but can potentially occur unexpectedly and lead to automation surprise. (Chapter 15) *See* **automation surprise**.

Monitoring. Continually watching, observing, keeping track of, or cross-checking aircraft flight and systems instruments, changes in aircraft performance, changing weather conditions, conflicting air traffic, and other aspects of a flight. (Chapter 14) *See* **attention** and **vigilance**.

Monocular cues. A variety of distance and depth perception cues—sometimes called *object-centered* cues or *pictorial* cues—that allow a person with only one eye to perceive three dimensions because these cues exist in the environment, not in the eyes. (Chapter 12)

Most Wanted List of Transportation Safety Improvements. First introduced in 1990, this is a list of 10 priority transportation safety issues the NTSB would like government and/or industry to address for the upcoming two years. (Chapter 1)

Motion parallax. A motion cue to distance perception. The apparent motion of stationary objects as one moves past them. Objects that appear to quickly move past you are perceived to be closer than objects that move slower or barely at all. (Chapter 12) *See* also **edge rate**, **motion perspective**, and **optic flow**.

Motion perspective. A motion cue to distance perception. The phenomenon of an outward expanding visual field as you move directly toward an object and a contracting visual field as you move away from it. Pilots use this cue when conducting approaches and landings, keeping the aim point in the landing zone stationary while other elements appear to move radially away from that spot. (Chapter 12) *See* also **edge rate**, **motion parallax**, and **optic flow**.

Multi-function display (MFD). Any physical display unit, other than the PFD, used to present information, on which the layout may be reconfigured. (Chapter 15) *See* **primary flight display**.

Near midair collision (NMAC). An incident associated with the operation of an aircraft in which a possibility of a collision occurs as a result of proximity of less than 500 feet to another aircraft, or a report is received from a pilot or flight crew member stating that a collision hazard existed between two or more aircraft. (Chapter 6)

Nearsightedness. Clear vision for close objects and blurred vision for distant objects results when an image is focused at the front of the retina. (Chapter 6)

Night blindness. Reduction of visual acuity at night caused by a variety of conditions, including a Vitamin A deficiency. (Chapter 6)

Noise. Any loud, unpleasant, or unwanted sound that interferes with communication and/or contributes to fatigue and hearing loss. (Chapter 7)

Nonconsolidated sleep. Obtaining sleep during multiple short periods. (Chapter 10)

Normative conformity. The tendency, because a person wants to be accepted by the group, to conform to group norms and expectations, even though he or she may privately disagree with them. (Chapter 18) *See* **conformity** and **informational conformity**.

Normative decision-making models. Decision-making models that describe how decisions should be made to arrive at the best possible choice. This often involves rational, logical, analytical, and sometimes mathematical/ statistical reasoning to arrive at the best possible outcome. (Chapter 17) *See* **descriptive decision-making models**.

Norms. The unwritten rules of expected behavior dictated by the majority of the group. (Chapter 18)

Nystagmus. Rapid involuntary back-and-forth eye movement caused by an automatic vestibulo-ocular reflex that creates an apparent back-and-forth movement of the visual scene that can last for several seconds after recovery from significant angular accelerations. (Chapter 9)

Obedience to authority. Complying with the requests or orders of an authority figure. Compliance is generally not a problem if doing so doesn't jeopardize safety. It is a problem, if it does, or could, jeopardize safety. (Chapter 18)

Obstructive sleep apnea (OSA). A sleep disorder that involves interference in breathing several times during a sleep period, causing fragmented sleep and reduced blood-oxygen flow to vital organs. It can lead to variety of long-term health problems, including persistent sleepiness when awake. (Chapter 10)

Occurrence. An aircraft accident or incident. (Chapter 1) *See* **aircraft accident** and **aircraft incident**.

Optic flow. The apparent motion of elements as we move past them, primarily in our peripheral vision, which is dependent on our speed and our distance from them. A faster flow rate of terrain elements generally occurs at lower altitudes and a slower rate at higher altitudes. (Chapter 12) *See* **edge rate**, **motion parallax**, and **motion perspective**.

Optimistic bias. Compared to others, people generally believe they have a greater likelihood of experiencing a positive event, and are at less risk of experiencing a negative event. That is, they are more optimistic and less realistic, about certain things in life. (Chapter 17) *See* **ability bias**, **invulnerability**, **impulsivity**, **macho**, and **resignation**.

Optokinetic cervical reflex (OKCR). Also known as *head tilt reflex*. In visual meteorological conditions, there is a natural human tendency to align our head with the visible (or perceived) horizon even though the aircraft itself may be in a banked turn. A sloping cloud layer or a false horizon (in VMC), or when flying in and out of IMC while turning, conflicts with the actual alignment of both the aircraft and earth which in turn can contribute to or exacerbate the leans. (Chapter 9)

Outside-in attitude indicator. Eastern-style attitude indicator that displays a moving miniature airplane on a stationary horizon. It conforms to the principle of the moving part in that it represents what happens in the real world by providing a bird's eye view of someone who might be outside and behind the aircraft; however, it violates the principle of pictorial realism. (Chapter 15) *See* **principle of the moving part** and **inside-out attitude indicator**.

Overconfidence bias. People are generally more confident in the accuracy and assessment of their beliefs, decisions, and abilities than is warranted. (Chapter 17)

Oxygen ear. Delayed ear block that occurs after landing from breathing 100 percent oxygen in flight. Because the excess oxygen is slowly absorbed by the tissues in the middle ear, a partial vacuum is created causing the eardrum to bulge inward that causes ear pain. (Chapter 5)

Oxygen paradox. Occasionally the administration of oxygen during an extreme hypoxic event results in further incapacitation of the hypoxic individual. (Chapter 4)

Party-line information (PLI). Information provided by all participants communicating on a single radio frequency. Analogous to old party-line telephones where several people shared the same line, PLI enhances a pilot's situational awareness by providing the location of other aircraft, weather phenomena that may affect their flight, runway information, and other activities in their vicinity. (Chapter 13)

PAVE model. An FAA basic systems error-model used to understand the context of flight crew error: the **P**ilot, **A**ircraft, en**V**ironment, and **E**xternal pressures. (Chapter 2)

Perceptual error. Failure to correctly interpret stimuli (inputs) received from the outside world through our senses. (Chapter 2)

Periodic limb movement disorder (PLMD). Unconscious involuntary leg twitching or jerking that repeats periodically throughout the sleep period causing fragmented sleep and excessive sleepiness during the day. (Chapter 10)

Personal weather minimums. Minimum weather conditions, usually in terms of visibility and ceiling values, below which a pilot will not attempt to fly in. These are generally above regulatory minimums and are dependent of a variety of factors (day or night, mountainous terrain, familiarity with geographical area, etc.), including your own flight experience, ability, and comfort levels. (Chapters 6 and 9)

Photopic vision. Day vision involving only cones. (Chapter 6) *See* **scotopic vision** and **mesopic vision**.

Physical ergonomics. The study of the effects of physical load (or stress) on the human body, including the role and effects of human anatomy, anthropometry, physiology and biomechanics. (Chapter 3)

Physiological deficient zone. Pilots and passengers flying in this zone—between 10,000 and 50,000 feet MSL—in an unpressurized aircraft will experience hypoxia and DCS. (Chapter 4) *See* **physiological efficient zone** and **space equivalent zone**.

Physiological efficient zone. Human functioning is generally unimpaired between sea level and 10,000 feet MSL, with the exception of possible trapped gas problems and diminished night vision above 5,000 feet MSL. (Chapter 4) *See* **physiological deficient zone** and **space equivalent zone**.

Physiology. The study of the ways in which the human body and its various systems function. (Chapter 3)

Pictorial display. Information on a flight deck display is presented graphically and spatially in analog format to more closely symbolize the analog reality it is designed to represent. (Chapter 15)

Pictorial realism. A display or control that is designed using the principle of pictorial realism looks like what it is supposed to represent. For example, an attitude indicator "looks like" what the pilot would see when looking out-the-window straight ahead. (Chapter 15)

Plan continuation error Also known as *continuation bias*. The decision to stick to your plan to continue a course of action even though the evidence suggests you shouldn't. (Chapter 17)

Population stereotypes. Culturally agreed-upon understandings of what certain locations of switches, direction of switch movement, symbols, shapes or colors mean. For example, in North America, the color green means safe or go, yellow (or amber) means caution, and red means danger (or stop). (Chapter 15)

Positional alcohol nystagmus (PAN). Nystagmus induced by alcohol diffusing into the semicircular canal membrane increasing sensitivity and movement of the hair cells in the canals that detect acceleration. (Chapter 11) *See* **nystagmus**.

Preoxygenation. *See* **denitrogenation**.

Presbycusis. Hearing loss that occurs in old age. (Chapter 7)

Presbyopia. Vision problems associated with aging, but primarily the gradually decreasing ability to focus on close objects because of the hardening of the lens. After about age 40, this results in the near-focal point moving outward, requiring corrective lenses to clearly see objects up close. (Chapter 6)

Pressure vertigo. Also called *alternobaric vertigo*, pressure vertigo is a temporary dizziness or spinning sensation induced from higher-than-normal middle ear pressures from an ear block or from performing a Valsalva maneuver. (Chapter 5)

PRICE check. A checklist acronym to use when using oxygen. Check **P**ressure gauge, confirm pressure **R**egulator working, check oxygen flow rate on **I**ndicator, ensure hoses, mask, etc. are properly **C**onnected and check **E**mergency supply of oxygen (required by airlines). (Chapter 4)

Primary flight display (PFD). A single physical unit that provides the primary display of all the following: altitude, airspeed, heading, and attitude located directly in front of the pilot in a fixed layout in accordance with 14 CFR §23.1321. It may provide other information pertinent to guidance and fundamental control of flight of the airplane, such as critical engine parameters. (Chapter 15) *See* **multi-function display**.

Primary optimum field of view (FOV). The angular extent of the display(s) that can be seen from the design eye reference point when a pilot is properly seated at their station that can be accommodated with eye rotation only. The primary optimum vertical and horizontal visual FOV is 15 degrees above and below the normal line-of-sight and 15 degrees either side of the normal forward line-of-sight of the aircraft. (Chapter 15) *See* **design eye reference point**.

Principle of the moving part. Symbols on displays should move in the same direction as the part that they represent. (Chapter 15). *See* **inside-out attitude indicator** and **outside-in attitude indicator**.

Proactive interference. Occurs when previous information/activity stored in long-term memory interferes with the recall of new information in working memory. (Chapter 16) *See* **retroactive interference**.

Procedural memory. Recalling from long-term memory with little or no conscious thought, how to perform some skill, like hand-fly an airplane. It is often referred to as muscle memory, and is about "remembering how" to do something. (Chapter 16) *See* **semantic memory** and **episodic memory**.

Proficiency. Compared to meeting currency requirements, which is a level of pilot performance that meets legal requirements, proficiency means being very good at flying, performing at a high level of competence and skill. (Chapter 14)

Prospective memory. Remembering to perform an intended action in the future. (Chapter 16) *See* **retrospective memory**.

Proximity compatibility principle. Several different displays that are frequently required to be compared to one another to obtain an accurate and complete perception of the situation are physically located in close proximity to each other. (Chapter 15) *See* **integrated display**.

Psychology. The scientific study of human behavior, or human thought and behavior. (Chapter 3)

Purkinje shift. A shift in sensitivity to the blue-green end of the visible color spectrum occurs when changing from cone vision (photopic vision) to rod vision at night (scotopic vision). (Chapter 6)

Radiotelephony (RTF). Standardized words, phrases, and techniques used to enhance communication between flight crew, ATC, and other aviation personnel. (Chapters 7 and 13)

Readback-hearback problem. A pilot incorrectly reads back a clearance and the controller doesn't catch it. This contributes to the pilot and controller each having a different understanding of what the pilot is supposed to do. (Chapter 13)

Recognition-primed decisions. Quick and effective decisions made by experts who are able to rapidly match patterns in their environment with information and experiences stored in their LTM. (Chapter 17)

Redout. Visual blurring and reddening of the visual field that occurs when exposed to negative vertical G_Z of approximately -2.5 G_Z to -3.0 G_Z. These values depend on the G-onset rate and individual tolerance. (Chapter 8)

Redundancy gain. Attention and monitoring performance is enhanced when more than one modality and one type of stimulus is used. (Chapter 20)

Relative brightness. A monocular cue to distance perception. Darker objects are perceived as being smaller and further away while brighter objects are seen as larger and closer. (Chapter 12)

Relative size. A monocular cue to distance perception. An object of known size is perceived as further away when it casts a smaller image on our retina appearing smaller. (Chapter 12)

Resignation. One of five "hazardous attitudes" identified in the FAA's aeronautical decision-making literature, which is the attitude of giving up too easily, believing that you are helpless. The antidote for such thinking is "I'm not helpless. I can make a difference." (Chapter 17) *See* **ability bias**, **optimistic bias**, **impulsivity**, **invulnerability**, and **macho**.

Respiration. The process by which a living organism exchanges gases with its environment. (Chapter 4)

Retinal disparity. A binocular cue to distance perception. Each eye sees a different image of the same object when closer. (Chapter 12) *See* **binocular cues**.

Retroactive interference. Occurs when new information/activity interferes with the recall of previously learned information or material to be remembered. Distractions are a common cause of this type of memory interference. (Chapter 16) *See* **proactive interference**.

Retrograde amnesia. The unusual loss—either temporary or permanent—of memories of past information that was acquired, or events that occurred, before the onset of amnesia. This is caused by some kind of physiological stress to the brain and is more than simple forgetting. A significant percentage of pilots who have experienced G-LOC failed to remember the event and circumstances leading up to it. (Chapter 8)

Retrospective memory. Recalling previously learned information. (Chapter 16) *See* **prospective memory**.

Risky shift. The tendency of an individual's viewpoints and opinions to shift towards greater risk while participating in a group than when acting alone— especially if that person's views and opinions leaned toward risk before interaction and discussion with the group took place. Group decision making leans towards greater risk than that of its individual members if most of the group members' viewpoints and opinions were somewhat risky before group interaction and discussion took place. *See* **conservative shift**. (Chapter 18)

Rods. Receptors in retina of eye that convert incoming light energy into neural impulses during night (scotopic) vision. (Chapter 6) *See* **cones**.

Role. A set of socially defined norms that define how people in a given social situation should behave. The captain has one role, the FO another. (Chapter 18)

Roll upset. *See* **airplane upset**.

Runway excursion (RE). A runway excursion occurs when an aircraft departs the end (overrun) or the side (veers off) of the runway during takeoff or landing. (Chapter 1)

Runway incursion (RI). A runway incursion is the incorrect presence of an aircraft, vehicle, or person on a runway. (Chapters 1 and 6)

Runway visual range (RVR). An instrument-derived measurement of atmospheric opacity converted to an RVR visibility value that represents the horizontal distance a pilot in a moving aircraft should see when looking down the runway from its approach end. (Chapter 12)

Safety management systems (SMS). A formal, comprehensive, and systematic approach to managing safety and assuring the effectiveness of safety risk controls in an organization. SMS incorporates procedures, practices, and policies into normal day-to-day business processes that are used to plan, organize, direct, and control an organization's business activities in a manner that enhances safety and ensures compliance with regulatory standards. (Chapters 1 and 20)

Sampling rate. The frequency with which a pilot directs his or her gaze and attention to the various flight instruments and associated flight guidance automation indicators and, if operating in VMC, the external environment. It is recommended during high areas of vulnerability to increase the sampling rate. (Chapters 14 and 15) *See* **areas of vulnerability**.

Satisficing. The search for alternatives is stopped when an option is found that *satisfies* the decision maker's most important criteria. (Chapter 17)

Scotopic vision. Night vision where only rods are activated. (Chapter 6) *See* **photopic vision** and **mesopic vision**.

Sector whiteout. *See* **flat light**.

Selective attention. The stimuli in the environment one attends to. Using the light beam of a flashlight as a metaphor, it is the location at which one points the beam. (Chapter 14) *See* **focused attention** and **divided attention**.

Self-imposed stress. Activities that you as the pilot can generally control—lifestyle choices you make, such as what you eat, drink, smoke, or otherwise ingest (medication,

drugs) and your level of physical activity—that could lead to impairment or incapacitation. (Chapter 11)

Self-serving biases. Biases, such as the optimistic, ability, choice-supportive, and overconfidence biases, that serve to protect our egos and self-esteem by painting an overly positive view of ourselves. (Chapter 17)

Semantic memory. Conscious recall of facts, concepts and ideas from long-term memory. It is a type of explicit or declarative memory because the memories can be verbalized (declared). (Chapter 16) *See* **episodic memory** and **procedural memory**.

Sensory cues. Characteristics in the environmental stimuli that are received by our sensory receptors (visual, auditory, cutaneous, olfactory, vestibular, etc.) that aid us in accurately perceiving the outside world. (Chapter 12)

Sensory memory. Sensation of sensory inputs are retained, or stored, momentarily after the stimulus has stopped. (Chapter 16)

Sensory modality. The sense through which different kinds of stimuli (inputs) are received. For example, light is received by the visual sense, sound by the auditory sense, odors through the olfactory receptors, etc. (Chapter 14)

Shape coding. The shaping of a control to look and feel like the device it is supposed to control. For example, a flap control looks like a miniature flap and the landing gear control looks and feels like a tire. (Chapter 15)

SHELL model. A systems model used to describe the various components—software, hardware, environment, liveware (others), and liveware (crew)—that could be involved in errors committed by flight crew members, who are only one component of the overall system. (Chapter 2)

Short-term memory (STM). *See* **working memory**.

Signal-to-noise ratio (SNR). In auditory perception it is the ratio of the signal (message) to the noise. Speech is generally not heard when the SNR is less than 1, it is heard when the SNR is greater than 1, and it can be heard if it is 1 provided the hearer hears the context of the message. (Chapter 7)

Single-pilot resource management (SRM). The art of managing all onboard and outside resources available to a pilot before and during a flight to help ensure a safe and successful outcome. (Chapter 17) *See* **crew resource management**.

Sinus block. *See* **barosinusitis**.

Situational awareness. The perception of elements in the environment within a volume of time and space, the comprehension of their meaning, and the projection of their status in the near future. (Chapter 14)

Situational stress. Short-term stress that results from demands placed on the body by the immediate task at hand (e.g., handling an in-flight emergency). (Chapter 19)

Skill-based error. Error involving attention, memory, and psychomotor technique skills, such as stick-and-rudder hand-flying skills and knobology skills. (Chapter 2)

Sleep debt. The accumulation of sleep loss over several days. If you need 8 hours of sleep a night, but only receive 7 each night for three nights, you have accumulated a sleep debt of 3 hours. (Chapter 10)

Sleep fragmentation. Interruption of a normal sleep period from waking up and going back to sleep several times during the sleep period. (Chapter 10)

Sleep inertia. Sleep inertia (also termed sleep drunkenness) refers to a period of impaired performance and reduced vigilance following awakening from a regular sleep episode or nap. This impairment may be severe, last from 15 to 30 minutes or more, and may be accompanied by micro-sleep episodes. It is usually more pronounced after waking up from a long sleep or nap (more than 30 to 40 minutes) and during the primary and secondary window of circadian low (WOCL). (Chapter 10)

Slip. A properly formulated action that is unintentionally not carried out as planned or intended. *See* **mistake** and **lapse**. (Chapter 2)

Social influence. The actual or perceived influence exerted by other people to feel, think or behave in a certain way. (Chapter 18)

Social loafing. Group members expend less individual effort to accomplish a goal than they would if they were acting alone. (Chapter 18)

Social psychology. The scientific study of how people's thoughts and behaviors are influenced by others. (Chapters 3 and 18)

Somatogravic illusions. Illusions involving the otolith bodies and the somatosensory system and include the false climb, G-excess and inversion illusions, and the false sensation of a straight climb while established in a prolonged turn. The false climb illusion is also often referred to as the "somatogravic illusion." (Chapter 9) *See* **false climb illusion**.

Somatogyral illusions. Vestibular illusions primarily involving the semicircular canals include the leans, the graveyard spin, the graveyard spiral, and the Coriolis illusion. (Chapter 9)

Somatosensory illusions. Illusions resulting primarily from the somatosensory system (also called the proprioceptive or kinesthetic sense) and are often called somatogravic illusions. (Chapter 9)

Somatosensory system. Postural sensations derived from receptors in the skin, muscles, joints, and tendons that respond to gravity and angular or linear accelerations (or G-forces). This is also called the *proprioceptive* or *kinesthetic* sense. (Chapter 9)

Sound frequency. The physical characteristic of sound that produces the physiological and psychological sensation of pitch and is measured in Hertz (Hz), or cycles per second. (Chapter 7)

Sound intensity. The physical characteristic of sound that produces the physiological and psychological sensation of loudness. It refers to the amplitude of a sound wave and is measured in decibels (dB). (Chapter 7)

Space equivalent zone. Flight above 50,000 feet is completely inhospitable to human survival when flying in an unsealed cabin or without the use of a space suit. (Chapter 4) *See* **physiological deficient zone** and **physiological efficient zone**.

Spatial disorientation (SD). Incorrect perception of your orientation with respect to the position of your aircraft in space. Specifically, it is an inaccurate perception of the aircraft's attitude, direction or motion as a result of faulty or inadequate information provided by your senses. (Chapter 9)

Special issuance. Authorization for a U.S. medical certificate, with a specified validity period, to an pilot who does not meet the established medical standards but demonstrates to the satisfaction of the Federal Air Surgeon, through a special medical flight test, practical test, or medical evaluation that the duties authorized by the class of medical certificate applied for can be performed without endangering public safety for the validity period of the authorization. (Chapter 11)

Splay. The convergence angle of parallel lines (like runway edge) that appear to converge to a single point in the distance. The larger the splay (angle) of a runway, the lower the approach angle. (Chapter 12) *See* **linear perspective**.

Staggers. A Type II DCS symptom that involves neurological disturbances that result from nitrogen bubbling in the brain, eyes, spinal cord, and peripheral nervous system. (Chapter 5) *See* **bends**, **chokes**, and **creeps**.

Stagnant hypoxia. Any situation that interferes with the normal circulation of the blood arriving to the body's cells. Positive G accelerations ($+G_Z$) will bring about this condition. (Chapter 4) *See* **hypoxia**, **hypemic hypoxia**, **hypoxic hypoxia**, and **histotoxic hypoxia**.

Standardization. The designing, making, and arranging of displays and controls to conform to a specified standard of design according to good human factors engineering principles. Standardization of flight crew behaviors is also included in SOPs. (Chapter 15) *See* **standard operating procedures**.

Standard operating procedures (SOP). Written best practice procedures that are applied uniformly and consistently by flight crews within a flight operation that involve all aspects of flight operations including normal, non-normal, and emergency-procedures. (Chapters 1, 2, 16, 17, and 20)

Startle reflex. A surprised reaction that results in an involuntary delayed response, no response, or even an incorrect response. (Chapters 9 and 14)

Statement of demonstrated ability (SODA). A medical waiver that is granted to a pilot whose disqualifying condition is static or nonprogressive and who has been found capable of performing pilot duties without endangering public safety. (Chapter 11)

Status. The prestige bestowed on individual members by the group they are in. (Chapter 18)

Steam gauges. An informal and somewhat pejorative term that refers to mechanical or electromechanical instruments that display information in separate individual displays often in analog format (sometimes referred to as *round dials*). (Chapter 15)

Stepped-on transmission. A radio transmission that is blocked or garbled from someone else transmitting at the same time on the same frequency. (Chapter 16)

Stereopsis. The brain fuses the two disparate images of a single object that is located close to the eyes into one 3D image. (Chapter 12)

Sterile cockpit rule. 14 CFR §§135.100 and 121.542 prohibit crew members from engaging in nonessential activities (including extraneous conversations) that could distract them from completing the essential duties required for the safe operation of their aircraft during the critical phases of flight: all ground operations—taxi, takeoff, and landing—and all other operations (i.e., climb, descent, approach) below 10,000 feet, except cruise flight. (Chapters 1, 14, 16, and 20)

Stimuli. Plural of stimulus, which is any action or agent that causes activity in an organism. This is primarily input or information in the environment (sensory cues) that stimulates activity in the visual, auditory, cutaneous, olfactory, vestibular, olfactory, and other senses. (Chapter 3)

Stress. The body's response to any stressor, or demand, placed upon it. (Chapter 19) *See* **life stress** and **situational stress**.

Stressor. Any environmental, physiological, psychological/cognitive, or social demand placed upon the body and/or mind. (Chapter 19)

Sudden decompression. A depressurization of an aircraft cabin in which the cabin pressure equalizes with the outside ambient pressure in 0.5 to 10 seconds (rapid decompression) or less than 0.5 seconds (explosive decompression). (Chapter 4)

Surface structure. Term used to describe the sequencing, or phonological arrangement, of sounds and words used by the sender. The receiver of the message only has access to the surface structure, not necessarily the deep structure (true meaning), and must infer what the sender meant. (Chapter 13) *See* **deep structure**.

Swiss cheese model. The popular name for James Reason's organizational accident model. The model gets its name from the idea that defenses are like several slices of Swiss cheese that are lined up to block fallible decisions and other actions made by people in the system, yet these may still penetrate through the holes in the cheese causing an accident. (Chapter 2)

Synergy. The total performance of the crew is greater than the sum of the individual performance of each crew member. (Chapter 19)

System. A set of components that act together as a whole to achieve a common goal. A system includes several subsystems—people, equipment, facilities, tools, procedures—in which the human operator is just one component in the overall system. (Chapter 2)

Terrain awareness and warning system (TAWS). A generic term used to describe an alerting system that provides the flight crew with sufficient information and time to detect a potentially hazardous terrain situation and avoid CFIT. The most popular TAWS is the enhanced ground proximity warning system (EGPWS). The older GPWS is based on the use of radar altimeters and provides warning and guidance features related not only to high closure rate to terrain, but also for such circumstances as descending at an excessive rate, a negative climb rate after takeoff, improper configuration during landing, etc. EGPWS enhances GPWS functionality by integrating a database of obstacles and worldwide terrain, thus allowing for a look-ahead feature as well as graphic terrain depictions on airplane navigation displays. (Chapter 1)

Texture gradient. A monocular cue to distance perception. The texture of distant elements appears finer (smaller, closer together, and denser) while the texture of closer elements appear coarser (larger, farther apart, and less dense). (Chapter 12)

Threat. Any condition, event or error outside of the influence of the flight crew that increases the operational complexity of a flight, can lead to pilot error and requires attention and management if safety margins are to be maintained. (Chapter 20)

Threat and error management (TEM). A risk management strategy that involves using countermeasures to detect, avoid or mitigate the threats pilots face and avoid, detect, correct (or capture) and mitigate the errors that they make. (Chapter 20)

Time awake. The total time since waking up from your sleep. Also called time since awakening (TSA). (Chapter 10)

Time of useful consciousness (TUC). *See* **effective performance time**.

Tinnitus. A perception of noise, ringing or buzzing in the ears even when no external sounds are present. There are several possible causes of tinnitus, but a common cause is hearing loss from exposures to loud sounds. (Chapter 7)

Tooth block. *See* **barodontalgia**.

Traffic-alert and collision avoidance system (TCAS). *See* **airborne collision avoidance system**.

Trans-cockpit authority gradient. *See* **flight deck authority gradient**.

Transfer of learning. *See* **transfer of training**.

Transfer of training. Also called *transfer of learning*. When prior learning in one environment either contributes (positive transfer of training) or interferes (negative transfer of training) with learning and performance in another. For example, negative transfer of training occurs when a pilot learns to fly an aircraft with the landing gear handle located to the left of the throttle/pedestal centerline then checks out in another aircraft were it is located to the right of the throttle/pedestal centerline. (Chapter 15)

Transportation modes. Different means of traveling from one location to another—land (road, off-road, rail), water (ship, boat), air (fixed-wing, rotary-wing, glider, airship, balloon), space, cable, and pipeline. (Chapter 1)

Trapped gas. Gas volumes in various body cavities expand with altitude in accordance with Boyle's Law. If this gas is unable to escape, pain may result in the middle ears, sinuses, teeth, and/or gastrointestinal tract. (Chapter 5)

Type I DCS. Pain-only physiological symptoms of DCS such as the bends and skin manifestations. (Chapter 5)

Type II DCS. Severe symptoms of DCS such as the chokes and neurological disturbances. (Chapter 5)

Type I SD. Unrecognized spatial disorientation. You are unaware that you are experiencing SD and will base control of your aircraft on a false perception of your attitude. (Chapter 9)

Type II SD. Recognized spatial disorientation. You are aware that you are experiencing SD and may or may not base control of your aircraft on a false perception of your attitude. (Chapter 9)

Type III SD. Incapacitating spatial disorientation. You are aware that you are experiencing SD and it is likely you may be unable to properly take positive control of your aircraft. (Chapter 9)

Unaugmented flight. *See* **augmented flight**.

Uncontained engine failure. An engine failure in which engine debris is not contained within the engine case (housing) or does not exit via the exhaust section, but exits in unpredictable directions at high speeds posing a threat to other airframe components (including aircraft controls), nearby engines, the cabin, passengers, and crew. (Chapter 4)

Uncontrolled flight into terrain (UFIT). Collision into terrain as a result of LOC-I. (Chapters 1 and 20) *See* **loss of control in flight**, **controlled flight into terrain**, and **spatial disorientation**.

Undesired aircraft state (UAS). A safety-compromising position, condition, or attitude of the aircraft resulting from ineffective threat and/or error management by the flight crew. (Chapters 2 and 20)

Unintended injury death. Deaths due to accidental or unintentional causes and do not include deaths caused by disease, aging, suicide, or homicide. (Chapter 1)

Unsafe acts. Unintentional errors (mistakes, slips and lapses) and deliberate violations (noncompliance with regulations, rules, and procedures designed to ensure safe flight operations). (Chapters 2 and 20) *See* **error** and **violation**.

Unusual attitude. *See* **airplane upset**.

Valsalva maneuver. A method to clear an ear or sinus block by pinching your nose shut with your fingers and quickly and sharply exhaling while not allowing any air to escape from your mouth or nose. (Chapter 5)

Vestibular apparatus. Located in the inner ear, this organ consists of three semicircular fluid-filled canals that roughly align with the three axes of flight (pitch, yaw, and roll) and respond to angular acceleration, and the otolith bodies (*saccule* and *utricle*) that contain a flat, plate-like membrane that activates sense receptors in response to linear acceleration. (Chapter 9)

Vestibular illusions. Illusions resulting from limitations of the vestibular apparatus located in the inner ear—the semicircular canals and the otolith bodies. (Chapter 9)

VFR flight into IMC. Visual flight rules flight into instrument meteorological conditions. For pilots who lack sufficient instrument flying skills, this often results in an accident caused by SD resulting in loss of control in flight or CFIT. (Chapters 1, 9, and 17) *See* **instrument meteorological conditions**, **loss of control in flight**, **spatial disorientation**, and **controlled flight into terrain**.

Vigilance. Sustained attention. In aviation it is often called *monitoring*. (Chapter 14) *See* **attention** and **monitoring**.

Violation. Deliberate noncompliance with regulations, rules and procedures that are designed to ensure safe flight operations. (Chapters 2 and 20) *See* **error** and **unsafe acts**.

Visual acuity. The ability to see fine detail. (Chapter 6)

Visual ambiguity. Impoverished environmental conditions that occur at night, in haze or at high altitude that limit the amount and quality of information needed for our visual brain to make accurate perceptual assessments of the outside world. (Chapter 12)

Visual blind spot. If an object falls within the visual blind spot of an eye it will not be seen by that eye because there are no visual photoreceptors located where the optic nerve exits the eye, about 18 degrees from the center of vision. Another visual blind spot exists in the center of vision (foveal vision) in each eye during pure night vision. (Chapter 6) *See* **central vision blindness**.

Visual flight rules (VFR). Regulations which prescribe minimum weather conditions in terms of visibility, ceiling, and distance from clouds so a pilot relying on outside natural visual references to maintain flight can successfully do so. For example, basic weather minima for operations in U.S. Class D airspace are ceiling no lower than 1,000 feet AGL and visibility no lower than 3 SM visibility. (Chapter 1) *See* **instrument flight rules** and **visual meteorological conditions**.

Visual illusion. The misperception of visual cues in the environment. A relatively common type in the flight environment is a runway illusion that occurs during a landing approach in conditions of visual ambiguity (e.g., at night, poor visibility, and over featureless or snow-covered terrain) that can trick a pilot into seeing something that isn't there. (Chapter 12) *See* **visual landing illusions**.

Visual landing illusions. A variety of illusions on landing approaches caused by varying runway shapes and dimensions, runway lighting and atmospheric conditions that convince a pilot that they are higher or lower than they really are. (Chapter 12) *See* **visual illusions**.

Visual meteorological conditions (VMC). Weather conditions where VFR flight is permitted. (Chapter 1) *See* **instrument meteorological conditions** and **visual flight rules**.

Visual perception. As opposed to visual sensation—the detection of visual stimuli—visual perception involves the interpretation of those raw visual inputs. (Chapter 12)

Willful noncompliance. *See* **violation**.

Window of circadian low (WOCL). Individuals living on a regular 24-hour routine with sleep at night have two periods of maximum sleepiness where core body temperature is at its lowest point in the daily cycle (circadian low). One WOCL occurs at night, roughly from 3 a.m. to 5 a.m. (primary low), a time when physiological sleepiness is greatest and performance capabilities are lowest. The other is in the afternoon, roughly from 3 p.m. to 5 p.m. (secondary low). (Chapter 10)

Working memory. Working memory (sometimes called *short-term memory*) is where we consciously process sensory inputs from our environment and stored information retrieved from LTM to engage in most mental processes. Retention of attended sensory inputs in working memory is limited in the amount of information that can be stored at any one time (about five to nine items) and is temporary (lasting for maybe 15 to 20 seconds) depending on the degree of rehearsal. (Chapter 16)

Index of Aircraft Accidents and Notable Incidents

Index

D

Dalton's Law 58

dark adaptation 101–102, 104, 108, 110

dark-night conditions 9, 145, 155, 162, 208, 236, 239, 241

decision making 333–356

  accidents/incidents involved in 21, 46, 77, 162–163, 171, 174–175, 181, 199–200, 333–337, 344, 352, 364–367, 372–373, 377, 394–395, 398, 412

  errors 14, 21, 344, 395

  fatigue and 171, 173–176, 181

  improving 352–357

  information processing 339–340

  satisficing 343, 351

  uncertainty and 340–342

decision-making biases and heuristics 46, 343–351, 356–357

  illusory correlations 344

decision-making models 338–340, 351, 353

  compensatory 339–340, 353

  descriptive 338, 343

  heuristics 351

  non-compensatory 339–340

  recognition-primed decisions 353

decompression sickness (DCS) 42, 81–84, 87–89

  cause 81–82

  predisposing factors 83–84

  symptoms 82–83

  Type I, II, and III 82–83

deep and surface structure. *See* Chomsky, Noam

defenses-in-depth 26

defining event 8

  most common 8–11, 11–13

dehydration 67, 138, 186, 192, 214–215

denitrogenation 88

Denver, John 29, 41

design eye position. *See* design eye reference point (DERP)

design eye reference point (DERP) 41, 245–246

diet and nutrition 138, 190–191, 212–213

diffusion of responsibility 371, 375, 380

disorientation stress 159

displays 282–294

  analog 41, 287–290

  digital 41, 161, 287–290

distance/depth perception 224–229

distraction 9, 44, 124, 170, 175, 263, 267, 269–272, 318, 322–323, 411–412

  management 275–276, 327, 418–419

disturbance stage of hypoxia 63–64

duck-under phenomenon 239–240

E

ear block 85–86, 90

Ebbinghaus illusion 231

effective performance time (EPT) 65–66

electronic flight bags (EFB) 9

elevator illusion 158

emergency medical services operations 368

empty-field myopia (dark-focus) 98, 103, 109, 226

engineered materials arresting system (EMAS) 21, 348

engineering reliability analysis (ERA) 31

English language proficiency 255–256

ergonomics. *See* human factors

error. *See* human/pilot error

escalation bias 46, 346–347, 356

event cascade 414–415

evolved gas. *See* decompression sickness (DCS)

exercise 70, 84, 89, 188, 191, 213, 402

expectation bias 233–234, 243, 254–255, 258

explosive decompression. *See* sudden decompression

F

false climb illusion 131, 145, 155–156, 158–159

farsightedness 107–109

fatigue 169–192. *See also* sleep

  accidents involving 169–177

  acute 185–186

  causes of 177–186

  cumulative 186–187

  defined 173, 186

  effects of 173–177

Fick's Law 61

field of view 97

fight or flight response 396

finger trouble 21, 296–297

five M model 28

flat light 223, 242–243, 246–247

flicker vertigo 105

flight control/flight guidance system 294–295

flight deck authority gradient 390–392

flight duty period (FDP) 178, 187

flight envelope protection 295–296, 300, 304

flight operational quality assurance (FOQA) 6, 15, 17, 416

flows 6, 21, 326, 417

fly-by-wire technology 295–296, 304

forgetting 29, 32, 45, 124, 174, 313–328, 398–399

  deferred tasks 322, 326–327

  task overload 270–271, 323–324

  time pressure 323, 327

framing bias 46, 345–346, 356

fundamental attribution error 334, 370

G

gambler's fallacy 344

general aviation accident record 5–6, 8–11

general aviation (GA) 3, 4–5

geometric/optical illusions 230–234
- horizontal-vertical line illusion 230
- irradiation illusion 232

G-induced loss of consciousness (G-LOC) 129–130, 135–141

glass cockpit 161, 293

glassy water 243, 246

Graham's Law 59, 61

graveyard spin 152–153

graveyard spiral 147, 151–154

grayout 129, 134, 136–139

ground proximity warning system (GPWS). *See* terrain awareness and warning systems (TAWS)

group cohesiveness 369, 371, 394

group influence/pressure 46, 365–366, 369, 378–379
- accidents/incidents involving 363–368, 370–373, 376–378

groupthink 371–373, 375

G-time tolerance curve 135–136

H

hazardous attitudes 349, 354–355

head tilt reflex 152

hearing and noise 115–128
- aircraft noise sources 118–119
- auditory fatigue 121
- auditory system 116–118
- effects of noise 115, 120–122
- hearing loss 121–122
- hearing protection 122–125
- noise defined 115

hemoglobin (Hb) 61–62, 68–71

Henry's Law 81

heuristics 343–345, 351

hindsight bias 334–335, 364

histotoxic hypoxia 69, 71

home-drome syndrome 238

homophones 252–253

human-centered design 38–39, 47, 282

human factors 37–47
- defined 38, 47

human factors analysis and classification system (HFACS) 20–28

human-machine interface 37, 282–287
- controls 37–38, 41, 282–284, 290–295
- displays 41, 282–293, 304

human/pilot error 19–33
- defined 19, 411
- handling and proficiency 411–412, 416
- models of 24–31
- procedural errors 412
- resource management errors 27, 412
- skill-based error 21–22, 24–25, 27, 341
- technique error 21
- unsafe act 20, 26–28

human reliability assessment (HRA) 31–32

hurry-up syndrome 323

hypemic hypoxia 63, 68–70, 203

hyperventilation 66–67, 74

hypoglycemia 138, 213–214

hypoxia 62–71, 73
- altitude thresholds 73
- avoidance 74–78
- defined 62
- effective performance time 65–66
- histotoxic 63, 69, 71
- hypemic 63, 68–70, 203–204
- hypoxic (altitude) 63–67, 70, 77, 138, 413
- severity 69–71
- signs and symptoms 64–65
- stages of 63–64
- stagnant 63, 69, 134–135
- types 63, 67–69

hypoxic (altitude) hypoxia 63, 70, 77, 138, 413

I

illusions. *See* approach and landing illusions, spatial disorientation (SD), and visual illusions

illusory correlations 344

illusory pyramid illusion 232

immediate action items 328

IMSAFE checklist 215

inattentional blindness 266, 273

incapacitation 54, 67, 69, 76, 81–83, 135, 139–140, 200–202, 216, 390

indifferent stage of hypoxia 63

information processing 24, 43–46, 173, 223, 252, 264–265, 339–340, 400

inner ear. *See* auditory system

insomnia 180–181, 184–185, 188, 215

instrument meteorological conditions (IMC) 8

integrated displays 287

interface coding 37, 283–287
- color coding 37, 284
- location coding 284–285
- population stereotypes 284, 289
- shape coding 37–38, 283–284